YEARS of WRATH, DAYS of GLORY

Memoirs from the Irgun

YEARS of WRATH, DAYS of GLORY

DAYS of GLORY

Memoirs from the Irgun

by

Yitshaq Ben-Ami

Robert Speller & Sons, Publishers
New York, New York 10010

©1982 by Y. Ben-Ami
ISBN 0-8315-0185-5
First Edition

Printed in the United States of America

To The "Anonymous Soldiers"
of the Hebrew Revolution

Acknowledgements

My thanks to Dr. H. Merhavia in Jerusalem for his encouragement, and to Yisrael Medad for his research assistance. In New York, I was helped by Mark Teich, who brought order to chaos and by Herbert Druks and Eliahu Matzozky. My gratitude to Samuel Merlin and Miriam Chaikin for their patience and assistance. Special thanks to my friend Dr. Irving Shendell who helped bring this work to completion.

Note: Some family members portrayed in this story are composites. Also, all dialogue is based on the author's best recollection of conversations in which he participated or as they were reported to him.

CONTENTS

Part IV: Darkness Descends

Part V: The War of Independence

LIST OF ILLUSTRATIONS*

*Note: Pictures appear opposite page number.

Foreword

In the early 1920's, in Palestine, the poet Uri Zvi Greenberg warned about terrible events to come. In the early 1930's, Abba Achimeir, while a political prisoner in a Jerusalem jail, feverishly scribbled manifestoes in his cell, calling for a Hebrew Revolution. In the mid-1930's, Jabotinsky sounded the alarm and called upon the Jews of Eastern Europe to leave the turbulent continent and save themselves.

When the menace became reality, the European Jews began to flee. Helpless, confused, they scurried from border to border like frightened animals. Gates were slammed in their faces. The world turned a deaf ear. Here and there, unique acts of heroism by individuals in last-minute attempts to save a few.

Some students and workers in Palestine as well as in the Diaspora responded to the call for national renaissance and revolution, but most respected leaders displayed defeatism and collapsed. Then came the final chapter—the exterminations—the horredous statistics.

Those were the 1930's and 40's which I lived through; these personal memoirs tell the story.

YEARS of WRATH, DAYS of GLORY

DAYS of GLORY

Memoirs from the Irgun

Part One: Ancestors

I

Tales My Parents Told Me . . .

My *maternal* great-grandfather, Dov Gedaliah, lived on the outskirts of Brisk (Brest-Litovsk), where Poland, White Russia and the Ukraine meet. By the end of the 18th century, Brisk had a large Jewish population eking out a living as middlemen and small tradesmen. Dov Gedaliah's son, Zeev Arieh (Leib), was born in 1845, went to *Heder* and Yeshiva, and was considered well-educated by the standards of the day.

Czar Alexander I's call for Jews to settle on the land had appealed to Dov Gedaliah in his youth, and he encouraged his son Zeev Leib to become a land-lease holder. For the next twenty years Zeev Leib built a substantial farming enterprise. He was remembered as a charitable man. My mother described him as short and solid, with a red beard and blue eyes, an almost slavic physiognomy. These features persist in our family.

During Zeev Leib's years on the farm he acquired the title of "Reb," akin in the Jewish communities of Eastern Europe to "Don" in the Spanish world. Zeev Leib's farm prospered, and his family grew until his children numbered six. The rabbi in Grodno was his mentor. The education of his children he left in the hands of young tutors who, in addition to their textbooks, brought books and pamphlets expounding new ideas that were piercing the darkness of Jewish life in the Pale.

Czar Alexander II had ascended the Imperial throne in 1855 and his policies spread the enlightenment, *Haskala,* into the Pale. Zeev Leib came across many new thoughts, including Rabbi Zvi Hirsch Kalischer's "Emunah Yeshara" (1843). Here he read that salvation would not come through the Messiah's great shofar

1

blast, miraculously transporting the miserable Jews to Zion, but "by generating support from philanthropists and gaining the consent of nations to the gathering of the scattered of Israel . . ."

Grandfather Leib was a fully observant Orthodox Jew who spoke vernacular Yiddish and prayed in Hebrew. Since childhood he had prayed three times a day for the restoration of Jerusalem. Though a farmer in the freezing north, he celebrated the feasts and farming holidays of sub-tropical Zion. Reciting the *piutim* of ancient Hebrew poets, he gave thanks for both his crops and those gathered thousands of years ago. A man who worked the earth with his hands, he sang and danced like all good Hasidim; he sat on the synagogue floor on the Ninth of Av and wept for the destruction of the Temple.

But deep in his heart gnawed uncertainties about the future of his family. His children were growing up, and their young teachers had exciting ideas about education and the world outside the Pale.

Zeev Leib saw clouds rising on the horizon. He tried to share his fears with his wife, Batya, but she was burdened with raising six small children and running the household. She did her chores, read her prayers and slept peacefully. Whatever was to be would be.

Zeev Leib's soul-searching came to a critical head as tensions developed across the land and the position of the Jews became threatened.

* * *

In the Ukrainian city of Kharkov, southeast of Grodno, lived the family of my *paternal* great-grandfather, Shneour Levi Yitshaq. They had moved there from Vitebsk in northern White Russia. No physical description exists of Shneour Levi, but his will, clearly written and luxuriant in flowing Hebrew, gave a good representation of his spirit.

Great-grandfather wrote: "Love and respect the Almighty. To achieve this, my beloved children, you must set aside time for study, even if only for a few minutes. A day should not pass without your having studied. Whether it is the *Mishna* or the law of *Gemara*, in no way forget your daily psalm—it is precious to the soul of Israel.

"Remember, a man is known by Kisso, Kosso, ve Kasso—how

he behaves in matters of money, drink and anger. Therefore, be conscientious in your dealings with men, be truthful and righteous to the end. An angry man is like a worshipper of idols, so sleep over your anger at least one night. Set aside a part of what you earn with God's help, to help the needy. Beware of intoxicating drinks . . . Do not imbibe except for your health or to celebrate happy events or on the Sabbath and holidays."

He echoed the central themes of Hasidic *Habad's* teachings:

"Watch over your sons and daughters. Give them the best and most righteous teachers. Do not economize on this. Watch, especially in their teens, with whom they associate; keep them away from bad company. Watch over their manners and language, that they should follow in the path of the Torah and wisdom and be without blemish. Do not say that you are too occupied with your daily livelihood and warn your wives to abide by this. Pray for this since it is in your life!

"My dear children, what is the lot of man for all his travail? Not money, fancy clothing, precious jewelry, or glory does man acquire to last forever. Wealth is taken away from man or man is taken away from his wealth. Even when he leaves his possessions, it is uncertain how his heirs will manage them. Therefore, the important thing for a man to leave his children is his teachings.

"All that I say is not my invention: this is the basis of life for any man of Israel—to learn from God's teachings and guide himself accordingly.

"My beloved ones, I and your mother, may she rest in peace, have gone through a lot of suffering for you. But all I ask is that you observe the anniversary of my death according to our tradition . . . ask for mercy for my soul and my spirit. Do it for the glory of the Almighty, and my soul, too, will benefit. . . ."

Great-grandfather had the reputation of being a learned and pious man. He taught, and served in the *Beth-Din*, the Jewish community court. When the large fairs took place in the town of Kharkov, great-grandfather settled disputes among the thousands of Jewish merchants who attended.

I reread the yellowing, fragile pages many times, yearning for the forefathers I wished to have known. A life of pain was reflected in great-grandfather's will. When the family lived in the Vitebsk area, my grandfather Shmuel, Shneour Levi's son, was kidnapped at the age of seven and taken to serve in the army of Czar Nicholas I.

One night, exhausted from grieving, my great-grandmother fell into a profound sleep. She dreamed that her Shmuel was at the town's railroad station awaiting transportation to a military camp.

She arose at dawn as if possessed, dressed quietly, and walked in a trance to the station. There, among a dozen youngsters, was Shmuel. The group was sitting on the platform, guarded by two slumbering, drunken soldiers. She moved up quietly to the group, took little Shmuel by the hand and walked slowly away. Once out of sight, they ran as fast as they could back to the *Shtetl* where the child was hidden by relatives for weeks. Nobody came looking for him. One Jewish boy more or less apparently didn't matter to mother Russia.

On another occasion, great-grandmother was going through final preparations for the Sabbath. She had swept the floors, fueled the large clay oven, placed the white Sabbath cloth on the table and on it two candlesticks and the two *chaloth* (breads) which she had baked. She covered the *chaloth*, and went out to do her last-minute chores.

She returned an hour later. Glancing at the spotless white cloth and the two covered *chaloth*, she knew that her meticulously laid table had been disturbed. She lifted the cloth that covered the breads, and there between the beautifully braided *chaloth*, on a bloody rag, lay a human fetus. She froze, paralyzed with horror. Then, like an automaton she picked up the bloody bundle, walked to the oven and threw it into the fire.

A few minutes later there were knocks on the door. Still stunned, she walked to the door and opened it. Outside stood a young Russian peasant woman accompanied by the village policeman and a few other peasants. The woman pointed to my great-grandmother: "She's the one! She stole my baby!" The policeman pushed into the room, and searched, overturning objects and knocking the *chaloth* onto the floor. The peasants stood in the doorway, hissing curses. Not having found any evidence, the policeman strode out of the cottage muttering about the "dirty Jews . . ."

This was an attempt at "blood libel," the centuries-old accusation that Jews used the blood of Christian children to bake their bread.

Great-grandmother died soon after. Shneour Levi remarried, and moved south with his family to Kharkov in the Ukraine.

It had only recently become possible for Jews to live in Kharkov, which was outside the Pale. In 1859, Alexander II had granted Jewish merchants the right to settle in Gentile areas; in 1865, he extended this freedom to various craftsmen. But not until 1868 were the Jews allowed to build a synagogue in Kharkov, or form a community council.

As the years passed and Shneour Levi's health deteriorated, his oldest son, Shmuel, became the head of the family. It was Shmuel who kept his father's *Habad* tradition alive among them, and it was he who, in the last years of his father's life, moved the family back north, to the village of Viazma near Vitebsk, so they could be close once again to the *Habad* land.

It was a big move, not just because it restored the family to their Hasidic roots. Large numbers of Jews had been living in the district since the sixteenth century (the first synagogue was constructed in 1627), and there were many more opportunities for them than there had been in Kharkov. A new railroad was built in 1860, and commerce flourished in and around Vitebsk.

In the first two years back in the *Habad* land, Shmuel married grandmother Haya Frieda Cohen, the daughter of a rabbi from the nearby town of Orsha. Her ancestors, descendants of Don Isaac Abravanel, had migrated there from northern Italy—two hundred years earlier, passing through the Rhineland and Poland. The marriage was arranged by their parents through a matchmaker. Grandfather Shmuel made his fortune in flour-milling and distilling alcohol, and he and my grandmother had eight children—four boys and four girls. Along with Russian, they spoke Yiddish at home, prayed in Hebrew, and the *Habad* tradition was always with them.

The next several years were relatively calm years of peace and prosperity for the family. During these years of the enlightenment, Jews in the west joined gentiles in an "age of optimism." For the first time, Jews in Europe migrated freely, moving to the great cities: Berlin, Paris, Vienna and Budapest. Freedom and brotherhood were descending on earth, presaging the Messiah. A generation before, Byron had written in his *Hebrew Melodies*:

> Tribes of wandering foot and wary breast,
> How shall ye fly away and be at rest!
> The wild-dove hath her nest, the fox his cave
> Mankind their Coventry—Israel but the grave!

But now the world seemed to open its arms to Israel. All it had to do was shed its medieval garb, polish its tongue, walk out into the sun and the world would be its playground!

Suddenly, every field of endeavor seemed to cry out for Jewish professionals who rode the crest of the industrial and liberal revolutions—the Rothschilds and Oppenheimers, the Poliakoffs and deHirsch, the Bleichroders and the Pereiras. They ran textile mills and lumber mills, financed railroads and became international merchants. The New World discovered that the Jew could be productive. They painted, invented, wrote, acted on the stage; they were praised in the gentile press. Their success triggered jealousies, but nothing could impede the belated Jewish Renaissance.

My maternal and paternal grandparents somehow combined tradition with the demands of modern life, managing bountiful livelihoods without abandoning their heritage. Both Zeev Leib who worked the soil in Grodno and Shmuel who operated his flour mill in Vitebsk were able to make their Russian and Hebrew cultures work together, enhancing their business acumen by the practices of *Habad*. They followed a narrow path winding through the stirrings of Russian nationalism and the Hebraist Abraham Mapu, the anti-clerical pronouncements of Y. L. Gordon and the call for Jews to identify with the revolutionary Left. Friends and relatives were dressing in Western garb, converting, losing themselves in the larger cultures, and it tore at the hearts of Zeev Leib and Shmuel.

The honeymoon with Czarist Russia did not last. Slowly Russian enlightenment was drowned in Russian nationalism, and the cycle of love and hate for the Jews repeated once more.

The Czar now ruled most of the world's Jews. Poland had been incorporated into the Empire after 1863, and Romania (Moldavia and Wallachia) was a protectorate. Anti-Semitism began to manifest itself in these countries in brutal and vulgar forms. But the more refined and threatening versions appeared first in the West. The first anti-Semitic international was formed in Dresden in 1882, and the bells started tolling for European Jewry. My grandparents heard the tolling.

II
Kill The Jews. . . .
(1881-1882)

Gentile tradesmen and professionals grew to resent the successful "enlightened Jews" in their midst. The assassination of Czar Alexander II of Russia by political terrorists in 1881 ended the period of relative liberalization, and ignited the fires. Mobs plundered and burned Jewish homes in more than one hundred and sixty towns and villages. They murdered, raped and mutilated children. Some of the pogroms went on for days while local authorities stood by and watched.

There were now three possible paths for the Jews—the New World, deeper integration within Europe, or Hebrew national rebirth. East and West, Jewish liberals and reformers stopped in their tracks to ponder. After countless generations of bloodbaths, not only the Orthodox believers, but also the intelligentsia—students, doctors, writers, the very ones who had broken away from the Pale to carry the torch of enlightenment—began slowly, hesitantly, to consider a future linked with national rebirth and return to Zion.

In 1882, with the Jewish blood staining the roads in the Ukraine and the south of Russia, Leon Pinsker, an assimilated physician decorated by the army, wrote his *Auto-Emancipation*, attempting to analyze the psychology and mechanics of anti-Semitism. The non-Jewish world, wrote Pinsker, saw the Jews of the diaspora as ghosts roaming the earth. Their unnatural, uprooted existence aroused fear. The fear caused suspicion, which in turn bred hatred. The salvation of the Jews, therefore, would be brought about only by giving the ghosts substance, by giving them a homeland.

The task, declared Pinsker, had to be undertaken by the Jews themselves. Instead of the elusive "civic emancipation" they sought for so long, they should secure their own territory and develop it through their own initiative with their own resources. Since the modern world had denied them a chance for normal living, they should return to their past and their ancient home. The Jews had to realize that relationships between people were based not on love, but respect. And respect would come only when the Jews were self-reliant, strong and the masters of their own destiny. This was no longer a mystical longing for Zion. *It was the answering cry to a need for survival.* Pinsker's *Auto-Emancipation* became the catechism of the nationalist movement among the Jews.

Slowly, very slowly, individuals gathered around *Hovevei-Zion* (The Lovers of Zion), the first important Zionist group. Students and other youths formed the *Bilu*, a student movement that drew its name from the initials of the Biblical verse, "Oh, House of Jacob, come ye and let us Go." (Isa. 2:5). Societies and small organizations, newspapers and periodicals, many in Hebrew, mushroomed all over the country. In the twenty years following 1882, twenty-five thousand people left the unbearable conditions in Russia, Poland and Romania and went to Palestine. This was to be called "the First Aliyah," the largest *Aliyah* (ascendance) so far. Even so, it constituted only a fraction of those who emigrated—one million went to the United States alone.

* * *

Grandfather Zeev Leib's family was not directly affected by the pogroms because they took place mainly in the south of Russia. But the attacks could occur any time and any place. The pogroms were precipitated by national planning. What happened yesterday in Kiev and Odessa could happen tomorrow in Grodno and Vitebsk, and *all* the Pale suffered.

Though Zeev Leib's farming operations were doing well and his family was comfortable and happy, he was terrified that the 1881 pogroms would come to Grodno.

Zeev Leib began taking the wagon into Grodno in the middle of the week, when no market day was being held. He told his wife, Batya, he was attending meetings with his childhood friend

Mordechai Diskin. The meetings, he told her, were under the auspices of "The Society for Settlement in Palestine."

He had heard of these meetings before 1881, but now he wanted to know more. He told Batya about a man named Fishel Lapin who had gone to Palestine from Grodno almost fifteen years ago and now lived in Jerusalem. Lapin had been writing to his friends and family, urging them to join him. And just a few years ago, a group of respectable Jews from Grodno had raised money and bought a tract of land in Palestine in a settlement called Petah-Tikva. Did Batya know, he asked, what Petah-Tikva meant? The gate to hope. What did she think of that? he persisted. The gate to hope. Couldn't she see it? Jewish farmers working their lands without fear, in the land of Zion?

Batya listened to his ramblings, at first without much concern. But by 1882 they became more frequent. Grandfather went to the Grodno meetings more frequently, returning more and more agitated, twirling his beard, his cheeks flushed and his blue eyes lit up with excitement.

A few days later Zeev Leib repeated a dream to Batya. His father had come back to him and told him "Leib, the time has come to go to Palestine."

"Bashe," Zeev Leib said, "I cannot go on like this. It has been on my mind ever since father spoke about Zion and Jerusalem when I was young. I'm worried about what is happening—this Czar, let his name and memory be wiped out forever! This farm is mine. I work hard and I make things grow. But sooner or later someone will come and kick us off our land, us and all the other 'dirty Jews,' and where will we be then? I *am* a Jew, and a Jewish farmer should live in Eretz Israel. I have no desire to go to America. We will go to Palestine and shall make it into a land of milk and honey, like it says in the Bible, like it was once. . . ."

Grandmother sat frozen. She knew the kind of man Zeev Leib was, she knew his stubbornness and determination. She realized this was the end of their pleasant life in Grodno.

Thousands of Jews lived in Grodno and thousands more all around the district. There had been no real trouble for decades. It was a respected Jewish community with a tradition four hundred years old. A synagogue and Jewish cemetery had always existed. Some of the first new books in Hebrew had been published in

Grodno a hundred years ago. It was a center for learning and her children, from two to twelve years old, were getting a good education. How could they just pack up and go to Palestine?

She had heard of a few men who raised money and spoke of Palestine, but all pious Jews sang of Zion in their daily prayers, and there was always money being sent to the poor Jews in the Holy Land. Why did they have to *go* there? Could they grow things there? Would they even be able to get land? Would there be peasants like the *mujiks* to help with the plowing? Were the Turks who ruled Palestine any better than the Russians? Weren't there pogroms in Palestine too?

Batya did not argue with her husband. She did not ask him the questions she asked herself. A good Jewish wife obeyed her husband, so she pressed her hands together and rocked back and forth, praying silently to the Almighty. At last, she asked haltingly, "Zeev . . . why don't you ask your *Rebbe*? You always say he is wise . . . Why don't you go and tell him what you hear in your dreams?"

Zeev Leib did go to see his *Rebbe*, who was a leader in the local *Habad* group. A good Hasid was expected to seek his *Rebbe's* guidance on such important questions, and also to obey his advice. He came back and told Batya, "The Rebbe said no! He said I shouldn't listen to my dreams. It isn't time to go to Palestine. We have to be patient. We have to *wait*. . . ."

"Do you know what else our beloved *Rebbe* said? That we are to stay here and *suffer*. Our suffering will 'make us ready' for the Messiah. Only then will He lead us to the Holy Land. . . ."

Zeev Leib looked at Batya, and his heavy hands tightened into fists. "Bashe, I'm not going to wait for the Messiah. If He is to come, we have to help Him. Why should any of us suffer more than necessary? Why should the Messiah want more blood to be spilt? What kind of Messiah would want that?"

Batya knew it was no use to argue, though she was terrified. When news spread that Zeev Leib was leaving, members of the family tried to dissuade him. There were stories, they said, about families who came back from Jerusalem, from Jaffa, from Hebron. To exist there, people had to live off *Haluka*, off charity. "*Haluka*,—the life of beggars." But Zeev Leib would never live off charity, so maybe they would not live at all. What would the future be like now, giving up their home, their friends and family? . . . Batya had heard enough about Palestine, and it did not sound like Paradise, it did not sound as if milk and honey flowed there. The *Rebbe* had said that life there was very harsh. Everything was coming to an end. . . .

Batya had her own prayer book. When the chores did not crowd in on her, she tried to pray daily as well as on the Sabbath and Holy Days. She needed strength, so she turned to her God, the "Master of the Universe," to whom any Jew in need could turn. She poured her heart out in her prayers, showing God all the emotion she couldn't show to Zeev Leib. Years later, when I carefully turned the pages of Grandmother's crumbling prayer book, the stains on many pages looked like tears.

III

To The Promised Land

". . . I have set before thee life and death . . .
therefore choose life, that both thou and thy seed may live . . . "
(Deut. 30:19)

The pogroms continued through the spring of 1882, followed by draconic anti-Jewish laws. The Jews of Russia as if in a state of shock failed either to respond or to comprehend the far-reaching implications of the assault on their existence. Many went west and many thousands crossed the Atlantic. However, only a handful saw their future in Eretz-Israel. Though the first *Aliyah* (1882-1890) eventually included about twenty-five thousand Jews, only a few hundred went to Palestine during early 1890. Of these, most settled in the major towns; but some headed for primitive, isolated farm settlements. Zeev Leib was among them. He gave up his leases, sold the house and raised 5,000 rubles; he bought seeds and farming tools and left Grodno forever.

The point of departure was Odessa, the major Russian port on the Black Sea. It was one of the centers of world commerce and culture, with a large educated class and respected Jewish community. Dr. Leon Pinsker, the author of *Auto-Emancipation*, lived in Odessa, and Zeev Leib hoped to meet him, but there was not enough time to locate him or the *Hovevei Zion* (Lovers of Zion) committees and Zeev Leib contented himself that they would meet one day in Eretz-Israel.

They found the small, rust-covered tramp steamer that was to be their home for the next two weeks. The ship would be stopping first in Constantinople, then at some islands in the Aegean before moving on to Jaffa. Zeev Leib went up on deck and sat down on a closed hatch at the stern, feeling absolute exultation. At last he was on the way to Petah-Tikva! There was no soil he could not work, and he felt confident that all would go well, if he and his family could only keep their health. He had believed all his life that God had meant that tiny land for his people.

IV

The Promised Land

*"By the sweat of your brow,
shall you get bread to eat . . ."*

(Gen. 3:19)

Zeev Leib's boat arrived in Jaffa harbor in 1882. Gazing toward the shore, Grandfather could see low, spare houses, scattered minarets, and in the background, whitish-gray buildings in a pyramid-like cluster.

Zeev Leib knew Jaffa was a very old city which, according to tradition, was founded by Japhet the son of Noah after the great flood. Three thousand years ago when the Israelites came out of the desert, the tribe of Dan had settled there and became sailors and fishermen. So content with their seafaring lives were they that when Deborah called upon the tribes to join her against Israel's enemies, the tribe of Dan "remained in ships." King Solomon brought timber rafts there from Lebanon, to use in building the First Temple.

The arrival of a ship from Odessa and other ports was an event, and the narrow, dirty pier was packed with people. There were Arabs, hawkers, beggars and Jews—some there to meet the arrivals, others to board the ship back to Russia. As the family climbed up the few slippery steps, Zeev Leib noticed some Jewish families sitting on bundles and boxes. He had heard about Jews who were leaving Eretz-Israel. They could not adjust to the rigors of life, or to the humiliation of *Haluka,* the charity raised abroad and distributed here to the needy and unemployed.

Though he would have liked to ask them a hundred questions, Zeev Leib avoided looking at those dejected figures and instead

15

went to see to his boxes and crates.

The family settled in one of the few Jewish inns that Jaffa had to offer, a cramped, malodorous place a few blocks from the pier. It made Zeev Leib that much more anxious to reach his new land in Petah-Tikvah, where he could breathe the fresh, sweet air he had heard about. In the next several days he went to Jerusalem to pray at the Western Wall, attended several meetings of the local *Hovevei Zion* to whom he carried letters of introduction from Grodno, and located his friend Mordechai Diskin, who had left Grodno for Petah-Tikvah only a short time before. Mordechai's enthusiasm was running high, and Grandfather could hardly wait to get behind a plow.

Petah-Tikvah, originally founded in 1878, was the first agricultural settlement in Turkish-ruled Palestine. Its idealistic Orthodox Jews came out of old Jerusalem's claustrophobic city alleys. Their first settlement was plagued by internal quarrels and a bad harvest, and devastated finally by malaria. The settlement was abandoned after a couple of years, but the settlers returned in 1881, this time putting some distance between themselves and the Yarkon River, the source of the malaria and infected water. With a loaded cart pulled by mules, the family headed for their new home. There were about a dozen homes in the settlement, mere lean-tos, and a few more substantial mud-brick homes. After enjoying hot tea, bread and salt settlers' wives brought as welcome gifts, they unloaded their belongings and slept under the sky.

Batya had heard discouraging tales at the inn in Jaffa. She already knew about the settlers' initial failure two years ago, and the problems they had with bad drinking water and malaria. Now she looked at the few mud-brick houses and shacks and remembered their home outside Grodno. Zeev Leib spoke in a low voice and told her that the next morning he would go by rented cart to Jaffa to buy lumber for their new home. The home he said that God willed him to keep as his, where his children and grandchildren would live through the centuries, cultivating the land and bringing forth the seed of Israel. . . .

Next evening he returned with the lumber, and only then did the leaders of the settlement tell him that he could not erect a permanent structure without a permit from the Turkish officials in Jaffa and furthermore, that the Turks granted no permits. Never hesitating, he drove stakes into the ground, laid out the boards in a makeshift roof and bought straw mats from the local Arab tenant farmers.

For the three years that followed, the family lived in this ramshackle shack, no better than a large lean-to, with a scrawny cow, a donkey, goats and chickens sharing their roof. The settlers knew now to avoid river water, and quinine became the lifesaver. There was no doctor in the settlement. For medical attention they had to travel or send a rider to Jaffa or Rishon Le Zion, to bring the doctor back, or to the hospital in Jerusalem. The trip took two days; often, one simply walked.

Zeev Leib threw himself into working his land with a passion. The two older boys helped, first Ovadia and later Dov as well. The children took to their new life happily. Batya rose with the first rays of dawn, and worked alongside Zeev Leib until the stars came out, a routine she would keep for the next forty years.

It took years to adjust to the scorching summers, to the spells of *Hamsins*, hot stifling winds blowing in from the desert and gusts of winds and rain blowing in from the sea during the winter months.

Zeev Leib raised wheat, which was then hauled to the German settlement of Sarona to be milled. The winter months were hard because rains came down torrentially and the Musrara Wadi dry bed overflowed, blocking the path to the mills. Some winters the family had to eat home-crushed wheat at nearly every meal because it was the only cereal available.

Thefts by Bedouins took place regularly. Zeev Leib, and his son Ovadia, established a reputation as tough fighters against marauders. But the heat and humidity, especially in the summer months, were not so easy to combat. Temperatures soared over a hundred degrees for weeks on end. Malaria was a constant threat, and they had to guard their health rigorously. For three years, Zeev Leib was too proud to buckle under these hardships, and refused to leave his hut on the small tract of land. But finally, he gave in to Batya's wishes. They rented a single room in one of the permanent buildings of the colony, and worked their new land for the next three years, until Grandfather at last obtained the permit to build a permanent structure. With an ecstatic feeling of having finally found a home, he put up his own small building on his own land. It would remain in the family for fifty years, being enlarged to accommodate the births and marriages of each new generation. It became the gathering place for holidays and family events, and would one day be the site of my Bar Mitzvah and celebration.

The settlement did not prosper. Funds were always low, the crops were sporadic, and even when they were good the thefts, illnesses and natural cataclysms made life hard. When the settlement was on the verge of folding once more, Baron Edmond de Rothschild's philanthropic organization made twenty-eight farmers eligible for financial assistance. Zeev Leib was one of the candidates.

The help came just in time, and the lucky farmers planted citrus fruit groves, almonds and a vineyard. They imported heads of cattle for both dairy and meat. Just when the family appeared to have been blessed, scarlet fever struck. Zeev Leib's youngest daughter became critically ill. A rider was sent to Rishon Le-Zion, but by the time he returned with the doctor, little Chaya'leh was gone.

For months, Zeev Leib hardly spoke. Batya, who with her stoic acceptance of life's tragedies could endure more suffering, tried to console her distraught husband. She shared with him the strength she drew from her simple faith and religion, but Zeev Leib could not free himself from guilt. Had he not brought all this suffering on his family, they would still be enjoying the comfort and security of the farm outside Grodno . . . A man with six children and a good wife should never have acted so rashly. He should have questioned more, and come to see the country himself before uprooting the family. Why had he been so irresponsible? He had seen the others who went and returned. Even some of the most fiery members of the Zionist "Bilus" had come back to Russia— temporarily, they said; but nevertheless they had returned. And most of *them* were young men who did not even have families to keep alive. But he, Zeev Leib, had not wanted to see; he, the stubborn Zeev Leib, had not listened to his *Rebbe*, he had to pull the Messiah on with his own hands.

This dialogue with himself went on for several months. His health deteriorated. But he was not ready to give up fighting.

The same night he came home from a month's stay in the Jaffa hospital, there was trouble with Arab thieves. Zeev Leib insisted on watch duty, despite the pleadings of his family and the other settlers. They knew he was trying irrationally to atone for his sins. He spent the entire night standing vigil in the colony's wheat threshing yard, and when he came home in the morning, he was raging with fever. "Leave me," he said. "Leave me alone. I am all right." Two days later he died.

* * *

By the 1870s, the enlightenment had swept into my *paternal* grandfather Shmuel's home. My grandfather's brothers were now clean-shaven and well-groomed, "Russified." Grandfather himself, in a concession to being "a Jew at home and a man outside the home," had shed the long back Hasidic overcoat and spoke as much Russian in the home as Yiddish.

But contrary to his brothers, Grandfather never gave up his attachment to *Habad* or his yearning for Eretz-Israel. He continued to wear his beard, though he kept it trimmed and dignified, and he continued to study the precepts his father had passed on to him, the words of the *Admor*, Rabbi Shneour Zalman: "The love of Zion must be a fire burning in the heart . . . a true Jew must go to Eretz-Israel, and if there are obstacles, he must overcome them all and go."

When the pogroms of 1881 swept over the south of the Pale, Grandfather Shmuel remembered the advice in his father's will: "May no alien influence ever overcome your children, and may they never be hurt by evil laws." Russian chauvinism was being glorified to new heights by Dostoyevsky, and his pupil, Pobyedo-nostsev, the Czar's all-powerful advisor, was bent on putting the Jew in his "proper place." He made his intentions for the Jews clear: "One-third will die out, one-third will leave the country, and one-third will dissolve in the surrounding population."

Grandfather Shmuel was neither a socialist nor a revolutionary, but he saw where things were heading.

Hovevei Zion was active in Vitebsk, and Shmuel became involved with the organization, merging his old Zionist heritage of *Habad* with the Zionism of the young Hebrew enlightenment.

In 1884, the leaders of *Hovevei Zion* gathered in Kattowicz for an historic meeting. Thirty-six delegates attended, and all spoke loftily about their dreams of settling in Zion.

But the meeting ground to a standstill, bogged down by trivial issues such as whether one or two delegates should be sent to Palestine. There were no tangible results and in the coming months, though its members worked diligently to raise funds, less than 20,000 rubles, hardly enough for any meaningful emigration, were raised. Wealthy Jews looked at them as fools and dreamers and offered little or no assistance.

As the "evil laws" took firmer and firmer hold in Russia, Shmuel grew impatient and decided to take matters into his own hands. In 1891, with his wife Haya Frieda's approval he liquidated his business, packed up his eight children and an orphaned granddaughter, and headed for Jerusalem.

They followed the route of most East European *Olim*, traveling on small cargo ships carrying humans and cattle, from Odessa to Constantinople to Jaffa, an exhausting, terrifying storm-ridden voyage. After twelve bewildering days in grimy dungeon-like holds they landed, filthy and half-alive, in the port of Jaffa.

* * *

When Grandfather Shmuel landed in Jaffa in 1891, immigration of Jews was officially forbidden; but it was not difficult to buy off and inveigle one's way past the authorities, and it did not prevent families from reaching Jerusalem. The most powerful weapon in the Ottoman Empire was the clinking of the *Bakshish*, the bribe.

By now, the country had about twenty-five Jewish agricultural settlements populated by more than six thousand farm families. Jerusalem had the most Jews, a majority of the population since the 1830's. Over twenty thousand Jews lived in the narrow, crowded alleys of the Old City. Hundreds moved outside the walls, establishing small communities. The first was the Mishkenot Sha'ananim quarter in 1860, just outside the Jaffa Gate. Help for these ventures came from abroad. Leading the efforts were Queen Victoria's favorite, Sir Moses Montefiore, generous individuals like Judah Touro, a New Orleans friend of the Rothschilds and a handful of other prosperous Jews across the diaspora.

When Shmuel and his family arrived, it was natural to look for a home in Old Jerusalem, the center of Jewish life.

The son of Shneour Levi could not see himself living anywhere but in the Old City, near the Western Wall, where the First Temple had stood.

The Jewish quarter, squeezed between the Armenian houses and the Western Wall, was overcrowded. The family settled in the middle of the Moslem quarter, in a small area around Hebron Street open to Jews. Over the centuries, parts of Hebron Street had turned into an open sewer, a source for the disease and plagues that hit the city regularly. These were the only parts available to Jews.

The Jews of Jerusalem were a vital community. A majority were now actually self-supporting, active in trade, crafts and services. Secular schools had been established, and the Jews were once more changing the small, dormant town into a pulsing city, as David had done three thousand years ago.

Jerusalem was the heart of Jewishness for Grandfather Shmuel. For the millennia it had represented the Jews' spiritual and national hearth. Their yearning for it was an emotional, almost mystical one. Its pull affected both religious and non-religious Jews alike.

Families had come back, in handfuls or in large numbers again and again throughout the centuries, though the non-Jewish world did its best to keep the Jews and Jerusalem apart. From Babylonia through pagan and Christian Rome, the City of David was repeatedly destroyed, its Jewish inhabitants exiled and forbidden from returning there. As if the outside world resented and feared that unique spiritual union, Jerusalem was always enlisted in the very process of humiliating the Jews. Even when banned from living in the City, Jews were permitted to visit their past glories, to shed tears and bemoan their fate. Christians and Moslems exulted in displaying an exiled Jew sobbing in front of the Temple's Western Wall (what the non-Jews named The Wailing Wall), atoning for his crimes against Christ or his rejection of Mohammed. But simple men and women, as well as teachers, poets and rabbis, did not stop "ascending" to Jerusalem, and a century did not pass without Jewish presence there. Even after the crusaders massacred most of the Jewish and Moslem inhabitants in 1099, a residue of Jews were left, and when Saladin conquered Jerusalem in 1191, Jews erected a synagogue and developed a community that has endured.

When Grandfather Shmuel came home to Jerusalem, he went

to pray at the beautiful Hurva, the synagogue founded by Rabbi
Yehuda Hassid in 1700 and completed shortly before the family's
arrival. (In 1948, when the Jordanians occupied the City, the
Ramban's Synagogue was turned into a cheese shop and the
Hurva was destroyed.)

As soon as Shmuel settled the family in their quarters off
Hebron Street, he set out to familiarize himself and his sons with
the City. They walked high and low over narrow, teeming streets
and under arches dating back to before the Crusades. They gaped
at the native merchants sifting their grains, and at the bright
colors of the oriental bazaars. They saw open sewers, and in them
little children whose sore, swollen eyes were covered with flies.
They visited the Bikur Holim Hospital and the Etz Haim Yeshiva;
they mingled with fez-crowned Arabs and Turks, Christian pilgrims and priests, hawkers, beggars and cripples and Jews of all
traditions. They visited the new cleaner Mea Shearim settlement
outside the walls, and listened in awe to the residents' stories
about the dangers of life away from the sheltered Old City.

For better or worse, none of these impressions changed
Shmuel's decision to settle in the Old City. In his mind, if a Jew
was to return home, there was no other place for him but Jerusalem, as near as possible to the place of the Temple.

Those first weeks were like a dream for Grandfather. The fetid
alleyways and the dilapidation of the Arab, Armenian and Jewish
quarters were not truly visible to him. They had no reality in the
powerful light of his spiritual home. He was in a state of ecstasy,
and his constant discourses to his children abounded with elo-
quent stories from the Bible, the *Midrash* and the tales of Hasidim. In his stories, David and Solomon had never sinned, had
nary a blemish; the men who built the City and the Temple were
the holiest, godliest, most perfect of men. Ezra and Nehemiah,
who rebuilt and defended the Second Temple, and the great
Hasmoneans . . . even Herod was seen in a heroic light, with no
mention of his infidelity and tyranny.

After three years, the family at last found a small, two-room
apartment just off the "Jewish Street," a few minutes walk from
Habad Synagogue. It was built of limestone and Jerusalem stone,
plastered over and white-washed.

The laundry and other family chores were done in the yard,

where the children played. Across the yard, near the cistern, was a small, open-air kitchen where cooking was done on a clay-covered stone hearth over coals bought from a special store which also supplied kerosene for the lamps. The water came from the cisterns in the courtyard or from the community well, and was stored in large earthenware jars. Haya Frieda learned how to direct rain water into the proper cistern. When the water was hauled up or hand-pumped, it had to be filtered through a white cloth to eliminate tiny worms and dead insects.

My father, Menahem Mendel, had reached twenty, and some of his sisters were older and marriageable. While Grandfather worked at setting up his distillery, Grandmother Haya started the search for suitable husbands. Our family came with good credentials, and soon two of the daughters were married. One moved to Haifa and the other to Be'er-Tuvia, a young settlement in the south founded by Jewish farmers from Romania and Russia.

In a short time Grandfather had his distillery working, producing good brandy and vodka. They acquired some repute, for when the Russian Consul inquired from which distiller he could order spirits for the Russian colony in Jerusalem, the visitor referred him to Grandfather as one of the best in all of Russia . . .

The family seemed to be settling down. Grandfather, the dreamer-industrialist, was determined to show that Jewish families in Jerusalem did not have to live off *Haluka*. Observant, God-fearing Jews, living by centuries-old laws and traditions, did not have to be *Luftmenschen* ("people living on air"), leading a life of unreal absorption in the Talmud. Professional acumen that kept them alive, sometimes even successful in the Pale, could achieve that and more in Eretz-Israel. He had risked his life savings to prove this, and it was on the verge of coming true.

Then catastrophe struck. It was Grandfather's wont to oversee everything that happened in his distillery, and when something went wrong, he would try to solve it himself before delegating the task. One day, as he was repairing a defective valve in the plant, the boiler exploded, and Grandfather was burned over most of his body. He died within the next few days.

The sudden tragedy shattered the family. Shortly after, most of the children left Jerusalem, scattering across the land—with future generations settling all over the country from the Negev to the

Golan Heights, from Jerusalem to Rosh Hanikra.

Within five years, Grandmother Haya Frieda joined "Reb" Shmuel in their resting place, the *Habad* section of the hillside on Mount Olive, overlooking the glories of the Temple Mount and the whole of their beloved Jerusalem.

V
Standing Tall

One of Shmuel's sons, my uncle Meir Rosin, took up sign painting to support his real loves, sketching and painting. His paintings were among the first displayed in the Bezalel Art Museum (1906), and his model of the old Hurva Synagogue is today in the Museum of the Old City in Jerusalem. Meir's brother, my uncle Zalman Levi, inherited his Grandfather Shneour Levi's love of modern Hebrew and became one of the first teachers in the land. He taught the language to the children of Rishon Le-Zion for some forty years.

My father left the City—its crowding, commotion and dejected thousands—and cutting himself off from the *Habad* community, went to the plains for a new life. In the village of Rehovoth, following his natural mechanical bent, he began to repair farming machinery and work in the orchards.

The thirty thousand Jews in Palestine in the early 1890's were broadly divided into Sephardim and Ashkenazim and divided further by economics, social class and traditions.

The initial founders of a village would generally be from one country; both Petah-Tikvah and Rishon Le-Zion were settled mainly by Russian Jews, while Zichron Ya'akov and Be'er-Tuvia were settled by Romanians. But a slow influx of Jews with different backgrounds followed until ebullient Hasidim would be wed to dour Lithuanians and recently arrived Ashkenazim would take Sephardic brides.

There were some good farmers among the pioneers, like Zeev Leib who had worked Russian and Romanian lands, but even they were new to the climate and the soil; they planted the wrong crops in the wrong way at the wrong time and had many failed harvests. Local Ottoman officials constantly invented ingenious new restrictions on the settlers, always at the ready for bribes. Whatever financial reserves the settlers had brought with them were quickly consumed.

Disease, especially malaria, took a continuous toll. Eventually they planted eucalyptus groves to drain the marshes and malaria greatly decreased. They dug canals to channel away stagnant waters. Methods of cultivation improved, and some farms began having small success.

My father, feeling stifled, moved again, from Rehovoth to Jaffa and apprenticed himself to Mishli, the town's leading watchmaker. Father lived in an ugly, dirty little room near the railroad station, walking each day to Mishli's shop on Jaffa's main commercial street. He worked hard, studying Mishli's every gesture, and within months he was able to open his own small shop on Boostros Street in the heart of the city. Before long the shop developed into a social center. Father was a gregarious man who could tell a story while keeping his eyes fixed unwaveringly on the inside of a watch. His friends were Jews, Christians and Arabs alike, and he did an excellent business.

* * *

Meanwhile, my mother, Zeev Leib's daughter Sara, grew up in Petah-Tikvah eight miles north. When Grandfather had brought the family to Palestine she was ten; she was sixteen when he died. She and the older brothers helped Grandmother Batya to carry on with the groves and fields. Ovadia, the oldest, also took on odd jobs with other settlers to help tide over the family between harvests. Baron Edmond de Rothschild's help to Zeev Leib had kept the family together, and its farming tradition alive as well. Edmond de Rothschild was committed to transforming the *Shtetl* dwellers of the Pale into farmers in Eretz-Israel. When first approached in 1882 he donated large sums to the settlements and personally planned and supervised programs to train the farmers. He helped develop schools and community projects, financed the drainage of the swamps in Petah-Tikvah, and he gave money to fight trachoma and typhus.

Grandfather had never known that his name was on Rothschild's list, and in one respect it was just as well; he was so proud he might have refused. After he died, however, Grandmother Batya had no hesitation about taking the funds. She felt immense gratitude for the "known benefactor," and that gratitude was passed on to all the children and grandchildren of Shmuel and Zeev Leib.

The settlers might have failed if not for his financial help and professional guidance. The Jewish Colonization Association (ICA) he created replaced wooden plows with modern implements, demonstrated the need to plant second crops, furnished the settlers with better seeds, and its agronomists showed them how to make the seeds grow.

* * *

In the early 1890's the Odessa office of *Hovevei Zion* had guided more than three thousand Russian and Romanian Jews to Palestine. Jaffa became a boom town, full of lonely bachelors who outnumbered prospective brides.

Father had heard from friends about Zeev Leib's daughter Sara, living with her widowed mother, sister and brothers in Petah-Tikvah. Mother's beauty had attracted suitors from as far away as Jerusalem and Hebron, and she was also the daughter of a respected *Habadnik* farmer. Father's friends introduced him properly to Grandmother Batya.

Father was a tall, handsome young man. Clean-shaven except for twirling moustaches, he had dark hair combed neatly to the side. He wore hard collars, flared ties and a watchchain across his vest. He had come a long way from his family's lean years in Jerusalem. By hard work and modest living he had become his own master.

When they met in the early '90's, my mother was twenty and he was twenty-three. It was no longer their parents' tiny *shtetl* world. They did not need a matchmaker. Three weeks after their first introduction they were married and they settled in Jaffa.

The *Yishuv* was growing. In 1897, Theodor Herzl formed the World Zionist Organization, and for the first time "return to Zion" went beyond dreams and the hymns in prayerbooks. It grew into an international movement for a renascent Jewish nation and its own state. When pogroms swept Russia again in the years from 1903 to 1905, it launched the Second *Aliyah*.

At the turn of the century there were seven thousand Jews in Jaffa, and by 1903 there were thousands more, all squeezed into the limited urban area of Jaffa. The absentee Arab landlords let the Jewish residences slowly go to ruin, and the neighborhoods grew noisier and dirtier each year. The streets and alleys were strewn with garbage, and became more and more hazardous to the inhabitants' health. It began to feel to my parents as if they had never escaped the alleys of Jerusalem or the old *shtetl* of the Pale. In 1906, they joined fifty-nine other families from all walks of life in Jaffa and formed a society called *Ahuzat Bait* (housing estate), to found a new, suburban garden community for Jews. It was strictly a self-supporting enterprise. The sixty families deposited 100,000 francs at the Anglo-Palestine Company, obtained a construction loan from the Jewish National Fund in Cologne and purchased twenty-five acres of land.

In April 1909, the founding families dressed in their best holiday attire, gathered on a sand dune to draw lots for their parcels. My parents drew number ten, on what was to become Herzl Street; and by 1910, thirty years after Zeev Leib reached the port in Jaffa, my parents had their first solid stone home in Palestine. That same year, the *Herzlia* Gymnasia, the first modern high school to teach in Hebrew, laid its foundation stone on Herzl Street, symbolizing the birth of a new community.

The suburb was officially named "Tel-Aviv," for hope emerging out of the ruins of the past (Ezekiel 3:15). When Herzl died in 1904, efforts to obtain a political charter for return to Zion were dropped. Full-scale political Zionism, demanding unlimited immigration, was replaced by the more modest "brick by brick Zionism"—the concept of the few chosen, educated idealistic individuals who would build an exemplary society.

The return-to-Zion movement became dominated by cultural Zionists like Ahad Ha'am and Weizmann and ultimately by Socialists who would rule Zionism for decades to come. Unlike Herzl and his political Zionist followers who called for immediate, full-scale return to Zion, these post-Herzl Zionists did not respond sufficiently to the physical dangers faced by the Jews of Europe. By the time World War I broke out in 1914, there were eighty-five thousand Jews in Palestine, a vibrant community but small and defenseless.

Family with maternal grandmother, Batya Yatkovsky.

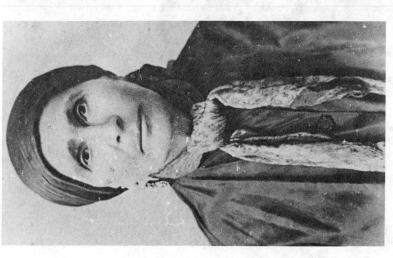

Paternal grandmother, Haya Frieda
Cohen, of Orsha.

Zeev Jabotinsky as an officer in the Jewish Legion (1917).

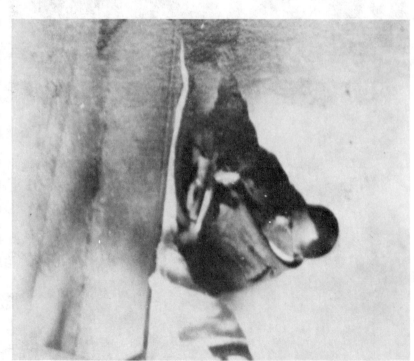

Zeev Jabotinsky in his Acre fortress jail cell.

Part Two: The Young Years of Palestine

I

The Great War

My first childhood memory is of the British attacking Palestine in 1917. I was four years old and I remember running in the dark as shells arched overhead in beautiful red and yellow balls, almost searing the leaves of the eucalyptus trees towering over us. The leaves fluttered horribly in the wind, sounding like an ocean whipped by storm. My mother led me with one hand, supporting my seventy-five year-old Grandmother Batya with the other; the ground shook under us as we ran. We only had to cross to the opposite side of a wide dirt road, but those few yards seemed to take hours.

We climbed down into the cellar of a building made of stone— our bomb shelter. The small cellar was packed with other members of the family and neighbors, and we could feel the tension as we sat pressed together in tight groups, on wooden benches. Most people were calm, expressing a mixture of exhaustion and resignation; at moments they almost looked bored. The last few years had taught them a stoicism which enabled them to keep their sanity. The shelling continued monotonously from the southwest. The British navy, lying off Jaffa, was slowly crumbling the Turkish lines. My parents and I had taken refuge with my grandmother in Petah-Tikvah in March when the Turkish commandant Djamal Pasha ordered us out of our home in Tel-Aviv. The Turks feared Jewish support for the British, so expulsion constantly hung over their heads. As the British drew near to Tel-Aviv, we were evicted from my birthplace, the home on Herzl Street.

In November, the battle line moved to Petah-Tikvah. Fighting became part of our daily life. During the day, we hid from the

Turks who were trying to expel us once more to the rear of their lines. At night, we sought safety from the bombs of the oncoming British, while praying for their arrival. During the day, our men were forced to dig trenches for the Turks. During the night, unearthing our guns, they guarded their property from the Turks and looting Arabs.

A volley of bombs fell near our shelter and the walls vibrated. I had no idea of why any of this was happening; I only knew I was afraid of all the noise—and I couldn't really remember any earlier time in my life when I hadn't been afraid.

A few days later, the *Da'alal*, (official town crier), came to Grandmother's door shortly after the evening's bombardment by the British. We had only just returned from the shelter. The *Da'alal* appeared regularly twice a day, bringing instructions from Turkish headquarters in Jaffa. We dreaded his visits, since he inevitably bore orders for us to quarter Turkish officers, help the troops prepare their defenses or do any of a thousand things that further limited our freedom. The *Da'alal* was a small, swarthy Sephardic Jew who wore a long, striped, dirt-stained, dusty robe and carried an official staff, trying to lend dignity to his position. He pounded loudly on my grandmother's terrace floor, and when we assembled, he made his announcement in a hoarse, dramatic voice. All refugees were to leave the colony within twenty-four hours and move north.

That night my family held council in Grandmother's small rooms. I could not understand what they said, but I listened to their low, urgent voices far into the night. Grandmother clutched me against her side as if afraid to put me to bed out of their sight. They talked straight through to the early morning hours as I slept in Grandmother's arms.

I understood years later some of the reasons for our latest deportation. Britain had issued the historic Balfour Declaration a few days earlier, supporting "the establishment in Palestine of a national home for the Jewish people." This declaration had reinforced Jewish support for the British and the allies. Trained Jewish combat battalions led by the rising Zionist leader Zeev Jabotinsky were on their way now to Palestine, one of them under the command of the British Colonel John Henry Patterson. These developments had convinced the Turks that they had to rid the front of the Jews as soon as possible.

Petah-Tikvah had become a refuge to many Jewish families throughout the war zone. When they were evicted from Tel-Aviv or Jaffa, they came to Petah-Tikvah. The roads and settlements farther north were already overcrowded with refugees and they were terrified of what the Turks would do to them once they were on the road. Other expelled Jewish communities had started out safely enough with laden carriages or mules. But once they came to a major crossroad, their carriages and animals were confiscated by the Turkish Army, and they had to abandon most of their belongings and continue on foot, with no idea where their next stop might be.

They became wanderers in their own land.

Early next morning, Mother took me to the old back wing of Grandmother's building. In this same spot thirty years earlier, Grandfather Zeev Leib had set up his temporary shack out of loose boards and straw mats.

To reach Grandmother's small room my mother and I had to climb a wooden stairway. We entered through the kitchen where rows of shining copper pots hung from nails. On the floor stood a large, tall, earthen jug, from which water was drawn by a two-handled copper dipper. There was a small wooden table, and simple unadorned wooden chairs. My mother hurried me across the creaking wooden floor to Grandmother's bedroom, separated from the kitchen by a partly drawn curtain. We knocked on the wooden frame and I could hear the rustle of her long black skirt as she approached the door. I could almost see her slow, precise movements. Grandmother ushered us in and quickly drew the curtain behind us. The shutters were tight, and before Grandmother said another word, she warned me to keep quiet. I knew enough to obey. She was a tiny, but stalwart woman, and I and the twenty other grandchildren were in complete awe of her. In her three-quarters of a century, she had endured things that the rest of us could not even imagine. Our parents held her in the deepest respect, and it was to her room that they came in times of trouble, not so much for her wisdom as for her warmth and sympathy, which made all problems less difficult.

Grandmother explained to us that the Turks intended to search every home for refugees and send them north by force. We would be no exception. Trying to soothe away our fear, Grandmother kept her kind, wrinkled face composed, and she repeated the plan to us calmly and methodically. Mother and I were to hide behind the wardrobe next to Grandmother's large brass bedstead. When the Turkish soldiers knocked on the door, Grandmother would do her best to dissuade them from searching the apartment. Father would take care of chores in the barn and when danger approached he would climb up and hide in the hay loft. We sat in Grandmother's room with the lights off the entire day. It was dark and bewildering to me, and I kept wanting to run away as fast as I could. Sometime during the afternoon a patrol of soldiers stopped in front of the house and I heard them knocking on the main door not far from our hiding place. My mother, following instructions, led me into the tight space between the wardrobe and the walls. Grandmother hurried to the main entrance.

We stood there in total darkness, my mother's hand gripping my shoulder. Before Grandmother returned it felt like hours. It turned out that the all-powerful *Bakshish* had worked its magic. The Turkish officer readily accepted Grandmother's argument that gold coins would be more useful to the Ottoman Empire than a couple of Jews. The officer went off a little richer and we were saved.

In a matter of weeks the British Imperial forces galloped into Petah-Tikvah, their horses drawing their artillery triumphantly behind them. Grandmother put up a refreshment stand in our courtyard and the women served orange juice and cake under the eucalyptus trees, to the tired, dusty Australian and Indian soldiers. The turbaned, big black Sikhs frightened us at first, but their smiling faces assured us they were friends. They lifted us onto their horses and let us hold their spears, which won us over for good. The Australians played with us and gave us chocolates and biscuits.

In December 1917 the refugees from Tel-Aviv were permitted by the British authorities to return to their homes. Father secured a wagon drawn by two mules, and we piled on all our belongings. Grandmother came down from her room to bid us farewell. She had on her black holiday silk with the usual dark kerchief around her small wrinkled face. Thin and frail, she was still the anchor of the family and her farewell blessing left us all in wonderful spirits.

II
The Hill of Spring

My parents walked most of the seven miles back to Tel-Aviv. I sat atop the cushions and blankets that covered our belongings, holding tight to a rope tied around the mountainous pile. The journey was thrilling to me. It was an amusement park ride: perched high above the luggage, wobbling and rolling as we jolted over rocks and bumps. When the cart caught in sand dunes, we clambered down to push. There were jokes at my expense, for all the pushing power I could generate at four years old.

We caught up with other wagons returning to Tel-Aviv, and friends shouted greetings and congratulations. Every time we stopped to water and rest the mules, the other wagons would halt. People would clasp hands again for the umpteenth time, trading gossip as if they had never left their town. The war was over and we all felt ourselves part of the victory. We were reunited, returning home.

Suddenly, instead of endless stretches of sand dunes heralded by a few scraggly vineyards, a small garden town sprang up. My parents told me it was our home, Tel-Aviv, "Hill of spring." There weren't more than ten short streets and a hundred houses then. But they were surrounded by green gardens and trees shaded the streets. Through the center of the city ran Rothschild Boulevard, and towering over the unpretentious little houses at the head of Herzl Street was the *Herzlia* Gymnasia. With its elaborate network of corridors, Gothic arches and sturdy oblong columns, the Gymnasia looked like part cathedral, part Turkish fortress.

We drove into Tel-Aviv and stopped in front of a two-story

stone building I didn't recognize. It looked strange and threatening after Grandmother's rambling country place. Father lifted me
from the wagon and led me into the house. When we entered a
small room overlooking the garden, I saw my bed and toys and
understood that we were back home. I wandered out hesitantly to
the backyard, and saw the small garden my father had cultivated
over the years. There were round, full, sumptuous pomegranates,
the *rimonim* of the Bible. There was the little orange tree bending
under the burden of its "golden apples." There were large lemon
trees, leafy banana, a tall mulberry tree whose fruit grew beyond
my reach.

The war still cast a shadow on our lives. Long rows of ambulances lined up in the street outside our home, waiting to discharge their wounded at the *Herzlia* Gymnasia, which had been
converted into a hospital. Lying in my own snug bed, I shuddered
at the moans and shrieks coming from the ambulances. I
remember the long rows of dirty, dejected Turkish prisoners,
mostly barefoot, who shuffled past our house. At the end of 1918
peace was proclaimed and the ambulances and prisoners slowly
disappeared. Tel-Aviv, in its small, quiet way, began to come into
its own.

It was a frontier town of barely a dozen streets which were our
playground. Whatever happened there—a new street laid out, the
first road paved, a new sidewalk built, a water pump installed or
foundations sunk for the main synagogue—each was a major
event in all our lives.

What an evening it was when for the first time electric street
lights went on! We gathered around the lamp post and stood
gazing at it in wonder. We had always used kerosene lamps in our
homes, and had only heard about electric lights. These brilliant
new lamps made us feel at once metropolitan. When my cousins
from Petah-Tikvah or Be'er Tuvia visited us, the street lamps were
inevitably the first topic for conversation. Home ceased to be the
only cozy spot during an evening as groups of us gathered at the
street corners. After supper, the children would run out to the
lamp post, staying there for all their games until bedtime. Since
the day we had returned to Tel-Aviv, I had been fascinated by the
imperious, stark white building that dominated the head of Herzl
Street. I repeatedly asked Father with impatience when I could

begin school. He smiled, stroked his moustache and said, "Wait, you will have time enough there. Once you start we will probably have trouble keeping you in. . . ."

But for the first time in my memory, father was wrong. Our imaginative young teachers made us feel part of their great experiment, and *Herzlia* became the center of our lives. The holidays we celebrated in school passed like a pageant through the year, commemorating our national past, its heroes and glory. Here in the homeland they seemed inseparable from our everyday lives. We lit the Hanukkah candles, we were told of the victories of the valiant Maccabees. We threw parties, traded gifts and paraded through the streets with torches, as a giant menorah shone over the municipal water tower. At the end of February, when the heavy rains ceased, we celebrated *Tu B'Shevat* (the New Year of the Trees). Children participated in the reclamation of the soil and planted saplings in the parks and fields. On Purim we heard the Scroll of Esther read in the Synagogue and celebrated the downfall of Haman, the evil counselor who plotted to kill the Jews of Persia thousands of years earlier. In later years, tourists would flock from all parts of the world to see our great carnival, the *Ad-lo-yada*. Children masqueraded in brightly-colored costumes and the adults lined the streets, cheering them on.

Passover in Palestine was an emotional time for my family. Remembering the exodus of our own fathers and grandfathers, we reenacted the age-old drama. We cleaned our home thoroughly, and I helped carry the utensils and pots out to the sand dunes, where we "kashered" them in large boiling pots. Then we picked up freshly baked matzohs at the bakery, carrying them home in laundered sheets. We took everything to Petah-Tikvah, and there at the seder with my grandmother, we read the Haggadah, drank the wine and recalled the "blood libels" and pogroms, the priests with crosses and incense leading *mujiks* against us to avenge Christ. The stories sounded remote and impossible, like the stories we read in school about medieval Spain and the Inquisition.

We celebrated and lit bonfires on *Lag B'omer*, this time commemorating the revolt of Bar Kochba, who had led the Jews back to independence in Jerusalem before being martyred by the Romans in 135 C.E.

These celebrations made us feel that two thousand years of
exile had never cut us off from our past. The first book we read
was a child's version of Genesis and Exodus, and at home or at
school the stories of the Bible were the ones we heard.

I met Tom Sawyer, Huckleberry Finn, and Little Lord Faunt-
leroy only years later. They were not as real or present to us, not as
natural as the stories of the Bible, which were part of Eretz-Israel.
We took extended field trips once a year and the country became
our textbook.

We were the first Jewish children in thousands of years who
shared in a widespread linguistic and cultural rebirth. I heard my
first Hebrew opera in Tel-Aviv at the age of ten. Literature,
mathematics, chemistry, physics and biology—all were taught in
Hebrew. It was a true, full-blown Renaissance in the early twenties, most of our school work was oral and the notes we took from
lectures became textbooks for the classes to follow.

From our first year in school, we were proud of our flag,
anthem and history. We accepted it as nothing remarkable, the
way children always accept their lives. We didn't know that only
twenty years earlier, Hebrew were considered a dead language, or
at best a "sacred tongue." Not until I traveled through the
diaspora as an adult did I feel the full thrill of having belonged to
the first generation of a reborn nation.

In a way, we were spoiled. Thanks to our strong identity, we
escaped many of the torments that Jewish children faced in the
diaspora. When our parents clashed with the Arabs in the 1920's,
we never saw it as gentile persecution from which we had to run;
we only developed a stronger national consciousness. We became
more certain that we belonged where we were.

In the early days, Jew and Arab accepted one another. Palestinian Arabs flocked to work in the growing Jewish cities and
settlements, and the Jews made friends with them. I met Arabs in
my own home in Tel-Aviv, in my grandmother's home and at my
father's shop in Jaffa. I never felt antagonism towards them, and I
grew to understand their economic and social plight. Even when I
faced attacking mobs of Arabs years later, I had no blanket hatred
for them

III
"Gateway to Hope"
(Petah-Tikvah 1921)

"And I will give her her vineyards for . . .
a door of hope . . . as in the days of her
youth . . . as in the day when she came up,
out of the land of Egypt."   (Hosea 2:17)

On Thursday, May 5, 1921, the streets of Petah-Tikvah
no longer basked in their morning serenity. The farmers
were not in the fields, but at the settlement's headquarters in tense
debates about the settlement's safety. Just the Sunday before,
news of battles between Jews and Arabs had first reached the
settlement.

My parents and I had been visiting Grandmother during Passover, planning to leave when the holiday ended five days earlier.
The reports kept Mother and me where we were, while my father
returned early on Sunday to his business in Jaffa.

After forty years in the settlement, Grandmother's relatives
constituted a good part of the population, and her house served as
headquarters for many of the farmers. Today, the gathering on
Grandmother's white-tiled terrace, which overlooked the main
street, was like a small Town Hall meeting. For a few days,
communications between Petah-Tikvah and Tel-Aviv were cut
off, and by the time we made contact, the Jewish dead in Jaffa
numbered more than forty. Most of them were recent immigrants
who had been trapped inside the Immigrant House in the heart of
the Arab city. An Arab mob suddenly swarmed the Immigrant
House, and those inside were totally unprepared to defend them-

selves. An Arab friend of my father's saved him from almost certain death. As the mob surged down Boostros Street, Father's friend raced ahead of them, burst into the shop, shouted to Father to lower the shutters and ran with him to a friend's apartment across the street. Father looked down helplessly from an upper story as Jewish merchants and passersby were clubbed and stabbed to death. The mobs surrounded isolated Jewish homes, murdered those inside, mutilated their bodies, ransacked and burned their homes. The mob raged for hours, until the Jews of Tel-Aviv could organize self-defense units. Finally, together with soldiers of the Jewish Battalion, they dispersed the mob and halted the massacres.

This was the second such attack in modern Palestine's history, and the second in a year. In 1920, the surge of Pan-Arabism began when an Arab mob ran wild in the streets of the old walled city of Jerusalem killing, burning and looting.

The Arabs in Palestine had many different backgrounds. There were the El Masris from Egypt, the Halabys from Northern and the Houranis from Southern Syria. The rootless nomadic Bedouins from anywhere—always ready to loot and steal from the settlers or other Arabs. The hard-working *Fellahin*, poor, sickly, illiterate tenant farmers, wanted nothing more than a chance to earn a living for their families. After a day's backbreaking work, they gathered on the village garbage mound to tell stories and smoke a cigarette. The city Arabs were both cunning and lazy. They lived by money-lending and other non-productive occupations. They spent most of their days in coffee houses off the main roads or on the wharves, drawing at their bubbling hookahs. They were ready at a moment's notice to make a deal with anyone, if it meant a few more *piastres* in their pockets. There were also more privileged Arabs: wealthy absentee landlords who lived in Beirut or Cairo, leasing land to tenant farmers who often ended up starving, Arab storekeepers and artisans, and the owners of the *Khans*, the overnight hotels scattered around the country. Many of these Arabs and Jews formed close friendships and after the first attacks in Jerusalem in 1920, these old settlers could not recover from the shock.

Despite the Balfour Declaration of 1917, favoring Palestine as a Jewish homeland, the friendly relations between Jews and Arabs continued relatively undisturbed until 1920. Feisal, the son of the respected Arab nationalist leader Sherif Hussein, welcomed the Balfour Declaration and was in favor of Jewish immigration into Palestine. Whatever place Jerusalem's Mosque of Omar occupied in the hearts of Moslems, Feisal believed the Arab's national interests were directed toward the traditional religious and cultural centers—Mecca and Medina, Baghdad and Damascus.

From 1917 to 1920, Arabs in Palestine accepted as fact that Palestine was to become a Jewish country. When Sir Herbert Samuel, a British Jew, was appointed as High Commissioner, the legend spread among the Arabs that at last the Jews were going to have their *Malek*, their "king." Many actually congratulated their Jewish friends on the happy turn of events.

Gradually, however, things went wrong at the "top." Local administrators of the British Colonial Office, with the tacit consent of London, began to institute anti-Zionist policies which were more than slightly tinged with anti-Semitism. General Allenby arrived to help see that the Balfour Declaration was carried out, but instead he spoke as if the Declaration never existed. The British governors and the military command simply refused to carry out London's orders to open immigration. To justify their hostile tactics they referred to the Jews as dangerous "Bolsheviks" and conspirators. The British military, plotting against the Jews and the French, aimed to build a puppet-ruled Arab Federation of Palestine, Syria, Iraq and Hedjaz. Feisal's abortive coup in 1920 against the French Mandatory administration in Syria was financed by British gold.[1]

The general unrest in Palestine fit into the Empire's schemes for future control of the entire Near East. Tension across the country mounted, until by the time of the riots in 1920 in Jerusalem, a strange, dull hatred appeared between Jews and Arabs who had previously been friends.

Herbert Samuel, the High Commissioner, finally stripped the Jews of their last hope for support from the local government. Although an observant Jew, he turned out to be above all a servant of His Majesty George V. His first act following the riots of 1920 was to grant amnesty to the chief instigator, Haj

---

[1] Horace B. Samuel, *Revolt by Leave*, The New Zionist Press, London, 1936.

Amin el Husseini, by appointing him Grand Mufti of Jerusalem for life.

In May 1921, Petah-Tikvah's Council had learned from friendly Arabs that agitators had traveled as far as Nablus, in the Hills of Samaria and to Tulkarem, all for one purpose—to amass Arabs for an attack on Petah-Tikvah. It was to be destroyed; its people massacred. Thousands of Arabs from different directions had been converging on the settlement over the past few days, by foot, by cart and on horseback.

The Petah-Tikvah Council called for a general mobilization. The men and older boys assembled in the center of the settlement, on the main street and on Grandmother's terrace. I knew many of them; they were from the first families of settlers.

Benjamin, a friend of my oldest cousins, was there with his father Yehuda. Though Yehuda was in his early seventies, he was still strong and erect, with a full white beard which gave dignity to his massive frame. He was reputed by Jews and Arabs alike to be a courageous fighter, and he stood there leaning on his rifle, his hands gripped firmly around the barrel. Over forty years before, he had been one of the six founders of the settlement, bringing his family to Jerusalem from a farm in Hungary.

Yehuda used to tell how the old Arab village, Melabes, looked in the 1880's, the abject Arab tenant farmers turned yellow by malaria, and their naked, pot-bellied children growing closer to death each day in their squalid huts.

When the settlers first planned to purchase the land, they asked a Greek physician from Jerusalem to inspect the site, and he reported that it wasn't fit for beasts. In all the hours he spent there, not one bird flew over. Surely the place was a graveyard, if even birds veered away from it.

The settlers did not listen to him. People called them "the insane idealists," but they gave up their homes and professions and moved to a place where they supposedly could not survive. Because of them, a wilderness not fit for beasts had become a home for men and women.

These and other tales were told about the settlement's early days many times. But one was particularly legendary. That was the story of Daud Abu Yousef, the Jewish Bedouin, whom only a few others besides Yehuda could still remember. Daud had appeared one day riding a pure-blooded Arabian mare. Galloping up and down the main street of the colony several times, Daud kept staring at the colonists with wild, incredulous eyes, as if they were a race he could not recognize. At last he dismounted and to their surprise introduced himself as a Jew, even reciting a Hebrew prayer to prove it. He told them that he belonged to a small tribe of Jewish Bedouins who roamed southern Arabia.

Daud was lean, quick, and strong, and he soon became watchman of the colony. He disdained guns, carrying a long sword instead. Once, when a group of bandits attacked the colony's cattle herd, he dashed to the spot from the other end of the colony. Brandishing his sword, he overcame the leader of the bandits and threw him howling across his horse. The band scattered in terror, and Daud brought his prisoner back as a trophy.

Daud played a musical instrument which he had fashioned out of a comb and some camel's hair. Playing the comb like an instrument, Daud drew enchanting strains from it, and won a reputation among the neighboring Bedouin tribes as a singer of romantic desert ballads. Sheik Abu Kishik presented him with a red saddle, red boots and belt as a token of appreciation, and it was common to see Daud, resplendent in his boots and saddle, piping his melodies at the neighboring Arab festivals.

Exactly a year after he had appeared, he mounted his horse and rode off, and that was the last they ever saw of him.

As the men of Petah-Tikvah assembled now on this day in May 1921, preparing to defend themselves against the attackers, some of them joked that they wished Daud was there to help them.

Avshalom, a battle officer in the Turkish Army, was destined to be a leader in the community. His experience had given him the poise and confidence needed to guide the settlers through this difficult time. Wearing an ammunition belt across his chest and a rifle slung over his shoulder, he asked:

"Why does the Mufti incite against us? For trying to make this something more than a desert? What have they created that makes them masters of this land? What have Arab invasions left behind here besides battlegrounds, marshes and graveyards?"

"And why do they see us as so priviledged?" asked young Benjamin. "We were so happy when the British overthrew the Turks. But the British have not made life so pleasant for us. They have given most government jobs to Arabs. How many Jews are in the police? How many in the courts? How many in the land registry offices?

"No more than a few," Avshalom joined in. "We pay 60 percent of the taxes, and get less than a quarter of the benefits in jobs, hospitals, public works and education."

"I say that even the Turks treated us better," said Benjamin.

"The British would like us better," said Avshalom, "if we *were* savages. Then they could civilize us." They all laughed.

The men grew grimmer as the morning advanced. The women brought out food and drink. Rifles and pistols the men carried were illegal, and if they were caught carrying them they could be sentenced to years in prison. The administration forbade owner-ship of arms by Jewish settlers, since "it was the responsibility of the government to assure security and order to the land." For some strange reason, though, during the past five days, not a single officer or policeman had appeared in the village. The local police, made up of a few Arabs and Jews, had essentially ceased to exist. The Arab police had bolted when the first news of the Jaffa riots reached the village. The Jewish policemen, trying to interfere as little as possible, kept to their quarters, leaving things to the settlers.

No laws could stop the men of Petah-Tikvah from unearthing their few hidden rifles. They posted scouts all around the settle-ments, and atop the water tower. They set up a receiving and transmitting station for semaphores manned by boy scouts. The moment one of the scouts spotted a movement in the fields or groves, they would signal the water tower, and a messenger would be dispatched to the local council a block away.

As the Palestinian sun rose high, a warm wind blew from the east, and some of the tension abated. Waiting for their orders, the men leaned against the walls, smoking their pipes or quietly conversing. If the attackers should come only from the camps of Abu Kishik to the west, Avshalom explained, the settlers could repel them. And if the Arabs of Feja in the northeast joined those of Abu Kishik, the settlers might well handle them too. But if the attacks came from the east at the same time, with the village of Yahudia and other northern Arab villages taking part, it would be impossible to put up a sufficient line of defense. There were not enough men, and not enough guns.

Some suggested they should abandon the farms on the out-skirts and fall back into the center of the colony, where the larger, sturdier stone buildings would give them better shelter. Others, especially those whose farms were on the outskirts, opposed this plan.

Avshalom's proposal finally won out. At first only the women and children would be assembled in the center of the village, in a few of the larger stone buildings. The men would stay on the perimeters and hold their positions as long as possible. If there should be imminent danger of being surrounded, they would retreat slowly toward the center of the village without exposing their flanks, and set up a defense line around the key buildings the families were in.

The council on the terrace adjourned. Some of the men walked to the council building. Others rode to their posts on the outskirts. A large group stayed near Grandmother's house. These were the reserve unit, about sixty men, who were to wait until the battle began. At the first sign of trouble they were to mount their horses and ride to the spot.

Abraham Shapiro was put in command of the reserves. He was an old-timer who in the smaller skirmishes scattered scores of trespassers by riding his horse wildly through their ranks. How-ever, any attempt today at such spectacular exploits would be doomed to failure. This was no longer a few individuals tangled in a brief battle. This was to be full-scale military warfare.

Before the men had even reached their posts, the alarm bell started tolling. A messenger dashed over to our terrace. The word passed among the women and children. They're coming! Abu Kishik and his tribe are advancing on the packing house through the fields and orange groves! Five hundred of them, and there may be more behind!

A column of thirty pairs of horsemen rode toward the threat-ened attack. No one cried out. The street became eerily quiet. With the men gone, those left behind suddenly felt naked and defenseless. We decided to leave the big family house and move to the stone building across the street, the one we had used for a shelter from the British bombs in 1917. There were about forty women and children in our family group.

In the stone house, my aunts placed our biggest kettles on the kitchen stove, pouring water into them and fanning the fires. We carried in more water from the pump in the courtyard. Some were bringing in large rocks, placing them on the window sills. Not quite understanding all these preparations, I asked my mother's permission to help carry the rocks, but she led me into a small room and told me to stay there with two young cousins. "And if you hear any shooting," she added, "get under the bed and wait till we come to get you."

Since I wasn't allowed to carry the rocks, I decided to see what it was like under the big bed. My two cousins, a boy and a girl my age, joined me lying on the dusty floor. Yoav proudly showed me his dirty hands. "I helped carry rocks. We're going to throw them at the Arabs if they get through. Did you see the water boiling in the kitchen? My mother says it's the best way to stop a mob."

Later we learned that more than three thousand Arab attackers from thirty-two villages had advanced on our settlement. They carried hand grenades and automatic weapons and brought carts, women and children to carry away the loot. Rocks and hot water were a pitiful defense. But lying there in the dark room, I was very excited and wanted to be part of it. I burned with envy that Yoav had gotten to carry rocks. I decided to get out from under the bed and go outside. Whether my mother liked it or not, I was going to bring in rocks, too.

As soon as I stood up, I heard shots. I scuttled back under the bed. More shots were fired. They seemed to come from the direction of the packing house. Suddenly, the sound of shattering glass filled the room. We ducked our heads and didn't look up once until my aunt ran into the room. "What happened?" we asked. Her face turned crimson. "Look what they've done!" she exclaimed. "They've broken my beautiful vase!" A bullet through the open window had struck the glass vase hanging on the wall over the bed, showering the bed with bits of glass.

Shortly after noon, the shooting died down, and we were permitted to join the rest of the family in the living room. The men had not yet returned, and there were rumors that there had been many casualties. We learned that a number of wounded men were brought to the council building where a temporary hospital was set up.

Our mothers put some food on a table for us in a corner and we swallowed quickly in silence. The women sat, waiting tensely for messengers bringing news. Every once in a while a volley of shots rang out. Whenever men brought the wounded in, they passed near our house but rode off without a word in answer to the women's questions. And each time they left, we would sit in a stony silence.

Finally a few riders came in, the younger reserves who had left from the terrace hours earlier. They were tight-lipped, and the women looked at them without daring to speak. The men walked in ignoring everyone, dropped their rifles and cartridge belts and sat down, staring into space. One woman brought in a pitcher of orange juice, and a few men drank from it. But none spoke. At last, one of my aunts approached Yosef, one of the youngest. "Did we lose many?" she said.

Looking down, his head in his hands, he muttered, "Four . . . four too many."

No one said another word. The women remained motionless. Faint noises of horse hooves could be heard approaching. One of the men woefully whispered: "I'll never forget the sight of him. Never . . ." Avshalom's brother, standing near one of the windows, turned ashen and abruptly walked out of the room.

Slowly the story came out. When the riders had reached the outskirts, the advance posts told them that hundreds of well-armed Arabs were grouping around the packing house, preparing to break through the lines into the heart of the colony. The Arabs had sent scouts, but the advance posts sent them running with a few well-aimed shots. Everything had been quiet; the Arabs were probably holding a council of war. Abraham, the veteran who commanded the reserves, called several leaders over and advised them of his plan—to ride into the open field, fanning out into a wide frontal line. Then, on signal, they would attack, riding as hard as they could and firing in unison, making as much commotion as possible. The Arabs had a wholesome respect for a mounted man with a gun, and in the past this gambit had always scattered them.

Some of the men pleaded against this. Maybe, they argued, the Arabs were just waiting for something like this. Maybe it was a trap. There were too many Arabs to frighten so easily, and once the settlers were out in the open they would be sitting ducks. Shouldn't they send a few scouts first?

Abraham insisted that they had no time to lose. They had to finish here and return to the center of the village to face possible attacks from other sides.

The order was given to mount and charge. The men climbed into the stirrups, fanned out one abreast of another, and slowly moved toward the open field, waiting for the signal. Suddenly shots came at them from all directions, one volley after the next—from behind every boulder, every tree, every fence, post or bush. Six of the riders were instantly hit. Two slumped off their horses onto the ground. The Arabs ran out from their ambush with blood-curdling screams. The settlers could not even see them through the clouds of dust.

The order was given to retreat to the orange groves. Either not hearing the order, or ignoring it, Avshalom charged forward. He galloped about two hundred yards, shooting left and right, headed directly toward the packing house where the Arab leaders were believed to be. Half a dozen Arabs leaped from ambush on top of Avshalom's horse. He emptied his gun at them, hitting two, then swung at their heads with his empty pistol. They pinned his arms back and dragged him from his horse. Some of the men started to his rescue, but were ordered by the commander to retreat and take shelter. Praying that by some miracle they might find Avshalom alive, they fell back to their original positions, carrying their wounded.

While the dead and wounded were taken to the rear, the defenders changed their tactics. This time, they left their horses behind and didn't make a sound, but held their fire. They had a few good rifles which, in the hands of the sharpshooters, would give them an advantage. Running from bush to bush, or crawling on their stomachs, they gradually improved their defense line. This time the Arabs were caught by surprise. Still celebrating the earlier rout of settlers, and the capture of two houses on the edge of the settlement, the Arabs concentrated on looting. The accurate fire threw them into a frenzy and within an hour, they turned around and fled.

While looking after the Arab wounded, one of the men came across the body of Avshalom. His abdomen had been slashed open and his shoes stuffed into the gaping wound.

When the defense posts on the perimeters reported that the Arabs were returning to their villages, the settlement felt safe. When evening came, they buried their dead. There were no speeches or tears. The settlers marched silently to the cemetery in final tribute. We grieved, but we felt more pride than pity for the dead.

They had not been murdered in their beds, nor burned and torn apart by shrieking mobs as their forefathers in Russia had been. They had not died defenseless. They faced danger and death as free men, and as free men they fell.

IV
On Learning

There is a bit of folklore handed down by the Rabbi Zvi Hirsch Kaidanower of the 17th century.

"When the time has come for the child to go to school . . . the father should rise early . . . and take the child . . . to the house of the teacher. Whether the father is . . . a great man, an elder, or a master, he must not be ashamed to take his son to school this first time. . . . On this errand the mother or father has the duty of shielding the child with a mantle so that nothing unclean in the world can lay eyes upon it. . . . Then a slate shall be brought on which the aleph-bet is written . . . and the child shall repeat the letters after the teacher. . . . Thereupon, the father should take the child again and carry it home, in such manner that the child may see nothing unclean. And it is right that on this day both father and mother fast and pray that the child may prosper in the Torah and the fear of God, and live in good wishes all his days and years."

When I was five years old my mother took me by the hand and walked me to the nursery school. It was a few minutes walk, just behind the imposing *Herzlia* Gymnasia at the head of our street. The nursery was a small, typical, one-story house made of sandstone, with a red-tiled roof. We walked up a steep set of steps; at the top was a tiled terrace and a large room. My mother introduced me to the teacher, then kissed me, and abruptly left.

My parents had infinite respect for education, and they made sure their only child had the best. They knew no better way to show their love than to obey the words in Great-grandfather Shneour Levi's will: ". . . watch over your sons and daughters with wide open eyes . . . do not economize . . . but obtain for them the

48

best teachers available. . . ."

Through the centuries, the Jewish people acquired respect for worldly goods. Money could buy them safety or escape, and sometimes even respectability. But there were always Jews, teachers or simple men and women, who eschewed material wealth, insisting that what mattered, what was uniquely Jewish, was the continual quest for knowledge. We were the people of the Book, of the Bible, of the Prophets. Some even claimed that "the chosen people," Jews, did not need to concern themselves with the base physical world.

Certain men, especially *Hasidim*, like Rabbi Shneour Zalman of Lyady, combined the best of both philosophies, forging a compassionate and workable code of life for the simple man. In this code, study, prayer and good hard labor all had equal shares. My parents' love and respect of learning filtered down from Rabbi Shneour Zalman through Great-grandfather Shneour Levi, who lived by Rabbi's *Habad* precepts.

From nursery school on, my education was totally in Hebrew. Even Rabbi Zalman and Great-grandfather never dreamed of such a thing. The average immigrant Jewish family out of the Pale did not teach Hebrew to its children. It was still the language of prayer, not to be defiled by daily use. Eliezer Ben Yehuda did not inaugurate secular Hebrew until the start of 1881, and when he did, he was condemned by pious Jews, denounced to the Turkish administration and sentenced to a year in jail. This did not temper his single-minded championing of Hebrew as a modern national language, and after his release he coined new words, composed a modern dictionary, and continued to teach the language.

Four preparatory years then eight years of gymnasia, were all taught in Eliezer Ben Yehuda's modern Hebrew. I entered *Herzlia* at the age of six. When I was ten, I heard my first opera in Hebrew, "La Traviata." My classmates and I were taken to gaze uncomprehendingly at Reuven Rubin's exhibition of flaming red and brown landscape paintings of Eretz-Israel. We watched the pioneer dancer Baruch Agadati as he leaped and whirled through Hasidic and Yemenite folk dances. We read Victor Hugo and Shakespeare and Romaine Roland all in Hebrew translations and in the upper grades we read them again in their original language. By the time we graduated, we knew Arabic, English and French.

Our teachers literally inundated us with learning; guided, punished and cajoled us, trying to mold us into cultured members of a new Hebrew nation.

We grew up knowing nothing about Christian holidays. We hardly knew any Christians. My father had a few German business friends who were Christians, but I never even entered a church until I visited Jerusalem's Old City in the late 1920's. My parents did not implant hatred of Christianity in our minds, but they did keep away from it, perhaps remembering centuries of persecutions; and as a child I never knew one denomination from another. There were no Christians in Tel-Aviv for us to have any understanding of their religion. In Jaffa we skirted their forbidding churches, we saw the clean-shaven men and the strangely dressed priests and nuns, but they were not part of our lives. Our own world, revolving around young Tel-Aviv and the farming settlements of the coastal plains, was all-absorbing.

As the twenties rolled on, the Jewish community across the land grew. The new friends I made in school, from Poland, Russia and Germany, described to me the rising anti-Semitism and repression which had forced their families to emigrate. Before long, I could measure the troubles in Europe by the new settlements, streets and faces. Strangers shared my courtyard. Distant cousins who spoke only Yiddish and Polish arrived from Grodno and moved into our house. We expanded the second floor and moved upstairs, while the room I was born in was converted to a pharmacy. The cousins, who complained constantly about the conditions, finally went back to Poland.

* * *

On Shavuot, 1926, my relatives came from all over Palestine for my Bar Mitzvah in Petah-Tikvah. We held the services in the old synagogue which Grandfather Zeev Leib helped found, and I sat with my uncles near the pew of honor at the eastern wall which the men of my family had occupied for decades. I had studied my *Haftara* for months, but when the time came to read it from the raised platform in the center of the synagogue, the cantor and beadle decided they could not trust me to recite the chapter from Ezekiel which was the portion for that Sabbath. Wounded to the heart, I was permitted to read the blessings only. The cantor recited the chapter. Probably out of sheer spite, I can still recite my *Haftara* today word for word.

The religious ceremony was followed by a celebration in Grandmother Batya's family home. Grandmother died six years before, but her children, grandchildren and great-grandchildren were there, and even some of Zeev Leib and Batya's surviving friends put in an appearance at the sprawling old three-winged house.

My first forays into political activism were in an after-school club at *Herzlia*. We gathered in the late afternoons to argue the merits and failures of our teachers. We felt *Herzlia* was foisting too general and European an education on us, when we wanted to search deeper into our Jewish roots. One of my friends, an apprentice printer at his father's shop, suggested we put out a periodical, and the principal gave us the use of a basement. At that time we were immersed in the humanities so we named our paper the "Classicon."

I plunged into writing with a passion, often neglecting my studies to work on an article. It was so wonderful to be writing something *substantial*, something that would be seen by more than a teacher! It gave me a heady feeling of truly being able to affect things. We distributed the paper to most of the student body and it created quite a stir. Here were the most dedicated pioneers of the Hebrew national revival being reproached by their pupils, no less, for failure to expose us sufficiently to Judaic lore! Rebels themselves against the traditionalists, they were getting criticized for carrying their rebellion too far . . . I wrote proposing that we add to the curriculum a class on the history of Zionism, and on current Jewish events throughout Europe. We wanted to know our generation's place in Jewish history and our relation to the Jews of the diaspora. We wanted to understand the political origins of our life in Palestine and the social structure of our society, we were starting to shed our innocence.

V
Political Awareness

As Britain tilted away from the Balfour Declaration, it declared the "Protection of Arab Rights" as the major responsibility of its mandate in Palestine. Then Herbert Samuel adopted the principle of "economic absorptive capacity" as a guideline to restrict Jewish immigration.

In 1922, Colonial Secretary Winston Churchill's White Paper formally and unilaterally partitioned the original Palestine Mandate area and created the protectorate of Trans-Jordan. This reduced the Jewish national home promised in the Balfour Declaration five years before, from forty-four thousand to ten thousand square miles. The maneuver simultaneously solved a number of vexing problems for the British: it compensated Faisal and the Hashemites for the loss of Syria by giving them a new territory to rule; it clipped the wings of Jews who wanted larger colonization and immigration; and it gave the British easier control over unruly Bedouin tribes by leaving the policing of the areas to a Bedouin chieftain.

In those relatively quiet years from 1922 to 1929, the Jews in Palestine did not comprehend how calamitous those developments would be for Jewish life in Palestine and Europe.

The "Classicon" that my friends and I published was the closest I had come to politics, and it whetted my appetite. I was not yet fifteen years old when I started attending the Saturday afternoon "Circle" meetings at my schoolmate Sarah's home. The "Circles" were part of a Zionist Socialist youth movement concerned with social issues, political ideology and the economic structure of the community. We went deeply into the essays of Ahad Ha'am,

52

whose work held sway over Zionist thought.

They also had a special significance for me. As a young boy, I had known an old man who lived in a small, white house next to the Gymnaṣia. The shutters of the house were usually closed, and the garden in front of it was always choked with weeds. Once in a while the old man emerged and leaning on his cane, walked slowly, to our school yard. He would sit on a chair, taking in the sun and smiling benignly as he watched the children through his heavy glasses. This was Asher Ginzberg, known by his pen name of Ahad Ha'am. Our teachers admonished us always to treat him with great respect, as he was a very important man. It was a little hard for us to believe. As we watched him leaning on his cane, his bald head glistening in the sun and the veins delicately outlined in his high forehead, he seemed to be the mildest creature in the world.

However, his teachings were powerful in their effect on Zionist thinking. His amalgam of lofty spiritual values and pride in the uniqueness of Jewish ethical heritage appealed to our young idealism. Ahad Ha'am believed that Jews had a distinctive consciousness of national survival, every bit as powerful as the individual ego's instinct for survival. This national instinct, Ahad Ha'am felt, had to be nourished by a renascent spiritual center. But, he said, this did not necessarily mean a Jewish *state*—as a modern political entity. Founded on pure justice and morality, this center would give strength, pride and fulfillment to the masses of Jews across the globe. It would represent a cultural rebirth leading to a gradual physical rebirth. Once the highest ethical and spiritual standards were achieved, this nucleus living in Eretz-Israel might one day evolve into a true Jewish State, one that rejected the gross world of power and physical force, thereby serving as an example to all humanity. When the spiritual core was wholesome, not only the Jews but the entire world's problems would be helped.

These were captivating ideas to us; they simplified complexities, and promised a clean, sweet, moral world free of political danger and economic inequities.

When we discussed Ahad Ha'am in the "Circle," I always had in my mind an image of that kindly old man innocently watching the children in the schoolyard. I imagined him as peaceful with himself in the serene twilight of his life and wanted to feel as satisfied that I had done my best for my people when I reached his age.

Sometimes my "missionary zeal" made life difficult for my family. My own mother's brothers were among those who hired Arabs rather than Jews to work on their farms and when I remonstrated with my mother about that, she insisted that her brothers would ruin themselves economically if they depended on Jewish workers. Her answer gave me little satisfaction. How could we refuse to give employment to our own people? Would the settlers have survived Zeev Leib's days if they had not helped one another? Would our family have survived if Baron Rothschild had not helped us?

"We are not Rothschild," Mother answered. "Let them struggle as we did and they will manage."

Our "Circle" did not agree. Children of the middle class, we condemned our parents' "indifference" to the growing social problems. Quoting Ahad Ha'am, and our Socialist leaders, we vowed that the injustices and inequalities of the diaspora would never be repeated here. And as we slowly brought the masses from the Pale to Palestine, we would have to re-educate them or they would continue to live as they always had. In *Hachshara* camps, we would train them as farmers and craftsmen preparing them for our new egalitarian society.

Like Ahad Ha'am, we felt that all of this had to be a gradual process. The last thing we wanted was to revive the philosopher Max Nordau's ideas about "dumping" half a million Jews "cold" on the beaches of Eretz-Israel. Nordau, Herzl's chief lieutenant, had believed that the problems with the Arabs and the British could be solved easily by mass Jewish immigration and a resulting Jewish majority and the prompt creation of a Jewish State. In our mind, though, there was nothing so magical about a majority or a state—Nordau's "State" would be full of "air people" like the ghettos of Eastern Europe—people wandering around homeless, rootless and probably half-starved.

And, as for the "Arab problem," we would not solve it by creating a Jewish majority, but by forging links to the Arab worker who was exploited by the Arab effendi class. The effendis, supported by the Imperial Colonial power, were the main beneficiaries of the Jewish-Arab conflict. But with solidarity between

"The Circle" (Zionist-Socialist) youth group. Author top, second from right.

A meeting of the student fraternity El-Al (December 1935), celebrating Eliezer Ben Yehuda's birthday, presided by Prof. Joseph Klausner. Author bottom, second from left.

Students' conference in Tel-Aviv, August 1931.

the Jewish and Arab workers, we would one day overcome the capitalists and the British imperialists. Arabs and Jews would live in harmony, in a moral, prosperous Socialist society guaranteeing freedom for all citizens. Whether these two nations lived together or side by side did not matter, they would still be equal.

Our "Circles" were not unique in their Jewish and Zionist Socialist thinking. By the end of the nineteenth century, half of the Pale's five million Jews were proletarian, and out of their class a powerful drive for social justice emerged. Jews constituted almost half of the delegates to the Second Russian Social Democratic Party Congress in 1903, and shortly after, the Jewish Social Democratic Party (the Bund) was formed. For the "Bundist" ideologues Zionism was sentimental claptrap, "Bourgeois Utopianism" created by Jewish capitalists and spoon-fed to the workers to misdirect their struggle and keep them in their place. Rich Jews were enemies of the working class just like rich non-Jews, and the battleground for survival was right there in the diaspora.

In 1905, Ber Borochov laid the groundwork for Marxist Zionism. Borchov maintained that ultimately the Jewish masses had to create their own just society outside of the diaspora. To achieve economic independence as well as political independence, they had to carry their class struggle to Palestine. The writer A. D. Gordon also believed that the economic and ethical uplifting of the Jew has to take place in Palestine and he offered himself as an example. Like Tolstoy, Gordon left a comfortable, sedentary life in Russia to become a laborer. He formulated his "religion of labor"; manual labor would transform the Jews out of the Pale into constructive individuals who could build a healthy, permanent nation.

At our Friday night gatherings, we heatedly debated the theories of the many Zionist philosophers. The meetings, in the modest cabin behind the *Herzlia* gymnasia, attracted young people from several high schools in the city. We invited speakers who represented the whole gamut of views within the Labor movement, from Meir Yaari of *Hashomer Hatzair* on the far left, to Itzhak Ben Zvi[1] on the right. Wiry, energetic David Ben-Gurion came; so did stuffy Moshe Shertok (Sharett)[2] and fiery young Israel Galili,

---

[1] He became the second President of Israel (1952).
[2] The first foreign minister of Israel.

who eulogized kibbutz life. We drew from all of them and from all sources of Zionist history, though our deepest affinities were for Ahad Ha'am, Borochov and A. D. Gordon.

In 1928, I spent the summer near Rehovoth on Kibbutz Na'an, a communal settlement of the *Hanoar Haoved* ("working youth") movement. Kibbutz Na'an was preparing to move to its own land and join the larger kibbutz movement. We lived in temporary wooden huts, and since the kibbutz was broke, as most were in those years, we city kids got an excellent taste of the demands of communal farm life.

As an only child from a comfortable home, I was struck first by the total lack of privacy. We lived four or more in a room and when we worked or ate, there were always scores of others rubbing elbows with us. We rose at five, breakfasted on bread, crushed eggplant and tea, worked for hours under a broiling sun in the groves and lunched again, mostly on eggplant. All of our wages went to the kibbutz. I thought of A. D. Gordon and Tolstoy, and felt extremely virtuous. I was contributing my share to the religion of labor and to the establishment of a just society.

My parents were amused, but also somewhat concerned. Father came to visit me on the kibbutz and asked about my budding political interests—my plans for higher education. I answered that I was not so sure I wanted any. He wanted to know what I was doing in a hot, stark wooden barracks eating as badly as a newly-arrived immigrant *halutz* and working without pay. I answered that he knew better than I that the farming tradition in our family went back generations, and if it was good enough for Shneour Levi and Dov Gedalia, why shouldn't it be good enough for me? And furthermore, I asked, hadn't he worked in the orchards of Rehovoth thirty years earlier? He countered that he had had no choice, and that he saved every penny he could and gotten away.

These arguments continued with my father even after I had returned to *Herzlia* for the school year and not until I was about to graduate, did we strike a compromise. I would go to Italy to study agriculture.

Once my parents agreed to my pursuing agriculture, I was more than satisfied, even if it meant a few more years before I could actually live on a farm. After all, I reasoned, if A. D. Gordon had been a graduate agronomist, he would have contributed that much more to his Kibbutz Deganya. I couldn't have been happier, but then my idyll was shaken in August of 1929 when new communal conflicts broke out in Jerusalem.

The Western (Wailing) Wall, the last remnant of the Temple, had been known as a Jewish place of prayer in the Middle Ages when Sultan Selim, the Ottoman conqueror of Jerusalem, had dug it out from the dung heap and turned it back to the Jews. However, beginning with the nineteenth century, the worshippers met constant interference from Moslem leaders. In 1928 the British police, at the request of the Mufti of Jerusalem, removed the flimsy partition between male and female worshippers because the Moslems considered the partition a breach of the ruling that no changes were to occur in procedures or services at the Wall. This began a series of harassments by the Moslem custodians of the area against the Jewish worshippers. Jews were stabbed or beaten going to or coming from prayers. On the ninth of Av, the anniversary of the destruction of the Temple, Jewish nationalist youth organized a demonstration and marched to the Wall. Our Labor Zionist youth kept away, heeding the words of Moshe Beilinson, one of Labor's leading ideologists and an outspoken secularist: "The value of the Western Wall is great, but we should not forget that in our national rebirth, other values occupy the central position—*Aliyah*, labor, land."

Within ten days of the demonstration, Arab gangs assaulted Jews and invaded Jewish settlements throughout Palestine on the premise that the Jews intended to attack the holy El-Aqsa Mosque. Within five days, one hundred and thirty-three Jews were killed and four hundred wounded. The Arabs lost one hundred and sixteen. My uncle Shraga, in Be'er Tuvia, was in critical condition, and Father's old friend Broza, a veteran farmer near Jerusalem, was seriously wounded. Ten settlements had to be given up altogether, following massacres in Hebron, Safed and Jaffa, where elderly, defenseless people were tortured and murdered. Hebron's Jewish community, the oldest *Habad* community in Palestine, was completely destroyed. Hebron, the city of Abraham, thus became off limits to the Jews who had lived there almost continuously for thousands of years.

When Dr. Chaim Weizmann, president of the World Zionist

Organization, attempted to meet in London with Colonial Secretary Sidney Webb, he was kept waiting while Webb's wife Beatrice, a leading socialist like her husband, said to Weizmann: "I can't understand why the Jews make such a fuss over a few dozen of their people killed in Palestine. As many are killed every week in London in traffic accidents."

These incidents were disturbing. They presented an unprecedented test to my Socialist ideology. How could our sister Socialist in London be so callous? Weren't we all supposed to be humanitarians? And didn't she know that *her* people who were responsible for maintaining law and order had failed completely? That in fact they often had helped cause the attacks by instigating certain incidents?

And how realistic, really, was our dream of a harmonious co-existence of Arab and Jewish workers? The Arab workers and peasants we had invited to join us had ended up murdering us. Berl Katznelson, the venerated labor leader, had said that improved working conditions would bring the Arab masses closer to us, but it wasn't the case. Our help raising their standard of living, had drawn to Palestine Arabs from Egypt, Syria and Lebanon.

The Arab population was thus rising 5 percent each year. And look how "close" to us it had made them! Could we believe David Ben-Gurion when he said that only the upper strata of Arab society feared Jewish immigration and development? Were all the murderers only riff-raff paid by the Mufti and his followers? Or was there a malignant pan-Arabism growing among the Palestinian Arabs?

We debated these questions in our "Circle," but when all was said and done, we clung to our basic convictions. Perhaps, we reasoned, it was true that the Jewish nationalist demonstrators were as much to blame as the Arabs for the attacks. Perhaps they never should have demonstrated at the Wall. As Moshe Beilinson had said, the symbols of the past were not as important as the present and future. As long as Jews could immigrate to Palestine and be permitted to buy land and build our new society, we must live in peace with the British and our Arab neigbors.

Besides, now that the Socialists under Ramsay MacDonald, were in power in Britain, they would sooner or later acknowledge the justness of the Labor movement in Palestine.

A Socialist colonial secretary could be an improvement on a Conservative one, if we only gave it time. What was called for was patience.

I went along with the "Circle's" thinking and consciously still accepted their thinking. But after a visit to my Uncle Shraga in the hospital, there was a gnawing doubt in the back of my mind.

VI
Uncle Shraga of Be'er Tuvia

I entered Uncle Shraga's room at the Tel-Aviv hospital, where he had been brought a day earlier. Shraga's head was swathed in bandages with only his face and beard visible. His right hand, also bandaged, lay over the covers, heavy and motionless. He was in his sixties—a small, thin man with a short, graying beard and shining blue eyes. He looked like thousands of other older Orthodox Jews one met in Jerusalem or Safed—except for his crystal clear eyes. They mirrored a man with a guiltless, happy soul.

It was a little over a year since I had last seen him. He and his wife, my father's sister, lived in a small, bare, single-story white house in Be'er Tuvia. Be'er Tuvia was not a prosperous village. The southernmost of Jewish settlements, founded some forty years earlier, it had never grown like the bigger plantation settlements farther north. Almost two hours' ride from the next Jewish settlement north, it never benefited from the occasional waves of immigration into the country. It developed little beyond what it was originally—about twenty homes on either side of a single street.

In spite of its sleepy atmosphere, or because of it, I loved Be'er Tuvia. It was as if the early pioneer days had been preserved intact there for me. Be'er Tuvia looked the way Petah-Tikvah supposedly had when my father was courting my mother in 1895. It conquered malaria, which had almost forced it to be abandoned, but electric lights had never reached Be'er Tuvia.

The nearby Arab lands were brown and dry, but the houses in Be'er Tuvia were surrounded by flowers and vegetable gardens

and separated by bright white picket fences. Up and down the little
street grew great arching mulberry trees which the children ransacked during the fruit-bearing season.

At the top of the street on a small eminence rising above the
homes, stood the synagogue—a small, plain stone building. On
Friday nights and holidays, its candle glow shimmered far out
into the dark. The observant farmers reveled in the chance for
moments of rest.

I studied Shraga's face as he lay dozing in his hospital bed. I was
extremely nervous about what to do or say when he awoke.
Shraga's field had been trampled and burned by the Arabs, his
home looted then destroyed. And the final blow—his right arm
had been mutilated when he tried to defend himself. He would
never be able to use the hand again. How would Shraga react
when he knew he could no longer work his fields?

I remembered visiting him in Be'er Tuvia on Shavuot a year
before. I jumped off the truck which brought me there, and waited
by the pump house until a herd of cattle went by. The pump house
was also the post office, town council and bus stop—in short, the
public center of the settlement, second only to the synagogue. But
it was deserted now and as the cattle kept ambling by, I could find
nobody to identify the house. Finally a few children came running
down the street. They stopped and smiled at me. "Shalom," I
answered their smiles. "Come, show me my Uncle Shraga's
house."

"Oh, Shraga," said one of the boys, his face lighting up. "He
reads the Torah and blows the shofar on the High Holidays."

The youngsters, eager for any new excitement, accompanied
me to Shraga's courtyard and right up to the very doorstep. They
did not leave until Shraga actually came to the door. Shraga's
children were scattered all over the country and he and his wife
lived alone, so they were delighted to have me share their holiday.
It also happened to be my birthday.

That evening the crowded synagogue sparkled; light from a
dozen tapers reflected off the spotlessly white walls. A modest
candelabra hung from the ceiling and the women had sewn and
embroidered the curtains of the Holy Ark where the Scrolls of the
Torah were kept.

Shavuot was the feast of the first fruits and green twigs and branches bedecked the walls, lintels and pulpit. The settlers were grateful for the modest harvest their labor had reaped, so Shavuot had special meaning for them. Joyously, they read the familiar words of the Torah: "Thou shalt keep a feast unto me . . . the feast of the harvest, the first fruits of thy labors which thou hast sown in the fields."

Late that night Shraga and I sat on straw-backed chairs cracking almonds in the backyard. The air was good, scented with flowers, and millions of stars studded the ceilingless sky of Palestine.

My uncle spoke about his problems which were always the same. High prices and need for an improved water system so the villagers could expand their crops. If they were going to survive, they needed to raise more fruit, vegetables and poultry. If the government would build a paved road, they could ship some of their daily produce into town.

"Why don't you quit?" I suggested. "Sell the land and house. Get the few pounds they are worth and move north where conditions are better. You could open a small store and be free of these endless worries."

"Everybody in the city—even most of my family in the settlements—thinks we're all *schlemiels* out here. You're not the first to tell me that," Shraga smiled. He paused, searched for the right words. Then he began slowly. "You, the native born, forget the things that brought your grandparents here. You have never even been to Europe and you take your comfortable life for granted. Let me tell you some of what I lived through." Shraga hesitated again, as if bracing himself against the memories.

"Remember the Kishinev pogroms? The newspapers stirred up the old 'blood libel' claiming that the Jews had been responsible for murdering a baby Christian girl, and for the suicide of a Christian woman in a Jewish hospital. Both incidents were later proven to be no fault of the Jews. A delegation of leading Jews had gone to the governor to warn him of a repetition, and the chief of police had been warned. Everyone promised that it was all under control." My uncle's smile turned to one of bitter irony. "In a sense, I suppose everything *was* under control. It had all been methodically organized from the first. Then all that was needed was final provocation—somebody fired shots at the crowds near the cathedral. Suddenly groups of hoodlums came running from every direction. . . ."

He was silent for a moment, then continued. "The first Jew was killed that afternoon and the sight of his blood sent his murderers into ecstasy. They swept through the city like a brush fire, slaughtering men and women in their path as they ran down the streets. They raped old women and girls no more than twelve or thirteen, then they choked or stabbed them and mutilated their bodies. The Moldavian peasants, brought into town especially for the pogroms, fought over the dead bodies. . . .

"We had no weapons to defend ourselves and the police for all their promises, never lifted a finger except when *we* tried to organize for self-defense. They even joined in with the mobs. They burned down our synagogues and homes, trapping Jews in the buildings and letting them roast alive. Bands played waltzes in the city gardens; the Bishop of Kishinev came to bless the rioters. It did not stop until late at night of the second day. When it was over, the Jewish streets were empty, littered with broken furniture, goods and disfigured bodies.

"After that, my brothers and I made up our minds to leave. All our hopes for better times, for humane government, assimilation and brotherhood . . . they had all been fantasies."

"But why didn't you go to America," I said, "where you might have had some peace?"

"Peace is more than just physical security. The Jews in America are still a minority and despite all they have, their lives are still dependent on people who can turn on them at any time. Here we don't need anyone to protect us because we protect ourselves. They may have easier lives but they are still not masters of their fate. This land is mine. I worked it and tilled it and there is no power on earth that can take it away from me. Not as long as I can push a plow and guard my farm."

I sat in his hospital room waiting for his eyes to open, and his words kept ringing in my mind: "No power on earth can take it away from me."

At last Uncle Shraga opened his eyes and, after a moment, recognized me. He gave me a brief smile.

"How are you?" I asked, approaching his bed. "Are you in pain?"

"No," he answered softly. "The pain is almost gone, except my hand." He looked into my face. "You know about it?" I nodded and felt relieved that I wouldn't have to pretend.

He was silent for a moment, closing his eyes. "It means the end for me. I'll have to move north and spend my days studying the Talmud. You know what our wise men said? 'He who owns no land is no man.' What do I have to show for my entire life? I have nothing. All I am is a cripple."

I answered quickly. "Uncle, you've lived your life as you chose to, which is more than most can say. You have done more than your share. Now you can give the younger pioneers a chance to take over. You know that plans for resettling Be'er Tuvia have already been made. In a short while it will be rebuilt?"

He stared at me hard. "No, tell me."

"A group of veteran agricultural workers of the *Moshavim* cooperative movement are taking over. At first, thirty families will settle there, and soon it will grow. There will be a paved road a new well and water pump."

Uncle Shraga tried to sit up. His cheeks were flushed and his eyes regained some of the sparkle I had known. "So, at last they're going to build Be'er Tuvia. It had to take something like this." He smiled at me. "Maybe all our troubles had a purpose. May God forgive me. I should not have been so bitter."

Uncle suddenly looked as if I had poured new life into his veins. He wanted to know about any further outbreaks, how the rest of the country was doing—whether the attacks were over, whether there were many casualties. "Did you know our doctor?" he said abruptly. I nodded. "A good man," said Shraga. "He was killed attending a wounded Arab. We warned him not to go out into the open. He refused to listen. 'They all know me,' the Doctor said. 'There isn't an Arab in twenty miles who has not come to me.' Five minutes later, an Arab stabbed him to death."

I was glad that Shraga's brothers, Joshua and Menahem, came in at that moment. They were three very different men. Shraga was the mystic among them, the dreamer whose reasons for coming to Palestine were the most symbolic. Joshua, the oldest, was the pragmatist who had come to Palestine simply to make a better life for himself. He was strong, solidly built and fearless. He lived in Rehovoth, one of the older colonies of the country, and he had built a successful farm there. Of the three, he was the only one who had farmed before. Menahem, the youngest, was the scholar, who had gone to a university in Berlin.

Though he always kept apart from politics, Menahem would argue in the best Russian intellectual tradition. One Friday afternoon, about a year before this visit to the hospital, we were sitting under an olive tree in his courtyard in Rishon. Menahem listened tolerantly to my passionate Socialist rhetoric, which he considered teen-age growing pains at best. But he could not keep a small smile off his face, and finally he broke in. "At your age," he said, "I was as radical as you and carried the world's injustices on my own conscience. But I'm amazed at the indifference some of you show toward our own heritage. You're all well enough informed on economics, social philosophy and political science, but you treat lightly the very things that Jewish life was based on for centuries. You read Marx, Engels, Hegel and Spencer, but how about our own ancient philosophers? What about the Pentateuch, the Prophets and the rest of the Bible?

"Our people had plenty to say about the world and the universe. And the Bible was full of dreams about social justice. You don't believe the Jews are the Chosen People—well, neither do I. But three thousand years ago, our ancestors were the first to give the common man a cohesive faith around a one and only non-tangible God."

"But of what importance is monotheism today?" I cut in.

He seemed to ignore the interruption and went on. "Our second great contribution was the Prophetic message. Where is there a greater cry for social justice than in the words of the Prophets? They lashed out at all who oppressed, took a bribe or turned aside the needy at the gate! The Torah's command, 'Thou shalt love thy neighbor as thyself,' was the touchstone of our heritage.

"We founded it three millennia earlier on this soil. Freedom? Jews even treated their slaves as humans who had rights. Slaves rested together with their masters and their work was not humiliating or cruel."

"And social justice?" I wanted to know.

"After fifty years all land had to be returned without charge to its original possessor. And 'Thou shall not . . . gather every grape of thy vineyard, thou shalt leave for the poor and the stranger.' It was a duty to lend money to the poor, without interest. And we were expected to offer them at least one tenth of our wealth. We never accepted that man is only materially motivated. Look at our concept of the Sabbath. Everyone was given a day of rest to find a purpose and search for answers beyond the most bestial survival. We even gave our animals a day of rest. It was Hillel who said, 'Do unto others as you would have them do unto you.'

"We formed these concepts as a free people. Tragically since then, as a minority we've lost a lot of our ability to think creatively, without inhibitions. In the few centuries before the Romans scattered our nation, we did more of lasting original worth than in all the centuries since."

"But we can't go back to before the Temple fell," I said with great seriousness.

"No, and I'm not saying we have to shut out the modern world." He smiled. "I'm just saying Marx isn't the cure-all. Jews allowed too much bondage into their souls and I'm saying look into your heritage."

Then Uncle Menahem said the words he was probably reaching for all along. "And perhaps, before we worry so much about social justice and the fate of the world, we Jews need to learn to survive. We need to solve our own critical problems and secure our freedom as a nation."

Now, as I watched Menahem chatting with his brother Shraga in the hospital bed, his words took on a strange, disturbing new strength for me. Once again I had a glimmer of doubt about the policies of my "Circle." Was it true that Shraga was lying there because Jews like myself were not "solving our own problems?" Would my family and relatives be driven off their lands while I attended meetings on universal Social Justice? Why wasn't the *Yishuv* better prepared to protect Be'er Tuvia and Motza and Hulda? As the brothers traded information about the Arab attacks, the questions continued to rankle in my mind.

Before the afternoon was over, I had pieced together the story of the Siege in Be'er Tuvia.

When the first rumors of trouble in Jerusalem and Jaffa had reached the little village, it started preparing for the inevitable. The council posted guards at the ends of the colony and dug out their few rusty Turkish guns. They soon understood the extent of their danger. On the first night, they chased away a group of Arabs who brought their cattle to graze on the Jewish fields. On the second night, prowlers set fire to an old house at the edge of the colony. The settlers intensified their vigil. Men stood guard at night and worked during the day, a few sharing the day watch with women and children. Rumors kept reaching the village and there were moments when they almost wished that the attack would start.

It was not long in coming. On Friday and Saturday, they noticed unusually heavy traffic around the village, and city-dwelling Arabs, like birds announcing a storm, were seen visiting the nearby Arab villages. It could mean only one thing—the village *fellaheen* were being incited to violence.

At noon on Sunday more than three hundred Arabs converged on the tiny colony. The bell near the synagogue summoned everyone to their posts. The guards opened the single, sealed ammunition box allowed to them by the government. They had a total of five shotguns, two pistols and four rusted "illegal" Turkish rifles. The British police who supervised and occasionally cleaned the rifles had told them that the box contained twelve rifles, but eight had inexplicably disappeared.

The farmers of Be'er Tuvia had never before prepared for such a concerted assault by the Arabs. They had lived as neighbors since 1887 and any trouble in the past had been settled by racing out on horses and scattering the marauders with sticks and stones. But from their posts, the colonists now saw mounted Arabs coming at them in droves, brandishing swords and rifles and screaming imprecations at anyone who lagged behind. Small groups of Arab women and children waited back in the distances with sacks and donkeys.

Moments later, the Arabs had spread all over the fields. They advanced slowly, one small group at a time, apparently intent upon penetrating the settlement in successive waves. When they reached the first guard post, the lone settler on duty fired. The Arabs stopped. The leaders renewed their incitement, and after a half hour of hesitation, they were again on the move. This time they opened fire on the houses at the edge of the settlement. The farmers were forced to abandon their outposts and fall back.

The settlers retreated to two houses in the center of the colony

from which all approaches were visible. The houses were protected only by the stone fences that surrounded them. It was late
afternoon. The attackers advanced on the outlying farms, feeling
their way cautiously. Each time an Arab exposed himself, a shot
rang out. This hide-and-seek continued for about an hour. Then
the attackers decided to smoke out the colonists.

They crept to two of the defenseless farms and soon the settlers
saw a spiral of smoke. The evening breeze was blowing and the
settlers knew the conflagration could quickly spread out of control over the entire sun-parched community. They would be
forced out into the open and certain death. The settlers held
counsel and decided to risk putting out the blaze.

Five men were chosen, Shraga among them. They did not take
arms; if one of them were caught by the Arabs, it would mean one
vital gun less, a gun that the settlers' wives or children might use.
So the five men armed themselves only with sticks, pitchforks and
shovels. The remaining men covered their advance.

The five crawled and jumped from fence to fence until they
reached the farms on the outskirts. They broke down the burning
walls of the houses, entered them and began to extinguish the fire
with sand. When the fire was finally under control, the five started
their retreat. At this point the Arabs spotted them and attacked in
a swarm. The five held them off with stones as they ran, and their
fellow settlers laid down a selective cover of fire. They were on the
verge of reaching safety, when suddenly one of them remembered: "The synagogue, the Torah Scrolls!" In their retreat, they
had forgotten the Scrolls which now would fall into the hands of
the Arabs to be burned and desecrated. Uncle Shraga led the
return for his beloved Scrolls. They reached the synagogue safely,
but as they emerged, they were set upon by Arabs who had
reached the adjoining courtyards. The settlers covering the five
men dared not use their guns lest they hit one of the men. Three
men carrying scrolls reached the defended farms, but Uncle
Shraga was caught by the mob. The colonists came charging to his
rescue, firing at the Arabs at close range. The Arabs scattered long
enough for Shraga to be rescued, but he had been slashed by
knives and was bleeding profusely.

The settlers withdrew to the cowshed, which was built of stone
and would give them better protection. They carried a few mat-

tresses, food, several buckets of water and the Torahs. That was all they could save of forty-six years of labor.

As night fell, the Arabs tried again and again to penetrate the courtyard around the cowshed, but each time a few well-aimed shots drove them away. The houses throughout the rest of the settlement were burning on all sides and by the lights of the fires, the settlers saw Arabs emptying their houses of everything of value.

The gunfire exchanged by the settlers and Arabs kept growing in intensity. By midnight, ammunition was running low. The settlers knew they would receive no mercy from the Arabs and their only, faint hope was that daybreak would bring rescue. Though they did not want to raise the horrible possibility until the last moment, the men kept two pistols aside with a few rounds of ammunition so that if help did not come, they would have the option of suicide to avoid rape and torture. The women and children would be given first choice. Then the men.

In a final, drastic move, they decided to cease firing gradually to give the impression they were out of ammunition. If the Arabs then became bolder and attacked in force, the settlers would let them advance into close range. Then they would open fire as if their stores of ammunition were unlimited.

Incredibly, the plan worked. The Arabs attacked the cowshed *en masse* but were met by such a sudden storm of bullets they turned and fled. They spent the rest of the night away from the cowshed, ransacking the rest of the village.

The men kept posts in the loft all night, while the women, children and old men stayed downstairs.

Early the next morning, the settlers faced each other in despair. After twenty-four hours of relentless attack, things were only worse. Word had spread that there was still loot in the Jewish settlement and more Arabs were arriving from all the surrounding villages. As they discovered how thorough the looting had already been, they became enraged that nothing was left for them. They bore down to vent their fury on the Jews. The settlers refused to give up, but sent a bullet at anyone who came within sight of the cowshed.

Suddenly the staccato spatter of a machine gun was heard approaching from the main road. In moments, over four hundred

Arabs were fleeing as fast as they could. The settlers were saved by a British sergeant, twelve Arab policemen from Gaza and a single Lewis gun.

Under guard, the settlers buried their dead. They put a few green leaves on the fresh mounds, bowed their heads for a few moments, then boarded trucks brought by the police. They left Be'er Tuvia with nothing but the clothes on their backs.

VII
Dialogues in Portici
(1930-1931)

The *Lloyd Triestino*'s small passenger-cargo vessel edged slowly towards its poorly-lit pier in Brindisi. I had finally cut the cord with my reluctant parents and was on my way to Italy to study agriculture. I stood at the railing, looking with some disappointment at the pier with only a few customs men and a pair of rifle-toting *carbinieri*. I didn't expect Brindisi's waterfront to be Paris or London but still it was a disappointing first view of Mother Europe.

Throughout the five-day voyage, my excitement had known no bounds. I was going to bring back to Eretz-Israel technology which Zeev Leib and A. D. Gordon had never even imagined—an updated agriculture which would feed all of our people, allow greater immigration and improve everyone's lives.

As the ship pulled up to the gloomy pier I tried to contain my excitement by thinking about what the next few months would bring. Here I was at seventeen on my first trip from Palestine and arriving in the land of one of the oldest civilizations, one that dated back to ancient Rome and the land of one of the oldest Jewish diaspora communities.

I settled in Portici, a small suburb of Naples built over the old Herculaneum. The Vesuvio towered over us and a few kilometers away lay Pompeii. I.found lodgings with a typical Neapolitan family run by "Mama." There were other lodgers—five students from Palestine, an Albanian and several Italians.

On my fifth day in Portici we were joined by a new student from Riga, Latvia. Mordechai N. was small, no more than five feet three, slightly stooped, with a long hooked nose and a permanent apologetic smile.

We, the other *Sabras* at the house, laughed at the poetic Hebrew he spoke—the equivalent of Shakespearean English. He did not say that the train arrived late, but that "the iron deliverer came tardy at the crossroads." As our friendship developed, I influenced only the Hebrew he spoke, corrupting and colloquializing it, while he in return changed many of the beliefs I cherished most.

I had noticed in his lapel the emblem of *Betar* (Brit Trumpeldor, the nationalist youth organization of the Jabotinsky movement)—a seven-armed candelabra. The rest of us were opposed to the ideas of Zeev Jabotinsky and I told Mordechai he would find himself a minority of one among the Jewish students in Portici. He smiled and said he was prepared for it.

"In Riga, the Jabotinsky movement is the strongest group in town. I can take it," he said.

The Jewish community of Riga dated back to 1536. When the Democratic Republic of Latvia was established in 1918, an autonomous Jewish school system was created in which secular courses were taught in Hebrew and Yiddish. Mordechai was a product of that dual cultural life, and of the community's traditional Zionism.

We spent many evenings together reading the latest papers from Palestine. Most of the news was negative. The emissary from London, Sir John Hope Simpson, had concluded there was no more land available in Palestine for sale to Jews and that at best the country might be able to absorb only 100,000 new immigrants, half of which had to be non-Jews. Simpson also stated that the country had no industrial potential. He disparaged all the innovations the Jews had introduced and ignored altogether the steady influx of Arabs attracted to Palestine because of the economic opportunities opened up by the Jews.

Thereafter, the British Colonial Secretary, Lord Passfield, issued a White Paper accepting Simpson's recommendations, in effect abrogating the terms of the Balfour Declaration.

Mordechai and I were astounded when we read of it. I was further surprised to hear him say it was useless to hope for a change in British policy at this point. He was a follower of

Jabotinsky. And I knew Jabotinsky to be an advocate of closer ties with Britain, even to the extent of having Palestine become a Seventh Dominion within the British Empire.

I asked Mordechai to explain himself.

"You people believe in building up the land acre by acre, cow by cow. You ridicule Jabotinsky for trying to secure a political charter for a Jewish homeland."

He had not answered my question. "I was speaking of Jabotinsky's affection for the British," I said.

"I have trusted Jabotinsky's political judgment till now," he said. "But we are approaching a showdown with the British."

I let him speak on and soon an argument broke out, he calling spiritualist-Socialist-Zionism anachronistic and I demanding to know how he can call a modern national renaissance, which sought to build a just society, anachronistic. I reminded him of the daily sacrifices that our pioneers made in the arid fields and the rocky hills and sand dunes.

"That is not the point, Yitshaq," he said. "You work hard, but you do nothing to help our hard pressed people the world over. . . ."

"What have you done in Eretz-Israel?" I asked irritably. "What settlements have you established? What land have you reclaimed?"

He answered calmly, saying that the Jabotinsky movement was not involved in social experiments; they would not allow themselves to be side-tracked from the main goal—moving the threatened Jewish masses of Europe, educated and uneducated, trained and untrained, to Eretz-Israel.

"Will your masses be willing to sleep in tents on the shores, and eat bread and water like other pioneers?" I asked.

Mordechai smiled faintly and leaned forward. "You just can't see what's happening, can you?" he said. "I come from Latvia, a liberal democratic Republic. Yet I wouldn't bet a penny on what will happen to the Jews there ten years from now. We are sitting on a volcano. Remember what we saw at the Herculaneum? Plaster figures of people who were trapped and engulfed in hot basalt. That's how I envision the end of the Jews of Europe."

Mordechai's words upset me. "In another ten years, maybe twenty or forty, the Jews will become a respectable percentage of

Palestine's population," I said.

"We can't wait," he answered. "The League of Nations recognized Palestine as our national home ten years ago. That is our history, waiting. Now the British have changed their mind about the Balfour Declaration. They are closing the gates to the land. Are we supposed to wait again? Or do we do something about it? The borders of Palestine must be kept open. It is a matter of life and death."

Subsequently, Prime Minister MacDonald backed off a little from the White Paper's immigration and land restrictions, in an effort to appease the Jews of Palestine.

The discussions continued. Another time, as Mordechai and I sat on the pier in the evening, we again spoke of the masses, he wished to bring them to Palestine and I claimed that they wouldn't come.

"In 1917-20, when the Balfour Declaration opened the doors of Palestine, our people did not come pouring in from the diaspora," I said. I told him I thought Zionism was an idealistic movement of the few, that it was not for the masses.

Mordechai looked out to sea. "The purpose of our national rebirth in Palestine is the survival of not a Jewish elite but of the Jewish people," he said. "Nationalism of a new, vicious type is sweeping Europe. You cannot survive by waving the Book of Isaiah or Marx's 'Das Kapital' at the world. Sooner or later, your just society will have to face enemies with weapons, and it had better be prepared for it.

"We Jews have a toehold on freedom now, and we not only dare not lose it, we desperately need to expand it at any cost. It is a lifesaving mission. The only way to save our people is by taking them off the volcano. *Now.*"

The sun was setting and the fishermen were drifting in from the Bay of Naples. Mordechai seemed exhausted. I wanted to continue the discussion, to warn him about the dangers of militarism. But I could not speak.

Mordechai gathered himself for the last fusillade:

"We Jews have always been masters at abstract intellectualizing. Over the centuries we were ostracized, degraded and assaulted, but we were stubborn and stiff-necked and we survived by our wits. We lived lower than worms, but we were still arrogant to claim by inverted reasoning that we survived because we were a chosen people. Look at the Assyrians and Babylonians, we said, look at the Carthaginians and Parthians. They had all been mighty empires and where were they? But we Jews had survived!

"But I ask you, at what price? What did we prove? That we can adapt ourselves no matter how much we suffer, no matter how many of us are killed? We actually glorified a diaspora existence. We accepted the abnormal. We declared that we 'liberated ourselves from land and territory!' Is that all we have to show for our national genius? For two thousand years most of our creativity has been used for running, hiding and surviving!"

As I listened, I felt a flood of affection for this frail man. What an unlikely revolutionary! How many thousands were there like him, sedentary but intense intellectuals, heirs to centuries of mysticism and intense Talmudic debate who broke with tradition and came up out of the squalid cities and ghettos ready to man the barricades of many causes and many nations? But he is a revolutionary of the Jewish cause.

I knew he had breached my defenses—everything I had seen the last several months—the attack on Be'er Tuvia and all the other Arab riots, the erosion of the Balfour Declaration, the recent "White Paper," the continuous newspaper stories reporting on economic upheavals and rising political unrest throughout Europe—it all fell into place.

Adolf Hitler had seemed a caricature to me, a Charlie Chaplin who had everybody in Germany duck-walking; but suddenly I saw nothing funny . . . Mussolini at least had once been a Socialist who had cared about the downtrodden—but this man with the ridiculous forelock and moustache, who showed such hatred for Jews, socialists, communists and capitalists alike—what would he ultimately lead to? Mordechai seemed to have read my mind. "European nationalism will convulse the continent. Poland, Russia, the Baltic States, Romania, Germany—they will all spew out their Jews. We must secure a haven for the Jews, for those willing to make the choice now before they are spewed out and for those who will soon be forced to flee."

By spring 1931, I was no longer the innocent, sheltered seventeen-year-old expecting all of Europe to embrace me in the struggle for universal brotherhood.

What had we in the "Circle" been hoping for when we sang "The International" and displayed our red flags? Had we really expected the Russian Marxists to rush forward to clasp our hands? Had we really expected the British Socialists to come to our rescue and think of us as their brothers?

Europe and the rest of the world had become too preoccupied with its own problems to worry about the future of a few Jews in a desert thousands of miles away. How naive we had been! We sang songs about universal justice and love, dreaming when we should have been alert, objective. Our "brothers" were not going to lead us at all. *We had to lead ourselves.*

By the end of the school year (June, 1931), Portici and the Naples area had lost their charm for me. There was little cultural or political life, and I considered transferring to the Agricultural College in Florence after returning from my summer vacation in Palestine. Tuscany's agriculture and climate did not exactly match Palestine's but it was far more in tune with my intellectual growing up.

Before Mordechai returned to Riga, on our last Sunday together, we went to the main square for a few glasses of local wine. Mordechai raised his glass and smiled softly. "I have not been feeling well," he said. "It's my chest. Had I grown up in Tel-Aviv and rowed in the Yarkon river and swum in the Mediterranean, I would have lungs like yours." He glanced away. "I'm not sure whether I'll be able to come back next year. My uncle wants me to go to a sanatorium."

I was aware of Mordechai's frailty but this was the first I heard of his illness. I tried to comfort him, and said I thought a few months in the mountains would do him a world of good and that he was sure to be back here for the fall semester.

Mordechai smiled sadly and said: "What about you?"

"What about me? I'm fine. . . ."

Mordechai grinned. "I know your health is fine. Daughters of Israel, beware." We both laughed and ordered more wine.

"What I meant," Mordechai said, "was what you had decided about our discussions . . . or whatever you choose to call them."

In my mind, I had already decided to look up acquaintances in the Jabotinsky movement and do some reading.

"I accept what you say about the dangers that threatened our people," I said. "The British will not help. But where do we go from there?"

Mordechai was silent for a few moments. Then he spoke slowly.

"We Jews everywhere are facing grave times and we are not prepared for them."

For two thousand years—since the loss of our independence—we have been exiles. We suffered terrible defeats. Our last great political-military leader, King Agrippa, was poisoned by the Romans (44 CE). Then came the zealots' revolts and the Temple was destroyed. Finally, Bar Kochba's rebellion was crushed (135 CE). These defeats traumatized us permanently. We lost our home. We never forgot that more than half of the Jews of Judea were killed, enslaved or exiled. We came to abhor arms. We became unlike all other people. Ever since, we have been a dispersed—I would say crippled—people, held together only by the threads of our spiritual heritage. It held us together but never led us home.

"Overwhelmingly we opted for dispersal. Even as recently as 1917, when the British made it possible to return home, the Jews of the diaspora chose to stay in exile. By 1920 the British reneged on their promises and it was too late.

"Now the Labor Zionists think that by obtaining a few thousand immigration certificates from the British, by gaining permission to buy some land, they will eventually build a society of select Jews who will live in harmony with all their neighbors. But, this is all fantasy.

"First of all, the British don't want us to build our ideal society any more. They want just enough of us in Palestine to keep us and the Arabs at each other's throats. Divide and conquer is the rule of all good empires. As long as they can keep the Jews and the Arabs off-balance, they can have oil and all the other resources of the area at their disposal.

"Second, those Zionists who still talk in terms of 'selecting' Jews for immigration to Palestine are living in another world. Germany and other European nations will not let Britain rule the world alone; vicious nationalism and a deteriorating economic situation will lead to war. And the Jews will be blamed for it, as they always have been. As tensions mount hundreds of thousands will be clamoring to enter Palestine, and 'selection' will be out of the question. The British will see to it that Arab reactions are prompt, violent and in the interest of 'security,' the door will once more be slammed shut on the Zionist dream.

"When this happens, the only thing left for us Jews will be armed revolt."

That frail, stooped, ailing, Jewish youth of Riga paused, then said: "Yes. We will rebel against the British Empire and force it out of our Eretz-Israel. . . ."

I had guessed this was where Mordechai's lecture was heading. But still, the abruptness of his words "armed revolt" caught me by surprise. Even the people who called for national rebirth the past fifty years looked upon arms only as self-defense. *Hagana*, or "defense," is what the armed units of our communities were always called. Jews had not used armed resistance for two thousand years, and now—rebellion against the mighty Empire!

Mordechai was sitting up erect as a drill sergeant. All of his timidity and physical weakness were gone and his eyes looked straight and hard at me. Then, as if he were aware of what was passing through my mind, he let his apologetic smile soften his features. "Here you are," he said, "still wobbly on your political Zionist's legs, and I go trying to make a revolutionary out of you.

"Yitshaq," he went on, "I'm not sure we will meet again. . . . You were patient and open-minded with me, not hostile like some of the others at the house. Now go back and talk to our *Betar* people in Palestine. Find out more about our 'Labor Units' and about Trumpeldor's original ideas on pioneering *and* military preparedness.

"Promise me one thing. Don't be discouraged by the tiny toehold political Zionism has in Eretz-Israel; we have an enormous reservoir in the diaspora. There will be millions to back us up, *if* we are ready to act."

* * *

I returned home to Palestine and Mordechai returned to his uncle in Riga, whose address I did not know, and then to a sanatorium. I never heard from him again.

Part III: The Making of a Revolution
I
The Seeds of Revolution
(1931-1932)

As my ship neared the shore of Palestine, I rose early to go on deck to watch the approaching skyline of Jaffa and Tel-Aviv. The small, dirty, bustling pier was little different from when my grandparents had landed half a century ago. As I mounted the few slippery steps from the landing boat to the pier, I smelled the aroma of lamb roasting on charcoal, and the stench of dung and rotting garbage in the gutter. I heard the vendors clinking their brass cups with the sweet tamarind drink and the shouts of the fishermen and vegetable sellers. It was as I remembered, all unchanged from my childhood, and I was happy to be home.

My parents was waiting at the dock. They both seemed to have aged terribly in the short time I had spent in Italy. The climate, sickness, their early struggle for survival had suddenly left an imprint, or perhaps with the ten months separation, I was seeing the relentless passing of the years for the first time. From our letters, I knew that Father was to stop working soon, and Mother had developed acute diabetes. I felt a lump in my throat as I embraced them.

After my first joyous hours of homecoming I felt a letdown. I tried to rationalize it as something to be expected, but depression bore down on me whenever I looked at my parents.

Since I had been to Rome and Paris, the little enclave of Jewish Palestine, once my whole world, struck me as small and limited. The streets of Jaffa and Tel-Aviv, my father's store, our home—all had shrunk amazingly, as if I had grown two feet taller. The newspapers and the issues they dealt with, all the problems of the

Yishuv seemed reduced in scope and importance. Disregarding it I tried to gather myself for my first ventures into political Zionism.

I accepted more and more the basic premises of political Zionism—the essential problem for the world's Jews was the homelessness of its masses and the only real solution was the physical ingathering and rebirth of the nation as an independent political entity—a Hebrew State on its own land. To achieve this we had to obtain international recognition of our right to quick, unlimited immigration, and to large-scale settlement. And if Britain and the League of Nations which had entrusted Palestine to the care of Great Britain would not act, we, the Jewish youth, would have to act alone.

Though I still believed strongly in universal social justice and in a restructuring of the world's economic systems, I knew I had to put those beliefs aside. What was needed now was a single-minded dedication to Jewish survival. I recognized the danger facing Jews all over Europe, and I saw in this danger, the single, overwhelming issue facing me as a young Jew in 1931.

Once I got over my initial surprise at Mordechai's reference to "armed revolt," the thought of physical resistance never bothered me again. I had grown up free from inhibitions on the subject of using force because I had seen my own family resorting to it time and again in order to stay alive. When challenged for its survival, my generation had to use all available means. Rather than sit and wait to be annihilated, we might have to raise our weapons first—whether or not this was a "Jewish" way of thinking and even if our people had not done such a thing for two thousand years.

I started to attend small Revisionist Zionist meetings, at which Abba Achimeir and Y. H. Yevin often spoke. I read all of Achimeir's articles in the weekly, *Hazit Ha'Am* ("The Nation's Frontline"), and I met with Achimeir and some of his associates in the *Hazit Ha'Am* cluttered editorial offices, a few minutes walk from our home on Herzl in Street in Tel-Aviv. I remember him as a thin, almost fragile, slightly bent, and bookish-looking man in his mid-thirties with a keen, analytical mind. He was a clear, concise lecturer who used no subtleties and pulled no punches. Born in Russia, he had attended my *Herzlia* Gymnasia in 1912-14, and had a Ph.D. in history from the University of Vienna. He was intimately acquainted with the leaders of the *Yishuv* from the twenties onward. Originally he had been a follower of the Labor Zionists, but eventually he had left them and had gone his own way.

Achimeir and a number of his associates were the first political prisoners of the British jails in Palestine. They had been arrested on October 10, 1930 when they organized a demonstration against a leading Socialist, Dr. Drummond Shiels, the Deputy Colonial Secretary.

The demonstrators had booed Shiels and carried placards demanding free Jewish immigration and major changes in Colonial Office policies. They shouted criticisms at the leaders of the *Yishuv* for toadying to the British. This was unheard of in Jewish life. Jews staging protest demonstrations in the Holy Land? In Tel-Aviv? In Jerusalem? Jewish demonstrations against a "friendly" British—Socialist government? The uproar in the Jewish establishment in Palestine was immediate. The Jewish commander of the Tel-Aviv police arrested Achimeir and the other leaders and had them beaten badly. The Hebrew press resoundingly condemned the demonstrations, and the Labor Zionists, incensed after years of Achimeir's criticism, demanded that they be punished severely.

The small demonstration left an impression far beyond its scope; it marked the first symbolic act on the road towards rebellion against the British. In his cell in Jerusalem, Achimeir wrote that Zionism was in crisis because Zionist leaders had failed to realize that the creation of a State was the main goal, and it had not prepared its youth for the sacrifices this will require. The establishment had not even broached this possibility, fearing that the sacrifices it would entail would cause the Jews of the diaspora to turn their backs totally on Zionism.

Eleven days after the demonstration when Achimeir was released, he predicted that the fight against the British would now assume, step-by-step, the character of a revolt. Achimeir bluntly taught that all the British laws enacted in Palestine were contrary to the original spirit of the League of Nations Mandate and the Balfour Declaration.

But in 1930-31, few Jews saw it that way. The Labor establishment clung to the notion that the Jews were a moral, spiritually superior people and not meant to be law breakers or revolutionaries. Consequently, any solutions to "the Palestine problem" had to be worked out peacefuly and gradually with the British.

Achimeir disagreed. No race of people, he said, were specifically spiritual or moral. All qualities were latent in all people, and external forces brought one or another to the surface. Secular and religious impulses, physical and spiritual impulses, vied with each other continuously, and the Jews were no more restricted to spiritual values than the ancient Greeks had been limited to aesthetics. If the Jews did not see themselves as a physical people, it was because the Romans had convinced them of it when they destroyed the Temple and the nation.

Along with Achimeir, the poet Uri Zvi Greenberg and Dr. H. Yevin formed the core of Zionist activism. Among them I met men who became my close friends for life. Some, like Arieh Ben-Eliezer, Shlomo Harari, and later Eri, son of Zeev Jabotinsky, eventually became legends who spent years in prisons and exile camps for serving their people. But in the early '30's, they were penniless youngsters, full of vigor and aflame with dreams of the national renaissance.

Uri Zvi Greenberg was a guiding light to us. He was a political polemicist in poet's guise. He was a gushing, spouting volcano who thundered about his people's moral and political degradation through the centuries. In his poems, he likened the *Senbalats*, the ancient Biblical collaborationists who opposed the rebuilding of the Walls of Jerusalem by Nehemiah, to the modern Socialists. Greenberg blasted the *Senbalats* for having sold their people down the river. His fiery nationalism, unlike Achimeir's, drew on religion and mysticism. He pointed at Jewish heritage, at the covenant and berated his fellow Jews as blind and stupid for not seeing the omens of the terrible days to come.

In the '20s and early '30s, Uri Zvi's poetry and his dire warnings were said to come from a demented mind. His visceral, expressionistic pounding poetry shocked the Socialists, and haunted and captivated those who were committed to oppose the establishment.

Yehoshua Herschel Yevin's pragmatism and logic balanced the acid pens of Achimeir and Greenberg. In measured, dispassionate words, Yevin preached for military preparedness:

> Fifty more settlements aren't worth the sacrifice and investment if they cannot be defended. There will be no future to national hopes if repeated Arab riots regularly cause the dispatch of British Commissions who, without fail, advise retreat from British obligations under the Mandate.... There will be no national future if the *Yishuv* depends for protection on British bayonets. Hebrew independent military power must be built now, brick by brick.

This took me back to when I was only sixteen, and the 1929 Arab riots had destroyed my Uncle Shraga's Be'er Tuvia. Those events had sowed the first seeds of political doubt in my mind.

Yevin, like Uri Zvi and others, had also been affected by the 1929 riots which caught the Jews unprepared—without weapons and without training. The riots were followed by systematic erosions of the trust handed to Britain under the Mandate, and 1929 became a revolutionary milestone in Jewish thinking.

Among the youth in Palestine, 1929 brought forth two historic answers: Achimeir's small group of "revolutionaries," and then unknown to me, the *Irgun Zvai Leumi*.

The critical events of 1929 also decisively changed the structure of the *Haganah*, the Jewish Underground Defense Units overseen by Labor. Despite ten years of existence, the *Haganah* had been unprepared for the attacks and though acts of heroism by its members abounded, so did massacres of defenseless Jews throughout several settlements. Ferment inside the *Haganah* mounted, as did Labor's determination to tighten its control. Those commanders who found Labor's growing stranglehold on the *Haganah* unacceptable, chose to leave it.

In April 1931, the *Irgun Zvai Leumi* was founded in Jerusalem. In the *Metzuda*, the underground organ of the *Irgun* (which appeared from 1932 to 1934) Dr. Yevin expressed the *Irgun*'s ideological links with revolutionary Zionism:

> There is nothing holier than safeguarding Jewish homes... Jewish lives ... Jewish land ... Our Hebrew youth must prepare, train, and be willing to give up all ... Not only life itself but also all the 'humanitarian' ideologies that ask us to treat our enemies as our brothers ... each one of our young people must know that he is contributing with his devotion, with his steadfastness, with his

blood—toward that magnificent edifice, Hebrew independent power in the homeland. Without it, it will not be rebuilt. . . .

In September 1931, I attended a university student conference in Tel-Aviv. It was organized by the student fraternity of the Hebrew University, *El-Al*, under the auspices of Tel-Aviv's grand old Mayor, Meir Dizengoff.

Now at the student gathering, Dizengoff welcomed us and spoke about our duties to the community as future professionals, academics and leaders. We were its guardians and economic providers. Though he did not know it, the young man sitting next to him on the dais, David Raziel, would one day be the commander of the *Irgun*, and scattered around the room were Hillel Kook, Haim Lubinsky and Moshe Galili, all of whom would play important roles in my life, in the *Irgun* and in the struggle for independence.

II

"We Are Anonymous Soldiers . . ."

In the summer of 1932, I joined *Betar* (Brit Trumpeldor), the
political Zionist youth movement which had been formed in
1925 under Zeev Jabotinsky. I spent the evenings in a training
course for future instructors. The key points of our philosophy
were these: the urgent creation of a Jewish state; the ingathering
of the Jewish masses in Zion in the shortest time possible; the
physical survival of the Jewish nation, above all other social or
political concerns; and military preparedness, not only for
defense, but when necessary, for liberation.

I went back and reread about the final centuries of Hebrew
national life, from the time of the Maccabees in 167 BCE to the
final rebellions in Galilee in the second, third and sixth centuries
CE. When they ended, the Judeans had lost their state, their
freedom and millions of their people.

This search into history was important, I believed, because we
could not reemerge as a nation unless we recognized the forces in
ourselves which had brought our nation down.

As I dug deeper into the history of the Judeans' downfall, I
knew that class and factional interests, along with fanatic religious intolerance among rival Jewish sects, had fed fraternal
hatreds which gradually bled the nation until it was weak and
ready for liquidation.

But even as a child, straining to read the book of Lamentations
on Tisha B'av by the flickering candle light, I was bitterly angry at
all the Jews who had fought each other instead of their common
enemy. The Sicarii, the Zealots and the "moderates" were all busy
killing each other, when most of the country was already

overrun by the Roman armies of Vespasian and Titus. I hated the stories about the internecine wars and the feeling would stay with me for life.

Now I saw that our people were once again under siege; I could no longer accept an ideology that considered the small Jewish bourgeois in Palestine to be an enemy whose small factory or orchard should be damaged or burned down if he did not accept the rule of Socialist-dominated Federation of Labor (*Histadrut*). Labor was determined to rule the *Yishuv* and I foresaw even worse confrontations to come. A few followers of Achimeir played with ideas about different totalitarian state structures, but many more in Labor, with its growing power, spoke and acted as if another dictatorship, the dictatorship of the proletariat, were already at hand. By now I was certain that this was not the road to survival. With *Betar*, however, and its emphasis on pioneering immigration and national service coupled with military disci- plines, I felt at home. I knew that sooner or later, *Betar* would merge with the activist followers of Achimeir, Greenberg and Yevin; I only wished that it would happen soon.

I did not go back to Italy that fall. Father's health had deter- iorated alarmingly and for that as well as other reasons, I stayed home and registered for the next term in the school of biology at the Hebrew University of Jerusalem. Among other opportunities my studies gave me the chance to become more deeply involved in the nationalist movement.

* * *

In August, 1932, Shula, a young friend who like myself was being trained as a future *Betar* youth leader, said she would like to see me after the *Betar* meeting. We left the clubhouse and walked up King George Street. I had known Shula for the past four months. This particular evening Shula pointed towards the center of town, saying that she preferred a more lively environment. At a certain point she turned, looked at me tensely and said: "How much do you know of unofficial activities outside *Betar*?"

I smiled. "Of course I have known about the *Haganah*. . . . We all know that there are underground groups at work and I noticed that many of our members disappear early some evenings, while others show up late. My guess is that there is activity . . . underground?"

Shula smiled back. "I did not expect you not to notice, after four months." She hesitated a moment, then continued. "Some of us are working outside *Betar*, in a completely separate, apolitical military organization. I have been permitted to ask you whether you are ready to consider joining the *Irgun . . . The Irgun Zvai Leumi.*"

I had wondered often about those who came in late to the club, usually several of them together, all wearing bright clean khakis shirts and pants. They always seemed especially sparkling on those evenings; now I knew what it all meant.

"Tell me some more about it, please," I said.

Shula pulled me a little closer as we walked towards her bus stop. "I don't have the right to tell you more. You'll find out soon enough. I just need your agreement to appear before some people and then we can talk some more." I nodded.

She kissed me goodbye, squeezed my hand, and ran after the bus. For the next twenty-four hours I thought long and hard. The little that Shula had told me, suggested that this was the opportunity I had been waiting for ever since my last talk with Mordechai in Italy when we discussed the possibility of using "armed resistance" to overcome British control. I was already becoming a bit frustrated with the limits of *Betar*, and felt that the *Irgun* might offer me a chance to be more "active."

A few days later, Shula gave me further instructions, and that night I walked alone up Bograchov Street, which was completely deserted, to a small, dark building which turned out to be an elementary school. On the other side of the building I located a closed side door. I stood beside it and whispered the password. The door opened. I entered a dark room. A young man whom I could hardly see took me by the arm and directed me to a low chair near the wall. He whispered to me to sit down and wait. As I got accustomed to the darkness, I realized I was in a kindergarten room seated in a cramped little child's chair, and all around I could make out toys, books and decorations. I smiled to myself at how appropriate it all was for an aspiring underground revolutionary—admission on the kindergarten level.

A few moments later, a twin ray of light reflected on the floor and a young man came out of an inside door. The guard led him towards the exit. He went out, then a few moments later the guard came up to me and pointed towards the half open door. In silence, he motioned for me to go in.

I entered a larger room with a desk covered with a green cloth on one side, and on it was a lamp pointed towards me. Three people sat behind the desk. The windows were covered with blankets.

The person seated in the middle pointed to the single chair facing the lamp. I sat down, straining my eyes to identify them. Two men and one woman. Finally I recognized the one in the middle as Moshe Rosenberg, one of the veteran leaders of the Tel-Aviv *Betar*. I could not identify the other two.

Moshe looked down at a sheet of paper in front of him. He cleared his throat, stared coldly at me as if we had never met, and said:

"You are Yitshaq R.?"

"Yes."

"Do you know why you are here?"

"Yes."

"Do you know what is expected of you?"

"Not exactly."

"Well, you'll find out." For the first time, he smiled slightly. "You have been recommended for the *Irgun*. We have investigated you and are willing to consider your admission. But first we want to ask you several questions. . . . Are you aware that your joining may entail extreme dangers? Second, are you ready to accept the *Irgun*'s military discipline? And thirdly, are you ready to swear allegiance to us in our pursuit of a free nation of Israel in its own homeland?"

Everything had happened so fast my head was spinning, and yet I felt no hesitation. I was certain at that moment that I had guessed correctly about the nature of the *Irgun*; in a sense, I had been heading towards this ever since Mordechai had won me over to nationalist thinking. *Betar* had been my training ground and the *Irgun* was the natural evolution.

I weighed all of these factors and then answered: "Yes, I am. I'm answering affirmatively to all three questions."

Moshe nodded, sat back and then, with his heavy Russian accent said:

"Why do you want to join the *Irgun*?"

I was somewhat taken aback. It would be ludicrous for me, the uninitiated novice, to deliver an oration on Zionist history or on my personal political evolution in recent years. Anything I said about the need for military strength in order to gain statehood would sound trite, though I had really been waiting for this moment for almost two years—ever since my discussions with Mordechai. Moshe knew me and had heard me instruct young-sters in the *Betar*, and probably read the articles I had done for various *Betar* publications. I had a growing reputation in the organization as a debater and I knew I did not need to try to impress them with my eloquence. My answer had to be short and to the point. I fidgeted in my chair, struggling for the words, while the three patiently kept silent. I could almost feel them chuckling to themselves, enjoying my discomfort . . . the loquacious instruc-tor, so full of advice all the time for new members, but now at a loss for words. I cleared my throat.

"I believe that we, the youth, have to serve our nation and our homeland, like the youth of all other nations. Military service is what every country, if it hopes to survive, requires of its people. We are a nation on the way to independence and statehood, and I'm willing to serve like young men everywhere else."

It wasn't an ingenious statement, but it was all I felt I could say. I prayed that it was enough.

Moshe actually looked relieved. He had probably been worried I might make some lengthly pronouncement. He had never been a great one for speeches and without uttering a word, he looked to his right and left. The other two shook their heads to indicate they had no questions.

"All right. We have no further questions. You will hear from us. Of course you understand that you will not discuss what you heard or saw tonight with anyone?"

I said yes and he nodded towards the exit. As I rose, he said, "Shalom, Yitshaq," and I saw a fleeting, friendly smile on his face.

I walked home alone. I did not feel especially elated or ebul-lient. I knew I had undertaken a step which would gravely affect the course of my life. I thought about my parents. Though at this point they did not even necessarily know much about the *Haganah* or that an *Irgun* existed, sooner or later they would guess what I had become involved in. My father and I had never discussed the current activism in Palestine, but he had often spoken of *Samo-ob-Rona*, the Russian name for self-defense. He had known about arms and weapons since his youth in Russia and the confrontations in Rehovoth and Petah-Tikvah. He had told me that even before the turn of the century in the Old City of Jerusalem, Jews had kept arms. The pistols were nicknamed "shmerls" after two courageous Jews who had settled in Jerusalem early in the 1800s.

I wondered how my parents would take it if they knew I had become involved in something beyond "self-defense." Father's health was worrying me more and more and Mother also was not well. If I got into trouble, what would it do to them. I tried to push these thoughts out of my mind. Whatever happened, I had to let events take their course. A week after my interview, Shula said: "You've been accepted. Report next Thursday to this address— it's a doctor's office—at eight in the evening. Wear khaki shorts and a plain shirt. Better shine your shoes." We both laughed. She gave me the password and I memorized the doctor's address. "Shula," I said, "I want to talk about it with you before I . . . I just want to know more about what I'm getting into."

She threw back her head and laughed: "You know as much as necessary . . . and the time will probably come when you will know more than you want to. You know we are all vulnerable. Anything may happen suddenly. The less we know individually, the better off we all are."

My swearing in was a simple affair. Twelve of us initiates reported Thursday evening to the doctor's office. Two officers were present—one the *Sgan* (non-commissioned), a young man about twenty, and the other a section commander quite a bit older. His name was Shmuel Katz, and I had known him for some time in *Betar*. Shmuel was a lanky, taciturn man and I had thought of him as rather lackadaisical. He turned out to be a tough, no-nonsense officer who knew his weapons and strategies and his politics well.

The twelve of us lined up: construction workers, office workers and two students. A few came from *Betar* or the Maccabee sports organization, and had some basic training, but some had never stood in military formation.

Shmuel made a short statement. "Men," he said, "you have been accepted into the *Irgun*. We are a volunteer military organization and expect you to behave like good soldiers. You will receive the best military and weapons training we can give you, but it will not be easy. We may even lose some of you. You will have to give the *Irgun* priority not only over private life, but over your life itself. You can still change your mind. Any questions?"

There were no questions.

"Stand at attention!"

Those of us with civilian backgrounds straightened awkwardly.

"Repeat after me: We swear allegiance to the *Irgun Zvai Leumi*, in Eretz-Israel. We shall be ready at any time to act for the rebirth of the nation of Israel in its land. To live and die for it!"

We repeated, sentence by sentence.

Shmuel went down the line and shook each man's hand. Then he departed. The *Sgan* took over and our basic training started. Teaching us to stand at ease and at attention, he corrected our posture, the placement of our feet and the position of our heads, over and over for the rest of the evening.

Weeks passed before I ever touched a pistol. Many of us had never held a weapon, and the *Irgun* knew that to mold us into fighters, they had to work with us slowly and methodically instilling in us respect for weapons and confidence in ourselves. We met one night a week, and Saturday mornings. Any more would have been too obvious and raised too many questions. One night a week we had close order drill; the next we had basic training in small weapons, at first using only a blackboard. We were shown manuals on small and heavy weapons, and we learned about explosives. Saturday mornings we spent on the beach marching, practicing close order drill again and again until we were ready to scream.

When we finally graduated to the actual use of weapons, we faced special problems. Rifles were very hard for us to transport and handle except in the suburbs, and even then our supply was always limited. We could not fire rifles or pistols in the cities; we had to go out to remote areas in deserts and caves before we fired a shot. Only on the rarest occasions, and only in the remotest, most forsaken area, were we able to practice with explosives. Under British law, we could have been thrown in prison for possessing a weapon. Within a few years, the punishment became death. We had to keep the strictest secrecy at all times, and we never even dared to tell our closest friends and families what we were up to, though of course in time they sensed it.

Between my *Betar* courses and my two times a week with the *Irgun*, I had little or no time for any social life. The girls I was able to go out with often had to wait until late at night before we saw each other, so I could finish my evening's training. The *Irgun* and *Betar* had become my entire life.

* * *

By the time I was assigned to an *Irgun* unit in Jerusalem a year later, I had learned quite a bit of history of the *Irgun*. Its nucleus had been formed from a breakaway group of officers and instructors of the Jerusalem *Haganah*. They had chafed at the *Haganah's* static defensive concepts, at the inadequacies of military training and at the lack of proper weapons, as well as at the internal political undercurrents which weakened the organization. The Socialist Zionists, through the Federation of Labor (*Histadrut*), dominated the *Haganah*. Since the early twenties, their goal, in conjunction with the moderate cultural Zionists, had been to dominate the *Yishuv*. Together they had steamrollered all opposition.

Socialist Labor never recognized that the prompt creation of a strong national army was a prerequisite to the future state. In their eyes, anything beyond a civilian militia for self-defense was considered chauvinistic, anti-socialist and latently fascist.

When Abraham Tehomi and most of the officer corps of Jerusalem seceded from the *Haganah* in 1931, their departure was actually welcomed by the top echelon of Labor, which never again permitted non-socialist elements to become an important factor in the *Haganah*. The *Histadrut*, led by Ben-Gurion and a few key associates, gained administrative and ideological control of the *Haganah*, never to relinquish it.

Prior to 1929, several youth groups of Jabotinsky's followers organized in cells, gathered weapons and helped in the defense of

Tel-Aviv. They were led by 'Irma' Helpren and Moshe Rosenberg, also originally Jerusalem *Haganah* men.

By 1929, they had trained several groups, acquired a fair supply of weapons and built a disciplined cadre. Other non-socialist groups gathered impetus during these same years in Haifa, Safed and in the Sharon district. When the large Jerusalem officer group broke away from the *Haganah*, the various independent units coalesced into the *Irgun* in April 1931.

The beginnings were modest. "Civilian committees" were created for the purpose of maintaining contact with the communities and the "national institutions." Most important, these committees raised the funds necessary for arms acquisition and the maintenance of a small-salaried staff. The actual results of all this were meager: the nationalists were long on idealism but short on means. Furthermore, the leadership of Labor saw to it that activists in the *Irgun* lost jobs and income, and the limited funds they could amass came from their ranks, from friends and family, and from some non-socialist circles worried about the growing partisan character of the *Haganah*.

The *Irgun* saw itself as a non-partisan National Army in the making. Its stated belief was that military preparedness should be put above party politics, and its first concerns—tough training and strict military discipline. Its publication, *Metzuda* (The Citadel), called for a synthesis of the fighting traditions of the ancient Hebrews with modern professional military training and the techniques of liberation armies around the world. Professor Joseph Klausner, under the pen name *Hamitboded*—"The Loner"—wrote in the fall 1932 issue dedicated to the Bar Kochba rebellion eighteen hundred years before:

> Bar Kochba rebelled against mighty Rome. For three years the Jews fought . . . They lost half a million people . . . and kept on rebelling, again and again.
>
> Was it the proud spirit of Bar Kochba that the stubborn Jews took with them into exile, which sustained us throughout the centuries, despite all attempts throughout the generations to wipe us out? . . . Conquered Bar Kochba is as dear to us as the conquering Judah Maccabee. . . . The spirit of Bar Kochba calls to us—young Jews, be strong! Don't give in to spiritual or physical lethargy, to compromise or defeatism. Don't abandon your people to shame and degradation. Freedom is acquired in blood; a home-

land is secured through sacrifice, and even the vanquished, in the battle for honor and liberty, are the conquerors . . . heroes . . . command eternal life to the people!

The *Metzuda* was read to the ranks from a handful of multigraphed copies. We did not know the authors until years later—Klausner, Yevin, David Raziel, Abraham Stern, H. S. Halevy. These men lived according to the words they wrote and some of them and their children also died by them.

My beloved teacher, Professor Joseph Klausner, was perhaps the most unique voice of all in the early 1930s. In the Hebrew University of Jerusalem, that citadel of socialist and cutural Zionism, the thinking of a man who could see national glory in the defeat of Bar Kochba was received with sneering suggestions about senility. The intellectual elite could not conceive of excellence that was not Marxist-rooted. Klausner was both anti-materialistic and anti-Marxist. He drew his models for social justice from the Bible and the rest of our Jewish heritage. He believed that lasting social justice would come not through violent revolution, but through a long evolutionary process of humanity. This brought down on him the wrath of the socialist establishment that preached class struggle.

Despite it all, Klausner brought up several generations of youths that listened to his words. As early as 1906, Jabotinsky had read the writings of Klausner in Odessa and twenty-five years later our small group of students still followed his basic teachings. However, in the 1930's we were a decided minority compared to the socialists.

Klausner and Jabotinsky made us proud of our national history. They fought against those equating the struggle for Jewish survival with chauvinism, or even worse, with fascism. Klausner taught us that the Hebrew renaissance would, make us better humans, more effective contributors to the family of nations. Believing that Hebrew nationalism was in no way regressive, that in fact it was an essential stepping stone to the successful life of twentieth century Jews, Klausner and Jabotinsky argued vehemently against the assimilationists; against Zionists who attached apologetic codicils to national assertiveness; against the spiritualists who felt the "trappings" of an army and a state, and a government would detract from pure humanitarianism.

The ideological challenges raised by Klausner and Jabotinsky were debated for years, and their views were adopted in the *Irgun* and the *Betar* by the dedicated few. The elitists sneered at them, and the masses would not follow their teachings until years later—too many years later.

III
Going Underground

While our teachers lectured and declaimed, landed in prison and went on hunger strikes, we young men and women quietly embarked on the dreary, lonely life of building the underground. Like most revolutionaries, we were long on sacrifice and commitment, but short of means to fulfill our commitments.

When Tehomi and his colleagues left the *Haganah*, they controlled the unit's weapons in Jerusalem. However, Tehomi felt that in stepping out of the frame of the establishment, he could not expropriate "public property"; so the weapons were returned to the *Haganah*. The hundred members of the new organization started with ten pistols borrowed from individual owners. They used wooden pistols for training. The Tel-Aviv district fared better. There, the underground groups that Helpren and Rosenberg formed around the *Betar* managed to purchase thirty rifles from Circassian villagers in Trans-Jordan. Rosenberg arranged for acquisitions of fifty handguns from Germany that were slipped through customs in Jaffa with a shipment of spare machine parts.

To raise equipment we required funds, and to raise funds we needed outside support. So the *Irgun* went out to the Jewish community of Palestine for help, always stressing that our goal was to build a well-trained, non-partisan national military organization which would not be crippled by politics. Tehomi and his colleagues hoped we could eventually guide the *Haganah* towards this goal as well, and that we would one day merge into one organization. To secure the widest public support, we formed "civilian committees" of public figures from inside the leadership of the *Yishuv*. Those figures ranged from Rabbi Meir Berlin, leader of the Orthodox Mizrachi, to Dr. Emanuel Neumann, a General Zionist leader from the United States, and non-political men like Dr. Edouard Joseph, a leading surgeon in Jerusalem.

Thus the non-partisan character of the *Irgun* continued widening for almost four years, to membership of almost four thousand men and women. It also generated additional funds and arms. But within the framework of this organization, there were seeds of conflict. The upper level of command in the large cities still hoped for a return to the *Haganah* and believed that ultimately they could turn the *Haganah* into the future national army. On the other end, those of us preparing militarily for a revolution preceding independence, hardly expected to wean the *Haganah* away from the pacifism imposed on it by socialist labor. These divergent views boded great upheavals within the *Irgun*, but in the later years from 1933 to 1937, the *Irgun* grew impressively.

* * *

New recruits met once every two weeks; reserves met once a month or less; and noncoms and officers spent most of their evenings performing their various duties. In addition, they underwent advance training, often in the orange groves of outlying communities. Saturday mornings were devoted to close order drill, usually at 6 a.m. on the beaches, on athletic fields and secluded spots among groves. Communications were mostly by word of mouth. The noncom or the unit head advised the first man in the unit where and when the next training would take place. He had one to two hours to advise the man next in line. Everyone was expected to leave his workplace or studies or whatever he was engaged in, to advise the next man. Usually, by the end of the day, the unit knew the evening's password and when to meet. We used private homes, offices and schools for the training sites, and during the meeting the sites were guarded by men of the same company, which meant extra duty. We knew members only from our own company, usually composed of two to four units. As tensions built up in the country, we had to perform extra duties in defensive positions, as messengers, drivers and clerks at headquarters. Every so often we would make special weekend trips out into the desert to practice with explosives. The Friday before these journeys, we had a curfew of 10 p.m., and officers would literally send men to our homes at night to make sure we obeyed it.

This was the routine in Tel-Aviv, and it continued in the fall of 1933 when I moved to Jerusalem. I headed the *Betar* youth, and was eventually appointed to head the entire Jerusalem branch of *Betar*. I had an ambitious schedule, attempting to concentrate on my studies, head the *Betar* and carry out my *Irgun* responsibilities evenings and weekends. Not surprisingly, I did not do too well at the university. Along with my lack of time, I also developed doubts about my future plans. Political events were moving fast. Hitler had come to power in Europe and the struggle in the Zionist movement intensified both in Palestine and Europe. I began to wonder if I would ever have the chance to carry on my grandfather Zeev Leib's tradition of farming. My father had bought a small orange grove as a lure, thinking it would wean me away from a future on a kibbutz; he did not realize how much my life had changed in two years. I had moved from the socialist dreams of high school days to the activism of Achimeir and then to the national revolutionary *Irgun*. I was drifting farther and farther away from my parents without their knowing it. It was a painful time for me, because I knew they were not well, but I was too involved to do anything about it.

Then, in the winter of 1933, Father suffered two heart attacks within three days. I returned to Tel-Aviv. I saw at once that there was not much hope for his recovery. He looked weak and gray, and in the evening as I went out to perform my *Betar* and *Irgun* duties, I was afraid he might not be alive when I returned home.

My mind kept running over all the ways I wished my father and I had been closer. There had never been much of a dialogue between us on ethical or abstract matters. He watched and advised me about my health and manners, and about my choice of friends; but his life had always been devoted to earning a living for his wife and child and he had never had time for "causes." I was grateful that he gave me the best of homes and educations. I had never known hunger, never had to support myself with a day's labor in the groves of Rehovoth. And though Father would have liked for me to follow in his business, he knew I would not. I could never see life the way he and Mother did—as one continuous battle for material security.

On the gray morning of Father's third day of confinement, he stopped me with these surprising words' "There is one principle I wish you to follow in your life . . . never hurt other people." He was alluding to Hillel the Elder, for whom the essence of the Torah was: "What is hateful to you, do not do unto your neighbor." Somehow in my father's mind the links had been reestablished to his grandfather Shneour Levi, who said in his will over a half century earlier: "Be righteous before God and before man."

I listened, feeling frightened. I somehow sensed that these were the last words I would ever hear from him. Father was quiet, his eyes wide open as if staring at some distant scene. Then he tightened his hands on mine and whispered: "It is so dark. . . ."

It was all over in a flicker. My heart froze to stone. I patted and kissed his forehead, smoothed out the cover, and went out to the terrace to tell Mother.

Years later, I read that before his death Shneour Zalman of Lyady, the father of *Habad* Hasidism, had said to his grandchild: "Do you see the ceiling?" And answering himself, he had said in a breaking voice: "I cannot see anything any more. I can only see the spirit of everything and the power of God to create and animate."

To this day, I wish I knew what Father saw in that last moment.

* * *

I stayed in Tel-Aviv through that summer. In the fall I returned to Jerusalem and changed to the School of Humanities. I knew that from now on, whatever studying I engaged in would be politically oriented.

Weakened by her diabetes, Mother died of pneumonia twelve months later. It was a long, trying illness which I could literally see consuming her face and body. She had always been as resilient, stubborn, and strong as her father, Zeev Leib, but now I could feel her just withering away, becoming more emaciated and lighter in my arms every day. When her suffering finally came to an end, I was almost relieved. For the first time, the hopes and dreams my parents held for my future no longer mattered. Whatever they had planned for me would only be a memory. I was alone and my future was subject wholly to what I made of it.

Jerusalem was my only home and I threw myself into my political obligations harder than ever. The *Irgun* and *Betar* became my family and a replacement for all my former personal ambitions.

On the surface, the country was quiet. The *Irgun's* last full mobilization had been in 1933 when I spent several weeks in a "defensive" position on a border between Jaffa and Tel-Aviv. A *Nekuda* was an apartment or home where a defensive unit was stationed. The number of men and women assigned depended on the degree of tension and mobilization. The weapons were usually kept nearby in an adjacent house or apartment. If trouble developed, the men fetched the weapons and went to the street. Both *Haganah* and the *Irgun* used this basic system in the urban areas, from 1929 to 1936.

During these years, an attempt was made to unify the *Haganah* and the *Irgun*. The effort collapsed after Socialist Labor attacked a parade of *Betar* youth on the last day of Passover, 1933. I was twenty years old and in charge of the young *Betar* units ages twelve to fifteen. We marched up Allenby Street from the sports field of Tel-Aviv to the clubhouse in the center of town. Suddenly a rain of rocks, bricks, old iron bed parts and steel scraps hit us. The youngsters were knocked to the ground, attacked and their shirts were torn off. By the time we reached the clubhouse many were bleeding and in shock, and some were suffering from concussions. The attack had been organized by the top people in the *Haganah*, and Labor, including Dov Hos and Rose Cohen. The ranks of the *Irgun* now overwhelmingly vetoed a merger with the *Haganah*. The negotiations broke off. The Socialists and the nationalist camps continued to function, watching each other with suspicion, with the Socialists strengthening their control of the Jewish Agency and all other institutions.

In the next few years, with Hitler in power, Jews tried to leave Europe in increasing numbers. Immigration to Palestine rose from twelve thousand five hundred in 1931 to sixty thousand in 1935; there were not many other countries, however, which were opening their doors to the refugees. Just as Mordechai had predicted two years earlier, the Jews in Europe were isolated and made more and more vulnerable.

During those years, we continued our work, intensifying our drills and our accumulation of arms. I was accepted for training as *Sgan*, and from then on training took up at least four evenings of my week and a half-day Saturday.

My training group, the seventh in the *Irgun*, had more permanent meeting sites than the rank and file. We met at the Spitzer School in the *Bokhara* quarter, at the Alliance School, and in the office of Dr. Edouard Joseph. The course was supposed to take six months, but unexpected political and security problems disrupted our training, and it lasted almost a year and a half. The intensiveness of a *Sganim* course sometimes hurt families and careers, it was so exhausting and time-consuming. But there was no complaining. We chose this way of life voluntarily, and there were seldom any defections from the ranks. The more the *Irgun* grew, the more selective became the admission process. We impressed the pressures and dangers on the potential recruits, and a few had second thoughts before the swearing-in. We reviewed potential recruits in the *Maccabee* and *Betar* youth organizations, and in schools and places of work. Prior to approaching candidates we would discuss them with the head of our unit. Once the recruits were placed in the admissions channel, we lost contact with them. We might come across them years later, in defense positions or, in unusual cases, where larger groups engaged in field training.

In Jerusalem, I gradually came to know the top echelon of the *Irgun*—if for no better reason than that I owned a car. Between 1934 and 1937 this was a vital asset to the *Irgun*. Because of my car, I got to see the inner workings and the key people of the organization. So I could be ready for emergency transports of men and equipment, I spent days and nights at headquarters during times of tension and I established friendships with key veteran commanders.

One man I came to know was David Raziel, or "Razi" as we called him. I first met him in 1931 at a student convention in Tel-Aviv, and again at the Hebrew University in 1933, but we did not become close friends until later through our *Irgun* activities. He was the son of an Orthodox family that came to Palestine from the Vilna region (Lithuania), when he was a child, and he grew up an observant Jew. He had rugged features, a heavy-set body, and a quick sharp laugh. He studied philosophy and mathematics, but his great devotion was to the rebirth of Hebrew military tradition.

As I came to know him over the years, he became more and more a unique phenomenon in contemporary Jewish life—the dedicated academic and the consummate military man.

In the most difficult situations he had a cool mastery of his emotions, yet, as a young man, he was often quick-tempered and snappy. He was generally short on idle conversations and abstract ideology, yet at odd moments he could be extremely verbose. He researched military literature scrupulously and composed manuals on weapons, tactics and training. As he rose in the *Irgun's* hierarchy, those he helped train gained a reputation for their outstanding battle readiness. Razi tolerated no mediocrity in himself or any of us.

I once went to see him in his room when he was quartermaster in Jerusalem. He was at his desk and as there was no free chair I moved to sit on his bed. Smiling, he stopped me, bent down and pulled out a homemade mine. He carefully placed it in the corner. Then he said: "You and your hundred and eighty pounds. You'd better lose some weight. Now you can sit down on my bed." Later he explained that he was building a prototype mine activated by weight and delayed action. The mine was still at a stage where he felt that if anything went wrong, others might be hurt; so he intended to do the testing himself. He then inquired whether I would "volunteer" for a trip to the desert next Friday. At about three in the afternoon we met at the designated point. Razi came to the car with two large, bulky rucksacks and a water canteen. He inspected my shoes approvingly. "Let's get going," he said. "We have half an hour of driving and three quarters of an hour walking. I would like to be back home before Shabbat." He suggested that I watch my driving speed, since we did not want any traffic cops after us.

We took the road to the Dead Sea and drove about six miles. The farther we went, the more the usually taciturn Razi unwound and began to talk. He bemoaned the advantage the *Haganah* had over us with their kibbutzim and other settlements in which city trainees and regular members could have unlimited field

"The Anonymous Soldiers"

Yaakov Raz. Mortally wounded during counter-terrorist action.

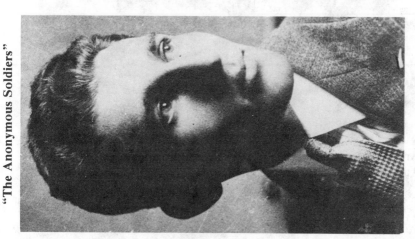

Abraham Stern, who led the *Lehi* (Lohamei Herut Israel).

David Raziel, *Irgun* Commander 1938-1941.

Group of Jerusalem Irgun officers on a tour of the Galilee (1935). Author first from left.

Irgun officers and *Sganim* on a training mission on the outskirts of Jerusalem (1938).

training. "And yet," he said, "I'll wager they're not doing much more training than they did before 1929. If only we in the *Irgun* had so many acres to drill our men!" Razi was one of the veterans of the *Haganah* that had split in 1931 and one of the first graduates of the *Irgun's Sganim* courses. He always believed that intensive military training was the primary contribution he could make to the soldiers of the *Irgun*. This devoted student of the Talmud now devoted his life to what Nehemiah described as the "holding of the spears." We talked about the lack of automatic and heavy weapons, ammunition and funds. "Whether we have funds or not," Razi said, "we will manage. We will simply manufacture what we cannot buy." I looked skeptical, and he laughed his short, hacking laugh. "Don't be a pessimist. Four years ago we had only ten pistols. We are not terribly prosperous but we have made some progress. Wait till you see what we have in the sacks."

We turned off the main highway onto the road that led to the Monastery of the Good Samaritan. Then Razi pointed out a narrow footpath and we stopped the car. There was not a living soul in sight. The sun was hot and the reddish rocks and the hard, flat barren patches of soil reflected the heat mercilessly. We picked up the rucksacks and climbed up to the summit of the hills to the East. From the crest we could see the outline of the Jordan Valley and farther south, the Dead Sea. We descended into the valley, located a small cave and crawled in. It did not appear to have been visited by the local goats or their young Arab shepherds. Razi instructed me to place the sacks in two separate places in the cave. We covered them up with rock and soil, camouflaging them as best we could. Then we crawled out. Nothing moved in the heat, although a weak breeze was building up from the mountains of Moab across the Jordan. We walked back to the crest and down to the car.

I gathered my courage to say something to Razi that I had felt a long time. We in the ranks had a favorite complaint—too much close order drill. I had years of it, hour upon hour every Saturday on the beach in Tel-Aviv, on the Maccabee soccer field in Jerusalem and in any number of gyms. I did not relish the thought of yet another session tomorrow. "Razi," I ventured quietly, "aren't we perhaps overdoing close order drill?" Razi laughed sharply again. "Sure. On purpose! Are you satisfied with the discipline in *Betar*?

Don't you think that our youth are far from being the soliders we need? We are not building just another *Haganah*. We are laying the foundation of our national army. We start with amorphous human material and turn it into a disciplined body. What's better than close order drill? We Jews have forgotten how to act as a single unit, obeying Jewish orders."

I regretted having said anything.

"But we need more field training with weapons. . . ."

Razi cut me short: "You'll get it when we have more. We can't afford the wear and tear, or the risk of exposure when we carry them to and from training places. And you know as well as I, that bullets spent carelessly now may make the difference in real action. We don't do enough with weapons, but we do what we can do."

I remained silent and when I stopped in front of Razi's house in Jerusalem, he did not get out. He looked at me, smiled and stretched his legs. Then, looking straight ahead, he said: "I read your article the other day in the *Hayarden*, about your disappointment with the physical conditioning and *esprit de corps* of the young *Betarim*, especially the city youngsters. You must have had quite a disappointing experience in the summer work camp in Zichron Yaakov. But the problem is deeper, you know. It is not merely physical training and camaraderie we need. We have to bring up our youth so that offering their lives becomes instinctive. We all could die peacefully in bed, but shouldn't we rather try to stop bullets that are meant to annihilate our people?"

Next morning at sunrise, we filed out from our meeting point through eastern Jerusalem, past the Hebrew University on Mount Scopus and continued eastward. We walked in small scattered single file groups carrying water canteens and light food and wearing a motley assortment of hats and garments. We carried a few Bibles and a couple of pistols for emergency—pistols could be disposed of quickly in an encounter with the authorities.

It took us almost four hours to reach our small cave. On the way we exchanged greetings with a few Bedouin goat herders. In the desert there was either banditry or fellowship.

Razi and two instructors dragged the rucksacks out of the caves. There were half a dozen small weapons. Some bags of ammunition, grenades, dynamite, blasting caps, fuses and wire.

We had new German Mausers and long-barreled Parabellums, some adjustable for automatic firing. We also had Austrian Steuers dating back to 1918 and some smaller Italian Berettas.

Lookouts were posted on the western and eastern ridges, and we spent the following two hours doing target practice. Automatic firing was new to us, even to some veteran commanders. We were permitted a short burst per person. We then watched grenade-throwing demonstrations with both dummy and live grenades. A short lecture followed on mines and demolition.

By noon we were finished. The sounds of firing and explosions died down. There were no signs of warning from the lookouts. We were far enough from the highway, no passing cars could have heard us.

We picked up the empty shells and stored them in the cave till the next morning when I would drive back with a colleague to pick them up. We started our leisurely hike back to Jerusalem. Another day's training was done.

* * *

A future liberation army could not function without weapons and arms acquisition became our most primary task. The man who immersed himself in it was our first commander, Abraham Tehomi. He had been appointed *Haganah* Commander in Jerusalem following the 1929 riots, which had exposed serious defects in the *Haganah*'s structure and training. In a short time the Jerusalem *Haganah*'s membership rose to over a thousand disciplined men and women. Party politics ultimately forced Tehomi and his associates to leave and to form the nucleus of what became the *Irgun Zvai Leumi* which they hoped would remain apart from political intrigues.

Tehomi was the archetypal underground commander. His right hand had been injured in a traffic accident, and he wore a black band around the fist to cover the scars. His black hair, combed to the side, always fell over his squinting, penetrating eyes. When he looked at you, you felt your innermost soul being examined. Tehomi was a tense man who moved furtively. He sometimes would enter a darkened meeting room and leave it without our ever noticing his presence. He always had an air of conspiracy about him and not many knew it was largely a cultivated image. Underneath it all, he was an easygoing, charming, good-humored individual.

From the moment Tehomi was appointed commander of the *Irgun* he concentrated on arms acquisition. He was as successful as he could have been, given our limited means.

One day in 1935, the instructor of our *Sganim* course, Eli Ettinger, an aspiring painter by profession, said that he had a "pleasant" surprise for us. By this time we had had eight long months of training, interrupted repeatedly by tensions and mobilization around the country, and we were constantly repeating a number of subjects. We had more than perfected our knowledge of small weapons; we could take apart three different automatic hand guns, mix up the parts and put them back together in five minutes in total darkness. We had reached the point where we felt little more could be taught us within the limits of what we had available to us. And we complained about it.

As we sat down to a weapons lesson, Eli reached for an unusually large package and unveiled what looked like a Thompson machine gun. We gaped at it in pure exhilaration. Here was the perfect urban weapon, suitable for both defense and attack. Small, dismountable, with a cylindrical magazine, it could hold forty-five or more rounds. We were mesmerized. Eli smiled then quickly dismantled it, and our love affair with the "Washington" was launched.

Tehomi has secured the "Washington" in a somewhat unusual way. He had visited a floating exhibition of Finnish products aboard a schooner docked in Haifa, and in the weapons exhibit he noticed a sub-machine gun—an almost identical copy of the United States Thompson, which sold on the world market for a hefty forty pounds Sterling. The Finns priced that gun at twenty. Tehomi immediately went to Finland and established a channel, and the shipments started arriving just before the Arab riots of spring 1936. We named the weapon the "Washington" in honor of the American Revolution.

The "Washington" soon became an important part of our budding arsenal. We were also blessed with a flow of small weapons which came from the Polish government. Since the twenties, Moshe Rosenberg, our "grand old man," had devoted most of his energies and endangered his modest import business in "accumulation of iron." Rosenberg sometimes quoted Jabotinsky's novel *Prelude to Delilah,* in which Samson blinded, shorn and degraded, speaks to the small Israelite boy who has sneaked through the Philistine lines to see him. Samson gives the boy a message to bring back to the Israelites: "Tell the people three things: let them choose a leader; let them learn to laugh; and let them gather iron."

For Tehomi, Rosenberg and many others, Samson's words became the code to live by. Our military strength grew and we were even able to sell part of our shipments to settlements who were short of weapons. Ironically, even the *Haganah* bought some of the "Washingtons" from us. They did so even as the British Zionists who backed them were denouncing Colonel John Patterson for raising funds on our behalf. The funds were used to buy the "Washingtons."

Gradually we built the foundations of a military industry. We convinced small metal shops to cooperate with us, reconditioning ammunition, and using spare parts to repair weapons and produce grenades and mines. The owners, foremen and workers ran grave risks to help us.

Many of our best instructors gave their lives in the process of amassing weapons. Menahem Strelitz, who helped develop a rifle-launched grenade, died in 1936 when a grenade he was testing exploded. My good friend Arieh Yitshaki, who had trained with me as a *Betar* instructor, was blown up in the workshop he built several houses away from our home in Tel-Aviv.

Though our responsibilities and our sacrifices multiplied with each passing year, we never felt we were doing anything above the call of duty. What we did feel, acutely, was that we were racing against time.

IV
Assignment in Galilee

The relatively peaceful years of 1930-35 were nearing their end. Nazism was on the rise and those European Jews who saw the threat arrived in Palestine in growing numbers.

By now the Mufti of Jerusalem, Amin el Husseini, had gradually disposed of competing chieftains and clans and created the "Arab Higher Committee," over which he had complete control. He established contacts with fascist Italy and Nazi Germany and enlisted the support of Fawzi-el-Kaukji, a mercenary Iraqi officer of Syrian descent, who in turn recruited volunteers from Iraq and Syria. The goal was a holy war against the Jews. The foundations were laid for future generations of strife between Pan-Arabists and the Jews returning to Palestine.

For the Jewish nationalist youth, the issues were clear. Palestine was our home, historically and morally. The Arabs in Palestine had no roots there. They were merely a residue of hundreds of years of transitory invasions, and the wandering of tribal groups. We recognized their right to live in civil and religious freedom, but in our minds, only the descendants of the ancient Hebrews had a past and a future irrevocably linked with this land. Only they had throughout history lived here and only here as a nation.

The fathers of Arab national rebirth had discovered the limits of Pan-Arabism in 1916, when Pan-Arab dreams succumbed to internal and foreign intrigues and Arab groups fragmented and sprouted various local ambitions. The Pan-Arab dream was still latent and would probably revive sporadically in generations to come. We saw ourselves facing continuous clashes with those aspirations, clashes where no reasoning, and certainly no weakness, would help solve the conflict.

We also were certain that Britain would not keep the pledges she made in the Balfour Declaration. Britain was unwilling to erode relations with Arab potentates; it feared the loss of lives in armed clashes and the loss of resources. Not only had we lost Britain as an ally; in fact, we guessed that soon she would declare war on the national aspirations of the emerging Hebrew nation. Brtain tightened the immigration laws of Palestine precisely at a time when nazism in Germany was on the rise and their vicious brand of anti-Semitism was spreading.

Jabotinsky stated in August 1932, "Several million Jews out of European Europe will have to evacuate their large areas of residence and form the national Hebrew State in Palestine." Tragically, even as late as 1936, all Jewish leaders, Zionists, and non-Zionists alike, denounced the Evacuation Plan as outrageous and criminal. The Jews themselves around the world did not see or refused to admit the mortal danger their people were facing. The Jewish opposition to the concept of evacuation formed a wall of resistance. To reach the masses in Europe, to gain support from the community in Palestine, to ask for help from the affluent Jewish communities of the West, we had to break through this wall. This was Jabotinsky's mission.

The answer given by our handful of young people in Palestine was to build our military strength—to counter Pan-Arab assaults; to break down the immigration bans so that our people could be saved; to force the British to eventually quit the country. Such acts and concepts had been foreign to Jews for two thousand years and was still rejected by Socialists, the middle class and the cultural Zionist establishment.

Eventually, the poisonous atmosphere inside the Zionist movement and the rapidly growing dangers in the world led Jabotinsky and his followers to leave the Zionist organization and form the New Zionist Organization (NZO) in 1935. This left Socialist Labor in unchallenged control of the Jewish Agency and the World Zionist Organization. They had both financial power and control over the immigration certificates handed out by the British and only one independent body remained outside their control in Palestine—the *Irgun.*

In 1936, the Jerusalem Mufti's "Arab Higher Command" organized a series of riots against the Jews. Our answer was to increase our arms and manpower. The Jewish Agency answer was to develop with British consent an auxiliary police to protect the settlements (it excluded *Irgun* members whenever possible). At a time when Arab-Jewish tensions were mounting, and the *Irgun* growth was hampered by limited funds, the non-Jabotinsky elements in the *Irgun* reached the conclusion that the *Irgun* had gone as far as it could as an independent body and a merger with the *Haganah* was unavoidable. The Zionist leadership still had illusions that some accommodation with Britain might result from the Peel Royal Commission which was then holding hearings. The Zionist leadership hoped that sooner or later it would assume semi-official status in Palestine's government and the *Haganah* would be legalized. The "moderate" elements in the *Irgun* were inclined to concur.

Jabotinsky agreed to *Haganah-Irgun* merger negotiations, but opposed anything but full parity in the command of a united military organization. The Socialists, of course, wanted the Jewish Agency to control the organization—but political Zionism had good reason to distrust such control; among others, they did not intend to submit to another partition of the country like the one in 1922, when Winston Churchill severed the eastern portion of the Mandate and gave it to the Hashemite family of Arabia.

The *Irgun* command decided to hold a plebiscite about whether to join with the *Haganah* or remain separate. The plebiscite took place on Saturday, April 24, 1937, and as a result, after six years of independent existence, the *Irgun* was split. Fifteen hundred men and women, headed by Tehomi and most veteran commanders went back to the *Haganah* with the hope of perfecting it as a military organization, and they took with them most of the weapons. Some eighteen hundred, mostly youths in their teens and twenties, remained in the ranks of the *Irgun*, myself amongst them. We did not believe that the *Haganah* could be freed from a defensive mentality nor from socialist control and turned into effective, military organization. We felt that our former colleagues would quickly be assimilated and disappear into the *Haganah*'s "civil militia" structure without any demonstrable effect on it. This is what ultimately happened.

We now had to rebuild the organization. We had lost all our commanders in the major cities, most of the company commanders, all our civilian local councils and their financial support, and most of our equipment. But we were left with the youth and a few of the higher command. With the divisive element gone, the ideologically committed core of the *Irgun* could now focus on its long-term goals.

* * *

Shortly before, Dr. Shimshon Yunitchman, who headed the "Labor units" of *Betar*, asked for help in revitalizing the *Irgun's* organization and training in the Galilee. Command had been handed to a veteran *Irgun* officer, Joseph Duckler, who was tubercular. As a full-fledged *Sgan* I was assigned to perform the functions that Duckler's health would not permit.

Galilee in spring, the hills were covered with golden flowers, the grass a deep green, and small streams could be heard bubbling. For a native of the south like myself, it was a feast for the eyes and ears.

I settled down in Rosh Pina where I had a small room in a house next to Ja'una, the Arab Village. It had once been an office for Baron Rothschild's old administration, the ICA. Rosh Pina was an old, non-communal settlement populated by second and third generation Romanian, Russian and Polish immigrants out of the first *Aliyah*. Like other such settlements—Mishmar Hayarden, Yesod Hama'alah, Metullah—it was in dire financial straits. All of them lagged behind the country economically, and in proportionate sharing of national funds. Outside the Socialist camp, they were on the bottom of the list for help from the labor-dominated Jewish Agency. Throughout the years, they had come to depend on cheap Arab labor. They found themselves further ostracized on that account, and even more dependent on Arab labor because of their deteriorating financial resources.

Plugot Ha'avoda, a two-year national service obligatory for *Betar* immigrants, supplied workers to individual farmers in these old settlements. The farmers were poor so the *Betarim* worked for the same low wages as the Arab workers. We considered Rosh Pina and the others, especially those in the Galilee, precious symbols of the pioneering past as well as crucial to our national security.

All through the years I had been an enthusiastic supporter of the *Plugot*. As head of the Jerusalem *Betar*, and a member of the *Betar's* national leadership, I had argued that the same two-year service should be obligatory on our Palestinian *Betarim*. Like Eri Jabotinsky, who headed the *Betar* from 1935 on, I saw in the *Plugot* an important contribution to military security. The *Plugot* gave its *Betarim* personal fulfillment while serving the national interest, and it induced many of the youths to live on the land.

On this point, I disagreed with Achimeir who saw the masses in the cities as the base of the Hebrew Revolution. He proved to be wrong about this. The selfless, idealistic youth from the *Plugot* played an exemplary role when battles came to a head in later years.

My priority assignment in the Galilee was to train the small group of *Sganim* candidates who I felt were the backbone of any military organization. They were a group of eager, bright young men chosen from the various units in the Galilee. They were already trained in the use of small arms, explosives and grenades, and they had studied the one "Washington" that had been allocated to Rosh Pina.

For many months during 1936, the Galilee was a main staging area for the bands of Fawzi El-Kaukji the Iraqi officer in the service of the Mufti of Jerusalem. In the isolated regions of the Galilee, especially in the old, small, underpopulated Mishmar Hayarden and Yesod Hama'alah settlements where the dozen or so young men and women of the local "Plugot" constituted almost the only young element, there was a heightened awareness of the need for military preparedness. The young *Betarim* knew they had to redouble their efforts.

With more attention now paid to the Galilee, morale rose. Training, combined with guard duty, followed each day's work and though food and lodgings were barely livable, there was little complaint. Over the years, many families in the settlements had either moved away or simply died out, leaving their deserted houses. Our *Pluga* occupied these houses for their training sites. Malaria was still a threat and sometimes I would come to a settlement on my appointed visit and find one of the men down with a soaring fever, apologizing profusely that he could not attend the training.

Shortly after arriving in the Galilee, Commander Joseph Duckler took inventory of our weapons and ammunition. The situation was pitiful. Except for the legal rifles assigned to the auxiliary watchmen, we lacked enough weapons to arm even our small units in the *Plugot*. We did not know exactly what weapons the *Haganah* possessed in their communal settlements, but based on past experience, we were certain their supply was dangerously inadequate. If the local Arabs brought in men and weapons from Iraq and Syria, the Galilee would be used as a transit and staging area and turned into a stronghold. Our units, underequipped, isolated way up in the north, with exposed communications and limited manpower, would be critically vulnerable. Duckler urged Tel-Aviv to review our needs but the situation in other areas was not much better. Across the land the *Irgun* was growing in numbers, but as usual, the organization was desperately short of funds. What use was it to train the youth and not be able to arm them?

In his last months as commander before returning to the *Haganah*, Tehomi had complained bitterly to Jabotinsky, but it did not help. Jabotinsky was already practically carrying the budget of the movement alone, through his personal public appearances all over the world—while the Socialists, who claimed to represent the proletariat, had Jewish capitalists as their main backers.

A great part of the weapons we used were borrowed from the settlements or municipalities. We owned outright barely a fifth of what we would need in time of mobilization. There were weapons available for us to buy—from overseas, the Arabs or various entrepreneurs—but we just did not have the funds. . . .

Duckler sent me to Tel-Aviv to argue for additional allocations of arms. I came back with a little ammunition, some supplies to build our own hand grenades and half a dozen handguns. It was the best I or anyone else in the Galilee could do.

My daily travels gave me time to reminisce, and often during a long, lonely night drive from Metullah to Rosh Pina, I tried to relieve the monotony by mentally flashing on and off chapters of history. The Galilee always touched a special chord in me. Next to Jerusalem, it was the place where I had the most powerful mystical feeling of having been here in an earlier life. It had been the home of the Israelites continuously for almost two thousand years, from the time when Joshua helped conquer it in the thirteenth century BCE, up to 614 CE, when the Galileans still rebelled against Byzantium. And in the city of Peki'in lived one tiny Jewish community that had never left the land. From an early age, when I first came to the Galilee, I felt as if history were looking down on me from the towering pinnacles of rocky Gush-Halav, from Yodefet, from the Hermon. I swelled with pride at my Israelite ancestors who settled on the forbidden mountains while the Canaanites inhabited the comfortable valleys, and I felt ashamed of the Galileans who had fought each other while Vespasian was marching to conquer them in 67 CE. The Galileans had been so busy with their fraternal wars they could muster no offensive threat, but only some last-minute defense. Vespasian picked off their cities one by one.

I always had ambivalent feelings toward Josephus Flavius, the Galilean traitor-general, turned historian and Jewish apologist. I identified him in my mind with present Jewish leaders and academics who distorted contemporary history for their own purposes. It was safe enough, after the defeat by the Romans, for Josephus to claim that it had made no sense to rebel. However, had the Galileans and Judeans not fought each other and, instead, engaged in proper preparations for the war, history would have followed a different course. History appeared to repeat itself.

Late one evening, driving home to Rosh Pina, I saw an Arab couple waving at me. The man was dressed like a simple farmer and the woman had on the customary blue, embroidered dress of the Palestinian peasant. I slowed down. The woman was crying, holding a young boy of about five in her arms. The child was moaning, and the man said the boy had been bitten by a snake. They had tried the usual remedies and salves but his leg was turning blue. Could I drive them to the hospital in Safed?

It never occurred to me that I might refuse them a ride. I opened the door, and the woman and child sat next to me. The man climbed into the rumble seat. When I had dropped them off and was driving back, I thought about the irony of it all. Here I sat, a beautiful target on the twisting road from Rosh Pina to Safed, one of the choicest locations for murderous attacks by Arabs on Jewish traffic. I had instinctively answered a human appeal for help, and I hoped that the small boy would live, but one day that same boy might do his best to see that I and my people perished. It struck me once again that for all the hatred our two peoples had built up over the generations, I never could look upon an Arab as an enemy. The growing hatred never seemed anything but a tragedy to me. As Jabotinsky only a short time before had declared to the Peel Commission in London, we wished our Arab neighbors no ill. The country could accommodate millions of Jews and Arabs, all we asked of the Arab nations was that out of the vast lands they did and would control, they leave one little strip of soil for the Jews who had no other safe haven on earth. Why wasn't this as understandable as my delivering a sick boy and his parents to the hospital?

* * *

One evening as the sun was setting behind the western mountains, I dismissed the *Sganim* group early and walked home to prepare to drive north for training. I was resting before departure when suddenly the door opened and without an apology, Joseph Duckler strode in, grim and flushed. "Yitshaq," he said, "you are not going to Yesod for training tonight. We have trouble."

In a few words he told me what had happened. The herd of cattle and sheep from Ja'una had climbed the main street of Rosh Pina as usual after returning from the grazing fields to the southeast. But once the dust raised by the animals settled, Shmuel G., one of the young men in the settlement was found lying on the stone steps leading to the schoolyard. He had been stabbed several times. Two things were certain. First, that it had been done by Arabs; in that tiny settlement every Jew knew where his neighbor was at the time of the murder. And second, it had to have been done with the *Mukhtar*'s full approval or it could not have been carried off so cleanly, with the murderer escaping so easily.

I pulled on a shirt and we walked down to the schoolyard where earlier I had spent hours giving the men close order drill. We went to the steps. In the descending darkness we could see fresh blood stains. After the initial excitement, the farmers had returned to their homes for supper and except for the two of us, the street was deserted.

Smoke rose from the courtyards where the evening meal was being prepared, and all around us it was deadly quiet. Every once in a while a dog would bark, and then the unearthly silence came again. Not a living soul was to be seen.

We walked back into our house without speaking.

"Let's go to your room," Duckler said. He sat down in the one available chair and was silent for a few moments. Then he said: "We have to decide what our reaction to the attack on Shmuel should be."

"That's our problem," I interrupted. "We're always reacting."

Duckler gave me an angry look. "I know our problem better than you. I want to discuss whether we should do something out of the ordinary . . . now. . . ."

My mind was racing. Duckler continued as if talking to himself: "From the viewpoint of our relations with Ja'una, it's difficult to relate this act to them. The village has no reason to start trouble with us right now. Unless this was done by an outsider and the *Mukhtar* (village head) was coerced into having the villagers hide him. I'm meeting later with the *Haganah* commander and the settlement's security committee; but the questions remain: are we going to act independently and how?"

Duckler's point was this: *Havlaga*, or self-restraint, was the official policy of the establishment. Whatever atrocities the Mufti's high command or Kaukji's bands committed, the *Haganah* officially practiced non-retaliation. For a number of months the *Irgun* went along but when individual commanders disobeyed the dictum, certain higher officers of the *Irgun* joined in favoring reprisals, either retaliatory or preventive. When Arabs threw a bomb from the Jaffa-Lydda train passing through Tel-Aviv, several unit commanders sprayed the train with automatic gun fire the following day. When an Arab village harbored terrorists who had fired on Jewish buses, *Irgun* men attacked the village to force it to expel the attackers. These retaliatory acts became a major point of disagreement within the *Irgun* and were one of the basic points of disagreement preceding the split. We were aware of ferment within the *Haganah* as well; we knew of several incidents during the past months where *Haganah* men acted without approval of their command, to retaliate for acts of terror.

So, while the *Irgun* was torn by internal discord on the issue of

Havlaga, we here in tiny Rosh Pina had to decide whether to risk the repercussions of breaking official policy.

Hesitantly I said to Duckler: "Your meeting will end by sending a warning to Ja'una's villagers that if anything else happens, their herd will not be permitted to pass through the settlement. This will stop them for a few days and then something like this may happen again. Whatever we do should be felt throughout the region."

Duckler looked at me in silence and waited for me to elaborate.

"I suggest we enter the village and blow up the *Mukhtar*'s house," I said. "We are prepared for something like this. Some of the boys know the 'Washington' inside out, and Arieh is particularly good at demolition. I think he used to work in a quarry. I can have them all ready to go in a few hours."

Joseph listened without a visible reaction. He continued to draw on his cigarette, then finally put it out and rose. "I'm going to the meeting, I'll be back in about an hour. In the meantime, see that the 'Washington' is dug up and made ready. Also get all our small weapons ready. Forget the explosives for the moment. I'll make up my mind by eleven o'clock." He looked at his watch. It was past eight. "We have enough time. Did you post additional watch?" I nodded.

I sent for two of the young *Sganim* trainees and we went together down the steep incline to the home of the Widow Rochelle, where I had my meals. As she served the omelet and salad, I told them about the possible plan. They were both experienced members of the Rosh Pina unit and knew the location of the *Mukhtar*'s house and the alleys leading to it. We discussed the approach, the placing of the explosives and withdrawal.

By the time Rochelle served our tea, we agreed that we could carry out the plan successfully, depending on several "ifs." The biggest "if" was whether Joseph would give his approval. I hinted, not too subtly, that any independent action by one of the boys would be dealt with immediately. I told them to report back at eleven. One of them put his hand on my shoulder: "Don't worry, *Yihye beseder*; everything will work out fine."

At nine-thirty Duckler was back in my room. He looked somber and pensive. "I have thought over your suggestions," he said. "I'm going to go with the security committee's decision. It was decided, for the time being, to bar the Arabs' herd from passing through the settlement. The auxiliary police would be posted at the head of the street before tomorrow dawn. There will also be further negotiations; someone will probably come from the District Commissioner's office in Safed. The usual routine. Incidentally, they wanted to know what we plan to do. I told them that we would post additional guards along the line facing Ja'una, and in other areas entrusted to us. The *Haganah* commander did not seem completely convinced that we could react so 'judiciously.' But the sad fact is that I do not believe we can do more now."

Instinctively I gestured with my hand as if to say "here we go again."

Duckler showed his temper. "Wait and hear me out. This isn't just another small local incident. What happens here now has major implications. With our measly weapons and a few dozen men and women, we can't just take everything into our own hands. First, we don't even know why the Arabs attacked Shmuel. Was it a provocation? By whom exactly? Are those who did it sitting in the village waiting for our reaction? Are they Kaukji's men or other outsiders? How many of them are there? We're pretty sure that neither the shepherds or the local Arabs did it.

"Second, if we entered the village, would our action begin and end with blowing up the *Mukhtar's* house? I agree that your idea is good because if the stabbing was done by outsiders, they had to blackmail the elders first; and if we show that we can punish the *Mukhtar* and his elders as well as the Mufti's gangs, we discourage future blackmail. It would convince them that we were well armed, strong and willing to fight.

"But what if we met resistance and a long battle developed, we would have everybody down on us. The police, the *Haganah*, the *Irgun* command, and the security committee of all the settlements from here to Metullah!

"Third, we're just beginning to build our strength here in the Galilee. We have one 'Washington' and a few dozen handguns. You came back with practically nothing from your pilgrimage to Tel-Aviv. If everybody turns against us, what can we achieve? We need time, maybe another year, and we need safe places outside the settlements; we need hiding places in the mountains mostly for the weapons, but also for ourselves. The Galilee is not going to have peace for a long time, and we can't permit one incident, even a murder, to affect our plans for the future."

I knew Duckler would be blunt and unbending but I was even more impressed by the force of his clear, terse logic. He had probably walked around thinking for some time before entering the room. I did not attempt to argue. I knew the discussion was over.

We carried out the orders of the security committee. Our men were all assigned posts in case of a confrontation next morning. Weapons were readied and ammunition distributed. Nothing happened. The Arabs did not try to bring their herd down the main street. A few short weeks after, they were allowed to resume their regular route and relations with Ja'una were patched up. Shmuel died from his wounds and became one more on the growing list of casualties during the so-called "1936-39 disturbances."

Soon after the murder of Shmuel, Duckler handed me a circular from *Irgun* headquarters dated Tel-Aviv, April 23, 1937. "The *Irgun*," the circular read, "is grounded in the conviction that the Hebrew State will not materialize without an independent, national military entity. The Jewish Agency, on the contrary, hopes to obtain a measure of internal freedom at the price of submitting to foreign rules and 'cantonization' of the land. The *Irgun* is faced with a choice—either submit to the Jewish Agency and thus to the foreign power, or ready itself for intensified sacrifice and growing perils.

"We believe in the destiny of our movement and in its power to rebuild an independent Hebrew State. We believe in the willingness for sacrifice of the youth of Israel; their lives are dedicated to the creation of the sovereign Hebrew power!"

I folded the manifesto carefully and placed it into my shirt pocket. I climbed up the hill overlooking Rosh Pina and the valley beyond it and settled on a rock to read the circular again. The Golan hills were slowly turning purple as dusk settled on the valley below. I could see the carts of the farmers slowly making their way back to Rosh Pina across the freshly plowed fields, and the sheep and cows of Ja'una climbing up Rosh Pina's main street. How thoroughly this idyllic scene contrasted with the fiery declaration in my hand! If only it was all as simple as those valleys and pastures, if only I could have followed my dreams and settled on the land, helping my people of the diaspora to find peace on the soil of Israel!

Even at that moment I knew there was no alternative. History had charted an irrevocable course for us and there was no time left for other choices. To survive we had to fight.

I carefully put away the circular planning to read it to every unit from Metullah to Safed. In my mind, it was the announcement of the War for Independence. I did not know at that time that it had been written by David Raziel, the eventual head of the *Irgun*, and by Abraham Stern, who would one day lead the Lehi-Stern Group, which splintered off from the *Irgun*.

Joseph Duckler had been prophetic when he warned me about underground action without proper training and careful planning of safe refuges; he was spared himself from having to deal with the tragedy which occurred in Rosh Pina in 1938 after he had been transferred to Jerusalem to head the intelligence section.

Months of increased Arab gang attacks all over the Galilee came to a head when David Ben Gaon, a veteran of the Rosh Pina Unit, was killed while plowing in the western Galilee. His death precipitated unauthorized retaliation by three members of the Rosh Pina *Pluga*. Without their commander's knowledge, they took some handguns and a grenade out of the cache of the *Irgun* and ambushed an Arab bus on the Rosh Pina-Safed road. They threw a grenade which did not explode and fired their guns without hurting anyone. They were caught when they hid in a deserted building not far from where the attack took place. The countryside along that stretch of road was totally barren, and there was no nearer Jewish settlement than Rosh Pina! They were tracked to the ruins of that building and arrested within an hour. One of them, Shlomo Ben Yosef, became the first man from the ranks of the *Irgun* and *Betar* to be executed by the British.

Ben Yosef had grown up in Lutzk, Poland, and had belonged to the *Betar* since 1929. In Poland he went through *Hachshara* agricultural training in preparation of *Aliyah*. He never would obtain immigration certificate from the Jewish Agency, but came to Palestine through *Ha'apala*, our "illegal immigration program." In Palestine he joined the Rosh Pina *Pluga*, and shortly after, joined the *Irgun*.

Joseph Trumpeldor, after whom *Betar* was named, was mortally wounded in an Arab attack in 1920. Seeing the stricken looks on the faces of his comrades, he said: "Never mind. It is good to die for our fatherland."

Before going to the gallows, Ben Yosef wrote on the wall of his cell, "I die without regrets . . . because I'm dying for our fatherland." On the morning of June 29, 1938, at exactly eight o'clock, when the British sergeant walked into his cell, Ben Yosef stood awaiting him with a smile. The hangman followed the sergeant in. They tied Ben Yosef's hands behind his back, and he walked towards the gallows with his head high. His last words were "Long live Jabotinsky!"

On the day Ben Yosef was executed, Jabotinsky wrote, in Yiddish, to Ben Yosef's mother in Lutzk: "I do not deserve that souls such as your son should die with my name on their lips. But as long as fate shall permit me, his name shall live in my heart, and his pupils, more numerous than mine, will lead the way for a generation.

Lead the way Ben Yosef did. His execution, which Colonial Secretary Malcolm MacDonald said was intended "to teach the law-breaking elements a lesson that will frighten and subdue them," instead wiped out the last hesitations in the minds of the *Irgun* Command. All-out military action against the British and against the terrorist Arab High Command was now unavoidable. Even more important, Jabotinsky finally reached a point in his political thinking where he recognized that the years of hoping for an understanding with Britain had now ended.

Ben Yosef's dignified death became a legacy for Jewish youths around the world. It launched the *Irgun* on an irreversible path of military activism.

Ben Yosef was buried on the hill southwest of Rosh Pina, where I had sat reading the manifesto written by Raziel and Stern: "We believe in the destiny of our movement . . . in its strength to reinstate our independence. . . . We believe in the youth of Israel's readiness for battle and sacrifice!"

V

Ha'apalah—Piercing The Blockade

> Behold, I will bring them from the North
> country, and gather them from the coasts
> of the earth, and with them the blind and
> the lame, the woman with child and her
> that traveleth with child together. A great
> company shall return thither . . . I will
> cause them to walk by the rivers of waters
> in a straightway, wherein they shall not
> stumble: For I am Father to Israel . . .
>
> (Jeremiah 31.8)

In June, 1937, Zeev Jabotinsky's son Eri, the head of the Palestine *Betar,* came to visit me in the *Betar* work camp I headed in Zichron Yaakov in the district of Samaria. Eri and I sat outside my tent under the stars to discuss the purpose of his visit. A few weeks earlier, a small, two-masted, fifty-ton sailboat had safely landed in Palestine carrying fourteen "illegal" *olim* (immigrants) mostly from the Vienna *Betar*, along with some youths from other Zionist groups. The prime mover behind the venture was a swashbuckling young man, Moshe Galili. Galili had pierced the British blockade of the coast with a motorized sailboat, the "Kosta," which sailed out of Piraeus. Following Galili's lead, we could now test the chance of achieving ultimate mass repatriation of Jews from Europe to Israel.

Eri folded his legs underneath himself in Middle Eastern style, and spoke to me with dry, solemn precision. "As you know," he said, "we in *Betar* no longer receive any immigration certificates from the Jewish Agency, even though candidates for immigration in the ranks of *Betar* and other sympathetic youth movements are growing steadily. The Left has not organized an 'illegal' immigrant vessel since 1934 and they still cannot see Hitler's influence throughout Europe as the threat to the Jewish masses. They have adapted to the British certificate system beautifully. It permits them to 'select' the immigrants, thus not only increasing their followers in the country, but also giving themselves and the British a perfect excuse to exclude our *Betar* youth and other Jews not aligned with left Zionism. If it is not too late, it's time for us to try to open the gates."

Eri and I both knew that this was easier said than done. Immigration to Palestine, though practically uninterrupted throughout the centuries, had never been easy. The doors had seldom been completely open to the Jews, and even when the ruling powers had been willing to permit *Aliyah* as in the time of Don Yosef Nasi in the sixteenth century, or intermittently under the Turks, the Jews had never been ready to respond as a unified body. A few scattered Jews came to Palestine while thousands remained where they were or sailed for other countries.

When my father's family had come, immigration was closed but adults could legally be admitted as "pilgrims." However, their children would have put them into immigrant status, so they had to smuggle the children in under the benches of the landing boats. The Arab stevedores who rowed the boats to the jetty were paid so much per child and the officials who counted heads on the boats were bribed as well. They would wave the boats ashore as the children crouched under the cross planks, peering out between the dirty, billowing trousers of the seamen. Once on shore they were lifted out from under the benches and immediately rushed onto the pier amid the omnipresent throngs.

The present immigration quota, imposed in 1920 by Herbert Samuel, was only sixteen thousand five hundred Jews a year, supposedly the "absorptive capacity" of Palestine.[1]

The Zionist leadership concurred with Britain's "absorptive capacity" policy in a communication sent by Dr. Weizmann to

---

[1]Some of us are convinced the initiative came from Weizmann. He knew that funds were not available for settling large numbers of immigrants, and that there actually were not many candidates.

His Majesty's Government in 1922. Weizmann, like Samuel a
follower of Ahad Ha'am's selectivity in picking Jews for *Aliyah*,
pledged that the Zionist establishment would act according to
Samuel's policy. This sacrificed the original main goal of the
Mandate—free mass Jewish immigration to Eretz-Israel and rees-
tablishment of an independent Jewish State. Max Nordau,
Herzl's close collaborator, raised a solitary vehement protest that
Weizmann's gesture threatened the survival of the Jews; but the
powerful culturalist-Socialist coalition overrode all opposition.

When Eri and I finally paused in our discussion, dawn was less
than an hour away. Eri gathered his thoughts, then came to
the heart of the matter. "We should have called for a showdown
long ago. The closing off of Jewish immigration wiped out any
legal right the Mandatory power has here. We should have confronted them then and there, and openly attempted to transport
thousands here by any means we could. We can't wait any
longer."

Eri had believed for a while now that the *Irgun*, his father, and
the entire political Zionist movement were dragging their feet. He
had been ready to declare the Hebrew Revolution before 1935. In
his fearlessness, he was not always so attuned to niceties like
timing and he was often too impatient to distinguish attainable
goals from dreams. But now he was making frightening sense. As
Eri's father had suggested, "the only choice left to us was to break
Britain's immoral and illegal immigration laws any way we
could." The Socialists had joined the British in refusing us our
proportionate number of immigration permits, and if we were
ever going to have the power to force the gate open for mass
repatriation, we had to have more nationalist youth in Israel
before nazism spread across all of Europe.

Eri and I agreed, given the *Irgun*'s limited budget and manpower, that the brunt of the "illegal immigration" would have to
be organized in the diaspora; we here in Eretz-Israel could contribute the support and the bases.

"We cannot continue to argue abstractions," Eri said. "We
must go out to the diaspora and organize, and the youth will
respond and follow. Let them draw their inspiration from us in
Palestine. I intended to make this my main endeavor from here
on, even if it means spending years away from my home. My time

as head of *Betar* in Eretz-Israel may be nearing the end of its usefulness anyway. My father, the *Irgun* and *Betar* are becoming closer and closer identified, and there soon may be no difference between underground and overt activities. In another year I will probably be forced to go underground, to jail or back to the diaspora."

"The air is clearer now," Eri said. "The *Irgun* is now a fully politicized army of liberation. There is no more ambiguity at the top. With Moshe Rosenberg, David Raziel, Abraham Stern, Hanoch Strelitz, and Aron Heichman, it has a high command with straightforward aims and broader horizons. We are finally released of all the limitations the moderates imposed on us and we are free to begin *Ha'apalah* and build military bases in eastern and central Europe. The fate of the nation will be decided by Hebrew weapons on the soil of the fatherland, as the *Irgun* recently declared."

We talked about the routes Galili proposed and the methods we would use—such as "boy scout" disguise to hide the movements of our young people. We knew, though, that large-scale movement could not be kept camouflaged for long.

Then Eri came to the point of his visit. "The first step I propose is that you go to Vienna as liaison for the *Irgun*. We need someone with your diplomatic abilities. Establish contact with *Betar* and the New Zionist Organization and gather candidates for immigration. Help coordinate the movement of immigrants until they board the vessels and act as liaison with the landing operations here in Palestine. Involve the *Irgun* as deeply as you can in all the phases of *Aliyah*."

The longer I listened, the more excited I became. I knew that the Jews were in constantly greater danger but we could turn these dangers to our advantage—if we could obtain cooperation from the governments of central and eastern Europe who wanted Jews out of their countries as much as we wanted them in ours. I could do more abroad than right here. I was beginning to lose my effectiveness in Palestine: I was recognizable, and it was more and more difficult to act both overtly and covertly. I had been imprisoned twice for leading *Betar* marches and my movements in Jerusalem were under continuous observation. I could go underground outside of Jerusalem but very soon the Criminal Investigation Department would catch up. It was difficult to disappear underground in such a small country, especially when my *Betar* activity put me in the public eye.

"I'm interested," I said to Eri. "When do you think I should leave?"

For the first time, Eri allowed himself a grin. "Next week!"

The first rays of light appeared over the hills of Samaria, as Eri crawled into my tent for a short catnap. I went over to wake the cook.

The following week I reported to Raziel in Jerusalem. It proved to be the first of many consultations we would have on *Aliyah* matters in the next several years.

Raziel felt that we should immediately start laying the groundwork for the land operations. He instructed me to meet with Eliahu Lankin prior to my departure for Vienna. Lankin headed the *Irgun* in the Samaria district in central Palestine. The Zichron Yaakov settlement, perched on a hill in Samaria overlooking the Mediterranean, was ideal for communications with seagoing vessels. The district's population was friendly to the *Irgun* and the nationalist movement and it could provide us with critical transport, security and hiding areas. It was the natural starting point for landing operations.

We could not hope for help from settlements controlled by the Socialists, conveniently coexisting with the certificate quota system of the British. They were still awaiting the Peel Commission's rulings on the future of Palestine and arguing among themselves about the "morality" of activities like illegal immigration. They did not want to deal with smugglers and other "unsavory elements," and it was clear that we were going to have to act alone. As quickly as possible, we would build the landing operations in the Sharon and Samaria ourselves, from Nathanya to Zichron Yaakov.

Before flying to Europe, I spent time with Eliahu Lankin in Zichron Yaakov. We decided that while I would help set up the immigration activities in Europe, Lankin would take on the organization of the landings. Lankin was not only the *Irgun* leader in Samaria, but also officially the head of Zichron's "watchmen's unit," and in my work at the labor camp I had come to know him fairly well. He could lose his temper over trivial matters, but in crises he was a cool-headed, fearless man. I was convinced he was the perfect man to work with, and when I flew to Austria in July I was confident of our success.

* * *

When I reached Austria the people of Vienna in 1937 led normal lives. Most of the populace managed economically, and the socialists and communists stayed essentially underground. A semi-fascist "Vaterlandische Front" corporate regime ruled the country. However, Austria's six million inhabitants were broken into many extreme factions, from outright Nazis in the south to active communist cells in the capital, and the cultural gap between cosmopolitan Vienna and rural regions like the Burgland was almost unbridgeable.

The majority of the two hundred thousand Jews in Vienna lived comfortably. Some of the wealthier families were thoroughly assimilated while the poorer ones like those in the Jewish quarter around the Hotel Central where I stayed, seemed to have just emerged from the ghettos of Galicia.

In a tradition that went back to Herzl, the Viennese Jews had several active Zionist groups, youth movements and student clubs as well as a Jewish community council with a Zionist majority. They had a substantial record of achievements in the nineteenth century Hebrew enlightenment. In 1937, they gossiped, flirted, argued and philosophized, but their ideological fervor began and ended in the coffee houses.

Avowed anti-Semites such as Mayor Karl Lueger in Herzl's era, or more discreet ones like the semi-fascist Chancellor Engelbert Dollfuss, had not kept individual Jews like Arthur Schnitzler, Arnold Schoenberg, Heinrich Neumann, Siegmund Freud, Stefan Zweig and many others from excelling in music, literature, medicine, law, finance and trade. And in the Second District, Vienna's Jewish Quarter, the poor "Jews of the East" still maintained their traditions with little interference from the non-Jewish world.

To establish a "cover" for my stay in Austria, I registered as a student at the University of Vienna. I managed to attend only a few lectures, but it was sufficient for me to notice that pro-Nazi sentiments had spread steadily throughout the University. The anti-Semitism first showed itself with a passing phrase or insult; later demonstrations and fist fights broke out in the halls.

Despite the Austrian civil wars in 1934 between socialist armed units and Dollfuss' milita and Dollfuss' assassination by the Nazis, it seemed impossible to arouse among the people I met a feeling of crisis. The non-Jews believed that France and Britain would never permit a German takeover of Austria. Even if Hitler did take over Austria, they said, "The Austrians could never be made to goose-step."

My newfound friend Dr. Paul Haller, a leading activist in the "maximilist" wing of the Jabotinsky movement, disagreed. He claimed that the Austrian Nazis were very much in evidence and dangerous and he predicted they would eventually do the dirty work for the lowest of the German S.S. The Jews in Vienna and elsewhere in Europe, Haller felt, were simply closing their eyes to reality. They proved it by never taking Haller seriously. He lectured and politicized in the cafes until he was blue in the face, especially on the subject of the emerging Hebrew revolution. For everyone but his small circle of friends this was enough to brand him as an eccentric at best and a madman at worst.

At first I resented sitting in a comfortable cafe, listening to this small, delicate philosopher revile the "bourgeois nationalist movement," lumping together *Betar*, the *Irgun*, all the Hebrew nationalist groups in Eretz-Israel and the diaspora into one colossal failure. "You're going nowhere," Haller would chastise me bluntly, wagging his almost transparent, thin fingers: "You're doing nothing of real importance."

Five weeks earlier I had been living in a tent in the hills of Zichron Yaakov, and before that, in a small, spartan room in the upper Galilee. For five years now I had been with men like Moshe Rosenberg, David Raziel and Joseph Duckler, leading a life of rigorous military discipline and continuous exposure to danger. We risked arrest with practically every move we made and helped people avoid being jailed and killed. We essentially had no life outside our work for the *Irgun*, and every hour of our every day was in one way or another, dedicated to the rebirth of the nation, so I was in no way ready to hear Haller's criticisms about how we were "doing nothing."

Yet I knew Haller was basically right: though we raced to train our soldiers and scraped together weapons, we felt virtually helpless before an approaching apocalypse. We simply did not have the funds, the arms or the boats, and we had largely failed so far to raise the alarm among the Jews back home or here in Europe.

"You *Irgun* boys think of your Herzl and Jabotinsky as such powerful leaders?" Haller said to me one day. "Well, right here in Vienna in 1897, our own Dr. Schalit, an inveterate Zionist who wasn't aligned with a specific movement, proposed to Herzl that fifteen hundred to two thousand armed volunteers land and occupy Jaffa, establish their national identity and proclaim their historic right to the land. Herzl rejected it. He saw political action as the only route to national rebirth. Well, now Jabo thinks the same way. He's trying to dicker with the British the same way Herzl tried to dicker with the Turks. Unless he and the *Irgun* see the light soon, everything will be lost."

Haller, however, was a little behind schedule. We were already deep in serious negotiations with Poland and Czechoslovakia for widespread "illegal immigration," and military assistance. Still, I fully agreed with Haller's perpetual anger at the failure of the "establishment" to react to developments in Europe. "I don't read Hebrew," he said, "but, I read enough of European Zionist publications to know that they don't realize what is happening. Austria is simply going to crumble and after it, the rest of central Europe. A few more years and the Nazis will control Europe. What is the Zionist establishment doing? What are you doing?" Then he relaxed and smiled at me. "Don't take it personally. You're just the first Hebrew revolutionary I've had a chance to argue with."

* * *

I did most of my work in the heart of the Viennese ghetto, where we hoped to lay the foundation for mass emigration. My identity was kept a secret and the name I used in Austria was Ben-Menahem. My papers said I was a journalist and student.

We quickly established a staging camp near Vienna at Kottingbrun. In the past, *Betar* has used the area as a summer camp. The first groups of *Ma'apilim* ("illegal" immigrants) started arriving from Poland and the Baltic states. Some local youngsters joined them but few Viennese parents wanted to give their consent for the voyage.

By the end of August we had fifty-four "boy scouts" on their way to Albania, all dressed up in blue-gray uniforms for their "Mediterranean" tour under the leadership of Moshe Galili. I flew back to Palestine and arranged with Lankin for their "reception" on the coast of Tantura. Lankin enlisted the head watchman of nearby Benyamina, and together they were to meet the incoming sailboat, the *Artemesia*.

For two nights, Lankin and the small *Artemesia* missed their rendezvous. For forty-eight hours, Lankin could not sleep, I felt heartbroken to see him return at dawn haggard and depressed, to Benyamina, where I waited for him.

On the third night the contact was made at last; the landing went off without a hitch before dawn. I went to the orange groves where the *olim* had been taken to wait the buses; to establish credibility it was considered advisable for the *olim* to see me once again, since I had been introduced to them as the *Irgun* delegate in Kottingbrun. We had to prove that our operation was part of an organized, responsible effort if we were to win the confidence of the thousands of *olim* to come. Within days, postcards and letters with greetings from Eretz-Israel reached towns and villages from Vienna to Riga, telling families and friends that the youngsters had landed safely.

Buoyed by our first success, I returned to Vienna. The time had come to begin planning larger-scale movements, so I went to Poland.

***Irgun* coordinated "Illegal" immigrants 1937-1940.**

A review of young *ma'apilim* Greece, 1939.

Group of *ma'apilim* on their way to a Mediterranean port (1938).

A tramper used for *Ha'apalah* work in 1938.

Ma'apilim landing in Palestine in the late 1930s.

VI
The "Sans Culottes"

Early one morning, in November 1937, after endless passport and customs inspections, my train crossed into Poland. Tired from the stuffy all-night trip from Vienna in the crowded railroad car, I looked out on the bleak snowbound countryside, feeling thankful once again that I had chosen to remain in the *Irgun* when Tehomi and others returned to the *Haganah*. As Eri Jabotinsky had predicted the split had proved to be a blessing in disguise. Our leadership had immediately assigned more and more commanders and cadres to work in Europe: While I had gone to Vienna, many top officers had gone to Poland to follow up contacts that Vitold Holienicki, the Polish Consul in Palestine, had established; the goal was purchasing arms and training officers in Poland. David Raziel had approved my visiting several communities to enlist *Ha'apalah* candidates whom I would channel through Vienna to the Mediterranean, and then to Eretz-Israel. I would spend three weeks in Poland before returning to Vienna.

I was grateful fate had brought me to Poland, and I looked forward to the visit as if it were a homecoming. Indeed, the Pale of Settlement had been the home of my ancestors for centuries, and I had as good a grasp on the history of Polish Jewry as I did on the history of Palestine. The Jews had first settled in Poland in the fourteenth century in the era of Casimir the Great. They had skills which the country needed, as well as financial contacts all over Europe, so they were welcomed into Poland and treated decently.

Becoming middlemen between the serfs and nobility, Poland's new citizens helped it become "the second Babylon"; within a century, Poland took over the leadership from Spain in Jewish learning.

The relative peace lasted until 1648, when Bogdan Chmielnicki led his cossacks and the peasantry in attacks on Jewish villages throughout the Pale. The Jews in Poland hardly had time to count their dead and wounded before the Polish armies seized the chance and swept down on the stricken villages to complete the cossacks' work.

The Jews slowly set about rebuilding the ruins, but the eighteenth century ushered in the worst religious persecution against them since the Spanish Inquisition. Once again they were accused of blasphemy and ritual murders and to pay for their "crimes," they were tortured and burned by the thousands. Pope Clement VIII had to intervene to end the violence. The Jews fled into mysticism and ultimately *Hasidism* as a refuge from their travails. In the latter part of the eighteenth century, when Poland was partitioned by Russia, Prussia and the Austro-Hungarian Empire, the essentially autonomous life of the Polish Jews began to break down. Russian and Napoleonic occupation slowly brought the enlightenment into the Pale, and the hold that *Hasidism* had on Jews gradually weakened. Well on the road to secular political life, Polish Jewry played a major part in the Hebrew national rebirth. In 1862, H. S. Slonimski founded the Hebrew nationalist periodical *Ha-tzephira* in Warsaw, which became a daily under Nahum Sokolow in 1874; *Hovevei-Zion* also built a center in Warsaw.

From the time of World War I, the Jews of Poland were the heart of European Jewry. Russia, the other great Jewish community in Europe, retreated into itself after the pogroms in the 1920s, until it was almost entirely isolated from the outside world. The three million Jews in Poland, however, with their creativity in so many areas, formed the core of the Jewish renaissance in Europe, and gained a leading position among their people.

* * *

As I entered Poland, I felt for the first time that not only was I undertaking one of the most important tasks of my life, but I was actually reaching back beyond my own life into history. Though my grandparents had left the Pale sixty years ago, it was as if the gap in time did not exist, and I had the sensation that every Jew we lost or saved in Poland would be literally my own brother.

My first stop in the provinces was in Czenstochowa. I was met at the station by a young man named Yasha whom I remembered as the "stowaway from Czenstochowa." I had first met him a few months earlier in the station in Vienna, when a group of young Polish *ma'apilim* were getting off the train for the short stopover before sailing to Palestine. The head of the group had discovered a "stowaway" on the train, a young man without money, papers or belongings, who had been smuggled into the car by his friends during the stop in Czenstochowa. For over twenty-four hours he crouched under a bench covered by the knapsacks of the *ma'apilim* who never gave him a way to the head of the group. They knew that he would never agree to carry Yasha over the two frontiers since it would endanger the passage of the entire group. The border inspections had not discovered him, however, and despite the harsh words the group leader directed at him at the railroad station in Vienna he was grinning from ear to ear.

The leader decided to send him back to Poland. It took several days for the Polish Consulate to issue a passport for him, and during this short stay, I got to know him. Yasha was a graduate of a Hebrew high school and now worked on a small Jewish paper in Czenstochowa. Versed in Hebrew as well as Polish literature, and a member of the *Betar* for the past six years, he explained to me that his decision to try and attach himself to the group of the *ma'apilim* had not been the lighthearted prank of an irresponsible youngster, but an act of desperation. Yasha had no money to pay for his transportation, nor were his papers in order. He was afraid that he would waste his life in the cramped editorial room of his little paper and he felt trapped and despondent. He had accompanied his friends to the station and when the train started to pull out, he jumped on it.

Now, months later, walking from the station into the city, we both smiled at the incident. "You know," Yasha said, "I'm all ready to leave with the next group of *ma'apilim*. I've saved two hundred *zloty* during the past three months."

"When will the next group be ready?" I asked. "It's ready now," said Yasha in a more serious tone. "It's larger than our quota and larger than our funds can handle; the economic situation is deteriorating. The Endeks, the anti-Semitic National Democratic party here in Poland, is making sure that we choke economically. They are the strongest opposition party in the Parliament. We've had a number of clashes with them. I was almost knifed in a brawl after returning from Vienna. The authorities don't want to let things get out of control in town yet, but in the provinces everything is going to hell. Let's cross to the other side of the street. We don't want to get into trouble."

I looked around surprised. There was no sign of any excitement.

"What's the matter?" I asked. "The Endeks made a rule," Yasha said with a queer smile, "that Jews must walk on the right side of the street only. Jews who disregard the regulation get thrown off the sidewalks. It's the old ghettoizing tactic. Some of us intentionally walk in small groups on the forbidden side, looking for trouble. But you and I shouldn't try it now, we have more important things scheduled for the evening."

We left the main street and entered a small Jewish restaurant on a dreary side street. The proprietress, a hefty woman, gave us a hearty greeting. "I thought you would never come!" she thundered over the counter. "Hurry up and get yourself a seat!"

Yasha winked at me. "This is 'Mama,'" he said. "What a cook! This is a special dinner tonight for my guests. Here comes my cousin Joseph."

Joseph was a short, thin, bookish-looking young man in spectacles who smiled as he shook hands with me. "How glad I am to meet you," he said. "There's so much we want to hear about Eretz-Israel, *Ha'apalah* and the *Irgun.*"

We sat chatting awhile, then Joseph suddenly turned to Mama. "Would you believe it?" he cried, "This fellow has never been to Poland before!"

Mama placed a platter of steaming chicken on the table, wiped her face with her apron, straightened her skirt, looked down and shook her head: "What a lucky fellow."

Yasha waited until she had gone before he explained. "Her husband was killed seventeen years ago. Remember when Poland regained her independence and the freedom fighters came home? The first thing they did was make a pogrom. That was when she lost her husband, in Lvov, in 1918. She hasn't felt 'Polish' since."

I asked Joseph what the Jews were facing in the countryside.

"I live about an hour's ride away" he said. "But it seems a different country. There is some semblance of government here, but in the rural districts, it's anarchy for the Jews. Jews are robbed, beaten and killed. The police do nothing. In some of the villages Jews shut themselves in their homes at sundown and when dawn breaks, they are thankful to still be alive. In one village near mine, several hundred Jewish families don't even leave their homes during daylight anymore. The slogan of the Endeks is starve the Jews and no one sells food to them. Government statutes keep us out of civil service work, schools, the professions . . . out of almost every realm of endeavor. We're literally being finished off by government regulations."

Yasha took up the story. "The masses are poverty-stricken and illiterate. The Endeks must gain political popularity and face the social problems. So as always, the Jews somehow end up the scapegoat."

"The prejudice against the Jews is centuries old," Joseph took up. "The children learn anti-Semitism from the first moment they can understand what is said to them. The Endeks point to the little the Jews still possess to arouse jealousy so the people will vent their bitterness on us instead of facing their real ills. The Jewish issue is the Endeks bestselling point in their efforts to gain control of the country."

"The 'liberal' elements in the country don't exactly rush to our defense either," Yasha cut in. "The intelligentsia is silent, either out of fear or because they share the views of the Endeks when it comes to the Jews and the labor party was trounced in the last election, so they have no power to help us even if they want to."

Two men hurried into the restaurant, one holding a handkerchief to his face. Mama rushed to help him into the back room.

"What happened?" Yasha asked the other man.

"He was walking on the forbidden side of the street. A few gangs of Endeks are out and there isn't a policeman in sight."

Yasha nodded towards the back room. "That's what I mean. These gangs are students from rich families. We Jews are no more than a peg to hang their hostilities on. I want out! And I don't give a damn if it fulfills their hopes. I'm going and so is Joseph and thousands of other young Jews. We have nothing left here but misery. That's why we need you."

* * *

I arrived at my next stop, Thomazsow Mazovietzk. It was already dark when I stepped off the train into the small, dark station. I was met by Moshe, a friendly, intelligent, young man of about twenty-one who wore a leather jacket and went bareheaded.

There was a clatter of horse's hooves and a coachman pulled up at our side. "Avrum," Moshe introduced me proudly. "This is Yitshaq Ben Menahem from Palestine." He turned to me. "Avrum's the best coachman in town."

Avrum's eyes could hardly be seen under the shawl that covered his head and face. He looked down curiously from his high perch: "Step up and make yourself comfortable," he said in a bass, hoarse Yiddish. "This is an honor."

We settled back in the open carriage, covering our legs with the heavy blanket which Avrum produced from under his seat. He urged the horse on and we turned into the slushy road leading into town. As soon as the horse had begun his steady pull, Avrum turned around. "Where do you come from originally did you say?" he asked.

"From Tel-Aviv. I was born there."

"No!" It took Avrum a moment of silence to recover. "You're actually a native Palestinian?"

"Born and bred."

"You don't say?" he was still amazed. "You must know my cousin Esther Rabinowitz. She's been living in Tel-Aviv about twelve years. She has a bakery there."

"No," I laughed. "I don't. There are more than one hundred and fifty thousand inhabitants in Tel-Aviv now, and the name Rabinowitz isn't exactly rare. Is she from here?"

"No, from Lodz. You know, when she left for Palestine, I almost went with her . . . I've wanted to ever since the end of the war. Can you use coachmen there?"

I assured him we could.

"I thought so. After all, Jews do all the work there, don't they? I'm sure that I could be of use. But you know how difficult it is to get an immigrant's certificate. I am not so young anymore, and they say they need young, strong pioneers. I could go as a 'capitalist' if I had twelve thousand *zloty*, but who has so much money? Why should I need money to go to Palestine? I have a strong pair of hands and I would make enough to feed my wife and children. I'd certainly make no less of a living than here."

He was quiet for a moment. "Some living. The Polish coachmen drive the few Jewish ones out of the business. They don't let us stop in the center of the city, and even at the station we can't leave our carriages for a moment or something will happen to the horses. We pay high taxes for our licenses but things keep getting worse. Isn't it so, Moshe?"

Moshe nodded. "Not only for you, but for all other working Jewish people. I'm a house painter and only the bits of business I get from Jews keep me going. If I didn't have my parents to give me room and board, I could never make it."

Avrum shook his head. "I tell you, it's all part of a plot. Hey, giddap, keep going," he shouted to the horse; it had fallen into a slow step, slogging its way through the mud. Avrum turned back towards us. "You know what they write on the walls? Jews to Palestine! They want to take our living and then force us to leave ... and why shouldn't we leave? Our children are running around with bare feet. I can't give them enough to eat or a proper education. When people go to America, nobody asks them for money. And Palestine is our country. I always gave what I could when the boys raised money for Eretz-Israel. Are only the rich supposed to go there?"

I explained to Avrum that the immigration laws were not made by the Jews, but by the British; and rich Jews probably were not so anxious to go to Palestine.

"Of course you're right. It's the poor Jews who want to leave, the ones who suffer the most. The well-to-do live in the big cities and think their money will keep them safe. Fools! In the last war, in Warsaw, we all got it, rich and poor alike, even those who 'didn't look like Jews.' They found us and yanked us out of our homes."

We arrived at a small side path and Avrum stopped the coach. I pressed his hand in farewell and a moment later he and his coach disappeared into the dark down the deserted street.

Moshe and I walked about two blocks down the dirt path to a small white house with an unpainted wooden door. He pushed to door open and we stepped into a large, warm, whitewashed room where it seemed Moshe's whole family had gathered. His father was a man of about fifty, small and dark, with a graying beard and earlocks. He had on a small *yarmulke*, and he was sitting at a table poring over a book. In a corner, Moshe's mother, a little woman, her hair covered with a kerchief, busied herself at the stove. A girl was knitting in the other corner glancing through a paper propped on another small table. The room served as kitchen, dining room and living room, but it was cozy and comfortable, neatly arranged and very clean. It struck me that Grandfather Zeev Leib's home near Grodno half a century ago might have looked like this one.

We had a hot meal of potatoes, borscht and herring, and then all of us launched into a friendly but somehow tense conversation about life in Poland versus life in Palestine, and then about the international situation. Through it all Moshe's father presided over the table with the customary authority of an Orthodox Jewish father. When he expressed feelings that seemed old-fashioned or over-cautious, the brother and sister exchanged looks, but never spoke up in disagreement. Moshe's mother took little part in the conversation, but his sister voiced her opinions strongly on most of our subjects. She seemed to think much in unison with her brother.

When dinner was over and the table cleared, we sat back for a short rest before Moshe and I left for the meeting. Moshe, who had been fairly taciturn and a little restless during dinner, glanced towards me, took a deep breath and spoke in a low voice. "Father, I plan to go to Palestine. This time I mean it."

A dead silence fell over the room. His father's face reddened. He shifted the *yarmulke* atop his head and fixed his eyes on Moshe, his face tight and hard. Moshe's sister started to wipe the dishes energetically. Now I understood the tension I felt all during dinner. There had been a long-standing conflict between the Orthodox father and the militant nationalist son. It was, of course, partly my visit that brought the disagreement to a head, and it made me feel uneasy.

When Moshe's father finally regained some composure, he said in a strained voice: "You know how I feel about it. Why do you bring it up now?"

"Because I'm leaving in a few weeks."

His father was silent. He again adjusted his *yarmulke*. He cleared his throat and tried to reason with Moshe, "Look here you have a roof over your head and you know I can still feed you even if you do not work all the time. I have a store, a little one, true, but thank God we are not starving, and . . ."

"That is not the point," Moshe interrupted.

"What is?"

"We've discussed it hundreds of times."

Now his father's face flushed, and he raised his voice. "You want to be a pioneer, a *chalutz*, eh? To end your days as an ignorant laborer among the godless *shkotzim* there, without any feeling of Jewishness in you!"

"The *chalutzim* in Palestine are as good as any Jews who go to synagogue three times a day here," Moshe said quietly.

His father's voice grew even louder. "I work all my life like a slave, building up a business, saving *zloty* after *zloty*, all to give you something to hold on to. And you want to run away! Isn't my home good enough for you? Isn't Mother's food good enough?"

Moshe bit his lips. "You know I appreciate what you and Mother have done for me, it's not that."

"What is it, then? Your clubs and meetings? Your Zionism? Your sacred Jabotinsky? I always knew no good would come of it."

"It's this in a nutshell, Father: I'm sick and tired of this town, this country and this life. I want to get out of here. I just can't stand it any longer."

"You cannot stand it any longer? What was good enough for me, my father and my grandfather is not good enough for you?"

"It isn't good enough for me and neither was it good enough for you. We should have left long ago, as Yitshaq's grandfather did. I want to go to a country which I can feel I'm part of, where nobody will be able to throw me out whenever they feel like it!"

"God has banished us from our land, and only he can take us back, in good time, when the generation deserves it!"

"God helps those who help themselves."

"Don't blaspheme the Lord at my table!! Who taught you to

talk that way?" His face was crimson.

Moshe's mother rushed from the room holding a handkerchief to her eyes; Moshe's sister could not sit still any longer. "Father, Moshe meant no disrespect. You just refuse to understand. It's *our* life. We look around us and there is nothing here to build a future on. It isn't even safe for us anymore."

"What security have you got in Palestine" her father tried to reason. "More Jews are being killed there than in Poland. I read the paper. Why risk your lives?"

"If things continue the way they're going Moshe will have to join the Polish Army. At least in Palestine, if he has to fight, it will be for his own country's future."

"If he will be drafted in the Polish army, he will have to go like everybody else. I won't give him my permission to go to Palestine. If he goes, I'll no longer have a son. God will give me strength to overcome it." He got up and left the room.

Moshe, his sister and I remained silent several moments—then Moshe looked at me with tired eyes. "You'd never believe such conversations could go on nowadays. Most of our boys have the same trouble, especially those in Orthodox families in the small towns. How can our parents be so blind?"

"They're like the slaves who wanted to return to Egypt," his sister lamented. "They are blind fatalists and take everything as God's will. If they are faced with death, they'll say that God wanted it so. No matter how we argue, there's nothing we can do for them. We'll have to leave our fathers and mothers and go our way alone."

Moshe pulled himself together. "It's late. Let's go." We left without saying goodbye. His sister turned down the flame in the kerosene lamp, threw a glance at the bedroom, sighed and walked out with us into the cold.

We reached a small house on a side street. Only the cellar lights shone. "This is our clubhouse," said Moshe. He led us down several steps into a large, brightly lit room with pictures of Herzl, Jabotinsky and Trumpeldor on the walls. About twenty young men and five girls in their late teens and early twenties were seated in a circle on wooden benches. They were plainly dressed but they radiated brightness and enthusiasm. Most of them, Moshe told me, were workers and artisans; the ones who had wanted to try their luck at higher education or at white-collar jobs had left for the big cities.

A young man came to greet us. Moshe introduced him as Zalman, the head of the branch.

"We're very happy to have you with us," Zalman said. "I hope your visit will at last help us solve our problem. Please be seated."

"*Chaverim*, friends," Zalman began, "headquarters in Warsaw has sent *Irgun* delegate Yitshaq Ben Menahem to confer with us on our problems, especially *Aliyah*.

"We have to speed up our plans. Some of you have finished your military training and others have occupations of importance for the economy of Palestine. We're ready for *aliyah*. Our chances of receiving certificates through the Jewish Agency are nil. We are not members of the World Zionist Organization and we are last on the list to receive certificates. We cannot sit waiting and hoping; anything may happen in Europe and our chances of reaching Palestine would be gone altogether. It is our primary duty to prepare ourselves for immigration in the shortest possible time. We must reach Eretz-Israel by any means available, in other words, through *Ha'apala*. That is why Yitshaq is here."

I described *Ha'apala* as completely as I could—the hardships they would face during the trip, the danger they might be in on the coast of Palestine and their chances for imprisonment or worse. I assured them that the *Irgun* needed young men and women with their training. We had a severe shortage of manpower and they could play an essential role in times of trouble. They would at the very least serve two years in *Plugot Ha'Avoda*. I also went into detail about the Galil, Samaria and the old city of Jerusalem.

When I finished, Zalman asked for questions. A young boy stood up and said: "I have one question. When do we leave?"

Everyone laughed. Zalman turned to me smiling: "You see all of us are determined to leave but money is a serious problem. Is it true that the trip costs two hundred and fifty to three hundred and fifty *zloty*? And that neither Warsaw headquarters nor our Tel-Hai fund can extend any help to us?"

I nodded.

"Then the problem is to raise the money through our own means. Do you have any suggestions?"

Moshe asked for the floor. "I know that most of us do not have even twenty-five *zloty*. We have temporary jobs with no steady income, no savings, and no wealthy organization to back us up. We are determined to leave in the shortest time possible and that is all that counts. So I suggest we pool all our funds and organize ourselves into a temporary 'commune' to seek work for every member, including both part-time and extra employment. After allotting a minimum for individual existence, all monies would be turned over to the common fund. We have to face this problem not as individuals, but as a unit with a common goal—*Ha'apalah*."

The discussion continued for another half hour, then Zalman formally closed the meeting. The members gathered around me with questions about Palestine, the *Irgun* and internal politics. Then the younger ones began to dance the *Horah*, and the melodies of the new Palestine resounded in the streets of poor, beleaguered Mazovietsk.

I returned to my hotel with Moshe and Zalman and we sat at a large table in the dining room and sipped hot tea. Moshe and Zalman were in high spirits.

"You don't know how long we waited for this," said Zalman before leaving. "Some of us spent years in *hachshara* retraining camps working like slaves to qualify for immigration. Then we were denied certificates anyway because those who doled them out didn't like our political views. We faced opposition in our homes, at work and among our friends in the Zionist Youth Groups. But we knew the day would come when we didn't have to ask permission from anyone to go to Eretz-Israel. Now you are here with us, and you've given us the chance we were waiting for. We won't let anything stop us now. We'll see you in Eretz-Israel soon."

Knowing that the *Ma'apilim* would have to pass through our transit camp outside Vienna, I smiled and answered, "I'll probably see you before then."

* * *

I spent several weeks traveling from town to town, recruiting immigrants for the next voyage. I spoke night and day to the *Betar* groups, and their loved ones, trying to convince them that the gates could be forced open. We managed to gather about one hundred candidates from Poland.

We used Kottingbrun as a staging area, since Austria was holding an International Fair and tourist visas were easily available. We dressed the young men and women in blue-gray uniforms once more, and Galili again led this group of one hundred and twenty *olim* through Durazzo, Albania, where they received an unexpectedly emotional welcome from the few Jewish families living there. After taking the *olim* into their homes for food and drink, the families closed their shops and accompanied them to the *Artemesia*, now embarking on its second voyage. On the pier, the men, women and children embraced and sang the *Hatikva*. As the *olim* sailed close to shore, the tiny, forlorn Jewish community lined up on the dock waving, tears running down their faces.

We had established credibility now and our communications were functioning much better, so there was no need for my returning to Eretz-Israel to see the boat in. I stopped in Austria to continue my work, and soon was advised that the boat had arrived safely in Tantura.

In February 1938, I went to Prague, Czechoslovakia for a consultative assembly of the New Zionist Organization, where both *Betar* and *Irgun* delegates participated in the planning of overt and covert actions. *Betar* was mobilizing more and more of its leaders to participate in the *Aliyah* work: Mordechai Katz represented the World Betar London; Eliahu Glaser out of Prague was in charge of Central Europe; Israel Epstein and Menahem Begin were to head the activity in Poland. Hillel Kook came from Eretz-Israel and Zeev Jabotinsky was there personally, participating in the consultations on security and immigration. One man was missing—Eri Jabotinsky. He was detained by the British administration in November 1937 and sentenced to three months imprisonment in the Fortress of Acre where his father had been jailed in 1920. Eri's prediction to me five months earlier about his imminent detention came through. He was in good company—Abba Achimeir and other leaders of the *Betar* and the Jabotinsky movement were with him.

The committee dealing with immigration decided that I was to remain in Vienna to continue coordinating the sailings with the landing operations. The *Irgun* assigned "pilots" experienced with the sea and the coast of Palestine, to participate in the sailings. We considered the lack of funds, the difficulties with transit visas and laid plans to solve these problems. Certain tensions surfaced during the committee meetings. Diaspora *Betar* was taken to task by the *Irgun* men for not responding radically and intensely enough to developments in Eretz-Israel and for lagging amateurishly behind the military training we were giving our men in the homeland.

After my travels in Europe, I was fully persuaded that the time had come for a total mobilization of our youth in Europe.

VII

"Die Strassen Frei"
("Clear the streets for us . . .")

In the two months preceding the Prague conclave, Vienna had bristled with rumors and anxieties. During the late evening gatherings with Paul Haller at our regular cafe, we lowered our voices and nervously exchanged news from all over town—from the university, from law offices, from newsmen—and the overwhelming feeling was that Austria was reaching a point of no return. Mussolini by now had dropped his guise of benevolence altogether, and he was moving steadily closer to Hitler. His empire-building crusades, first in Ethiopia, then in the Spanish Civil War had strained Italy's economy and political position and had left her unable to protect Austria.

When the German envoy in Vienna, Franz Von Papen, was fired by Hitler for being too moderate, even the most nonchalant Viennese had to admit that a crisis was imminent. Dr. Kurt von Schuschnigg, the Austrian Chancellor, was "invited" to Hitler's mountain retreat in Berchtesgaden. The Fuehrer harangued him for hours about Germany's greatness and Austria's insignificance. At the end of the meeting Hitler gave Schuschnigg an ultimatum to turn over his government to the Austrian Nazi Party or face a German military attack. Schuschnigg had no alternative but to sign the document Hitler thrust in his face. Austria's independence was, for all intents and purposes, ended.

Four weeks of turmoil followed. The Germans conducted maneuvers along the Austrian border to test the Allies. Hitler kept protesting that all his efforts were aimed solely at bringing Germans and Austrians closer together. Britain's Prime Minister

Neville Chamberlain believed him and took no steps to protect Austria. The French, who were trapped in a continuous economic crisis, also did nothing. As for Mussolini, he became a full partner with Hitler in the Berlin-Rome axis. Austria was left on her own.

One of Schuschnigg's concessions to Hitler was to appoint a Nazi, Seyss-Inquart, as Minister of Internal Security in Austria. The Austrian Nazis felt secure enough to come out of hiding and thousands demonstrated in the city of Gratz against the government and raised the Nazi flag over the city hall. Chancellor Schuschnigg announced a plebiscite for March 13th to vote on whether or not Austria should "rejoin" the Third Reich. Demonstrations broke out throughout the country. Nazis, Schuschnigg supporters and Social-Democrats marched and shouted slogans. The Nazis marched with awesome discipline, while their leaderless opponents appeared irresolute and disorganized.

Jews were afraid to be out in the streets of Vienna after dark and the evening sessions of our *Ha'apalah* activities broke up shortly after supper. On March 10, three days before the scheduled plebiscite, I went home directly from the cafe, deciding to stay indoors and communicate with our *Betar* and immigration activists by telephone. We agreed to hold a meeting the following evening at a Student Cafe across the street from my boarding house.

The next afternoon curiosity got the better of me and, prior to the meeting, I detoured over to the center of the city. Nazi mobs were all over, shouting "Sieg Heil," while the Austrian police stood by smiling. Though the Nazi demonstrators were no more violent than previous ones, I had a peculiar feeling that a major new development had taken place in the past twenty-four hours.

I felt as if I were sitting in a car about to plunge over a precipice, unable to stop it, yet morbidly fascinated by the inevitable impending disaster.

At that early evening's meeting, we made hasty preparations to destroy all files and literature from the offices and clubhouses of *Betar* and the New Zionist Organization, especially on our anti-Nazi boycott activities from years past. We briefly discussed how we could coordinate activities once the Nazis and Gestapo had entered Vienna. Agreeing to keep in constant touch by telephone we parted tense, but not shaken or frightened. We, Jabotinsky's disciples, had been among the few "Jeremiahs" who predicted these developments all along and now that they had come to pass, our reaction was almost matter-of-fact. We were simply embarking upon a new phase of action.

On March 11, the German army marched into Austria. Hitler came to Vienna and reviewed the delirious Austrians. Within weeks, almost forty thousand Austrians, Jews and Gentiles, were in jail. It became dangerous to walk in the streets without a swastika pin in your lapel. If you looked Jewish, you might be stopped by uniformed men, by men with armbands or by youths wearing white knee-socks, the Nazi symbol of those who had been Nazis when nazism had still been illegal in Austria.

My phone rang incessantly with reports of arrests of acquaintances and friends. My landlady, a Jewish woman, came to my room to ask me not to use the phone—"the *Polizei* might be listening and she did not want to get into trouble." I tried to explain to her that the Nazis would be glad to see the Jews emigrate, but she was adamant, and from then on I had to make my calls from the cafe across the street.

Before the week was over, I was advised to meet other *Ha'apalah* activists in a cafe in the Jewish "Second District."

Haller, my friend Tury Deutsch and a few others were "invited" to Gestapo headquarters for a meeting with Dr. Lange, head of a special unit on Jewish affairs. They asked me to come along. Sooner or later my presence in Austria would have to be explained to the Gestapo and it might as well be now.

The Gestapo headquarters in the heart of the city was in an exclusive nineteenth century mansion that had formerly been owned by the Rothschilds; part of the Nazis' sense of "irony" involved taking over residences of prominent Jews for their headquarters. We were stopped at the gate by two SS men in black uniforms and were directed to a small office. We were left to cool our heels until, finally, Dr. Lange strode into the room, wearing a crisp uniform, his boots polished like mirrors. To our surprise, he was polite, well-mannered and calmly reassuring. He said he understood we were involved in helping Jews emigrate to Palestine with British approval and that he had no objection to our activities. In fact, he would assign several of his subordinates, among them Adolf Eichmann, to supervise us. With that he turned on his heels and left.

At that time and for many months to follow, the Germans accepted our "Underground Railroad" as a means of achieving a Germany that would be "judenrein" (free of Jews). Ironically, this lifeline would utimately be severed not by the Nazis but by the Allies with the tacit acquiescence of Washington.

* * *

Late one night in April, 1938, on my way home I heard a gruff voice shouting in the darkness: "Sind Sie ein Jude?" A group of young Nazis in a car had stopped alongside a boy and his girl-friend. The boy's reply was drowned out in a hail of Nazi fists and boots. The Nazis drove away guffawing loudly, their arms extended in the "Heil Hitler" salute.

I helped the young man's girlfriend lift him from the gutter. Blood trickled from his swollen nose and his arms were lacerated by the Nazis' boots; but what stuck in my mind was the astonished look in his eyes—he simply could not grasp what had happened to him. The girl was weeping quietly, pressing her clenched fists to her mouth to stifle her sobs. Supporting the boy on either side we took him home.

Every time I went out on the street now, there were similar incidents. That morning they had tortured an old man in the building of the Jewish community center. They forced him to polish their boots with a prayer shawl taken from the synagogue, and they kicked him, spat in his face, and knocked him to the floor.

I had seen Nazis shout with laughter as they forced young girls to take off their skirts and scrub the same square foot of pavement for hours on end, crawling on their knees under the whip of a member of the Hitler *Jugend*.

They had rounded up men and marched them half-naked in the streets, putting top hats on their heads which read "I'm a Jewish swine, hit me!" They had broken into homes and looted them, leaving feces on the beds. Jewish fathers, brothers and husbands, often failed to return home, and their families never heard from them again.

The night I saw the boy beaten I couldn't sleep. I sat at my window ledge trying to cool my head in the April breeze. In this once-festive lighthearted city an unearthly quiet now reigned. The celebrations which began with Chancellor Schuschnigg's resignation had quickly subsided. Traffic had almost entirely stopped, and the streets were empty and dark. Here and there a police car sped to some unknown destination, and periodically I could hear the rhythmic sound of boots, and voices singing the S.A. marching song, which proclaimed: "Die Strassen Frei!"—Make way for us!

One night I went to my friend Fritz' home to find how far along he was in his efforts to get out of Austria. I had spent many evening with him. We had taken drives out to the countryside and, with his wife, Johanna, had often gone to the theatre and their favorite Rathskeller.

Fritz was not a Zionist, nor was he interested in Jewish affairs. He had been a Socialist but the Dollfuss crusade against leftist movements had weaned him away from politics. His disinterest in politics of any kind probably drew me to him all the more. It gave me a haven from the endless turmoil of meetings and debates.

I knew Fritz had gone to American and British Consulates to see about securing an immigration visa and I was anxious to know what he had been able to accomplish. He slowly began his story. After leaving the consulates, he had been held up by two storm-troopers, beaten and thrown into a truck with more than thirty other people. He had thought to himself: "This is the end. But my good luck star did not desert me," Fritz went on. "All that happened was that, for seven hours, I had to wash and polish the cars and trucks of the German battalion stationed near B Bridge. But that wasn't the worst part. They had also picked up two bearded old Jews, and they kept pulling their beards, pushing them, throwing water at them, and tripping them, as their comrades sat around enjoying the circus show. I was outraged that I could do nothing to help these two old men.

"But you should have seen those two patriarchs! I don't know if they were rabbis or just Orthodox Jews. The inner strength they showed was far beyond that of most younger men. They never lost their dignity for a moment. Their clothes were wet, their coats were soiled, but they smiled softly, as if none of it mattered. I was puzzled and my bitterness almost turned to envy.

"At the end of the afternoon, I realized that they were doing what I've never been able to do; they were praying. All through the afternoon they'd been praying silently, their lips hardly moving. They were totally oblivious to where they were, as if they left this physical world."

Fritz was quiet for a moment, then he gave his wife a queer half-smile. "Johanna, you'll shake your head when I tell you this: I've been an agnostic all my life. All I've ever believed in was pure reason. But in the past few days, I find myself pronouncing the name of God."

The last several weeks under Nazi rule had done something to Fritz that thousands of years of Jewish history could not—it had taught him what it meant to be a Jew. The Chinese whose homes and properties were burned by Japanese invaders could still retreat and live among their countrymen. When their country was invaded and their people were massacred by Mussolini's fascists, the Ethiopians still remained in their own land. Other peoples suffered revolutions, invasions, upheavals, but they were able to stay in their own country. But when the Nazis came into Vienna. the Jews were left without a straw to clutch. The culture to which they had so richly contributed was no longer theirs. They were cast out of human society.

Fritz resumed in a slow, disjointed monotone. "I can't walk about for fear I'll be picked up. I can't stay home because I feel I'll go insane. I shudder when the bell rings that the Gestapo is at the door. I'm afraid to use the phone, meet a friend, go to my office, stand, sit, sleep, keep awake or commit suicide.

"How can the people here do this to me? I fought for them; spent more time among the workers in *Wiener Neustadt* than in my own home. I tried to give their children food and education. I tried to help them organize, defend their rights and work for a better future. I never wanted to go to Palestine. I had no feeling for it. I was an Austrian, and these were my people. But I see now that something was always wrong.

"I never told you before why I dropped out of the Social Democratic movement. It wasn't because we had to go underground. I didn't mind the danger or the hardships. It was because I was Jewish. It was the way my friends reacted to the anti-Semitism of our enemies . . . the way they avoided sending Jewish speakers or representatives to a meeting where the other side might capitalize on it. As if this bigotry wasn't part of our cause! They just tried to sidestep the issue instead of facing it. How could I reconcile this with all the Socialist ideals had fought for? And the indefineable feeling of not belonging. I was an Austrian, a liberal, a fighter, just as they were—but in addition I was also a Jew. And though it wasn't 'wrong' or 'shameful' to be a Jew, it still made me . . . a little different."

The longer Fritz talked, the more shrill his voice became and I could see he was struggling to fight off hysteria.

"I can't believe it's happening!" he said. "There are moments when I pray I'll wake up and find it was all a nightmare. Bank accounts and property confiscated! My friends and relatives taken away! I stood for two and a half days before the British, American, Chinese and Siamese consulates, and every one said that the earliest I could get a visa was a year or eighteen months from now. No one can help. I might be arrested or murdered and I can't do anything!"

He buried his head in his hands, then raised it and shook it slowly. "It's hard to believe that somewhere people lead normal lives. It seems impossible that I'll ever be able to walk down a street and talk to friends."

Then suddenly, as if remembering something he had seen, he tensed and muttered through his teeth, "If I could only get a chance to face them man to man, with a gun in my hand, I'd show them how it feels!

"Does anyone outside the country realize what is going on here? My friends in the Socialist International, do they understand the danger? What are they thinking of in London and Paris? That this maniac is going to stop here? That he just wants the return of his 'separated brothers'? No! There will be his 'brothers' in Czecho-slovakia, Poland, Russia, Switzerland, and Balkans and in the colonies in Africa! These youngsters marching around the streets singing '*Heute gehort uns Deutschland, morgen die ganze Welt!*' they are not just mouthing words!"

Fritz jumped up, walked over to the window, and held the curtains apart. He looked out into the dark, sprawling city, and the last words I ever heard from him were: "I can hear it coming. It will be the worst thing any of us have ever known. And there won't be a person in the world who isn't touched by it."

The next evening the telephone in the hallway rang suddenly and jerked me out of a revery. "It's me, Johanna," I heard an anguished voice say, "please come over right away. They took Fritz away a few moments ago."

* * *

The annexation of Austria by Nazi Germany had brought about a dramatic change in the attitude of Viennese Jews toward *Ha'apalah*. Prior to March 12 it had been almost impossible for younger people to obtain their parents' approval to join our groups, but now we had hundreds of candidates.

All of the Jews in Vienna were pursuing exit permits and visas and long lines formed in front of all the consulates. Chances for visas were slim and our activists ran into continuous problems attempting to secure the transit visas we needed to continue our work. Nonetheless, some visas to Italy and Greece were still obtainable and trafficking in travel papers for Jews had become a profitable business. Some consular employees had pity for the frightened, dejected individuals they faced and did what they could.

As the months passed, the particular destination ceased to matter and Jews swarmed to any consulate rumored to be granting or selling visas.

The more the Nazis tightened their grip, the faster the number of candidates for our *Ha'apalah* increased. Eichmann helped us: he wanted the Jews out and we were ready to accommodate him. Knowing that this was, to say the least, a tenuous accord, we raced to expand our activities.

The chartering and piloting of our boats was still done by Moshe Galili. He was then in Greece negotiating for several sail boats. We kept our lease on the camp in Kottingbrun and assembled immigrant candidates from all the branches of the Austrian *Betar* for the next sailing. We also located an inconspicuous site in Greece for a staging area.

The evening meetings at the few cafes still open to Jews were now strictly business sessions. Abstract discourses on revolutionary Zionism had been forgotten, and Haller, Deutsch and Perl were involved in day-to-day planning. We organized a trip to Berlin to learn how much cooperation we could expect from the nazis. Then we had the first of several clashes with Lange's chief subordinate, Adolf Eichmann. While Lange seemed calm and rational, Eichmann's moods were unpredictable. He would rave and rant during the meetings, threatening us and shouting hysterically. He seemed to be purposely imitating the mannerisms of his Fuehrer. Yet despite all the pyrotechnics he cooperated with us. Besides, his reputation as an achiever was growing.

In consultation with *Irgun* headquarters in Eretz-Israel, and with *Betar* world leadership in London, we decided that we could not continue Galili's limited "boy scout" approach to our *Ha'apalah*. A few well-trained uniformed youths passing for boy scouts on a tour of the Mediterranean would not work anymore. Gates were being slammed shut in the face of Jews around the world, and we had to deliver as many as we could, as fast as we could, any way we could.

As Galili was securing the boats for the Austrian groups, we also chartered a vessel for a group out of Poland. It became imperative to assign more *Irgun* pilots to head the future groups, and David Raziel, moving up in *Irgun* hierarchy, sent Shmuel Tagansky and later Nathan Kalfus and Shlomo Trachtman to pioneer these operations. Joseph Kremin, a veteran commander, was assigned full-time to coordinate all *Ha'apalah* work from the Palestinian side.

The Gestapo authorized the opening of an office in Vienna specifically for *Ha'apalah*. The number of *Aliyah* candidates immediately rose to thousands. To start with, we were allocated twenty pounds sterling per passenger, a sum which the Gestapo continuously reduced in the following months. The bank drafts were usually drawn on various accounts of the Bank of England, which gave me great personal satisfaction.

I was instructed by Tel-Aviv and London to go to Fiume, Italy, to help charter additional vessels. From there I was to proceed to Paris to consult with *Betar* and N.Z.O. representatives.

On April 30, 1938, I left Vienna, nine months after Eri Jabotinsky and David Raziel had sent me to first meet Moshe Galili. The few of us had then been regarded as madmen who were willing to subject Jews to all sorts of hardships and dangers, all for the dubious goal of getting into Palestine "illegally." But now, thousands were lining up outside our office in Vienna, and even that was only the beginning. We needed much more than we had; we needed boats and men to guide them. We needed tighter organization run by more experienced men.

Not only did the Zionist establishment fail to help us, they actually increased their opposition. The Chief Rabbi of Berlin, Dr. Leo Baeck, telegraphed the Zionist organization head-quarters in Vienna to oppose our activities. He told them that the Mandatory Power would deduct the number of our immigrant *Ma'apilim* from the immigration certificates granted to the Jew-ish Agency. Moshe Shapiro, of the Jewish Agency, had to come to Vienna with certificates for sixty immigrants, when some hundred thousand Jews were seeking to leave.

One day, Paul Haller, Deutsch, Dr. Perl and others of our people were invited to meet with my former Hebrew University teacher, Norman Bentwich, a veteran of the Zionist establish-ment. Bentwich, who was introduced to our people as represent-ing the Jewish Agency, was accompanied by several people, including a shadowy character named Gildenmeister who repre-sented himself as a humanitarian but was reputed by some to be a Gestapo informer. His specialty was said to be keeping track of Jews who attempted to save some of their properties or savings. Another man with Bentwich wore the lapel button of Nazi party men.

Bentwich did not begin the conversation on a friendly note. "Those of you involved in the illegal immigration must stop. You are committing a major crime!"

Haller answered sarcastically: "Yes, well, we happened to go out on the street and saw Jews being chased like rats, and we jumped to the rash conclusion that perhaps someone ought to do something."

Bentwich fumed: "Your crimes are threefold: first, you have no chance to bring these people safely to Palestine; second, Palestine cannot absorb them; third, you are officially acquiescing to the expulsion of the Jews!"

"And you're a murderer!" Perl exploded at him. With that, Haller and his colleagues walked out of the meeting. Haller phoned his liaison man in the Gestapo and told him about the meeting, saying: "We know the Zionist leaders are against us but what about your man who was there? Are you going to halt our work?"

The Gestapo officer asked for a detailed description of those present and then promised to phone back shortly. When he called, he started by saying: "Do you want us to expel that British agent Bentwich?" "He does not concern us," Haller answered. "We know what he stands for. Do you authorize us to continue our work?"

"Of course," assured the official, and with unusual politeness added "good luck."

In June I was back in Eretz-Israel to prepare for the landing of three hundred and eighty Austrian *Betarim*, many of whom were my friends. I again spent the night before the landing in the village of Benyamina on the coast, and before dawn went to the meeting place in the orange grove. where the buses that were to carry and disperse the *Ma'apilim* in many directions were assembling. The landing was carried out without a hitch.

With the landing of the three hundred and eighty *Ma'apilim* we terminated our cooperation with Moshe Galili: Our larger mission called for new kinds of expertise. I had come to know Galili well in the past nine months and I admired his courage, but we could not go along with his political fantasies. We had to think and plan rationally, but Galili was consistently spontaneous and romantic. His slogan was *Af-Al-Pi*—"Despite it all!" and he dreamed of thousands of disciplined freedom fighters, youths from all parts of the diaspora, sailing towards Eretz-Israel, well armed and trained, carrying banners and flags and military bands and daringly outwitting the police launches.

It was a beautiful dream and we were working towards it, but first and foremost we had to save as many Jews as we could.

VIII
The Voyage of the Melk

In early October, 1938, I was back in Vienna. I found the Jewish community was almost completely destroyed. Jewish shops and cafes I had known had all been "liquidated," and on the main streets, boarded-up windows stared at me where elegant interiors had once glittered. Scarcely a Jew appeared on the streets, and the expressions of the non-Jews were frozen and impassive.

But Vienna was now performing a new role in Jewish history. Eichmann was doing so well in clearing Vienna of Jews that a central office for Jewish emigration was established there under his direction.

Shortly after I arrived in Vienna, an "action" took place throughout German territory, during which fifteen thousand Jews of Polish nationality were rounded up and dumped on the Polish border. It was part of Germany's intensified efforts to extrude the Jews from its territories which challenged us to expand our *Ha'apalah* work.

Shortly before midnight, on November 4th, I entered the desolate Customs House on the Danube, to await the arrival of the men and women of our "underground railroad." What the British in Palestine called "illegal" immigrants, and what we called *Ma'apilim*, or "those who scale the mountains," had been officially designated as "Juden transporte" by the Gestapo. This was the first time we were going to use the Danube for our transit and I was tense. We had taken exceptional precautions to keep secret the route of these immigrants, yet we were still not certain whether their passage from Vienna down to the Black Sea would escape interference. The Danube wound through several nations on its way to the sea, and any one might try to stop the boat, though the Danube shipping laws said it could not be stopped.

The idea of using the Danube had been born in an emergency. The group leaving tonight had made a previous trip scheduled to go through the Aegean Sea, but when they arrived at the Italian border, the authorities refused them passage. Although the *Ma'apilim* possessed Italian transit visas, they did not have immigrant visas to final destinations, and the Italian authorities who knew by now where these groups of Jews were heading, did not want hundreds of refugees on their hands in case they could not land in Palestine and the Germans would not allow the immigrants back. The long train, overcrowded with hundreds of weary men and women, was stranded for more than three weeks in the fields near the Italian border. When all hope for securing transit through Italy had vanished, the train had no choice but return to Vienna. This incident strained relations with the Gestapo and endangered our work in German-controlled areas.

Our office staff in Vienna settled down around a map to find another means of escape for these immigrants, as well as for the thousands to come. It was then that we "discovered" the Danube. The Danube was recognized as an international waterway by a special accord ratified in 1923, and traffic on it was to be as free as on the high seas. Even without visas to final destinations international law specified that immigrants could not be detained.

The Greek and Turkish ship owners swore that this was our solution, and the Gestapo in Vienna confirmed our evaluation of the Danube Accord. They agreed to permit Jews to immigrate via the Danube, but warned us that if other countries breached the Accord they would take drastic action against us, the organizers and the "transport."

We decided to take our chances and we chartered a Danube vessel called the *Melk* which would take us as far as the Black Sea. There we would meet a tramp steamer piloted by an *Irgun* man who would take the immigrants the rest of the way.

Since this was our first voyage down the river and we needed close coordination with the pilots in the tramper, I was assigned to accompany the *Melk* to the Black Sea.

When the train pulled up near the Vienna Danube Customs House, five hundred and fifty disoriented people dragged out onto the platform. Dozens of S.S. men emerged from trucks parked outside the building.

The train that discharged these passengers at the Customs House had made one of the shortest trips in railroad history. Pulling out of the main station in Vienna a few minutes earlier, it had traveled exactly a mile and a half. With the cooperation of the German authorities, we had succeeded in hiding the route so well that even those who knew of the group's departure believed they were heading again toward Italy or Yugoslavia.

This time we were taking no chances, and each passenger's passport bore an immigrant visa to Liberia. To further formalize the operation, we had printed special railroad tickets which read "Liberia Transport." As we all knew, Liberia's name came from the Latin root for "liberty." The passengers unloaded their few belongings and carried them into the Customs House, lining up in groups along the walls for inspection. The Nazis allowed Jewish immigrants to take only as many possessions as they could carry. All that each one had was a knapsack containing some clothing and the most vital necessities. A few youngsters had also brought musical instruments. That was all.

Scores of Gestapo agents moved through the crowd, accompanied by local customs inspectors, as S.S. men surrounded the buildings from the outside. As if anyone wished to escape! The Gestapo ripped bags apart and searched the emigrants' pockets, making sure they had not cheated the Third Reich by taking anything of value. The Gestapo agents enjoyed themselves immensely, swearing at the emigrants, mocking and imitating them, calling them names, pushing them and poking their ribs. They were very much amused.

Dr. Lange and Adolf Eichmann were there to supervise the emigration. From time to time they paused to listen to the reports of their subordinates, nodding approvingly as their underlings clicked their heels and saluted.

When the last group boarded, I went down the gangway to join them. The Gestapo agent stopped me and asked for my papers. Noting that I was a Palestinian "journalist," he raised his eyebrows. "Where do you think you're going?" he asked. "You do not belong here, you cannot get on this boat." It finally took a personal intervention from our contact man at the Danube

Steamship Company, Mr. Bischof, with Dr. Lange, to let me through. The Gestapo agent shrugged his shoulders, muttering, "I can't understand why they need a newspaperman to cover a ship of pigs."

As I started once more toward the boat, I was stopped again, this time by a customs agent and an S.S. man. They took me into a closed room and for ten minutes methodically searched everything from the inside of my heels to the lining of my hat, as well as my hair and ears. Finally, having run out of places and people to search, they let me go, and I boarded the boat.

The *Melk* had once been a Danube pleasure boat, built to accommodate about eighty people for a holiday jaunt of eight or ten hours, and there was supposedly cabin space for only sixteen people. Into this boat we loaded five hundred and fifty passengers, who would have to live on it for at least two weeks. But despite the confusion, the strain on their faces began to lift. Just being out of sight of the Nazis was enough to revitalize their spirits.

A few minutes later, the boat headed toward the middle of the river. Only the few who were standing outside the corridors could see Vienna for the last time. Their faces mirrored both sadness and relief.

I stood at the rail on the upper deck of the *Melk* and watched the lights of Vienna disappear. What would have happened to these people on board, I wondered, if they had remained in Austria? And what would happen to thousands of Jews in the near future if we could not expand our work? The Zionist establishment still fought us at every turn and we never knew from one day to the next where we could get funds to expand our activities. The new *Irgun* pilots joining these voyages left their families and careers and received no salaries or benefits for all their sacrifice. They were all in danger of being blacklisted in Palestine and arrested whenever they returned from a trip.

Our *Ha'apalah* activities were starting to assume huge proportions, and even though we finally had full cooperation from the central and eastern European governments, we were chronically broke. The nationalist movement never had funds for settlements, land or vocational training. Now the little money raised went first to our immigration work.

"Official" Jewish organizations like the Joint Distribution Committee and the labor-controlled Jewish Agency denied us financial support, claiming that they could not engage in "illegal activities." Somehow, no matter what happened in Europe, they could not comprehend that "illegal" or not, our work meant life or death to thousands of fellow Jews.

There was no sign that our relationship with the establishment would change. In early October, another attempt to create a rapport between the *Haganah* and the *Irgun* had been personally vetoed by Ben-Gurion. Cracks were appearing in the stubborn opposition of Zionist Labor to *Ha'apalah*. The British were still giving out a few immigration certificates, and some in the *Haganah* finally woke up to the facts of life and sent their representatives to Vienna. But through it all, they clung to their belief in "selectivity" of immigrants, and refused to accept the principle of mass immigration.

As conditions in Europe became more menacing, unscrupulous individuals in various countries had begun to engage in this human traffic for profit. Some honest but irresponsible people had also plunged into immigration traffic and failed horribly, endangering the lives of their passengers. All of this was injuring our reputation and slowing down our work. We could not stop these individuals and our answer was to try and intensify our own activity.

Since the summer, an expanded effort by the *N.Z.O.-Betar-Irgun* coalition had gained us new offices in central and Eastern Europe. Immigrants registered with us and we gave them medical examinations to be sure they could endure the rigors of the trip. We instructed them about finances and baggage, and briefed them on the inevitable hardships and dangers ahead. We also opened small offices in western Europe where we raised funds from a few concerned individuals, some of whom also volunteered to act as liaison officers, using their western passports to cross borders more and more impassable for Jews.

Once the would-be immigrants completed their registration at the local offices, they were assigned into units and subunits as in the military, with a commander at their head, guard units and various other officials all selected from among the candidates. Members of youth organizations were mixed with other immigrants to help maintain strict discipline during the voyage under the often critical conditions. Once aboard the seagoing tramps headed for Palestine, they were joined by a member of the *Irgun* who then had overall authority up until the moment of the landing. He controlled communications with the coast of Palestine, designated the landing spot and gave emergency instructions.

The landings in Eretz-Israel were well organized. The large ships would stop outside the territorial waters, then transfer small groups into sailboats equipped with motors. The sailboats would glide onto the beach, discharge their *Ma'apilim* and return for another load. With this method, in the event of arrest by British patrols, we would lose only the smaller boats, and only a few of the *Ma'apilm*. This also saved us the hundreds of thousands of dollars the shipowners would charge us if the ships were confiscated.

The scale of our activities in the underground railroad had developed from a trickle to a flood. The *Melk* was just one of several groups at that moment on move to ports all around the Black Sea and the Aegean.

* * *

Early the first morning on the *Melk*, I walked into the Commander's cabin. Unshaven and red-eyed, he grinned at me through a haze of smoke. Everything was organized. The expanded kitchen already working at full steam, with two large wood-burning ovens on either side of the deck. The infirmary's first patients were already lining up with sore throats, colds and headaches. All the food was kept in one place under guard to prevent "raids" by the younger *Ma'apilim*, whose quest for adventure, even under these trying conditions, we knew would be irrepressible.

The transport commander was a thirty-two year old engineer from southern Austria. Despite his youth and amiable nature, he could be hard as nails when necessary. The job demanded the skills of an army officer, a naval expert, a community leader, a social worker and a psychiatrist.

As the transport staff assembled to meet with the commander, the cabin seemed ready to burst. There were twelve on the staff: two doctors, the head of the guard unit, a former champion prizefighter, the chief cook, once a chef in a famous Viennese hotel, a young woman in charge of the women aboard, a secretary, the commander, the second-in-command, and four more men charged with miscellaneous duties. Most of them were young, and in their sports clothes, boots and military belts, they looked fit and capable of meeting any contingencies that might arise.

We docked in Bratislava for a short stopover to pick up a small group of *Ma'apilim* registered with the Bratislava office. The local authorities were nervous and discourteous, and we stayed no longer than necessary.

The depressed atmosphere of the night before was disappearing from the ship. Most of the emigrants were relaxing on the upper decks, sitting or standing in groups, sunning themselves and chatting quietly. The men had shaved; the women had freshened up. Hot tea and a few hours of sun seemed to have cured their colds, and already the *Melk* was becoming home. Although the leavetaking of their families and homes yesterday had been agonizing, and the boat and its meager accommodations depressing as well, they were escaping from a nightmare to a new life, and healthy optimism began to take hold of their spirits.

The boat traveled at full speed along the green, luxuriantly wooded shores of Slovakia. We passed the local barges and small boats, and their crews gaped at our boat with its large swastika painted on the hull, and its decks dark and overflowing with human beings. It was a sight to which they would grow accustomed in the months to come, but now it was new and strange and they could not understand. They stared at us in stony silence until we were gone from their view.

As I stood looking at the local boatmen fade into the distance, a man with thick white hair and a slightly stooped back joined me at the rail. "Wonderful what potency lies in this medicine called hope," he said, smiling. "Everyone seems to have taken a liberal dose." He inhaled deeply. "They can already smell the air of Palestine."

"Can there be Jewish nostrils to go with the Jewish nose?" I said.

His name was Dr. Brill. I had first met him in Vienna in the summer of 1937. We struck up a friendship based on a common interest in Palestinian archaeology. Dr. Brill had accumulated half a dozen doctorates in such fields as chemistry, biology, history and archaeology. All in all, he seemed the perfect personification of the absent-minded professor. He could read Aramaic inscriptions fluently and he was thoroughly at home in Greek philosophy, but he frequently forgot what day of the week it was, or what he had set out to do that morning. He had a fine sense of humor and was an unsurpassable conversationalist. Once he got started discussing recent excavations in Palestine, I could not stop him and never wished to. I always found these talks with him a balm for whatever struggle I was facing.

Now, as we looked out at the fading wake of the boat, breathing in the fresh air blowing in from the wooded shores, he said: "Under the conditions on this boat, you can learn more about human nature than you would from the best academic program in psychology. Some seem to lack the proper community spirit," he chuckled. "But the greatest problem was with the Burgenland boys. They're armed with knives, like the good tough farmers they are. We told them bluntly that they could not walk around carrying those things and would have to surrender them to the guard unit. They did so, but only after we argued with them at length, and finally had to call upon their Rabbi to intervene. He is probably their only authority on Jewish matters. They're a most interesting lot."

We went across the deck to a corner where about a dozen young "Burgenlanders" were sitting apart from the others. The only Palestinian Jew they had ever seen was the *shochet* (the animal slaughterer according to Orthodox tradition) who had visited the villages once a week, a wizened old man with a beard and sidelocks. That was how they imagined all native Palestinians must look; it took them some time to recover from their amazement when they learned that I too had been born and bred in Palestine. They were also amazed to hear that there were farmers in Palestine and that for three generations my people had been Palestinian farmers.

As the voyage progressed, we became good friends. They were good, hardy, simple people. Their communities had existed for more than four hundred years. In years past there had been a strong Orthodox Jewish tradition in Burgenland. However, some families, mostly farmers, lived scattered among the non-Jewish population with little or no Jewish education, and only a scant Jewish consciousness. Some Jewish chidren intermarried with Christians. These farmers never went to synagogue except on the High Holydays, and even then, less for any spiritual commitment than for the rare chance to meet with relatives and friends from farms and villages scattered around the countryside. Some remembered a few words of prayer from their Bar Mitzvah, but most read from the German translation of the prayer book. They were cut off from Jewish life in the big cities and knew very little about Palestine, but contributed generously when the Rabbi made an appeal during the Holydays to help the Jews "over there."

With the *Anschluss* their harmonious lives changed suddenly. The Germans garrisoned in the province quickly started a violent campaign of anti-Semitism and many young native Austrians and local Nazis followed their lead. The elders simply did not dare show any opposition to the New Order, and in a few weeks, the Jews were hermetically isolated from the rest of the community. Shortly after came the shock from which many of them would never recover: they were told that they had to leave. The government confiscated their lands and properties, and within a few days, all the Burgenland Jews had to leave for Vienna. "The Gestapo in Vienna will have money for you and take care of you," they were told.

Once in the city, they received several marks a day for food and their fare to Palestine was paid by the Gestapo. Altogether, for the forty Burgenlanders on the *Melk*, the Gestapo had probably spent ten thousand marks. The property that was taken from them was worth many millions of marks.

What shook them most deeply, though, was being so cruelly wrenched from everything they had ever known. Their fathers, grandfathers and great-grandfathers had worked these lands and passed them on, and in one fell swoop they were gone. Even the family cemeteries were destroyed by the Nazis. Nothing was left. They bombarded me with questions. What was the climate in Palestine? Did my family actually own a citrus grove? They wanted to know all there was to know about the soil and water. Would they be helped to a new start? They had no tools or seeds or cattle. How would they be received? What did it mean to travel "illegally"? The whole lot of them, with their rabbi had been brought under Gestapo surveillance, directly from their rooms in Vienna to the train which dropped them at the *Melk*. They had never even had a chance to learn the nature of the trip they were taking.

In spite of all they had been through, I felt no great sadness as I looked at them. They were here, alive and hopefully, safe. I could already see the whole strong, vigorous little community happy and free, bringing in the harvest from the mountains of Galilee or the valley of the Sharon.

* * *

On November 9, 1938, we approached Budapest. Earlier in the day we had watched Hungarian artillery and cavalry move along the banks into Czechoslovakia. Hungary had joined the Nazis in the dismemberment of Czechoslovakia under the Munich agreement two months earlier. Budapest was fully illuminated as we approached, and its brilliant lights and the music that drifted to us on the river were a violent but welcome contrast to Vienna a few night ago. Midnight was approaching and the boat was quiet as it slowly edged in toward our berth. Most of our passengers were fast asleep.

Lilting gypsy music continued to float in from the city. Budapest was celebrating the "return" of the *Komora* region to the motherland from Czechoslovakia. Before long Hungary would take back Transylvania from Romania, and the next day the Romanians in turn would grab a chunk of Bulgaria. Bulgaria would invade Greece, and Italy would march into Yugoslavia, and around and around they would go, while Hitler's Germany waited in the wings, playing them off against each other until they were all ripe to be overthrown. When he marched in, millions of Jews would be the first to suffer for it.

"Why are you grimacing?" a woman's voice sounded near me. "Did you swallow something bitter?"

"No," I answered looking up. "I hope I'll never have to." It was Bertha, a medical student who had recently worked in our Vienna office. She was an intelligent, serious young woman who had been in her fifth year at the University of Vienna at the time of the

Anschluss. She had joined the group bound for Palestine the moment her parents gave their reluctant consent.

"Are you all right?" she asked in surprise. She sat down near me. "It's stuffy downstairs." She looked at the lights. "Happy Budapest," she said. "Like Vienna before the Germans."

Bertha was slender, tall and dark, with smooth skin and strong, even features. She had beautiful dark eyes and thick black hair which she wore in a braided half-arch. When she mentioned Vienna, I said: "Bertha, take my advice. When you reach Palestine, stop talking about Vienna! People won't appreciate hearing 'back there in Vienna we had beautiful streets and homes and museums and weather.' You're going to be a Palestinian now, not an Austrian, and stories about how well off you were before will only antagonize people you should be trying to make your friends."

Bertha was stunned by my sudden tirade, and I instantly felt guilty. Poor thing! Why did she have to be the victim of my irritation? All day I had been rankling about a dispute that morning among some of the older passengers. A group of Viennese had said they had heard that former Russian and Polish Jews in Palestine were unfriendly to recent German-speaking immigrants. An elderly man shot back that the Viennese had not treated him so well either when he settled in Vienna twenty-two years earlier. Then someone originally from Berlin muttered something crude about *Ostjude,* or "Jews from the East." The conversation had irritated me thoroughly. Would these people cling to their diaspora memories to the end of their days? Were they going to Eretz-Israel to start over, or just to carry their regionalism with them? "Polish-Jews." "Austrian-Jews." "German-Jews." Couldn't they fling aside these hyphens and accept each other simply as fellow Jews?

"I don't know what caused this outburst," Bertha answered calmly, "but I certainly don't intend to go around in Palestine repeating to myself, 'Oh where are the snows of yester year!?' and neither do the others. But it's only a couple of days since we left, and whatever Austria did to us in the end, it was our native country! We can't just instantly lock a door in our hearts and say, 'it never existed!' And if we talk about how much better things were back there, well, they were. I know what will happen. Nice people will invite me to their homes, discuss their problems, their jobs, their worries, and I won't be able to sympathize with them at all, because I have nothing. I'll feel foreign to them and beneath them. I'll want to tell them that we had homes too, nice ones; that we had businesses and professions, and used to go to the theatre and opera, and on vacations. And what will be so wrong in saying that, if it's all we have to keep our self-respect? Or are we supposed to constantly play the poor, grateful refugee, so benumbed by the generosity of our hosts that we can't exhibit the smallest scrap of pride or say a word beyond 'thank you, thank you!?'"

"I don't disagree with anything you've said," I answered, "But why do almost all the recent immigrants concentrate together in the cities and insist on speaking German or Polish or Italian instead of trying to be part of their new land?"

Bertha shook her head. "You're not very tolerant, Yitshaq. Try learning a new language in six months, after you've used your mother tongue for thirty or forty years. Try changing your habits, your tastes, your profession and everything else you've ever known. Wait till you're middle-aged, then pack your suitcase and go to Finland. I'd like to see how fast you readjust!"

"Yes," I admitted, "and my Russian and Polish grandparents were not better in the beginning. But don't you think that you central European Jews should make a special effort to integrate faster? You were the last to come to Palestine as pioneers, your immigration started on a large scale only when Hitler came to power."

"You had better check your facts," Bertha interrupted. "Some of the first settlers were Hungarian, Austrian and German. Some of the leading doctors, scientists and teachers who came to Palestine forty years ago or earlier were from Germany. It was not a mass movement, but you never had a mass movement out of eastern Europe either. After the war there were no more than six hundred thousand Jews in Germany. There were over *three million* in Poland. And the Jews in the West never suffered the way they did in Poland and Russia. Central and western Europe never had pogroms on the scale of those in eastern Europe. So, we didn't have the same 'idealism.' Common people simply are not born idealistic. They had good lives, so why should they have left their countries? And how could they have foreseen that it would suddenly all end."

"Herzl did," I broke in. "Right in your own Vienna. So did Nordau in Hungary, and so did Jabotinsky in Odessa, when everything was easy and comfortable—right before the 1905 pogroms. Why didn't the Jews in the West listen, when it affected all their lives? Even the Zionist leaders couldn't find the time to think about what was developing."

"Some did and some did not," Bertha answered quietly. "Some emigrated to Palestine or to Argentina, but others believed in assimilation, liberalism and baptism. They made mistakes just like the rest of humanity, and all that matters is that we try not to make them again. It took pogroms in the last century to send your grandparents to Palestine and it took Hitler to send me there. What does it matter who was kicked out first? We have a common past and future. There are millions of Jews still in Europe— they're what we have to worry about, not what's been done in the past."

I started to reply, but I realized that Bertha had made her point. I smiled at her and said simply, "Of course you're right."

IX
The Crystal Night

We eventually docked in Budapest, and "Herr Direktor" Bischof came aboard. I had spoken with him last in Vienna when we boarded the *Melk* and the Gestapo high brass gathered to inspect us. Since the return of the ill-fated train from the Italian border, we had heard about friction within the Gestapo concerning money allocated for our "transport" charters, as well as what to do with Jews who were sent back to Germany and Austria from foreign ports. Eichmann was threatening to deport all of us to Buchenwald. However, some of the top men in the Vienna Gestapo had high stakes in the emigration, and Bischof, a Director of the Danube Shipping Company and an expert on the international transit on the Danube, was called in to handle our movement. When I had been pulled aside at the dock in Vienna, it was Bischof who took my passport to Lange and got it approved, stamped and returned to me. When at the last moment another officer barked at me, "Report to Headquarters the moment you are back in Vienna," Bischof whispered to me: "Don't worry. You'll make it to the sea, and everyone will be in seventh heaven."

As soon as Bischof came on board now, he took me aside and we were joined by other members of the command. In a low, solemn voice Bischof described the events of the evening before.

On November 7th, a young Jew named Herschel Grynszpan had shot and killed a German Embassy counselor in Paris to protest the increasing deportation of Jews to concentration camps. Hitler was enraged, and ordered Goering and Goebbels to organize a pogrom throughout the Reich. Scores of Jews were killed, and many more were wounded. More than a hundred

169

synagogues were destroyed, many dating back to before Germany existed. Countless Jewish homes and businesses were destroyed and so many windows were shattered that the entire episode was called *Kristallnacht*, a reference to the glass that covered the streets in Jewish neighborhoods. The damage was estimated at twenty million marks. Bischof had seen the attacks break out in Vienna; he had also kept track of developments since, by radio and in the Budapest newspapers. He told us everything he knew, and as he talked the circle of people kept growing around us. Some of the crew joined and listened impassively, until Bischof glanced around guiltily as if he had said too much. Bowing stiffly, he abruptly broke away from us and went about his business. He looked exceptionally haggard and gray. I knew his secret—he had a Jewish wife.

Slowly the listeners drifted back to their allotted spaces. Bischof's report had left them tense with worry for the friends and relatives they had left behind. The future looked like a long nightmare: deportations and dislocations; trains to whispered-about camps; daily disappearances of Jews; and now overt, full-scale attacks with scarcely an effort by the Nazis to hide exactly what they were doing. They were dropping away the last vestiges of pretense and what could come next was too horrible for us to imagine. If the West kept finding reasons not to intervene, if they let Hitler calmly march into Czechoslovakia and randomly kill Jews, then he was not going to stop until he had taken over all of Europe.

Finally our boat left Budapest and a few of us sat in the dark on the damp deck as the city lights gradually disappeared behind us. None of us were capable of small talk or philosophy any more, and every question we posed to each other was on the same subject: How much time was left? What could any of us do? And unbeknown to the others, I asked myself the critical question: How soon could we be ready to move tens of thousands of armed men off the coast of Palestine to face the British warships? The Poles promised us weapons and training camps, but it would take a few more years to prepare and it did not look as if we had a few more years.

As we talked that evening on the *Melk*, we did not know that on that very day, the Mandatory power had issued a circular to all coastal police stations in Palestine: "The following vessels are preparing to sail from Greece to Palestine: *Eli, Draga, Artemisia.* The destination is Caesaria. Motorboats to intensify patrolling. District stations to patrol the coast." As Hitler watched the world's reaction to his *Kristallnacht*, Britain laid the groundwork to intensify its intervention against the Jewish immigrants along the Mediterranean. It was doing its best to make sure that Hitler's noose would not slip.

* * *

To our left lay the fields of Romania; to our right the wooded hills of Yugoslavia. Young people sat in a large circle at the stern singing Viennese, Hungarian and Hebrew songs, playing guitars and accordions. The music and the bright day restored a semblance of optimism to the group. The older people traded stories and discussed their future plans. Several days had passed since we left Budapest and we had not yet stopped at another port. We had been isolated from the outside world long enough now so that people were starting to have a sense of unreality. Having suddenly lost everything that made up the framework of their lives they felt as if nothing ultimately made sense any more. They were thankful for their escape, yet uncertain and understandably nervous about the future. Circulating from group to group, I became an information bureau for them, trying to put their minds to rest and keep them grounded to the earth. Yes, their professions would be useful in Palestine; yes, they could settle on the land; yes, they could live in a remote colony or in a larger city.

At this point I headed off to be alone at the bow, but Dr. Brill was at my side before I had a moment to relax. Dr. Brill hesitated a moment and then said: "I was in the radio room a few moments ago. Bad news. Even worse than Bischof told us."

We headed for the radio room and had the whole story a few minutes later. Jews in nearly every city of Germany and Austria had been attacked.

Dr. Brill's brother was still in Vienna with his family, and so were many of his friends. As he listened to the radio he said in a low voice, "We have to try and save as many as possible . . . I only pray to God that the Germans don't decide to stop emigration."

"I don't think they will—not yet," I ventured. "They're still trying to make the world believe that they're as human as anybody else but just have different political views. They'll let the Jews out until Hitler engages in an all-out war. We have to work fast—at best we have a couple of years."

Dr. Brill nodded. "I hope we have as long as you say. You know the Gestapo has already reduced the traveling expense money they let Jews take out of the country. You told me that because of the increased danger of confiscation, the price of the boats keeps going up? How can we pay when the Germans are letting us have less?"

"We have to raise money abroad—even if the organized Jewish charities won't help us. Since we're not 'legal' enough for them— we'll have to find other ways."

Dr. Brill smiled bitterly. "We try to save lives and they worry about technicalities. Why don't they stand up and shout to the whole world that what's 'illegal' is closing immigration to Palestine. It breaks international law and contradicts the very pledge made by the Mandatory power.

"Why don't they just fling the few miserable certificates back in Britain's face and tell them we don't need their permits to bring Jews to Palestine."

I shrugged my shoulders. "The big charitable Jewish organizations say this is all 'political' and they're not interested in politics. They say they have to deal with governments, not fight them."

"I would say," Dr. Brill began, "that these 'charitable' organizations are more political than charitable. What do they want the Jews to do? Bare our necks to the hangman and roll our eyes piously, murmuring: 'We agree to die peacefully rather than disturb the political setup'!?"

I tried to calm him. "I understand that a special delegation may go to the United State to raise funds for *Ha'apalah.* Colonel Wedgwood, Colonel Patterson and Commander Locker-Lampson have been mentioned as possible participants. They and other good Englishmen are anxious to save Britain from history's judgment."

Dr. Brill shook his head. "They'll have a tough job on their hands. No matter how inhuman and corrupt laws are, the Jews in power seem to have an aversion to breaking them. I was in the

United States two years ago. American Jews won't get it through their heads that millions of people's lives might depend on what they do. They just want to give a little gift and that's enough to salve their conscience."

By now Dr. Brill and I had depressed each other thoroughly, and we fell into a silence. As I leaned over the rail, watching the water of the Danube rushed by, I tried to fight off my mood. There was too much to be done and all my deepest convictions precluded my surrendering to hopelessness. Every moment that I or the rest stood still, more Jews would face a grim future.

* * *

Two days later we stopped at Giurgiu, a dirty little port on the Romanian side of the Danube. We remained in Giurgiu for three days, while a thick, heavy fog covered us like a cloth.

The Romanian police placed a heavy guard around us as if we had the plague and no one was permitted to board or leave the boat. All five hundred and fifty of us were caught in a floating cage. Still, I never heard a single passenger complain.

Our second night in Giurgiu was Friday, the Sabbath eve and the transport staff planned for a special program. After dinner, shaven and washed we assembled on the lower deck, young and old jamming into every available inch of space. The girls had cleaned the area thoroughly, and even hung up a multi-colored paper chain which they had found somewhere. A long table improvised out of various pieces of furniture was covered with a spotless white cloth and adorned with candles. The transport commander, the rabbi from the Burgenland, a cantor and members of the staff seated themselves around the table. Then the program opened with a Sabbath evening prayer by the cantor. Next, several members of the transport started playing their instruments and in moments everyone around the table was tapping their feet and singing along. Whether they knew the words or not, the way their mood rose in such a short time was a small miracle. Then the commander invited the rabbi to speak.

The young rabbi was small and pale, with a short, tapering brown beard. Because of his spiritual strength and his almost tragic devotion to his flock, he had earned the respect given to a much older man. He refused special accommodations and slept together with his Burgenlanders on the cold, damp floor of the rear deck. Never forgetting that he was the spiritual leader of his community, he constantly set an example for all others. The transport staff felt that the passengers should be told about the scope of the tragic events in Germany and Austria and the rabbi was chosen to give them the news.

The rabbi stood a moment, solemn and still, and the Sabbath gaiety quickly died down. The passengers looked up and waited tensely. The rabbi slowly glanced from one corner of the hall to the other, as if trying to discover whether they could stand the truth. Then he spoke: "We Jews of Germany and Austria lived with Christian neighbors for many centuries, sharing their happiness and sorrows. When peace was our fate we were thankful and when hatred and destruction befell us, we prayed forgiveness for our destroyers. We never faltered in our belief that we were all part of the true 'master race'—the human race. Our great teacher, Hillel, taught us to 'Love peace, seek peace, love mankind.' He told us also that God had granted men the wisdom to choose between good and evil.

"I know it has become difficult to believe in Hillel's teachings when the Nazis have made a mockery of good and evil." Here, the rabbi took a breath, then continued quietly: "From Frankfurt to Gratz, from Nuremberg to ancient Worms, from Stettin to Salzburg—our homes and synagogues are burning from fires set by the Nazis. Thousands of our brothers have been massacred by mobs and the House of Jacob in Ashkenaze has ceased to be. We should tear our clothes and put ashes on our heads and call, 'How doth the city sit solitary, that was full of People.' We should cry, 'Behold, Oh Lord, if there be any sorrow like unto my sorrow.' We feel like shouting, 'Wherefore came I forth out of the womb to see labor and sorrow; that my days should be consumed with shame?'"

The rabbi paused as if waiting for someone to answer. Then he said, "And yet, we cannot yield. We cannot betray all that we believe in. We must survive, and with our survival we will prove the power and the glory of the human spirit which is part of God, which cannot be destroyed by man. We have a new life to build, a new world for our children and we will not lose faith in God and man, as long as we draw strength from our heritage. 'Israel shall blossom and fill the world with fruit!'"

The rabbi paused and then apparently deciding he had said all he could, merely raised his hand and said *Hatikva*. Slowly, one voice joined another in the Hebrew national anthem, at first sobbing but then rising loud and strong to the sky.

X

The Shaved Heads

On our third day at Giurgiu, with the fog still enveloping the *Melk*, I talked with the *Glattkoepfe* or "shaved heads" as we called them on board. There were four of them, their heads all shaven at Buchenwald Concentration Camp. They had been brought to the *Melk* by S.S. men a few minutes before its departure.

Their passage had been arranged by their families but the "shaved heads" never had a chance to thank them or say goodbye.

It had taken the *Glattkoepfe* four days on board before they began emerging from their shells. They sat apart from the others, each in his own world. They obeyed all orders but when anyone approached, they looked up with eyes full of fear and suspicion, like starved, beaten dogs roaming the outskirts of a city. They could not comprehend that the rest of us might be something other than torturers. Nearly a week passed before they could digest anything but bread and tea. Then slowly they began recovering, walking about hesitantly and listening to the conversations on the fringes of groups. I succeeded in engaging one of them, Professor Kohn, in a more or less coherent conversation. In his late sixties, he was the oldest, yet strangely he seemed in better condition than the others.

He was a very short, slightly paunchy man, whose naturally bald head had not really had to be shaven by the Nazis. His face could be baby smooth and placid one moment, then wrinkled, misshapen and tragic the next. Although his eyes never teared, he was forever wiping them with his hands, a nervous habit he seemed to have acquired at the camp. Only nine months earlier, he had headed a department in the medical school at the University of Vienna and had lectured to hundreds of students from all over the world. I was the first man to whom he had talked in months who did not verbally or physically abuse him.

Professor Kohn spoke in a low, dispassionate monotone.

"I used to lie on my straw sack for hours, trying to understand my arrest. I was never interested in politics or public life. I could trace my family back in Vienna over two hundred and fifty years, and neither I nor anyone else had been very active in Jewish affairs. Even the week before I was arrested, when funds from Jews were being sought to save the Schuschnigg regime, I did not contribute. I felt Jews should not take a political stand, even against Hitler. Nevertheless, they arrested me among the very first.

"I found out why months later, at camp. A student I hardly remembered had failed to pass one of my examinations. I do not know if he was a Nazi then or became one later but when I was arrested, he was there in the uniform of an officer of the Elite guard. 'There's one Jew,' I heard him gloat, 'who won't bother Aryan students any more.'"

Professor Kohn wiped his eyes with the back of his hand, but his face was devoid of emotion. His eyes stared directly ahead. "I spent eight months in the camp and my only crime was trying to enhance Austria's reputation in world medicine, but what do they care about the rest of the world? There would not be a Buchenwald if they cared about the opinion of the world." A tremor momentarily took hold of the professor, and he waited a moment until his head stopped shaking from side to side. "There must be a streak of madness in a people that can produce such pathological individuals. Our camp commandant was a big man, a drunkard, with a vicious temper. His hobbies were music and torture. Sometimes he combined them. In his honor a Buchenwald anthem was written, and once, when hundreds of us were lined up to witness the murder of one of the prisoners, he ordered us to sing it. When we kept silent he threatened to shoot us, so we sang. The man who had been chosen randomly to be the morale-builder, an old man, was already out of his mind with pain. Nails has been driven into his feet and hands. He was flogged by two of the guards, then bloodhounds were brought into the court. The commandant led the singing with his hands like a conductor.

> Oh Buchenwald, I can forget thee never
> My fate has made it plain to me
> That none who have known thee can ever
> Know what is meant by liberty!

"When we had finished, the bloodhounds were let loose on the crucified old Jew. They tore him to shreds and we were forced to watch to the last moment."

"Were you ever tortured?" I asked.

"No, nor were the other three released with me. I do not think the Nazis would release anyone they tortured—if he survived, he would be either crippled or insane. They would not like such examples of their 'new order' out in the world. I was not hurt but I felt as if everything I saw happened to me. Our labor group, and all other labor groups with intellectuals in them—rabbis, ministers, professors—were put under the control of convicted murderers, thieves and rapists. There was always the threat that at any given moment, our supervisors might decide to kill or mutilate one of us for their entertainment. And when someone else was chosen for it, you always felt that the next time it could be you. There we were, in the middle of the forests where Goethe once met Schiller and it seemed the more intelligent any of us were, the more viciously he was treated by the Germans—as if they were trying to show that the spiritual side of man was weak and the bestial side strong.

"They even tried to 'educate' us! They had us read the *Voelkischer Beobachter*, the party organ. When that didn't make us see the beautiful light of nazism, they confined us in pitch black rooms for days on end. Prisoners went insane there; once twenty men opened their veins and bled to death. The only one who survived was left a raving lunatic. The Nazis flogged him to death in front of all of us so we would know that they were the only ones to decide who should die and when. They placed a 'Jehovah's Witness' in a barrel full of human ordure and taunted him, 'Call Jehovah now! Maybe he will help you!' One old Jew who dared to complain was forced to cut out his own tongue. Then he was left bleeding in the latrine, where all those who had gone insane were kept."

No longer able to endure the old professor's narrative, I looked at my watch as a pretense, excused myelf and walked unsteadily up to the commander's room. The commander offered me a tumbler of brandy, and I was grateful for it, but the nagging thought stayed in my head: If only every Jew in Europe could hear with his own ears what the Nazis had in store for him.

XI
The Tramper

On November 16, we reached the port of Sulina, where the Danube flows into the Black Sea. According to the latest instructions from Vienna, this was our point of rendezvous with the tramp steamer. So we dropped anchor in the middle of the river. We waited until nightfall but the tramp steamer did not appear, and we hastily called a staff meeting in the commander's cabin.

We decided that early in the morning we would secure permission for the transport commander or myself to go ashore and try to contact our people in Vienna or Athens. There was a chance that the vessel was not coming at all. The captains of these tramp steamers had been known to change their minds and balk at the last minute, contracts and advance payments notwithstanding. If this was the case, we would have to arrange to purchase additional food, have more money sent from Vienna and have the central office immediately secure a new vessel. The owners of the *Melk* (the Donau Schiffahrt Gesellschaft) and the Gestapo would both give us serious trouble and the credibility of our people in Vienna would be damaged. It would be that much more difficult for the group of *olim*. We emerged from the commander's cabin in a black mood, and that mood soon spread to the passengers. In a short while, the entire transport knew that something had gone wrong. Conflicting rumors traveled back and forth over the ship and that night not many people slept. The transport commander, his aide, the cook and his helpers never even went to bed. They checked the provisions and prepared lists of supplies we would need in the event of a long delay.

Early the next morning, the Sulina representative of the Donau Schiffahrt Gesellschaft boarded the *Melk* with good news. The vessel had run into official difficulties in clearing Constanza, the chief Romanian port on the Black Sea, where it had stopped to notify the authorities of its route. Everything had been ironed out and our *Ma'apilim* would be transferred to the steamer in a few hours. Last night's anxieties disappeared as if carried away by the offshore wind.

At noon the tramp lurched into sight from around the point. A cheer went up and we all watched eagerly as it approached. But as the vessel neared the *Melk*, our smiles slowly disappeared and we had a sinking feeling the time for celebration was still far away.

The ship was no larger than the *Melk*, which was only a riverboat and her deck no higher than the *Melk*'s upper deck. The top of the vessel and its sooty black funnel were the only parts of her that looked anything like a ship. She was ugly, dirty and unpainted, a tramp in the truest sense. She came up to us with excruciating slowness, listing heavily on her side. A bridge was thrown across the two decks, in what should have been an historic moment. For the first time, the underground had sidestepped the extreme difficulties of obtaining transit visas; it had delivered its immigrants from the heart of central Europe directly to an ocean-going vessel.

What was on our minds, however, was whether or not we would successfully complete the voyage. Group after group lined up and had their knapsacks inspected, while their quarters on the *Melk* were checked for any forgotten items. Then they marched off over the bridge to the *Draga*.

I crossed over to inspect accommodations, if such they could be called. The immigrants' quarters were in the freight holds. The two available cabins were immediately assigned, one as sickbay and the other as headquarters for staff members on duty. Everyone from the transport commander on down was to sleep in the hold for the entire voyage, which might take weeks. There were three levels in the holds. The air on the upper floor was bad and on the lower ones it was worse. It was hot and stifling and I could only imagine what would happen in a storm, when the hatches would have to be closed. I went back on deck, almost falling off the narrow, shaky ladder in the dark.

At the stern I found the washrooms, no more than wood and canvas loosely nailed together. These "facilities" consisted of a large barrel fastened to a pump which supplied fresh sea water, I could see a tough job ahead for the sanitation staff.

Sulina was the end of the journey for me; I was to head back for Vienna to start arrangements for the next transports. I felt buoyed up to now that everything had come off more or less according to plan, and as I looked at the passengers boarding the *Draga*, I could see they were in better spirits. It was starting to dawn on them that whatever the conditions on the *Draga*, they were at last completely out of German territory and in another week or two, they would reach Eretz-Israel.

Before I returned to the *Melk*, I went to meet with the captain of the *Draga*. It was probably a mistake, because the visit gave me doubts which jostled my brain all the way back to Vienna. The captain was a short, stocky man with the apple-shaped nose of a chronic alcoholic—the archetypical master of a tramp ship. Fumes of liquor seemed to emanate from everything in the cabin. The captain shook hands jovially with me, saying, "Don't worry, don't worry, don't worry, we'll deliver them safely—only there are so many!" He waved to a crew member in the cabin—"Hey! Tell the *passengers* not to crowd together on the starboard side. We might capsize."

I thought he was joking, but when I glanced out the porthole, I realized he was not. The men and women had all gathered on one side of the *Draga*, some to call goodbye to the *Melk*'s crew, while others just stared transfixed at the purple swastika painted on the *Melk*'s hull. The weight of five hundred people had the *Draga* listing more perilously than ever; she indeed look ready to capsize. I turned a worried look toward the captain and he let out a belly laugh, "Never mind. She's a good ship. Been all over the world with her. Brought grain to the Loyalists in Spain"—he winked at the word 'grain'—and "food for the Italians in Eritrea during the Ethiopian war; we even went to South America." I did not dare ask him what his cargo to South America might have been.

I told the transport commander that he might do well to keep an eye on the captain and his crew, and he assured me that he was ready to handle them in any emergency. The Athens office had warned us of the captain's weakness for alcohol, but they assured us that he was otherwise reliable and had the trust of the ship's owners. I made a mental note that from now on we must bring our *Irgun* pilots out to Romania. We just could not entrust future groups to men like that captain, even for part of the voyage.

I said emotional farewells to the transport commander, Dr. Brill, the rabbi, Professor Kohn, Bertha and the others I had come to respect and love and as I returned to the *Melk*, they stood by the bridge, waving their hands and shouting *Shalom*. Slowly the *Draga* turned and moved out to sea. Bent on her side, she looked like an old beggarwoman looking for scraps on the sidewalks. But if she made it to Palestine, her name would sound as beautiful as 'the Mayflower' to the descendants of those she carried.

*   *   *

The voyage back to Vienna was lonely and uneventful for me. I was the only passenger on the *Melk* now and I kept to myself, away from the crew, as much as possible. After the excitement of the last few weeks, and my fleeting sense of victory at the transfer of the *Ma'apilim*, I had come back down to earth quickly, and already felt numb with hopelessness. My "victory," I saw, was a delusion: the five hundred and fifty passengers were not even the tip of the iceberg. Millions needed to be saved and our funds were non-existent.

I tried to find an answer, any answer, to our financial straits, and only one kept recurring to me—the United States. Where else were there so many of my people so well off financially and so far removed from Hitler they did not have to worry from day to day about their own safety. It occurred to me that at this point I could be far more useful on a fundraising mission to the United States than I could be in Europe, trying to organize voyages without funds. I decided to speak to David Raziel about it once I got back to Palestine.

Back in Austria I met with Eichmann's assistants at the new Gestapo headquarters in the Metropole Hotel. The talk was brief and to the point. They would allocate foreign exchange funds whenever a group was ready to leave and all other conditions would remain unchanged. The emigrants would be permitted to take what they could carry, as long as they had paid their taxes, their exit permits were in order, and no gold or valuables were taken out. They wanted the Jews out, and how, at least for the present, did not matter to them. Eichmann, as he had promised Berlin, was doing his best to rid Germany entirely of Jews. Despite Eichmann's promises, it had become clear that since the "Crystal Night" pogroms, we could not keep our headquarters in Vienna. The city was now dead for its Jews. The one hotel still available to them, the Hotel de France, had its own cafe and a few Jews still dropped in for coffee and the latest rumors. But it was not safe—a Gestapo raid could take place at any time and the Jews sat on the edge of their chairs, their eyes on the door ready to grab their coats and run.

Most Jews stayed off the streets, and out of public places except to search for exit papers and visas or when they had to report to Nazi officers.

We began to shift our *Ha'apalah* activities to Warsaw, Bucharest and Prague. We considered establishing a central office in Zurich, Switzerland in order to have a neutral haven when the situation worsened on the continent. We proceeded to liquidate the Vienna office. I phoned Hillel Kook in Warsaw, and Eri Jabotinsky, who had been recently released from the British jail in Acre and was now in Paris. I expressed to Eri my feeling that with funds as low as they were and with things deteriorating for the Jews so quickly, it might be time for us to try a serious fundraising effort overseas. Since my work in Vienna was done, I offered to lead a fundraising mission to the United States. I was told to go to Zurich, then to Warsaw and that my idea would be considered later. For the last time, I said goodbye to the handful of friends I still had in Vienna and took the train to Zurich.

* * *

Late one afternoon in February, 1939, I was back in Palestine, walking down Ben Yehuda Street in Jerusalem. I had just obtained my visitor's visa to the United States, and I was preparing for final meetings in Switzerland and Paris. My mind was whirling with the details when suddenly someone caught me by the arm. "Well, well, look who's here!"

"Dr. Brill!" It was my turn to be surprised. "What are you doing in Jerusalem?" Then I laughed. "What an absurd question. Why shouldn't I expect to find you here? Let's go into Cafe Europa," I said excitedly. "You're the first one of the five hundred and fifty I've seen here!"

"Eretz-Israel is a big world," he answered with a smile.

Dr. Brill had not changed much since I last saw him aboard the *Melk*, except that he was happier. He was teaching chemistry at the Hebrew University on Mount Scopus. With all his Ph.D.s, he had spent the last several years as a sort of intellectual dilettante; but now, in Eretz-Israel, he was settling into a focused, pragmatic way of life and was negotiating for a position at the Sieff Institute in Rehovoth. He was doing research on a process for producing alcohol fuel from seeds and he hinted that it might be of great importance in case of war.

"Maybe," he joked, "Lange wouldn't have been so anxious to kick me out if he had ever learned about my work. Maybe he would have made me an honorary Aryan. Now I suppose we'll just have to use my findings against the 'Master Race.' He leaned back in his seat and lit his pipe. "You know what happened after you left us in Sulina, don't you?

"As night fell and our boat was struggling towards the Bosphorus, all hell broke loose. One of the regular Black Sea storms hit us. I managed to climb up to the captain's cabin and found him dead drunk in his bunk: 'Let them all go to hell!' he bellowed. 'The *Draga*, the Jews, the agent who told me to do this goddam job! Filling this little boat with all these goddam Jews! We'll never make it! We'll all drown!' Then he roared with laughter. 'Don't look so worried; we've had this many times before; we carried six hundred head of cattle from Constanza to Beirut! His talking about us in the same breath with cattle was the final straw for me and I left him.

"We were grateful to God when day broke and we were nearing the Bosphorus. The sea grew calmer and we started to relax. By the time we entered the Bosphorus, most of the people gathered enough strength to climb to the deck. What a sight! They looked yellow, they were dirty and unshaven, their clothes were disheveled, and straw was stuck in their hair. And the smell... when the Turkish inspectors boarded they were overwhelmed. They checked the boat's papers quickly and just said 'All right, none of our business, but you can't stop in any Turkish port. We don't want any trouble with the British. And then they left as fast as they could.

"By morning, we entered a small port on one of the Greek Islands, where we were supposed to rendezvous with the *Irgun* pilot who would guide us to our landing in Palestine. We stopped there for four days. The climate was heavenly. We sunned ourselves, and some of the boys even dived overboard for a swim. The local authorities treated us well. They guarded the boat rigorously so no one would sneak ashore but they permitted a few staff members to leave the boat for fresh supplies. I'll always remember the help the Greek and Turkish people gave us. The common people with whom we dealt received few material benefits from the 'transport,' and yet they showed a true concern for us. I even saw tears in the eyes of some of the officials who got a glimpse of our holds below.

"The last two days in port, our people grew restless. Rumors spread that the captain was holding out for more money. People were afraid that no one was coming to lead us to Palestine, and that we might stay here for months. Tension mounted on board.

"Then in the early evening of the fourth day, a boat suddenly sailed into view. As we watched it enter the harbor, I could have sworn it was the twin sister of our boat. It approached slowly, listing on her side; it looked like one wisp of air would have made her collapse. She came to a halt nearby and a small boat was lowered, carrying two sailors and a young man in shorts with a small bag slung over his shoulder. As they came up to us, the young man stood up and shouted *Shalom*!. Our people crowded along the rails, slapping each other on the back and kissing each other. They threw their hats in the air, cheering at the top of their lungs. In one swift moment, the word *Shalom* had told them they were not forgotten.

"When the young man stepped on board, he was immediately taken to the staff room where we all introduced ourselves. His name was Shmuel.

"We all liked him," Dr. Brill continued. "He had just returned from landing another group of five hundred immigrants and the boat that delivered him to us was the same one that had carried them. He spoke about the plans for our landing so matter of factly, that we felt an instant sense of relief from all our fears.

"That evening after dinner, Shmuel assembled us on the aft deck, and made one of the shortest speeches any of us had ever heard. In his broken Yiddish, he asked for patience, saying 'I am making this trip for the third time, not because I have to, but because it is my duty to help our people. We are anxious to have you reach our shores safely, and we know you will make our task as easy as possible.' That was all."

"On the fourth day we saw the blue-gray coast of Eretz-Israel in the distance. The sea was calm, and we hoped the landing would be easy.

"The sun had already set when the ship's engines finally stopped, and through a slight white mist, we could see the lights of Palestine. Our Commander climbed atop a pile of ropes and announced to us that in an hour a schooner equipped with a motor would reach the *Draga*. It could accommodate about forty people comfortably, but because we needed to move as quickly as possible to avoid patrol boats, it would have to carry more than two hundred and fifty. All the passengers would be brought to shore in two trips. They would stand the entire time, about an hour, and keep completely quiet. No matches, no flashlights.

"When the Commander finished speaking, many of us hugged each others' hands in excitement. We were finally on the threshold of our freedom, and some actually sobbed out loud.

"About two hours before midnight, we heard the low hum of motors, then minutes later, we heard voices shouting in Greek. A small fishing boat came up alongside. We stood tense for over half an hour, whispering to each other, thinking that something had gone wrong. Suddenly we saw a sharp point of light blinking rapidly on the coast, in a series of short and long flashes. It stopped, started, stopped, and started again, then finally stopped for good. The few city lights we had seen were gone, and darkness enveloped the coast.

"Shmuel came and told us that the coast was clear. A group of young men would meet us on shore and distribute us to Tel-Aviv, Haifa, and settlements in between. 'But let me warn you,' he said; 'there is a possibility of being overtaken by police patrol boats. They might shoot to make us stop. Try to stoop as much as possible but please remain calm. If you lose self-control, you might cause the boat to capsize. I will go in the first trip and after unloading, I'll return to the *Draga* to pick up the rest of you. Please keep cool and obey instructions. *Shalom* again to all!'

"Shmuel went down the ladder and we followed him filling the boat to the brim. We just stood there in whatever spot we first settled down, our knapsacks on our shoulders or at our feet. The motors started, the ropes tying us to the *Draga* were cut, and we turned towards the coast; in a few minutes the *Draga* was out of sight. We hated every minute on that floating junkyard, but now we would have preferred it to this flimsy sailboat with no room to move and only a thin layer of wood separating us from the dark water. We traveled about half an hour. Three flashes pierced the dark, then again three more. The boat turned towards the lights. We were so low in the water that the offshore waves seemed to come down on us like crumbling mountains. We were all drenched and afraid we would capsize.

"Finally we touched bottom. Shmuel leaped into the water and waded ashore. A moment later, two men on horseback trotted into view from inland. At first we weren't sure if they were *Irgun* or British. Half an hour later, soaking wet, we were all on the beach. We didn't have a moment to celebrate. A dozen people were awaiting us, the two horsemen among them.

"We left the beach in a long file, walking three abreast. Two more riders joined the others and the four of them strung out alongside us as we marched. We slogged over the sand, passing through some orange groves, and reached a small eucalyptus forest. We were told to rest there and wait for buses that would come at dawn. A few hours later, word came that our second group had also landed safely.

"By now dawn was breaking and the first glorious rays of the sun appeared over Samaria. The smell of fresh earth rose up pungent from the ground.

"For the first time I could make out the faces of our guides. They stood around chatting and laughing, some in riding breeches, others in khaki shorts, with white or khaki shirts open at the throat. They were all under thirty. Shotguns were slung over their shoulders and pistols were stuck in their belts. As I listened to them laugh I remembered all the downtrodden, broken Jews we had left behind. I remembered the Gestapo agents kicking us the last night in the customs house and I remembered a Gestapo officer's remark: 'We will get you all in Palestine, all in one place, and it will be that much easier to dispose of you.'

"But looking at those guys, I knew that if the Nazis came to Palestine it would never be like it had been in Vienna. We would meet them head on with whatever weapons we had and we would not be humiliated here, on this soil. We would face them as men."

XII
The Political Salon
(Warsaw, December, 1938)

In December, 1938 I was in Poland again. We had a thousand immigrants en route to Constanza, another group assembled in Warsaw and three groups sailing on the Mediterranean. Both the scale and tempo of our work had grown steadily.

I was to meet key people in the capital to review future plans for moving immigrants through Romania. We needed to tighten coordination between the *Irgun* pilots and the various other groups of people involved at all stages of the transit. Conditions were becoming critical on the coast of Palestine and we had to make some important decisions. I was met at the station in Warsaw by Hillel Kook, the new chief *Irgun* delegate in the diaspora and the liaison officer to Jabotinsky. Abraham Stern and Haim Lubinsky were also expected to arrive from Palestine. Kook and Eri Jabotinsky reached a tentative agreement on coordination of the *Ha'apalah* work between the *Irgun* and *Betar* and Zeev Jabotinsky scheduled a conference to, among other things to improve all aspects of administration, finances and the charter and purchase of vessels.

We recruited and organized immigrant groups in Poland, Czechoslovakia, Romania and the Baltic at a continuously faster pace. We combined young people unable to pay their share of the transportation costs with applicants who could afford to pay more than their proportionate share which helped solve the problem of transporting the penniless youngsters out of impoverished Poland. The Polish authorities agreed to convert Polish currency, equivalent to twenty sterling per emigrant and this helped, but did not solve the basic lack of funds. Attempts by Zeev Jabotinsky and the N.Z.O. in London to obtain funds from Jewish relief institutions and wealthy individuals ended mostly in failure. I came back from fundraising trips to Zurich and Paris badly disappointed. By now I was convinced that *Ha'apalah* would fall short of even the most modest goals.

At our meeting, Hillel Kook discounted my sense of foreboding: "We've made great headway in Poland. This country is at our disposal. Arms, training camps, full cooperation with exit papers, passports, rail transport and everything else. Another couple of years and we'll be ready to mount a serious military campaign to open the gates of Eretz-Israel."

"We don't have a couple of years," I argued. "I've lived almost eight months in Nazi-occupied countries now. The Germans are intoxicated with their success and the democracies in Europe are unstable and militarily impotent. Their people are hopeless and about ready to throw in the towel. Hitler can smell victory; he'll soon move."

"If you really believe that, what do you suggest?"

"There is one wealthy, aware Jewish community still left in the United States. I want to go there. If I can mobilize significant funds, we'll be able to buy anything that floats. And we have to change our basic approach to *Ha'apalah*. Anything minimally safe for sailing should be acquired. Never mind avoiding the British. In special cases we still can do that with small sailboats we use for the landings. We need to buy larger boats and pack them with *ma'apilim*, and if we're cornered by the British patrols, we'll just have to beach the boats, destroy all papers and scatter. The time for traditional *aliyah*, even our own *Ha'apalah* is over. Remember Nordau's plan in 1919? As Jabotinsky preached for years, we need now *mass evacuation*, with no concern for the immigrants' political ideologies and apart from our military plans. . . ."

Hillel was not convinced. Eri Jabotinsky saw it my way and we all decided that after more consultations in Warsaw, I should return to Palestine to present my views to David Raziel.

In fact, we made great progress in Poland through 1938. Jabotinsky established top contacts with the Polish foreign office and military, while visits to Poland by Abraham Stern, Haim Lubinsky and Kook constantly expanded our activities. The

Polish army supplied *Irgun* warehouses in Warsaw with the first shipments towards a goal of twenty thousand rifles, ammunition, machine guns, grenades, explosives and other supplies to be shipped to Palestine.[1] After Stern's and Kook's visits to Poland, *Irgun* cells, drawing mostly on *Betar* and affiliated veterans' organizations, spread throughout Poland and into Lithuania with a central command in Warsaw.

Officers from Eretz-Israel came to take charge of the network, laying the groundwork for training of *Irgun* officers by the Polish army. A course made up of twenty-five top *Irgun* officers, selected in Palestine by the high command, was scheduled for early 1939 in the Carpathian Mountains. It would create a top corps of underground fighters which could perpetuate itself through the military struggle in the years ahead. Another training course taught by the veteran *Irgun* officer Aaron Heichman was scheduled in Zupiowka, Poland for non-commissioned officers selected from local cells.

By the fall of 1938, *Irgun* delegates finally penetrated circles of assimilated upper class. Circulation of tens of thousands was achieved by our Yiddish-language paper *Die Tat* ("Action"), only the youth and the impoverished masses had gathered under Jabotinsky's banner, but now even the more "secure" Jews could not escape reality.

An activist group that sprang up in Warsaw opened a social club called "Jordan," and published a Polish-language bi-weekly called *Jerozolima Wyzwolona* ("Liberated Jerusalem"), which displayed on its masthead the *Irgun* emblem—the map of Palestine with a rifle superimposed on it. Beside this emblem were the words: "Only thus." "Liberated Jerusalem" was aimed at the assimilated upper class. Circulation of tens of thousands was achieved by our Yiddish-language paper *Die Tat* ("Action"), published since July and directed to the masses of Polish Jewry.

The militancy of Hebrew revolution was now overtaking Jabotinsky's political Zionism. Jews in central-east Europe were running out of time and patience, and to keep hoping for eventual accommodation with the British or the civilized West was more of a luxury than they could afford. The *Irgun* sidestepped Jabo-

---

[1] A small part of which reached Palestine in 1939.

tinsky's venerated political activism while it merged Achimeir, Yevin and U. Z. Greenberg's revolutionary prose and poetry with the activism of Raziel, Stern and Eri Jabotinsky. An armed showdown with Britain and the Pan-Arabists in Eretz-Israel seemed more and more possible—if we could only obtain sufficient funds, we felt we could land tens of thousands of *Irgun* soldiers from the diaspora on the shores of Palestine, force Britain to open the doors to the Jewish masses and at last settle our disputes with the Arabs.

In September, 1938, the world conference of *Betar* in Warsaw endorsed the militant stand of the charismatic leader of Poland's *Betar*, Menahem Begin, who called upon *Betar* to move away from traditional political activism:

> "We are standing on the threshold of the third phase of Zionism," Begin declared. "After 'Practical Zionism' and 'Political Zionism' the time has come for 'Military Zionism.' Eventually, military and political concepts will merge, but . . . if we create our military strength, the salvation of the diaspora will come. The world is indifferent . . . its conscience ignores what is happening to our people. The League of Nations is impotent. We cannot continue on this road. We want to fight!" Begin declared. "To win or die!"

* * *

Shortly before I returned to Palestine, I met Dr. Eryk Strassman and his wife, Lillian, at the Jordan Club to arrange an informal gathering to recruit non-activist assimilated Jews. The Strassman home had become the home-in-exile for David Raziel, Abraham Stern and all *Irgun* delegates to Poland. The Strassmans were deeply involved in the negotiations with Polish authorities, especially with the army, and they conducted a continual political education campaign among the upper circles of Warsaw Jewry. They were more than eager to set up an evening for me with several of their acquaintances.

A few days later, Vitold Brant, a friend of the Strassmans, met me at the pension in Warsaw. As he and I drove to the meeting in his car, he let me know that it would be just a small, informal group.

"We have some interesting people here tonight," Brant said to me as we entered the living room. "The heavy man over there is Aaron Schlossberg, one of the country's leading industrialists. Donated a million *zloty* recently to purchase planes for the Polish Air Force. He's a strong opponent of Zionism, though he makes small contributions to the Palestine funds. The attractive couple near him are Mr. and Mrs. Korn from Bydgoszcs. They have no opinion one way or another about Palestine or Hebrew nationalism. I hope you'll win them over. That thin, intense man with the glasses across the room is Dr. Pfeffer, a staunch Bundist [Jewish Socialist Party of Poland] and a vehement opponent of ours. I invited him so conversation wouldn't lag."

I gave the group a short description of what I had lived through for the past year, and I touched briefly on the *Irgun*'s history and activism. I told them that hundreds of thousands of people, had nowhere to go but Palestine, and no way to go but through the underground. All other doors were closed to them. We were doing our best, but we needed their active participation.

Aaron Schlossberg, the heavy-set industrialist, spoke up without preliminaries: "The stories our Palestinian friend has told us are heartbreaking. I think we should help emigration to the utmost of our abilities. I contribute a thousand *zloty* to save these helpless people." He sat back to dead silence.

Brant cleared his throat. "I didn't ask you to my home for the purpose of raising funds, my friends. I just wanted you to spend a few hours looking at our problems in the light of events in Germany and Austria."

"I really don't see how these events could affect us directly," Dr. Pfeffer remarked, "except that we have to intensify our fight against fascism, and cooperate with the liberal forces in our country to keep the Nazis away from our borders."

"Don't you think," asked Brant, "that Jews face definite dangers in Poland that existed before fascism was ever born? And don't you think we might still face them when fascism and nazism are gone?"

Dr. Pfeffer shook his head. "Extreme reaction and insularity have always been the enemies of the Jews. We have to fight in solidarity with the non-Jewish working masses of Poland."

"It can't be solved through the workers," Schlossberg gruffly interposed. "The government is what counts, and the army. We have to prove our undeniable patriotism.

"Nobody can doubt our patriotism," said Mr. Korn. "The Jews of Poland contributed thirteen of the forty million *zlotys* raised for civilian defense. But still our children are assigned benches in the universities and my son has been thrown out of school altogether."

"It's the capitalists' fault," Pfeffer said acidly.

"Our students belong to too many radical groups," Schlossberg countered.

"Or maybe they try too hard to excel in their studies?" said Mrs. Korn hesitantly.

"Don't you think our problem goes further than whether or not we have a socialist government or whether we're in good favor with the generals?" prodded Brant. "Don't you think there is something fundamentally unhealthy in our position? We're a minority of only ten percent of the country; not strong enough to affect legislation, but we constitute thirty percent of the city dwellers where Jews face disastrous economic conditions."

"That's exactly why our problem is tied up with the interests of other oppressed groups," said Pfeffer. "We have to unite with them and fight for equal rights."

"Won't that be dangerous, though," Korn asked, "to identify with Ukrainians and White Russians clashing with the government?"

"Definitely," said Schlossberg, "we should keep away from any troublesome elements."

"All the oppressed should stand by each other," Pfeffer repeated.

"I also disagree; conditions are not so bad for us," said Schlossberg. "We've had no serious problems since Pilsudski's regime."

"Mr. Schlossberg," Dr. Pfeffer intoned coldly, "if you think the Jewish masses here have decent lives, you're living in a different country. The civil service is closed to us. It is impossible for a Jewish worker or small merchant to earn a living."

Mrs. Brant jumped into the conversation. "Anti-Semitism goes further than the government. What about the worker who comes into the cities searching for jobs, or the farmer who moves to the small town and resents Jews who are competing with him in the trades and in crafts?"

"That antagonism exists only as a result of the capitalistic society," Pfeffer asserted.

"Can't you admit that it's more than an economic problem?" said Brant, exasperated.

"Of course; it's also a matter of re-education," said Pfeffer, "but as long as the masses are exploited, the Jews will suffer as the scapegoat."

"Why didn't the Jews' problems in Russia end with the Revolution?" Brant shot back.

"You know that as a Socialist, I'm opposed to communism," Pfeffer replied. "But the fact is that the Revolution did solve most of their problems."

"Then why," said Mrs. Brant, "are there still trials of anti-Semites in Russia, and why was a Jewish republic formed?"

"Prejudice cannot be eradicated overnight. Biro-Bidjan was formed to give Russian Jews a territory of their own, where they could develop their culture."

"Then you admit that Jews have a national culture to develop in their own country?" said Brant.

"Not necessarily our own country. Poland is my country! Whatever I consider my ethnic culture, I should be able to pursue right here. My Jewishness is not tied to a state."

"We are getting nowhere," Brant said politely. "You believe, Dr. Pfeffer, that the cure-all for our ills would be a socialist government. I cannot agree. As long as we are ten per cent of the population, we will always be exploited by someone for political ends. Even a Socialist government might—in humane language— *advise* the Jews to look for another country. Liberals and reactionaries will both try to reduce our numbers, though their methods will vary in subtlety. Nationalists will see us as an obstacle to the unification of the state. The masses will see us as unwelcome foreign competition."

"What do you suggest as the cure?" Korn asked.

Ready to bring the discussion to an end, Brant looked Korn in the eye and said simply, "Evacuation."

"My friend, you're always bringing that up." Korn, his face reddening said: "You know I'm a Zionist, I contribute funds to help the poor people who want to go to Palestine. But Jabotinsky's hysterical calls for mass evacuation have been discredited by all responsible Jewish leaders. I'm a Pole by nationality and citizenship and I don't want to go anywhere else."

"My friend," Brant soothed, "you can always stay. But there should be unlimited evacuation for those who wish to return to Hebrew national life in Palestine.

"To put it bluntly, we are not welcome here so why should we stay? I'm not bitter but there is nothing to hold me here. I want my children to grow up in a healthy atmosphere, not in a place full of pathological hate for them. I want them to feel part of their country and its past, as any Polish boy is part of this land and its past, with no one daring to question it.

"Mr. Korn, you live only fifty miles from the German border, so you should have some idea what is happening. The Nazis are making it permissible for the rest of Europe to mistreat the Jews. If war breaks out and Germany conquers part of Eastern Europe, what will happen to us is only too obvious."

Later that night, after the guests had left, I stayed to talk with the Brants. Though we had expected only so much, we were all disappointed. Beyond Mr. Schlossberg's offer of a thousand *zlotys*, we had not really convinced anyone. How different these Schlossbergs and Korns were from the young Polish *Betarim* I had recruited a year before, who had no question for me but "when do we leave." The people I had spoken with today, for all their status, for all their education, pigheadedly clung to their beliefs, but it was precisely these narrow "self-interests" which would very possibly cost them their lives.

Mrs. Brant said to her husband with a faint smile, "They will not understand and will not change. They're shortsighted, deaf and blind; they've created a vacuum to live in, and can't tell what's good or bad for themselves, or what's immediately threatening their lives. Schlossberg will keep contributing to all national drives and have his name mentioned in the papers as a great Polish patriot. Pfeffer will continue his sincere, hopeless fight for socialism. And Korn, the 'Zionist,' will never get off the fence. We haven't the time to win these people over. We have to spend our energy trying to save the poor who don't have the money to delude themselves that everything is fine and help the young whose heart guides them toward national rebirth and revolution."

* * *

As my train was racing back across the Polish border, I pondered over how different my first trip, only one year ago, had been! Hitlerism had been confined to Germany then, with only a few signs of international crisis. The people of Europe, with the exception of Spain, had hardly felt the New Order. The *Irgun* had audacious plans; it was coming of age and out to win over the diaspora. The Polish government was finally listening to Jabotinsky, and major breakthroughs in immigration seemed right around the corner.

But since then, the annexation of Austria, the Munich surrender, the ceding of the Sudetenland to Nazi rule became facts of life which made the rest of the continent look vulnerable, helpless and confused.

Even Jabotinsky's ten-year plan, of moving one million Jews out of East-Central Europe, outlined as recently as a year ago in the N.Z.O. conclave in Prague, now appeared hopelessly out of step with reality.

When I had commuted between the big cities of Lodz and Lvov, and small communities in Thomazow, Piotrkov and Biala, I had seen how the people struggled to find the tiniest bit of security and freedom. I had joined with them in their homes and clubs and I was with the lucky young ones aflame with their ideals when they set out in those miserable boats to escape to Palestine. I met them in the trains and stations, singing and laughing as if the heavens had opened up to them, and I turned my face away when men and women wept in our offices because they did not have the few *zlotys* necessary for the trip. The Jews of Poland, the hundreds of thousands of small storekeepers, artisans and unemployed workers; the brilliant intellectuals and the handful of rich; and the Orthodox—the poor *shtetl* dwellers in their medieval garb—what hadn't they tried to keep alive? And yet how many would survive?

When I had been a student in Portici, I had my doubts when Mordechai predicted an apocalypse for Europe. I did not doubt it any longer. I saw what had moved my grandparents and hundreds of thousands of others to travel to a faraway land to fight against insuperable obstacles. I knew now why they were willing to pay so dearly for freedom.

Part IV: Darkness Descends

I

Mobilizing for the Eleventh Hour

I was in Paris in February, 1939 when a special meeting took place in the offices of Simon Marcovici-Cleja, a baptized millionaire of Romanian origin who had suddenly rediscovered his Jewish ancestry. He was one of the very few wealthy individuals who helped in our *Ha'apalah* work. The meeting was mostly meant to eliminate the rising tensions between the *Irgun* leadership, *Betar* and the political leadership of the N.Z.O., including Jabotinsky. The top personalities of our movement were present: Zeev Jabotinsky, David Raziel, who came out of Palestine on board one of our boats, and leaders of the *Betar*, the *Irgun* and the N.Z.O. We hoped to eliminate our frequent petty frictions.

What surprised and disheartened me was that many of those present seemed to feel no sense of urgency to concentrate on specific timetables for radical action. I did not know where the responsibility for this lay. Maybe because Jabotinsky did not believe that a new world war was likely to break out, or because by February, 1939 he did not as yet consider military action against the British as likely to succeed. But there were heated debates about the political-ideological link between the N.Z.O. and the *Irgun* and about whether the *Irgun* had the right to independent political activity; and there was a lot of jockeying as to who would supervise our meager funds or whose authority would stop where on *Ha'apalah* and training. What the participants did not stress was the urgency of the impending national crisis. One saving grace had been that Zeev Jabotinsky and David Raziel, who met for the first time, established a warm rapport.

We came out of these meetings hoping that internal problems

and disputes between *Irgun* and *Betar* cells in the diaspora would be eliminated. If we were to wage a successful war against British rule in Palestine, we would have to be mobilized together. The *Irgun* was to become the highest rung in the *Betar* structure, with Zeev Jabotinsky as Commander-in-Chief. The world *Betar* leadership created a military command headed by Mordechai Strelitz, a member of the *Irgun* high command in Palestine, who was to go to Poland to assume his duties. The commander of the *Irgun* in Eretz-Israel also became, *de facto*, the head of *Betar*. He would function underground for the duration of the battle for independence, while the world *Betar* immediately undertook all necessary steps to evolve into a national army in Palestine with its reserves in the diaspora. All *Betar* members eighteen or older would join the reserves in the diaspora and the active *Irgun* ranks in Palestine. Menahem Begin, emerging as a popular militant leader of the youth, was appointed head of *Betar* in Poland, which had the largest, strongest national following in world *Betar*.

These were great leaps forward for the Jabotinsky movement (or "Herzlian movement," as we called it then), and we hoped that at last political Zionism had finally graduated into revolutionary Zionism.

It was also an ideological leap for Jabotinsky. The non-Jew Josiah Wedgwood's simple message to us about fighting for our freedom had apparently touched the anglophile Jabotinsky, who until recently could not see his way beyond diplomacy and political persuasion in the struggle for independence. Jabotinsky had also been stirred by the execution of Shlomo Ben Yosef and British police torture of *Irgun* suspects. Our young leadership—Raziel, Stern, Shmuel Merlin, Ben-Eliezer, Begin—had put mounting pressure on Jabotinsky as did veteran Achimeir followers like Joseph Katznelson who had recently joined the *Irgun*. By early 1939, he and the *Irgun* leadership agreed, in principle, that there was little other realistic alternative except work towards an armed uprising. The British believed for a long time that we were utterly incapable of such action; as one of their foreign office memos of February, 1939 stated: "Unless Jewish immigration to Palestine is stopped, we will face troubles. . . . The Jews will *shout* their protests. . . . (However), the Arabs are likely to act."

What was gratifying to me was that after the Paris meeting,

Ha'apalah was seen by all involved as every bit as important as the armed action for which we were preparing. Jabotinsky's political Zionists in the N.Z.O. were told to mobilize towards a military build-up: recruitment, training, weapons acquisition, and sea transports but also intensify the mass *Ha'apalah* efforts. All told we concluded that Wedgwood's goal of forty thousand Hebrew soldiers who could break the British stranglehold on immigration was attainable, as were our other goals which depended on help from the governments of Poland, Romania, Lithuania and Czechoslovakia.

We knew the 1916 Easter Revolt in Ireland had failed tragically despite the intense self-sacrifice of the rebels; we knew that no amount of commitment was enough without proper preparation. The fine details of our plans had not yet coalesced, though our direction had become clear. For the scale of activities we were now projecting, we needed financial resources which we did not possess and human reserves which we did.

In the weeks after the meetings in Paris ended, I had become more and more convinced of a seemingly unbridgeable gap between our political analysis and prognosis and our chances of mobilizing within the proper time limits, the means necessary to end British rule. The atrocities being committed by the Nazis might convince some of the Jews of the West to help us, but my experiences with the wealthy Jews in Paris, Switzerland and Poland, had not offered much encouragement. I could not see us keeping pace with the mounting threat of the Nazis. Our idealists and idealogists would not flinch to offer their lives, but they were not the ones who knew how to mobilize the physical means.

Ultimately my personal doubts did not matter. Our Paris bene-factor, Marcovici-Cleja, made it possible for Col. John Patterson, Robert Briscoe and Haim Lubinsky to leave immediately for the United States and I was to follow the next month. To secure my visa to the United States I returned to Palestine.

* * *

Haifa, a small hotel in the "German Colony." The sun was low over the Mediterranean and it was pleasantly cool. The working day was nearing its end, so the traffic was heavy below near the port area. One would never guess that this was a country in a state of siege. It was February, 1939, and there were twenty thousand British soldiers and police in Palestine; four or five thousand armed Arabs reinforced by mercenaries from Iraq and Syria; more than two thousand armed *Irgun* men and women; and many more in the *Haganah* and its auxiliaries. For most of the guests assembled at my small peaceful hotel, the country's tension seemed to have been put out of their concern. Not for me.

Having completed arrangements with David Raziel for my trip to the United States, I suggested Izhak Zarzewsky to replace me as coordinator for *Ha'apalah*. His appointment was now final, and I had been relieved of my duties in Europe.

In the past year I had no chance to think through political events affecting Palestine in depth. The rush of daily emergencies absorbed my full attention. But now, back in Palestine I felt certain that, as Jabotinsky recently predicted, nothing would come of the pending partition plans. Nothing would come of the Zionist establishment dreams of a truncated miniature nation. Arab intransigence and British colonial designs would undoubtedly make a lie of the Mandate once and for all. Malcolm MacDonald, the Colonial Secretary, had made this clear enough in his speech to Jewish leaders a few days ago in London. Britain wanted to protect its oil interests in Iraq, keep its naval base in Alexandria and maintain complete control of the Suez Canal— and in their decision-making, nothing else ultimately mattered. MacDonald had put it a little differently by saying that the Middle East was the "achilles heel" of the Empire. The British had to take all precautions to keep the area strong. What mattered to the British were their physical and economic interests— humanitarian concerns and international commitments be damned. And any Britishers who felt differently would not be heard. Josiah Wedgwood had recently written: "I want to see in Palestine once again a fighting nation, free and courageous like the Maccabees. . . . An army of forty thousand fit to defend what is dear to them and to me. . . ." The *Irgun* disseminated this message, which the British administration banned.

As I strolled down Hadar-HaCarmel towards the railroad station, I felt a smile break out on my face. How odd Wedgwood's message must have sounded here in Haifa, the stronghold of Socialist-Pacifist Zionism, where the philosophy of *Havlagah*, of dealing softly with Arab terrorism and the British, held sway. An English non-Jew preaching Hebrew Revolution? Here, *Irgun* men were kidnapped and tortured, and turned over to the police by the *Haganah*, while Wedgwood, a Socialist himself, supported breaking British laws. He knew what Britain had once solemnly promised, and he called upon us to fight for our rights against his own country. The Zionist establishment thought he was a madman or a traitor. David Ben-Gurion exploded when he read Wedgwood's words. He cabled the Jewish Agency in London to approach British Labor immediately to muzzle comrade Wedgwood, and stop his support of "the Jewish Fascist Organization."

Walking past the port area, I saw several British patrol boats tied to the pier, probably the ones that would go out and search for *ma'apilim*. They were causing us a lot of trouble. The British were mobilizing to make the country safe from additional Jews and the chances for confiscation of the ships was increasing. However, even the *Haganah* and the establishment were beginning to dabble in *Ha'apalah*, so perhaps the pressure would be eased at our disembarkation points. We were presently "subsidizing" certain police officers; hopefully that might keep them more cooperative, but my briefings in Jerusalem had indicated that more and more British agents were in Greece trying to interfere with boat purchases, and now that the Danube was established as an open route, we could expect diplomatic intervention in Romania and Bulgaria, the countries along the route. Finally, if worse came to worst, the British might attempt to shut the country to all Jewish immigration, legal and illegal. King George's private secretary advised the foreign office: "The King has heard ... that a number of Jewish refugees from different countries were surreptitiously getting into Palestine and he is glad to think that steps have been taken to prevent these people leaving their country of origin. . . ."[1]

Gradually, the entire political and military picture became more critical. If Ibn Saud, King Gazi of Iraq, Emir Abdullah and the other Arab leaders invited to London joined with Britain in

---

[1]A. J. Sherman, *Island Refuge* (London 1973)

rescinding, or at least negating, the Balfour Declaration and the Mandate, then the Mufti and his cohorts would further increase their attacks on the Jewish population, and seek to liquidate once and for all the embryonic Hebrew nation. We would then be forced into more violent action. With the pressure in Europe mounting relentlessly, how much longer could we wait before an all-out showdown? For a hundred years this catastrophe has been coming. And now the Jewish leaders had to beg and weep for help from an indifferent world. Our leaders still did not want to accept what was staring them in the face.

In the morning before my flight to Venice I was rather nervous. I had been making so many trips back and forth between Europe and Palestine that I was sure my "Ben-Menahem" identity would not fool the C.I.D. too much longer. Ever since my two arrests in 1935 and 1936, the C.I.D. had watched me closely, but by some miracle they had never connected my birthright name, Rosin, with the journalist Ben-Menahem.

My luck held out again and I got through immigration control and police check without any problems. My seaplane soon was skimming over the quiet water of Haifa Bay, and when we were airborne, I caught a last glimpse of the Carmel and the coast to the south. I recognized the two small islands off Tantura where we had landed our first *Ma'apilim* in 1937 and 1938.

As I leaned back in my seat, my mind lingered over earlier years in *Betar* and the *Irgun*—the early thirties, so recent and yet so distant. I recalled Yaakov Raz, who had died a few months ago in a Jerusalem hospital. In 1934 he had been one of my young trainees in the Jerusalem *Betar*. We had instituted a system of small local clubhouses where youngsters, mostly from poorer homes, could gather in the evenings for lectures, sports and socializing. I met Yaakov at one of the lectures. A native of Afghanistan who had lived in Palestine since childhood, he was olive-skinned, freckled, and very small and thin. His family was among the poorest in the Bokhara quarter and he worked in a grocery store to help them get by.

Our "young *Betar*" had adopted colorful hats and scarves, and I remembered coming to the Bokhara club one Sabbath eve, and seeing Yaakov all aglow in his uniform, his face scrubbed, his hair neatly combed. His instructor whispered to me: "That uniform is the most important thing in his life. He saved up for it from tips he got for deliveries and collecting empty bottles."

Yaakov soon had joined the messenger unit of the *Irgun*, and shortly thereafter, the regular units. By 1937 he had already been part of several dangerous missions which he had executed without hesitation at great risk to his life. In July, 1938, as a retaliation for Arab attacks, he carried out an assignment to plant explosives in designated Arab sites in Old Jerusalem. On his way out of the Old City, he was discovered and attacked by Arabs. He was pummeled and stabbed, and left for dead. The police found him and transported him, under arrest, to the hospital where he remained under police guard and continuous interrogation for twelve days. The interrogation often went on for twenty-four hours at a time, but he did not break down. Finally he took advantage of a lax moment by the police watch, tore off his bandages and bled to death, taking his secrets with him. U. Z. Greenberg paid homage to him in a poem which ended:

> A marble statue will not be erected
> But in the garment of the Redeemer
> The name of the Avenger Raz will be woven
> And when all the blood in avenged, so will his be. . . .

I kept plumbing my memories of the past. What good would all these martyrdoms do if we could never carry our message beyond the poor masses? The Jabotinsky movement had always belonged to the proletariat—but what use the blood offerings of Yaakov Raz and thousands of youths like him, all risking the death penalty every time they carried a weapon, if we could not obtain help from our more comfortable Jewish brothers? And how could I presume that I would succeed with the wealthy Jews of America when I had failed with those in Europe?

I remembered my last trip across western Europe a few months back, when Eri Jabotinsky had introduced me to his father in Paris after my return from the *Melk* voyage. As Zeev Jabotinsky listened to our reports about the obstacles and dangers his youthful followers faced, I felt that I detected the slightest hint of embarrassment or guilt in him. He could not give us the funds, the weapons, the boats we needed, and in his diffident manner he seemed to be saying: "I brought them into this, I asked them to stand up tall, fight and die, and all I can give them is slings." He had never forgotten that Trumpeldor could have been saved if weapons and manpower had been supplied to him. And what had Shlomo Ben Yosef carried—a grenade that did not explode, a handgun that could not reach a target?

Staring out over the water now without really seeing anything, I thought back to the way Jabotinsky had acted during the Paris Conclave—his doubts and reservations in response to the pressures the *Irgun* put on him for military action. It occurred to me now that his hesitation was, in great measure, tied to his uncertainty that we could mobilize the finances. We had the reserves of idealistic manpower in the diaspora. The Polish Army allocated to us large quantities of material. But we needed funds to prepare for action. The fact was that we spoke a language most Jews did not understand and Jabotinsky knew it.

I had admired Zeev Jabotinsky from afar for almost eight years. As early as 1932 he had asserted that historic hatred and economic conditions would ultimately make Jews' lives unlivable in Europe. "Several million Jews will be forced, in the very near future," he had written, "to evacuate the main centers in eastern Europe and to institute in Eretz-Israel a national state."

Still, in the late 1930s, he had been criticized by many among us for letting history pass him by, for naively persisting in his belief that the British could be won over by diplomacy. Finally, though, in recent months Jabotinsky seemed to have crossed the Rubicon. After the Nazis takeover in Austria and the Munich capitulation he had come to see our urgency, acknowledging that the militant platform of the "maximalists" and the *Irgun* was the only course to be pursued. At last sowing the seed for mass *Ha'apalah* and armed landing and rebellion in Palestine, he said: "An updated Nordau Plan [immediate transfer of hundreds of thousands of Jews to Palestine] is now the only course that can come under consideration."

When Eri had taken me to that first meeting with his father, the strongest impression I came away with was that Zeev Jabotinsky was above all a compassionate human being. There was no lordliness about him; he talked and listened to Eri and me for hours, showing us the same warmth and respect we showed him. Since I was from the "front lines," he wanted me to tell him about all my personal experiences, about the *ma'apilim* and their behavior on the boats, the conditions they had to face and how those conditions affected their state of mind. He wanted to know how the Germans were with us, what the tiniest procedures were, what went wrong and why and what proposals I had for the future. Though he asked all his questions with a certain gentle restraint, I could feel his intensity, as if in my every word he was looking for clues to the future.

Finally, in early 1939, he had given the *Irgun* command his unconditional directive that he would support armed rebellion— he would sail with the youth and see that the national flag was raised over Jerusalem.

My plane was over the Adriatic now, nearing Brindisi. I had first crossed this sea towards Europe in the *Lloyd Triestino* vessel eight long years ago—eight years that seemed like many hundreds in their impact on Jewish history. In the rush of events, I felt that I had lost my innocence, my faith in the goodness of men and workings of the world. It had been a long journey from my dialogues with Mordechai in Portici to the realization of his worst predictions only seven years later; it had been a profound difference between talking revolution and becoming part of one. David Raziel was aware of this, and saw to it that we remained constantly involved in all aspects of the battle. Even those of us on special long-term missions in the diaspora were, when briefly visiting home, sometimes suddenly directed to front-line operations in Palestine. Raziel was molding us into a tough, hardened revolutionary army.

* * *

It turned out that my anxieties on passing through the inspections leaving Palestine had not all been unjustified. I found out shortly after reaching Venice that if I had left Haifa a week or two later, I would not have made it safely. The C.I.D. received a report at their headquarters in Jerusalem, containing a list—headed by the names Zeev Jabotinsky, Eri Jabotinsky, and Joseph Katznelson—of those who had participated in the Paris Conclave earlier that month. On that list was my real name, as well as my *Ha'apalah* alias, Ben-Menahem. At the bottom, handwritten as if it were an afterthought, was the name of David Raziel, "from the *Irgun* command." The intelligence work had been sloppy: several facts in the report were wrong, and some names were even spelled incorrectly. Dr. Arieh Altman, who headed the N.Z.O. in Palestine, was described as "ex-*Irgun* commander"; he had never been commander, nor even a member of the organization. We were grateful for the poor job the C.I.D. had done.

What disturbed us, though, was that clearly there were leaks or informers somewhere within our organization. Consequently, steps were taken to strengthen our intelligence. My old commander from the Galilee, Joseph Duckler, was put in charge. His innate skepticism and conspiratoriality made him the perfect man for the task.

By March I was with Eri Jabotinsky in Paris, helping him prepare an outline of future *Ha'apalah* plans. They were to be submitted to Zeev Jabotinsky and the coordinating committee now heading our immigration work. I also spent my last weeks on the continent working with Eri, 'Irma' Helpren, Benjamin Payn and others to raise funds for chartering more boats. Frustrations were our daily fare.

One afternoon, we met with Madame Helene Allatini at the Café *Colisée* on the Champs Elysées. Madame Allatini was an attractive, sophisticated woman, related to the Paris Rothschilds and we hoped she would open their doors to us. She had helped many refugees who passed through France and were stuck there with no place to go.

Eri prodded me to tell her about my personal experiences with *Ha'apalah* in Austria and on the Danube. We impressed on her that we could quickly turn our work into a mass movement, if we only had the funds. We could have a multitude of seaworthy trampers converging from ports all over Europe to the shores of ̈alestine. The Germans would not, at this point, interfere. We ̈ad centers of activity in Bucharest, Prague, Warsaw and Zurich, but the Joint Distribution Committee still refused to contribute to our "illegal immigration" and would not help to charter or buy the tramp vessels. The Zionist establishment had half-heartedly sent several immigrant groups themselves, and still adhered to their policy of selecting the elite few whom they considered politically fit for immigration.

We did not really have to convince Helene Allatini. She asked about the conditions on the boats, saying that the J.D.C. and the Central Jewish Committee called our trampers "unfit for cattle."

In a controlled tone I explained to her that we did our best to get the *ma'apilim* to Palestine as safely as our funds and conditions permitted. Undoubtedly there would be some tragedies, but we could not turn down even the elderly if they were waiting at the ports, on barges on the Danube or on islands in the Mediterranean. We were improving communications and we would do our utmost to see that no boat sailed without one or two *Irgun* "pilots," but we needed help. We had a lot to correct—but to make these corrections we had to have funds.

Madame Allatini gave me her hand and said:"I'll do my best to have your people meet with Robert de Rothschild."

Eventually, Benjamin Payn, the executive secretary of our benefactor Marcovici-Cleja in Paris, and 'Irma' Helpren had a number of meetings with Robert Rothschild, the most influential Jewish leader in France. It took weeks of repeated visits by Payn and Helpren to gain some modest personal donations by Rothschild, and even then, Rothschild could not convince his fellow Jewish leaders or any of the charitable institutions in France to help us. He did attempt to bring Payn, Helpren and Yaacobi, who eventually coordinated our *Ha'apalah* finances, together with Dr. Chaim Weizmann in an attempt to find common ground on immigration efforts, but Weizmann ended the meetings by expressing to Rothschild his wariness of us: "When you soup with the devil, you've got to have a long spoon." Weizmann must have been enamored with this phrase, because he repeated it to Helpren and Yaacobi when Robert Rothschild had them meet once more. This time, Weizmann also complained at length about the terrible conditions on our boats and Yaacobi answered that the conditions were bad indeed, but preferable to remaining in the countries the immigrants were escaping from. Weizmann went on to say that not all of these immigrants formed an altogether satisfactory element, and that furthermore, they were difficult to absorb. He admitted that hundreds of thousands of German Jews were then seeking refuge in Poland, Czechoslovakia and France—but they were "adding to the anti-Semitism" in those countries and he did not see how they could be admitted in such numbers into Palestine.

There was nothing new in this. Up until 1936, Weizmann had rejected most of the Jews in the diaspora from his selected elite fit for settlement in Palestine. The Socialist youth trained in the *Hachshara* camps were admitted under the limited British immigration quotas, and that was all. However, by 1937, even Dr. Weizmann came to realize that the Jewish masses did indeed face a physical threat to their survival. Before the British Peel Commission in 1937, Weizmann admitted for the first time that six million Jews needed to emigrate from Europe. He told the Commission that being a scientist, he was acquainted with certain physical laws which showed that only about two million youths could be saved. "And the rest?" the Commission members asked.

Weizmann, heir to Herzl and leader of the World Zionist Organization answered: "The old ones will pass; they will bear their fate . . . They are dust, economic and moral dust in the cruel world."[1]

For over thirty years, Weizmann had led the Zionist movement according to the spiritualism of his mentor Ahad Ha'am, telling Jews from Warsaw to Bucharest to Berlin they had to mend their ways and correct their ideologies or they would not be welcome to the pure, just, utopian society in Eretz-Israel. And even now, as history was proving the cataclysmic error in the socialists'-spiritualists' beliefs, and as Weizmann begged the Mandatory power to help save the Jewish youth by partitioning Palestine, he could not give up his vision of an exemplary society: "Only two million youth would be saved and all others would simply become dust." The final irony was that the British were not willing to provide even the scraps for which Weizmann would have been grateful; they would not take steps that were unacceptable to the Arabs, and as Jabotinsky had predicted, partition never materialized. Instead, the White Paper of 1939 laid down a ground plan for the liquidation of Zionism.

* * *

Because Weizmann denigrated our work to Robert Rothschild, many of our best plans fell through. Our veteran member, Reuben

---

[1]The *Kongresszeitung*, August 5, 1937—XX World Zionist Congress, Zurich 1937.

Franco, had found a navigation company ready to sell us four tugs, eighteen Danube vessels and three trampers with which we could have moved a wave of four thousand or more people per trip. To buy the vessels we needed only thirty thousand sterling— less than ten sterling per Jew!—and yet we could not afford to purchase. And when the S.S. *Pilsudski* became available to us, a ship that could carry up to ten thousand immigrants, we could not buy it either. It would have served as a "mother ship," delivering food, water, and medical supplies to the schooners, but we could not come up with the two hundred and fifty thousand dollars, even though we had twenty thousand members of the Polish *Betar* alone ready for *Ha'apalah* on a few weeks notice, and tens of thousands of Jews registered in our offices in Poland, Romania and Czechoslovakia. And the worst part of it all was this: during those same years between 1937 and 1940, the *Haganah*, guided by the Socialist leadership of the Yishuv who did have the money needed, moved only about six thousand immigrants; less than half of what we did.

East and west, our *Ha'apalah* still faced violent condemnation from everyone, from the assimilationist "Bund" to the Zionist Abba Hillel Silver, to the ultra-Orthodox *Agudath Israel*. Noah Prilutzky, leader in the Yiddishist movement in Poland, said: "While Jabotinsky wishes to empty Poland of a substantial number of its Jewish population, I wish we had seven million Jews here so we could fight anti-Semitism even more vigorously."

In New York, Stephen Wise, the most politically prominent rabbi in the United States, called Jabotinsky a "traitor" for preaching "evacuation" from the ghettos of Europe. *Davar*, the Socialist-Zionist daily in Palestine, said that by working with the Polish government on annual emigration quotas, Jabotinsky was "joining hands with the *Endeks*, the pogromizers of the Jews of Poland." And even in the last Passover services held in the great Tlomacka Synagogue in Warsaw in 1939, the Chief Rabbi, Moses Schorr, attacked Jabotinsky's call for mass immigration.

Well-to-do non-Zionists like Robert Rothschild, who had the means to turn our plans into reality, became aware of the physical threat to the Jews but still, whenever we approached them, they looked for approval from the Zionist establishment. And that approval never came. Had Weizmann maintained even a neutral posture, the French Rothschilds and their contemporaries would have helped, but instead Weizmann urged all his followers to fight us. Madame Allatini raised only pitiful amounts and Robert Rothschild donated a thousand pounds sterling here and there, but that was all.

When young, ebullient, Reuben Hecht came out of the Palestine *Irgun* to establish our offices in Zurich, I went to call upon his father, Jacob Hecht, a Rhine shipping and grain magnate, and one of the wealthiest Jews in Switzerland. Known to be a generous philanthropist, Direktor Hecht told me bluntly that he was disowning his son Reuben for his insane involvement in smuggling Jews into Palestine.

Robert Rothschild escaped from France before the advancing Nazis. His wealth and properties and his magnificent art collection were expropriated and he spent the war years in New York in modest surroundings. Helene Allatini, helping Jewish refugees and the Jewish underground to the end, was turned in by a refugee who was a Gestapo informer. She and her husband disappeared in the extermination camps. Jacob Hecht's substantial German holdings were confiscated by the Nazis. Wizened and mellower when I saw him again in 1960, in Basle, he told me: "My son, Reuben, the *Irgunist* was right and I was wrong."

Late in March, 1939, when I boarded the *S.S. Manhattan* bound for the United States I saw my journey to mobilize funds as almost our last chance. My cabin mates were Sicilian, Anatolian, and Greek peasants, and they were all in happy and ebullient moods, all eager and excited at the prospect of reaching the United States. Wondering why I was so subdued, they shared their wine with me, offering a "toast to America." I drank with them, trying to buoy my spirits and brace myself up for my last-ditch effort with the Jews of America. But when it came my turn to propose a toast, I was at a loss.

II
Mission to the U.S.A.

Just before sunrise on March 30, my cabin mate, a peasant from a small Sicilian village, nudged me awake: "*Amico mio, alzati. Siamo a Nueva York!*" In moments, off the port side, the Statue of Liberty came into view, its torch reaching high into the flaming crimson sky. I thought of the statue's inscription written by the compassionate Jewish poetess Emma Lazarus:

> Give me your tired, your poor,
> Your huddled masses yearning to breathe free.

Lazarus had also written prose about many of the saddest chapters in Jewish history and I wondered how she would have described the last several years, or what vicious irony she might have seen in her inscription gracing the gateway to the United States—only recently the government had refused to allow several thousand German-Jewish children to be admitted into the country even temporarily. When I had heard this what flashed back in my mind was the scene of hundreds of thousands of Austrians screaming *Sieg Heil* to Hitler on the Vienna Ring. If several thousand children were too much for this great country, how could I delude myself that in America we would find the understanding and help we needed?

My spirits had not risen when in Vienna when I had read about the Evian Conference, a major international project assembled because of growing pressures for havens from Nazi persecution. The conference, proposed by the United States, ended up a disappointment when America's contribution essentially went no further. The French ran the show and the British made sure that

Palestine was never even mentioned.

About the only thing all participants agreed on unanimously was that a refugee problem existed! And though every one knew that the European refugees were ninety-nine percent Jewish, the Jews were never mentioned. The American, Myron C. Taylor, who chaired the conference, managed to deliver his opening address, outlining the gravity and magnitude of the tragedy, without using the word "Jew" once. William Green, the President of the A.F.L., showing no more sympathy than British Labour to the Jews of Europe, expressed conditional approval of the conference as long as it did not raise the United State immigration quotas.

The State Department, using some fascinating logic, had briefed United States delegates prior to the conference, stressing that they should not encourage official assistance to refugees, since it would encourage the Germans to banish all the Jews under its rule, as well as convince other European nations enthusiastically to do the same. And what would the democracies of the world do if they had to absorb eight or ten million Jews?

So the conference had come and gone, and doors remained closed to Jews. In a disdainful, sarcastic speech delivered in the Reichstag a few weeks later, Hitler had spoken some of the truest words he ever uttered: "It is shameful to observe how the entire democratic world dissolves in tears of pity, but then . . . closes its heart to the poor, tortured people."

And now, sailing up the Hudson in the shadow of the torch of liberty, I wondered if America or any other country was truly left to us as a citadel of freedom.

* * *

Haim Lubinsky, the ranking *Irgun* officer of the mission to the United States, met me at the landing, bubbling over with energy. In one month here, he and Robert Briscoe, a member of the Irish Parliament and one of the most fiery activists, had addressed dozens of groups in and outside New York. And so had John Patterson, the seventy-year-old former commander of both the Zion Mule Corps and the Jewish Legion during the first World War. Patterson, a Protestant Irishman, had teamed up with

Robert Briscoe, a Jewish Irishman and a veteran of the IRA, to head the *Irgun* fundraising mission to the United States. They came armed with letters of introduction to the Jews of America from my former teacher, Professor Joseph Klausner, and Rabbi Moshe Avigdor Amiel, the Chief Rabbi of Tel-Aviv. Robert Briscoe, however, did not need any introductions to the Irish Americans.

I spent my first evening in America listening to Lubinsky and Patterson. Lubinsky held the floor with his bursting staccato, while the ramrod Patterson, once a lion hunter, patiently waited his opening to interject bits of wisdom. What they told me about their progress was not encouraging. Following up the limited leads of Jabotinsky and his followers, they found the Zionist movement, and particularly the "Revisionist" or symphathies for Hebrew nationalist rebirth, neither strong or popular in the United States. Two of the strongest Jewish organizations here, the American Jewish Committee and the Jewish Labor Committee, were traditionally, sometimes vehemently, anti-Zionist. Most Zionist groups were under the autocratic rule of Jabotinsky's opponent Stephen S. Wise. Those friendly to us like Jacob de Haas and Justice Louis D. Brandeis were in retirement or dead, so our warnings, exhortations and appeals were falling mostly on deaf ears. The traditionalist "Young Israel" had struggled to scrape up contributions of a few thousand dollars for us; the funds had to be acknowledged personally by Rabbi Amiel. Beyond this, only insignificant amounts had been raised.

With the help of Rabbi Louis I. Newman,[1] our people had held meetings in several synagogues and private homes, espousing free immigration to Palestine for the Jews of Europe. Listening to Patterson, Briscoe and Lubinsky, some individuals were sincerely moved. They went back to their homes and offices, called their rabbis or heads of their fraternal lodges and asked if they should help us. Who are these people? they asked. Who is Jabotinsky? What is the *Irgun*? And the answer was always the same: "Don't touch them."

Briscoe was asked by Jabotinsky to try and interest President Roosevelt in an emergency project to move two million Jews out

---

[1] Of temple Rodeph Sholom, New York City, the only Reform leader to extend a helping hand in that community.

of eastern and central Europe, but he never managed to obtain a
hearing. James Farley, the top Democratic politician in the
United States, arranged for him to meet Governor Herbert Lehman, Felix Frankfurter and the retired Louis D. Brandeis, but
Briscoe was never allowed into the White House. The delegation
also tried to win over non-Zionists and the assimilated American-
ized Jews, far removed from their heritage. In the past few years in
Poland and central Europe, we had had some success mobilizing
similar groups of Jews, whose minds had finally been opened to
our "Jeremiahs" by the rise of Hitler and who were now ready to
respond to our call for activism. We hoped that these same
catalysts would work for us here, in a way that no amount of
pleading by Jabotinsky or Herzl had done. As things turned out,
these non-Zionists, along with a smattering of observant,
Orthodox Jews, some recent immigrants from eastern Europe
and a few warm-hearted non-Jews, would give us far more support than the established groups of our "Zionist" brothers ever
did.

Within the first weeks after my arrival, Lubinsky took me to the
home of the noted journalist John Gunther and his Jewish wife,
Frances. The Gunthers' home was one of only a few "respectable"
homes open to us. Addressing a number of guests, Lubinsky
delivered a short talk describing the situation in Nazi-controlled
lands and in eastern Europe. Then I answered questions on
Ha'apalah and British policies and our reactions to them in
Palestine. When the meeting was over, some of the guests promised to help financially.

We stayed behind with Frances, John and Harry Louis Selden,
a young editor who was gradually becoming involved in our
work. He and Frances were good examples of the non-Zionist
neophytes we were recruiting.

Our conversation was somewhat subdued. We had expected
more substantial results. Frances had even invited the author
Edna Ferber, whose backing supposedly would have been important, but Miss Ferber bowed out at the last moment. It was just as
well, because she turned out to be one of the most rabid antag-
onists of Hebrew nationalism.

We stayed up late that night, in the Gunthers' apartment. John
and Frances Gunther were sophisticated, worldly people and

John had a position of high respect in international journalism. With complex world events crowding in on the insular Americans, Gunther's books were welcomed as straightforward answers to incomprehensible developments.

Gunther did not feel personally involved in what we were saying or doing but he reacted to the problems of the Jews as he would to any other serious human problem and left the nitty-gritty of Jewish matters for his Jewish wife. Frances was small and frail with a slow, halting, small voice. They both knew so much about international politics that we could speak in a kind of shorthand, as if we were using headlines. In this way the Gunthers were unique. Americans were not well-informed about the world. In 1938 Senator Robert Reynolds of North Carolina, upon returning from "Hungria," (sic) announced that it was wrong for Hitler to have annexed the "Sudan."

That evening, the Gunthers tried to educate Lubinsky and myself about American politics and about what part Jews played in it. My image of a rich, generous Jewish community with a proud and strong ethnic consciousness was quickly deflated. We were not, as we had hoped, going to find a Brandeis or deHaas in every town. It was almost fascinating to hear the Gunthers and Harry Selden tell us about anti-Semitism in America; about the South and its persisting prejudices, about widespread prejudice against *anyone* of a "less than pure" American origin; it was so far removed from my knowledge of American history and the vision of a pluralistic land I learned from Professor Kovner in Jerusalem. John Gunther reminded us that as early as 1797, Congressman H. G. Otis from Massachusetts had said: "When the country was new, it might have been good policy to admit foreigners but it is so no longer." I thought back to my bunk mate on the S.S. Manhattan the peasant from the little Sicilian village who had wiped away his tears as he looked up at the torch of liberty.

The American Revolution and the French Revolution were the two pillars on which we had based our own quest for independence, but now we were seeing that neither of our models had stood the test of time. The one in Europe had already crumbled, so what would prevent the other from failing here? At best, what could we realistically hope for from a country that professed no great love for the Jews?

"Are you familiar," Frances Gunther wanted to know, "with the racist theories of Lothrop Stoddard of Columbia University, of Hendrick of Yale, of C. Conant Josey of Dartmouth? And there are a host of others, with prestigious institutions like M.I.T. and Stanford and the American Museum of Natural History connected to them." These were men who, in writing and even before congressional committees, expounded theories on superior and inferior races—the Jews among the latter. "Don't be fooled," Frances went on, "this is not a liberal pluralistic society—regardless of your book-learned, rosy impressions. It is a cruel country full of paradoxes and contradictions. Look at the Irish. They came here poor, uneducated, starving refugees, and they clawed their way up to blue collar and middle class respectability. So where do they stand today politically? They're the main backers of anti-Semites like Father Coughlin and Joe McWilliams."

"And our own Jewish-Americans?" Harry Selden broke in. He banged a cigarette against the pack as he raised his voice: "The German Jews who first came here in the nineteenth century weren't so happy with the thousands of bearded and caftaned east European Jews who came later and clustered in ghettos. The German Jews wouldn't mix with them. My friends," he pointed at the two of us, "you have your work laid out. Neither the Jews or the non-Jews are ready for you. We're just coming out of a long, debilitating depression, and a large part of our work force is still unemployed. The natural isolationist sentiment in this country is being fanned and financed by the Germans. The Jews, as usual, are splintered, split, and frightened and can't take the definite strides in any direction. And in Washington, from Roosevelt down to the lowest State Department official, no one will stick out his neck."

"At the White House level," John Gunther offered calmly, "Briscoe, if he ever manages to reach it, will have to put up with passivity. But at all other levels of the State Department you'll face active opposition. Too many of the Near Eastern experts served in Arab lands, or were connected with the oil companies or the American University of Beirut. They're at home with the Arabs and that's whose side they're on." John stood up and continued in a thundering voice, pointing a finger at us: "Your only hope is to generate enough public opinion to pressure Congress. If you push hard enough, the government will bend. But you have to reach the multitudes, not just Zionists or Jews. And unless you work non-stop, you won't achieve a thing." With that, he left the room.

Throughout her husband's speech, tiny Frances Gunther had sat listening with her hands in her lap, looking as helpless as a hurt bird. Now, searching for words in a barely audible voice, she asked us what we intended to do.

It was past midnight and we were all dead tired but Haim Lubinsky gave her an answer: "What we don't know about American political and community affairs we will learn. If we need more manpower for our campaign here, we'll send for it from Palestine. We're at the eleventh hour and we have no choice but to keep trying. If the Jews of Europe are permitted to be destroyed, Jews all over the world, and millions of non-Jews as well, will follow to their destruction. No oceans will protect Americans or any of the human race from what is happening in Europe. We will go out to the streets, carrying this message to Jews and non-Jews alike."

* * *

In April, 1939, Robert Briscoe was ready to return to Ireland, and we came together at the bar of the Hotel Taft to wish him a good trip. Our old soldier John Patterson suggested a "nightcap," an expression I had never heard before. The idea of a good stiff drink appealed to all of us.

John Gunther's prediction had come true. Briscoe had failed to have an audience at the White House or even at the highest levels of the State Department. Jabotinsky had requested him to join the delegation, specifically to attempt to interest the White House in a modified Nordau Plan—a million Jews or more, moved to Palestine over a two year period from central and Eastern Europe, the first phase of evacuation. "Jabotinsky," said Briscoe, "had no doubts that Palestine could absorb the millions anxious to flee." Briscoe paused a moment, then added softly: "Jabo was so apprehensive by then that he wrote to me[i] saying that this was

---

[i] In the fall of 1938.

only the first step, that large-scale action was required soon."

But, no one was ready to extend a hand for an international effort to evacuate the Jews from the "zone of Jewish danger." Very few responded to the emergency that loomed or even acknowledged its existence.

Briscoe told how when he had come to the States, the Irish-Americans James A. Farley, Postmaster General under Roosevelt, and William O'Dwyer, later Mayor of New York, introduced him to Governor Herbert Lehman. Lehman, an assimilated Jew, said he was worried that our campaign was embarrassing England, which was already on the spot because of mounting German aggressiveness. Jim Farley said to Lehman, "Governor, England had been on the spot for the last thousand years and is likely to be for the next . . . Do you people think you can wait that long for a solution to the Palestine problem?" Briscoe made little headway with Lehman, and did no better with other prominent American Jews like Felix Frankfurter, and the eighty-three-year-old Louis D. Brandeis. Brandeis had asked Briscoe all manner of questions about the military resources of the *Irgun*, about their financial means, about the *ma'apilim* vessels. Then at the end, Brandeis only said that he was sorry, but that he would not be able to help, that he had "seen too much bloodshed and violence." But before Briscoe left, Brandeis admitted: "If I were a young man like you . . . I would be with you."

The *Irgun* delegation had been in the United States over eight weeks, but we had raised only pennies for our *Ha'apalah*. Having been confronted with indifference, suspicion, and worse, we now were uncertain as to how to publicize an activity labeled "illegal" by Britain, and so many Jews.

In the United States, where Jews still lived peacefully in a society ruled by law, they were not ready to hear us tell about breaking British laws. They did not have the sense of emergency to push them into dealing with "common criminals," as so many of our Zionist brothers referred to us. Most groups actually refused to hear us, and even when they did let us speak, they did not listen.

By now, Robert Briscoe was an expert on all of this. He had been both a "lawbreaker" and a fundraiser for years. He had rebelled against the laws of Britain ever since he fought with the

IRA and twenty years ago he had been sent to America to raise funds for the IRA's struggle to free Ireland. He had done well on all counts. This time he was returning home in failure. Neither he nor John Patterson had been able to break through the apathy and antagonism with which the most influential Jews in America had confronted them. He was going back to his post in the Dail in Dublin, to take up once again the leadership of the Fianna Fail Party, and Patterson planned to return to Britain in June. Lubinsky was heading back to Palestine, while I would remain here alone until a decision was reached in Eretz-Israel about the future of our work in the United States.

Briscoe looked us over and smiled, his dark eyes flashing their usual optimism, then he spoke quietly in his deep baritone, carefully articulating each word. "You fellows think we Irish had it easy? It was not the multitudes who helped us, but only a handful. No one was waiting on the streets holding out his checkbook. We talked and scrounged and cajoled and robbed, and we were ostracized by our own. And there were plenty of opponents and informers from within. Our internal problems were as threatening as those created by our enemies. Then, as now, a few compassionate outsiders helped."

Briscoe reflected a moment, then smiled and continued: "There isn't an Irishman in America today who doesn't boast of supporting us twenty years ago. And twenty years from now, most American Jews will tell their children how they helped illegal immigrants, how they helped build up the rebels' arms, in short, how they brought about Hebrew independence."

It was comforting enough to sit there in the bar of the Hotel Taft and talk about twenty years from now, but I suddenly heard myself say: "Who cares what anyone says in twenty or thirty years from now? Who of us will be here to hear it? Our people have substituted pronouncements for deeds since time began. Living in the diaspora warped us until we called our illusions and inertia spiritual greatness. We still look for shelters and escape everywhere, hedging, procrastinating, and over-intellectualizing instead of acting. We live in a physical world, yet we reject the physical as the way of the gentile while expecting to survive in such a world."

Patterson sighed. He ordered another round of drinks, then

looked me in the eye: "Why do you persist in equating the 'diaspora mentality' with physical debility? What about the men who fought with me in Gallipoli and in the heights of Samaria? What about those in the Royal Fusiliers who took the Jordan Passages? Where did they come from? From the diaspora! from Whitechapel! From Russia! What about Shlomo Ben Yosef and Yaakov Raz and the *Irgun*? So what if your teachers told you to rely on the word of God? I taught my boys to read the Hebrew Bible and that's where they drew their courage from! Who else but the ancient Hebrews had a greater tradition of fighting for freedom and their land? There was no one of greater courage than Joseph Trumpeldor in Gallipoli, and my boys in the Royal Fusiliers were given special honors by the Commanding Officer, General Chaytor, who told them: 'By forcing the Jordan fords, you helped in no small measure to win the greater victory . . . at Damascus!' And Theodore Roosevelt also wrote to me in 1918: 'Congratulations on leading . . . one of the most important . . . incidents in the whole war. To have the sons of Israel smite Ammon on hip and thigh.' My Whitechapel tailors and Russian ghetto immigrants chased the Turks from the Mountains of Moab, even though you Palestinians still aren't allowed to live there. So our problem [Patterson always spoke as if he were a Jew himself] is not a shortage of youth ready for sacrifice, but in the thinking of the Jewish leadership and their disciples. Ghetto life hasn't killed Jewish courage, it has deadened the Jewish ability to think politically. To acquire and defend a country requires willpower, astuteness and perseverance, as well as courage. Diplomacy has to work together with physical might. Can the Jews manage this? I pray they can. My experiences with Weizmann and the High Commissioner Herbert Samuel were deeply disappointing. I warned Weizmann that General Bols, the first military Governor of Palestine, was an avowed anti-Semite, but Weizmann insisted that he was a fine gentleman, and Bols proceeded to do everything he could to wreck the Balfour Declaration, and Samuel supposedly a lifelong Zionist, turned out more Imperialist than the Britishers!"

In 1939 it was impossible to bring together great masses of Jews in isolationist America to hear about the sins of the British in Palestine or the dangers that Jews in Europe faced. Patterson and our small groups of concerned Jews and non-Jews had managed to draw a few small meetings, while the great majority—the religious bodies, the socialists and the cultural Zionists—backed away, considering the views of Patterson, Wedgwood and Briscoe, anathema. Those who attended our meetings were considered dupes of the "Fascist" Jabotinsky. Ben-Gurion, the Socialist leader, regularly called Jabotinsky "Vladimir Hitler" and the N.Z.O. "NAZO."[1]

How embarrassed I was for my people that Patterson had to experience all this Jewish internecine warfare. More than ever now, we shared his fears about the ability of our people, and above all, of our leaders, to deal with the real world.

I had come off the boat ready to deliver our message. From Galilee, from the jails of Jerusalem, from the heart of Europe's ghettos, from the barges of the Danube and the trampers on the Black Sea. I wanted to grab the Jews and shout: "It's almost too late! Help us! All we ask for are pennies. If every Jew in America gave us one dollar, we would build a bridge of ships over the Mediterranean. We would send anything that floated. We would put the British, the League of Nations and the diplomats who wined and dined at Evian all to shame; we would force them to let the Jews into Palestine and anywhere else that shelters can be found. Please just listen without fear, without prejudice. If you help, the British won't be able to block us!"

But we were never given a chance. A solid wall of indifference and hostility shut us out, though it would not in the end shut out the inevitable. My impulse was to leave the country when Patterson and Briscoe did, to go home and simply say it had been no use. But I remembered that I had come thinking it was our last hope—and I could not afford to give up a last hope so easily. After all, I had been here only a few months! I thought of young Raz in his glowing uniform on Sabbath night, shy Shlomo Ben Yosef sitting on the floor of the staging camp outside Vienna with his fellow *Betarim*, taking in my every word about the *Irgun* and its future plans, of Mordechai in Portici eight years ago, who knew he would never make it to the fields of Eretz-Israel. What right did I have to quit when all of them had come to the very point of death still confident and full of dreams?

---

[1]Joseph B. Schectman: *Fighter and Prophet*, Vol. I, p. 248 (New York 1961)

I went back to the daily routine. During Patterson's and Lubin-sky's last weeks in the United States, we formed the "American Friends of a Jewish Palestine" and opened a small office, trying, with a handful of good men and women, to win some support from the American people.

III

From Diplomacy to Rebellion
(The White Paper, 1939)

On February 23, 1939, the British revealed that another White Paper would be forthcoming this time repudiating any obligation towards Jewish Statehood, and setting up a gradual program to establish Arab rule. The Paper stated that armed Arab attacks represented the will of the Arab population of Palestine to resist domination by the Jews. No mention was made of the fact that Arab armed gangs from outside Palestine were involved, or that a reign of internal terror had been instigated by the Arab Higher Committee. The Paper limited Jewish immigration to seventy-five thousand over a five year span. The country would slowly be prepared for self-rule with population ratios frozen at present levels.

For all intents and purposes, this was official British acknowledgment that its promise in the Balfour Declaration and its obligations under the Mandate were now abrogated. British ruling circles saw this as the only logical move towards securing Arab loyalty in the growing world turmoil. The Jews in Palestine and Europe were not considered a human resource for any purpose, military or otherwise, nor were the Jews of the United States seen as a political factor. The Arabs, however, sat on oil and on the route to India. British self-interest meant pacification of the troublesome Arabs and ignoring the powerless Jews.

This final slap in the face was the ultimate proof of the bankruptcy of Weizmann's leadership and the policy of passive dependency on British pledges.

The impotency of the Zionist establishment in the face of

British edicts had never been so obvious. The *Haganah* still had
no substantial *Ha'apalah* organization; its very ethics prevented it
from countering Arab terror and from considering serious armed
resistance to British rule. The leaders of the *Yishuv* also felt that
resistance to Britain might deplete the *Yishuv*'s economy, as well
as the small incipient military nucleus of the *Haganah*. A British
officer, Major Charles Orde Wingate, assigned for three years to a
special duty in Palestine, became a close friend of the *Haganah*
leadership, but when he himself proposed armed resistance to the
British administration, the friendship of the *Yishuv* establishment
cooled off in a hurry. Wingate had to leave Palestine and his
passport was stamped forbidding his reentry.

Although spiritualist-Socialist Zionists had never aimed at
solving the physical problems of existence of the Jewish masses,
they were now suddenly faced with no other choice and they were
unprepared. As the vise closed in on the Jews of Europe and the
British shut tight the doors of Palestine, the Zionist leadership
faced a dead end in its relationship with Britain.

Jabotinsky, who predicted that the Peel Commission's recommendation for a tiny Jewish State on the Plains of Palestine
would come to naught, offered an alternative. For years he had
urged the Jews to develop pride and self-reliance, and told the
youth to "learn to shoot" in preparation for the return to Zion.

In the early thirties he had cut to the heart of the matter:

> Either Zionism is morally good or it is morally bad . . . this
> problem should have been solved before we became Zionists . . . If
> it is just—justice must be achieved without regard to anyone's
> agreement or disagreement . . . Popular slogans are used against
> Zionism: democracy, the right of a majority . . . [i.e.] since the
> Arabs are presently a majority in Eretz-Israel, they have the right
> to self-determination . . . [However, this] does not mean that he
> who grabbed a piece of territory must always remain its owner and
> he who was forcibly expelled from his land should be the eternal
> wanderer.
>
> There are between fifteen and sixteen million Jews in the world.
> Half of them today lead, in plain terms, the life of homeless dogs.
> There are thirty-eight million Arabs. They occupy Morocco, Alge-
> ria, Tunis, Tripoli, Cyrenaica, Egypt, Syria, Mesopotomia, and
> the whole of the Arabian Peninsula—an area (excluding the
> deserts!) as large as half of Europe . . . Eretz-Israel is only one
> hundred and seventieth the size of the vast area on which the Arabs

have settled . . . But when a homeless Jewish people demands Eretz-Israel for itself, it is regarded as 'unethical' because the local population finds it unplesant. . . .

To take a piece of land from an overendowed nation in order to provide a home for a wandering nation is an act of justice . . . a sacred truth which must be accomplished by force, nevertheless remains a sacred truth.

When Jabotinsky saw that the Jews of Europe were a step away from annihilation, he conceded that the only hope of survival would be armed action.

Slowly probing the possibility of an armed uprising, he first raised the subject with a group of *Irgun* leaders who visited him in Egypt in July 1937. (Because of his "militancy," the British in 1930 had banned Jabotinsky from entering Palestine.) He asked the leaders about the potential manpower for military action against the British and what the likely reaction would be from the Jewish establishment. He emphasized that he would give the ultimate approval for military landings and revolt only if he participated in person.

In 1938, the *Irgun* began insisting on serious preparation for military action against the Mandatory power. All barriers to immigration were to be torn down, and a widespread campaign would be launched to enlist and train diaspora youth for the coming battle of liberation. To our way of thinking, Jabotinsky's Zionism, based on cooperation with Britain, was no longer feasible. A strong part of him still inclined him to try diplomacy first, and to put his faith in "civilized" Britain. A nineteenth century liberal more than a revolutionary, his admiration for democratic British tradition did not let go of him until conditions became critical in Europe in late 1938.

At the February 1938 convention in Prague, the N.Z.O.'s platform had called for the transference of a million Jews to Palestine over the course of ten years. We *Irgun* men knew that we did not have ten years to spare. In the months after the convocation the *Irgun* moved ahead, continuing to build its bases in Palestine and eastern Europe, accumulating weapons, creating a cadre of trained officers and rank and file. We had also moved thousands of "illegal" immigrants into Palestine.

Throughout those months, the *Irgun* pressured Jabotinsky to take the only logical step beyond political Zionism—revolutionary Zionism. He talked with the Jewish masses in the "zone of danger" in Europe, and with the young leadership of the *Irgun*—constantly weighing the forces Hitler had set loose on the continent versus Britain's policies. Gradually he came to believe what we were saying. After the Nazis' ruthless attacks began against the Jews in Austria, Britain clamped down tighter on immigration, and Jabotinsky was appalled.

By the end of 1938, he gave in and placed himself at the head of the Hebrew Revolution. From that point on he became in fact the Supreme Commander of the *Irgun*.

Jabotinsky was familiar with Garibaldi's "March of the Thousand," which had helped accomplish the unification of Italy; he had also studied the consequences of the failed 1916 Irish Easter revolt. He knew that armed landings in Palestine and a declaration of Hebrew revolution would not instantly result in the creation of the Hebrew Republic—but it would at least break the pattern of Jewish passivity.

When Briscoe's mission to the U.S.A. failed, Jabotinsky warned once again that "we cannot go back to a normal agenda .. . the alternative [to action] is destruction! ... memorize this word: D-e-s-t-r-u-c-t-i-o-n."

The Jewish-Zionist leadership, at last seeing the catastrophe approach, could resort only to begging the British to help, and when the British ignored them, some in the ranks of the Socialists were ready to turn toward resistance, and breaking the British blockade. But still the traditional Zionist leadership, led by David Ben-Gurion, overruled them. As late as the Zionist Congress in Zurich of August 1939, on the eve of the war, Rabbi Hillel Silver stood up before his colleagues to oppose *"Ha'apalah"* and warned against any "hasty, immature ventures in Palestine."

* * *

To celebrate the forthcoming British White Paper, the Arab High Committee organized demonstrations and attacks on Jews throughout Palestine. The *Irgun* reacted with armed attacks throughout the country, attempting to show the British that the pressures the Mufti and Kaukji used could be brought into play even more resoundingly by the Jews. In a speech before the House of Lords, days after the White Paper had been issued, Josiah Wedgwood defended our course once more: "The law is inhuman and they [the Jews] consider it their duty to break the law. I hope they will all unite to do so." The Jews did not unite, but we were gratified that the *Haganah* began slowly to increase its *Ha'apalah* work.

The *Irgun* command had met to decide on policies for the near future. Raziel presided. He had returned from the Paris conclave on February 22nd, traveling on the passport of Shimon Tchurkai, an *Irgun* soldier who, a few months earlier, had been kidnapped from watch duty by an Arab gang and murdered. With Tchurkai's passport in hand, Raziel was detained at Lydda Airport for interrogation but his identity was not discovered. After dusk, he managed to escape from the detention room, and with the help of some Jewish supernumerary police at the airport who dressed him in one of their uniforms, he made it safely to Tel-Aviv by evening of the next day. In a letter to Jabotinsky he related lightheartedly: "The C.I.D. has distributed the pictures of my passport to the police and to army intelligence, whose agents have become a multitude. They now have my picture with a moustache and without one. The only way for me to eliminate my identity is to have my head removed."

At the meeting of the *Irgun* command, aggressive counter-terror action against the Arab gangs was planned, as well as sabotage actions to disrupt Britain's ability to govern the country. On the 27th, which came to be known as "the Black Day," the *Irgun* set off bombs in Haifa, Jerusalem and Tel-Aviv. The casualties numbered over a hundred.

On May 9, 1939, Raziel was arrested when a local plane he was on, flying the Tel-Aviv and Haifa route, made an unscheduled stop at Lydda where the plane was searched by the C.I.D. It was a serious blow to the *Irgun* and lowered and weakened our cohesiveness. Raziel was a natural leader who enjoyed our unchallenged respect and trust, as well as our deep affection.

The head of the C.I.D., Giles, a tough intelligence man, led Raziel's interrogation. The *Irgun* engaged a lawyer, Asher King, a "respectable" *Haganah* man, to represent Raziel. King's main goal was to have Raziel administratively detained under the Emergency Regulation for suspected "political activities," rather than remanded for trial as an *Irgun* officer for which he could be sentenced to death. It took a number of sessions between Giles and King to work this out. At Raziel's first interrogation, he had told Giles: "I'm David Raziel, head of the *Irgun Zvai Leumi* in Eretz-Israel," to which Giles responded: "We will bring you before a military court and you will hang." According to King, Raziel then calmly answered: "It is obvious that you won't . . . If you touch a hair on my head, you and your assistants will be shot and killed . . . And I can assure you that my men are better marksmen than yours!" Raziel was not tried, but instead was administratively detained and sent to the Acre Fortress to join dozens of other *Irgun* suspects. A plan to arrange his escape never materialized because of events which intervened.

The imprisonment of Raziel and the subsequent shifts in the higher command of the *Irgun* did not slow down the plans the *Irgun* command had agreed upon as reaction to the White Paper. I and other delegates throughout the diaspora continued receiving our communications regularly, by courier or by post, often through neighboring countries. We got regular intelligence reports on German and Italian activities, on the Mufti's cooperation with these powers and on British intelligence. Two of our men, Mark Margolov and Joseph Raphaeli, had infiltrated the C.I.D. Raphaeli was eventually discovered and arrested, but, because he was an American citizen, he was permitted to leave for the United States where he joined our delegation.

Our twin campaigns against Arab terror and the colonial administration did not slow until September. Our men blew up government installations, electrical installations, postal and telephone services, broadcast studios, railroads and administrative headquarters. The attacks on the Arabs were in areas used as bases for attacks on Jewish settlements or transportation.

By now, with the probability of Palestine becoming an Arab State, there were no gaps between Jabotinsky's thinking and that of the *Irgun*. The developments in the last several years prompted Jabotinsky to write:

One does not depend on the enemy's righteousness, but only on making it physically impossible for him to kill our people and to burn our homes. . . .

None of this meant that Jabotinsky condoned indiscriminate killing. In a directive dated June 24, 1939, he instructed the *Irgun*:

Cancel operations if they endanger women and children. . . . Avoid mass retaliation. . . . Old people, women, and children should not be hurt. Distribute, in Arabic, warnings that it does not behoove Arab men, these days, to send their women to the market.

Irgun attacks on Arab market places received harsh criticism at home and overseas, but we knew that weapons were being smuggled into Palestine in vegetable trucks, and that the same method was being used to bring weapons from the countryside into the towns. We knew what villages sheltered Arab terrorists and yet the British and Arab policemen made no serious attempt to block roads and paths or verify the contents of crates and sacks that came in from the country early each morning. We had no choice but to uproot the weapons ourselves.

The British administration now dropped Jewish immigration even lower than the White Paper quotas of fifteen thousand annual admissions. "Illegal" immigration from this point on exceeded the number of legally admitted persons, proving our point that more Jews could reach Palestine without British approval than with it.

I read the world press and confidential reports from Palestine, watching Hitler's advance in Europe. After the Nazis took over Czechoslovakia, it seemed only a matter of time before Poland's turn came. War seemed more and more imminent, but strangely Jabotinsky did not consider it inevitable. The son of nineteenth century European liberalism could not accept that, after the horrors of the Great War, Europe could again engage in mutual genocide.

These misgivings, however, did not affect Jabotinsky's prognosis of catastrophe for the Jews of eastern Europe. He repeated his warning to the Jews of Poland:

It is three years . . . I continue to warn you that a catastrophe is coming closer. . . . My heart bleeds that you, dear brothers and sisters, do not see. . . . Listen to me in this eleventh hour; in the name of God! Let anyone of you save himself as long as there is still time. . . .

And while he pleaded with the Jews of Europe, the *Irgun* in Palestine tried one last time to be heard by the British. In the underground English language publication *The Sentinel*, it reminded Britain that the Jews in Palestine were a military resource available to fight Hitler and that the sooner Britain made peace with the Hebrew community, the better for the democracies. Obviously, the more Jews there were in Palestine, the larger the reservoir for future allied power.

To most of us in the *Irgun*, it seemed too late for such an appeal, too late to convince Britain that giving in to Arab terror and closing the shores of Palestine would not subdue the sheiks and kings who respected strength above all. But a handful of our friends, Patterson, Wedgwood and others, still hoped that the Colonial Office could be ruled by the common sense and decency of the British people. So we ran the articles, without placing any great faith in them, and Britain only redoubled its efforts to liquidate the hopes for our national rebirth.

Jabotinsky campaigned throughout east and west Europe and the few of us in the United States continued to search for help from any source. Jabotinsky and his political emissary in Poland, Dr. Joseph Schechtman, repeatedly had long talks with the U.S. ambassadors in London and Warsaw, arguing for several millions of Jews to be removed to Palestine immediately under international auspices.

The diplomatic efforts led nowhere, but nevertheless they were a constant irritant to Ben-Gurion and Weizmann. There was not much they could do to stop Jabotinsky. They could, however, take steps against our stepped-up armed resistance in Palestine.

In June and July, 1939, two public proclamations were distributed by the Jewish Agency and its affiliates. They were signed by hundreds of the establishment's leaders and functionaries, the list headed by Henrietta Szold, S. Y. Agnon and Berl Katznelson, who considered themselves the ethical teachers of the *Yishuv*. "Thou shalt not kill," they declared, "is a commandment out of the roots of an ancient people. . . . We shall not build our national future by imitating the worst of the gentiles . . . Let us stop this evil at its beginning. Isolate it. Let the *Yishuv* unite to defend the national homeland from the terrorists from within, as from the enemies from without."

The June 21st proclamation stated that the purpose of the *Irgun* was "not to fight the Mandatory power but to weaken the *Yishuv* . . . to take over its control." It might have been flattering for the twenty-five hundred members of the *Irgun* to be credited with such political ambitions. Actually, our thinking and the establishment's were worlds apart, our people had never faced such an ominous threat to their existence, and unprecedented actions were called for. We hoped that partisanship would be buried—that the time had come for Jews to stand up together to throw off the British overlords. Still no Zionist leaders issued a call to rally for the national survival. Instead, they rallied to stifle Jabotinsky. The leaders of the *Yishuv* sounded the alarm about a danger not from the Nazis, not from imperial Britain, but from the solitary exiled leader who had correctly predicted the threat the eastern European diaspora faced.

He and his pupils were the danger! Our youth were offering their lives for what was ours by right and the *Yishuv*'s leaders could only say that we were "imitating the worst of the gentiles." By trying to destroy us instead of the enemy, by condemning the use of force and all the attempts we made to rescue our people, the *Yishuv*'s intellectuals helped turn the Jews into the most vulnerable of living beings.

* * *

On August 31, 1939, the *Irgun* high command (Stern, Kalay, Heichman) met in Tel-Aviv to review the world situation. Their focus was on the plan for armed landings and revolt in Palestine. It would require an intricate, tightly coordinated action of both the diaspora reserve forces and the *Irgun* forces in Palestine, the latter securing the beachhead for the landings from Europe.

Jabotinsky had spent some time now preparing a detailed plan of operations which he outlined in six coded messages, and Haim Lubinsky, who had met with him in France on his way back from the United States, brought in most of the plan to the meeting. A series of secret consultations had already taken place between

N.Z.O. leaders, *Betar* and *Irgun* delegates, and in July a special committee had been formed to deal with the maritime aspects of the operation.

Many wheels were already turning when Stern, Kalay, Heichman and Lubinsky sat down to review the details in Tel-Aviv.

The members of the High Command knew the weapons and material available in the *Irgun* both in Palestine and Poland. The Polish Army had committed itself to supply the Irgun with twenty thousand rifles, as well as machine guns, grenades and small weapons. A small part had already reached Palestine. More than five thousand rifles and miscellaneous material had recently been delivered to the main *Irgun* warehouse in Warsaw, and limited funds were available for vessel purchases. Robert Briscoe was to leave shortly for South Africa and others for the United States to help raise additional funds.

The manpower required was estimated to be in the tens of thousands. Much would depend on the ships we acquired and on the weapons we got to Palestine prior to the landings. Our fighters would face over twenty thousand British soldiers, as well as the police. Still, our limited objectives were within our capabilities: securing a beachhead, defending the road to Jerusalem, occupying government headquarters in Jerusalem, raising the blue and white flag over the Jerusalem Citadel.

If all went according to plan, Jabotinsky would land with the main force and from Jerusalem declare a Provisional Hebrew Government of Palestine; hopefully this temporary government would hold out long enough to negotiate an agreement with the British. If the action failed, a government in exile would continue to function abroad. In the meantime, it would establish for the record the precedent of Hebrew statehood.

At the meeting some misgivings were raised that the *Irgun* could be crushed in this confrontation with the British, and that Jabotinsky might fall in the battle. Abraham Stern objected to the entire project, seeing it as a mere propagandistic gesture which could produce no enduring effects. But the high command accepted the plan in principle. Lubinsky was to leave the next day for Europe, carrying the approval of the basic plan to Jabotinsky. David Raziel, in the Sarafend detention camp, was to be consulted before the plan went into action. A tentative date was set for October.

However, as the Command was nearing the end of their discussion summarizing their conclusions before rising from the table, a single knock was heard and the door burst open. The house was surrounded by plainclothesmen and uniformed police. All present were arrested. Within twenty-four hours, they were transferred under heavy guard to the Central Prison in Jerusalem. Six hours later, the German Army invaded Poland. World War II had begun.

IV
War

By the summer of 1939 Jabotinsky's followers in Europe numbered as many as a million, including some one hundred thousand men and women in *Betar* alone, also in veteran and student organizations, and smaller groups involved in daily actions. At the core of these were approximately fifty thousand members of the *Irgun* in Palestine, *Irgun-Betar* military cells in eastern Europe, and small groups of *Ha'apalah* activists across the continent. All of these concentric bodies had worked feverishly through most of 1939: we had obtained arms from Poland, with more promised, and in the not-too-distant future we could have had thirty to forty thousand men ready for a landing in Palestine. But the morning the German planes bombed Poland, they were at least months ahead of our best laid plans, and they destroyed the fragile structure we had so carefully and dearly built for saving our people.

On September 1, 1939, the day the Germans invaded Poland, David Raziel, was still in the British detention camp at Sarafend, southeast of Tel-Aviv. Several other top commanders were with him or in other prisons. Within a few days, the Palestine C.I.D. intensified its campaign to round up and detain "enemy suspects," which meant any and all *Irgun* adherents. Ironically, the first shots fired by British soldiers following the Polish invasion killed two *ma'apilim* on September 2nd, on the vessel *Tiger Hill* as it landed fourteen hundred escapees from eastern Europe on a Tel-Aviv beach.

However, after prolonged negotiations, a gradual release of *Irgun* detainees commenced. Raziel was released in October, and he immediately resumed his position as head of the *Irgun* and *Betar*. Haim Lubinsky was among the last to be released in June 1940. Our training courses and our accumulation of weapons actually intensified, in an attempt to keep the shreds of the military and *Ha'apalah* organization together.

On September 2, the day after the invasion of Poland, Jabotinsky issued the first of several statements to the effect that Germany was the number one enemy of the Jewish people. That same day he addressed Anatole de Monzie, a member of the French Cabinet, proposing the formation of a Jewish army—not just a few units or battalions of Jewish soldiers, but the nucleus of a true national army—which would fight alongside the allies. From this day on, Jabotinsky and Patterson, with the help of Wedgwood and other sympathizers in Britain, conducted a campaign to convince Britain and its allies to start immediate recruitment and mobilization of Jews worldwide. Volunteers would come from wherever they could be found, from the millions of Jews scattered throughout the free world, as well as Palestine. Jabotinsky envisioned a body of a quarter of a million men which would eventually grow to half a million. In December, Dr. Weizmann submitted a proposal of his own for the formation of a single Jewish Division to be included in the Empire forces. Neither plan made any headway with Churchill or other British leaders. Whatever sympathies Winston Churchill might have shown for our cause before he assumed leadership of the government, never progressed beyond the oratorical. When the campaign for a Jewish army finally began to gain some support due to simultaneous pressure in the United States and London, Churchill wrote to Lord Moyne, the Colonial Secretary: "Tell Dr. Weizmann that the Jewish Army plan is to be postponed for six months . . . the only reason to be given is the lack of equipment." This would become the stock answer for the duration.

In September 1939, making little headway in London, Jabotinsky and Patterson decided to visit the United States to extend their campaign. Jabotinsky issued an appeal to the Jews worldwide:

> A brutal enemy threatens Poland, the heart of the Jewish world dispersion for nearly a thousand years . . . France, all the world's fatherland of liberty, faces the same menace. . . . England has

decided to make their fight her own; and we Jews shall . . . never forget that for twenty years, until recently, England was our partner in Zion.

The Jewish nation's place is, therefore on all the fronts where these countries fight. . . .

We swallowed hard when we read Jabotinsky's statement about "England . . . our partner in Zion." But nevertheless, on September 13, our American Friends of a Jewish Palestine submitted a memorandum to Lord Lothian, the British Ambassador in Washington, suggesting that in view of world developments, Great Britain now recognize the *Irgun* as a legal entity, help arm it and permit it to participate in the defense of Palestine. The offer was curtly rejected in a communication from the Embassy dated November 20, 1939. Later, when British fortunes were at a low ebb, when their last troops were fleeing Dunkirk, leaving their weapons behind, we repeated our offer that the *Irgun* be given a role in the defense of Palestine. The answer from the Secretary of the Embassy said in part: "There can be no possibility of H. M. Government in the United Kingdom recognizing the 'Independent Jewish National Army,' which is an illegal organization concerned with political terrorism in Palestine."

Watching events in eastern Europe I knew that my worst fears were being borne out. I had to battle with myself not to be paralyzed. Though I managed to carry on my work, I was torn two ways at once. My pessimism told me that we had already lost the battle; yet somehow I continued to function, performing to the best of my ability, hoping against hope that some Jews could still be saved.

Our small remaining group in the United States did its utmost to raise funds for *Ha'apalah*, but we always came up short. Joseph Katznelson, our coordinator, based in Warsaw, fell gravely ill and during the siege of Warsaw, we practically lost all contact with Poland. A central *Ha'apalah* committee was formed in Bucharest and it seemed that every message we received from Eri Jabotinsky in Romania or Rudi Hecht in Switzerland or Eliahu Glaser the veteran *Irgun-Betar* leader now in Paris, was the same: "Help! There is so much we still could do, but the costs are running away from us!" They reported that the British were intensifying their campaign against our *Ha'apalah*, aiming to close every exit out of

France, the Balkans, the Black Sea. Ironically, the Germans were continuing to permit the departure of Jews from German-occupied lands and until October, also from the Reich proper.

Practically every country refused the Jews admission. Once the war was well under way, the United States followed Britain's leadership and closed its doors to all immigration. It appeared as if keeping the Jews in Europe became a central part of Britain's war effort. It looked as if the entire British diplomatic corps was mobilized to prevent Jews from reaching Palestine. The rationale, both in Britain and the United States, was that Jews worldwide could always be counted on to help win the war. They had no choice but to be selflessly on the allied side; that they would precipitate domestic anti-Semitism and represent an economic burden to the country which took them in. Thus, if it became necessary, they were expendable.

Our small group was aware of all of this, but we were not yet ready to say it aloud. We had only one priority—to save as many lives as we could—and we could gain nothing, as yet, by pointing an accusing finger at the leaders of the free world.

In July, 1939, I was joined in the United States by Arieh Ben-Eliezer, whose friendship, dating back to 1932, had always been a great source of moral and emotional strength. His arrival, more than anything else, helped me to keep going.

A few months later, Alex Rafaeli and Samuel Merlin came as well, both with years of experience in public information. Ben-Eliezer and Rafaeli had been sent by Raziel to join me both in our fundraising campaign, and in a broader campaign to educate the American public.

We struggled and scrounged and sent our people in Europe pennies, saving a few thousand people while millions of others were dying; but as is said in Jewish tradition, 'one life saved was a world saved,' so we kept on.

* * *

On November 17, 1939, thirty-two *Irgun Sganim* candidates, chosen from around the country, graduated their training course at Mishmar Hayarden in the Galilee. Just a few years earlier I had helped train the first six *Sganim* candidates in Rosh Pina, when the entire *Irgun* unit in Mishmar Hayarden numbered less than a dozen men and women armed with a few handguns.

The thirty-two went out to "celebrate" their graduation on Sabbath morning, November 18th, by engaging in demolition exercises. The sounds of the explosions were heard by an Arab policeman on duty at the Jordan Bridge near Mishmar, and the British police, armed with machine guns, surrounded the group and arrested them. The four girls were sentenced to two years imprisonment, and the men were given five to ten years. Not until early 1941, when the war in North Africa was going badly for the Allies, with the Axis in Africa, and the Arabs on the Axis side, the detainees were released.

But during 1940, the British government, freed from League of Nations supervision, implemented the 1939 White Paper to the fullest degree. Immigration was shut down completely, and the Jews of eastern Europe, caught between the Nazis and traditional Russian anti-Semitism, had nowhere to go. The democracies throughout the free world refused to open their gates.

On the shores of Palestine, *ma'apilim* were shot and killed, vessels were confiscated, the *ma'apilim* exiled to Mauritius. *Haganah* members were imprisoned in cells alongside members of the *Irgun*. The Zionist Establishment was stunned. In their vocabulary, they had distinguished between their "pure" weapons and ours and they had actually come to believe in these semantics. To the British, keeping vigil over the military potential of the Jews in Palestine, this distinction had never existed. Weapons in the hands of Jews, any Jews could be expected one day to turn against the administrators of the White Paper. Expecting from Jews the same reactions they faced from the Irish, the British did not understand the thinking of Ben-Gurion and his co-leader Sharett, whose later memoirs revealed sincere shock and disbelief that the *Haganah* had been referred to as "bands," or that officials of the Palestine administration felt Jewish weapons might one day be used against the British.

The White Paper and other new laws prohibited land acquisition by Jews. The Zionist establishment reacted with demonstrations and mass meetings similar to those our Achimeir and his followers had held ten years earlier at the Western Wall and throughout Palestine. The *Irgun* did not participate in these current demonstrations, believing that at this point in time such displays were meaningless: "The policy is an offspring of the 'self-restraint' policy of the last few years, the one rewarded by the White Paper. . . . These new 'Nuremberg' laws will be repealed only in fire and blood . . . the day will come when the people of Israel will terminate these cruel laws instituted against them in the land of their forefathers." (*Irgun* High Command circular #100; March 29, 1940, affixed on the walls of Palestine.)

In 1940, ideological and tactical disagreements, aggravated by individual ambitions and personality clashes, threatened the *Irgun* once again. A dissenting faction was led by Abraham Stern, a number of veteran commanders and some of the rank and file, though most of the organization backed David Raziel. Tactically, the key difference between Raziel and Stern was their different feelings about the "cease fire" with Britain, which Jabotinsky had defined and Raziel concurred with. Stern said this concession should never have been granted to Britain without reopened immigration and substantive allocation of arms to the Jews of Palestine. Ideologically, the Stern followers felt that the *Irgun*'s ties to Jabotinsky were injuring its ability to develop into a non-partisan national army, and that links with any "legal" movement like the N.Z.O. or *Betar* made it that much more difficult to function as an effective underground organization.

Stern and his circle also wanted to engage in independent political and agitation activities. They and others believed that the Jabotinsky movement, as well as the top leadership of the *Irgun* was suffering from political hardening of the arteries. In moving away from Raziel, Stern wanted to create a body committed totally to immediate armed resistance against the British, regardless of what was happening in the war against the Nazis. This he did forming what eventually became known as Lehi—"the fighters for Israel's freedom." When Raziel reported it to us in New York, we found it deeply disturbing. We also received an emotional, bitter letter from Stern. Kook, Merlin, Ben-Eliezer, Rafaeli and I met and despite the confusion created by Raziel's and Stern's different accounts, we did not let the split affect us. We remained loyal to the *Irgun*.

During the winter of 1939-1940, our delegation to the United States had grown to five people. The latest arrival in June out of

London was Hillel Kook who assumed the name of Peter Bergson. He had been acting as liaison officer with the N.Z.O. and senior *Irgun* officer in Europe. Kook took over as head of our delegation and under his authority we functioned much more effectively. We accepted his suggestions as the next thing to commands though we were on a civilian mission involving public relations and political activities, we still considered ourselves a unit of a liberation army, and we kept a strict hierarchical discipline within our ranks just as we had in Eretz-Israel. It was the ultimate source of our strength. Our attitude was the same as that of all nations in time of war—accept discipline or accept defeat.

Not that everything went smoothly among us. We never lacked for arguments. We disagreed, sometimes vehemently, about each other's analyses of events, about policies, tactics, and specific courses of action. But eventually a consensus always emerged, and when it did, we all adhered to it regardless of whether or not it led to bruised egos. It enabled our small disciplined group to achieve the impact we eventually had.

Sometimes, as in later years, we were temporarily cut off from home base, becoming a sort of "lost battalion." When the command in Palestine was almost dormant, we simply took it on ourselves to proceed the best we could. Then, when closer contact was reestablished with Palestine, it was as if a hiatus never existed, although tactical differences surfaced time and again.

When the *Irgun* split, those of us in the United States sided with Raziel, with whom most of us had been on very close terms. Zeev Jabotinsky, who had arrived in New York shortly before Kook's arrival, showed us his instructions to Tel-Aviv, reconfirming Raziel's appointment as head of the *Irgun*, and we agreed with the view the two of them shared on full collaboration with the Allies. We advised Raziel that he had our full trust, and we never deviated from the principle that we were delegates of the *Irgun*.

From the time Jabotinsky reached New York, we established close cooperation with him. In March 1940 we put at his disposal the small organization we had built over the past year. He was preparing a concise treatise, *The War and the Jew*, calling for the establishment of a Jewish army to help combat the Nazis; in it he demanded the end of Jewish homelessness through the creation of a State in Palestine. Our American contacts arranged for him to meet with the press and leading political writers. But it was tough going. Isolationism was widespread and American Jews, frightened by growing anti-Semitism and by a pro-German campaign in the United States, were fragmented rather than united. They were not eager to speak out for fear it would feed the fires of anti-Semitism.

Jabotinsky's campaign in London had ended unsuccessfully after about six months. He realized that the British government would not budge. In his book he explained Britain's intransigence: "Once a nation received recognition as a partner in a fight, it could not be prevented from presenting and pressing its demands . . . as equal partners." Official Colonial policy precluded that the Jews would have that chance. When the war was won, Britain aimed to create an Arab-Palestine which they woulc dominate, and which would serve as Britain's guardian of the Suez Canal, the Empire's lifeline.

Yet until the end of his campaign in the United States, Jabotinsky maintained in his heart a vestige of his faith in the British fairness and common sense, believing that a Jewish Army could not be created without Britain's consent. When Jabotinsky scheduled a mass meeting for June 25, 1940 at the Manhattan Center, the British Ambassador in Washington instructed its New York Consulate General to be officially represented. This directive was withdrawn after a delegation headed by Rabbi Stephen Wise formally requested the British Ambassador not to make any gestures of sympathy to Jabotinsky's campaign. The timid establishment explained this request in their organ *New Palestine*, intimating that Jewish volunteers from the neutral United States would be "mischievous in their effect upon the status of American Jews."

Jabotinsky tried to counter such a fearfulness of official American Jewish circles by putting Jewish survival above partisanship. He addressed an urgent appeal to Jewish leaders like Justice Brandeis, Paul Baerwald, a key leader of the Joint Distribution Committee, editor Abraham Cahan of the *Daily Forward* and many of the most influential United States rabbis. Jabotinsky proposed the immediate formation of a World Jewish Committee to "concentrate the core and defense of the interests of our people in the eastern hemisphere." Jabotinsky truly hoped that the leaders would at last respond, and that "in the face of dangers never yet paralleled in our history, a common platform could now perhaps prove easier to find than ever before." Scarcely a single recipient of the letter had the courtesy to answer it.

The last time I saw Jabotinsky he looked tired and gray. I attributed his appearance to the troubles with the split of the *Irgun*, to the slow progress here, to the bad news from Europe, and to his separation from his beloved wife, whom he had to leave behind in the London blitz. Then on August 3, while visiting a *Betar* summer camp in New York State he died of a heart attack.

Losing him was, for all of us, like losing our father. We were intellectually and emotionally tied to him as our leader and teacher, and his death created a vacuum in our hearts that we knew could not be filled. He had died when we needed him more than ever, and we felt a kind of desperate abandonment.

Standing with thousands of others outside the funeral parlor on the Lower East Side in New York I felt orphaned, and a bitter anger welled up in me. Fate had taken Jabotinsky from our people at the most crucial time in our history. The Nazis had starved and dislocated entire communities in Poland and central Europe and hundreds of thousands of Jews were already dead. Jabotinsky was the one leader who could have injected pride and courage in the Jews around the world; despite the opposition and indifference he encountered, he could have rallied thousands of people to halls in New York, Philadelphia, Chicago and Los Angeles, sounding the alarm and awakening America's conscience. He could have reached the White House and represented the Jewish people not just as another pleader but as an acclaimed national leader. Young Jews from all backgrounds would have rejected their country's isolationism and joined Jabotinsky's Jewish army. And if the Jews were going to survive beyond the war, Jabotinsky would have been the one to prepare and lead them towards nationhood. The one leader who may have moderated the catastrophe, was gone.

* * *

Once Abraham Stern and his followers had seceded from the *Irgun*, David Raziel gradually re-established his dominance;

however, several veteran commanders and officers withdrew from active roles in the organization—some after almost ten years of constant sacrifice. Conflicts of loyalty, battle fatigue, imprisonment and all the daily stresses of underground life had taken their toll. A vibrant younger generation was coming from the ranks, and the withdrawals were an acceptable, natural part of the process in a revolutionary movement.

As the war spread, we were faced with the possibility tht the Axis powers might win. In 1940 a neutralist government came into power in Iraq and the British still hoped to maintain a toehold there through the Foreign Minister, Nuri Said, a British sympathizer. However, the situation changed radically when a pro-Nazi coup took place in Iraq on April 5, 1941, under the leadership of Rashid Ali. The British-Indian forces landed in the city of Basra and reinforced their airbase in nearby Habanya but the German planes came to the aid of Rashid Ali's government by strafing and bombing British positions, then landing in the Baghdad area. British intelligence was in the dark as to the whereabouts and effectiveness of the Iraqi Army. The British were left extremely vulnerable to surprise attacks.

At this point, incredibly, the British who had for years supported the Arab cause to the detriment of the Jews, approached the Hebrew Underground to help them battle against the Iraqis. David Raziel was asked by British headquarters in Cairo whether the *Irgun* could help to destroy the stocks of aviation fuel in Baghdad. Raziel promptly answered yes, provided the *Irgun* might also have a chance to "acquire" the Jerusalem Mufti, who had taken refuge in Baghdad. The British answered that they themselves could not participate in such a venture; but they implied that they would not interfere if the *Irgun* tried to capture him.

Raziel called in Yaakov Meridor, a key *Irgun* commander, and proposed that the two of them carry out the mission, along with two men who spoke Arabic. Meridor tried to persuade Raziel not to participate personally in the mission but to no avail. As always, when it came to a risky operation, Raziel wanted to test the conditions himself before sending his men out for action. He also had doubts that the British would provide the right explosives and timers in the right place, and he felt that the only way he could be sure was to be there. On May 17, 1941 he and Meridor boarded a "Dakota" plane in the south of Palestine, carrying with them a hundred pounds of explosives and other material from the stocks of the *Irgun*. That evening they landed in Habanya, the British airbase which was under siege by Iraqi units and under continuous bombardment by German planes. The confusion was total. A day earlier, an Indian unit of the British had captured Faluja, and Iraqi outpost on the road to Baghdad, and what the commanding general wanted now, even before Raziel was to blow up the storage tanks, was information from the major of the Indian unit on the whereabouts and combat potential of the Iraqi units facing them. There was no radio contact and he had no reliable scouts or units that could infiltrate Arab lines; his command in Habanya was not even capable of locating a couple of *Galabayas* (traditional Arab peasant shirts) the two *Irgun* scouts needed as a disguise. The Arab Legion of Trans-Jordan could be enlisted only for a non-critical guard duty assignment, protecting the foreign minister Nuri Said Pasha. In its hour of need, Britain had no consequential friends among the Arabs, who had been friendly only as long as the tides of war ran for Britain. Even the skeptical Raziel had not foreseen all this confusion.

On May 20, Meridor, with his companion Sica, crossed the flooded Euphrates in a small boat, and located the major in command of the Indian unit. Unfortunately, the major could tell them little about what lay ahead towards Baghdad. At the same time Raziel and another *Irgun* scout, Tarzi, went with a British major and a driver to try and find a land approach to Faluja. They were unsuccessful, and then on the way back to Habanya, three German Heinkel planes attacked their vehicle. Tarzi was unhurt, but the driver lost both legs, and Raziel and the British major were killed instantly.[1]

Thus, on that dusty road to Baghdad, an era in the history of the *Irgun* ended. David Raziel, our most effective military leader, had been with the *Irgun* since the time of the first *Sganim* course in 1931, and he had authored together with Abraham Stern the first Hebrew literature on weapons and military concepts for our

---

[1] There are historical researchers who believe that Raziel was purposefully killed by British planes.

youth to follow. To improve our weapons, he had worked and experimented on them with his own hands. He had led men on the beaches when our *ma'apilim* were clawing up the dark sand dunes of the Sharon; and to the very end, he would not send men to battle unless he shared their dangers. This was why we loved "Razi" and this was why he fell.

Raziel was a combination of *Safra* and *Seifah*, a scholar-warrior like those who had disappeared with the ancient Judeans. He had gone on his mission carrying his phylacteries and *talit* (prayer shawl), and Meridor brought them back to Raziel's parents. Raziel had always been at home with his people's past; he belonged to the ancient world of the Euphrates, the Jordan and the desert, where Abraham had travelled on his way from Ur-Kasdim. They were part of Raziel's covenant with the God of the ancient Hebrews. It was most fitting that he died in the old land of the Euphrates and the Tigris.

The rest of the mission was carried out without casualties. It took the British three more days to locate the Arab dress required for Tarzi and Sica. They went out on reconnaissance posing as Palestinian Arab war refugees, and they made it to the outskirts of Baghdad. After a week they returned, reporting that the Iraqi army no longer existed. The flooding of the dams on the Euphrates had destroyed all its equipment, and within two days, the British reopened their campaign and took Baghdad quickly.

With Hitler now concentrated on his Russian campaign, Britain asked for and received full cooperation from the Jewish Agency, which made available special units under Yigal Allon and Moshe Dayan. The casualties were heavy. In one incident a unit of twenty-three men, engaged in an amphibious operation, disappeared without a trace. The *Irgun* cooperated with the British for the duration of the Mesopotamian operation, as well as later operations in North Africa; with the Free French in Lebanon and Syria; our intelligence sections in the Balkans and Istanbul supplying important reports on German movements and activities, both to the British and to partisans in the Baltic countries.

* * *

For two years after Raziel's death, our group of five *Irgun* delegates in the U.S. were on our own. Some sporadic communications continued with the N.Z.O. in Palestine and with small groups in Romania and the Baltic countries, but the passing of Raziel and Jabotinsky gradually severed our last links with traditional Zionism. From then until the fall of 1943, we drew up our own battle lines and tactics, even our own grand strategy. We ventured into ideological refining of the relationship between the Jewish diaspora and the emerging Hebrew nation.

We gradually took on additional manpower and divided responsibilities. On the diplomatic and political fronts, Kook led a campaign in Washington. Merlin gathered around him an outstanding group of writers, editors and scholars, some of whom, like Michael Berchin, a veteran journalist, and Aaron Kopelowitz, an analytic political thinker, were veterans of the Jabotinsky inner circle. Together with the novelist Konrad Bercovici, editor Harry Selden, Nathan George Horwitt and Professor Pierre Delougaz, they formed an unequalled group of political analysts and communications experts. When we enlisted Ben Hecht, a brilliant dramatist, our chances to be heard increased tenfold.

Still, it seemed that in all we attempted we were carrying the banner for our fallen leaders. Merlin often solved our internal debates by saying: "If Jabotinsky were alive, he would do it this way or that . . ." and we would pause and ponder. The teacher was not with us but his teachings were.

We gradually widened our campaigns for a Jewish army and for the rebirth of the Hebrew nation in Eretz-Israel. But the going for us was harder than ever. We defined, we explained, we argued and counter-argued, but for the most of the war years the concept of a Hebrew Republic of Palestine, with its own government, army and navy, flag and anthem, was as alien to most American Jews as a proposal from Christian missionaries to solve the "Jewish Problem" by mass conversion.

We went out to conservative synagogues, where we were faced with the traditional pacifist cultural Zionist's reactions: "Who needs an army? A state? We are a people of the spirit!" We went to the Reform temples, where oftener than not the rabbis and trustees were embarrassed by us: "We are Americans! Why should we join a Jewish army? What is this talk about a Hebrew republic? Judaism is only a religion." Orthodox congregations were more sympathetic, but in no hurry: "Don't rush things. The Almighty will help us when we deserve it." They collaborated with us on straightforward rescue missions and relief, but like the others, they relied heavily on the gentiles to save our people.

We carried on, gaining a few friends here, a few converts there, but few "respectable" well-to-do Jews gave us their support.

The basic message we delivered again and again, in a hundred different forms, was that the Germans had disenfranchised European Jews as citizens and left them homeless. The Jews in Palestine were also disenfranchised: the British had announced plans for an Arab-ruled Palestine where the Jews would have no more than minority status, which was better than the fate of their brethren in Nazi lands, but still, after all we had achieved in Palestine, it was far less than we had to accept. We had a right to our nationhood and our homeland like any other people, and we demanded that this be recognized. It would to the Allies' benefit, because we required a national identity to participate in the war, and to offer our voices in the councils of the allied powers. We needed an army, weapons and supplies to help defend the six hundred thousand Jews of Palestine and the millions of Jews in Europe; and we could not leave it to others because ultimately no other nation would help us. Up to Pearl Harbor we called on American Jews and Jews worldwide to join our national army, to fight the Nazis and regain dignity and the respect of the world. Our greatest recruiting achievement was winning back assimilated Jews like the writer Ben Hecht to the fold. We had first approached Hecht after reading his column in *PM* (an afternoon liberal paper published in New York). In 1941 he said:

> I write of Jews today, I who never knew himself as one before, because that part of me which is Jewish is under violent and ape-like attack. My way of defending myself is to answer as a Jew.

We went to see Hecht at the Algonquin Hotel suite. Charles MacArthur, the husband of Helen Hayes and Hecht's collaborator, sometimes sat in, shaking his head in disbelief, listening to our excited dialogues and gentle bickerings as if we were all crazy. Hecht at first thought we were somewhat mad as well, but we gradually won him over, and he ultimately became our most important exponent in America.

After Hecht joined us, Senator Guy Gillette, Louis Bromfield,

Will Rogers Jr. and numerous other political and literary figures followed him into the ranks of our supporters.

Once we had defined our goals, we launched our campaign. By December 3, 1941, we had inaugurated the "Committee for a Jewish Army" under the honorary chairmanship of Dr. Samuel Harden Church, president of the Carnegie Institute, and Col. John Henry Patterson, with Pierre van Paassen as National Chairman. Shortly after Pearl Harbor, we amended the name to the "Committee for a Jewish Army of Stateless and Palestinian Jews." On January 5, 1942, in a full-page advertisement in *The New York Times*, our first public statement stunned Jews and non-Jews alike, made Washington uneasy, outraged the British and irritated the Zionist establishment. The ad was headlined "Jews Fight for the Right to Fight," and it bore the signatures of people such as Louis Bromfield, Ben Hecht, Melvyn Douglas, Lion Feuchtwanger, Bruno and Waldo Frank, Frances Gunther, Max Lerner, Reinhold Niebuhr, Abraham L. Sachar, Paul Tillich and Lowell Thomas. Many congressmen and senators also signed as did all of us, including Eri Jabotinsky and 'Irma' Helpren, who soon went to London to organize our campaign there.

The ad was repeated in *The New York Sun, The Philadelphia Record,* the Yiddish *Forward,* Philadelphia's *Evening Bulletin, The Washington Post* and other papers. We continued using this technique of full-page ads until we ended our activities in the United States. It was without precedent among Jews to campaign on such a large scale of public agitation. When we brought into the open the subject of a Jewish army the reports about the Nazis' attacks on Jews were hidden away as small news items in the back pages with the religious news, next to the obituaries, as if Hitler himself had chosen the location. Since 1933, owing to the Nazis' worldwide propaganda, the word "Jew" connoted the lowest species of animals, creatures that only knew persecution and deserved no better than pity. The non-Jewish world was tired of reading about our plight; it was not news anymore. The only place Jews were mentioned loud and clear was in the German-American *bund* meetings, by Father Coughlin, Joe McWilliams and other anti-Semites. In good company, the word "Jew" was spoken quietly, the way it had been in Vienna in early 1938.

When the United States entered the war, this did not change

much. The Germans kept hammering about the "Jewish War," and the message was perpetuated here by many in the "America First" movement. After Pearl Harbor, anti-Semitic attacks were toned down but hit more deeply. There were now millions of Americans in the service, and casualty reports kept coming in. Americans were still not enthusiastic about the war, and it was not too difficult to spread the word that somehow the war was the fault of the Jews. So, the Jews in America kept an even lower profile, as did the press and the government on all Jewish matters. Our ads, slogans, demonstrations and lobbying before Congress were upsetting indeed, because they deprived everyone of the fantasy that Jews simply did not exist.

Gradually we were welcomed into the homes of people in Chicago, Los Angeles and Philadelphia who had never been involved in any sort of Zionist activities before. Because our finances were always a catastrophe, and because we were still forbidden from traditional Zionist homes, synagogues and organizations, these few hospitable environments were true havens for us. Sometimes we just needed a good, warm meal. Some of our men literally were going hungry.

We were always on the verge of bankruptcy. Every ad was paid for with whatever the preceding one generated, and our small offices were maintained on a shoestring budget. I remember coming to the office early one morning and finding Arieh Ben-Eliezer there—he had arrived from out of town the day before and was too embarrassed to mention to the secretary that he had no money for a hotel room. He had slept on a desk.

However, we continued our campaign, laying out our plans as if there was no financial problems, and we did our best to carry them out, straining to cover the deficits.

Our campaign for a Jewish army lasted almost three years, reaching the highest levels in the United States government. Since Churchill had claimed lack of equipment as his reason for not helping us, we asked the American government to equip our army, and to appoint an American officer to prepare it for battle under the Allied command. We argued that we could mobilize one hundred and fifty thousand to two hundred and fifty thousand men and women. We proposed also that channels be established to help Jews escape from Nazi occupied lands to special assembly points and recruitment centers. We urged Washington to influence Britain to accept this plan, especially in view of the critical situation in north Africa and the Near East. 'Irma' Helpren formed a committee for this purpose in London, under Lord Strabolgi and other friends of ours in Parliament and the House of Lords, but all this was doomed to failure. The British were committed to preventing Hebrew political rebirth, and a fully-trained Jewish *army* could only be a threat to them.

In the end, as John Patterson had suggested after our first few months here, the Jews could not think *politically*—and lacked the vision to grasp the opportunity we pointed out to them. Neither the Zionist or non-Zionist leaders could comprehend that such a tangible achievement now would have immediate consequences for Jewish survival in Europe and Palestine for decades to come.[1] They could not conceive of Jews as a military asset; and because they did *not* believe in or campaign for an *army*, the White House, supported by Great Britain, opposed our campaign, and the chance for the Jews to defend themselves against the Nazis with their own air force and commando units was lost.

---

[1]Zionist defeatism is expressed in this item from the minutes of a Z.O.A., National Administrative Council meeting 3/8/42: "Neither the United States Government nor the British Government are going to give a Jewish Army to Ben Ami. . . ."

V
White Stones Along the Danube

Way back on March 15, 1939 at dawn, the *Wehrmacht* crossed the peaceful Czechoslovakian border and raced unhindered towards Prague. By seven in the morning they entered the capital without a shot having been fired. The Czech leadership had followed the advice of the leaders of France and England to "recognize the legitimate rights of the Germans in the Sudetenland" and rid themselves of "the demographic problem" meaning the large numbers of Sudeten Germans. In the process, they also lost their independence.

The day before, the three top men of our *Ha'apalah* work, Joseph Katzenelson, Izhak Zarzewsky and Abraham Stawsky arrived in Prague and checked into the Hotel Excelsior. They scheduled a conference with Eliahu Glaser, the head of *Betar* in Czechoslovakia and the key man of our *Ha'apalah* work in central Europe. They carried with them working documents, vessel charters, bank deposits, correspondence with government officials.

Glaser's first reaction to the German invasion was to get our three men out of the country. With great difficulty, he obtained train tickets to the Polish border at Bohomin. From there he hoped they could walk across the border since all train movements were stopped there by the invading Germans.

During a hasty meeting, it was also decided that Glaser, while a Lithuanian citizen, was nevertheless in an exposed position as head of *Betar*, and should leave the country at once for Paris, and from there go to southern France, where alternative exit ports were to be secured for our *ma'apilim*. Glaser's duties in the area would then be taken up by his deputy—Naftali Faltin.

In the next few days, thousands of Jews flocked to our office in Prague. Suddenly we were not lacking for *Ha'apalah* candidates. Our Danube underground route became the main avenue of escape for east European Jews, and Britain intensified its efforts all over the Mediterranean, the Danube and the Black Sea to halt our rescue work. By 1940, the banks of the Danube were dotted by white gravestones of would-be *ma'apilim* who had died on shipboard. The winter, the lack of food and medicine, the poor living conditions on board took their toll, mostly of the older men and women and young children. A rabbi said over the fresh grave of a passenger: "These white tombstones are the milestones of our road to Eretz-Israel."

Our *ma'apilim* drifted down the Danube on rickety barges, on wobbly tubs unfit for any cargo, and the Jews along the shores of the Danube came out to help and feed them the way their ancestors had helped Jewish refugees over the centuries. In Novisad and Orshova, in Sulina way down on the river delta, the last port on the Danube, they all came to help, weeping for themselves because they were staying behind, and for those who were on their way to freedom.

Once, while two of our river boats were tied up on the Danube in Yugoslavia, a Jewish woman of modest means died in town. In her will, she left instructions for all her possessions to be distributed to "the people on the two boats on the Danube."[1]

From the day Prague was taken, up to 1940, we participated in the movement of fourteen vessels that carried twelve thousand people out of Europe.

The outbreak of war struck a terrible blow to our work. The difficulties of obtaining boats and of moving people across borders became almost insurmountable. Shipping patrols tightened, and as conditions for the Jews in Europe worsened, so did the conditions under which the *ma'apilim* traveled. Still, thousands chanced the dangers and survived.

When our top *Ha'apalah* coordinator, Joseph Katznelson, fell ill and died behind the German lines in occupied Warsaw, a new central committee was formed in Bucharest. Eri Jabotinsky, Reuben Franco and J. Meissner took charge.

---

[1] This contrasted with the indifference and lack of compassion shown to *Ha'apalah* by most Jewish leaders and even the Jewish masses in the U.S.A., during the 1930s and early 1940s.

My friend Izhak Zarzewsky continued his *Ha'apalah* work in occupied Warsaw until February 1940. Though escape out of Poland had become almost impossible by then, Zarzewsky and his small group of co-workers managed to arrange travel documents for hundreds who reached Italy. Among them was Lillian Strassman, the assimilated upper-class Jew who edited our Polish language paper and helped our work so much in Poland. Reuben Hecht concentrated his activities in Yugoslavia until he and his wife were almost captured in Zagreb by the Gestapo. Hecht then moved his base of work to Zurich. Abraham Stawsky spent his time between Greece and Paris, where Eliahu Glaser joined him shortly after the fall of Prague.

Robert Briscoe went to South Africa to help raise funds, but he faced the same obstacles there that we were facing in the United States. The *South African Zionist Review* attacked him and our *Ha'apalah* work, describing our vessels as "coffin ships," and advising the community that "these people are dumped into Palestine without regard for their usefulness to the country. No screening or selection is attempted . . . Some of them are Viennese prostitutes . . ."

During those critical months, the horror stories from Europe were filtering into the papers and on the radio, the largest Jewish community in the world could not seem to hear us, because the diatribe against us by the Zionist leaders had left them deaf.

* * *

On December 26, 1939, John Gunther at the request of his wife went on the air over a national network and spoke about the plight of our immigrants on the Danube:

> This is the night after Christmas . . . It is quite fitting to talk about Palestine tonight. The greatest Jew in history was born there some nineteen hundred and forty years ago. Incidentally, it's a little-known fact that Jews are not allowed in the Church of the Nativity at Bethlehem. Nor, of course, can Jews visit one of their greatest monuments, the Rock of Abraham, which is the holy Moslem Area. . . .

Gunther went on to speak about the 1939 White Paper and how the British had reneged on their promise of the Mandate. The Mandate Commission of the League of Nations, Gunther explained, had in fact refused to accept the White Paper, but that had made no difference to the British who proceeded with their intent to close down Jewish immigration to Palestine. Gunther finished his broadcast by describing our efforts to rescue our people despite the British laws:

> They looked at Europe; they could not endure the appalling things that were happening to Jews there, they decided to get them to Palestine because it was the only place to go—all the other places were closed. . . .
> The Gestapo . . . gave these miserable people a choice. Either they could go to the concentration camps at Lublin from which they would quite possibly not emerge alive . . . or they could leave with the clothes on their backs . . .
> The work of the Jew-runners, as the "extra-legal immigration directors" might be called, is fascinating. They have to hire boats at steep prices, though the extra-legal immigrants are very poor. They have a hard time. I shouldn't be surprised if they have babies being born tonight in the humblest surroundings. Perhaps even in a manger . . .

It was an emotional broadcast, and we listened to it tense and silent. I had with me the latest cables from Eri Jabotinsky, Reuben Hecht and Willy Perl in Bucharest and Zurich asking for help. But in the days to come, as far as we could discern, the broadcast did not result in a single offer of help or one penny from the public.

In New York, Stephen S. Wise, Rose Halprin, the leader of Hadassah and Henry Montor, head of the United Palestine Appeal, issued instructions to the Jews of the United States not to contribute funds to us, or to help in any way the several thousand "unselected" immigrants assembling in the Danube Delta. Their justifications were outlined in a detailed document marked "Personal and Confidential," sent out by the Executive Director of the United Jewish Appeal.

* * *

The story behind these several thousand "unselected" *ma'apilim* was complex.

Throughout 1939, headquarters for our immigration work were located alternatively in Warsaw and Prague, Paris and even London. Within certain bureaucratic limitations, these facilities gave us freedom to travel and transfer funds. By March the Prague office had already moved three groups of *ma'apilim*. The gradual dismembering of Czechoslovakia, had begun in September the year before, and the young people, who saw what happened to the Jewish community in Austria, needed no further incentive to risk *Ha'apalah*. The three groups from Prague landed in Palestine and were quickly absorbed, and the Bucharest office soon advised Prague to prepare five hundred more *ma'apalim* as the core of a larger group. The *ma'apilim* were assembled from all parts of the country. They passed an initial medical examination, then were assigned to different work units—security, food and general duties.

In the middle of preparations, the Germans entered Prague. From then on the *Betar* command in Czechoslovakia had to carry the burden of feeding and lodging this group under the nerve-wracking scrutiny of the Gestapo. The Germans themselves were confused about how to proceed: the Gestapo, under Eichmann's direction, wanted all Jews out, but the army was not sure it should be sending thousands of young, able-bodied Jews to the Near East.

It took most of April to establish relations with the Prague Gestapo. Before we could move the five hundred *olim*, the Gestapo made our people face reams of paperwork and acres of administrative red tape. It took weeks of work. When Prague finally advised that it was ready to move the five hundred *olim*, Bucharest answered that they could not locate a boat.

As the summer wore on, the Bucharest office was pressured by Warsaw to accept the largest number of *ma'apilim*, while our Vienna and Bratislava offices were being pushed by the Gestapo to ship out their groups immediately. The whole of central Europe was under Nazi control, and tens of thousands of Jews were crowding our offices from Vienna to Warsaw to Bucharest.

To complicate our problems, the British intensified their campaign against *Ha'apalah* in Greece and Romania. The Greek shipowners had responded by upping their rates. Romanian authorities required visas for our transports, as well as other "papers" to prove that Romania was conforming to international laws. We had to prove that specific vessels were available for the *ma'apilim*. For all this, of course, we needed additional funds:

for bribes, for down payments of vessels that often did not materialize, for visas—the list was endless.

Finally, the situation with the five hundred stranded Prague *ma'apilim* became desperate. Eichmann came to Prague and called in Faltin, the head of *Ha'apalah* and warned that if within fourteen days the five hundred were not on their way one out of every ten *olim* and the administrators would be shot. Faltin phoned Bucharest, Paris and Warsaw while the Gestapo listened in, but no one had encouraging news. In September, when war broke out, boats became scarcer and the charter rates quadrupled. By October, the Czech *olim* had used up almost all their subsistence money. In New York we were still unable to come up with any substantial financial help. The Gestapo repeated their threats to begin killing, and this time, since we were already beginning to learn about atrocities in occupied Poland, we believed them.

Despite warnings from Bucharest, Faltin decided to charter two small Yugoslav boats and move them to the border port of Moldova Veche.

Faltin told Bucharest that all but six pound sterling per passenger of his budget had been consumed in food and lodgings. This was not enough to charter a vessel. At best, the money might be used as a down payment. However, it became a "Catch-22" because even the six sterling in foreign exchange would not be released to us unless the Gestapo was shown evidence that a boat had been chartered. A year earlier, the Gestapo had accepted my word in Vienna that we had a vessel for the *Melk* group, and had actually transferred the exchange ahead of our departure, but now we were placed in an impossible position—no boat and no funds.

Someone in the Bucharest office finally remembered that we still had an unsettled contract for a small tramper, the *Nalko*, which we had originally been seeking for a Polish group of *ma'apilim*. Eri Jabotinsky confirmed to the Romanian Tourist Bureau that the *Nalko* was under charter to our headquarters. He did not mention that we had no final agreement with the owners of the *Nalko*.

The Germans were satisfied. Before our Bucharest headquarters could even approve Faltin's departure, they received his cable that he was preparing to move his people. Eri Jabotinsky answered that if Faltin moved the people before funds were transferred, Headquarters would wash its hands of this group, and Faltin would find himself marooned on the Danube. "Read my letter," answered Faltin. "I know I'm getting you into trouble. Don't judge me by the standards of other countries—we are not masters of our souls! I trust you. *Betar* will not let us down!" Faltin's message was clear. There was no other choice. He knew, as I knew from my experiences in Vienna, that like the devil, the Nazis could only be argued with and stalled for just so long.

Eri's colleague, Reuben Franco, a *Betar* and *Irgun* man originally from Bulgaria, knew the Danube well. He told Eri that Faltin's *ma'apilim* faced a possible catastrophe. "Eri, they will die like flies on the Danube, and you will be blamed!"

Eri threw his cup of coffee at the wall of the hotel lobby, stalked out and bought a train ticket to Moldova-Veche.

Eri managed to persuade the police chief of Moldava to help and eventually a Romanian barge, *Spyroula*, was chartered. The five hundred *ma'apilim* were transferred from the river boats without interference by the police and proceeded down the river to Giurgiu. These five hundred would be the nucleus of the *Sakarya*.

The preparations for a *ma'apilim* group from Austria had not been much easier. In Vienna in the fall of 1939, several hundred *Betarim* and other young people were awaiting transportation; Eichmann had permitted about a hundred *ma'apilim* to travel to Brun to join the Czech group. Also, Dr. Willy Perl, originally part of our Viennese group, decided that he could do much better independently chartering boats and beaching them with their passengers on the shores of Palestine. He did not worry about follow-up relations with different government bodies as we did, and it was possible that he was right, so we did not argue with him too much. Other private entrepreneurs had tried the trip in recent months, and most had managed to get the vessels to the shores of Palestine.

Perl, with his associate Mandler in Prague, assembled eight hundred *ma'apilim*, most of whom paid for their own transportation. Perl managed to charter a solid Danube vessel, the *Saturnus* and proceeded down river to the Delta. Just as Faltin did with our

Prague *olim,* they left without knowing that a sea-going vessel would be waiting for them at the mouth of the Danube. The Gestapo had threatened them, too, and they opted not to delay their departure.

So, as winter closed in, both the Prague *olim* and the Austrian *olim* were floating downstream, with no guarantee that they would even be able to reach the Mediterranean. For all thirteen hundred of them, this uncertainty was better than the certainty of going to Lublin.

Our recent experiences with the Romanian authorities did not offer much encouragement. A transport of twelve hundred of our *olim,* mostly young *Irgun-Betar* members led by Menahem Begin, had recently been stopped at the Polish-Romanian border at Schnyatin. A few hundred somehow got through into Romania and made their way to embarkation ports, but all the rest had their Romanian transit visas cancelled. They were returned to Poland and the Baltic States.

Nevertheless, as we felt time running out, none of us wanted to be responsible for stopping any group that could get out of Nazi-controlled areas, regardless of what awaited them down the road.

One more effort brought about the exit of two hundred Viennese and four hundred Hungarian *olim.* This group was organized in cooperation with *Agudath-Israel,* with whom we had already collaborated on the emigration of the *Burglanders* on the *Melk* a year ago. Reuben Hecht managed to convince the Hungarian Foreign Minister and the Jewish Community Council in Budapest of our past success. Funds were provided by the Council, and foreign exchange by the Central Bank. The six hundred Hungarian *olim* chartered the Danube ship *Grien* and sailed on Christmas eve. Now nineteen hundred *ma'apilim* headed down river, anchored and waited in Sulina.

Several hundred additional candidates—Romanian Jews and others who managed to infiltrate from Nazi-occupied Poland were also cleared by the Bucharest office. The urgency to secure a sea-going vessel became greater than ever.

Our people in Bucharest joined efforts with the Perl representatives, promising Perl that we would arrange for the landings in Palestine, and eventually they secured a Turkish vessel named the

Sakaraya. Perl's eight hundred *olim* from the *Saturnus*, the only group that still had funds, transferred three thousand pound sterling out of Prague, and their representative paid it to a local ship broker who undertook to deliver the *Sakarya* by about November 18th.

The weeks that followed were critical, especially for the *Saturnus* group, which was on board a German Danube vessel, flying the swastika and captained by a Nazi. He advised his passengers that his orders were to return to Austria before the river began to freeze; he would do so, he said, "with or without his passengers."

Most frightening were the days between November 18 and December 10, when we had no evidence, and no assurance that the *Sakarya* would appear, and when depressing rumors were abounding all across the Balkans. Press stories appeared that *ma'apilim*, upon approaching Palestine, had taken over boats, shot their captains, and thrown them overboard. The stories in the Balkan papers were embellished and exaggerated, but several boats, like the *Parita*, were actually beached on the rocks of Tel-Aviv, which left the owners with a total loss, and far less inclined to charter their boats for such purposes again. Captains and crews caught by the British were imprisoned in Acre Fortress for periods up to six months. With each press report the picture looked grimmer.

In addition to our fears for the passengers on the Nazi ship *Saturnus*, we were increasingly worried that Faltin's Prague *olim* on the barge *Spyroula* would be in danger from exposure to the harsh winter now descending on the delta. The *Spyroula* had two large, shallow, holds used to carry bulk cargo like coal or grain. Three wooden platforms were built for the passengers in each hold, the lowest just off the floor and the highest, two feet from the ceiling. That group was made up mostly of *Betarim* and other trained Zionist youths, so the discipline, hygiene and morale were high throughout the three and a half months on the barge. A voyage of two to three months on a barge or tramper crowded with hundreds of strangers, all of whom were exposed to violent weather and countless other dangers, normally caused severe tensions among *ma'apilim*, and often harsh disciplinary measures had to be taken by transport commanders. But not so on the

Spyroula.

Eri Jabotinsky, who spent a great part of his time on the *Spyroula* told me of one incident when a wedding took place on the barge and the cake ran short of fifty portions. A scuffle ensued at the queue, and the command resolved to forgo dinner for themselves, since the incident represented a failure on their part to imbue the group with the proper spirit. In response, the rest of the transport unanimously voted to skip their own evening meal. The entire group fasted, spending the evening singing and listening to Eri's stories about Eretz-Israel.

However, no matter how disciplined the passengers on the *Spyroula* were, the approaching bitter winter was a serious threat to their health and safety.

Then the Nazi captain of the *Saturnus* advised the passengers that ice had been sighted on the Danube. As he had already told them, he was sworn to return to Austria with or without them, before the river froze. Their lives now immediately depended on the arrival of the seagoing *Sakarya.*

It was not a safe bet that the ship would ever come. Ever since we had plunged into our *Ha'apalah* work, we knew we would not be dealing with the most moral individuals; sometimes the greatest hope we had was "honor among thieves." Down payments were misappropriated, contacts disappeared, and sometimes we were blackmailed outright in the small ports of the Aegean. Jews were contraband, the only help we could get was from smugglers and bribed officials. And all along, British agents haunted us throughout the Balkans, closing one avenue of escape after another. They induced the French government to confiscate the *St. Brience,* a boat we had chartered for a group from Slovakia, and they intervened in Romania to block the group of twelve hundred *ma'apilim* on the Polish-Romanian border, most of whom eventually died at the hands of the Nazis.

Knowing all the factors which could have prevented the arrival of the *Sakarya,* Eri was ecstatic when the *Sakarya* appeared on the horizon on December 10, twenty-three days behind schedule.

It was a three thousand ton ship that had been built in Germany forty years before. Originally a coal carrier, it had holds about two stories high, accessible only by steep and dangerous ladders.

Everything inside and out was covered with a thick layer of coal dust.

The ship anchored outside Romanian territorial waters; because of British demarches, we no longer could transfer immigrants within territorial waters, as we had done with the *Melk*.

The transport command wanted to start immediately building bunks, ladders, kitchens and lavatories, but the young owners of the Turkish ship, Avni and Kemal Bey, who had come on their boat, were not ready. Avni, twenty-eight and Kemal, twenty-three, had apparently expected a long, haggling delay, because they brought along a most attractive and intelligent lady named Leyla, whom they identified as their "cousin." She was the only one of the three to speak a European language.

Weeks of "negotiations" with the owners ensued, during which time we were forced to allow "adjustments" in our formal charter. The amount originally agreed upon, 6750 pound sterling, was upped to 12,000, 17,500, then higher and higher.

Deperate cables and phone calls from Bucharest went to all our world-wide organizations in London, New York, and South Africa, and newspaper articles appeared with headlines like "Jews freezing on the Danube." By now there was no reason to keep this operation confidential. The overriding aim was to extricate the people safely from the delta. Funds were at last contributed by the N.Z.O. of South Africa and by the Jewish Community Council of Bucharest. We in New York had played a minor role in all of this. Even at that, the Jews in America, like most Jews elsewhere could not admit the danger, though the press and radio reported events on the Danube, the borders of Poland, Romania, Czechoslovakia and Hungary.

When Reuben Hecht had cabled from Bucharest begging us for ten thousand dollars, Arieh Ben-Eliezer and I contacted two wealthy anti-Zionist Jews—Lucius Littauer and David Donneger. We pleaded with them for help, asking them to forget their prejudices and react as if the people on our boats actually were en route to Paraguay. "Please!" we implored, "just help them out of Europe."

They helped—without waiting for the approval or imprimatur of Stephen Wise and Hadassah. They called Rabbi Louis I. Newman to ask if he would vouch for the funds reaching Romania and he said he would. So with their help, and a bit more from some of our own followers, we raised the $10,000. On January 19th, I cabled Reuben Hecht the money. It had arrived just in time to end the haggling with the owners. During the final negotiations, the captain of the *Saturnus* received his final order to return to Vienna within twenty-four hours, "with or without passengers." With this threat hanging over the transport, the owners of the *Sakarya* finally agreed to accept a second down payment of 3750 pound sterling and they permitted the eight hundred people of the *Saturnus* on board. But luck smiled also upon the *Spyroula* people. A few days earlier, the command had succeeded in chartering a barge with a heating system, the *Stefano*, so at last the *Spyroula* with its exposed holds was given up, just because ice covered most of the area.

On December 30th, when the *Grien* arrived with the six hundred Hungarian and Viennese *olim*, it was not so lucky. Overnight it was frozen solid with ice.

Eri, Glaser, Faltin and five others now constituted a transport command, and during the last month of wrangling with the owners, they had bunks built along the bulkheads of the vessel with balconies and access stairways. Three kitchens were constructed, (one kosher), twenty lavatories, and a ventilated storage area for food. There were cooks, a medical staff of fifty-two doctors, and a cadre of young men who did everything from maintaining order to administering first aid.

While we were finishing negotiations with the Beys, the problem of supplying and feeding almost two thousand people on the river was enormous; but somehow, throughout the ordeal, hardly a meal was missed. Any sickness or suffering was due more to the weather and the "accommodations."

In the end, to find the *olim* some protection from winter, our people arranged for the *Sakarya* to enter the shipping canal and tie up indefinitely at the Sulina wharf, allegedly to take on water. The area was better protected than the mouth of the Danube Canal.

By mid-January, 1940 most of the money asked by the owners was raised and *ma'apilim* from the *Grien*, the *Stefano*, (those formerly on the *Spyroula*) as well as four hundred additional others, came on board the *Sakarya*. Some were actually smuggled

The Danube barges on which *ma'apilim lived during the winter of October 1939-Jan. 1940 (Sulina, Romania).*

Sulina, February 1, 1940. Ma'apilim left behind as the *Sakarya* pulled away from its pier.

On board the *Sakarya* **on the way to Palestine (February 1940).**

Tel-Aviv's Chief Rabbi confirms receipt of $1500 from Young Israel for our *Ha'apalah* work (6/1/39). It was one of the largest single contributions obtained in the U.S., in 1939.

M. A. A M I E L
CHIEF RABBI
of Tel-Aviv & Jaffa District

אמיאל אברהם מרדכי
הרב הראשי
לפתח תקוה, ת"א ויפו ־יפו

Tel-Aviv, the _____
2, Maimon Street

[Hebrew handwritten letter]

Rescue of Refugees

To the New York Herald Tribune:

The letter in your issue of Sept. 14, signed by Rabbi Newman, illustrate, the growth of a legend. His story of the rescue in 1939-'40 of the several hundred refugees marooned on cattle boats and freighters at the mouth of the Danube, who were subsequently transferred to Palestine, is correct, save in one important detail —it was not Jabotinsky and his associates who were responsible for rescuing these refugees, but the Haganah—against whose leadership Jabotinsky carried on a prolonged and bitter struggle.

RABBI LEON M. ADLER.
Brooklyn, Sept. 21, 1948.

Myths that never die, the "establishment" version of the *Sakarya* voyage.

aboard without the command's knowledge, and two hundred others thronged on the dock in the last hours before the *Sakarya* sailed, but the owners, who counted heads continuously, refused to let them abroad.

On February, 1940, under gray skies and a biting wind, the *Sakarya* cast off, the last the Jewish passengers saw of Europe were scores of shivering, bedraggled fellow Jews standing on the snow covered pier. Twenty-three hundred people were crammed into the three holds of the *Sakarya* but somehow major conflicts never occurred. Despite engine troubles, storms and heavy fog, the boat managed to reach Istanbul on February 7th. The local Jewish community sent provisions, including mountains of oranges, which looked to the passengers like manna from heaven.

When the ship got into the Aegean, the boilers broke down and the *Sakarya* had to put in at a small port near Gallipoli, where twenty-five years earlier, Jewish soldiers had fought gallantly under John Henry Patterson. The transport command decided to hold a ceremony honoring those Jewish soldiers. Eri Jabotinsky later described the strange contradictions in the scene:

> Here were Jews escaping on a Turkish ship from Germany, honoring the memory of their brothers who died in British uniforms fighting the Turks; and now going to Palestine with the help of Germany, against the will of Britain, with the intention of joining the British army to fight against Germany. . . .

On the first sunny day of the voyage, thirty-seven couples were married by Captain Ali. He issued impressively proper marriage certificates and the transport spent a festive evening.

On February 10, 1940 the pleasant, sunny trip was interrupted. A British warship camouflaged as a freighter accosted the *Sakarya*, firing a shot over the bow. An armed party boarded the vessel. After several hours of negotiations with the captain and "cousin" Leyla, the warship left a party of sixteen soldiers, two sailors and a young lieutenant on board. The captain was ordered to proceed southwardly, towards Palestine. Leyla, in a master stroke, had obtained a document with these words: "I . . . ordered the Captain of the S.S. *Sakarya* to proceed to Haifa. He refused to do so and produced a contract to the effect that he was to proceed to Alexandretta, where he had to transfer the refugees he had on

board to ships bound for South America. He consented to proceed to Haifa only under compulsion."

This document saved the captain of the *Sakarya* from imprisonment and the *Sakarya* from confiscation.

Passengers and escort got along without serious incident.
When one of the British sailors asked Eri what his function was on
the vessel, Eri said he was a journalist traveling to gather material
for a book. "What is the title?" he was asked. "*Mare Nostrum,*" he
replied.

In the afternoon on February 13th, the *Sakarya* anchored near
the docks in Haifa.

Eri, the only Palestinian among the *ma'apilim*, was immediately whisked off to jail for "bringing Jews illegally to Palestine." After nine days he was sentenced to be detained for the
duration of the war. Before being transferred to the detention
camp, he was interviewed by a C.I.D. official, a Mr. Mosgrave,
and he repeated the same words he had said a few months back to
a British Embassy officer in Bucharest: "You Colonials make
laws. We consider these laws illegal. You rule our actions illegal
and punish us when you can . . . we will continue to break your
laws."

The twenty-three hundred "illegal" Jews, along with beautiful
Leyla, were interned by the British and spent several months in
detention camps. All were released by August 12, 1940, except for
six Hungarian Jews. Disobeying the orders of the command, they
would not part with their Hungarian passports and they were
deported by the British back to Hungary. It was hard to say what
was more incredible, the pettiness of the captors or the self-
defeating obstinacy of the Hungarians.

For twenty-three hundred men, women and children, however,
it was the beginning of a new life. One man eventually commanded the *Irgun* unit in Jerusalem during the War for Independence. Others rose to positions of command in the army, navy
and government of Israel. One, Dov Gruner, an *Irgun* fighter and
a veteran of the Jewish Brigade, went to the gallows in 1947.

* * *

On February 1, 1940, the day the *Sakarya* had sailed from
Sulina, the United Palestine Appeal circulated from New York a

four-page paper signed by Henry Montor, its Executive Director. The document contained the following comments:

> Selectivity is an inescapable factor in dealing with the problem of immigration . . . many of those who have been brought into Palestine by the Revisionists have been prostitutes and criminals...
>
> The increased incidence of crime in Palestine in the past year is the most tragic reflection of the haphazard and impossible guidance of unregistered immigration . . .
>
> A great many of the passengers were old men and women . . . who were obviously not fit for the hazardous journey.[1,2]

Ironically, and for the wrong reasons, the British Foreign Office and the Colonial Office contradicted these sentiments in a joint memorandum: "The N.Z.O. is the principal body . . . which possesses an illegal military organization in Palestine . . . [whose] immigrants are carefully picked and trained young men of military age . . . not the old men and women and children . . ."

In a way, both the Zionist establishment and the British were partly right: we took very well trained youth for whom we could find space, as well as any man, woman and child we deemed able to stand the voyage. We asked the ones with means to pay for their voyage plus a little more, so that the penniless ones could also sail. We certainly were not concerned with whatever their past professions may have been.

When I read Montor's letter in New York, our twenty-three hundred "unselected" Jews were alive and well in the British detention camps of Palestine, and Eri was secure in a Haifa jail cell he shared with two Jewish thieves. When the thieves found out why he was with them, they gave him their woven sleeping mat and the best location in the cell next to the window.

* * *

Our last independent efforts had partial success. The *S.S. Pancho*, with five hundred and fourteen *ma'apilim*, sailed from

---

[1] Document in the writer's possession.
[2] In a private dialogue with Zeev Jabotinsky (September 1939, London), Berl Katznelson, the venerated Socialist-Zionist Leader, denied that Labor's philosophy is based on "selective" immigration.

Bratislava on May 18, 1940. It took the *Pancho* four months to reach the Black Sea. And then the Italian-ruled Dodecanese Islands off Turkey by early October. On the tenth of the month it foundered. The *ma'apilim* were rescued by the Italian navy and later interned in Italy. They eventually reached Palestine, with offical immigration certificates in 1944-45.

In a joint effort with our political opponents of the extreme left, the *Hashomer Hatzair*, we got seven hundred other *ma'apilim* safely to Palestine in July, 1940. And later, our people in Romania joined with the other Zionist groups to help a smattering of Jews to emigrate.

The British now attempted to stop the trickle of *Ha'apalah* that was still being conducted by local Zionist groups in the Balkans and the *Haganah*.

On November 19, 1940, Dr. Weizmann cabled from London to Ben-Gurion in Palestine:

> Lord Lloyd informs me ships now at Haifa are being followed by another contingent about eighteen hundred now at sea which may be followed by yet others.
>
> Government opinion is that this action may be prelude to wider and more systematic efforts by Nazis now in control of Romanian ports.
>
> This aims first at getting rid of Jews, second at embarrassing British by creating conflicts between Government and ourselves by introduction of German agent provocateurs and using this for propaganda among Arabs.
>
> You must try to prevent rise of feeling which may complicate situation.

Ben-Gurion answered Weizmann assuring him that whatever *ma'apilim* are reaching Palestine are: "mainly trained *Chaluzim* and capitalists . . ." and that whoever is a suspected agent should be interned.[1] In fact, the *Haganah*'s "Rescue Committee" landed only two more boats with twenty-six hundred people.

The official "Rescue Committee," which represented all Zionist Groups, sent via Turkey, mostly with British sanction, about three thousand immigrants to Palestine from March, 1941 to

---

[1] Robert Szold papers, Zionist Archives, New York.

December, 1944. This was all the entire Zionist movement managed to save out of Nazi-occupied lands in those years.[1]

* * *

One of the worst calamities was the loss of the *Struma*, a forty-eight foot riverboat. Eight hundred *ma'apilim* and *Ha'apalah* activists sailed on her, including a hundred *Betar-Irgun* people. The ship broke down after leaving Constanza and drifted on the Black Sea until it reached Istanbul, where it was placed in quarantine. For the next five weeks, the boat stayed in quarantine while Jewish organizations all around the world appealed to the British government to grant the passengers immigration permits to Palestine. Even Stephen Wise overlooked his reservations about "unselected" Jews and personally cabled the *Struma* passengers that immigration certificates would be forthcoming. But Churchill, and the British government viewed giving in on a single "illegal" ship as endangering the interests of the Empire; the Turkish authorities finally towed it back onto the Black Sea and left it drifting. The following day, February 24, 1942, the vessel exploded. All except one passenger drowned. The cause of the explosion, a torpedo or a mine, remained a mystery, and Germans, British and the Turks all blamed each other.

By the end of 1940, our mass rescue work was nearing its end. Our mission in the United States was a financial failure. Our east-central European organization was in ruins. There was not much we could do. The only regret we had was that we had not had the money and support to break more "laws" during the critical years 1937 to 1940. The British suffered for it as much as we did. Their pro-Arab policies brought them no recompense. The Arabs did not lift a finger to help the Allies. They acted according to their narrow self-interest, shifting and adapting according to the fortunes of war. Once the Allied position became precarious in North Africa, the Pan-Arabists and the Mufti turned actively to Hitler.

Had the British permitted into Palestine the hundreds of

---

[1] Yaakov Esabi: *A General Survey of the Periods of Ha'apalah* (The Zionist Council of Israel, undated).

thousands of Jews who were ready to leave in the late 1930s, the war may not have been so protracted, and countless lives might have been saved. In Poland alone, the *Brit-Hahayal*, an organization of Jewish war veterans, had over one hundred thousand men registered for military action in Palestine. *Betar* had an adult membership of seventy thousand in Europe. Other organizations could easily have raised another hundred thousand men of military age, and with their families, these would have constituted a reservoir of more than half a million people, who would have loved nothing better than the chance to fight Hitler. As things worked out, though, most of their lives were just thrown away.

VI

Eichmann, Wdowinski, Ben Hecht

Historians have pinpointed two critical dates in the extermination of European Jews. The first, January 20, 1942, was the Wannsee Conference, where mostly second-echelon Nazi officials met in the Wannsee Suburb of Berlin to lay the foundation for the extermination of the Jews.

The second, to which Jewish historians attached great importance, was the time when Jewish leaders of the major Zionist and non-Zionist bodies first realized that the Germans were carrying out a methodical mass extermination of Jews. These two dates trivialize and obscure the issue. The Jewish leaders helped seal the fate of European Jewry when they ignored our warnings of the growing emergency, and when they grasped the enormity of the tragedy, they still reacted ineffectually. In 1943, the veteran Polish Socialist leader Samuel Zygelbojm witnessed the annihilation of the Jews in the Polish ghettos, and his despairing response was to commit suicide.

It would be an oversimplification to pinpoint the Wannsee Conference as the critical point in the destruction of the Jews in Europe. The German's genocidal policies were not formulated at any given moment, nor was support for them ever unanimous or irreversible. They were evolved gradually by increasingly psychotic officials and bureaucrats, and ignored consistently by cynics and bigots on the Allied side. Until 1941, and as late as April, 1945, there were German officials ready to deal for Jewish lives.

Historians often point to statements made by Hitler in 1919 that his objective was the complete elimination of the Jews. True,

271

these statements grew in vehemence with each passing year, but Nazi policy was still ambiguous and contradictory throughout the early years of the Third Reich. As late as 1938 and 1939, when I was working in the countries that had fallen under Nazi domination, I was convinced that the Germans were determined to rid Europe of the Jews, but that they did not contemplate mass annihilation. The idea grew on them as they observed the passivity of the nations around the world.

We, the disciples of Pinsker, Herzl and Jabotinsky, felt all along that we were racing against a possible explosion, but the Germans took their time. They constantly increased the pressure on the Jews but nevertheless kept the doors open and for several years allowed them to leave. And though, in January 1939, Hitler told the Czech Ambassador, "The Jews will be destroyed here," Eichmann, with Hitler's and Himmler's approval, prepared a plan for the resettlement of four millon Jews to Madagascar.[1]

The most important years were the late thirties, especially the few years before the Wannsee Conference. Germany still wanted the sympathy of the world, especially the United States. Hitler invested heavily in overseas propaganda in an effort to keep Britain and the United States away from his expansionist progressions. The Germans at first thought the Jews had a certain negative, nuisance value because of their protests to the world about Nazi mistreatment. Germany still needed friends in the western world. They still had room to say to the democracies: "If you feel such sympathy, then *you* take them," as Hitler had said after the Evian Conference in 1938.

But as the years passed, it became clear to Hitler that the Jews did not even have this value; nor could they be used as collateral for bargaining. Because the Jewish establishment did not have the courage for an all out rescue campaign and the nations of the free world did not care—the Jews of Europe gradually became worthless to the Nazis.

* * *

Berlin, Wannsee.
On July, 31, 1941, Goering had Reinhard Heydrich, one of

[1] For differing views on the "sincerity" of the M Plan, see: Hannah Arendt's *Eichmann in Jerusalem* and Nora Levin's *The Holocaust.*

Himmler's favorite S.S. officers and head of the Reich Security Office, prepare the "final solution of the Jewish question." When the Germans invaded Russia, their Einsatzgruppen killed hundreds of thousands of Jews. But from now on it was to be done scientifically and efficiently. To achieve this "final solution," the Germans had to gather and isolate the Jews. Eichmann acquired that experience herding Jews towards Poland. Now.he devoted months to perfect the means of mass liquidation. On October 31, 1941 Jewish emigration from German-occupied lands was finally banned. Heydrich and Eichmann were ready. The war in Russia was progressing satisfactorily, and when Pearl Harbor turned the United States into a belligerent, there was no longer any need for the Germans to worry about propaganda. From that point on they could do what they wished to the Jews. Heydrich assigned Eichmann to prepare the agenda and statistics, and dispatch the invitations to the Wannsee Conference.

Eichmann had climbed high on the ladder of the Nazi hierarchy since I had seen him walk into the old Viennese home of the Rothschilds in 1938. He seemed then an insignificant figure, servile and obsequious to his superior, Lange, who treated him with disdain and there was nothing particularly memorable about him. Only in my later dealings with him did I become aware that this mousy-looking man was an unpredictable, vicious, psychotic whom one dared not cross. He appeared to thrive and grow more powerful as the Nazi policies became increasingly brutal. But not even in my last encounters with him on the pier at the Danube in November, 1939, did I foresee the crucial and terrible role this former traveling salesman would play.

On January 20, 1942, Heydrich sat down with fourteen men, including the head of the Gestapo, Heinrich Mueller, undersecretaries of state, high police, and S.S. officers to carry out Hitler's fondest wishes. Heydrich, the opening speaker, introduced himself as the official charged with "the definitive solution of the Jewish problem." The participants were told that since the assumption of power by the Nazis, more than five hundred and thirty-seven thousand Jews had emigrated from Germany, Austria and Bohemia-Moravia, but that since 1939 "restrictions or bans on immigration hampered the immigration efforts exceedingly." Heydrich told of problems with foreign currency exchange and taxes imposed by the countries which received the immigrants. His conclusion was that now, due to wartime conditions, the dearth of shipping, and "continually intensified restrictions," emigration was obviously not only a problem for Germany, but also for the countries of destination and it was no longer worth the effort to continue. Since Germany could not afford to waste its funds for the war effort on feeding and sheltering the Jews, the only choice was to carry out the "final solution." Hans Frank[1] spoke openly of what it meant: "to take measures which would lead somehow to their annihilation."

Eichmann, the fawning bureaucrat who had been so successful in removing Jews from German lands in 1938 and 1939, was given a key role. Eleven million Jews, in Britain, Switzerland, Sweden and Turkey, as well as in eastern Europe, were to be murdered.

The conference went smoothly. The participants were aware that the plan represented the wishes of the leadership and would be carried out. Even the civil servants there, some of whom were not avowed Nazis, raised no objections. Heydrich was pleased. Under his and Eichmann's leadership the "final solution" had already been achieved for a million and a half Jews in Europe and Russia.

* * *

WARSAW. 7-9 MURANOWSKA

In 1938 I became friends with a Polish psychiatrist, Dr. David Wdowinski. He was a highly cultured, sensitive man with a charm and vitality that offered me an antidote to the frustrations of our *Ha'apalah* work. In his youth he had been sentenced to death by the Polish authorities for organizing the Jewish self-defense during a pogrom in Lvov. He also played an important role in the Polish Jabotinsky movement, which he helped found in 1926 together with the Hebrew poet Yaakov Cohen. He criss-crossed Poland with Jabotinsky in the campaign for the evacuation of east European Jewry, spreading Jabotinsky's message, "Liquidate the diaspora or it will liquidate you." In 1938, David admonished me to ignore all obstacles—the hostility of "official" Zionist

---

[1] Head of the Government-General, Poland.

bodies, the indifference of well-to-do Jews, and the opposition of intellectuals—because the masses in the ghettos who were living through the emergency, would listen to us and follow.

After the invasion of Poland, I often thought about David and what fate had had in store for him. It took five years before I found out.

In 1939, when he was forty-four, he headed the psychiatric department at the Czysta Hospital in Warsaw. The hospital had a capacity of twelve hundred patients. But, by 1940, the hospital had become an intense microcosm of the Warsaw ghetto, and was caring for some three thousand people, almost three times its capacity. At this point the Jews were not yet being killed scientifically, but only in sporadic outbursts by the German Nazis, Polish and Ukrainian anti-Semites and Lithuanian collaborators.

David, already a long-time Jabotinsky activist, moved into the ghetto and gradually assumed an important political role in nationalist circles there.

Since both he and his wife were physicians, they were allocated three rooms for the seven members of their families. By mid-1941, four hundred thousand Jews were crowded into the ghetto and as it grew more crowded and unhealthy, by 1941 forty thousand died of typhus. The Jewish police kept things running for the Germans, sometimes selling out their own people for a pittance. Raids were made frequently by the Jewish, Lithuanian, and Ukrainian police. To protect themselves, the Jews built tunnels and bunkers for escape and eventually to fight from.

The worse conditions became, the more undercover activities in the ghetto increased. Clandestine radios were constructed to monitor the BBC broadcasts. When Roosevelt and Churchill's "Atlantic Charter" had been announced, promising "The Four Freedoms" in the post-war world, the Warsaw Jews heralded it as a new Magna Carta for humanity. The ghetto survived on hope.

In the winter of 1941-42, Jewish emissaries disguised as Polish workmen slipped into the ghetto and reported that the Jews in Vilna, Bialystok, Lvov and Brest-Litovsk were being systematically exterminated. In April, 1942, two *Betar* members from Lublin reached David and reported to him that the Lublin ghetto's forty thousand Jews had been annihilated. The "final solution" was under way. David called upon several Zionist leaders in the ghetto: Dr. Ignaz Schiper the noted historian and a former member of the Polish Parliament; Bloch, who headed the Jewish National Fund; and David Guzik, who had represented the American Joint Distribution Committee. He urged them to form a non-political, non-partisan armed self-defense force. He warned Dr. Schiper that the Nazis would try to kill all the Jews in Europe. Dr. Schiper looked at him with a benevolent smile. "You Jabotinsky people are always so excitable. It's impossible to liquidate half a million people. Hans Frank, the Governor General, has personally told us that the ghettos of Warsaw, Cracow and Radom would be left alone. The Germans wouldn't dare destroy the largest Jewish community of Europe; they have to consider world opinion."

David came away from these meetings in despair, convinced that the Jewish people, and above all their leaders, had been emasculated over the centuries, and had lost their ability to react to anything. Even at the brink of death, they could not admit the mortal dangers facing them, and for the few who had warned them in the past—Herzl, Nordau, Jabotinsky—they had shown nothing but distrust and animosity as they now did to David.

In the summer of 1942, the underground N.Z.O.-*Betar* in the Warsaw Ghetto arranged for a memorial on the second anniversary of Jabotinsky's death. Just a few days before the liquidation of the Warsaw Ghetto began, thousands gathered to pay their respects, and the great synagogue on Tlomacka Street was packed. Those who came were the Jewish masses, who only now at the twelfth hour were beginning to hear his words: "Liquidate the diaspora or it will liquidate you."

But the Zionist leaders did not attend. David invited all of them, but only one came; even at this late date, Jabotinsky was still anathema to the Establishment, though everything he had predicted was coming true.

The German "actions" in the ghetto progressed and by the end of July, hundreds of thousands had been shipped to Treblinka. David's mother died on the bare floor of a make-shift hospital, while waiting to be shipped to the camp. Among those taken to Treblinka were David's revered teacher, Mendel Shapiro, the father-in-law of Sholem Asch. Ironically, only a few years earlier,

Asch, one of the great twentieth century writers of the diaspora, had violently denounced Jabotinsky's evacuation proposals. (Early in 1940, he apologized to Jabotinsky for his earlier attacks, and in 1956, in Israel, he was to recant publicly his opposition to Jabotinsky's warnings.)

In the last months of 1942, three hundred thousand Jews were "evacuated" from Warsaw to extermination camps; only fifty thousand Jews were left alive. A few escapees from Treblinka had returned to the ghettos and by their eyewitness reports confirmed once and for all the real purpose of the Nazi "transports," putting an end to the illusion that the deportees had only been "resettled" at "labor camps."

Military resistance groups were finally organized; but even now, the Jewish youth split along political lines. The left eventually formed the "Jewish Fighting Organization," (J.F.O.) composed mostly of Socialists and leftists, both Zionist and non-Zionist. David proposed a unified force headed by a non-partisan, non-political military expert, but the left insisted that one of their political leaders be appointed, and that *Betar-Irgun* members could not join the force in units, but only as individuals. It was like the old pattern of negotiations between the *Haganah* and the *Irgun* with the Socialists still obsessed above all else with control. In the last desperate hours of the Warsaw Ghetto, rather than unite with the disciples of Jabotinsky, the Socialist-Zionists joined the militantly anti-Zionist Bund and the Communists under the banner of "We fight against fascism"; the Socialist-Zionists could not permit *Betar-Irgun* men to die under a common banner.

Jabotinsky's followers formed, in July 1942, "The Jewish Military Organization" (J.M.O.) patterned after the *Irgun* in Eretz-Israel, combining several clandestine groups that had existed since December of 1939 under the leadership of David Aplbojm. David Wdowinski chaired the J.M.O.'s political committee, and Paul Frankel, the former head of the Massada student organization, was appointed commander. Units of five to ten men were formed, arms were acquired from individual Poles and Germans and stored in bunkers. The location of headquarters and main weapons storage was Muranowska Street 7-9, from which a tunnel was dug to the other side of the ghetto wall. Via this tunnel, the J.M.O. formed auxiliary units in the few small factories just outside the ghetto, and made contact with Polish underground groups, whose officers helped and assisted it in accumulating arms, exceeding those of the numerically superior J.F.O. The underground published news bulletins, gathered through their own radio receiver, reporting and recruiting Jews to these activities all of which had the same ultimate purpose: to prepare the ghetto spiritually and physically for the final stand. The J.M.O. moved on its own, without consulting the "leaders" who had rebuffed David and his friends as "hotheads." In any event, there were not many leaders left.

The J.M.O. sought as many weapons as it could beg, steal or buy, taking money from Jews who still had it, whether or not they contributed voluntarily. Grenades and Molotov cocktails were manufactured and weapons were also obtained by killing policemen and Nazi officers.

The Germans blackmailed, bribed and physically coerced Jews to collaborate, and when these informers and provocateurs were discovered by the J.M.O., they were eliminated. *Zagiew*, a newly formed group of collaborators consisting of fifty-nine people, were systematically liquidated by the J.M.O. within three weeks. The Socialist-dominated J.F.O. used some of the same methods, their pacifist upbringing peeling away at last.

On April 18, 1943, the ghetto was surrounded. The German S.S., reinforced by Ukrainian, Lithuanian and Latvian units invaded the ghetto with armored cars and artillery. On April 19 the first shots were fired on the Germans by armed Jews. The J.M.O. flew the Zionist and Polish flags in Muranowska and kept them flying for days. The battle lasted for more than three weeks, as the "Polish National Army" radio and other underground stations reported to the world about the Jews' resistance. The Germans and their mercenaries burned and dynamited house after house, bunker after bunker, and their machine guns mowed down anyone who was caught. The various Jewish groups fought individually, unit by unit, with little coordination or general strategy, nevertheless inflicting heavy casualties on the Germans. While the Germans claimed only sixteen dead and eighty-five wounded, Polish hospital reports showed more than nine hundred Germans killed and a thousand more wounded. But it was not a military confrontation; a handful of Jews determined not to die without striking back. Even after the headquarters of the two Jewish fighting organizations were overrun and destroyed, sporadic fighting continued. Some individuals and small groups managed to escape and join the partisans in the forests.

On May 16th, somewhat prematurely, the Nazi Commander General Jurgen Stroop reported the Hitler: *"Es gibt keinen Judischen wohnbezirk im Warschau mehr."* ("There is no Jewish quarter in Warsaw anymore.") Still, Paul Frenkel and a few of his J.M.O. comrades managed to cross to the Aryan side, adjacent to the ghetto and continue their resistance until June 9 (possibly till the 19th) then, after a last, desperate fight, they were all killed. The Third Reich had won one of its most arduous major battles, against almost one thousand Jews who fought with little more than slings and arrows.

David and his wife, practically the sole survivors of the J.M.O., were caught and transported to the Lublin district. On November 2nd, the rest of David's relatives were killed. Of his entire family, he was the only survivor. He lived through eight different concentration camps, and later said that the human race was divided into two groups—"Those who had lived through the camps and those who had never been there." He saw children being loaded on cattle cars, asking their parents if they were going to Treblinka, and he saw Dr. Mengele at Auschwitz, standing rigid before a line of children, his index finger moving like a metronome; right for life, left for death.

* * *

NEW YORK. EAST 86th STREET

On a hot Indian summer weekend, in September, 1942, when our delegation met with a few colleagues for consultations, we were unaware of the one hundred and twenty thousand Jews of the Warsaw Ghetto who just then underwent a final "selection." Only thirty-five thousand were permitted to remain inside the walls, and the rest, twelve thousand people daily were sent to Treblinka. In one of the largest, smoothest operations the Germans ever mounted, their trains ran day and night, never stopping, carrying the Jews to the green, manicured lawns of Treblinka, where military bands played as the Jews filed into the efficient gas chambers.

In New York we spent forty-eight hours reviewing our plans for the future. We were far from the ghettos, but we had done our best to keep up communications, and we knew that everything was more critical than ever.

Arieh Ben-Eliezer, Sam Merlin, Hillel Kook, Alex Rafaeli, Aaron Kope and Professor Pinhas Delugasch all attended but Eri Jabotinsky did not join us because he was stationed in Los Angeles.

Kook presided and we discussed some minor points first, then the key issue surfaced. What was the best course of action we could take for our people in Europe? Should the campaign for a Jewish army remain the central theme? And if not, what should be our emphasis? Several of us felt that our campaign for a Jewish army no longer was the best way to try to save the Jews of Europe, but we were not certain what the best way was. We had only so much energy and little time left.

Among our delegation, I was the only one who had dealt personally with the Germans. In my encounters with the Gestapo and the S.S., I learned respect for German thoroughness, and I knew it was important to assess objectively just what they seemed to be planning next.

For those of us who had grown up in the Jabotinsky school of thought, hand-wringing had never been a tolerable solution. Our advertisements and appeals in the United States had always proclaimed "action—not pity!" But now, knowing this might be our last chance to do anything meaningful for our people in Europe, we felt tentative and confused, and it was hard to stave off hopelessness. We saw nothing around us that could bolster our spirits. The United States was at war with ever greater numbers of casualties. The draft was putting millions of people into uniform, and life or death concerns were becoming daily fare for almost all American families. As was only natural, the President, and the people of the United States were out to win the war in the shortest time possible, with the least casualties, and this was what occupied their thoughts. The survival of the Jews in Europe did not matter to the overwhelming majority of the American people. None of our attempts—via the press, radio, meetings or on the street—had mobilized Americans behind us, and now winning any real support seemed almost impossible.

The war had slowed our *Ha'apalah* work to a standstill. After Jabotinsky's death, we had focused on the campaign for a Jewish Army stepping up our efforts, particularly in the United States and England. It seemed the right goal at the right time because chances for *Ha'apalah* were so much decreased, and the news from Europe kept getting darker. We had gotten to the point where we felt no one would rescue Jews from the camps except Jewish soldiers and airmen. However, events in Nazi-controlled Europe were passing us by. Once again our prognosis and plans were proven right, but we were incapable of halting the horrors.

My personal belief was that our Jewish Army campaign was losing its relevance; what good was it to struggle for a vote in the council of nations through national participation in the war effort when soon there would be no Jews to represent?

We became embroiled in a heated debate, some of us inadvertently repeating the arguments that Dr. Schiper had given to David Wdowinski in the Warsaw ghetto: "Germany will not dare kill millions of civilians because world opinion would not stand for it. Besides, it is physically impossible to organize mass killings on such a scale."

We concluded with some basic policy decisions. We concluded that probably a million to two million Jews had already been killed, and that, unless the Allies acted immediately, most of the Jews under Nazi rule would be lost. We further agreed, that the key for helping the Jews in Europe lay in the hands of Franklin D. Roosevelt because the Allies would follow any forthright action the United States initiated. We hoped that, if we could mobilize enough support from the Jews of America, many political, academic and literary leaders would also respond to our appeals. We had already spent three years attempting to win over leaders in Washington and London. But now, with the truth about what the Nazis were doing known, we hoped for a massive rallying of Jewish forces, giving us far wider support than we had ever gotten for our controversial Jewish army.

We had no hard facts about the large-scale extermination, though they had been available to the State Department and to Stephen S. Wise for many months. Nor did we know that early that year the J.D.C. and others had been advised by Jewish leaders in Slovakia of a mass, systematic annihilation which could be halted only through payments of ransoms and bribes. Nor that the major Jewish organizations ignored other large rescue and ransom proposals earlier in the year, such as the "Europa Plan" offered by Rabbi Michael Ber Weissmandel of Bratislava.[1]

So, based only on meager information reaching us through the Jewish Telegraphic Agency and our own intuitions, we began to organize the first phase of our campaign. Sam Merlin, insisting that a campaign of this magnitude must be backed by a clear basic declaration of principles, took six weeks to prepare our "Proclamation of the Moral Rights of Stateless and Palestinian Jews." We hoped that this document would give us a solid moral foundation which could overcome the apathy and outright hostility we had experienced thus far.

In the "Proclamation" we made these central points:

> We shall no longer witness with pity alone, and with passive sympathy, the calculated extermination of the ancient Jewish people by the barbarous Nazis
>
> We recognize the right of these Jews to return to their place among the free peoples of the earth, so that the remnants of tortured Israel . . . may take up life as a free people . . . to fight as fellow partners in this war . . . in their own army, to which the United Nations High Command will assign them.
>
> Hundreds of thousands of Jews had perished as helpless martyrs in the war which Hitler is waging on Christian civilization . . . No other people have suffered, comparatively, so much loss of life . . .

In December, 1942, we placed the "Proclamation" as a two page spread in *The New York Times* and in papers across the country. Alongside it we ran a powerful drawing done by Arthur Szyk, showing a Jewish fighter on a ravaged battlefield, with an automatic weapon in his hands, and holding in his arms the body of an old bearded Jew. More than three thousand prominent Americans and European exiles signed the document, among them, Herbert Hoover, Clare Booth Luce, Eugene O'Neill, Taylor Caldwell, Aaron Copeland, Senator Harry S. Truman, Melvyn Douglas, Bruno Walter and Sholem Asch.

---

[1]S. B. Beit Zvi: Post Ugandian Zionism in the crucible of the Holocaust (Bronfman Publishing, Tel-Aviv, 1977)

With the universal prestige of the signatories, we aimed to counteract the inhibitions of Jewish leaders like Stephen S. Wise. Later, dumbfounded, we were to read a statement made by Wise to the American Jewish Conference in 1943: "We are Americans first and last; and at all times our first and sternest task, in common with all other citizens of our beloved country . . . is to win the anti-fascist war." We failed to see how there could be any conflict between saving the Jews of Europe and being good Americans or Englishmen but we did see how Wise's statement would provide the State Department and the Foreign Office with the alibi they needed not to act on behalf of the Jews.

Our immediate goal in 1942 was to take the campaign out of the synagogues and the Yiddish press, out of the back pages of the daily press, out of the hands of the traditional Jewish leadership, and to make it universal. Ironically, we, the Zionist "extremists," were the ones now calling for broad humanitarian rescue above all. Helping the Jews to survive was all that mattered now.

* * *

No one helped us more in our new campaign than Ben Hecht. None of us had any second thoughts about exposing the hypocrisy and inertia of the Allied leaders, but none of us could do it as effectively as Hecht, and the little that was ultimately achieved by the United States' War Refugee Board was due mostly to his militant involvement. While Stephen Wise was writing his naive "Dear Boss" notes to his idol, President Roosevelt, Hecht was lashing out as hard as he could with his barbed pen.

I first met Ben Hecht in the spring of 1941 in New York. I did not know much about him then except that he had written a number of plays, the most successful being *The Front Page*, which I had found entertaining but nothing more. But, in early 1941, Ben Hecht was the first in the general press to excoriate powerful Jews and the leaders of the free world for turning their eyes from the destruction of the Jews in Europe. In his daily newspaper column, Hecht poured out his anger at the hypocrisy of the gentiles and the cowardice of the Jews. During these same years, *The New York Times* was reporting only sporadically on the killing of Jews in Europe, in tiny, well-hidden news items.

Hillel Kook and 'Irma' Helpren had their first meeting with Hecht in his New York haunt, the "21" Club, and within a few weeks, we knew we had found a voice that would catch America's ear, a voice from outside the Jewish establishment, uninhibited by political and parochial interests. Hecht reacted to events in Europe with a fury commensurate to the enormity of the crimes. Our mission in the United States would not have attained the scope and intensity it did if not for Hecht's gifted pen.

Ben Hecht was rough to tangle with. He had a compassionate heart, covered up by a short temper, a brutal frankness and an acid tongue. Once he decided right from wrong on any issue, he mobilized all his faculties to fight for his beliefs with righteous fury.

At first, his interest in Palestine had been nil and his involvement in all other Jewish matters not much greater. He was about as assimilated as a Jew could be, having grown up in Racine, Wisconsin, and earned his first literary laurels as a Chicago reporter before making it to the top as a Hollywood writer, one who never publicly aligned himself with the Jewish people. But unlike many other creative Jews who lost their roots, throughout the Depression years Hecht had kept some seeds alive in his heart. When the first reports of unrestrained German assaults on Jews reached the United States in 1939, Hecht instinctively identified with the victims, and felt viscerally disturbed by the silence of the successful Jews among whom he lived and worked.

Hecht's mind was as sharp as his tongue. He said that he "wrote with a whip as much as a pencil," but the whip seemed more to me like a scalpel; sometimes it drew another's blood, sometimes his own. He had long been a cynic and a pessimist, but as he rediscovered his Jewish roots, I felt that for all his bitter frustration at the Jewish establishment he found a certain peace and a sense of identity he had never known. Though he would have chuckled at my saying this, no one could have been happier than Hecht when he discovered the stories of Sholem Aleichem.

When I saw that our "Proclamation" was not generating mass public response, I proposed that our delegation recruit Hecht's dramatic talents to break through the apathy and wariness of the Jews of America.

On a cold, icy January day in 1943, Stella Joelson, Saul Collins and I drove out to Hecht's home in Nyack. Though Hecht used the Algonquin Hotel in Manhattan as the base for most of his confrontations with the Eastern literati, he loved his place on the Hudson dearly. Stella Joelson and Saul Collins both had links to the theatre. As we analyzed the latest news from Europe about the extermination, and the recent perfunctory pronouncements by Roosevelt and Churchill, Hecht's clipped comments were like poison darts. We in the *Irgun* had been at work for ten years or more now and Hecht for three years, doing everything in our power, but we had still not succeeded in making ourselves heard where it counted. The Allies insisted that they could not be bothered with secondary issues because they had to concentrate on winning the war. They made no secret of it: saving the Jews of Europe was secondary on their agenda.

Late that evening Hecht agreed that a theatrical representation of the extermination might shake up the Jewish community and exert some pressure on the administration. None of us truly expected momentous results, but we had to try to wake up America. We were grasping at straws. Hecht had an inspiration for a possible dramatic presentation at Madison Square Garden which would also be shown in Washington and elsewhere if it proved to be effective. Thus, the pageant "We Will Never Die" was born. Our delegation came back to Nyack several times during the following weeks, watching in fascination as Hecht's abstract ideas gradually materialized. Hecht immersed himself in research, delving into Jewish history and lore with a vengeance, as if to punish himself for all the years during which he had ignored his heritage.

On March 9, 1943, forty thousand people came to see the pageant in Madison Square Garden. The stage backdrop consisted of two huge tablets three stories high inscribed with the Ten Commandments. Answering a roll call, the great Jewish figures throughout history emerged from the tablets one after another, each carrying a little candle to symbolize the contribution of the Jews to humanity's upward struggle. Moses first appeared, followed by Rabbi Akiba, Don Isaac Abravanel, Maimonides, Spinoza, Pissaro, Sarah Bernhardt and Disraeli. The roll call went on and on, as the stage and tablets shimmered with lighted candles. The staging under the direction of Moss Hart was awe-inspiring, and Kurt Weill's music brilliantly encompassed centuries of Jewish themes. At the climax, the narrator said, "The corpse of a people lies on the steps of civilization. And no voice is heard to cry halt to the slaughter, no government speaks to bid that the murder of millions end. Those of us here tonight have a voice. Let us raise it. Perhaps the dead will hear it and find hope. Perhaps the four freedoms will hear it and find their tongue."

When we staged the pageant in Constitution Hall in Washington, D.C., Ben Hecht added the following words:

> We, the actors who have performed for you tonight, are nearly done. But there is another cast of actors whose performance is not done. This cast is our audience . . . a notable cast, playing vital roles on the stage of history. It is to this audience more than to any group of human beings in the world, that the dead and dying innocents of Europe raise their cry "Remember us!" Two million Jews have been mercilessly destroyed in Europe. Four million surviving Jews are to be destroyed by Christmas, according to the pronouncements of the German government. To utter these words . . . here tonight is to summon you to action.

Eleanor Roosevelt was in the audience, that night, and in her nationally syndicated column for that week she wrote: "No one who heard each group come forward and give the story of what happened to it at the hands of a ruthless German military, will ever forget the haunting words: 'Remember us!'"[1] Chief Justice Harlan F. Stone and six other members of the Supreme Court attended that evening's performance, as did two members of the Cabinet, hundreds of members of Congress, as well as high government officials.

It was all extremely moving, but during the weeks that followed we waited in vain for any action by Roosevelt or Churchill. No immigration barriers were dropped, no gesture was made to show the Germans that Jewish lives mattered to the Allies; not a single serious warning was issued to the Germans; not a single specific

---

[1] The message did not come across to the establishment's historians. Leonard Slater wrote in *The Pledge* (Simon & Schuster, 1970): ". . . playing upon the American fascination with massed pageantry . . . forty thousand people . . . watched a line of shapely chorus girls waving papier-maché tommy-guns . . ." In fact there was no scene of "girls waving machine guns." There was a five-minute scene on the darkened stage, which portrayed a handful of Warsaw Ghetto fighters, matching their pitiful weapons against the Germans.

"We Will Never Die"—Madison Square Garden, March 9, 1943.

State of New York
Executive Chamber

PROCLAMATION

WHEREAS, nearly two million Jews in Nazi-occupied Europe have been murdered in cold blood by the minions of Adolf Hitler; and

WHEREAS, this mass extermination has been in accordance with the official Nazi dogma which calls for the complete enslavement or destruction of all other peoples in violation of the laws of decency and of humanity; and

WHEREAS, the Legislature of the State of New York has passed a resolution condemning these murders and denouncing this ruthless and wholesale murder as an act unparalleled in the annals of civilization; and

WHEREAS, on March ninth, nineteen hundred and forty-three, a Mass Meeting will be held in Madison Square Garden, New York City, in commemoration of the two million murdered Jews in Europe;

NOW, THEREFORE, I, Thomas E. Dewey, Governor of the State of New York, do hereby appoint and proclaim Tuesday, March ninth, nineteen hundred and forty-three, as a day of commemoration of the two million Jews who have been brutally massacred; and

GIVEN under my hand and the Privy Seal of the State at the Capitol in the City of Albany this sixth day of March in the year of our Lord one thousand nine hundred and forty-three.

BY THE GOVERNOR:

Secretary to the Governor.

Governor Thomas E. Dewey's proclamation on the occasion of the pageant "We Will Never Die" staged in Madison Square Garden, New York.

United States Senate
COMMITTEE ON FOREIGN RELATIONS

August 1, 1944

Mr. Harry Louis Selden
American League for a Free Palestine, Inc.
11 West Forty-second Street
New York 18, New York

My dear Mr. Selden:

On my return to the office today, my secretary called my attention to correspondence had with you during my absence and particularly referring to your letter of July twenty-fifth in which inquiry was made as to whether or not Dr. Stephen S. Wise was responsible for the introduction of the Gillette - Rogers Resolution in the Congress which resulted in the creation of the War Refugee Board.

In reply may I say that Dr. Wise had nothing to do with the development of action looking to the introduction of these Resolutions so far as I am concerned personally. My part in the matter came as the result of a meeting called by a group which was organizing a Washington branch of the Emergency Committee to save the Jews of Europe. As a result of conference held with this group a decision was reached to ask for the introduction of a Resolution covering the subject matter and Representative Rogers agreed to sponsor the Resolution in the House of Representatives and I agreed to sponsor such a Resolution in the Senate. With this sponsorship, I associated some of my colleagues. I had no conference with Dr. Wise on the matter until some time after the Resolution was introduced when Dr. Wise called at my office accompanied by two or three other gentlemen and discussed the pending Resolutions with me. None of these gentlemen seemed to be enthusiastic for the passage of the Resolution and the tenor of the conversation seemed to suggest their belief that the notion as proposed by the Resolution was not a wise step to take, although they professed very strong interest in everything that would look to the saving of the remnant of the Jewish people in Europe from destruction.

Very sincerely,

GUY M. GILLETTE

Senator Gillette and the War Refugee Board.

act of retaliation undertaken. When the Luftwaffe bombed the open cities of the British Isles, the Allies responded with dramatic swiftness, but when millions of Jews were being massacred, the Allies were masters of restraint and circumspection. The rails leading to the extermination camps were not bombed, nor were the camps themselves, and the trains to Treblinka and Auschwitz kept on rolling unimpeded.

There were chances to purchase Jewish lives from the Nazis with hard cash, food and trucks—but the Allies maintained that these expenditures would have reduced the chances for victory. To defend this inaction of the Allies, both the State Department and the British Foreign Office circulated internal memos insisting that the reports of atrocities committed by the Nazis were being greatly exaggerated. When there was still time enough to take Jews out of the Balkans, Hungary and Slovakia, and place them in temporary camps in Canada, the United States and Australia, British Foreign Minister Anthony Eden claimed that there was no transportation available for the refugees; besides the Germans would plant agents into the transports. And the State Department's main objection was that thousands of Jewish refugees would aggravate food shortages in the United States. This sounded like Hans Frank, the Nazi Governor General of Poland, who, in December, 1941, had complained that "the Jews represent for us too extraordinarily malignant gluttons."

Breckenridge Long of the State Department, known sympathizer of totalitarianism, also feared that agitation to save Jews would only strengthen Hitler's claim that this was a "Jewish war." The reality was that, by ignoring the Jews, the Allies were proving Hitler's theory that the Jews were of no value and stoking the fires in the extermination camps.

However, our "Proclamation" and "We Will Never Die" did prepare public opinion for more concrete action. They brought America's Jews into the streets and halls asking for action and attracted the attention of the press, making Roosevelt uncomfortable, and irritating the British. And at long last they prodded the Jewish establishment, especially the Zionists, to start imitating us with rallies, pressure on the administration and organized political lobbying. In short, they finally made the fight to save Jewish lives "respectable."

By January 1943, Roosevelt and Anthony Eden felt the mounting pressure of public opinion sufficiently to arrange for a conference in Bermuda to tackle the "refugee problem." On the eve of the Bermuda Conference, we ran an ad in several major papers containing an appeal by Ben Hecht to "The Four Freedoms, Care of the United Nations leaders," in which Hecht reported on the latest news from Romania: "Romania was willing to 'sell seventy thousand Jews at $50 apiece.'" The State Department and the Jewish establishment denied that such an offer existed. Stephen Wise actually called our appeal "a hoax on the part of the Hecht group." Furthermore, he estimated the total cost of assembling, transporting and ransoming seventy thousand Jews to be about thirty million dollars, which was "prohibitive." This was reminiscent of Eliezer Kaplan, the treasurer of the Jewish Agency Executive, who, at a meeting in Jerusalem in 1942, complained about Yizhak Greenbaum having spent 100 pound sterling on cables to leaders in the diaspora, attempting to corroborate information on the extermination. Kaplan insisted that 50 pounds sterling would have sufficed.

By the fall of 1943, when the United States Government and Stephen Wise finally admitted that such an offer had even existed, it no longer did.

On April 20, 1943, as the Bermuda conference was to open, we ran a full page advertisement in the *Washington Post* with this headline: "On the field of battle, soldiers die . . . on the field of massacres, civilization dies!" We proposed that the conference create a United Nations agency staffed by military and diplomatic experts who would embark on a two-pronged program: first, to follow up immediately all possibilities of rescuing Jews by taking them "to Palestine or to any temporary refuge;" and second to create immediately a Jewish Army of stateless and Palestinian Jews. This army would include "suicide" commando units which would raid deep into Germany, and air squadrons for retaliatory bombing. On April 30th, at the conference's end, Myron C. Taylor cabled Hull, Long and Sumner Welles, the top echelon of the State Department, saying: "The Bermuda Conference was wholly ineffective as I view it, and *we knew it would be.*" As a tactic to delay public outrage the final report was withheld until December, although Jews were being annihilated at the rate of two hundred thousand or more per month. It was while the representatives of the Allies met in Bermuda that S.S. General Jurgen Stroop opened the final offensive to liquidate the Warsaw ghetto. While the handful of Jewish resistors in the ghetto flew their banner "We shall fight to the end," the representatives in the splendid Hotel Horizons talked, and talked to the end. And later, Richard Law, the top British delegate at the conference, made his report to the British Cabinet:

> The Americans . . . dare not offend 'American' opinion (which is fearful of alien immigration) . . . if it comes to a showdown, Jew and Gentile, I am satisfied that their internal position is such that they would have to tell the Jewish organizations to go to hell.

He was right. As recently as July, 1942, one American in six had told pollsters that Hitler was "doing the right thing" to the Jews. Other polls reported that Jews were more unpopular than Germans or Japanese. Roosevelt knew all this, so United States immigration quotas similar to all other democracies stayed as they were.

The United States had admitted about one hundred and sixty thousand Jews between 1937 and 1943, and it did not want more.

And though the Arabs had turned against Britain in the war, the British held fast to their old excuse for keeping the doors of Palestine closed—they did not want to antagonize the Arabs. The truth was that whatever damage the Arabs were going to do in Syria, Lebanon, Iraq and Egypt had already been done.

But the Colonial Office already made plans for after the war. Surviving Jews, especially militarily trained, were potential enemies so of course it was safer to let them die than to create an army of them.

The Bermuda Conference had been only a flimsy curtain behind which Washington and London hid their inaction, and even tried to hide the facts of the extermination. As if this were the Evian Conference of 1938 all over again, Harold Dodds, the chief American delegate, never once mentioned "Jews" in his opening or closing remarks.

Through Hitler's reign of terror, the Jews were expected to do nothing but remain quiet, and the overwhelming majority did. As Ben Hecht wrote in 1943:

> Four million Jews waiting for death
> Oh, hang and burn out—Quiet Jews!
> Don't be bothersome; save your breath—
> The world is busy with other news.
>
> Oh world be patient—it will take
> Sometime before the murder crews
> are done. By Christmas you can make
> Your Peace on Earth, without the Jews.

After the Bermuda Conference, we headlined an ad in *The New York Times*, "To five million Jews in the Nazi death-trap, Bermuda was a Cruel Mockery." As we hoped we would, we touched a nerve, and a storm of protest against us broke loose, whipped up by Senator Scott Lucas, who had just returned from the conference. The debate which then broke out on the Senate floor revolved mostly around Senator Lucas' hurt feelings. Lucas declared before the Senate that no one could accuse him of not caring for the Jews of Europe, since "some of my best friends are members of the Jewish faith." In May, 1943, this was considered a forthright and courageous statement. Without knowing the facts or understanding the historic issues, Lucas' colleagues rose up on the floor and several, including Harry S. Truman, announced their withdrawal from the Committee for a Jewish Army. How could our ad have dared to state "It was almost improper to mention the word Jew?" Lucas called this a "diabolical untruth," and wanted to know how we knew what had been said or not said at the Conference. (We did have friends who had attended.) While Eichmann's Germans daily herded thousands into the shuttle trains to the extermination camps, while David Wdowinski and his comrades were retreating from bunker to bunker in the Warsaw ghetto, the members of the United States Senate were patting each other on the back in a show of support for each other's fine efforts.

On May 7, 1943, while the debate was continuing on the floor, Hillel Kook wrote to Senator Edwin C. Johnson:

> President Roosevelt called this a war . . . for the survival of human liberties; for the survival of human freedom; for the survival of world civilization and the dignity of the human race . . .

Let not the day of victory come and find seven million Jewish corpses in Europe.

When the day finally came, six million Jewish corpses were found.

VII

The Revolt

Nineteen forty-three was one of the most difficult years of my life; every day thousands of our people were being killed, and yet many people still saw the war and the extermination as two separate events. For the disciples of Jabotinsky, they were irrevocably linked. We never let up our agitation, no matter how much it disturbed the Zionist Establishment, the White House and the State Department. The British tried to ignore us, but nevertheless prodded the United States government to see that we were stifled, and the State Department, backed by the Jewish-Zionist Establishment, did their best to oblige them. But it did not work. With the war prospects looking better for the Allies, people were now listening to issues apart from the daily pursuits of the war, and we could see that we were at last having some impact.

Simultaneously, Ben Hecht's "We Will Never Die" was being performed, and our "Proclamation" campaign was in full swing. When Bernard Baruch phoned Ben Hecht and asked him on behalf of President Roosevelt for a respite in our advertisments and public demonstrations, we knew that the administration was feeling our pressure. When Rabbi Wise and Nahum Goldmann visited Breckenridge Long one of the main subjects of discussion was our campaign. The one issue on which the State Department and the American Jewish establishment were in complete agreement was their mutual wish to silence us.[1] By mid-1943, the

---

[1] According to the transcripts of these meeting, made public twenty-five years later under the Freedom of Inforation Act, Wise and Goldmann again stated that our "program of advertising and demonstrations were severely criticized by other Jewish organizations," and that only the American Jewish Congress and Dr. Wise were the proper persons with whom State should deal.

chairman of the Committee for a Jewish Army, Senator Edwin C. Johnson of Colorado, had called for an "emergency conference to save the Jewish people of Europe."

Oddly, Wise and Goldmann did not like the fact that our committee (and the conference) was a "body composed of a lot of persons who were not Jews."[1] Apparently, in their opinions, the killing of millions of Jews was only to concern Jews. We met on July 27 in New York, and emerged with a basic program of pressure for political and military action by the United Nations; approaches to Axis satellite governments to permit Jews to emigrate; and appeals to neutral countries to open their doors for transit and asylum. If we could carry through these concessions, we would have a chance to save countless numbers of Jews; the transportation panel of the conference stated that idle neutral shipping lying in United Nations ports was available for fifty thousand persons per month.

We summarized the proposals of the Conference in ads in the New York Times (8/30/43) and throughout the country. We captioned them:

"WE ALL STAND BEFORE THE BAR OF HUMANITY, HISTORY AND GOD!

"WE WILL ALL BE JUDGED IF WE DO NOT CREATE THE MACHINERY TO SAVE THE JEWISH PEOPLE OF EUROPE."

We listed twelve major recommendations for steps to be taken for rescue, refuge and retaliation.

The conference to Save the Jewish People of Europe definitely touched a sensitive chord somewhere, because while it was in progress Dr. Max Lerner, the resolution committee's chairman, received messages from President Roosevelt and Secretary Hull to the effect that "The rescue of the Jewish people of Europe . . . is under constant examination by the State Department." In reality, these messages amounted to delaying tactics, because as far as we could see, the "examinations" never produced any results.

---

[1]Documents of U.S. Government agencies, referred to throughout this work are available at the Institute for Mediterranean Affairs, 428 E. 84th Street, New York, N.Y.

Throughout those months in mid-1943 an informal dialogue continued within our delegation. Eri Jabotinsky insisted there was a conspiracy of inaction led by the British, abetted by the State Department and possibly the White House, despite its messages of good faith and cooperation. Eri predicted that nothing would result from our campaign in the United States unless we exposed this conspiracy and the Jewish establishment's acquiescence with it.[1] Eri further maintained that unorthodox steps had to be taken to attract attention to the events in Europe and the physical possibilities of rescuing Jews. He proposed setting up bases in Turkey and throughout the Balkans. Meissner, Ariel and other men of ours were still alive and active in Romania, and Eri felt that once in Turkey he could reestablish contact with them. Romanians were offering to "sell" Jews, and if they were willing, why wouldn't other countries be as well? What was happening in Hungary? Could we act there?

After David Raziel's death, our communications from Palestine were erratic, so we could not keep track of all that was going on at home. The remaining units of the *Irgun*—those who had neither enlisted in the British forces nor joined the seceding

---

[1] In a lecture at the Hebew University of Jerusalem in 1972, Sir Isaiah Berlin discussed Zionist politics in wartime Washington. Berlin had been Weizmann's friend and pupil, and had spent the war years in the United States as a "public information specialist" of the British Ministry of Information. Berlin was in charge of reporting to the Foreign Office about public opinion developments throughout the United States. In 1942 he happily reported to London that "Zionist attacks on the British government virtually died down, save for the campaign for a Jewish army, conducted most vehemently by revisionists and their allies, both Jews . . . and their liberal gentile sympathizers." In one of his reports, he referred to the impressive march of the rabbis on Washington, who in the fall of 1943 were received by the Vice President of the United States on the steps of the Capitol as "the notorious march of rabbis." He stated in a later report to London that "the quarrel is between the majority of American Jews and HMG, not between the American public and Britain." In his lecture, Berlin scarcely made mention of the key issue during those years, which from 1942 on caused an ever more acute confrontation between Britain and the Jews in Palestine and the United States: the gruesome news of the extermination.

Even as Jewish resentment was growing against British policies, Berlin reported to his superiors in London that Weizmann had frequently announced that as long as he was in charge of the movement, "there will be no breach with Britain."

In 1979 Berlin wrote to a research student in Jerusalem: "As for the Holocaust, I know no more than was printed in the American press, and that was astonishingly unprominent, despite Revisionist agitation, the real news of what was going on did not . . . seriously penetrate the general Jewish, still less non-Jewish, public until after the war." Berlin's paucity of information is the more fascinating since "the Zionists I saw . . . were Dr. Weizmann, Goldmann, Arthur Lourie . . . Eliahu Elath and Moshe Sharett (then Shertok)."

Lehi—were floundering, ideologically and organizationally. We had read issues of the *Irgun*'s new underground publication *Herut* (Freedom), and we saw in it the same sense of frustration with the Allies, and above all with Britain, that we in the United States constantly experienced.

Arieh Ben-Eliezer reminded us that he had close friends among the *Lehi* people who had split from the *Irgun*. The leader of *Lehi*, Abraham Stern, had been shot to death by British police in his Tel-Aviv home in 1942, so now was as opportune a time as any to reunite the underground. Ben-Eliezer felt that one of us must return immediately to Palestine to establish a closer interchange. I agreed, saying that otherwise we were in danger of becoming politically and ideologically a "lost battalion" here in the United States. We realized long ago that an Allied victory would not mean instant deliverance for the Jews; our only hope to save the remnants of our people and assure their future independence was to commence to make things as rough as possible for the British in Palestine, even if it took all our resources. The question was exactly how.

Hillel Kook agreed that while Europe and Palestine were the front lines, Washington and the United States were just as important, and that public opinion in the United States would play a decisive role. We were aware that the indifference and open hostility that non-Jews in the street showed toward Jewish issues, was being gradually replaced with feelings of guilt for what the Germans had been allowed to do to the Jews. One thing was clear—our work had to reach an even greater populace and Kook was just the one to do it. A master public relations man in the American mold, he had unlimited *chutzpah*. He had an ability to accept defeats with little emotion. He would retreat and lick his wounds, and the next day he would be ready for the next round. If he had any flaw, it might have been that he was slow to accept new ideas. He would ponder and stray and equivocate, but once he accepted an approach, he would carry it out tenaciously.

Sam Merlin's main recommendations were that we focus our energies on political education and public information; Hebrew independence and statehood needed to be popularized for the American public. We had to explain that the British had to get out of Palestine because they continued to occupy it illegally. The

Class A Mandate, linked to the Balfour Declaration, was meant to bring about independence to the reborn Hebrew nation. To focus the public's attention and to properly represent this historical act Merlin proposed a "Free Palestine Committee" along the lines of the Free French and other liberation bodies around the world. I agreed and also recommended a large-scale, non-sectarian "League for Palestine" which would back up the Committee's work. In a year or two the war would be over, and we had to be well under way by then, to face the British.

Alex Rafaeli pointed out the friendship and understanding we had found among Chinese, Indians, Koreans, Yugoslavs, Czechs and other exiles in the United States, and said that we needed to attend international gatherings to present the cause of Hebrew independence in a militant style, without the self-deprecating restraint of traditional Zionism. When the war was over, and the nations of the free world met to decide the future, we had to make sure that the reborn Hebrew nation was represented forcefully and with dignity.

Nor were we ready to give up our rescue work. We had to carry on relentlessly, and every soul we could save would be one more bit of help in overthrowing the British. Only by gathering up the remnants of our people, and tightening our contacts with the homeland, could we possibly have a chance to win freedom.

We knew we did not have reliable friends in the White House and the State Department, and that we had to try to work through Congress.

By the summer of 1943, the war was turning in favor of the Allies. They were even planning for the day their troops would land on the west coast of the continent. In a matter of months, they hoped that this "second front" would sweep over the Reich and join forces with the Russians who were advancing from the east, and shatter the Third Reich's dream of a thousand year reign. By then, we knew it would be too late for the Jews in Europe. Furthermore we did not see any chance of a basic change in Britain's policies after the war. As of 1943, they were again confiscating weapons from the *Haganah*. We were aware of Churchill's proclaimed sympathies toward the rebirth of the Hebrew nation in Palestine, but we doubted his resoluteness and whether he would face up to the Colonial and Foreign Offices. We remembered that Churchill had been responsible for truncating Palestine in 1922, and we had our reservations that he would be a steadfast friend in times of crisis. After the tide turned in North Africa in late 1942, we carefully watched the reactions of the British in Palestine; we felt certian that the moment the Colonial Office was again in a position to act out of strength, we would face the same policy that had given birth to the White Paper of 1939; control of the Near East by using local puppets and manipulating contradictory interests—true to the Roman Senate's old maxim—*Divide et Impera.* Perhaps the Jews in Palestine would be allowed to become a substantial minority, strong enough to deter Arab attempts to control the country and surrounding lands, but not strong enough to determine their own political future. I never believed that these policies were dictated by anti-Semitism, at the high levels of government, though it was well-known that most British officials liked the Jews less than they liked the Arabs. But contrary to United States officials and functionaries who were anti-Semitic out of sheer provincialism and ignorance, Anthony Eden and others at the top of the British hierarchy were above all Empire-minded. From Churchill on down, their first motivation over all humanitarian considerations was always national self-interest. Jabotinsky himself had not become convinced of this until 1938, and the Jewish leadership under Weizmann did not see it in so simple a light even now. But in the twenties and thirties, we in Palestine had seen how the British Colonials used Pan-Arabism as well as religious and clan interests, to strengthen their hold of the temporary Mandatory trust, with the ultimate goal of perpetuating British rule. "Colonial interests" were what had dictated closing immigration during the war, leaving millions of Jews to be murdered.

The riots of 1920, 1921, 1929 and 1936 in Palestine causing so much suffering to us, were also the direct result of the British machinations.

In 1937, the *Irgun* had voted for armed resistance against the British, but when the war broke out in 1939, defeating the Nazis became the priority; under Raziel's and Jabotinsky's leadership, a unilateral cease-fire had gone into effect. Our battle continued only through diplomatic channels and pressure groups like our delegation to the United States. Now, however, with the end of war against Germany in sight, it was time to prepare again for our ultimate goal: independence and statehood.

It was going to be difficult for us at every turn, though. The British were not all we had to worry about. As long as the war continued, the Colonial Office could convince Washington that it was vital for the Allies to keep the gates of Palestine shut, so the powerful Arabs would not be antagonized. Washington would go along quickly enough because the American policy was to court Saudi-Arabia and the other Arab potentates for their oil. The "Jewish leadership," concerned with keeping control over all Jewish affairs, would fight us tooth and nail. Only one thing really had changed—there were four million fewer Jews in the world, which made it easier for Britain to ignore the Mandate's obligations, and which must have eased Dr. Weizmann's mind about all the Jews "of Nalewki and Djinka" flooding Palestine, since most of them were dead. The British could now hope to show the world the "absurdity" of our desires: "Independence for a non-existent Hebrew nation? A nation of dead people?"

So, knowing that the British would never be talked into accepting Hebrew independence, knowing that Washington's political help would be at best minimal and knowing that our own brothers in the establishment would do nothing at all to help, we decided to chart and follow our own course. Armed struggle with the British was now unavoidable.

But we lacked the organization, the funds and weapons to mount a sustained military campaign in Palestine on our own. At some point, without moral, political and material support from the United States, we would simply come up short. If our revolution was to have a chance, we had to cultivate whatever support we could for it in the United States; if not from the government, at least from American Jewish and non-Jewish sympathizers.

If nothing else, our campaign in the United States had brought us a small devoted circle of friends, as well as a great deal of experience. We had a feel now for just what the people and the government of the United States would or would not do to help. It was not much help that we would get, but without it, we were doomed to fail.

We saw some proof of our limited success when Senator Edwin Johnson was approached by emissaries from the White House on

September 25, 1943. Johnson sent us a letter in New York with the following message:

> President Roosevelt invited King Saud of Saudi-Arabia to visit the United States. His son . . . and six princes will arrive in America about October 5th. Confidentially, The State Department is hopeful that no one in this country will raise embarrassing issues regarding Near East policy while our officially-invited guests are here, and that all organizations will refrain from public criticism and advertising.

Perhaps we were not really piquing the government's conscience, but we were becoming nettlesome enough to need to be silenced, even temporarily.

It took several months to get our plans underway. Arieh Ben-Eliezer left for Turkey via Palestine, officially to do rescue work; his main mission, though, was to prepare the underground for the coming revolution. Eri Jabotinsky was to follow him to Turkey to reestablish contacts for rescue work in the Balkans. We also decided that Alex Rafaeli and I were to join the United States Army; as we were of military age, we were having trouble explaining our presence in America without joining the Allied forces. We did not feel it was worth the effort, risk or cost to try and reach Palestine where we could have volunteered for service under British command.

It was difficult enough to obtain transportation for Eri and Ben-Eliezer to the Near East, and we were not sure how the British would react to any of us. We did not want too many of our people in the lion's den at once. While Alex and I went into the service, Kook and Merlin stayed in the United States to carry on their work, fighting off attempts to deport them as best they could. Up until the time we joined the army, Rafaeli took charge of mobilizing local activists to manage our spreading network of organizations, and I finished the "We Will Never Die" tour and helped strengthen our New York headquarters.

By November, Rafaeli and I were both in American army uniforms. The first phase of the *Irgun* mission to the United States was over.

* * *

On October 17, 1943, Arieh Ben-Eliezer reached Palestine and reestablished the link between our "Lost Battalion" and the homeland after more than two years of broken communications. In the following months he played a key role in revitalizing the *Irgun*, staying at Menahem Begin's side during the period when Begin assumed command, and helping him lay the foundations for the revolt.

Thousands of young Jewish Palestinians were now serving in the Allied forces, and more than a million Jews were fighting in the uniforms of a score of different nations. Units composed almost entirely of Jews suffered heavy casualties in the North African campaign. A thousand Palstinian Jewish soldiers helped defend Bir Hakim in June 1942 as part of a Free French Brigade.[1]

But, if nothing else, the Jews of Palestine in British uniforms received good military training and occasionally had a chance to "liberate weapons and put them away for other battles still to come.

When Ben-Eliezer talked to the young *Irgun* members in Palestine, he found that though their spirits were temporarily low, their dreams were still alive. The older members had drifted in different directions; some had entered the British forces, others, disappointed by internal feuding and embittered by a floundering leadership had withdrawn from all activities and a few had kept in touch with Yaakov Meridor, who was doing whatever he could to keep the *Irgun* alive. It was the emerging youth, though, in whom our best hopes rested, and Ben-Eliezer's reports of a nucleus more willing than ever to fight for freedom were gratifying. Herzl and even Jabotinsky had never hoped for a massive response from the masses. Herzl had believed that the Jewish people needed powerful leadership because they lacked political understanding and the ability to act forcefully; Jabotinsky had trusted the Jewish masses

---

[1] Although the Jews had begged the Allies in vain for rescue, they unwaveringly joined in to help the Allies defeat the Nazis. In Palestine, Hebrew youths voluntarily donned the uniforms of their British oppressors, while the police still barred the gates of their homeland, scrawling swastikas on their helmets and on the walls in Jerusalem and Tel-Aviv. Yet it took worldwide public criticism and intervention before the Free French admitted Jews as officers or non-commissioned officers to combat units. And when they established control in North Africa, they introduced quotas for Jewish physicians and other professions. In British units, Jews were often considered "former enemy aliens," and assigned to work battalions instead of combat troops.

and the youth more, but even he did not anticipate how selflessly they would respond to the call for revolution, how completely they would be ready to sacrifice themselves. Ben-Eliezer wrote to us that the spirit of Shlomo Ben Yosef was alive.

But when Ben-Eliezer went out to see the leaders of the *Yishuv*, the results were disheartening. He met with the *Haganah* leader Eliahu Golomb, a "friend" of ours from way back, and their first talk was amiable enough. Ben-Eliezer suggested an intensified joint effort on rescue work in the Balkans. He expressed his shock to have learned from Mr. Knox, the acting Secretary of the British administration, that thirty thousand immigration certificates had not been used. (Knox told him: "The Jewish Agency leaders said they knew about them but advised the administration that they were holding them back for use after the war.")[1] Ben-Eliezer proposed a joint campaign to create a Jewish air squadrons to bomb the extermination camps, as well as cities in Germany; he also proposed collaborating on massive civil disobedience in Palestine, ending in armed resistance if the British still kept the ports closed. He told Golomb how we were mobilizing public opinion in America to back these demands and actions, and in the course of the discussion he laid bare our plans and described in detail our political campaign in the United States.

Golomb was aware of a restlessness in the *Haganah* due to the unbending British policies and the defeatism of the Jewish Agency leaders. He knew that a group of *Haganah* men had contacted the *Irgun* earlier in the year with a plan to occupy the British High Commissioner's office (and take him hostage). Golomb listened carefully, probing him in a gentle, friendly manner.

The second meeting, however, took place in a different mood. Golomb attacked the *Irgun* delegation to the United States, saying that cooperation with us was impossible because of our aggressive, damaging independent activities in the United States. Ben-Eliezer could only guess whether their first meeting had been innocently friendly, or whether Golomb's only purpose had been to have Ben-Eliezer lay out our plans so that the Jewish Agency could fight us better. In any event, the discussions came to nothing.

---

[1] Draft of Ben-Eliezer's unfinished memoirs; Jabotinsky Institute, Tel-Aviv.

Ben-Eliezer then met with Itzhak Ben-Zvi, the head of the *Yishuv*'s Natonal Council, and the results were the same. Ben-Zvi maintained that the *Irgun* had no reason to exist, and we were only adversely affecting relations with the British. Our agitation in the United States, according to Ben-Zvi, was giving the Zionist movement a black eye, and killing its fundraising efforts. Ben-Zvi concluded that all our members should join the British army and submit to the parallel discipline of the *Haganah*.

Next Ben-Eliezer tried to revive relations with the *Lehi* but that proved a failure. There was still too much distrust between the two groups. The *Irgun* had no choice but to go it alone.

The question then became who would lead the *Irgun*. Meridor was undoubtedly one of the most courageous men we ever had, and since Raziel's death he had assumed many of Raziel's duties. But he lacked the magnetism necessary to lead us at this critical juncture in history. He himself admitted this in conversation with Ben-Eliezer. In his reports to us, Ben-Eliezer mentioned the possible choices for a new commander, among them Hillel Kook and Ben-Eliezer himself. In the end, though, the candidacy of Menahem Begin, the leader of the Polish *Betar* prevailed. But he adamantly refused to assume formal control until he obtained his official discharge from the Polish army.[1]

Most of us who were veterans of the Jabotinsky movement knew and respected Begin. A fiery orator with a sense for political foresight, it was he who at the world *Betar* conference in the fall of 1938, called for the evolution of political activism into "Military Zionism." After the German invasion of Poland, Begin had left Warsaw via Vilna and had gone through detention in Russian labor camps in Siberia. In 1942, he reached Palestine as a soldier of the Polish army in exile. His writing in the local *Betar* publications under the pen name of "Ben Zeev," attracted great attention from the leaders of the *Irgun*, and a consensus had emerged to choose him as commander even before Ben-Eliezer's arrival.

Begin adamantly insisted on an honorable discharge from the Polish army; Ben-Eliezer played a decisive role in this. After six

---

[1] Myths, especially derogatory ones, never seem to die, no matter what evidence is amassed to disprove them. In Howard M. Sachar's *A History of Israel* (Knopf, New York, 1976), page 266, he incorrectly reports that Begin, "upon reaching Palestine with this [Polish] force, promptly deserted.")

weeks of intensive negotiations with the Polish military, they agreed to honorable discharges for five men so they could help us promote the evacuation of Polish Jews who had found shelter in Russia. Begin was one of the five. In turn, Ben-Eliezer promised that we in the United States, using our contacts and experiences in the American political arena would do our best to win support for the London-based Polish government in exile. It was a good, sound political deal for all concerned.

Begin's discharge was a decisive step in our preparation for the expulsion of the British. He immediately moved from Jerusalem to Tel-Aviv, and went underground as commander of the *Irgun*. Ben-Eliezer, on the surface still functioning as representative of our United States Emergency Committee to save the Jewish people of Europe, spent months in intimate collaboration with Begin, in long nightly walks along the beach in Tel-Aviv, defining the future path of the revolution.

They agreed on several basic points: Our political aims would be realized only if accompanied by a military struggle; the British had to be made aware that they could not remain in Palestine except with the consent of the Hebrew population; we had to start immediately laying a foundation for a provisional Hebrew government; we had to ask the Arabs to avoid civil strife at all costs, either to join us in the battle or at least to stay neutral; we needed to intensify our efforts in Turkey, the Balkans and the United States to open the gates for immigration to Palestine. If everything worked out, the last step would be the establishment of the Hebrew state.

Ben-Eliezer later told me that at the end of their deliberations Begin showed him a typewritten text outlining a proposed declaration of revolt by the *Irgun*. Though Begin had drafted it months earlier it repeated almost verbatim the platform we had come up with in New York, as well as the one the two of them had arrived at in Tel-Aviv.

Now the plans began to go into action. A new command was formed: Begin, Ben-Eliezer, Lankin, Shlomo Levi and, after a short furlough, Meridor.

Ben-Eliezer then approached Professor Joseph Klausner, my old teacher at the University of Jerusalem, and asked him if he would head a Provisional Hebrew Government-in-Exile when the time was ripe for it. Klausner was venerated by the nationalist youth of Palestine, and we could think of no better candidate for the Provisional Presidency than the kindly historian who with such insight and exuberance had introduced us to the turbulent years of the Second Temple. Beginning with the first Zionist Congress, Klausner had fought for Hebrew independence for all his adult life.

Ben-Eliezer told him about our plans and Klausner and his wife listened with great emotion. The Klausners asked for a few days to think it over. At the next meeting, the seventy-two year old Klausner took Ben-Eliezer's hands, and in a trembling voice explained that he was heartbroken to turn such a great honor down, but he and his wife were simply no longer strong enough for strenuous traveling. Still, he would give the *Irgun* all the support he could. From my own experience with Klausner in the thirties, when I had invited him to participate with us in protest demonstrations in Jerusalem, I knew that if it had come to open rebellion, my frail, goateed teacher would have joined the youth on the barricades.[1]

The next step was a thorough public reeducation program. Amazingly, despite the war, people of the *Yishuv* were acting as if it were a time of plenty. General Rommel's defeat at the gateway to the Near East had somehow convinced them all their problems were over, and escapism was the order of the day. The atrocities in Europe were played down by the leadership, and though the people could not help but be more and more aware of the tragedy, they flocked to the theatres and movies, filled the dance halls and whooped it up at sports events. Ben-Eliezer wrote later: "The population was anesthetized. It was put to sleep by its own prosperity; by enthusiasm for the glorious victories of the Russian armies; by promise of a redeeming day of Hebrew renaissance after the Allied victory. We in the United States are shaking the rafters in congress . . . hammering at the public about the events in Europe, and here in the homeland the *Yishuv* leads an escapist, pleasure-seeking life."

The *Yishuv* had been virtually hypnotized by its leaders, and

---

[1] Professor Klausner lived to see independence gained in 1948. In the first presidental elections of the State of Israel he was the nationalist movement's candidate.

the *Irgun* saw that it would have to bring the people back to consciousness before they could comprehend a revolution. We would have to use body and pen and sword. Begin and Ben-Eliezer were assigned "the pen," and Meridor, Lankin, and Levi "the sword."

We all agreed that our declaration of revolt should have come much earlier, probably at the end of 1942 or early 1943, when the extermination was known as a daily, systematic process and Britain still showed no sign that it would alter its White Paper policy. But neither the *Irgun* nor the war situation had been ready for it. Now, however, North Africa and the Near East were safe, and for the British to use the Arab factor as an excuse was no longer defensible. The Arabs had already done whatever harm they could; from King Farouk of Egypt to Rashid Ghaliani of Iraq, they had made repeated overtures to the Axis and had often fought under its banner. In 1941-42, when the Arabs believed that the Axis would win, they welcomed it wholeheartedly but now that the Allies were winning, the Arabs were not about to bite the hand that might soon feed them. It would have been logical then, for the British to try and activate the emerging Hebrew nation as a full ally. But Churchill himself seemed adamant in his refusal to consider Hebrew statehood till after the war, never recognizing that the Allied war effort could have benefitted from an all-out mobilization of a proud Jewish people.

We unanimously agreed that our declaration of revolt could not wait any longer though we had a paucity of trained personnel and material. Only a few months earlier, a retaliatory attack by the *Irgun* on the pro-Nazi *Templer* colonists of Sarona[1] had been called off because of our limitations.

Four years after the cease-fire declared on September 1, 1939, by Jabotinsky and Raziel, the *Irgun* went into battle. It mustered four hundred men and women against the British Empire. Our weapons were several dozen handguns, some machine guns and a half a ton of explosives. The treasury contained approximately three thousand dollars. For communications we had a small

---

[1] The German Templer movement (1868), established German settlements, under Ottoman rule in Jaffa, Sarona, Haifa and Jerusalem which became centers of pro-Nazi activities in the 1930s.

transmitter and a paper called *Herut* which appeared intermittently. Training courses were going on in about a dozen towns and villages, and a few individual soldiers were scattered around the country.

But the *Irgun* had unlimited faith and it had at least one resource in abundance: the willingness of its soldiers to give their lives for independence.

* * *

The Hebrew revolt in Palestine was proclaimed on February 1, 1944, in a lengthy document posted on walls and kiosks throughout the country. Not many understood, though, that the launching of this war will end only with Independence.

The Proclamation of Revolt was divided in three parts. The first summarized and analyzed significant events in the first four years of the war; the cease-fire the *Irgun* had observed since September 1, 1939; the contribution the *Yishuv* had made to the war effort and actions by the Nazis and the British which had affected the Jews in Europe.

The second part was more emotional. It concluded that after four years of war and millions of its people dead, the Hebrew nation was not being given international recognition; it was still not allowed to form an army, and the gates to its homeland were still closed to survivors. Consequently, the British had no moral right to occupy Palestine and the armistice between its administration and the Hebrew nation was hereby at an end. "The war," the document announced, "will cause many painful casualties . . . but we shall go forward, knowing that we are faithful to our tortured and decimated brethren, since it is for them we are fighting."

Then the Proclamation defined the goals of the revolution: the government of Palestine was to be turned over to a Provisional Hebrew Government; a Hebrew army would be formed; the Jews in Europe would be evacuated to Palestine; peaceful relations with its neighbors would be established; full, equal rights would be granted to the Arab population, and extra-territorial status

Press Conference (Washington, D.C., May 1944) announcing the creation of HCNL. This event was described by establishment historias—"[Kook] and his colleagues strode in wearing black shirts and boots . . ." (Am. Jewish Archives, Nov. 1976).

Headquarters of the Hebrew Committee of National Liberation, Washington, D.C., 1944.

Arieh Ben-Eliezer. Joined the *Irgun* in 1936. Member of the HCNL and the Irgun High Command (1943-48).

U.S. Senator Guy M. Gillette.

would be given to the holy places of Christians and Moslems.[1]

Coordinated military actions by the *Irgun* began simultaneously with the Proclamation. The actions were carefully planned to disrupt the administration in specific ways: British arms were confiscated, their immigration, income tax and land registry offices were bombed, as were C.I.D. Headquarters, police stations, rail transportation, army properties, aircraft and airfields. The attacks on government offices were usually carried out after working hours, and warning signs were first tacked on entrances of the buildings. It was a war in which unusual consideration was shown for human lives.[2]

By April, 1944, it was dawning on the administration and the Zionist establishment that the *Irgun* was capable of carrying out its revolt. The British began an all-out campaign to destroy the organization, arresting hundreds of *Irgun* soldiers and suspected sympathizers. One of the first arrested was Ben-Eliezer.

When Ben-Eliezer had returned to Palestine from the United States, we intended his stay to be limited. He would reestablish communications, help organize the command, and coordinate the new policies and military actions; then he would move promptly to Turkey to accomplish similar tasks in our rescue work. Once finished in the British sphere of influence, he would then travel back and forth between the United States and Europe, eventually to be joined by Eri Jabotinsky and others.

Our plans did not work out the way we hoped they would. Ben-Eliezer was afraid that it would seriously endanger our work if he disappeared underground; Kook and Merlin, by association, would become more vulnerable in the United States. He decided to stay above ground. By not going underground, he acted to shield his comrades. Neither I nor the others tried to dissuade him; I trusted his integrity and I had faith in his sound, intuitive judgment.

---

[1] This was the first national scale rebellion since the Bar Kochba Revolt eighteen hundred and twelve years before. The state which Bar Kochba had founded lasted only three years, then it was crushed by the Romans at the costs of hundreds of thousands of Jewish lives. The memory of that defeat lingered in the Jewish subconscious into the twentieth century, when key *Haganah* leaders like Eliahu Golomb publicly expounded the thesis that Jews had never rebelled successfully, and except for the Hasmoneans, would have to achieve their national aspirations "unlike other people."

[2] This has been amply documented, yet, today historians and the media still propagate the fiction that the *Irgun* indiscriminately caused the death of hundreds of civilians.

But we didn't know that the C.I.D. had told the Palestine Administration: "Ben-Eliezer came from the United States to reorganize the *Irgun*."

Ben-Eliezer never reached Turkey. The C.I.D. arrested him on April 17, 1944, and after months of isolation in the cells of the British Military Intelligence Center in Cairo, he was deported along with three hundred others to internment camps in East Africa. He became spokesman for hundreds of Hebrew prisoners who moved through the Kenya, Eritrea and Sudan detention camps.[1]

* * *

The C.I.D.'s evidence, provided by Yaakov Chylewicz, was a somewhat outdated list of one hundred and seventy-nine alleged *Irgun* activists. Chylewicz sold out his friends for 5,000 Palestinian pounds ($20,000) and shelter in the United States. American military intelligence and the State Department, working closely with the C.I.D., helped fly him out of Cairo and gave him a new identity in the United States. Perhaps it was he to whom the Justice Department referred, when it later advised State that since November of 1942 it had possessed information on our delegation's link to the *Irgun* but specific information could not be produced in court for fear of endangering their source.[2]

Eri Jabotinsky was not much luckier that Ben-Eliezer. When our Conference had decided that the two of them should both head for Turkey, Eri was overjoyed. As our roving delegate in the United States, he became increasingly unhappy. He felt like a deserter, playing bureaucratic games in comfortable America while others gave their lives. Now he would have a chance to be back at the battle ramparts.

Eri was a born rebel, at home in the hills of Galilee, the swamps of the Danube and the dank cells of the Acre jail. For him, struggle was as inevitable for natural survival as a heartbeat was to life. "We live not by passivity," he said, "but by continuous struggle. We will bleed and sacrifice." Nevertheless, when his wife

---

[1] In 1948, after four years in the camps, he escaped and reached Palestine and eventually he became deputy speaker of the Knesset.
[2] Also referred to in Justice Dept. internal memo (Laurence A. Knapp to Herbert Wechsler), 8/16/44, 149-893.

Aviva was expecting their first child, Eri explained, "It was no accident, we wanted a child regardless of what the future held for us."

Eri could not wait to reach Turkey and get over to Romania and the Balkans. We warned him that there were too many bureaucrats to deal with in the Balkans and he would be maligned and exasperated. He answered, "We must engage in 'non-diplomatic' activities." ·

Eri hardly had time to acquaint himself with recent events in the Balkans when Dr. Nahum Goldmann complained to the State Department that he could not see how Eri "could contribute in any way to the rescue of Jews from the Balkans, since the Jewish Agency representative, Mr. Barlas is the only person in Turkey who had the right to allot certificates for entry into Palestine." Incredibly, in May, 1944, the Jewish establishment still spoke as if the few paltry certificates the colonial office was handing out represented "rescue" work. Eri spoke French and Russian, he had invaluable experience dealing with the Greeks and Turks and Romanians in our *Ha'apalah* work, he had daring, imagination and courage—yet the establishment "could not see how" he could contribute to the rescue of Jews.

Friends of ours at the W.R.B. (War Refugee Board) helped facilitate his admission to Turkey. Although the State Department tried to prevent it, the W.R.B. arranged for him to take a United States Air Force bomber to Palestine, then proceed to Turkey.

Eri, who did not dispense compliments easily, said of his first contacts with Laurence A. Steinhardt, the U.S. Ambassador to Turkey: "Any backing that has been given our work by the local government is due solely to the personal efforts and prestige of Mr. Steinhardt."[1]

---

[1] The British Embassy in Istanbul constantly deprecated Steinhardt's and Ira Hirschmann's activities for the W.R.B., insinuating that their efforts in conjunction with the White House on behalf of Jewish rescue were motivated purely by political considerations; the United States presidential elections were taking place in November, 1944, and the British called their rescue efforts "a public auction for Jewish votes."

In 1941, Steinhardt as Ambassador to Moscow, wrote to Breckenridge Long in the State Department opposing the admission of Russian and Polish Jews into the United States. Long quoted Steinhardt as describing these Jews as useless, scheming and defiant "... the same kind of criminal Jews who crowd our police dockets in New York." In 1944, however, Steinhardt's conscience had caught up with him, and he was dedicated to rescuing the Jewish remnants.

Eri confirmed in his reports that Jews still could be freed from satellite countries like Romania, Bulgaria and Hungary, and he tracked down Romanian and Turkish operators and ship owners we had used years back. Almost openly, they helped Jews out of local areas occupied by the German military. However, they required a continuous supply of money. At one point, the Romanians had actually sold the Jew-running as a monopolistic "concession" to a veteran Greek trampship owner, authorizing him to transport Jews out of Romania.

Eri hit major stumbling blocks—first, the Turkish authorities were willing to grant transit visas to emigrants only if they held an end visa. But no end visas could be obtained from the British in Palestine, or from the great democracies because no one wanted to take in more Jews, not even temporarily. The British Embassy in Turkey strictly adhered to the White Paper's limits of fifteen thousand Jewish immigrants to Palestine per year, over five years. Because of problems with local hostile British administrators and shortsightedness by Jewish Agency leaders, some thirty thousand immigration certificates were still unused as of 1944 and yet the embassy clung to the cut-off date under the White Paper's quota. Finally, under pressure from Ambassador Steinhardt, they generously amended the quota to one thousand five hundred immigrants per month.[1]

During it all the deportation out of Hungary continued. Eri and his associates had managed to speak to Budapest by phone and Eri had never been as frustrated as during that period. He suffered a heart attack, his first of many to come, but within a short time he was back at work. The Allies claimed that no shipping was available for Jews; but they were available for hundreds of thousands of POWs, French children, Polish and Balkan refugees and Moslem pilgrims; Eri found several shipowners willing to transport Jews to Palestine for $500 per head, and he advised us that this could be reduced to $250. A Turkish vessel, the S.S. *Tari*, was ready to carry several thousand immigrants from Romania to Haifa every two weeks, and about sixty thousand people could be moved quickly. On December 4, 1944, he cabled us and asked for $250,000 as first payment; the Emergency Committee authorized

---

[1] E. Jabotinsky's Letters—Inst. Med. Affairs, New York.

the commitment. However, the British were adamantly opposed. Eventually Eri proposed that the *Tari* should sail to Palestine anyway, as a challenge to the Mandatory Power's blockade.

It was not difficult for the British to find out about Eri's dealings; he was under continuous surveillance by British and American intelligence.

It did not take the British long to ascertain that Eri was in contact with the Russians, negotiating to use the passenger vessel the *S.S. Stalingrad* to move immigrants from Black Sea ports to Istanbul and Palestine. The British may or may not have been aware of a confidential memo Eri had written early in September, 1941, circulated among our group and the N.Z.O., proposing that, in view of Britain's adamant backing of the Arabs, the time had come to investigate common ground with the U.S.S.R. Because of the war, there were hundreds of thousands of eastern European Jewish refugees in the U.S.S.R., and Eri's premise was that this would lessen Russian ideological opposition to Zionism. Eri assumed that ousting the British from Palestine and providing a home for all those refugees would seem an attractive prospect to the Russians. When formulating these ideas, Eri was unaware that we had had earlier contacts with the Russians. Back in the summer of 1940, the head of the *Betar-Irgun* organization in Lithuania, Joseph Glasman, had been approached in Vilna by agents of the Russian NKVD. The agents had asked him to help form partisan cells to fight Nazi Germany (at that time a Russian ally) in the event that the country was overrun by Germany. The agents showed a remarkable familiarity with Jewish and Zionist affairs in the country. When Glasman asked why they were approaching him and not the Zionist Socialists, their laughing answer was, "Oh, they are too pacifistic for us." Glasman and other of our people eventually were killed in the forests of Lithuania, fighting with the partisans against the occupying Germans.

After those meetings in Vilna, the Russian Communists had kept a close eye on events in Palestine, and by mid-1944, when the *Irgun*'s revolt was a fact, they were that much more interested.[1]

---

[1] The Russians eventually voted in the United Nations in favor of the creation of the State of Israel. They also allowed, in 1948, a limited but extremely vital supply of Czech rifles to be provided to the *Haganah*.

The British, however, before moving in, had to await a plausible excuse which they could impress upon the Turkish government. The government by then was listening to Eri about possibly receiving aid from the United States in exchange for permitting transit for substantial numbers of Jews, and the British were getting nervous. They acted at the first opportunity—the assassination of Lord Moyne in CAriro, on November 6, 1944, by *Lehi*, the Stern group.

The British filed criminal charges against Eri, linking him with with the incident. With the Allies gaining in the Balkans, the British had considerable weight and they put severe pressure on the Turks. Ehud Avriel, a top delegate of the Jewish Agency stationed in Istanbul, also played an important role in stacking the campaign against Eri, as did Nahum Goldmann and Arthur Lourie in Washington.[1] The Turks told Eri that they could not reject the British demand for his expulsion, since his Palestine passport bore the British imprint. He was put on a train for Palestine, and on arrival taken directly from the train to jail. Now the British and the United States State Department, and the Jewish Agency could breathe more easily. Out of the "six Palestinians," two were in British jails, two were in the United States Army, and only two left in the United States.

---

[1] FOIA document: memo from Gordan P. Merriam (State) to Louis Nemzer (Justice), dated 6/1/44 (p. 2).

The War Between the Jews

"Your destroyers shall go forth from you."

(Isaiah 49.17)

"It is unimportant whether we will fire the first shot in the Civil War. The propaganda apparatus is in our hands and we will instruct the recorders of history. You will always be the ones who started the war between brothers."

Eliahu Golomb, head of the *Haganah*, in a face-to-face conversation with Menahem Begin, 1944, Tel Aviv (as quoted in Yaakov Meridor's *Long is the Road to Freedom*; Achiasaf, Jerusalem, 1950)

New York, May 1943. I especially enjoyed the few days of leave because there was a possibility that I would be shipped directly into combat. I thought of it as time for *Heshbon Hanefesh*—"taking stock." I went to the New York Public Library and dug up the writings of Josephus Flavius, the Galilean Jewish officer who had joined the Roman enemy in 67 C.E. General Josephus Matityahu Ben-Yosef had left a detailed, though biased, record of the wars which the Jews of Palestine waged against each other instead of joining forces to defeat the invading Romans. He wrote that the Roman General Vespasian felt that "God was a better general of the Romans than he, for He was surrendering the Judeans to them without any effort on their part."

In 68 C.E., the Jews weakened themselves by splitting into three fratricidal camps. Soon only two factions were left to face the Romans. By 70 C.E. there were none. Only during the last days of the siege of Jerusalem and the Temple by Titus, the son of the newly anointed Emperor Vespasian, did the Jewish factions unite.

Josephus described it in his chronicles: "Both sides forgot their hatred and quarrels and formed one body . . . However, it was too late to matter."

Two thousand years later, when the Jewish people again came under mortal siege, the factions battling each other did not unite, not even at the end. When Hitler had risen to power in 1933, Jabotinsky wrote an essay called "Germany" in the Tel-Aviv paper *Hazit Ha'am*, saying that it was clear that the goal of the Nazis was the destruction of the Jewish people. He pointed to the Nazi platform, stressing that, while it contained contradictions and espoused unrealistic goals, the clauses concerning the Jews were crystal clear and could be carried out under any circumstances. From that date onward, his certainty of an approaching catastrophe dominated Jabotinsky's thoughts and actions. But the harder he and his followers tried to be heard, the harder their "brothers" in the Jewish establishment fought them and tried to silence them.

I spent most of the rest of my furlough in the library, briefly jotting down my own chronicle of the Twentieth Century's "War Between the Jews" as I had experienced it personally.

* * *

In the summer of 1933, when I was a political neophyte, I spent several days watching a trial in the small, uncomfortable court house in Jaffa. Listening to the convoluted legal arguments and watching all the puzzling procedures, I strongly felt the contrast between the drab, dirty streets of Jaffa and the studied decorum inside the courthouse. British justice was attempting to graft its Colonial tradition onto a semi-feudal society with its own traditions which went back a thousand years. I did not know the two accused men personally but I was aware that they were members of *Betar*. They were an incongruous pair, one tall and heavy-set, with a large slightly stooped body, small eyes, and an eerie smile, and the other short with touseled hair and a pale, taut face. The physical contrast between the two was never so great as when they were led in each day, handcuffed to each other, surrounded by British and Arab policemen. Their names were Abraham Stawsky and Zvi Rosenblatt, and they were the first men accused of committing a political murder in the history of the Jewish community of Palestine. When I was a small child, I had heard about an ultra-Orthodox Jew named DeHaan who had been shot because of his fanatic anti-Zionist stand, but no one ever spoke about that episode. Now the Jewish community of Palestine and the Zionist movement the world over was up in arms about what was in effect an attempt to try an entire political group for murder.

On Friday night, June 16, 1933, Haim Arlosoroff, a brilliant young Labor ideologist who was political director of the Jewish Agency, was shot and killed by "assailants unknown." The next day was the Sabbath. As no newspapers were published, rumors swept through Tel-Aviv, saying that Jabotinsky's followers were implicated in the murder and arrests had already been made. The men arrested were supposed to be members of the "maximalist" *Brith-Habiryonim*, a faction within political Zionism that followed the teachings of Abba Achimeir. Within forty-eight hours of the murder, David Ben-Gurion, at a memorial gathering for Arlosoroff in Warsaw, declared: "I have no doubt that this was an act of political terror." Simultaneously, the executive committee of the *Histadrut,* the *Yishuv's* General Federation of Labor distributed a similar statement.

Within a few days, two suspects were arrested and brought before a magistrate in Jaffa for preliminary hearings. They matched perfectly the physical description given to the police by Arlosoroff's widow.

Watching the proceedings in the stifling courtroom, I was unaware of the plots and counter-plots which had led up to this scene, but I personally knew enough adherents of the "maximalist" group to be absolutely sure that the charges were false. I had had my own arguments with Achimeir about his early flirtation with Italian fascism, but he and his followers, some my closest friends, were bitterly opposed to the sort of internecine political assassination. In the atmosphere of mass hysteria created by Labor following the murder, the *Irgun* command had nervously begun an independent inquiry and within a few days came to the conclusion not only that the "maximalists" had nothing to do with the murder, but that the charge was on the level of a blood libel. Labor was conveniently using the murder of Arlosoroff to defame the Jabotinsky movement.[1] The immediate effect of the trial was that in 1933, Labor's representation in the eighteenth World Zionist Congress went from 29 to 44 per cent, while Jabotinsky's following dropped from 21 to 14 per cent, also losing its moderate wing, which spun off under Meir Grossman.

That Zionist Congress was a sham. In the middle of a session on August 26, a cable was received by the presiding officer, advising him that Achimeir had "confessed" to organizing the murder. Although the cable was immediately disavowed as a forgery, it further fueled the campaign being waged by Labor. This was the last time Jabotinsky participated in a Zionist Congress. Although the Revisionist Zionist remained the second largest Jewish political group, both in Palestine and the diaspora, Jabotinsky was in fact eliminated as a threat to Labor within the Zionist organization. The Zionist movement lost Jabotinsky's vital leadership, and Jabotinsky found himself without the organizational and financial advantages of the Jewish Agency and the Zionist organization. The spiritualist-Socialist coalition sealed its iron grip of the Zionist establishment and institutions.

As David Ben-Gurion put it in his memoirs: ". . . they (the Jews of Europe) are coming to us because it seems to them that we are the pipeline for *Aliyah*. If we are not—they will turn elsewhere. Our ideology has attracted the youth in the past. Now there is a different decisive factor—*Aliyah*; and they will go to the place that has control of *Aliyah*."

Within a year of the trial, all the accused were freed for lack of evidence. Stawsky was the last to be released, and the day after he left his cell, Labor's daily, *Davar*, declared: "Stawsky is free—but

---

[1] Years later, investigative reporters for the leading papers in Israel (Tamar Maroz, *Ha'aretz*, July 20, 1973: *Forty Years of Mystery*) concluded that the murder trial had been purposefully and falsely staged by the leadership of Labor. The list of Labor leaders involved in the frame-up read like a Who's Who in Zionist hierarchy. In 1956, two *Haganah* men, Yehuda and Tuvia Arazi, finally made public what they knew about the case. Shortly after the murder Yehuda, a key *Haganah* operative in the Palestine Criminal Investigation Department, had identified the two Arabs who had killed Arlosoroff. He submitted the information to his superior in the police but neither Yehuda's superior nor Yehuda himself ever made it public. The document remained secret until after Yehuda's death. When the Arazis' declaration that "two Arabs were the murderers" became public, Labor refused to agree to a neutral commission to investigate the matter once more. But none of the facts were publicly known in 1933. Just before his own death in 1973, Tuvia Arazi went to the grave of Abba Achimeir to beg forgiveness for his long silence.

his guilt was proven."

From that point on, Labor always controlled immigration and the budget. Funds were never available to the Jabotinsky movement for any purpose, at any time. In 1935 Tehomi was enraged because our Tel-Hai Fund came up with so little money to buy arms. And young men who had served their two-year national service in our *Plugot* farm work units had no chance for funds to help them settle on the land. As for immigration, Labor's control prevented all Jabotinsky youth from being *Aliyah* candidates; and when we launched into *Ha'apalah* work in 1937, the Establishment, led by Labor, sought to cut us off from funds and sympathetic ears at every chance.

* * *

I remembered when we approached Robert Rothschild in Paris, in 1938 for financial help with our *Ha'apalah*, we were under extreme pressure to step up our work. But after we talked with Rothschild, he checked with his friends in the Zionist organization and was told: "There is no need to help them. The *Haganah* are doing all that is necessary." (According to official Zionist records published after the War, we now know that, from January to December of that critical year (1938), the *Haganah* organized only five small groups totalling 713 immigrants.)

The extent of the personal intervention by Dr. Weizmann during a follow-up meeting between Rothschild and our men Yaakobi and Helpren in Rothschild's home was described to me a few years after. "There was no use even to have begun the conversation. Before we had a chance to present our case, Rothschild said 'So you're the terrorists! Dr. Weizmann told me you're transporting people in boats not fit for cattle.' We knew Weizmann had killed our chances. Poor Yaakobi acknowledged that the conditions on the boats were bad, but he explained that nevertheless dozens of Jews had tried to smuggle themselves onto the boats, some even swimming the Danube delta, 'because Eastern Europe was burning under their feet.'"

* * *

I remembered in June, 1939, our delegation to the United States formed the "American Friends of a Jewish Palestine" (AFJP) to raise funds for immigration. We had a two-room office on Madison Avenue. All our costs were covered by two old friends of the movement. Whenever we went out to appeal to individuals and groups, we hit a stone wall of suspicion, because of the continual attacks on us by the Zionist Establishment.

We had hardly launched our fund-raising campaign in the United States when "the Emergency Committee on Zionist Affairs," a united front of Establishment Zionists from Robert Szold on the right to Haim Greenberg, editor of the Laborite *Jewish Frontier*, on the left, issued this statement:

> The American Friends of a Jewish Palestine and the "Tel-Hai fund" are appealing to the public for funds for purposes of immigrant transportation, agricultural colonization . . . and other activities. There is no public record by which the claims advanced . . . may be established.

The "Emergency Committee," including Stephen S. Wise, Louis Lipsky, and Dr. Solomon Goldman, had spoken. Our *ma'apilim* on the Danube, the *Betar* work units in the Galil, the Maritime School that 'Irma' Helpren headed—all these never existed! The public read these words and due to the authority commanded by the members of the "Emergency Committee," believed them; instead of helping our efforts, they bowed to the Socialists' dictate that "the needs of Palestine could be served best by making larger funds available to the Jewish Agency."

The Establishment's sabotage of our *Ha'apalah* work did not stop at choking off financially. What we did not know then was that as late on the Jewish European calendar as the summer of 1939 the Jewish Agency endangered the lives of Jews we were then moving out of Europe. In May and again in June 1939, Arthur Lourie, the political secretary of the Jewish Agency then in London, and Ben-Gurion's personal confidant, communicated to Sir Herbert Emerson (head of the League of Nations Commission for Refugees, London), the names of vessels we were then using from Mediterranean and Black Sea ports, to Palestine. To better help the British, he identified the countries of origin of our various transports which would then permit the British to start deportation procedures to return them to the Nazi-controlled lands.

Sir Herbert Emerson, although a League of Nations official, never ceased to act as His Majesty's loyal servant. He promptly forwarded the information from the Jewish Agency to the British Foreign Office. The latter was satisfied to learn from the Jewish Agency that our *ma'apilim* on the *Aghios Nicolaos* and the *Astir*, "phantom vessels" according to the Emergency Committee on Zionist Affairs in New York, carried 700 and 748 Jews out of Czechoslovakia and Danzig respectively. These Jews were saved from deportation to occupied Czechoslovakia and Danzig by Hitler's invasion of Poland.[1]

The failures of our United States delegation did not stop *Ha'apalah*. We moved one or more ships a month, carrying 500 to 800 passengers per trip. The boats were often nearly unlivable, but most made it to Eretz-Israel safely. Except for rare tragedies like the *Struma*, which sank into the Black Sea with 796 aboard, almost all our *ma'apilim* survived. But somehow none of this proved our integrity.

When the war broke out in Europe on September 1, 1939, our fundraising work immediately became more urgent. Eri Jabotinsky advised from Romania:

> ... the Germans are still permitting Jews to leave from territories under their control, and as long as this is happening, we will continue our work ... We must intensify our efforts to raise funds in the United States.

The appeals kept on coming. When Eri Jabotinsky and Reuben Hecht cabled us from Bucharest in November, 1939, asking for immediate help for the *ma'apilim* on the frozen Danube we mobilized all our supporters. Immediately, Stephen S. Wise issued a statement to the press that "the activities of independent organizations seeking to duplicate or parallel the work of the Jewish Agency are to be discouraged." The sum total of the Jewish Agency *Ha'apalah* work at that time was one *Haganah* vessel with 723 *ma'apilim*.[2]

---

[1] Foreign Office File 371/24o0/2829).

[2] Berl Katznelson, the venerated ideologue of Socialist Zionism, wrote about a meeting with Jabotinsky in September, 1939: "I don't want to discredit the Revisionists on one matter ... we cannot belittle people who, at this time, exert themselves to bring *olim* to Eretz-Israel."

On February 1, 1940, the day the *Sakarya* sailed, the United Jewish Appeal issued a carefully edited five-page letter, signed by its Executive Director H. Montor, announcing its policy towards our *Ha'apalah* work:

> Unregistered immigration . . . by individuals associated with the Jewish Agency for Palestine was based on a recognition of the fact that 'selectivity' is an inescapable factor in dealing with the problem of immigration to Palestine. By 'selectivity' is meant the choice of young men and women who are trained in Europe for productive purposes either in agriculture or industry and who are in other ways trained for life in Palestine. Sentimental considerations are, of course, vital and everyone would wish to save every single Jew who could be rescued out of the cauldron of Europe . . . I think it is fair to point out that many who have been brought into Palestine by the Revisionists . . . have been prostitutes and criminals. This particular affair could be satisfactorily liquidated if the American Friends of Jewish Palestine would cease its separate fund-raising activities at which it had already proved unsuccessful, and if it were to agree to 'selectivity' in immigration . . .

The Montor letter carried the names of Jonah B. Wise, Stephen S. Wise, Albert Einstein, Herbert Lehman and Edward M. Warburg, among other well-respected names; the document was a natural corollary to the longtime basic policies of the Zionist Establishment: first, that Palestine could not absorb the masses of Jews who needed saving, even if Germany was going to leave its exit doors open only a little longer; second, that the future of Eretz-Israel dictated absorbing only "selected" Jews who were physically and ideologically acceptable to the Zionist leadership; third, if we only agreed to disappear, whatever problems faced the mass rescue of Jews would be solved.

Stripped of cant, the message went back to Ben-Gurion's "Control immigration and funds, and you control the Zionist movement." If immigration to Palestine had been controlled that way in 1884 or 1891, neither of my grandparents, then middle-aged, with broods of six and eight children respectively, would have qualified, and their descendants in Israel today would not have numbered in the many hundreds.

Elsewhere in the United Jewish Appeal's document referring to their own *Ha'apalah* efforts through the *Haganah*, there were outright falsehoods. The UJA said: "Certain experienced persons would have brought together . . . during the past four weeks . . . some 2200 young men and women . . . on the Danube, for transport to Palestine." No record exists that during January, February, or any other month up until August 1940, there was any group of 2200 *ma'apilim* gathered on the Danube by the *Haganah*. The *Haganah* organized one group of 723 *ma'apilim* that landed on January 8, 1940, and that was it. The next 2300 *ma'apilim* on the *Sakarya* sailed under our auspices.

The facts were that, between July 1934 and mid-1940, the entire World Zionist Organization managed to bring into Palestine only about 6200 *ma'apilim*, though it had worldwide Jewish financial resources at its disposal. During the same period, we moved about twice that many *ma'apilim* with hardly any financial means whatsoever. We knew that if we publicly complained about the United Jewish Appeal's statements, we would not have been believed; so we made no outcry.

But when, to publicize the rescue work it was doing in Europe, the United Jewish Appeal took to using the picture of the vessel *Parita* that had successfully landed 850 *ma'apilim* on the Tel-Aviv beach in 1938, I could not restrain myself. I drafted a letter to the Executive Director of the United Jewish Appeal, saying: "As you no doubt know, neither the Joint Distribution Committee nor the U.J.A. had any part in the financing the voyage of the *Parita* . . . we do not object to the publicity given to the *Parita*, but would it be asking too much if in the future . . . a footnote be added that the Parita voyage was enabled through the 'American Friends of a Jewish Palestine.'"

In 1940 in the United States, the Emergency Committee for Zionist Affairs issued a 26 page booklet titled "Revisionism—a Destructive Force." In the booklet, the Committee reversed its previous 1939 statement that we lacked "any record" to substantiate our immigration work. Now we were slandered for actually having made the *Ha'apalah* voyages. "The conditions on their boats are revolting . . . They resemble concentration camps in that passengers were hung to the mast and were refused food in retaliation for criticism or complaints . . . The Revisionists . . . demand more money than necessary, using the surplus for their own party purposes."

The Emergency Committee's booklet, bearing the imprimatur

of the entire American Zionist leadership, ended by making appeal for "democratic America" to join with American Jews in putting a stop to us: "Revisionism is viciously Fascist, but lacking the sole asset of fascism—power. There is no room in democratic America for the empty slogans and destructive activities of Revisionism."

To seek the help of democratic America in their campaign to end our "Fascism," the Jewish Establishment turned to one of the oldest, most despised means in the diaspora—the informer.

On August 24, 1940, J. Edgar Hoover, director of the F.B.I. sent a memo to his New York office advising:

> Informant left the following note: Articles appearing in the Yiddish vernacular press, advocating the formation of secret Zionist Armed units for carrying out raids on Arabs in Palestine, appear to emanate from the office at 285 Madison Avenue. This Office appears to be occupied by one Y. Ben-Ami.

A link was now established between the Jewish-Zionist Establishment and the Roosevelt Administration with a common aim of ridding America of the "Fascist Revisionists." In the months and years to come, this would remain their emphasis over and beyond saving Jews from the extermination.[1]

* * *

In Washington, in 1941, when we launched our Committee for an Army of Palestinian and Stateless Jews, the Zionist Establishment became sufficiently concerned about our activities to consider a common effort with us. However, Arthur Lourie who now transferred to New York was General Secretary of the Emergency Committee for Zionist Affairs made it an overriding condition that such cooperation could take place only under the Emergency Committee's aegis.

---

[1] As recently as 1978, Melvin Urofsky wrote in his *We are One, America Jewry and Israel* (Anchor Press, Doubleday): "Several thousand Jews were indeed smuggled into Palestine (during the war years) . . . It was the *Haganah* and not the *Irgun* which ran the clandestine operation!" The over 3500 *ma'apilim* of the *Sakarya*, two sailings of the *Rudnicher*, *Delpa*, *Pencho* (the vessel foundered in the Aegean and the ma'apilim were interned in Italy), and the *Libertad* (jointly with the *Hashomer Hatzair*) do not exist in Zionist history.

Doubting their steadfastness or ability to comprehend the on-rushing horrors we refused to submit to their hegemony.

The Jewish leadership still refused to acknowledge publicly the reports filtering out of Nazi-occupied Europe. In New York, the editorial board of the Zionist-Socialist paper the *Jewish Frontier*, which led the attack on our activities in the United States, declared in 1942 that the Extermination were merely "The macabre fantasy of a lunatic sadist."

Haim Greenberg, the leading Socialist-Zionist ideologist in the United States, when criticizing our campaign to raise an army of "200,000 Palestinian and Stateless Jews," claimed that "by no stretch of the imagination can one identify 200,000 male Jews in the West who would fit this definition." At that time, the British were hauling thousands of German and Austrian Jewish refugees to Australian detention camps. The Jewish population in Palestine numbered over half a million, and more than 136,000 men and women had registered there for military service.

On April 17, 1942, a Philadelphia public relations man named Samuel Edelman[1] wrote to Secretary of State Cordell Hull:

> I would like to bring to the attention of the Department the agitation that is being aroused among Jewish circles by a small band of Palestinian Jews, urging the creation of a Jewish Army. This demand does not even have the support of the Zionist organization and certainly not of the educated classes of Jews in America. Nevertheless, this movement is gaining support from the masses, and it is a flareback against the British government.

Mr. Edelman, who described himself as "both an American citizen of the Jewish faith, and a former career consular officer who was on duty in Palestine many years," went on in the letter to identify "Y. Ben-Ami as a leader" of the movement, "in this section of the country." Edelman concluded by inquiring if it were possible "to start proceedings against him (Y. Ben-Ami) as an undesirable alien." The letter from Edelman triggered a long correspondence between the Department of State and myself, as to whether our campaign for "A Jewish Army of Palestinian and Stateless Jews" originated from or was conducted on behalf of a foreign principal.

---

[1] An old time anti-Zionist.

On September 1, 1942, Nathan M. Cohen of the United States Department of Justice reached a joint decision about us with Paul Richman, public relations representative of B'nai B'rith. They agreed "that the speakers of the Committee (for a Jewish Army) should be curbed somewhat in their denunciations of the British, who are now our allies." Mr. Cohen also told Mr. Dunn of the U.S. Military Intelligence: "Dr. Weizmann, head of the World Zionist Organization, is an extremely loyal British subject and is opposed to any movements [which] would in anyway embarrass the British government."[1] With Weizmann's loyalty to the British government, and Stephen Wise's loyalty to Roosevelt, it was difficult to find Jewish leaders loyal to Jewish survival even though, as Mr. Edelman pointed out in his letter, the Jewish masses instinctively looked for guidance outside the halls of the Establishment.

The persistent derogation of us by Jewish entities, and by individuals like Professor Hans Kohn, who, in a U.S. Department of Justice memorandum on December 8, 1942, was quoted as saying: "The N.Z.O. is advocating a sort of Fascist Jewish State" eventually led the Department to recommend that The Jewish Army Committee register as foreign agents. The memorandum recognized that no foreign principal exercised control over the Committee, but "if the Committee were required to register and made aware that its propaganda were under careful scrutiny . . . it would be less likely to stir up dissension among the Jews in this country." Apparently stopping Jewish dissension was more important to the Roosevelt administration than another 100,000 soldiers added to the war effort—soldiers with more motivation to fight the Nazis than all other Allied soldiers.

Cables and letters from London, Buenos Aires, and Montevideo concerning the formation of a Jewish army were intercepted by the combined United States and British intelligence efforts, neatly catalogued by Washington, and circulated back and forth between Britain and the State and Justice Departments.

Soon Justice tried a different tack. On June 16, 1942, Pierre van Paassen, the Chairman of our Committee, received a telegram

---

[1] Department of Justice memorandum Nathan M. Cohen to James R. Sharp. JRS:NMC-149-178, of 9/1/1942.

from the Russian-Jewish Anti-Fascist Committee, which urged us to join the campaign initiated by Soviet Jewry to present the Red Army with a thousand tanks. Justice quickly found out about the telegram and asked J. Edgar Hoover if he would investigate the Communist connection of the leaders of our Committee. Nothing got Hoover's immediate attention more than a hint of Communist subversion.

On April 13, 1943, Hoover submitted an unsigned, four page memorandum to the special War Policies Unit of Justice, citing "remarks by an Executive of the American Jewish Congress . . . which said that this group (Committee for a Jewish Army) was sponsored by a group of thoroughly disreputable Communist Zionists." In the memorandum, Hoover indicated strong suspicion that we were involved in political and financial racketeering, and said that his informant learned that "the American Jewish Committee, through its powerful Washington contacts, would see to it that all the senators and congressmen whose names appeared on [our] advertisments would withdraw."

A list of names designated as "Communists" and "Communist Connections" included Ben Hecht, Lion Feuchtwanger, Arnold Schoenberg the composer, and William Zorach the sculptor. Professor Max Lerner, Rabbi Raisin and the editor of *Aufbau* (a German-Jewish weekly appearing in New York) were listed as "fellow travelers." Ben Hecht was marked "Communist."[1]

Now Justice was faced with a difficult choice: should our "Fascist" character be stressed or our "Communist" character? The idea never occurred to Justice that possibly "the six Palestinians" were simply agents of Jewish misery all across Europe.

When our pageant "We Will Never Die" was about to be staged at Madison Square Garden on March 9, 1943, Governor Dewey of New York declared that it would be "a day of mourning to the memory of the millions who have already died." The American Jewish Congress wrote the Governor to cancel the day of mourning because "We Will Never Die" was being put on by "irresponsible" people, and because "such action would offend the great masses of American Jewry." On that same day, our supporters in

---

[1] Hoover to Lawrence M. Smith; 4/13/43; Dept. of Justice; Division of Records: No. 149-178 and F4173.

Congress passed the first official resolution in America condemning the Nazi atrocities—"the mass murder of Jewish men, women, and children." This, we assumed, was what the American Jewish Congress meant by "irresponsible."

On May 12, 1943, the Department of Justice asked J. Edgar Hoover "to obtain the assistance of the British authorities (in Palestine) in making the necessary investigation there," so that a foreign principal could be identified.

On October 6, 1943, with nothing concrete accomplished by the Bermuda Conference nor by the Inter-Governmental Committee on Political Refugees, Stephen Wise and Nahum Goldmann of the American and World Jewish Congresses respectively were to see Breckenridge Long at the State Department. After the meeting, Long reported[1] that he advised them that the Red Cross served as agent for the Inter-Governmental committee and was "taking food to certain remnants of Jews in Germany." Having achieved this momentous clarification, Wise and Goldmann "excoriated" our Emergency Committee to Save The Jewish People, saying they had "no sympathy with their methods or actions, and that they hoped the Department of State would recognize and deal . . . with the American Jewish Congress . . . Dr. Wise was the proper person with whom to deal." Long concluded that all Wise's and Goldmann's questions "were answered to their apparent satisfaction." The gist was that Goldmann and Wise were content enough as long as power remained in their hands, even if only "remnants" of the Jews in Europe were left. Two thirds were already dead.

On December 23, 1943, the Interim Committee of the American Jewish Conference, an umbrella group of major Jewish Establishment organizations, issued a four-page document which never once mentioned the Extermination, but instead focused on one limited goal: to stop our "attempt to establish a front against the Jewish Agency."[2]

---

[1] B. Long's "Memorandum of Conversation 10/6/1943."

[2] In 1967, Elie Wiesel asked why Stephen Wise, the leading spokesman of American Jewry, did not protest, march, fast daily, and do whatever else he could to save the Jews in Europe. Lillie Schultz, who had been Wise's assistant, told him: "Human beings have so much capacity . . . We were heroes fighting Hitler!" Nevertheless, Wise, Haim Greenberg, Marie Syrkin and Arthur Lourie all found the energy, time, and funds to fight our activities year in and year out, for more than a decade.

Throughout 1943, Wise interceded with Congressmen Sol Bloom and Emanuel Celler against every piece of legislation we attempted to initiate to save Jewish lives.[1] Our full-page ads, the "We Will Never Die" pageant, our mass petitions, and the Rabbis' marches on Washington were nevertheless slowly swinging members of Congress in our direction, and we even won some members of the Cabinet over to our side. The Jewish Establishment could not tolerate any of this.

When we learned, in February, 1943, that Romania would let Jews out for a price, and we said so in an advertisement in *The New York Times*, Wise immediately released a statement on behalf of the American Jewish Congress: " . . . no confirmation has been received regarding this alleged offer." He described our ad as "a hoax of the Hecht group." This, though the State Department had been aware of such ransom possibilities since February 10. On March 31, when Wise obtained confirmation from the State Department about the authenticity of this offer, he never issued a retraction. His original condemnation helped kill all response to our ad, and the money to save the remaining Jews was never really raised. They were caught by the Germans and sent to the gas chambers. In his autobiography, Wise placed the blame entirely on the State Department and the British Foreign Office.

* * *

When victory for the Allies over the Germans began to look feasible, we felt spurred on in our campaign, though we knew we were running out of possibilities. In November 1943 we published nationwide ads which featured Ben Hecht's "My Uncle Abraham Reports." Uncle Abraham was a ghost delegated by the millions of murdered Jews to represent all their ghosts at the conferences working "to make the world a better place to live." He would sit on the windowsill and take notes, then report back to his departed friends. He told them that for some unknown reason, their names were never mentioned—not in Moscow, not at 10 Downing Street, London, not at the White House, "'When we were killed,

---

[1] All source material is available in minutes of the House of Representatives hearings on the "Palestine Question," November 1943; Selected Executive session hearings (Vol. II, part II); Committee on International Relations.

we were changed from Nobodies to Nobodies. Today, on our Jewish tomb, there is not the Star of David but an asterisk.'

"Uncle Abraham has gone to the White House . . . is sitting on the windowsill two feet away from Mr. Roosevelt. But he has left his notebook behind."

Roosevelt did not like the ad; neither did the Secretary of State Cordell Hull. On August 6, 1943 Hull again asked Attorney General Francis Biddle if our Committee members were duly registered foreign agents, and if not, why not? The Attorney General answered again that the matter was under study.[1]

Finally, we gave the Department of Justice peace of mind. When our Hebrew Committee of National Liberation (HCNL) was founded in March, 1944, under the chairmanship of Peter Bergson (Hillel Kook), it applied for registration as a foreign agent, giving as its foreign principal "The Hebrew Nation which consists of those Jews in Palestine and occupied Europe who desire to belong to it." At long last it seemed the Department could close its thick files of arguments and denunciations and informants' reports. But the formation of the HCNL and the pending negotiations with Justice on our "Foreign Agent" registration caused the Zionist Establishment to launch its heaviest assault against us yet.

This campaign against us had grown in direct proportion to the recent steps we had undertaken and the progress we had made with the public and Congress.

Our first substantial success in the past year was to introduce in Congress, in November 1943, the Gillette-Rogers resolution calling for a "Presidential Commission to Save the Jewish People of Europe." The resolution was approved by a unanimous vote of the Senate Foreign Relations Committee. By January of 1944, the resolution led to the creation of the War Refugee Board, which eventually proved to be the only United States Government entity to help save substantial numbers of Jews from extermination. Still, those rescued were only a small portion of the ones who could have been saved, had the Board been created a year earlier.

Our second major step had been forming the Hebrew Committee of National Liberation. Paralleling the declaration of revolt by

---

[1] Department of Justice, letter of 8/25/43 (Reference # 149-718).

the *Irgun* in Palestine, it served notice on the Zionist establishment, on the British, on the State Department that once the war was over, Hebrew freedom and Statehood could not be stopped.

Consequently, cooperation in Palestine between the Establishment and the British to dispose of us became tighter than ever, while in the U.S. the internal memoranda of the Justice and State Departments reveal an indefatigable search for proof of our perjury and violation of the Foreign Agents Registration Act. Since November, 1942, Justice had been convinced that our delegation was in one way or another linked with the *Irgun*, but they lacked proof that could stand up in court. The Zionist establishment did their best to help them find it. During meetings with Eri Jabotinsky and Kook in February and March, the Foreign Agents Section of the Department of Justice kept insisting that we specify the foreign groups with which the HCNL was linked. Not until years later did we learn that they had an unsigned memo on which the name of a well-known Jewish Washington lobbyist was penciled in, as well as a report by the Chief of Near East Affairs of State about a May 9, 1944 meeting with Nahum Goldmann, the leader of the World Jewish Congress. Dr. Goldmann declared before Gordon P. Merriam, Chief of the Near East Division at the State Department, that "Bergson and his group (the HCNL) were perpetuating a gigantic hoax on the more guileless members of the Jewish community." Goldmann demanded of Merriam why, since the HCNL's connection with the *Irgun Zvai Leumi* was so well known, the government did not "either deport or draft" its members.[1] The report by Merriam complemented the unsigned

---

[1] However, when Morris D. Waldman, Executive Vice President of the American Jewish Committee visited the State Department on January 10, 1944, he suggested that Dr. Goldmann should not be recognized as a spokesman for American Jewry since he "is an alien." But Waldman did not overlook to suggest that "certain [other] alien Jews were very vocal in making their views known [Bergson and his group] and whether some way can be found to instigate an investigation to ... curtail his stay in the U.S. ... . [since] many of Mr. Bergson's activities were little better than racketeering." Waldman's obsession with classifying Jews carried over to his evaluation of Isaiah Berlin, the First Secretary at the British Embassy, whom he described "as an English Jew of Eastern European origin ... [who] was not regarded as a representative of the best elements among Jewry." E. M. Wilson summarized this meeting in a memo, without comments, copies of which, as always, were circulated to U.S. Embassies and consulates in Cairo, Jerusalem, Beirut, Baghdad and Jidda—especially since the purpose of the visit was to advise Wilson and his colleagues that the American Jewish Committee had decided to embark on "a publicity campaign in opposition to the pro-Zionist cause."

memo which contained most of Goldmann's arguments in a more journalistic style. The memo stated that we were "known to represent the *Irgun* . . ."

The memo went on for several pages, extolling the "democratic structure" of the *Yishuv* in Palestine, of the World Zionist Organization, and of all the major American Jewish organizations. Copies of Merriam's report were sent to the U.S. Consulate in Jerusalem, and from there found their way to the Criminal Investigation Department of the Palestine Police and the Colonial Office in London, leading to the arrest in Palestine in 1944 of our colleague Arieh Ben-Eliezer.[1]

Merriam's report gives the clear impression that the purpose of Dr. Goldmann's visit was not to urge the War Refugee Board to move Jews out of the Balkans, but to mobilize the Justice Department to "deport or draft Bergson."

Goldmann protested the "support the Bergson group received from the WRB . . . and that Mr. Pehle, the Executive Director of the WRB, has taken the position that . . . the 'Emergency Committee to Save the Jewish People of Europe' had inspired [and] led to the creation of the Board."

In fact, we had done our best to see that the WRB was staffed by sympathetic officials, mostly men from the Treasury, men free from the traditional antagonism or outright anti-Semitism of the staff of the State Department.

Dr. Goldmann reported that he had warned Pehle that, unless he disavowed the Emergency Committee, it would be necessary for the World Jewish Congress to denounce the WRB publicly. This was the same week in mid-May 1944, when the Nazis started moving half a million Hungarian Jews to Auschwitz. Dr. Goldmann further stated that Stephen Wise told Pehle that he regarded Bergson "as equally as great an enemy of the Jews as

---

[1]The campaign to discredit the HCNL never let up. In November, 1976 the American Jewish Archives (Hebrew Union College, Cincinnati, Ohio) published recollections by Rabbi Leon I. Feuer, who in 1943 took charge of the Washington office of the Emergency Committee for Zionist Affairs: "The Bergson boys finally overshot their mark by staging in the spring of 1944 a cheap melodramatic 'happening' the opening of a 'Hebrew Embassy.' To mark the event, they called a press conference . . . There was a flourish of trumpets, doors were thrown open. Bergson and his companions marched to the platform . . . dressed in black shirts and boots and proceeded to proclaim the Hebrew State . . ." This, in 1976, from the prestigious institution of the American Reform movement.

Hitler, for the reason that his activities could only lead to increased anti-Semitism." This was the same argument FDR and Cordell Hull had used to justify ignoring the Jewish plight for the past ten years.

Not satisfied with these various actions against us, the American Zionist Emergency Council sent on August 10, 1944 its Secretary Arthur Lourie and its counsel Irving D. Lipkowitz for a meeting at Justice.

Lourie and Lipkowitz delivered a fourteen-page document to the Department of Justice. It discussed the history of Zionism and the Jewish Agency, and culminated by repeating that our group represented no one, but was "associated with a small terrorist group called the *Irgun* . . . whose activities were condemned by the National Council in Palestine, the Jewish Agency . . ." etc. The *raison d'etre* of our delegation's existence was "to destroy the existing Zionist leadership . . . and to place ourselves in control of Zionist affairs."

With four million Jews dead, and millions more about to be killed, the Establishment was concerned, above all, with control.

* * *

I remembered the report from London in 1942-44 when we attempted to establish some rapport with Britain, especially when the tide of battle was running against the Allies in the Near East. The *Irgun* contributed some of its top officers and many rank and file soldiers to units in the British army, to intelligence work in the Balkans, and eventually to the British Jewish Brigade. We had even lost our commander David Raziel on a British mission. We had found friendship from Wedgwood, Colonel Patterson, and Lord Strabolgi.

In 1942 we sent 'Irma' Helpren to London to establish a committee to promote a Jewish Army. To introduce Helpren to the political arena in London, we sent a letter to all members of the House of Commons, signed by U.S. Senators Edwin C. Johnson, William H. Smathers, and James E. Murray, as well as William Green, President of the A.F.L., and Philip Murray, the head of the C.I.O. The letter asked the British Parliament for help in forming a Jewish Army.

On August 21, Helpren announced the opening of the London office, and on August 27, Professor Namier, the Jewish Agency representative in London, called at the Colonial Office requesting that the War Office have no dealings with our Committee. By October, the Jewish Agency had drawn up a report on our Committee, which was circulated among the highest circles of the government, attacking the manpower data we used and implying that 'Irma' Helpren was "politically affiliated" with the "Stern Group."

To get our campaign for a Jewish Army out of London, the Jewish Agency used every tack from condemning us to simply dismissing us. On November 22, Foreign Minister Anthony Eden wrote a letter to Lord Cranborne: "Pressure for a Jewish Army seems to have subsided somewhat in the United States and elsewhere."

Then, on December 10, 1942, the War Office issued a seventeen-page review of His Majesty's Government policy on the subject: "The Committee for a Jewish Army . . . is closely connected with the [aim of] creation of a Jewish State in Palestine . . . If H.M.G. were to enter into any discussions with the Committee, grave offence would be given to the Jewish Agency, which would probably be driven thereby to more extreme courses." It was sound political thinking for the War Office to stay on the good side of Weizmann and the Jewish Agency, because, as the memo went on to say, Dr. Weizmann "had been consistently moderate in his attitude and appreciative of His Majesty's Government's delicate position."

The memo then proceeded:

> Lord Halifax states that officials of the State Department are aware of the real objectives of the Jewish Army agitation, but profess to hold the view that we need not worry unduly about it . . . The sympathy expressed by Col. Knox (Secretary of the Navy), Mr. Stimson (Secretary of War), etc., is considered to have been due principally to benevolence, and a desire, in an election year, to avoid the risk of offending voters or being called anti-Semites . . . At no time has the State Department shown any sign of wishing to press H.M.G. in the matter of a Jewish Army.

Indeed, it never had had any such intention. As Secretary Hull, thoroughly briefed by the Jewish establishment, expressed it to

Attorney General Biddle: "The efforts of Mr. Kook and associates [are] designed to forward the political fortunes of a small but turbulent Jewish faction which appears to have little regard for unity between the principal Allies."

Earlier, on June 9, 1942, by which date H.M.G. was fully aware of the ongoing destruction of the Jews of Europe, Colonial Secretary Lord Moyne said before the House of Lords: "It is to canalize all the sympathy of the world for the martyrdom of the Jews that the Zionists reject all schemes to resettle their victims elsewhere—in Germany or Poland, or in sparsely populated regions such as Madagascar." By June 1942 Eichmann's *Einsatzgruppen* had been "resettling" Jews to Poland's extermination camps at the rate of thousands per day. Josiah Wedgwood explained Moyne's comments as colossal rationalization, because the government had its "horrid past to defend."

On July 4, 1942, the British Embassy in Washington recommended that the Foreign Office include this answer by the Prime Minister to a letter from our delegation: "The arming of the Jews in Palestine . . . is being actively implemented with the valuable help of the Jewish Agency." Three years after 130,000 men and women had registered in Palestine for service, only 12,000 had been admitted to, and carefully dispersed in, various British units in the Middle East.

* * *

My army furlough was ending in June 1943, and in the time left I tried to see events from a wider perspective.

In two thousand years of diaspora life, my people had lost many abilities necessary for national survival. In Western democratic societies, political disagreement is accepted as basic to the preservation of the system. In Palestine where I grew up, and in the world Zionist movement, political traditions were mostly of Eastern European origin—where political disputes were traditionally settled by force. Life in the diaspora so brutalized the spirit of the Jews that often force was used by Jew against Jew, instead of against the common enemies.

Informers, people who betrayed their brothers to save their own skin or win favor, were one of the results of this enslavement.

The Talmud consigned informers to *Gehinom* (hell). At certain times, the local Jewish communities in Spain were granted the right to judge informers and even condemn them to death. Special prayers denounced the *malshinim.* David Wdowinski used to expound on how the stresses of diaspora life and ghetto-dwelling made people into knaves.

Maimonides ruled that it is lawful to kill the informer anywhere, even before he has informed. Once, a known informer was executed on the Day of Atonement which fell on a Sabbath, at the hour of *Neila* . . . the holiest hour in Jewish tradition.

The return to Eretz-Israel did not eliminate the ghetto-dwellers' psychological impairments, as the constant attacks on us by the establishment so clearly revealed. After all these centuries, instead of factions compromising with each other to save people, Jews in power would not distinguish dissenters from the enemy, and in fact never stopped fighting harder against the "dissenters."

So, as I looked back on our works during the past few years in the United States, I could not admit to a great record of achievement. We had thought that a Jewish Army would give the Jews a better chance for survival, but the British could not risk letting Jews gather a body of military power and, since the British were too important an ally for the United States, America ultimately would not help us either. We had launched our emergency rescue campaign though probably too late. Even though we had met opposition every step of the way from our fellow Jews in the establishment, if nothing else, we had at least served as a stimulus, pointing to new approaches, and shaming Jews and non-Jews alike to look up, to take notice, and sometimes to act. Whether or not we succeeded, we had done our best.

IX
The Smell of Death

A troop ship in safe water can be almost as relaxing as a pleasure cruise. Under a summer sky, with a mild, cooling breeze
blowing from the southwest, the S.S. *Argentina* sailed eastward
through the Atlantic at a leisurely pace. It had once been a luxury
tourist liner in South America. Now painted gray, its identity was
camouflaged. It was part of a small, swift convoy of American
troop ships, but for all appearances it could have been out for a
holiday cruise. Even our escorting warships were out of sight.

We knew that battles were raging on the beachheads and hedge-
rows of Normandy and rumors abounded on the ship. Our commanders had not told us where we were headed.

My basic training as an infantryman had been arduous; eight
years passed since I had last undergone military training in the
hills of Judea in 1935. But I was in good shape now. As our Master
Sergeant had said in Fort McClelland, Alabama, before assigning
us to overseas duty: "Youse guys over thirty did okay. Six of you
are going overseas as A-1."

The *Argentina* maintained its southerly course and we were not
surprised when we made out the profile of the Rock of Gibraltar
off the port side. We were in the Mediterranean, or *Mare
Nostrum*—"our sea"—as Eri Jabotinsky called it. It looked as if
we were heading to Italy after all. We had heard speculations
about an invasion of occupied southern France and we guessed
that was our eventual destination.

On the last full day on board, the *Argentina* turned north,
towards the Straits of Messina. We were ordered to prepare for
debarkation the following day.

Our small convoy of troop ships now grew in numbers. We had slowed down, and freighters and tankers of all descriptions caught up with us. Warships appeared on the horizon. Vessels stretched from the horizon ahead, to the farthest point we could see to the south all steaming towards the Bay of Naples. We were nearing the war zone in the Rome area and we could feel a mounting tension.

The next morning, I recognized the Isle of Capri, and Mount Vesuvius. I was back in the land of my student days—Portici, south of Naples. We steamed past and tied up north of Naples.

* * *

A few days later, our L.C.I. (Landing Craft Infantry) softly touched the white sand beach between St. Tropez and St. Maxime on the French Riviera. The U.S. Seventh Army had invaded several days before and we were coming up as their replacements.

On the beach, we dug foxholes, camouflaged our positions and manned anti-aircraft defenses. A few older French resistance men who came to visit, wearing their F.F.I. armbands and lugging odd assortments of weapons, shrugged in mild surprise at our precautions, saying, "*Mais les Boches sont tous foutus*"—"But the Germans are done in." They were not completely right, nor were they far from the truth.

We moved slowly towards Grenoble, which was now to become the main replacement depot for the Seventh Army. Along the route we passed newly dug flower-strewn graves of French civilians and resistance fighters, hostages who had been executed within earshot of incoming Allied artillery.

* * *

On Rosh Hashana 1944, in Grenoble, five hundred Jewish American soldiers assembled in front of the mess. Under the curious gaze of the French who had not seen Jews in uniform or in such numbers before, we marched through the city streets to the University complex.

We packed into the hall, converted into a synagogue for the

holidays and were joined by a smattering of civilians. Bright lights and candles gave the sanctuary an appropriately festive glow, but the atmosphere was still sober and subdued. We all had families or friends in the still-occupied lands and we dreaded what we would find when we reached them.

I sat next to a father and two sons. The boys, in their late teens, wore brand new uniforms of the *Chasseurs Alpines*, the French mountain troops. They had qualified after having lived in hiding with an isolated French farmer for two years, then having joined the Resistance, they became excellent mountain climbers and scouts. The boys looked handsome, healthy and proud. They were among the luckiest Jews in Europe. The entire family was safe—their father, mother and younger sister.

They invited two of us to spend the holiday with them in the small apartment newly assigned to them in town. We enjoyed the traditional meal—wine, gefilte fish, boiled chicken, all the proper accoutrements and blessings. They described Paris after the occupation, speaking about good French people and bad French. About anti-Semites, informers, traitors, saints and angels. From time to time when a name was mentioned, I saw tears, but a holiday spirit of giving thanks prevailed. When the family inquired about Poland, which the parents had left in the twenties, I told them some of what I knew but I left even more out. They had family in Warsaw and I could not offer much hope. I talked instead about recent events in Hungary, because though the news was not much better, I felt it would hurt them less.

My mail from New York had led me to the conclusion that the battle for rescue had been lost in Hungary as well, but curiously, when I criticized the Allies for their failure to help, the French Jewish family had little to say. They had waited and prayed a long time for the Allies to roll back the German war machine, and they had become reconciled to the fact that the Jews would be ground into ashes in the process, as if it were predestined that the Jews had to suffer most in any crisis. Now that the family itself was delivered, it saw Roosevelt and Stalin as the great liberators and only felt gratitude.

I went to sleep on the kitchen floor. It was warm, dry and cozy, the aroma of the meal still wafted in the air, and I stretched out feeling relaxed and safe. Then, against my will, I began to think about what we would find farther north, across the Rhine, beyond the Danube. Knowing that it never had to have been that way, I cried for the first time in years.

* * *

In the winter of 1944 we moved north; we reached Epinal, not far from the border of Alsace, where I remained at the Replacement Depot for two months. It appeared that about half a dozen of us, all foreign-born, were being saved for special duties once we crossed into Germany.

We were temporarily assigned to an anti-aircraft position, on the roof of one of many deserted factories by the Depot, but we never saw a German aircraft. Soon enough, our holiday came to an end.

The Battle of the Bulge had begun, and across Luxembourg and Belgium the Third Army was in the thick of it. Before we could grasp the situation, our "Elite" group was on our way to the battle in a truck, bouncing up and down shelled roads full of holes.

As they attempted to break westward towards Antwerp, the Germans had sideswiped the Seventh Army. Several divisions suffered substantial casualties, and were pulled back to regroup and recuperate. I was now assigned as a replacement in an anti-tank platoon in a battalion of the Seventy-First regiment of the Forty-Fourth Division. It took our truck driver two days to locate regimental headquarters. For more than forty-eight hours we roamed back and forth on back roads, passing through deserted towns and half-razed villages between Alsace-Lorraine and the Saar. We slept in abandoned farm houses and piled up straw and rags over us to keep warm, since we could not light fires during the night. We were tense, cold and fed up with "C" rations, and we griped constantly as soldiers do when they are not in combat.

Shortly after we reached headquarters, we met units from the Grave Registration Section. They were following up reports of unidentified bodies, and their businesslike behavior was depressing. It made me look closer at my comrades, and I noticed "battle fever" on many faces: a certain paleness, a subdued expression, a nervous excitement in their laughter and gestures. In the months to come I saw this more and more. The fever reminded me of the *Irgun* back in Palestine in the late thirties. The men showed many of the same symptoms before we went out for action, and then as now, the symptoms usually disappeared once we were engaged in action. However, in my underground days, the battles were intense but short, while here combat often went on for days, until battle fever was only replaced by battle fatigue.

There were other differences between this and the *Irgun*. There was not the same sense of camaraderie here; we hardly knew each other. Almost half the men were replacements, and we did not have time to develop the closeness men had shared in the *Irgun*, where some were together from their first training to their final battles; nor was there the solid foundation of common experiences and years of cultivating common ideals.

Nevertheless, within a few weeks after a jeep picked up two of us from headquarters and delivered us to the anti-tank platoon, we had integrated into the unit enough to know who could be trusted, and that an infantryman's life was a monotonous, muddy gray experience, interspersed with short bloody episodes. Our platoon sergeant, Tom M.,[1] had no great love for Jews, but things changed between us. When I devised an effective method of blasting holes in the frozen ground for our defensive positions, he asked where I had gotten my expertise in handling explosives. When he found out, perhaps the rebels in his country's history inspired an empathy towards me and we quickly became good friends.

When we crossed the Siegfried Line, our sergeant, Tom M., stopped our gun-hauling trucks, broke out a case of wine we had acquired a few days earlier and instructed me to raise a toast to the defeat of the Nazis. I was the only Jewish soldier in the platoon. Once on the outskirts of Frankfurt, he came across a German Jewish girl who had survived by hiding with old gentile friends of her family. Tom collected sweets and cigarettes from the men, gave me his jeep and dispatched me to deliver the gifts to the small, dark-haired girl and the gentile family. The family welcomed me in, and in a shy whisper the girl told me how she had hidden for months in a closet during the last year of the war.

---

[1] An Irish American.

One day, as we were moving south towards the Alps and the Austrian border, Tom told me about a trainload of Jewish camp inmates that the Division on our Eastern flank had overtaken. There were two young Jewish girls off that train in the nearby village. "Why don't you drive over, take some food and chocolates and talk to them?" Tom suggested, avoiding my eyes.

When I located the girls, I soon understood Tom's embarrassment. They were in their late teens. They wore striped concentration camp clothes, but they looked comparatively healthy and well groomed. We spoke in Yiddish, and they told me they came from Slovakia and had been in German camps less than a year. As they talked, each blushing continuously and trying to hide behind the other, it dawned upon me how they had survived, and in such good condition . . .

There was not much I could tell them. I spoke about the war being over, about how they would now have a new life, and they kept smiling bashfully, saying very little. They never let go of each other's hands. In parting, they shook my hand timidly, and looked me over from the corner of their lowered eyes, mystified at this supposedly Jewish man in uniform who spoke their language and acted friendly.

As I drove back, a gnawing pain gripped me. Nazi pictures I had recently seen flashed before me. Jews in their caftans and boots and small caps: riding each other piggyback, their beards and side locks half shaved; rabbis with naked Jewish girls. I saw the faces of my Dov Gedaliahs and Schneour Zalmans, my Batyas and Chaya Friedas . . . my people.

I drove off the road, stopped the jeep and rested my flushed forehead to cool on the steering wheel. Will I ever forget the degradation of my people? Could I ever accept a possible recurrence? Despite David Wdowinski's comment, some who have never been inside a camp will not be the same either.

In the spring of 1945, southern Germany was lush with wild flowers; and as we went from one skirmish to the next, through the beautiful starbursts of color in the fields, it all seemed terrifically incongruous to us. We took things fatalistically, cracking to each other, "There is a war on, you know." Still, we had some bloody clashes and close calls.

One night southeast of Mannheim, we were crossing the

Neckar River and a barge canal parallel to it, when there was sniper fire. Our platoon, minus our anti-tank guns, hurried over a pontoon foot bridge. We dug in on the southern bank. Then our back-up division began advancing through our lines. It rained throughout the day, and the water rose, straining the bridges' flimsy wire supports. When the back-up division's soldiers crossed in too tight a file, carrying their battle gear, their weight snapped the cables. Out of the dark, we could hear the cries for help of the drowning men, but there was little we could do. We had no boats, we could not save them.

* * *

By April 1945 Germany was crumbling and each new city we reached was practically ours for the taking. We were mostly just mopping up. Our division was in between moves, bivouacked in farmers' homes near the city of Ulm. The farmers were moved into the barns, where their huge fat cattle were the most prosperous living creatures we had seen in Europe. These Germans had managed to live well enough while the rest of the continent was starved and pillaged, and we had no qualms about displacing them to the barns while we took over their clean and comfortable peasant huts.

I had gotten off guard duty in time for breakfast, so I gathered my mess kit, slung my carbine over my shoulder and trudged half-asleep up the main village road to our battalion kitchen. I had heard a rumor that fresh eggs had been delivered and it was worth the muddy and slippery uphill walk. Suddenly, Sergeant Tom came rushing down the hill, as excited as ever. "Roosevelt is dead. Just saw the *Stars & Stripes* . . ." he blurted out, and down the hill he went.

My legs began moving mechanically, and a great sadness came over me, not because FDR was dead. He had lived a good life full of personal and public battles, battles usually of his own choosing.

I felt bereft, not because of all FDR had accomplished, but for what he could have done but had not. For all his greatness, for all his deeds, he and his government to a large degree was responsible for the death of millions of Jews who could have been saved.

FDR had been at worst "a parlor anti-Semite." He had abandoned the Jews in Europe not so much from dislike of Jews as because, in his judgment, there were more urgent problems to worry about in the world. If six million Dutch people—his distant ancestors—had been threatened instead of Jews, he likely would have done no differently. The British, the State Department, FDR's highest military officers, including Eisenhower, convinced FDR that rescue efforts would adversely affect the war effort; and this was all that mattered to him. Between 1942 and 1943, FDR's efforts on behalf of the Jews had amounted to two formal statements that the United Nations would hold accountable the perpetrators of the crimes against the Jewish people of Europe.[1] The State Department proudly pointed out this to the co-chairmen of our Emergency Committee, Ben Hecht and Sigrid Undset.[2] Between the two dates the Nazis killed over two million Jews.

When Ben Hecht had blamed FDR's inaction on anti-Semitism, I pointed out to him that neither Churchill, with his sympathies for Hebrew national rebirth, nor Anthony Eden with his avowed dislike for Jews, had done any more or less to help the Jews.

The oil of the Near East had been one of the final factors keeping FDR from helping the Jews. Early in 1945, he met in Egypt with King Ibn Saud of Arabia; the Saudis were becoming important enough to be specially befriended by the President of the United States. FDR said later that in five minutes, he had learned more about "Arabia . . . the Moslem problems, the Jewish problems . . ." from this medieval-style Bedouin king than from "an exchange of two or three dozen letters."[3]

FDR assured Ibn Saud that he "would take no action which might prove hostile to the Arab people."[4]

So on that gray morning I gulped down breakfast absentmindedly, and filled with anxiety, walked down the hill to our farmhouse.

We were to move out of the village that night. Where to, we did not know, but we knew the war was coming to an end. The Russians were across the German borders, we were pushing east

---

[1] State Department statement of 12/17/42 and Secretary of State Cordell Hull statement before the Joint meeting of the Congress 11/18/43, reporting on the Moscow war crimes declaration (11/3/42), which actually omitted reference to Jews.
[2] Letter of 12/4/43 from H. Travers, Chief Visa Division, State Department.
[3] Sachar's *History of Israel*, p. 255.
[4] Roosevelt's letter to King Saud, April 5, 1945 (*New York Times*, October 19, 1945.)

and south, and it could not go on longer than a month or two. The Germans were almost inviting us into Berlin, while stubbornly fighting the Russians on the eastern front. Our guess was that they feared what the Russians would do to them far more than they feared what we would do. Once Germany surrendered, the battle for independence in Palestine would escalate. It could easily become a bloody war, and we would need vast public support in the United States. As I prepared my gear, I thought about the coming months. I was sorry for a leader of the free world who had not lived to see his victory; but I was also relieved to see him out of the political arena, because I was sure he would have been a mighty opponent in the years to come as my people were fighting for independence. I was reacting pragmatically to his exit from the political scene.[1]

* * *

By April it looked as if the German forces were collapsing faster than we had expected. On short notice, units were being rushed to points all over Germany to fill gaps and mop up. Our unit was somewhere west of Würzburg and moving south. Some staff members from the local field hospital discovered a magnificent wine cellar in Würzburg and we spent hours each day near their mess tent, bartering our souvenirs for Rhine wines.

Early one evening, an odd-looking man came up to me as I sat on a crate next to the hospital mess, sipping the light wine and chatting with a friend. I could not help but stare at him. At first glance, I thought he was quite old. The man wore an apron of sorts, and G.I. fatigues much too large. He was about five feet tall, with a large chest, short legs and stubble covering his wrinkled, ugly face. His ears protruded straight out from under his bushy brown hair, and then drooped like an elephant's.

He grinned, showing a big gap where his front teeth were missing. His skin was wrinkled but his eyes had a twinkle, and close up I realized that he was really young.

Suddenly he blurted out two words: "Cigarettes! Leica!" I continued to stare, trying to identify anything more precise about

---

[1] Later, the President's assistant, David K. Niles, remarked: "There are serious doubts in my mind that Israel would have come into being if Roosevelt had lived."

him than that he was some distant precursor of homo sapiens. He kept on grinning, and repeating "Cigarettes! Leica!" Then, instinctively, I murmured in Yiddish: "Do you speak Jewish?" The grin spread all over his face, and I saw that there was hardly a tooth in his head.

Neither his empty mouth or his downtrodden appearance seemed to make him self-conscious, and as soon as he knew he had a comrade, he was the personification of happiness. He launched into an exciting monologue in Yiddish, telling me his history, and I could hear the unmistakable accent of Galicia. As his story went on, he every now and then interjected questions and little business offers: "Do you want to buy a camera? Some schnapps? Where do you come from? Were you ever in Poland? When?" I motioned to him to sit down. He accepted a cigarette and took a few extras "for his friends." We sat talking for a couple of hours, until it was time for his kitchen duty in the hospital. Two days later he came to visit me in our unit's quarters, and under the curious gaze of my comrades we sat chattering for hours in Yiddish. We must have been a strange couple indeed, I with my muddy boots, grimy fatigues and several days growth of beard, and "Moish"—which was what everybody called him—with his pruny face, floppy years and great toothless grin.

Moish said that he came from a small village near Lvov, and that he had grown up in a traditional Jewish home. His father was a wholesale merchant of wheat and fodder. After Moish's Bar Mitzvah in 1939, his parents had agreed to his pursuing a high school education. Eventually he hoped to take up law, if the restrictions and quotas in the Polish universities allowed for it.

That was how Moses "Motel" Yosselevich had planned his future in the summer of 1939, but by September of that year, the Russians occupied Lvov, and two years later, when Moses was fifteen, the Germans occupied their little town. Originally he prepared to move in with an aunt in Lvov so he could enter the Lvov gymnasia but he never made it. Two weeks after the occupation, the Germans shot his father, a few months later his mother died from typhus. His two sisters, one older and one younger, left in an attempt to reach the aunt in Lvov and he never heard from them again. He refused to go to his aunt in Lvov, telling his sisters he was going to the country to work and live among the peasants.

By then he spoke fluent Polish, simple Russian and some Ukrainian.

Conditions around Lvov deteriorated rapidly, as the local population collaborated completely with the Nazis. All Jews had to wear the yellow badge, and many were shot and killed in the streets. The Nazis, happily aided by the citizenry, launched pogroms, confiscated Jewish properties and destroyed synagogues and Jewish cemeteries. By March, 1942, thousands of Jews were being deported to the Belzen extermination camps.

Moish did not wait for all these developments, but headed to the country and for months in late 1941 and early 1942 he moved from farm to farm, performing any and all chores, eating the simple fare of the peasants or stealing scraps. Some peasants suspected that he was Jewish and chased him away. Others did not care; they needed help so they let him stay.

Jews and non-Jews were fleeing the Nazis and the Nazis were chasing thousands who were roaming the countryside. Soon he was caught by a German patrol and sent to a collection point. At the age of fifteen he found himself in his first camp, Janowska, a notorious road camp. Then he was taken to Belzen, then back to Janowska. He was classified as a cook because he had acquired some kitchen experience during his months among the peasants. It ended up saving his life. Working around the camp kitchens for the following three years, he became a scavenger who fed on scraps.

Moish was only nineteen now; it was the year he had expected to graduate from the gymnasia and apply to the university. He talked about the past years in an even voice, describing the horrors as if they were simple facts. He hardly spoke of his parents or the rest of his family but he spoke frequently and enthusiastically about the future. Hour after hour I sat listening to him, only once in a while asking a question. Sometimes in the hours between his chores at the hospital, we would walk in the fields, and I would feel myself on the verge of reaching out to Moish. But always as I began to move closer, I suddenly found myself withdrawing from him, as if to maintain a clinical distance. He was the first camp survivor I had met after Hitler instituted the "Final solution," and inadvertently I was studying him, attempting to understand how a survivor acted, reacted and adapted. I kept trying to push away the questions in my mind which deeply disturbed me. Could I have survived the loss of my family? Would I have killed myself? Would I have joined the local partisans hiding out in the hills and forests to fight the Nazis? Could I have concentrated on my own survival, knowing that everyone dear to me had been killed? Moish had survived by singleminded determination, by clawing, scratching and grabbing at the garbage. Why?

Slowly the answers became clear to me. In a way it came down to this: he wanted to perpetuate his vanished family. Though he rarely mentioned his parents or his sisters, he constantly spoke about his future family. The future had become for him the replacement for his past and it was the only thing that mattered to him. He was going to move to New York where he had an uncle in the garment business. Originally a tailor, the uncle had become a successful business man and Moish was intent on doing the same. He was going to work for the uncle, learn the trade and build a great business for himself. Then he would marry and have at least four children, naming them after his parents and sisters. And he would definitely be rich.

When I asked Moish if he had any interest in moving to Palestine, he answered bluntly, "No. Too hard a life." Yes, he knew about the pioneers and all the rest but it was not for him. He had worked hard enough in the past five years just to survive. "Besides," he said, "it's too many Jews crowded into one small country. It would be too easy for the non-Jews to gang up again on the Jews."

It was not that I wanted to convert Moish into a Hebrew nationalist. But I wanted to see just what his experiences had done to him. I asked him if he felt more aware of his Jewishness now, and shrugging his hunched shoulders he answered that he had no specific Jewish consciousness. He did not believe in any kind of God; he did not believe in anything except his own survival and the survival and material success of the family he would build. He had survived by his own determination and neither God nor anyone else had contributed. Many continuously prayed to God for help, and where were they? To survive he stole when he had to, he lied, he ate garbage, he stepped on the dead bodies of those around him.

As Moish spelled out his life philosophy, his amiable toothless grin disappeared and he became stern, tight-jawed and hard. Even his wrinkles seemed to be gone. His face was a mask and the eyes looked past me. Again, he began to speak about children! I did not question him but I kept wondering what kind of children he would bring up with his view of the world. I felt a kind of visceral terror. Just six years before, little Moshe Mordechai Ben Avraham Yosselevich had been called to read the holy days *Haftarah*. He was scrubbed, combed, his face radiant, dressed in his best Sabbath clothes. From the women's section, Mama and his two sisters looked down, swelling with pride. Papa draped the prayer shawl around Moshe's shoulders, and the small synagogue filled with his high boyish sing-song. On that day, the day he was graduated to manhood, he was secure in the love of all around him, and survival was the last thing that could have entered his mind. I raised my eyes now and looked at the horrific caricature of a man sitting next to me, a dwarf, a physical and spiritual cripple. I turned my head away and looked out over the German fields into the distant woods. Suddenly, I felt I smelled the burning, the ashes drifting up the smoke stacks and settling on the lush fields and forests. The odor reeked in my nostrils.

I turned to Moish. I did not know what was going on in his mind, but I felt sick. I reached out and put my arm around his heavy, misshapen shoulders and gave him a hug. My brother, my own pitiful brother.

* * *

Late in April 1945 we crossed the border into Austria, moved through Salzburg, then south toward Innsbruck in the Tyrol. This was Nazi-land. Southern Austria had given the world Hitler, Eichmann and countless others like them. For me, the Tyrol did not mean skiing, music, and yodeling, but soil soaked with blood. I remembered the Austrian Nazi "illegals" of the southern provinces in 1937-1938, the Hitler youth with their ecstatic violent anti-Semitism. Now they were not to be found. To listen to them they were all "Austrians," now none of them had ever been Nazis! As everywhere else, the thousands marching and heiling youngsters, applauded by their elders, covered with flowers by their women, had disappeared into the woodwork. It had all been a mirage. Every village, every church steeple, every Bürgermeister's home now flew Austrian and white flags.

I wished we had reached Vienna before V-E day. But we were only as far as Ozthal near the Italian border when the armistice was announced. I was on a mission tracking some S.S. officers who were hiding in isolated farms high in the mountains. We identified them by the letters of their blood type which they had had tattooed on their arms. How arrogantly sure they had been of their thousand-year Reich; it had never occurred to them that one day this mark might betray them as clearly as tattoos betrayed the Jewish prisoners in their camps. When we caught them they claimed they had never been combat S.S.—they were scientists, administrators, technicians. When some showed me wounds they had received on the Russian front, I asked how they had managed to be wounded at their desk jobs. "Oh," they finally admitted, "after Stalingrad we all went to the front."

Overnight, after peace came, the world changed. Everything suddenly seemed quiet. We changed from fatigues to regular uniforms, we were served meals by Austrians and displaced persons. There were smiles on all faces. The Austrians were as effusive as if their side had won the war.

The Alps were beautiful in May. The tall, snow-capped mountains melted into bright green valleys. I walked up the paths alone, carrying my liberated German Schmeisser Automatic with Edelweiss flowers, in the muzzle. I sat atop the mountains and looked towards the west, towards Germany. I felt endless peace and quiet, I felt impervious and safe. But the longer I sat, the stranger the quiet became, the more it felt like emptiness and desolation. Gradually I realized that this was the peace and quiet of a cemetery.

Part V: The War of Independence

I

Armed Resistance—At Last!

The train pulled out of Kantara at midnight October 1945. Kantara, east of the Suez Canal, was the check point for all passengers and goods moving from Egypt to Palestine and the train was packed with military personnel, mostly Empire troops. Some were going on vacation to Palestine, some on assignments to the north, Syria and Iraq. Cairo was British headquarters for the Middle East and a major transit point also for allied troops. I had been granted a special furlough, and I was using the chance to visit Palestine.

A few uniformed Americans and civilians were on the train. I found a window seat, threw my gear on the overhead rack, and attempted to make myself comfortable for the six-hour trip to Lydda. The slow motion of the train and the cool, dry Sinai night air lulled me, but as I sat there on the edge of sleep, the past whirled in kaleidoscopic flashes before my closed eyes.

Palestine six years ago! Our last hurried meetings and decisions as war appeared a greater possibility. My constant feeling of foreboding and emergency. And wasn't it just yesterday that we met in Paris and planned the acquisition of vessels? How our pulses quickened when we heard the reports—"Poland gives us their all-out support . . . training, weapons, everything." All we needed was money, and we would land forty, fifty thousand people in Palestine. Raziel had said: "The day is not far off when we will bring Zeev Jabotinsky back to the homeland on our own cruiser." There were millions of destitute, desperate Jews at long last ready to come home, the masses, the ones Herzl and Nordau had wanted to lead and that Jabotinsky had given hope to.

Only six years, but now almost none of the millions of destitute Jews were left in the lands they had lived in for centuries. Zionism, above all, was supposed to have preserved Jewish lives, but it had failed. What good were ethics when there were none to heed them? What good was an "exemplary society" when the masses of the Jews were dead. What good was a revived language when six million dead would never speak it? Once a proud youngster had told Jabotinsky about his love for Eretz-Israel, and Jabotinsky asked him: "What is even more important than *Artzenu* (our land)?" The youngster shook his head in puzzlement, and Jabotinsky answered simply: "*Amenu (our people).*" We built schools and settlements and planted the land but we lost our people, the millions for whom the State would have become a haven and home.

Now our struggle to create the state was for the remnants, for those still alive who had no home or shelter. I had been requested by our people in New York to meet with Menahem Begin and try to coordinate our work more closely with the *Irgun* in Palestine. We had to strengthen the bridge of communications Ben-Eliezer had built between the homeland and the United States eighteen months ago, if the revolution was going to have a chance.

Someone lowered the window in my compartment and my eyes opened. The cool breeze blew in from the Sinai. Three thousand years ago, Moses had led the slaves, the beaten-down children of Jacob, out of their hovels towards freedom across this forbidding desert. I had heard the stories since I was knee high, and I had always been troubled by doubts and questions. Had they followed Moses out of their own free will? Had Moses really slain Pharaoh's overseer in a fit of anger, or had he done so calculatingly, in order to force a showdown between Pharaoh and the children of Israel. Did he have the right to endanger his people the way he did, first in Egypt, then in the wilderness, then in the conquest of Canaan? Would it have been better for him to have left them as they were, slaves rather than risk their lives in a "foolhardiness" and "irresponsibility" as the Socialists had accused us of when we declared our revolt or when we had packed immigrants onto rickety boats to try and free a few of our people?

Were the masses any less blind and reluctant than their descendants thousands of years later, the Jews of Poland and

Romania and Russia, who had chosen not come to Palestine in 1919 when they had the chance, prior to the restrictions imposed by the British?

Why, I asked myself, was Nordau not heeded when he urged the leaders to bring the Jews to Palestine quickly? Was it true, as Weizmann claimed, that the Jewish masses did not want to come? Were the "flesh pots" of Poland and Russia and the rest of the Pale so enticing that they would not see the hatred, and did not care if they were in danger? Did people always have to be dragged, or even forced, to see that freedom was their only way to survive? Even now, after most of their brothers had been killed, would they be capable of understanding a call for self-reliance? We did not have forty years now to wander in the desert—if we did not strike fast, the British would regroup their forces and the chance would be lost forever. The survivors in the camps in Europe, in northern Africa, in the Arab lands and the six hundred thousand in Palestine, the millions who constituted the new nation—would they at long last hear us now?

I lit another cigarette and took a long draw. The darkness deepened and the stars shone brighter. Dawn was getting near. The latest news from New York was that in the eighteen months since the *Irgun* had launched the revolt it had achieved much of what it set out to do by putting the British and the United States on notice that this time the Hebrew revolution would not cease until independence was won, and the state of Bar Kochba and the Hasmoneans was reestablished.

In Palestine, Europe and the United States, the Zionist Establishment still refused to admit their mistakes and once again mobilized their superior resources, not to topple the power occupying the homeland, but rather to destroy the *Irgun*. With the gas chambers still working the Establishment instigated their own version of the "St. Bartholomew night" against the *Irgun*, the pretext being the assassination of Lord Moyne by the *Lehi* group in November, 1944. The shooting of Moyne, the British Minister of State in Cairo, stirred the rage of Winston Churchill, but even his indignation had been exceeded by the Zionist Establishment. Headed by David Ben-Gurion they declared the "season" as it became known—on the *Irgun*.

In the week before Moyne's murder, negotiations had been

taking place between the *Irgun* leadership and that of the *Haganah*. Ben-Gurion demanded our political and organizational submission to the "recognized institutions," namely Labor and himself, and Begin's answer was: "We agree, if Ben-Gurion will head a Committee of National Liberation and launch the battle against the occupying power." Nothing resulted from these exchanges. Weizmann was again convinced that Britain would repay his moderation with a new partition plan in which the major part of western Palestine would comprise a Hebrew Commonwealth.

Begin and the *Irgun* leadership scoffed just as Jabotinsky had done in 1938 when Weizmann and his colleagues were led to believe that Britain would provide a viable partition plan. In February, 1944, the *Irgun* had been set on a determined course to expel the British from Palestine as fast as possible. This threatened Ben-Gurion and Weizmann, whose policies and power were rooted in compromise and co-existence with the British. The *Irgun* predicted that the short-sighted British would not extend even the modest gestures which would have satisfied the Establishment—slightly increasing immigration and other superficial concessions—and that nothing short of an inevitable military climax would achieve the Hebrew state. Although Ben-Gurion himself sporadically toyed with the idea of armed resistance, right now he was happy to use the enthusiasm of the left wing for an "Anti-fascist" crusade to benefit his own (*Mapai*'s) rule.

Ben-Gurion justified the "season" by stating that political means could be achieved either by diplomacy or by "terror," and that the two could not exist side by side. "Terror" was the derogation he consistently used to describe the Hebrew armed struggle for liberation and it served his purpose well. The appellation "terrorist" stuck like glue to the *Irgun*, and the powerful machinery of the *Histadrut* (Federation of Labor) joined the British in the war against us.

The brunt of the campaign was directed against the *Irgun*, not against the *Lehi*, since the *Irgun* was the one force that could threaten Ben-Gurion's political hegemony. Ben-Gurion knew that sooner or later the only alternative for Labor-*Haganah* would be to join in the battle for independence or the *Irgun* would lead the

PALESTINE

SIR,—In his speech in Parliament on Thursday, August 1st, 1946, the Colonial Secretary, Mr. Hall, denied the truth of Mr. Crossman's remarks and stated that neither the Jewish Agency nor Haganah had assisted the Palestine Police in discovering the mortars (nicknamed V3's), which were trained on the King David Hotel in Jerusalem. The truth of the matter can be seen from the enclosed extract from the *Palestine Post*:

June 17th, 1945.

"The Inspector General of Police wishes to express his appreciation to the Arab Customs Officer and to the member of the Jewish community who gave the information which led to the finding of the two batteries of mortars in Jerusalem on June 12th and 13th."

I am the "member of the Jewish community" referred to by the Inspector General of Police. I received the information regarding these weapons in my capacity as liaison officer between the Jewish Agency, which was actively and consistently working to break the terror, and the Palestine authorities, and I passed it on in the usual way.

It is also correct, as Mr. Crossman stated, that at first only the general location of these, as well as other mortar batteries trained on other Government buildings in Jerusalem, was obtained and passed on by me, but that Police or Army mine detectors were unable to locate them. Only later one of these batteries was found by chance by an Arab, approximately where previously indicated, and the other was found after additional exact information had been received. There were two or three other occasions when the authorities were warned by us about attempts to blow up the King David building.

TEDDY KOLLEK

Teddy Kollek turns over information on the underground's attempts to attack British installations in Palestine.

WARNING!

1. The Government of oppression should WITHOUT ANY DELAY evacuate children, women, civilian persons and officials from all it's offices, buildings, dwelling places etc. throughout the country.

2. The civilian population, Hebrews, Arabs and others are asked, for their own sake, to abstain from new and until the warning is recalled, from visiting or nearing Government offices etc.

YOU HAVE BEEN WARNED !

Warning issued by the *Irgun*, on May 12, 1945.

Menahem Begin, his wife Aliza and son Benajmin, (1945). Begin posed as "a Rabbi Sassover."

Members of the resistance exiled to Asmara (Eritrea). Ben-Eliezer, second from right, front row.

future actions alone. The only alternative, if Labor wished to keep control, was to eliminate the *Irgun* entirely. The order came down from the high command of the *Haganah*: the hunt was on.

This was the situation when I returned home to Palestine. In the last several months, the *Irgun* had suffered severely from the "season" attacks; its highest officers were being kidnapped, tortured, imprisoned for months without trials and delivered over to the British.[1]

One of our top officers, Eli Tavin, was kidnapped and held for months in a bunker on one of the communal settlements. Out of necessity, the organization had dug deeper underground, saving its resources, increasing its stores of weapons, recruiting additional soldiers and continuing its training, though for all appearances it had gone into hibernation. As its older, seasoned key people were eliminated by the "season," we brought up men from the ranks to fill vacant positions. Our supporters in the *Yishuv* had not deserted, and to the contrary, as the weeks and months passed, we had drawn greater admiration and strength from the population.

Despite the attacks, Begin proposed his "twin" policy, saying that there would be "no halt in the battle against the occupying power and no civil war!" Jewish manpower would not be wasted in pitting brother against brother: this was the real *Havlaga* or self-restraint, in the national interest. And, in reward, our base of

---

[1] The Jewish Agency's cooperation with the British was largely flouted before the public in Palestine. Teddy Kollek (later Mayor of Jerusalem) wrote to the *New Statesman and Nation* on August 10, 1946:

The truth [on Jewish Agency cooperation with the British forces] can be seen from the enclosed *Palestine Post* extract June 17, 1945:
The Inspector General of Police wishes to express his appreciation to the members of the Jewish Community who gave the information which led to the finding of the two batteries of mortars in Jerusalem [trained on the British Headquarters in the King David in Jerusalem].
I am the member of the Jewish Community referred to . . . I received the information . . . in my capacity as liaison officer between the Jewish Agency . . . and the Palestine authorities. . .

Teddy Kollek

Later Kollek told Arthur Koestler, the author, that he himself had turned over about one thousand names of *Irgun* and *Lehi* men to the British.

To establish the record for history's sake, Richard Crossman, member of Parliament, stated before the House (7/31/46): "More than one thousand men, members of the *Irgun*, have been handed over to the British authorities in Palestine by the Jewish Agency . . ."

support had never stopped growing.

My train slowed down in Khan Yunis to take on water. After six years, I was again on the border of Palestine. I looked out the window and saw the sun rising over Judea, shining down on the coastal *shefela*. I saw Rehovoth and a campsite where I had pitched a tent almost twenty years ago. I had scarcely had a moment for nostalgia while I was gone, but now it swept over me, and I felt the full weight of the six long years.

Twenty-four hours after my arrival I met with Begin. In Tel-Aviv I walked into the office of Dr. Yaakov Weinshall, one of our long-time activists. A top physician, he had enough energy to spare to develop into a political leader, author, lecturer and historian. He and his brother Abraham, a leading magistrate, and men like Joseph Klausner, U.Z. Greenberg and Dr. Yevin were all part of the intellectual elite which had kept political Zionism alive after Jabotinsky's death; they were the men Socialist historians clearly considered non-persons when referring to the "intellectually barren Jabotinsky movement."

Dr. Weinstall did a double-take when I came in. After giving me a smile of recognition, he arranged contact with Begin. A day later on the outskirts of Tel-Aviv or Petah-Tikvah—it was dark and the country had changed so much that I was unable to identify the neighborhood—I met him. I had last seem him, briefly, in Warsaw six years ago. As head of the *Betar*, he had been given the top assignment in our Polish *Ha'apalah* work, and I remembered him as a scrawny, bookish type, inclined to fiery oratory even in confined surroundings. I was impressed enough then to accept without reservations, his appointment four years later as *Irgun* commander. The man I met now, in far different circumstances, bore a physical similarity to the Menahem Begin of 1939, but the resemblance ended there.

Now in October, 1945, he was an underground leader whose life could be violently ended at any moment. He had declared war on Britain and had led the *Irgun* for eighteen months in a revolutionary war against almost one hundred thousand occupation troops. He had stepped into the void left by Jabotinsky and Raziel, and successfully defended the *Irgun* from the assault of the Establishment. I was in a state of awe and nervous expectation. Would I be able to communicate with the leader of the underground after having worked in the open for years?

I was not disappointed. In the following weeks we met several times, and struck up an easy rapport. I developed great admiration for Begin's intellect. He was not a field commander like Raziel or Meridor, but an ideologist, a political analyst who dissected policies and events for their short and long term effects on the historic process. And though, like Abraham Stern, he showed flashes of a certain mystical, messianic grandeur, it was his cool calculation and judiciousness which made him such an imposing figure. His gifted mind, combined with an ascetic readiness for supreme sacrifice, made him just the man to have assumed the leadership of the *Irgun*.

Begin had once written to us in New York: "I don't command ... although I'm called 'commander.'" He preferred, even in purely military affairs, to remain slightly aloof, leaving operational details to expert associates and functioning more like a chairman of a board where all operational plans were prepared by the respective officers and submitted for approval to the high command. Decisions were reached by consensus.

In military actions Begin played an essential role in the planning stages, working out proper timing of the actions to achieve maximum political reverberations. Usually, once the operations were approved, he gave the officers no interference and his involvement boiled down to trying to minimize casualties on all sides.

My discussions with Begin were intense. We usually met alone so we could have a free play of our ideas. My job was to help Begin and his associates understand the political scene in Washington, London and the United Nations, so we could best coordinate strategy between our delegation in the United States and the *Irgun* in Palestine. Begin and I did have some disagreement about the word "Palestine." In the United States, we favored using the English term "Palestine" as well as "*Eretz-Israel*" in Hebrew. We felt that giving up the term "Palestine" would allow it to be usurped by the British and the Pan-Arabists. We compromised on agreeing to use both Hebrew and non-Hebrew appellations for now; we would also use the terms "Hebrew Government" and "Hebrew Nation."

Begin stressed also that the distinction between Jews and

Hebrews should be understood in a positive and not an exclusive sense. The Hebrew nation was not going to isolate itself from or exclude the rest of the Jews in the world. Very much the opposite—the new nation would educate the diaspora and make it more aware of its national roots, the ultimate aim always being to expand the nation.

In European camps, there were only a few hundred thousand displaced Jews who had survived the extermination while another six hundred thousand constituted the vanguard of the nation in Palestine. However, Begin pointed out that the Hebrew nation included several million *de facto* citizens—scattered throughout Romania, Hungary and the Arab countries—who were prevented from entering Palestine by the illegal policies of the occupying power.

Most important was our agreement in principle that as the time neared for the final stage of the uprising against the Mandatory power, a provisional government would be formed, one part underground in Palestine, the other in the diaspora. To my persistent questioning as to when the *Irgun* would sponsor these moves, Begin answered that while it was becoming more urgent every day, we had to make sure our timing was right. Begin was adamant about timing. As he put it, if we were not careful, instead of freeing the country, we would "find ourselves in a bloody civil war." He became tense discussing this, raising and lowering both his hands, chopping the air, looking hard at me as if to impress his message indelibly. The gist was this: we would never give up our principles but we had to await the propitious time, and avoid giving our opponents an excuse for a fratricidal war. Since our inception, they had dubbed us fascists and claimed that our only real goal was to usurp control of the *Yishuv*. We did not want to prove them right. Consequently, even if we were going to be forced to act unilaterally one day, perfect timing was crucial, and we had to have dialogues with wider and wider circles.

Our meetings often ended over a glass of tea, a tall glass, steaming hot in the style of east Europeans. The dialogue would continue over the tea, and at these moments Begin easily slipped into a teacher's posture. I was fascinated by Begin's orations. Begin's intense dialectics sounded as incisive to me as Paul Haller's had in Vienna in 1937. Except now these were not exercises in the abstract. The concepts and options we discussed now were to be tested within months.

First of all, we would need international recognition and support: the HCNL would establish its European headquarters in Paris; our people had already begun building units in the D.P. camps and in the free communities of France, Italy and North Africa. In all these activities we knew we would have to act alone, without material help from any established body.

As far as the Establishment was concerned, Begin made it clear: he was ready to cooperate with the *Haganah* and even accept the leadership of Ben-Gurion and the Jewish Agency, but on one condition— that the immediate goal of the Zionist movements would be to throw off the British rule through armed struggle. Eventually Begin foresaw the possibility of an integrated military effort, but he believed that cooperation would still be possible on a limited basis or on specific operations. He pointed to recent dialogues he had with Golomb and Sneh, the top leaders of the *Haganah*, to show that this was not out of the question, especially in view of developments in London.

British Labor, under the leadership of Ernest Bevin, was developing irrational opposition to national Hebrew rebirth, and the fantasies of Zionist Labor about British Socialists' empathies was starting to be badly shaken. Soon the resentment and the tensions among the *Yishuv*—among the rank and file of the *Haganah* and even among the more extreme left *Palmach*—would force the Establishment to reconsider its pacifism.

And then? As Begin put it at one meeting: "Let's hope . . . we may sway them towards a united effort . . . for how long . . . ? No one knows. We will not bare our soul nor our organization before them . . . As they swing towards resistance, they may also swing away from it . . . Don't worry, we will not sell ourselves for a pot of gold." Here Haim Landau, Begin's chief of staff, smiled and pointed at me. "The only pot of gold we are looking for is to come from you fellows."

Begin and Landau and the others I met during these meetings always came back to funds. They recognized that our United States delegation's political and public relations successes had been important, and that both the British and the Jewish Agency had shown more restraint in their attacks on the *Irgun* because of our activities. But we were not providing sufficient financal help. The chances for weapons acquisition, for training and for large recruitment were there, if we in the United States provided the means. No matter what we accomplished in the United States, the center of the battle was in Palestine—and if our people lost the ability to fight with arms, no political campaign would secure our nation's freedom.

I could not disagree. I myself felt that our United States delegation was developing an over-emphasis on the political and symbolic aspects of the struggle, ironically tilting backwards towards Jabotinsky's old political Zionism when the time for it was past. Even though Jabotinsky had pointed out Britain's early abandonments of its political commitments, it had taken him twenty years to realize that political action by itself was not enough; it certainly needed political backing to succeed, but by now it should have been obvious to all of us that the crux of the battle was the military one in Palestine. It was true that without the political front the military one would fail, and we needed to achieve a synthesis, but we had to remember that everything we did was to support the military revolution. I felt that in the end, I, Begin and his comrades understood each other very clearly on all this.[1]

In one of my last meetings with Begin before I returned to Germany, I asked him if he minded if I met with Nathan Yalin Mor—then the key man in *Lehi*. Begin shrugged and said with a somewhat bitter smile: "Of course not. But remember . . . whatever he says or proposes is to be taken with great reservations."

This critical comment still rang in my ears when I was led to Nathan's room in Tel-Aviv in the working class home of a Yemenite family in the Hatikva quarter. To shake off any "tails," I had traveled via a long, circuitous route. I came to the meeting with ambivalent feelings. Like Begin, I had been prejudiced against the *Lehi* since the days of its secession from the *Irgun* in 1940. I had

---

[1] I was disappointed by Begin's *The Revolt*, Eli Tavin's *The Second Front*, and other memoirs later written by *Irgun* leaders. In theses books, our comrades on the home front did not give our 1944-48 campaign in the United States its due. In his correspondence with us, during the same years, Begin admitted that our work played an important role in deterring both the British and the Jewish Agency from all-out campaigns to destroy the *Irgun* in Palestine in the early stages of the Revolt.

been hurt and disappointed by the ease with which some of my closest friends discarded loyalty to Jabotinsky and his teachings. Men with whom I had shared dangers and tragedies shed their loyalties to David Raziel and the traditions of the *Irgun*, and I saw it as the result of personal ambitions and vindictiveness. I traced these conflicts back to 1938 when the *Irgun* was beginning to expand and increase its strength. Symptoms of a power struggle had begun appearing them, especially between Raziel and Stern; but I had hoped that these were solved at our Paris Conference in February, 1939, when we unified under Jabotinsky's command. I had felt then as if our dreams had all been realized, dreams of a proud, loyal Hebrew youth working towards a common goal of independence. The merger of the *Betar* and the *Irgun* was to be the foundation of the national revolutionary army.

Like many other *Irgun* veterans, I, too, had felt frustration with Jabotinsky in the late thirties for his reluctance to lead us into the final revolutionary phase; and I had my disagreements with him during my year of work in the United States. I too strove to maintain the *Irgun* independence from the Revisionist party apparatus and legal status but I never challenged Jabotinsky's leadership. But when Abraham·Stern ("Yair") and several of our top men on assignment in Poland spoke of Jabotinsky as the "old man, the old fashioned Zionist," and likened him to Weizmann, Sokolow and all the other vacillating, passive Zionist leaders, I resented it. Stern and the other dissenters were not ready to present Jabotinsky with clear-cut plans of action; when Jabotinsky attempted time and again to elicit these plans, they had nothing to offer beyond ideological generalizations. And in actuality, detailed proposals for an armed landing of tens of thousands of men led by Jabotinsky had been formulated by Jabotinsky himself. Back in 1937 at a meeting in Cairo, he had raised the option of an uprising. This was before Ben Yosef had gone to the gallows, before the *Ha'apalah* was developed, before help had been offered us by the Polish government. And though he recommended continuing diplomatic efforts to change British policies, he never ceased turning over in his mind the alternative of a substantial rebellion against the British.

But he would not proceed unprepared, under-armed, under-trained. He appointed commissioners to obtain funds, shipping, and additional governmental sources for weapons, and when gradually our resources increased and our probabilities of even limited success were better, he submitted his plan to the *Irgun* command. One of his central proposals was "Hold Government House in Jerusalem for forty-eight hours."

This was taken up at the ill-fated meeting in Tel-Aviv, on the night of August 31, 1939. Only one man, Abraham Stern (Yair), vigorously objected to the plan, calling it a useless gesture. The beginnings of the split had shown itself right there. And in September, 1939, when war broke out, I did not see an alternative to the unilateral cease-fire by the *Irgun*, declared by Jabotinsky and Raziel. So I came to this meeting with Nathan heavy-hearted. Since the *Lehi* had executed Lord Moyne, I had wondered what Jabotinsky's reaction would have been; I guessed that he would have applauded the "two Eliahus," the young men who had given their lives. But he also would have said that even though Moyne undoubtedly had been responsible for the death of hundreds of thousands of Jews because he denied them refuge in Palestine or anywhere else through the empire—even though punishing this man was emotionally understandable, it did not advance the cause of Hebrew freedom. Jabotinsky believed that Jews should use force, like any other nation, to safeguard survival. But selecting individuals as targets or shooting British soldiers and police at random? I remembered Jabotinsky's objections to the retaliatory *Irgun* policies of 1937-38. It had taken almost a year to convince him that the Arab population and the terrorist bands it sheltered must be made to understand that innocent Jewish civilians could not be killed with impunity.

All of these questions surfaced when I sat down with Nathan in the barren room furnished with a simple low iron bed, a few wooden orange crates used as bookcases, and a bare table with a couple of unadorned wooden chairs, under a naked light bulb. Nathan and I had met once before in Warsaw, where he was a senior editor together with Samuel Merlin, of *Die Tat*, the Yiddish daily paper of the *Irgun*.

I sat down across the table from him. A bottle of brandy was waiting for us, and in return I offered Nathan a cigar out of my army PX stock. Nathan came from Grodno, my grandfather Zeev Leib's home, so that two of us were practically "landsmen." We were of the same age and we talked easily. He asked when I had last seen his friend Sam Merlin, and I asked for news about my old friend Shlomo Harari who was in detention in Africa.

While Begin was ascetic, almost monastic, Nathan was a *bon vivant*, a displaced Left Bank intellectual. He was an amiable man and smiled easily. But he was by no means an easy fellow to bulldoze. He would listen attentively to his interlocutor, and if the person objected to any of his statements, he simply shrugged his shoulders and said: "That's the way I see it." Then he was ready for the next subject.

We covered several years of history, from the split between Raziel and Stern to the present, and many of the old differences cropped up: "Raziel was a military man with a limited political scope," Nathan said at one point, "but certainly not an innovator or independent thinker." Nathan went on to say that after Jabotinsky was gone, the Raziel faction stagnated, while *Lehi* remained flexible, innovative, and relentless. The cease-fire with Britain, had been a one-sided surrender on our parts, and Jabotinsky was gone, the Raziel faction stagnated, while *Lehi* remained flexible, innovative, and relentless. The cease-fire with had even sacrificed our commander Raziel, and for what? Britain had never even hinted at changing their anti-Jewish policies.

Nathan waved my objections aside, even before I concluded them. "I know, I know," he said, "we had to fight the Nazis. So what did we achieve? Six million dead! What did the Allies do for us? Nothing. The place for our youth was here, in the homeland, and that includes *you*." He pointed at my uniform. I tried to counter: "You don't understand. For three years we headed a campaign for a Jewish army and none of us ended up in a Jewish uniform . . ."

"To hell with these niceties." His hand came down flat on the table. "Our duty is only to our nation, the same as the British and everybody else. They fought for their survival. Our duty was to fight for our survival, right here! Instead, Raziel followed the political line of the N.Z.O.! And Menahem hasn't progressed much further."

There was nothing to be gained from these exchanges, so I held my tongue. I remembered a long letter to Samuel Merlin from Yair in the summer of 1940. He asked us to sever our link with

Raziel, and if need be also with Jabotinsky if he did not change his instructions appointing Raziel as *Irgun* Commander.

Neither then or after, had I personally ever regretted resisting Yair's call to "split and rebuild," and I did not feel like arguing now with Nathan; so I merely asked questions and Nathan answered. I asked him if the Moyne assassination had been a positive act in the War of Liberation, and he answered "Absolutely." Moyne, he explained was the personification of British imperialism in the Middle East. As Colonial Secretary earlier in the war, later as member of the House of Lords and finally as Resident Minister in Cairo, he had stonewalled every appeal to help our people in Europe. He had espoused a theory that European Jews were hopelessly mixed with Slavic blood and consequently could not, according to Moyne, be held Semitic. The only pure Semites were the Arabs, thus only they had historic rights in Palestine. To make sure not one crack was left open to the Jews he had the authorities in Turkey send the vessel *Struma* back to the Black Sea, where it foundered with its seven hundred and seventy passengers, and he had defended the cold-blooded murder of Abraham Stern by the Palestine British police in 1942.[1]

I poured myself another brandy as Nathan gave me his arguments. I could not defend Moyne, but neither could I defend the symbolic murder any more than I would have condoned the assassination of FDR. Moyne had been party to the deaths of millions of people, but he had not committed murder himself or even ordered them.[2]

To change the subject, I asked Nathan what the chances were now for close cooperation, or even a merger between the *Irgun* and *Lehi*. Nathan was silent for a moment, then answered slowly: "Coordination—possibly. Merger—no." Nathan explained that he felt Begin would never treat *Lehi* as equals; there was no mutual trust and too much bad blood. Besides, the *Irgun* had adopted too "gentlemanly" a style of dealing with the British

---

[1] Years later Nathan insisted to me that when Adolf Eichmann sent Joel Brandt to negotiate with the Allies on exchanging one million Jews for trucks, Moyne was stunned and reportedly blurted out: What would I do with a million Jews?" To Howard Sachar, in his *A History of Israel*, Moyne appeared as "a gentle and widely respected man."

[2] However, we in New York arranged for funds to be sent for the legal defense of Hakim and Beit Zuri.

when what was called for was a ruthless, bloody fight, the same treatment the British had inflicted on our people. *Lehi* was going to battle the British in Britain as well, and it would not stop until Palestine was rid of them. There was no compromise with British imperialism. Begin was still toying with the outdated Revisionist ideas of Jabotinsky and Raziel that somehow, somewhere, common ground could be found with "friendly" Britons. This was dangerous self-delusion.

When I asked Nathan why the *Irgun* was bearing the brunt of the "season," when *Lehi* which had executed Moyne was hardly touched, he offered the simple explanation that *Lehi* men were always armed and neither the police nor the *Haganah* were anxious to tangle with them. But he also agreed with me that the small, tight *Lehi* organization was less vulnerable to infiltration by informers, and he added coolly that *Lehi* "would execute informers without hesitation."

From there Nathan and I got into a general discussion about the Jewish malaise of informers, and how "Moses had been the first Hebrew denounced by his brothers." Before the evening was through, we talked about how the *Lehi* had evolved since the split, about actions they had carried out against the CID officers, and about the selfless dedication of the *Lehi* and *Irgun* youth. The conversation lasted past midnight, then we parted, shaking hands. We had not changed each other's views on basic issues, but we understood one another better, and more than ever I respected the courage of these few, lonely young men and women.

As I walked towards the door, Nathan asked unexpectedly: "Did Menahem say anything about developments on the *Haganah* front?"

I was surprised. "No. Nothing was mentioned."

Nathan smiled, "Why don't you ask him at your next meeting?" In effect, he was implying that certain important developments were expected in relations with the *Haganah*.

I did not expect to see Nathan again. I was sure that one way or another he would come to the same end as Yair. But somehow, as it turned out he emerged from the underground unscathed. The British never caught him. He was imprisoned by the Government of Israel after the assassination of Count Folke Bernadotte in 1948.

My final meeting with Begin took place towards the end of October, 1945 in the apartment of a family of *Irgun* sympathizers in Tel-Aviv. The encounter was short and to the point. Begin gave me a summary of the political situation. Our delegation in the United States was to establish closer coordination with the diaspora-*Irgun* in view of the military activities projected in Europe.

Then Begin came up with important news: Now that British Labor had declared an outright anti-Zionist stance, the local Socialists, and especially the *Haganah* had agreed in principle to coordinate with the *Irgun* and *Lehi* armed action against the British. This was despite the objections of Dr. Weizmann, still loyal to the British. The URM (United Resistance Movement) was to go into operation shortly, after final discussions on long-term goals and strategy. The *Haganah*, *Irgun* and *Lehi* would each take care of their own budgets and weapons acquisitions. Military action would be approved and coordinated by a central body, with the *Haganah* retaining the veto power.

I asked what would happen if the Jewish Agency's political leadership at some point suddenly decided to withdraw from the URM. Begin answered that all the pros and cons had been weighed. The advantages were greater than the dangers.

This was the first time the Establishment had ever embraced the concept of an armed struggle. Once, after the "Emergency Zionist Conference" in the Biltmore Hotel in 1942, Ben-Gurion intimated in private conversations that at a certain point in post-war developments, the *Yishuv* might have to resort to arms to achieve self-rule, though at present he was still willing to accept a partition, giving the Jews a small territory. Until now, that was the most militant statement he had ever made. Six years before the Biltmore Conference he had written in the *Haganah* organ "Bamahaneh": "The British will not do a thing for crazy people." We in the *Irgun* were the crazy people to whom he was referring.

As I expected, Begin did not feel that reunification with *Lehi* was feasible except as part of this wider agreement with all the armed groups in the *Yishuv*. He felt that the *Lehi* had too sectarian a philosophy, and could not be counted on to adhere to commitments. Their assassination of Moyne had taken place in the middle of negotiations with us, aiming at a merger, and we were never warned that something this serious was planned. *Lehi* had known full well that the police reaction could be disastrous to us, and when the "season" followed hard on the heels of Moyne's death, and centered on us, we were not prepared for it.

Begin also pointed out that inherently the strategies of our two organizations were at basic variance. *Lehi* was committed to continual small-scale clashes without necessary long-term planning. They saw themselves as the catalysts—"the yeast in the struggle," as Nathan put it—while the *Irgun* operated long-range, preparing for the full scale uprising, creation of a Provisional Government and expulsion of the British. We chose to be and were the real threat and alternative to the Establishment's political policies. It knew that if it continued its collaborationist policies with the British, we would act alone. While *Lehi* was the "yeast" we were the body and muscle who had to bear ultimately the responsibility for the revolution. "If the bread won't rise, we must constitute the rising bread," said Begin.

In a final burst of warmth before we parted, Begin embraced me and said: "We are proud of you in the States. You sent us Arieh Ben-Eliezer, who helped us reemerge as a fighting force, and with your help in mobilizing public opinion, we will surely win. You are our guarantee for survival, growth and success."

The new United Resistance Movement might not last, but Begin, Nathan and the thousands of other committed rebels would see the battle through to the end. Armed resistance was at last being accepted by the *"criminal fascists"; even if Weizmann got the Haganah* to withdraw from the common fight, the people would no longer see us as pariahs, and they would never again permit a "season." The Establishment could no longer point to us as the enemy; the days of collaboration with the British were coming to an end. That was the way it appeared to us as the year 1945 neared its end.

* * *

In the following weeks I was marooned at Payne Field outside Cairo, awaiting transportation back to my base in Germany.

Almost as soon as I had reached Payne Field, the Cairo press carried this news in bold headlines: "Terrorists strike all across Palestine!" For the first time since David's campaigns against the Philistines, all Hebrews were fighting together against the occupiers of their land. They were not calling one another "renegades" or "dissidents" or "terrorists" any more, and the weapons of the *Haganah* were not "purer" than any one else's. From dozens of bases, hundreds of men and women were going out to fight for freedom. My pulse quickened as I read the papers: "The railroads were damaged in a hundred and eighty points. The locomotive works in Lydda were blown up. The refineries in Haifa badly damaged."

The British had learned beforehand of the formation of the URM: *Haganah* counter-intelligence failed at protecting the new organization's secrecy, and the British intercepted and decoded messages sent by Moshe Sneh and Israel Gallili to David Ben-Gurion and other Jewish Agency leaders abroad. These letters discussed the forthcoming campaign.[1]

But even though they were forewarned, the British were taken by surprise by the scope of the resistance and by the smooth planning and strength of the attacks. The Hebrew Revolution proclaimed by the *Irgun* in 1944, now swept over the whole of Palestine.

* * *

At last I left Cairo. My plane refueled in Vienna, and I was sorry I could not go into the city to see the vengeance that had been wreaked on the hundreds of thousands who had cheered Hitler on March 11, 1938. How arrogant they had been then. Vienna of Sigmund Freud and Heinrich Neumann, sheltered from the music of Schoenberg, Mahler, and Mendelsohn, its libraries cleansed of Schnitzler and Kafka, now lay in physical and cultural ruin.

---

[1] They were later published by the British in the 1947 White Paper, "Violence in Palestine."

II
On Two Fronts

In March, 1946, I was on a troopship out of Bremerhaven, Germany, on my way back to the United States. It seems that critical moments in my life were always marked by ocean crossing. I would stroll for hours or lean against the rail on deck. I loved the sea: the isolation; nature in its rawest element, nothing but sea and sky in all directions. It cleared the mind. I always did my best thinking on ships.

I looked forward to the coming months. The war was over, and there would be no more distractions. In the last year, trying to survive from day to day, I had to suppress my deepest concerns; but now they all came rushing to the surface. With my visit home, my renewed contact with comrades in the struggle, my mind was racing as fast as events in Palestine. The URM was in full swing. The *Haganah* had attacked coastal stations; the *Irgun* had confiscated British weapons and payrolls. Together the *Irgun* and *Lehi* were attacking railroads, oil storage tanks and administrative offices.

Britain's Foreign Minister, Ernest Bevin, appeared before the U.N. General Assembly in January and drove a last nail into the coffin of the Balfour Declaration. He announced that Great Britain would "take steps in the near future for establishing (Trans-Jordan) as a sovereign independent state." On March 22, Great Britain and Trans-Jordan signed an agreement cutting off eighty percent of the original Mandate area from international obligations for a Jewish Homeland. This was in clear contravention of Article V of the Mandate: "The Mandatory shall be responsible for seeing that no Palestine territory shall be ceded or

leased to, or in any way placed under the control of the government of any foreign power."

This maneuver abrogated not only the Mandate but also contravened the U.S.-British Convention rulings of 1924.

Our friends in both houses of Congress stood up and urged the
government to oppose it, but to no avail. Secretary of State
Byrnes wrote to Senator Francis J. Myers defending Britain's
actions on the basis of Churchill's White Paper of 1922.

The new State of Trans-Jordan was established, consisting of
about three hundred thousand inhabitants, mostly nomadic
Bedouins. One clause in the agreement between Trans-Jordan
and Britain provided for the training of Trans-Jordan's Arab
Legion, and the staffing of its top command by British officers.
This provision guaranteed the British a military base for their
colonial interests in eastern Palestine.

In the United States, our people were putting more and more
pressure on Roosevelt's successor, President Truman, to do
something about the remnants of Europe's Jewry, and Truman
was sympathetic. But when his special emissary, Michael Harrison, reported to him that "ninety-five percent of the displaced
persons in the camps in the American occupied zones of Germany
and Austria wish to emigrate to Palestine," Foreign Minister
Bevin countered by promoting an Anglo-American Commission
of Inquiry (AACI) on the subject. This commission, composed of
six British and six Americans, drew America into making specific
recommendations, but left Britain the option of refusing those
recommendations. At this moment, while I was crossing the
Atlantic westward, the commission was traveling eastward to
Palestine.

As my ship moved closer to America, I read some references to
the commission on the daily mimeographed news bulletins near
the recreation room. The commission was holding hearings in the
Jerusalem YMCA. Outside, armed patrols guarded the entrances
and the streets, while inside Weizmann and Ben-Gurion testified,
as well as the opposition—Auni Abdul Hadi and Jamal el
Husseini (the cousin of Hitler's friend, Amin el Husseini). I wondered whether we presented our views to the Commission.

A band was waiting to welcome us on the New York pier. As we
disembarked, people threw streamers and confetti. It was good to

be back, safe and sound. But in my heart I felt that we Jews did not have that much to celebrate about. For the non-Jew, the war was over. The Americans, the British, the French, even the Italians and Germans were going home. But what about the remnants of our people?

A few days after my discharge from the army, a courier arrived from Palestine with a document hidden inside the heel of his shoe. It was a copy of the memorandum the *Irgun* had submitted to the American members of the AACI:

> We do not address our words to all members of the committee, but to the American members *alone*. It is absolutely useless to talk to the British. For twenty-five years the representatives of our people have been doing so . . . appealing to the conscience, the justice, and the humanitarianism of the British rulers. In vain . . . our fathers, our mothers, our sisters, our brothers, our children . . . our rabbis and sages were massacred with the complicity of the British . . . even now and in the future, the British are to be those who deprive us of our homeland and destroy our people . . . we are determined, in our relations with them, to use no other words but "Fight!"

For six single-spaced pages the document detailed British crimes against the Jews.

> Around Eretz-Israel as a whole, a close fence has been drawn, behind which sadists in military and police uniforms are committing their outrages, having been equipped, from the High Commissioner down to the last soldier, with unlimited power to arrest, to suppress, to shoot and to murder.

After quoting the Declaration of Independence, the document then added:

> Indeed, gentlemen, all the rights for which your forefathers waged righteous war, and for which they gave their lives one hundred and seventy years ago, are being denied to us by the British regime of oppression. There is neither life for us nor liberty, nor happiness, so long as this country has not been returned to its lawful owners: to the Jewish people, its elected representatives and its persecuted sons and daughters . . . in Europe, Asia and Africa.

The commission read the memorandum and did not understand it. Not even the American members understood that it was 1776 in Palestine.

The commission's major recommendations were that neither a Hebrew nor an Arab State should be formed in Palestine, and that one hundred thousand Jewish immigrants should be admitted. The commission conditioned this on the Jewish Agency's collaboration with the Mandatory Power "in suppressing the terror," helping the Mandatory keep law and order.

Eventually, the Anglo-American Commission's recommendation to admit the one hundred thousand European Jewish survivors was rejected by Bevin and Prime Minister Attlee. From the start, the commission had been a ploy by the British to swing the United States to their viewpoint; and when the conclusions did not suit them, they simply let those conclusions fade away, the same as they had done with the Peel Commission report in 1937.

Bevin was oblivious to all but his own concepts of policy. He and Britain failed to appreciate several important developments. One, with the war over, the people of the United States would no longer give unconditional backing to its war-time allies' policies. Second, perhaps even more important, Truman was a less sophisticated political man than Roosevelt. He had the basic beliefs of the Bible belt, and he was also impulsive, stubborn and unpredictable. In December 4, 1945 he told J. David Stern, the Philadelphia newspaper publisher and one of our leading activists, that he opposed the concept of a Jewish State as well as a Moslem or a Baptist—in Palestine, but favored Palestine as a home for the Jewish refugees. A year later, he wrote to King Ibn Saud that ever since World War I, the United States had unflaggingly supported self-government and a national home for the Jewish people in Palestine. Truman added that most liberated peoples were now citizens of independent countries, and since this was not yet true for the Jews, "it was only natural . . . that this government should favor at this time the entry into Palestine of considerable numbers of displaced Jews . . . to contribute their talents and energies to the up-building of the Jewish national home."

Whether or not Truman's words were a complete turnaround from the year before, they were a courageous stance to take with the leading oil rich Arab King.

A deep chasm was splitting the United States and Britain over the fate of the Jews of Europe. Attlee actually wrote to Truman that the Nazi concentration camps had housed people from many regions, and that "there appears to have been very little difference in the amount of torture and mistreatment they had to undergo."[1] Even British Jews had a distorted view of history: Harold Laski, a representative of British Labor, when sent to Italy to mollify a group of immigrants detained in ports on crowded ships at British request, told the immigrants that if not for the British, probably none of them would have been alive![2]

Regretfully, we did not have the means or the opportunity to place large advertisments throughout the British Isles, telling the real story.

The British were told by Attlee to consider the feelings of "ninety million Moslems in India." It was no surprise when Bevin proposed that the Jewish Displaced Persons of Europe should resettle in *Germany*.

When I rejoined our delegation in the United States and was brought up to date on recent events, I did not know whether to weep or laugh about it all. In Palestine it was a less complex proposition: There were a few thousand Hebrew soldiers ready for any sacrifice, and both our enemy and mission were clearly defined. Here in the United States, with our small delegation minus Merlin, who was now in Paris, and Ben-Eliezer in a detention camp in Eritrea, we had to face opposition from the British, the State Department, an unpredictable White House, the Establishment-Zionists, the anti-Zionists, and the "neutral, influential Jews." In certain aspects it was as if nothing had changed since 1943.

But in some ways we had made great progress. We had gathered around us a number of intellectuals who gave us their full support. They kept up an indefatigable lobbying campaign in Washington backed up by our offices, and young people all across the country. We published ads, put out a weekly paper called *The Answer* in New York, regularly raised funds, held forums and debates and distributed literature. Eighty percent of American Jews now declared themselves in favor of a Jewish State—a giant step from

---

[1] Bevin said in 1945: "everybody would be taken care of but the Jews must not push themselves to the head of the queue."
[2] Foreign office records 371 525!5.

the indifference and antagonism of 1939. So our chances were much better for a hearing.

Most of our delegation was back together: Kook and Merlin had more than fulfilled the hopes we placed in them when we scattered in 1943; Eri Jabotinsky, back from the British jail, and, Alex Rafaeli back from the wars. So, despite the odds against us, we felt a spirit of renewal. This time we knew we would succeed both in Palestine and the United States.

* * *

The confrontation in Palestine between the URM and British forces was developing into a bloody war, in which less and less consideration was given to human lives. The *Irgun* had never gone into battle with the intent of killing Britishers, but as the police and military took harsher and more vicious steps, the *Irgun* gradually gave up the discriminate, gentlemanly approach it had practiced since its announcement of the revolt in 1944. *Irgun* and *Lehi* men were now being tortured, flogged, shot randomly and even hanged. But still, they tried to avoid brutality as far as it was possible. When they launched bombing attacks against buildings that housed civilians, they issued advance warnings. While on missions destroying government facilities or otherwise disrupting government operations, they answered fire with fire. When their warnings to the British to curtail the floggings were not heeded, then and only then they inflicted flogging on British officers. And we knew that more cruel and tragic events were still to follow.

Historic roles were being reversed: for the first time in thousands of years, it was the Jews who were *acting* and the non-Jews who were reduced to talking and reacting. General Sir Frederick Morgan, the top British Relief Officer in Germany, complained that his territory had been invaded by thousands of rich, rosy-cheeked Polish Jews, with a "well organized plan to get out of Europe." He feared, he said, "a second exodus from Europe to Palestine." From Jerusalem, the newly appointed British High Commissioner, Sir Alan Cunningham, wrote to London: "Incitement by the local press and leaders is directed to inducing in the Jewish mobs a readiness to sacrifice their lives for the sole purpose of putting us in the wrong." Nevertheless, one of his lieutenants gave his own version: "H.M.G.'s policy has caused more than a flutter in both Arab and Jewish dovecotes. As always, the Jewish birds squawk loudest."

In early 1946, British hostility was directed less and less towards the *Irgun* and more towards institutions of the Establishment; Weizmann and his moderate colleagues, still attempting a dialogue with Britain, were doing the "squawking" and being insulted for it. Constantly describing the situation with innocuous terms like "squawk" and "flutter," the British seemed incapable of grasping that a full-scale national uprising was taking place before their eyes. A prejudicing anti-Semitism blinded British policy makers to the fact that Jews are capable of backing up nationalist rhetoric with physical sacrifices.

Ernest Bevin was the most tunnel-visioned of everyone involved. "Regarding the agitation in the United States," he said, "and particularly in New York, for one hundred thousand to be put into Palestine . . . I say with the purest of motives, that that was because they do not want too many of them in New York." As the *Lehi, Irgun* and *Palmach* continued to hammer away at British targets, Bevin only hardened his position, proceeding to try and paralyze the "respectable" Jewish leadership. He began imprisoning the top echelon of the Jewish Agency and the National Council, and hundreds of suspected leaders in the *Haganah* and *Palmach*.

In New York and Washington we responded by taking on the British in the press and Congress. The clandestine *Irgun* "Voice of Fighting Israel" broadcast the following message which we distributed widely in the United States:

> The arrest of the heads of the *Yishuv* . . . has but one purpose . . . to rob us forever of our only country; to turn us, as in the diaspora, into dust . . . In this situation there is no other choice but to fight . . . vacillation is a misdeed . . . delay—criminal.

At a press conference in Washington, Hillel Kook on behalf of the HCNL proposed:

> At the joint initiative of the HCNL and the *Vaad Leumi* (National Council of Palestine) or of either one, a Hebrew Representative Assembly shall convene. . . . It will set up a Provisional Government which will include the Hebrew partisans of Europe, Hebrew

displaced persons and citizens of Palestine, without reference to creed or descent . . .

The Provisional Government shall devote itself to: Repatriation, creation of a regular army, applying for a seat at the General Assembly, entering diplomatic, political and trade relations with all friendly nations in the world.

The leadership of the Zionist Establishment could not go along with us in such a bold and sweeping commendation. It would take them two more wasted years of floundering and agony before they would gather their courage to commit themselves to independence.

* * *

In July, 1946, when the URM was entering its eighth month of operations, the destruction of British military headquarters in the south wing of the King David Hotel shook Jerusalem, and had wide repercussions. The heavy casualties were the end result of a series of tragic missed signals.

Ironically, the President of our American League for a Free Palestine (ALFP), former Senator Guy M. Gillette, and the co-chairman, Harry L. Selden, had confirmed reservations for July 27th at the King David.

The activists who gathered around our cause in the ALFP, had been ceaselessly searching for ways to avoid the ever-increasing bloodshed. In December, 1945, Senator Gillette, J. David Stern, Professor Fowler V. Harper and colleagues had flown to London to meet with Bevin. With the gas chambers hardly cooled Bevin had presumed to lecture them on Jewish history and Jewish equal rights in the diaspora! He reminded them that Britain had been the first country in modern times to give Jews full citizenship rights, and he told them that Jews had to adapt themselves as equal citizens in the European countries in which they lived.

After he returned to the States, Gillette did not give up. He groped for a way to communicate with the local officials in Palestine, to convince them that the overwhelming majority of Jews in Palestine, in the displaced persons camps in Europe and in other diaspora centers wanted independence in their own country, for themselves and for generations to come. Our delegation in the United States acquiesced to Gillette, letting him pursue his negotiations. It was at this point that Gillette arranged his trip to Palestine, and booked the reservations for the King David Hotel. Harry Selden was less sanguine than Gillette about their chances of success, but he went along, knowing that his knowledge of the history of Britain's presence in Palestine, and his understanding of the legalities involved, would be invaluable if any serious dialogue developed.

* * *

In Palestine, the British and the entire *Yishuv* were now on a collision course. General Montgomery, Chief of the Imperial General Staff, visited Palestine and reported back to the Cabinet that the way to end the Hebrew resistance was a get-tough policy. He said he was fully prepared for "a war against a fanatical and cunning enemy who would use the weapons of kidnap, murder and sabotage." The Cabinet concurred, giving the High Commissioner authority to liquidate the "extreme elements" now supposedly in control of the *Haganah* and the Jewish Agency. The United States Government was to be informed, but not until the last moment, to prevent leaks to American Jewish groups.

On June 29, at 1:45 A.M., Attlee cabled Truman: "In view of the continuance of terrorist activities in Palestine, culminating in the recent kidnapping of six British officers, His Majesty's Government has come to the conclusion that drastic action can no longer be postponed." With the message, Attlee launched Operation "Agatha."

By "terrorists," the British now meant the entire *Yishuv*, with the exception of Weizmann. "Agatha's" dragnet was to put behind barbed wire anyone local British officials considered a "V·I·J" (Very Important Jew) including Rabbi Judah Leib Fishman, the venerated leader of the Orthodox *Mizrachi*; Wolfgang Von Weisel, a veteran leader of the Jabotinsky movement; the moderate Moshe Sharett; and Ben-Aharon of the left wing of Labor. Having broken the Jewish Agency code eight months earlier, and having tabulated and indexed all cable exchanges between Jerusalem and the Jewish Agency in London and Paris, the British had a good idea whom they were after and they arrested two thousand six hundred and fifty men and fifty-nine women.

The British acted like an occupation Army in enemy territory, which in effect they were, and they treated the Jews like a conquered people. A hundred thousand British soldiers and ten thousand police participated in the operation. In addition to the arrests, they killed three civilians and wounded hundreds of others. They discovered and confiscated arms—producing shops and ammunitions caches, and they captured hundreds of *Haganah* rifles. They considered it their chance to crush the moderate *Haganah* and almost succeeded. Before they were through, the core of the one element in the *Haganah* that counted militarily, the *Palmach*, was behind bars.

To justify the arrests, the British seized documents in the Jewish Agency building. Much later they admitted that those documents did not sufficiently incriminate either the official institution or the individual leaders; but at the time of the seizures, High Commissioner Cunningham advised London that ample evidence had been found to link leaders of the Agency with the illegal *Haganah*, and that they should begin court proceedings.

Their next step was to prove the link between the *Haganah*, the URM, and, of course, the "terrorists." Every child in Palestine knew that the *Haganah* was the military arm of the Establishment, and that the URM was an umbrella organization functioning with its blessing. The URM's communiques were read over the *Haganah* radio station. But to obtain hard documentary evidence of "terrorism," the British felt compelled to use all efforts.

Operation "Agatha" shook up the Agency's leadership, but it failed to destroy the *Haganah*, and hardly touched the *Irgun* or *Lehi*. Two prominent leaders of the *Haganah*, Dr. Sneh and Yizhak Sadeh, were not caught.

Strains were developing in relations among the URM's three underground groups, and it looked as if this unique collaboration—the first time since the Maccabees that Hebrews had fought as one for freedom—was coming to an end. Yalin of *Lehi* related later that he had felt for some time that the *Haganah* was preparing to back away from the armed struggle. However, when "Agatha" was launched on June 29, the immediate impulse in the URM was for armed actions against the British administration; and the go ahead was given, for the King David attack. The *Irgun* interpreted the message from Sneh and Sadeh to mean that damaging evidence had been found in the British searches through the Jewish Agency's offices and that it was urgent that this evidence reportedly kept at British headquarters be destroyed.

The *Irgun* had conceived a plan for the King David attack early in 1946, but the green light was given on July first. According to Dr. Sneh, the operation was personally approved by Ben-Gurion, from his self-exile in Europe.

Sadeh, the operations officer of the *Haganah*, and "Giddy" Paglin, the head of the *Irgun* operation, agreed that thirty-five minutes advance notice would give the British time enough to evacuate their wing, without enabling them to disarm the explosives. Giddy had memorized almost every nook and cranny of the building and he had done a careful survey of grocery and milk delivery schedules. It was the most well-guarded building in Palestine, but it had become thoroughly familiar ground to Giddy. In the *Irgun* unit specially assembled for the mission, there were twenty-three men equipped with one machine gun, four submachine guns, six pistols and 350 kilograms of explosives. The explosives were to be delivered in milk cans to the kitchen. Warning time was finally set at thirty minutes. Two young women were assigned to phone the switchboards of the Chief Secretary of the Administration, the French Consulate next door to the King David and the *Palestine Post*. Defensive units were assigned to several street corners leading to the hotel, and escape routes and first aid stations were laid out. Everything was ready to go.

Simultaneously, unbeknown to the *Irgun*, Dr. Weizmann had decided to halt the armed struggle of the URM. Weizmann's confidant, Meyer Weisgal, was sent as emissary to Dr. Sneh's home to demand that all armed resistance cease. Through Weisgal, Weizmann told Sneh that the fighting not only "corrupted" the Jewish youth, but also amounted to a declaration of war against Britain—a war the Jews could never hope to win.

Weizmann threatened to resign as head of the World Zionist Organization if his words went unheeded. With Ben-Gurion in Europe, and the cream of the Agency's leadership in detention,

Sneh gave in, accepting Weizmann's argument that yet another conference with the British in London would this time bring acceptable results.

Without divulging the pressure from Weizmann, Sneh sent notes to Menahem Begin on the 19th and 22nd, obliquely requesting that the King David operation be delayed.

The *Irgun* decided to proceed with the operation, with or without the blessing of the *Haganah*. The project was too far along. The *Irgun* also feared that the suggested delay was a replay of Weizmann's capitulation to the British in 1944.

The *Irgun* went ahead with the plan as originally agreed upon by the URM. On July 21, 1946, the *Irgun* soldiers, disguised as Arab delivery men, carried the explosives to the basement of the King David. While they set them up, other *Irgun* soldiers set off diversionary smoke bombs in the street. When the long fuses on the explosives were ignited, a few soldiers were left behind as guards until the last moment, while their commander went up to the street and gave the signal for the warning phone calls. The explosives blew up the entire south wing. Ninety-one people were killed, including British, Arab and Jewish civilians.

From that day on, Sir John Shaw, the Chief Secretary, steadfastly denied that he or any one else in authority in the building ever received the warning phoned in by the *Irgun* member Adina Nissan.[1]

A secret British report which was revealed later states that a warning was received by the telephone operator of the King David Hotel *two* minutes before the explosion; she immediately advised the hotel manager. No explanation is given in this police report, or any other official statements as to why the kitchen staff came out of the cellar twenty minutes before the explosion, and ran upstairs to the manager warning him that "Jewish terrorists left milk cans in the basement." Nor is any mention made of three

---

[1] On May 22, 1979, Lord Janner in the House of Lords read into the minutes of the record of a communication he received from one Dr. Crawford: "I'm writing to confirm that the officer who wrote to me in 1946, concerning the King David Hotel, was Major General Dudley Sheridan Skelton . . . In 1946, he was head of a hospital in Palestine, near Jerusalem, and was a frequent visitor to the King David Hotel; apparently he was there on the very day of the explosion . . . A warning was passed on to the officers in the bar, in rather jocular terms, implying it was a 'Jewish terrorist bluff.' But despite advice to 'ignore the bluff' he decided to leave and thus was out of the hotel when the explosion took place."

warnings that reached Police Headquarters prior to the explosion, either from the switchboard of the *Palestine Post* or from the French Consulate. These latter facts were all later corroborated by several other sources.

A recent investigation seems to present the likeliest reason of the tragedy. The fuses, calculated to burn for thirty minutes, through some error only burned for some twenty odd minutes. In addition, the *Irgun* officer supposed to give the signal for the phone calls was delayed three to four minutes from getting to the street. The result: only about seventeen minutes, instead of the planned thirty, remained after the *Irgun* gave the warning. This still would have been ample time for the British to clear the south wing, if they had chosen to.

When Senator Gillette and Harry L. Selden reached the King David on July 27, the building was half-ruined. Selden carried a letter from the manager of the Shepheard's Hôtel in Cairo to his colleague the manager of the King David, and he delivered it to the assistant manager, who happened to be at the front of the building. They struck up a conversation, during which the assistant manager said that on the day of the explosion, one of the phone operators had called him to report that someone had called warning that the building would be blown up in thirty minutes. He immediately phoned the British headquarters, but "he was thanked and told to ignore it . . ."

That same evening, Selden spoke with Gershon Agronsky, editor of the *Palestine Post*, who told Selden that he too had received the warning and passed it on to Sir John Shaw's office in British Headquarters at the hotel. A few days later the same report was given to Selden by the French Vice Consul.

Although the King David attack was a human tragedy, it had certain positive historic effects. For the first time it brought the whole issue to the British public with immediacy. It made the headlines of the British papers day after day, showing the people the tragedies their government's Colonial policies were producing.

The King David incident and the later execution by the *Irgun* of two British sergeants convinced the British public that the situation in Palestine could not go on.

The King David incident also brought the moderate wing of the

Establishment back into control of the *Haganah*. Dr. Sneh quit as head of the *Haganah* high command, and was replaced by Israel Galili, who in the months and years to come, would play a destructive role in relations with the *Irgun*.

With the attack on the King David Hotel, the URM came to and end. The *Haganah* lost its nerve for an all-out confrontation with Britain. In an interview with the paper *France Soir*, in Paris, Ben-Gurion declared that the *Irgun*, was "the enemy of the Jewish people." Weizmann, the devoted friend of Great Britain, had won one more battle.

* * *

In July, 1946, Jerusalem was not the most peaceful place to visit. But for Guy Gillette, a respected United States Senator from Iowa, and a close friend of President Truman, the visit to Jerusalem was like a pilgrimage. There was no other place on earth he wanted to be.

When Gillette had become full-time President of our ALFP in August, 1945, he chose this controversial and politically unrewarding task sheerly out of empathy. When Gillette and Foreign Minister Bevin held their dialogue in London in 1945, they presented a strong contrast in Christian philosophies: ingrained, irrational anti-Semitism on Bevin's part, and on Gillette's part deep affection for Jews based on the common, millennia-old Judeo-Christian heritage.

Gillette continued his active leadership through the first half of 1946, presiding over an "emergency conference" for Hebrew survival and heading an intensive campaign to prevent Bevin from establishing Trans-Jordan as an independent state. He sent a message to the American co-chairman of the AACI, Judge Joseph C. Hutcheson, pointing out that this unilateral action by Britain contravened its obligation under the Mandate and went against the policies set by the Anglo-American Convention of 1924. Gillette secured the signatures to this statement of leading senators and congressmen such as Arthur H. Vandenberg, Owen Brewster, Warren G. Magnuson and Claude Pepper.

Nothing helped. On March 22nd, while the AACI was reviewing Britain's performance as a trustee of Palestine, Mr. Bevin and

Ibraham Pasha Hashim, "Prime Minister" of the Abdullah Kingdom, signed the treaty creating the new State of Trans-Jordan on three quarters of the original Mandate area. On June 18, speaking on a national radio hook-up along with Senator Albert D. Thomas of Utah, Gillette said:

> It appears, from the study of Great Britain's record on Palestine, that she supports the lofty ideals of democracy provided they happen to coincide with the interests of the British Empire.

* * *

Gillette and Selden proposed a last-ditch trip to Palestine to plead with the High Commissioner, and perhaps modify the course of action the British Administration was pursuing. They also expected to find a way to meet with Begin and work out future policies. At the very least, they hoped to contribute to a better rapport with the Jewish Agency.

They failed on all fronts. At the very outset of their mission, the meeting with Sir Alan Cunningham, the High Commissioner reached the usual impasse when the High Commissioner stated that his function was to maintain a balance between the Arab and Jewish communities. When asked under what mandate he replied, "The White Paper." Selden countered that the White Paper was a unilateral British document, and that the League Mandate was the trust under which Britain was in Palestine at all. Cunningham inquired: "Do you expect us to enforce the Mandate at the point of a bayonet?" Selden answered: "You're enforcing the White Paper with more than a mere bayonet."

They fared little better with the Jewish Establishment. They were received courteously by the labor leader David Sprintzak at *Histadrut* headquarters, more warmly by non-Socialist community leaders at the home of the Mayor of Ramat Gan. They were honored at a dinner in Tel-Aviv by two hundred leaders of the *Yishuv* even after they were denied the right to visit the detainees in Latrun. The closest thing they had to success was being allowed a brief visit with *ma'apilim* kept on vessels in Haifa harbor, awaiting deporation to Cyprus. They were watched and pursued so assiduously by the C.I.D. that the *Irgun* deemed it inadvisable to arrange a meeting for them with the *Irgun* Command.

Selden left Palestine with a vivid picture imprinted in his mind of the gulf separating the British forces from the Hebrew population. Once, when riding the shuttle limousine between Jerusalem and Tel-Aviv, he was stopped at a roadblock by British soldiers. The soldiers proceeded to check the documents of the passengers, and as the woman sitting next to Selden extended her identification card, he noticed a tattooed concentration camp number on her arm. The British soldier checking her card had a tattoo on his arm as well—a swastika.

The impact of the visit on Gillette was more of a surprise—he came back a converted revolutionary. His eyes blazed as he told us his experiences in Palestine, and by the time he finished talking, we had established the theme of his future work for us. From then on his opening statement at public appearances was: "It is 1946 in America, but it is 1776 in Palestine!"

It was 1776 in Palestine, but the message of history was not getting across to the leadership. Weizmann was back in control, Sneh in exile, Ben-Gurion again in hibernation and Gallili in charge of the *Haganah*. Armed resistance was terminated; the Establishment went back to its old pattern of party politics and appeasement. Once again the *Irgun* and the *Lehi* were on their own, though they were now closer to each other than at any time since their split. It was as if the historic cycle had continued all the way around back to 1944.

The *Yishuv* was tired. The past nine months of curfews, bombings, arrests and searches had taken their toll. A compromise would have been welcomed by many in the desire to return to normalcy, but the myopic British did not offer one.

To strengthen the HCNL's political campaign, and tighten coordination with the armed action in Palestine and Europe, Samuel Merlin signed in Rome on May 1, 1946, a memorandum with Eli Tavin of the *Irgun* high command. It defined the political goal of the struggle as urgent repatriation to Palestine of all the "seekers of Zion." All Jews in Palestine and the diaspora who saw Eretz-Israel as their home and desired to liberate it were defined as "the Hebrew Nation." The HCNL is the political representative of the *Irgun*; the links between the *Irgun* and its delegates abroad are reestablished. The HCNL accepts the Irgun's supreme authority. The *Irgun*'s covert activities in the diaspora are directed by the *Irgun*'s diaspora command. The *Irgun* delegates are autonomous in their political work and shall participate in formulating the *Irgun*'s military and political policies.

It was a good working agreement which Begin hesitated to ratify. This failure would lead to considerable future painful friction.

In the summer of 1946, Begin wrote to us referring to the British-American Morrison-Grady plan whereby Palestine would be separated into four provinces, two under direct British rule, one under Jewish rule in Tel-Aviv and environs and one under Arab rule:

> We may be faced with additional dismemberment of the homeland which would result in the abandonment of greater numbers of our nation to life in the diaspora . . . If this development secures the support of the Agency people, then, especially then, it will be necessary (for us) to establish the Hebrew government of Eretz-Israel . . .
>
> A civil war can break out at any time within weeks or months . . . I have no doubt that your campaign in the United States . . . is one of the factors inhibiting the plotters.
>
> How long this will restrain them is impossible to predict . . . We did not give up our principles two years ago, after the Moyne incident, when Golomb threatened us with annihilation. We did not stop our struggles then and we won't now.
>
> But we cannot jump the gun . . . We cannot give the incitors the excuse to claim that we are not fighting the British but the *Yishuv* . . . Consequently, there will be no hasty formation of a Provisional Government . . . We will do so only if we are sure of the participation of others . . . or if there is no choice left.

* * *

Begin's messages as well as Bevin's political convulsions made it clear that we urgently needed to intensify our activities in the United States. Once again we appealed to Ben Hecht, and once again he came to the rescue.

In his play, *A Flag is Born*, which opened on Broadway in the fall of 1946, Hecht gave a powerfully moving presentation of the events that were taking place in Palestine. In no uncertain terms, the play revealed to Jews and non-Jews the causes and motivations for the battles growing in intensity in Palestine. The drama was directed, produced and performed by top artists and presented in half a dozen cities. Kurt Weill wrote the music, Luther Adler directed, and Paul Muni and Marlon Brando starred as the old man, Tevya, and the young man, David.

In the play, Tevya, an old Jew, wanders among the tombstones somewhere in Europe, wrapped in his prayer shawl; in a series of flashbacks, he recalls the stories of the ancient past and the horrors of the recent past. He is then confronted by a young man named David, who has despaired of ever reaching Eretz-Israel, and is ready to give up hope in life. Then the young soldiers of the Hebrew Resistance appear, seen through a gauze curtain. "The past is dead, David," Tevya says. "The whole black past of the Jews . . . Come, David—Saul and the Maccabees live again in Palestine. Their strong arms are bared again! We promise you an end of pleading and proverbs . . . We promise to wrest our homeland out of British claws . . . The English have put a fence around the Holy Land. But there are three things they cannot keep out—the wind, the rain and a Jew."

As the curtain slowly lowers, David picks up the torn, defiled shawl of the old Jew, and raises it until it becomes the white and blue flag of the reborn nation.

The British, to say the least, were not pleased by the play. *The London Evening Standard* wrote: "Forty-four thousand eight hundred people have already flocked . . . to see the most virulent anti-British play ever staged in the United States."

And they were joined in their ire by Judah L. Magnes, a respected American Jewish rabbi and teacher who settled in Jerusalem and was now president of the Hebrew University. Magnes wrote to Eleanor Roosevelt, one of the sponsors of the production, protesting her backing of a play at whose climax a group of armed Hebrew youth appear asking for support for the armed resistance in Palestine. Magnes asked: "Are you in favor of supplying money and arms for the terrorists . . . who are poisoning the minds and souls of the younger generation?"

* * *

A dialogue of the deaf

THE JEWISH LEGION
21 Hyde Park Street, W.2.

CALLING
ALL FAIR-MINDED PEOPLE OF BRITAIN
TWO BRITISH N.C.O'S WERE HANGED IN PALESTINE
DO YOU KNOW WHY?

DO YOU KNOW

THAT three young Jews, soldiers of the Irgun Zvai Leumi and prisoners of war, were hanged by the Palestine Administration the day before.

THAT none of these three prisoners of war had been found guilty of any crime punishable in this country by death.

THAT the UNO Commission asked that these executions should not be carried out until UNO had reached a decision on Palestine.

THAT the Superintendent of Acre Prison resigned rather than supervise these executions.

THAT the Irgun had repeatedly warned the Palestine Administration that if they persisted in hanging prisoners of war, they would be forced to do likewise.

THAT the death of these Five young men is the culmination of the infamous, stupid and unjust policy pursued by the Palestine Administration.

STOP BLOODSHED IN PALESTINE

CALL UPON YOUR M.P's TO DEMAND THE WITHDRAWAL OF BRITISH TROOPS FROM PALESTINE AND END THE WASTE OF BRITISH AND JEWISH LIVES THERE.

"RIGHTEOUSNESS ALONE EXALTETH A NATION"

The Jewish Legion, in London;

BRITISH EMBASSY,
WASHINGTON 8, D. C.

March 5th, 1945.

14 MAR 1945

Dear Department,

      Please refer to your letter U.126/16/73 of February 19th about the Hebrew Committee of National Liberation. We enclose herewith for your information a copy of our circular No.93 which we sent round to Consulates in this country on July 5th, last, giving them some guidance about this body. Our attitude is still as set out in that paper. We receive numerous communications from Mr. Bergson and his boys mainly in the form of violent protests against our Palestine policy, but we never acknowledge any of them. In fact we have made it a rule to have no communication with these gangsters. We are accordingly taking no action on your letter under reference.

      Yours ever,

John W. Russell

The British Embassy in Washington, D.C.

Young men and women of the *Irgun*, in a defense position (1947).

As the *Irgun-Lehi* coalition stepped up the battle in Palestine, the leadership of the Jewish Agency backed farther and farther away from the militant stand the *Yishuv* had taken for the past year. The militant "Biltmore platform" calling for a "Hebrew Commonwealth" was abandoned. Weizmann pleaded for a partitioned State of any size, for whatever compromise the British might offer. A serious split was developing between him and the Zionist movement in the U.S. which was starting to take a more assertive militant stand under the leadership of Abba Hillel Silver and Emanuel Neumann. The emergence of a militantly independent leadership was an unheard-of phenomenon till now in the American Zionist Establishment.

At the World Zionist Congress in Basle, Switzerland in December, 1946, the first since the war, Abba Hillel Silver spoke out forcefully against partition and in favor of renewing the Resistance. Weizmann exploded and accused Silver of spurious and backbenching military options: "World and political support means very little when you send other people to the barricades to face tanks and guns." A delegate on the floor of the Congress reacted to this by calling him a demagogue, and Weizmann rose to his full height and delivered the swan song of his long domination of Zionist Congresses: "I—a demagogue! I who have borne all the ills and travails of this movement . . . ! In every house and stable in Nahalal, in every little workshop in Tel-Aviv or Haifa, there is a drop of my blood . . . If you think of bringing the redemption nearer by un-Jewish methods . . . then you commit idolatry, and endanger what we have built."

Neither the pathos nor the prophecy worked. Weizmann's lack of political resoluteness finally had caught up with him. He was not reelected as president of the World Zionist Organization.

Neither Weizmann nor Ben-Gurion could block the path to resistance any longer. The young rank and file of the *Irgun* and *Lehi* unhesitatingly continued to offer their lives, performing deeds which Weizmann and Ben-Gurion damned, then standing up to the British officers and magistrates and delivering a message that became a part of the nation's heritage.

Yeruham Livni said to the British judges:

> You, the presiding officer, have said to your friends 'It is regrettable that what was done to the Jews in Europe could not be

> done here . . . I could then leave this cursed land and return home!'
> Sir, what is your natural right, to return to your home, is denied
> our nation . . . If you please, go home! Take with you your army,
> your police, your functionaries. Go home and return to us our land
> that you have usurped. . . . Go home and our people will come
> home . . . and there will be no cause for enmity between our people.

And when Debrah Kalfus, arrested following an *Irgun* attack
on the country's railroads, denied her guilt and accused the judges
of their own. Alluding to a BBC broadcast which called *Hatikva*
"a so-called national anthem," and the blue and white banner of
David an "unknown flag," she faced her accusers with a cool and
measured speech: "This is the basic conflict between the British
and the Jews."

Dov Gruner said: "When a regime in any country becomes a
regime of oppression, it ceases to be lawful. It is the right of its
citizens—nay—it is their *duty* to fight against it . . . No force in the
world can break the link between the people of Israel and their
one and only country!" Gruner concluded that, since the British
abrogated the Balfour Declaration and the Mandate, there was
no reason for their staying in Palestine.

Surprisingly, he received support from an unexpected source.
Following the roundups of Black Saturday and the King David
attack, an ambivalent friend of Hebrew independence, Winston
Churchill, said in Parliament: "The one rightful, reasonable, simple and compulsive lever we held and, if you will, still hold, was
and is a sincere readiness to resign the mission, to lay our Mandate at the feet of the United Nations Organization, and thereafter
to evacuate the country with which we have no connection or
tradition . . . We should now give notice that we will return our
Mandate to the United Nations Organization. . . ."

At long last Churchill was addressing the reality; but Bevin and
Weizmann were still not listening.

* * *

When I married in November 1946, my colleagues thought it was
an excellent excuse for a honeymoon trip to Palestine. We were
not sure of my standing in the current C.I.D. files in Palestine, or
just what information had been provided to the C.I.D. by the

British from the United States and the FBI. But we decided to chance it. Armed with brand new United States passports, and letters of introduction from half a dozen senators and congressmen, my wife and I flew to Cairo in January 1947, and from there to Tel-Aviv.

In fact, with the various border clearances and minor complications, the trip took three days, which gave me a good chance to prepare myself for talks with Begin and others. I was possibly not the best honeymoon company, because my mind was constantly awhirl with the political situation.

With the *Irgun* in Palestine irreversibly committed to armed resistance, we in the United States had plunged ahead in our diplomatic, public relations and fund raising efforts to back up the *Irgun's* campaign. We knew we would have our hands full with the Establishment's renewed compromising under the erratic Ben-Gurion.

Not until May, 1942, at the Hotel Biltmore Conference in New York, had Ben-Gurion at last come out officially for a "Jewish Commonwealth." Furthermore, largely due to the relative effectiveness of our efforts, did he (and eventually Rabbi Abba Hillel Silver) finally realize that the five million Jews in America were potentially a powerful political force—one which Hebrew rebirth could, actually must, rely upon for realizing its goals. Despite bitter oppposition by Weizmann and his followers, Ben-Gurion expressed the unmentionable in a memorandum to the Jewish Agency: "Our youth must be prepared to do everything possible when the right moment comes."

This was not the last of Ben-Gurion's turnarounds. In 1944, when Churchill and Attlee whispered grand promises in Weizmann's ear, Ben-Gurion's militancy evaporated once again. Churchill and Attlee swore that one hundred to one hundred and fifty thousand Jewish orphans would be able to come to Palestine at once, and up to one and a half million Jews by war's end. They also promised the creation of a Jewish State—and to cement their favor, Ben-Gurion launched the "season" against us in full cooperation with them.[1]

---

[1]Nicholas Bethell, *The Palestine Triangle*, pp. 161-163; M. Begin *The Revolt* (Dell, 1968) pp. 246; David Niv, *The Irgun Zvai Leumi* Vol. IV, pp. 92-93.

When Bevin and Attlee had gone back to the old Colonial path, Ben-Gurion appeared before the Anglo-American Commission of Inquiry and unequivocally defined the goal of Zionism as "Jewish Statehood." "We are not going to renounce our independence," he said, "even if we have to pay the supreme price." At that point, the *Haganah* had joined with *Lehi* and the *Irgun* in the URM.

Ben-Gurion, having lost his steadfastness once again, reverted to his old pattern, denying responsibility for the King David attack, so that once again the Establishment could sound the call to "eradicate the renegades!" But by then the *Yishuv* was not satisfied with the traditional leadership, and no longer amenable to the on again, off again policy of armed struggle against the Mandatory power. Thousands of Jews in Europe were still in camps, or in societies that were again treating them like animals, and the *Yishuv* would no longer endure it. At last, seeing all of this clearly, the *Yishuv* gave the *Irgun-Lehi* wider popular support than ever before, backing them with thousands of supporters, funds, shelters and recruits.

This was where things stood in January 1947, when my wife and I reached Palestine for a belated honeymoon. We passed all border check points without trouble, and registered in a small Tel-Aviv hotel. It was a typical drab drizzly Tel-Aviv winter evening, when we met Begin in a modest ground-level apartment, furnished sparsely with books strewn across a desk and several shelves. He rose from his chair smiling, both his hands outstretched in a warm welcome. The thirteen months had not visibly changed him. With him was Marek Kahn, an old friend from Warsaw and a veteran activist of the Jabotinsky movement. Kahn had developed into Begin's closest friend and confidant; he fulfilled the role with paternal affection and patience.

Begin, always the Old World European gentleman, kissed my wife's hand with a flourish. Kahn knelt on one knee to help her remove her wet overshoes, it was as if the lot of us had gathered for no more than a social event. It was hard to believe that these bespectacled, benign-looking, cultured individuals had their drab pictures displayed on police posters all across Palestine.

Sipping tea from tall glasses, we quickly laid out an agenda and guidelines for our meetings. To begin with, we needed to clear the air between the Command in Palestine and our delegation and the HCNL in the United States. By now the HCNL had expanded its activities to a Paris headquarters and other parts of the continent, and with Kook, Merlin and Eri Jabotinsky leading the way, was urging formation of a provisional government. For the present Begin kept an unequivocal stand against it.

For months, he himself had promoted the idea of a provisional government; in a recent *Irgun* memorandum circulated to two hundred and fifty leaders in the *Yishuv* and carried to delegates of the recent Zionist congress, he had sponsored a provisional government formed by a coalition of all Zionist groups. But he consistently refused to join the HCNL in such unilateral action. His major argument was that it would be Ben-Gurion's excuse to launch a civil war, once more railing against "fascists striving to capture control of the *Yishuv*." The Zionist Congress of December, 1946, overriding Weizmann, had narrowly backed Ben-Gurion in a declaration that Hebrew statehood should succeed the British Mandate. This turn of events left Ben-Gurion in control of the Jewish Agency and all security matters, at long last giving him the power to do us immeasurable harm. As Begin saw things, we had to move with careful foresight.

In our following meetings, some of which were attended by the *Irgun* Chief of Staff, Haim Landau, Begin repeated to me what he had written to us in the States over and over during the past year—that we needed all our strength, all our resources and manpower, to hammer away at the British occupation forces. He was convinced that by 1947 or the year after we would see the final days of British rule, if we dedicated ourselves to this goal. We are nearing the days of decision. We accepted that the battle would get costlier and bloodier every day, but the one thing we could not allow was a civil war. "But don't mistakenly conclude," said Begin, "that we will not be ready for such a final step—a unilateral declaration of independence—if Ben-Gurion and his friends don't do it. When the time comes, we'll let them know they have no choice."

Begin then stressed that we always had to remind our friends and opponents alike that the *Irgun* as a nonpartisan military entity had no internal political designs. There was time enough for ideological power struggles after the State was declared! The *Irgun* aimed at only one thing—freeing the country from the foreign occupation.

At this point in the conversation, Begin assumed a grave tone: "We are not interested in gestures but in facts, in deeds," he said. He was rebuking some of our actions in the United States, which he sometimes saw as no more than "gestures": the Washington headquarters of HCNL had been dubbed by the press the "Hebrew Embassy"; the HCNL itself had registered as "agents of the Hebrew nation"; and it had also given statements and interviews to the press and Congress, aiming to establish publicly the *de facto* existence of the Hebrew Nation. Begin had congratulated the HCNL on all of this, but deep inside he and the rest of the *Irgun* leadership in Palestine deemed these activities secondary to the military battle in Palestine, and they resented funds being spent on "gestures." They also resented that Peter Bergson (Kook) and others in the HCNL were receiving such a buildup which appeared to smack of personal ambitions for the future, rather than total commitment to the armed struggle.

I was not inclined to pursue this last point any further with Begin. Future events would take care of it.

Begin promised to continue urging the *Yishuv* leadership to aim towards creating a provisional government; he would not, however, commit himself to a timetable. I agreed to accept this course, but I was not too sure about my colleagues overseas.

Then we came to funds. Begin demanded that all funds raised by us should be remitted in total to the *Irgun*, and I did my best to explain that in the early years, as well as in recent months, most funds raised recently in the United States had been for immigration. We were also in debt, I explained, because we had purchased and equipped the S.S. *Abril* (later named the S.S. *Ben Hecht*), which had just sailed (December 26, 1946) for Europe from Staten Island. I repeated that throughout the years of our campaign for a Jewish army, and on behalf of vanishing European Jewry we were continuously short of funds, that our "Embassy" was a modest enterprise, mortgaged to the hilt with friends.

I could have told Begin that the delegation members in the United States were continuously penniless, that we never even received the pitiful $25 weekly allowance promised to us by two benefactors. We tried to cover our barest living expenses through a commercial enterprise that a friend had volunteered to manage, and other friends also slipped us onto their payrolls at nominal salaries. I myself had been lucky enough, with war-time controls over and the Palestine economy in better straits, to manage to transfer some funds from Palestine to cover my own living expenses for the balance of the year.

But I did not tell any of these particulars to Begin and the others. They were men whose lives were not worth a farthing if they were ever caught in the gunsight of a British policeman, men I might never see again. How could I tell them about rents and food, or that my wife was expecting our first child?

I promised that we would intensify our fundraising for the *Irgun*, not only in the United States, but also in South America and Canada. I vowed that funds raised for the *Irgun* would be personally handled by me, and transferred according to instructions from Avraham (Haim Landau), the Chief of Staff.

Then we took up the matter of *Ha'apalah*. We agreed that now we would have to leave this mostly to the *Haganah*. We did not have the means to organize mass operations. Some of the funds we had transferred to Europe a year before had been lost in three unsuccessful attempts to purchase boats in Italy, and in recent months, the S.S. *Ben Hecht* project had left us penniless. In the final analysis, the military activities were simply more important now than the immigration work, and we did not have the money or the manpower to do both. We in the United States would keep the stateless, displaced Jews of Europe in the public eye, but we were no longer in the desperate years of 1937-1940 when any Jew snatched away from Europe meant a life saved. Any ships we obtained from here on would be for transporting armed men as part of the military struggle.

We agreed that after my return to New York, we would submit more detailed plans for all of this, and that all such plans would be coordinated and approved by Eliahu Lankin who had escaped from the detention camp in Eritrea, and was now *Irgun* commander in the diaspora.

Begin and I held our last meeting on Sunday morning. He gave a summary of British policies; he saw no sign of Attlee or Bevin easing their policies; in fact they were hardening their military posture, with a buildup of troops and military enclaves. Their basic view was still that the Empire's security and Britain's welfare depended on Arab good will and oil, and thus on blocking Hebrew aspirations for independence.

The picture looked rather grim. Bevin was determined to let the Arabs take control of the country; he had said recently that he would put at the disposal of a puppet Arab State of Palestine more than one hundred thousand British soldiers and police-men. At best Bevin may come up with a crippling partition plan. Begin felt the same way he always had about it: "We shall op-pose it! We shall never acquiesce in partitioning of our home-land."

There was one more tactic Bevin might use if all else failed. Expecting the Russians to vote against partition, he might inten-tionally put the plan before the United Nations expressly so the Russians would veto it; the whole issue would thus be handed back to the British, giving them a free rein to pursue their Colonial goals.

But as Begin put it, "Whichever Machiavellian ploy Bevin uses, it really does not matter. We are going to make sure Britain gives up and gets out. In 1947, the initiative shall be ours."

Before I left, Begin reminded me one more time that public opinion was secondary, that what counted was "what the Nation was able to muster on the battlefield." I saw difficult times ahead trying to balance Begin's ideas that the armed struggle had to go forward at all costs, with or without a base of political and public support overseas, with the view of Kook, Eri and others, that the greatest practical results would come from the political arena. Begin pointed a finger at me and said: "The nation will need every man, woman and child who can bear arms . . . every gun, every bullet. When the time comes, the entire people must unite for the final battle." The message he wanted me to take back to the States was clear: No rushing into acts which might give Ben-Gurion the excuse to unleash the *Palmach* and *Mapai* for a civil war.

My wife and I shook hands with Begin, then Landau accom-panied us to the door. With hands outstretched, he said: "*Le hitraot* . . . till we meet again." Then he added with a small smile: "Try to get to your hotel promptly, and do not venture out on the street today." I understood his words to mean that "events" were to soon occur. I guessed it might be connected with the pending execution of Dov Gruner.

Gruner, a veteran *Irgun* soldier, had reached Palestine on the *Sakarya* in February, 1940. He had fought as a British soldier during the war. Then in early 1946 he was captured by the police during a raid on the fortified police compound in Ramat Gan. On January 24, he had been sentenced to death by a military court, his execution set for the 28th. Today, Sunday the 26th, London had refused to commute the death penalty.

The *Irgun* claimed for its soldiers the status of prisoners of war, combatants who according to the Geneva Convention rules could not be executed. The British claimed they were "terrorists" who broke their "emergency regulations." According to these regulations, anyone caught carrying arms was to be executed.

The Irgun countered by kidnapping two British civilians—a retired major and a high magistrate. It was the kidnapping of Judge Ralph Windham in Tel-Aviv that had precipitated our speedy departure from Begin's home that Sunday morning. Curfew had been declared instantly in Tel-Aviv, and we spent the rest of the afternoon and evening listening to the radio with our fellow guests in the hotel.

By the next morning, it was reported from London that Dov Gruner had been given permission to apply for an appeal[1] with the Privy Council; consequently his execution was being delayed. That afternoon, Judge Windham was released near Ramat Gan. This was the last news we had of the affair until we left Palestine.

As we traveled back via Cairo to Paris, I read the Hebrew papers of the past weeks over and over in disbelief.

According to the papers, Labor now claimed that the *Irgun-Lehi* leadership was composed of recent immigrants from eastern Europe who did not understand the *Yishuv*. They did not relate

---

[1] Gruner never asked for an appeal, and refused to do so up until the end, declaring that British laws and courts were illegal in the Hebrew homeland. The Privy Council ultimately rejected two appeals, one by the municipality of Tel-Aviv, and one by Gruner's uncle in the United States.

On April 16, Gruner and three other *Irgun* and *Lehi* men were hanged in the Acre Fortress. This time no date had been announced for their execution, for fear of *Irgun* action.

The next *Irgun-Lehi* men condemned to death cheated the hangman. On April 21, the eve of their execution, using grenades smuggled to them inside oranges, the Hebrew soldiers Meir Feinstein and Moshe Barzani blew themselves up.

to the blood that had been spilled in the valley of Yisrael, or the sacrifices that had built the kibbutzim in the Jordan valley.

I was shocked, for I had grown up along with the country. Every little suburb, every niche from *Mishmar Hayarden* to old *Be'er Tuvia,* was part of my youth and home to members of my family. We had graves scattered in a dozen settlements; my grand-fathers Zeev Leib and Shmuel had died here and little Rochelle, and others who had succumbed to malaria and typhus, and fallen to Arab bullets. How could anyone claim that we were strangers to the land? Once again we are dissipating our strength on inter-necine warfare.

The enemy was British imperialism, not the British people for whom we had felt only empathy for centuries. In some ways this imperialism was more formidable an enemy than the Germans. British officials of lower echelon initiated their own hostile actions and sabotaged directives from the very top. The order to fire on *ma'apilim* had come from minor officials of the Colonial Office and the Palestine Administration. The sabotaging of Churchill's strong recommendation to bomb Auschwitz origi-nated from functionaries of the Foreign Office and the Air Force.[1]

With the war won, there were Britishers who felt that their wartime sacrifices and their heroic stand entitled them to rebuild the Empire come what may. It was a stupid, bloody, and hopeless task. Here in Palestine it was evolving into an ugly war, with sadistic British soldiers and policemen recruited from the lowest elements, who behaved like S.S. officers. In the coming months the violence and the suffering would multiply a hundredfold, and it would end only when the British left our land. We had struggled and pre-pared for this since the early thirties, in Palestine and overseas, and from here on in, it would be the goal of our every waking breath.

Dov Gruner had said to the British officers who sat in judgment of him: "This you must know—there is no power in the world that can cut the ties of Israel to its only land. Whoever tries it will have his hand cut off, and God's wrath shall descend on him, forever and ever."

---

[1]Bernard Wasserstein, *Britain and the Jews of Europe 1939-1945*, pp. 307-320. Martin Gilbert, *Auschwitz and the Allies*, pp. 299-324.

This was the message I carried to Paris, Dublin and to New York.

* * *

In February, 1947, Paris was a focal point for our activities in Europe. The HCNL activists—Kook, Merlin (since March, 1946), Eri Jabotinsky, Albert Stara, Samuel Ariel and Reuben Hecht—were all working out of the Paris headquarters in the Lutetia Hotel. France seemed the best choice for a future government in exile. The overwhelming view here favored creating a Provisional Hebrew Government, with or without the Jewish Agency. The HCNL believed that such a *de facto* entity would put Britain on the political spot, elevating our "terrorism" to "National resistance," and our battle would be given legitimacy in the eyes of the world.

In France public opinion and the press were showing more and more sympathy to the Hebrew struggle. "The French League for a Free Palestine" had been established and enlisted the support of Jean-Paul Sartre, Simone de Beauvoir and others. Albert Stara had come from Egypt to edit *La Riposte*—the French-language sister publication of the ALFP's *The Answer* in New York. In addition to the European headquarters of the HCNL, Paris now also housed the expanding headquarters of the *Irgun* in the diaspora.

Irgun and *Betar* veterans of the Jewish Brigade and the British and Allied armies, together with *Irgun* and NZO men who had survived Nazi rule in Romania and Yugoslavia, reactivated the framework that had been dismembered when the Nazis swept over Europe in 1939. They received a major boost when Eli Tavin was released after six months of captivity by the *Haganah*. In early 1946 he was given the priority assignment of organizing the *Irgun* outside Palestine. Slowly, a modest network of cells, combat units and non-com training camps, were created throughout Germany, Austria and Italy.

Their first action against the British outside Palestine took place on October 31, 1946, when the *Irgun* bombed the British Embassy in Rome. This incident made the point that the battle would henceforth not be limited to Palestine, and gave Britain one more bitter pill to swallow.

Further attacks followed on British installations in Austria and Germany, coupled with confiscation of weapons and explosives. Scotland Yard asked for the cooperation of the French and Italian police, which led to widespread arrests of suspects in *Betar* camps all across Europe. Moshe Gallili, our old immigrant runner from the thirties, was arrested, and so was Israel Epstein, a veteran *Irgun* officer recently arrived in Europe. Epstein was killed shortly after, while attempting to escape. By December, the Italian police had arrested Tavin, and detained him for three months.

What the "*Irgun* in the diaspora" had lacked was a solid, tight, disciplined base; but when I arrived in Paris in February 1947, such a nucleus was beginning to form under the new leadership of Eliahu Lankin. Lankin had escaped from the detention camp in Asmara, Eritrea, fourteen months earlier, and after living in Addis Ababa with the constant fear of being turned over to the British, he had finally managed, with the help of the HCNL in France, to proceed via Djibuti to France, where he joined the HCNL headquarters. All the months Lankin had been a fugitive, we in New York, and Kook and Ariel in Paris, maintained contact with him, eventually securing official French authorization for him to come to France.

A number of *Irgun* members had escaped from the Asmara camp, and the British were so anxious to get them that they were willing to try anything. At one point they offered to trade the Ethiopian Emperor's mortal enemy, Prince Guksa, for our officers Zeroni and Gurewitch, whom the Ethiopians had arrested after they crossed the border from British-controlled Asmara.

As Tavin and his young comrades were being apprehended and put behind bars, the veterans of the thirties were returning to the front lines. Gathered at the Lutetia listening to my reports on the meetings with Begin were Merlin, Eri Jabotinsky, Lankin, Reuben Hecht, Ariel, Abrasha Stawsky—the old guard from the critical years of 1937-1940. We were only ten years older, and none of us had reached middle age, but hair was flecked with gray and brows were cut with furrows.

* * *

Before I returned to New York, Lankin suggested that I visit Dublin for a quick look at the group of *Irgun* volunteers assembling there. I phoned ahead to Robert Briscoe. I arrived just in time for a traditional Sabbath evening dinner.

The Sabbath candles were still burning on the festive table when Briscoe's son, a pilot, and two of his young friends retired with me to the study. With a sad-looking half-smile, Robert Briscoe excused himself, saying: "Nowadays when it comes to warfare, you young fellows have to carry on without me."

Till late in the night, the air still filled with the aromas of the Sabbath, we went over plans for an aviation school, the acquisition of weapons and explosives and bases for operations and supplies. With the front expanding across Europe, Ireland, so close to the British Isles, could become a vital link and transit point for operations. Back in Paris I reported to Lankin.

Lankin was consolidating the *Irgun* in a dozen countries now, and branches and recruits were multiplying rapidly, while Kook and Merlin focused on politics and public information. They were building up contacts in France and in other countries, for building up contacts in France and in other countries, for both moral and material support similar to the kind the Polish Government had offered us in the late thirties.

the United States, seeking funds, vessels, volunteers and supplies and I was promised that several young men and women would be sent from Palestine to help organize a framework for all of this.

III
On the Threshold of Freedom

Before boarding the plane back to New York, I loaded up with newspapers and magazines, and brought myself up-to-date on British policies.

Throughout the extermination, the Allied excuse for ignoring the Jews had been that their problems "interfered with winning the war." Now Britain's stated reason was sheer economic self-interest, morality be damned. Bevin had summarized his position in January 1947, in a cabinet paper to the Prime Minister: "Without the Middle East and its oil . . . [I see] no hope of being able to achieve the standard of living at which we were aiming in Great Britain."

Though the Empire was now to be retrenched and India was to gain independence soon, Palestine was to replace Egypt as the chief base for Imperial forces, protecting Britain's communications, oil resources and strategic positions in the Near and Middle East. But the road to it was devious.

On February 18, Bevin announced in Commons that the government is referring the Palestine issue to the United Nations, giving the impression that the government and the people of Britain were tiring of the Palestine situation and the economic burden it imposed on them. While supposedly giving up in despair, Bevin was actually trying to precipitate events that would permit Britain to create an Arab puppet state in Palestine. He guessed at the scenario: The Arab and communist bloc would oppose a partition resolution, while the United States stayed friendly to all concerned. Thus, partition would fail, and under British tutelage, the Arab majority of Palestine would be given control of the country and eventually rule it. The Jews would be relegated to small "cantons" in a plan similar to the Morrison-Grady plan Bevin had attempted earlier to push through the British Cabinet. Through it all, Bevin publicly projected the gallant protection of Arab rights as the reason for his policies,[1] while off the record officials stressed British and American mutual geo-political and economic interests in wooing the Pan-Arabists. This approach was looked upon benignly by the Secretary of Defense Forrestal, Secretary of State Byrnes, his Arab specialists—Loy Henderson, Gordon Merriam, Fraser Wilkins, Evan Wilson—and the oil executives of Aramco and Cal-Tax. The word was to spread: Jewish pressure in the United States was bad for national self-interest.

Bevin blamed American domestic politics for his troubles in Palestine. He proclaimed that he had a dialogue with Jewish representatives and that if left alone, they would accept his proposals for interim British tutelage over a five or ten year period. Incredibly even Ben-Gurion was ready to forgo the goal of Statehood and agree to the continuation of the British Mandate. Colonial Secretary Arthur Creech-Jones let the true hand show: "We are not going to the United Nations to surrender the Mandate . . . We are setting out the problem and asking their advice on how the Mandate can be administered."

A few weeks after he had referred the Palestine issue to the United Nations, Bevin announced that he would not be bound by the United Nations resolutions "unless they were unanimous." Bevin, and everyone else, knew full well that there was no chance for a unanimous vote.

Though freed of Weizmann's vacillations and at the same time prodded by Abba Hillel Silver's militancy, Ben-Gurion was still reacting to unfolding history. He hurried to London to speak with Arthur Creech-Jones, and try to win him over to a solution of partition. When Creech-Jones backed away from partition, Ben-

---

[1] Bevin stated: "The Arabs have been in Palestine for 2000 years" (sic). "Jewish immigration," he said, "was virtually an invasion." As King Saud wrote in his 3/10/45 letter to F.D.R.: "We have mentioned to Y.E. [and] to the British Government . . . the history of Palestine begins in the year 3500 B.C., its first inhabitants being the Canaanites, an Arab tribe . . . the Jews were . . . aliens who had come to Palestine . . . [and] had been turned out over 2000 years ago. . . ."

Gurion panicked. He feared harsh British military steps; unilateral action on cantonization; further restrictions on immigration, and worst of all, that the Jewish Agency's special status under the Mandate would be abolished. On February 13 he advised Bevin via the Lord Chancellor, William Jowitt, that he was agreeable *to what amounted to an historic abdication from Zionism,* and a retreat from his recent conversion to the goal of a Jewish Commonwealth, namely a limit of one hundred thousand immigrants over the coming two years, thereafter linking it to the country's absorptive capacity, to be determined by the British High Commissioner; also to end the "illegal" immigration. The *piece de resistance*—he promised that he would help eradicate the terrorists![1]

But still, Bevin would not negotiate. Meeting alone with a sullen Bevin, Ben-Gurion attempted alternatively to interest him in maintaining British bases in a partitioned Hebrew State's Negev. Still·Bevin would not negotiate. At this point Bevin was phobic about "this political fight for a Jewish State." As he saw it the proposition for one hundred thousand immigrants was merely the advance proposition in order that more millions can be poured in so as to get a complete Jewish State which "we have never undertaken to create." Ben-Gurion's improvisations and capitulations were inevitable because among others he underestimated the *Yishuv*'s readiness for sacrifice; because he neglected to develop its physical armed power and because he failed to understand the importance of Jewish and non-Jewish American public opinion. He also failed to grasp at the budding Russian sympathies towards anyone aiming at the ousting of British forces from any part of the Near East. When what seemed to him to be the crunch came. Ben-Gurion once again collapsed. He offered his capitulation to Bevin who arrogantly rejected it.

At that time we in the *Irgun* editorialized (*Herut,* February, 1947):

> The British pretend to present to the United Nations a case of two communities in strife . . . but we are changing this image. We shall continue to fight and send the message to the world that we

---

[1] PRO-London; PREM 8/627; memorandum Lord Chancellor; dated: 14-2-47.

are a nation, independent in spirit, fighting for political independence against an occupying power. Our goal is clear—Zion, in its historic boundaries is our home! Here we will ingather millions of our brethren, here we will build a free home, make it prosper and defend it, and fulfill our age old yearning for a better and just society.

* * *

My plane was delayed for refueling in Newfoundland. I used the time to summarize my impressions. Britain would give up only when faced with all out armed resistance. The *Irgun* sent the message that now was to time to persevere through the final and probably bloodiest phase of the war for independence. I drew attention to an almost overlooked but ominous statement uttered by Bevin that the creation of a Jewish State "would provoke a conflict in the Middle East which I do not desire to see." This altruistic sounding comment suggested to me that if, despite Britain's warnings, a Hebrew State would emerge, he was not only laying the groundwork for a parallel Arab puppet State, but that, on the way to achieve it, he was preparing the Eastern Mediterranean for a full-blown war. Begin had been right when he said "Britain will not fight fair and square . . . and at the end our future will be decided on the battlefields."

Ben-Gurion and colleagues refused to face or anticipate British plots. Consequently, the overall preparedness of the *Haganah* was sorely lagging. This would have serious consequences when the intensity of the *Irgun*'s battle drives the British from Palestine. This will occur though our resources are limited, though it may take months or years, and even if the *Irgun-Lehi* had to go it alone—with or against the wishes of the Jewish Agency. The only unknowns were when, and under what conditions, the British would depart. We knew they would not step down with a genteel, Victorian ceremony, but we also knew that thousands would join us when the final battle came.

We knew we could not rely on charitable contributions. We needed governmental help. We must intensify our political work in the United States, to seek supporters in France and Italy and throughout Western Europe and as Eri Jabotinsky insisted, even behind the Iron Curtain. To achieve all this we knew we would have to break through powerful opposition; but this was the least we could do when our people in Palestine were giving their all. And we also knew that we would not permit the Jewish-Zionist leadership to let this moment in history pass without proper action.

IV
A Yacht for the Poor

The day I returned to New York, the S.S. *Ben Hecht* sailed from Port du Bouc, a small French port near Marseilles. I scanned the report from Paris and Palestine with a certain anxiety, but ten days later, when she was arrested by two British destroyers as she entered the territorial waters of Palestine, I was relieved. At least the *ma'apilim* had made it safely.

Our involvement with the *Ben Hecht* went back about six months. When the American League for a Free Palestine had produced Ben Hecht's *A Flag is Born,* the play generated funds used for two purposes. Part went to the *Irgun* in Palestine, and the rest was used to test the legality of keeping Jews out of Palestine. We purchased a small ship called the S.S. *Abril*, planning to man it with our American crew before filling it with immigrants and sending it to Palestine. Our idea was to force the British to arrest United States citizens, then challenge their actions in the courts of Palestine, and if that failed, in the United States courts and Congress as well. We had apprehensions about the British treating *Irgun*-related passengers more harshly than other *ma'apilim*, so both we in the United States and Lankin in Europe issued instructions for only passive resistance if the vessel were captured. Possibly for this reason, the ultimate boarding and arrests took place without untoward incidents.

I had first seen the S.S. *Abril* tied at the dock in Brooklyn in October, 1946. We had moved her there after purchasing her at a government auction of surplus vessels. My initial glance at her was neither encouraging nor discouraging. The ship looked no more seaworthy than the floating hulls I had climbed aboard on the Danube eight years earlier.

A seven hundred dead-weight tonner, she was rusty and spotted with peeling paint, just about ready for the scrap pile. There was nothing left of the beauty she had in her days as a pleasure yacht, although she still had contours as sleek as a greyhound. It was fitting enough that Jewish remnants of the extermination used a German product to reach their new homeland. She was alleged to have been the private yacht of the Krupp family. Her twin diesels had been built at the Krupp shipyards in 1931.[1]

Julian Licht, our activist, the engineer who coordinated the refitting operation, assured me that by removing all extra partitions and bulkheads, he would enable her to carry over five hundred people without too much trouble.

Julian had thrown himself body and soul into this operation, obtaining a leave of absence from his employer, spending twenty hours a day on the dock, and chasing after parts, supplies and welders. Julian had recently received confirmation that his parents had been amongst the Jews exterminated in Riga. Outfitting the vessel became his personal tribute to the memory of his father and mother.

I climbed down to the engine room, then came back up on deck and went aft and stern. The more I saw, the more perturbed I was. We had paid $38,000 for this hulk as it was, and I shuddered to think what it would cost to refurbish it. I asked Julian for his opinion, he answered, "Possibly another $100,000 if we do the work ourselves." I was not convinced. We would need additional funds for fuel, food, transportation from Germany and Italy, assembly camps in France and any unforeseen problems. I was then responsible for the flow of funds—both towards the *Irgun* command in Tel-Aviv, and here in the United States as Executive Director of the ALFP.

It was chilly that fall afternoon on the small rotting dock in Brooklyn. I descended from the boat, I stuck my hands in my raincoat, picking my way carefully over the rubbish and pieces of metal strewn on the dock, I walked slowly up to the head of the pier. I stood there for a long time alone. Did we have the right to deprive the *Irgun* in Palestine of funds now? Would we do better

---

[1] Later she served for a short while as the flagship of the Israeli Navy.

to leave the breaking of the blockade entirely to the *Haganah* and devote all our meager funds to building the armed strength of the *Irgun*? But on the other hand we had to show them that if they did not act, we surely would, backing up with action our public campaign for free immigration. And also, we were gaining experience in moving people across the continent and running the present blockade for possible future armed landings. We must build a network in Europe capable of moving thousands of *Irgun* soldiers to Palestine when the final battle came.

We formed the "Tyre Shipping Company" to give a cover to the operation and when the crew was being assembled, candidates flocked to the office of the ALFP. Those most likely to serve reliably were sent to the "Tyre" office where they were screened again. We had to weed through fiery idealists and adventurers, crooks, informers and all other sorts. Interview followed interview until finally a crew of twenty was assembled. The captain was the most difficult choice, and even after careful consideration, the choice we finally made proved to be a blunder.

The crew was an odd melange of ancestries: there were Irishmen, Scandinavians, Italians, Jews and one black man. Except for one, they were all American citizens. They volunteered without pay, solely to participate in what they considered a just cause. Some came aboard to help rehaul the engines at the dock, and Licht, Dr. Irving Shendell, and the engineers often worked a twenty-four hour day. The FBI watched us from the beginning. The longer the vessel was tied up in Brooklyn, the greater the danger of the authorities blocking its departure. For funds we were forced to bring several important potential donors to visit the pier even though it was a breach of security.

An ill-timed poisonous barrage loosed on us again by the Establishment did not help matters. In the American Jewish Congress weekly, *The Jewish Frontier*, and in other establishment publications, Marie Syrkin, Jesse Zel Lurie, and others accused the "Bergson Group" of all the usual deadly sins. We were charged with hoarding hundreds of thousands of dollars to launch a government-in-exile for the sole purpose of usurping the position of the Jewish Agency. These proclamations hurt our fundraising badly.

In December 1946, I had the good fortune of finding in New

York one of my old "Jerusalem boys," Gershon Hakim, who in the mid-thirties, as a youngster of fifteen, had been a "runner" in the Jerusalem *Irgun*. He came to New York early in the war, and served in the United States army, then later started a business with his brothers in the fur district. With the revolt escalating, he wanted to do what he could do to help. I snapped up his offer quickly, and soon he joined the group handling the *Abril*. Gershon concentrated on completing the crew, assembling provisions, medicines, spare parts, securing fuel and generally readying the ship for departure.

Just before the vessel was to leave, the FBI came on board, "searching for arms." Instead, they found hundreds of lifebelts, which they reported dutifully to Washington. At last, the *Abril*, sailed on December 26, 1946 and headed for the Azores. Because of the captain's misjudgment, the vessel encountered rough seas and reached Marseilles six days late.

In Marseilles, Abrasha Stawsky awaited the ship. He had spent months in Europe helping to assemble the immigrants. The *ma'apilim* were gathered from the American zone in Germany, France and Italy, and their travel papers were prepared with visas to Boliva.

Almost immediately after the ship pulled into Marseilles, Stawsky and Gershon replaced the captain. When Stawsky and Gershon reached the decision, they invited the captain to a meeting on shore. He was surprised by being flash-photographed, then he was handed an envelope full of cash and told that if he valued his safety, he had better forget all he had learned or seen up to then. He was put on a plane back to the United States, and the first officer, Robert Levithan of New York, took over as captain.

On February 28, 1947, the *Abril* sailed from Port de Bouc. The police register read: "Name: *S.S. Abril*, seven hundred tons; crew: twenty-seven Americans, one Swede; Flag: Honduras; destination: Bolivia. Carrying six hundred and twenty Jewish immigrants of all nationalities." As the ship left French territorial waters, the transport commander announced: "This vessel is now renamed the S.S. *Ben Hecht*!" Great cheers went up, and the crowded deck rang with the *Hatikva*.

This time the passengers were not youngsters cast out of their homes, or the old and sick fleeing for their lives. Wallace Litwin,

The *Ben Hecht*, as delivered to a Brooklyn yard (fall 1946).

The *Ben Hecht* being refitted (November 1946).

The *Ben Hecht* prior to sailing from Port de Bouc (February 28, 1947).

The King David Hotel explodes. (Courtesy Jabotinsky Institute)

Before

During

After

one of the crew, later described them in a syndicated column carried by the American Newspaper Alliance:

> These were mostly young men and women in prime condition . . . filled with an unbelievable determination to get to Palestine . . . They had come from Poland, Greece, Germany, North Africa, Italy, France, Holland and Belgium. One tight little bunch were former Russian Partisans. Many were men who had fought well for their countries during the war . . . the unofficial leader, was a former bomber pilot.

On March 8th, two destroyers of H.M. Navy captured the *Ben Hecht*, arrested its passengers and crew, and transported them to a detention camp on Cyprus.

The ALFP launched a full-scale advertisement campaign for their release. We declared:

> Britain waives the rules! British jail American seamen in Palestine. Who is breaking what laws? These men fought alongside the British in W.W. II. Still fighting for freedom, they ran the *Ben Hecht* through the Royal Navy's illegal Palestine blockade. They were seized. Their crime: "Aiding and abetting illegal immigration"—the British say.
>
> Did the *Ben Hecht* crew violate the international pact of fifty-two nations? Or did they effectively fulfill President's Truman's repeated demand that Palestine's gates be opened "at once"?

On March 13, Congressman Hugh D. Scott, Jr. of Pennsylvania said on the floor of the House: "After repeated statements by the President of the United States, that this country desires the admission to Palestine of the Hebrew refugees now in displaced persons camps and after resolutions by innumerable American organizations a group of American citizens have been arrested by the British for trying to do their part in implementing that American policy."

Congressman John D. Dingell of Michigan carried the subject forward:

"The civilized nations of the world clearly set forth, in the League of Nations Mandate, their intent that Palestine become a Hebrew homeland . . . Britain concurred and eagerly accepted the Mandate . . . The freedom of the seas has a long history in America, from the shores of Tripoli to Leyte Gulf. I should not like to see that freedom abandoned under circumstances in which every precept of law, honor and humanity asserts its dignity."

In Palestine, the *Irgun* issued a statement which was later repeated in the March issue of our underground paper *Herut:*

> From the depths of our hearts, we congratulate our delegates and friends overseas, on the arrival of the *ma'apilim* ship, the *Ben Hecht*. Other vessels will follow.
>
> We say to our delegates and brothers overseas, multiply your efforts . . . *Ha'apalah* is part of the larger battle front!

Because of all the agitation, the British released the crew and let them fly back to New York. Mayor Vincent R. Impelliteri greeted them on the steps of City Hall. Addressing the crew at a welcome-home dinner which the ALFP threw at the Hotel Astor, Ben Hecht said in his inimitable style:

> Today there are only two Jewish parties left in the field; the terror-ists and the terrifed. You can dismiss the second party as a political force. People afraid have left few monuments to their existence . . . The terrified amongst the Jews will take their place in history alongside the terrified amongst the American Colonists in 1776. . . .
>
> These lads are Americans . . . the same sort of Americans who kept the lifeline to the British Isles open, when human liberty was endangered for our English cousins . . . It was an American boat, bought with American money.
>
> There is no Hebrew navy yet. There is no Hebrew nation in Palestine yet. There are no victories yet—there is only this: the air is clearing around a flag . . . victory is in us—and there is light ahead.

---

¹Jacques Mery, a French newspaperman who traveled with the *Ben Hecht*, wrote an emotional series of articles relating his experiences. When his editor insisted on editing the copy, Mery instead expanded the story into a full book: "Laissez Passer Mon Peuple." Albert Camus wrote in the preface: ". . . [This] book is an embarrassing book. It does not tell about all the persecuted . . . but only of one people who is a symbol of all the others . . . but I want to assure you they are not totally lost for us. The Jews are like all other people, says one of the personalities of the book, they have only one life. And the Old Sarah sighed 'I don't even own a Tomb.' I'm sure these small details, the idea the persecuted have had enough of being thus—will make for them, at last, some friends. They want their right to private graves as they have their lives, like the rest of the world. It is a good beginning . . ."

V
The Walls are Breached

In Washington, the ALFP work was now being carried on by our American friends headed by Maurice Rosenblatt. The organization had also grown to proportions that would have been unmanageable for our small corps of delegates from Eretz-Israel. We had branches all across the country, some one thousand activists and one hundred thousand supporters and contributors. In New York, Philadelphia, Chicago, and Los Angeles, the organization's chief officers—Harry L. Selden, Alexander Wilf, and Maurice Rifkin—were joined by several Palestinians, among them Victor Bennahum, a former *Haganah* activist, who had fought in the British Army during the war.

The British Embassy complained bitterly about our advertisements, and every aspect of the campaign. The State Department urged the FBI to discover misdeeds, and as in the past, the FBI obtained information from (to quote a memorandum to J. Edgar Hoover from Herbert Wechsler, Assistant Attorney General): "those organizations interested in Palestine, but opposed to the views and methods of the HCNL . . . among those the Jewish Agency for Palestine." A number of *Haganah* informers were planted among our activists, and FBI agents came to the offices of the ALFP and spent weeks scrutinizing the books and accounts. After one such visit in New York, they left a $20 contribution— "to help the good work you are donig."

Now the Jews in America understood our "Proclamation" of November 1942, which had asked that "an end will be put to the scandal of history of a great and ancient people compelled to haunt the corridors of time . . . as beggars." Now many finally had their fill of their "reasonable" and "moderate" leadership. They had had enough of the guile and evasion and hypocrisy that had surrounded the "Jewish problem" since the early thirties; they, and Jews all over the world, including hundreds of thousands of soldiers who had recently given up their weapons and uniforms, watched the resistance in Palestine, and saw the moment of fulfillment of all the old dreams coming near.

When we addressed Jews now, at meetings and in private homes, we could feel the differences in the mood. There was a fierce dedication and determination that had been missing only a few years before. I read it in the letters enclosed with single dollar bills coming in from all across the country, and I had seen it in Europe in the face of the youngsters who reported to the Paris headquarters, after smuggling themselves across borders defying arrest and risking deportation by the British military authorities.

Now no double-dealing by Bevin or General Barker or other British diehards could stem the tide. No matter how they tried to ignore the formidable coalition, they faced a new generation of Jews young and old, whether Palestinian, European or American. To make Palestine their own, they were willing to face British guns and courts and detention camps in Cyprus.

The cells of the resistance kept growing. The cruel, callous statements coming from frustrated British officials in Palestine were no match for the mordant Ben Hecht, for the incisive and bitter drawings of Arthur Szyk, for the music of Kurt Weill, the oratory of Will Rogers, Jr. and Guy Gillette, the unwavering support of other senators and congressmen, and former high officials like Fowler Harper and Harold Ickes. These combined forces behind the combatants in Palestine could not be matched by Britain.

Because we desperately needed funds, the British just as desperately tried to keep us from getting them. To support their campaigns attacking our "illegality," they enlisted the accommodating State and Justice Departments to gather evidence. For all their efforts, nothing outright illegal could be proven, even though their files on us swelled to gargantuan proportions, and the files were not closed until 1952.

Congressman Ray J. Madden of Indiana responded to these attacks by recalling "a statement by the British Foreign Minister that he would stake his political future on solving the problems of Palestine . . . he had succeeded only in discourtesy to the President of the United States, irritation to the American people, and the solidification of a determined resistance movement in Palestine . . . it is little wonder that the advertisements about which the British government so bitterly complains, appear in American newspapers."

When the British forbade the mention of the ALFP in the Palestine press, we saw that little had changed in the colonial mentality since 1937. Senator Warren G. Magnuson of Washington responded by asking the President to announce that unless large-scale emigration of displaced Hebrews to Palestine was undertaken within a stated period, the United States government would itself transport to Palestine such persons from Europe under the protection of the American flag. The Senator added: "Mr. President, this may appear to be drastic action . . . but the situation which it is designed to correct is one which has always had drastic consequences and which is certain to have consequences . . . even more tragic."

Magnuson's predictions proved to be accurate. The following months saw some of the bloodiest episodes in the history of Palestine. The *Irgun* bombed the British officers' club in Jerusalem, then the British encircled Tel-Aviv and imposed a continuous curfew on all three hundred thousand inhabitants. Twenty-four hours a day for several days, no one was allowed on the street. Sixty suspects were arrested, among them twenty-four alleged *Irgun* and *Lehi* men. In the next several weeks, the curfew nearly bankrupted many businesses and choked off any semblance of normal living.

By then, there were four *Irgun-Lehi* men awaiting the gallows in Acre prison, and two in death cells in Jerusalem. On March 21, the *Lehi* set the Haifa refineries on fire. The fires were still burning when not far away in the Acre prison, Gruner, Drezner, Alkochi and Kashani went to the gallows. To the end, Gruner called himself a prisoner of war. The Commanding Officer of the British Army, Lt. General Evelyn Barker snorted: "There was no war. Gruner was a criminal."

Palestine reverberated with the attacks on the British and groaned under the latter's castigations. Bevin stubbornly ignored the recommendations of the new United States Secretary of State, George C. Marshall, and as he had planned, referred the Palestine issue to the United Nations.[1]

We did not neglect the diplomatic front but the time was ripe to speak to the world and the Jewish people in a new language.

The HCNL sent a challenging message to Trygve Lie, Secretary General of the United Nations:

> The HCNL, acting as the Hebrew National Authority pending establishment of the provisional government of the Hebrew Republic of Palestine, respectfully requests that the Secretary General place the following proposal on the agenda . . . that a Hebrew national delegation . . . consisting of representative Hebrew leaders from Palestine and veterans of the Hebrew resistance against the Nazis in Europe . . . be granted a seat for the duration of the special session with full power of participation.

* * *

With all the ongoing diplomatic maneuvering there was no reason to halt the armed resistance; since the British did not indicate any willingness to open the doors of Palestine or cease military action, neither did the *Irgun*. The surprisingly hasty executions in the Acre prison had been carried out to demonstrate to the British public, as well as to the United States and the United Nations, that Britain still ruled Palestine. The *Irgun* decided to prove otherwise. One April evening, on a quiet sidestreet in Tel-Aviv, eight members of the *Irgun* command met to study and approve plans for an attack on the Acre prison. Begin opened the meeting by reviewing the latest developments in London and the United Nations. The group concluded that the time was ripe for another serious blow to British prestige and morale. "Giddy" Paglin, chief of operations, presented the details of his plan, and it

---

[1] During these months, Bevin's behavior bordered on the psychotic. Richard Crossman later described Bevin's state of mind during a meeting in August, 1947. According to Crossman, Bevin's main points sounded like the infamous anti-Semitic "Protocols of the Elders of Zion." Bevin claimed that the Jews had organized a worldwide conspiracy against Britain, and against himself personally. This hoax, he said, had been perpetrated mainly from America. When Crossman suggested that the Irish Republic might also have been "a racket operated from America," Bevin answered: "Yes, but they did not steal half the place first." Then, referring to recent *Irgun* actions, Bevin added that he would not be surprised if the Germans had learned their worst atrocities from Jews.

was quickly approved.

The raid was supposed to free exactly forty-one prisoners—eleven *Lehi* men, and the rest *Irgun* men, several officers among them. Dynamite and fuses, hand grenades, and civilian clothing were smuggled into the prison and stored in a secret tunnel. Minute preparations were made for transporting and hiding the escapees after the operation. A fortnight before the attack, the three top *Irgun* officers in the prison, had been informed of the plan and they briefed the other intended escapees one by one. Everything was set for May 4th. At 1640 hours on the 4th, a "British" convoy left Shuni, an *Irgun* base between Benyamina and Zichron Yaakov. Its travel orders gave Beirut as the destination. The convoy consisted of thirty-four soldiers in solid British army trucks, led by a "British" captain of the Royal Engineers. The captain rode in a jeep at the front of the convoy. He was a squat, powerfully-built blond who had spent six years in commando units in the British Army and the Jewish Brigade; for years now he had been the top *Irgun* combat officer. Other *Irgun* units involved headed elsewhere: one went to mine the roads leading to Acre. Another started a diversionary attack on an army camp on the outskirts of Acre. Finally an "army telephone repair" unit made its way through the heart of the Acre market to the prison, climbed ladders, and scaled the wall over the main gate. A few minutes later, their explosives went off. The walls were breached.

The battle raged inside the prison. Alarms were sounded in army camps as far away as Haifa, and British units rushed to the prison from adjacent camps. The mines, however, delayed these movements. The casualties were actually amazingly light until, after the escape had been completed, the getaway convoy accidentally ran into a group of British soldiers who were bathing in the vicinity, protected by fully armed guards. Most of the losses occurred in the exchange of fire which ensued before the convoy could escape.

When the raid was over, twenty-nine key *Irgun* and *Lehi* men had been freed, nine were dead and five had been arrested. "Shimshon" (Dov Cohen) the commander of the operation who had posed as a British captain, never made it back to the base.

The operation badly shook up the British, both in Jerusalem and London, and helped spark an unprecedented event in the

United Nations. A few days later Andrei Gromyko, the delegate from the U.S.S.R., delivered a speech in the United Nations on "recent events" in Palestine, observing that British colonial policies in Palestine were bankrupt. We had known that such a tilt towards "the aspirations of the Jews to establish their own state" had been developing for some time, but this was the Russians' first public expression.

It was not that the communists sympathized with Hebrew national aspirations. Ingrained Russian anti-Semitism, the vicious anti-Zionism of Jewish communists in positions of power, precluded this. But at that given moment, the Hebrew armed resistance, contrary to both Britain's and Ben-Gurion's expectations, was the strongest threat to the British administration's power; and if it could help expel the British from Palestine, why not use it? Impressed by the tenacity of the few Hebrew fighters facing all that British might, the Russians decided, at least for the time being, to cast their lot on the side of Hebrew rebirth. As seen from Moscow, the ouster of British power would create a convenient vacuum for Russia. Bevin, who could have still chosen to accept the fact of an allied Hebrew State in the Near East, chose to ignore basic geo-political considerations. On this as on many other critical matters, Bevin miscalculated.

At the time of the Acre attack, Ben Hecht was in a hospital recovering from serious surgery. From his bed he wrote "a letter to the terrorists of Palestine."

> My brave friends—you may not believe what I write . . . but on my word as an old reporter, what I write is true.
> The Jews of America are for you. You are their champion . . . Everytime you blow up a British arsenal, or wreck a British jail, or send a British railroad train sky-high, or rob a British bank, or let go with your guns or bombs at the British betrayers and invaders of your homeland, the Jews of America make a little holiday in their hearts.
> Unfortunately, the heads of nearly all the Jewish organizations whom the American newspapers call 'The Jewish leaders' are against you.
> Everytime you throw a punch at the British betrayers of your homeland, nearly all these Jews have a collective conniption fit. They rush in waving white handkerchiefs and alibis. They didn't do it—not they! Respectable people don't fight. They gabble . . .
> Right now, all the responsibility of the Jews is handsomely

engaged in cooing before the United Nations. The British put the matter . . . up to the United Nations because they are frightened of you . . . [they] figured the sound of gabble before a world court would drown out the sound of Hebrew guns in Palestine.

It has not and it won't!

The ad was carried as a news item by papers all across the United States, Canada, Mexico, South America and France. The British and the Jewish Establishment were apoplectic. In the United Kingdom, Hecht was blacklisted, while in Palestine, the *Irgun* distributed his message to the population at large.

Day in and day out, the *Yishuv* watched proud, knowledgeable, articulate young people willingly offer up their lives, and it made a profound impression. Gruner and his comrades, singing the *Hatikvah* on their way to the gallows, "Shimshon" leading his men over the Acre prison walls, Feinstein and Barzani blowing themselves up in the Jerusalem jail to cheat the British executioner—they set examples for the rest of their people, fanning the flames of the revolt.

* * *

On May 15, 1947, the United Nations Special Committee on Palestine (UNSCOP) was formed. Through it, Ben-Gurion and the Jewish Agency once again attempted to find a common language with the British. *Herut,* the underground paper of the *Irgun*, kept up a relentless attack on Ben-Gurion for these new attempts at capitulation.

> What will result from 'asking?' . . . What shall we do in the meanwhile, during the years it will take the United Nations with all its committees and inquiries to act—if at all?
>
> To all these questions, the chairman of the [Jewish] Agency does not have an answer. He promises that one of these days, in our lifetime—the Hebrew State will rise . . . In what does Ben-Gurion put his faith, if he wants to suppress this [our] battle?
>
> The gates are closed. The remnants of our people are being gradually demoralized in the camps . . . the *ma'apilim* are exiled (to Cyprus) . . . What do you propose to *do*—besides making statements?
>
> If our battle is not to your liking—where is your civil disobedience? Mass resistance? Where are your tax-strikes? Battles on the seashore?

How different a language Ben-Gurion spoke to the British than our young fighters did. Before Meir Feinstein and Moshe Barzani were sentenced to the gallows, Feinstein stood up in the Jerusalem military court and said to those sitting in judgment:

> Officers of the Occupation Army! You are attempting to establish a regime of the gallows in this country ... In your foolhardiness, you assume that such a regime will break a nation's spirit ...
>
> Don't you realize whom you are facing? ... We, who for years listened to the monotonous refrain of those rail cars that carried our parents, our brothers and sisters, the best of our people, to a slaughter unequalled in human history?
>
> We who ask ourselves daily why we were spared? We who should have been with them in their moment of truth!
>
> To this we have one answer—we were spared not merely to live in hopes and expectations or in bondage, awaiting new Treblinkas. We were spared to assure our people, our nation, of a life of freedom and honor, so that what happened there shall not be repeated!
>
> There is life worse than death and death greater than life ... And if you have not understood that, then your time has come to step down from the stage of history ... Assyria and Babylon, Greece and Rome, Spain and Germany, preceded you ... You shall follow them.

But none of this slowed Ben-Gurion's toadying to the British. Only one year after "Black Saturday," on June 12, King George VI's official birthday, the Union Jack flew from the Jewish Agency building in Jerusalem, next to the blue and white flag. Almost all the *Haganah* men jailed in Palestine were amnestied. In gratitude, Ben-Gurion had the *Haganah* blow up an *Irgun* munitions dump.

On June 16, the three *Irgun* soldiers who had survived their capture by the British after the Acre attack were sentenced to death by a military court in Jerusalem. Four days before, two British sergeants had been captured and were being held, with a warning to the British Army not to execute the *Irgun* soliders or the two hostages would be promptly executed as well. This was a last-ditch measure; first the *Irgun* had sent a message to UNSCOP asking that the three condemned men be called as witnesses, to "submit to the committee most important facts ... regarding the criminal behavior of the British 'security forces' towards prisoners and wounded." There had been no response.

On July 17, eight senators long involved with the Hebrew struggle for freedom introduced a resolution in the United States Senate. It proposed that the Secretary of State advise the British government that its actions in Palestine constituted a "flagrant violation of the American-British Convention of 1924." It also requested the British to abolish immediately the emergency regulations presently enforced by the administration, reinstating civil liberties. The resolution was still in the Committee of Foreign Relations when events superseded it.

When the *Irgun* abducted the sergeants, the British, with full support of the *Haganah*, combed the coastal areas, going from house to house. Their combined efforts to find the sergeants failed, but so did the appeal to the British by the *Irgun* to grant the condemned *Irgun* men prisoner-of-war status. On July 23, Haviv, Nakar and Weiss went to the gallows, singing the *Hatikvah*.

The next day, the two British sergeants were hanged. British rage and humiliation was without bounds. Anti-Semitic riots broke out in Liverpool, Manchester, Glasgow and London, and the hatred boiled over among the British soldiers in Palestine. On July 31, from the safety of armored cars, a group of soldiers and police killed five civilian Jews in the streets of Tel-Aviv, and wounded many others. No one was ever indicted or punished in any way. It was a neat little pogrom, British style, essentially condoned by the British administration. The High Commissioner wrote to the Colonial Secretary, explaining away the behavior of the soldiers and police: "Most of them are young . . . They have had to work in an atmosphere of constant danger . . . It was therefore understandable that the death of the two sergeants excited them to a pitch of fury."

The hanging of the British soldiers produced one lasting effect: from that day on, the British never hanged a single Hebrew soldier. The Resistance was generating respect as well as fear and anger. At the same time, the British showed the Jewish Agency and the *Haganah* their special gratitude for helping hunt the "renegades," by capturing the *Haganah* vessel *Exodus* and returning its *ma'apilim* to Germany.

VI

America Comes Across

One of the central roles now of our delegation in the United States was to explain why the bloody events in Palestine were occurring and what could make them come to an end. We did this through advertisements, with Ben Hecht's writings, with our weekly the "Answer," in the halls of Congress and on street corners. Young men and women addressed crowds, distributed literature, gathered signatures on petitions and raised what funds they could. Esther Untermeyer trained a group of theater people, among them Sidney Lumet and Marlon Brando, to help us in speaking engagements and other public presentations. For the first time since we arrived in the United States, funds trickled in and permitted us to transfer money to Europe and Palestine, as well as cover our investments in a new vessel we recently purchased. The average Jew and some non-Jews could not help but stop, ponder and react to the happenings in Palestine. The stranglehold of the Establishment on the Jewish masses was slipping.

Our campaign aimed at creating both grass roots and governmental support for the struggle in Palestine, working up from representatives in Congress to the White House.

It was hard, however, to tell how we fared on the highest levels. The Truman presidency baffled us. His simple activist notions of the chief executive's duties were best expressed by the rather trite sign on his desk: "The buck stops here." Jews, Arabs and their problems were familiar to him from his days as a senator. As chief executive he was exposed to continuous delegations of Jewish leaders with their internal bickering, and their oblique threats that his decisions could win or lose him Jewish votes. But he was a good Bible-reading Christian and believed in helping the under-dog and fighting injustice, so he could not merely dismiss the issues they presented. Possibly he wished Palestine would just disappear, but as a realist, he knew that he would not be able to avoid dealing with these problems for long. He tried to keep them as simple as possible, guiding and improvising, but sometimes in the late months of 1947, he had to indicate his preference. It became necessary to preserve the integrity of his personal inclinations while accommodating his cautious secretary of state, George C. Marshall; he also faced severe political presure from Democratic bosses.

Gillette, Selden and Rosenblatt gave us fascinating reports on the changing, contradictory moods in the White House and Congress. With Rabbi Silver and Emanuel Neumann now taking more militant stands than Ben-Gurion, the Jewish leadership was creating great tumult with their campaign for partition. Silver admitted to us that the *Irgun* was having "a more successful psychological effect" on the British and world opinion than the *Haganah*.[1]

Truman's vacillations reminded me of my spontaneous reactions that spring in Germany when FDR died and Truman assumed the Presidency. I was convinced then that FDR eventually would have developed into an all-out opponent of Hebrew statehood. But the State Department continued to be the center of opposition to Hebrew independence. The "Arabists" in State accepted hook, line and sinker, the supposedly "pragmatic" self-deceiving ideas espoused by the British colonials that a rational policy of co-existence could be worked out with an amorphous Arab-Islamic world.

President Truman and Secretary Marshall pursued their versions of an even-handed policy carefully. In May, Marshall brushed aside British protests about our activities, but then on June 5, Truman issued a statement urging "every citizen and resident in the United States to refrain from activity which might inflame the passions of the people in Palestine, so long as the United Nations was considering the Palestine problem."

Guy M. Gillette, Truman's old friend, quickly responded: "The

---

[1] Begin even reported later that Silver told him: "Without the *Irgun* the State of Israel would not have come into being." (*The Revolt*, Dell, New York, 1978, p. 412).

appeal would be much more effective if the President could prevail upon the British administration to refrain from further acts of hostility against the Hebrew people of Palestine and against the remnants of that people in Europe who are returning to their homeland on the basis of rights granted to them by international covenants, and violated by Great Britain, despite repeated requests by the President of the United States . . . The people of Palestine, left without any recourse to courts of law for redress of wrongs by an oppressive administration, feel that they have no choice but to meet force with force—as our forefathers did in 1776 . . ."

In any event, the British refused to follow Truman's request to "refrain from activity which might inflame the passions of the people in Palestine." In July they rejected the United States' request that they not return the *Exodus* and its *ma'apilim* to Germany.

And Marshall was not inclined to stand up to the British. He showed his hesitancy in a letter written by his legislative counsel: "It would be inadvisable for the United States Government to make specific recommendations (or) . . . take action . . . on proposals such as advanced by the HCNL (urging immediate repeal of British immigration policies in Palestine)."

Truman dropped two key "Arabists," George Wadsworth and Loy Henderson, from the American delegation to the United Nations General Assembly. But that was as far as he was ready to go. London was not adverse to further delays. Bevin continued to believe that the United States and the U.S.S.R. would ultimately reject partition and that the Palestine hot potato would be tossed back one way or another into his experienced hands. Bevin saw nothing to suggest otherwise. As late as July 1947, Marshall assured him of American cooperation in suppressing "illegal" immigration to Palestine. The State Department even went so far as to advise Moshe Sharett (Shertok), then in the United States, that unless the Jewish Agency stopped its "illegal" immigration, the United States would vote together with Britain in the United Nations against partition.[1] This unnerved the Establishment to the extent that the treasurer of the Jewish Agency, Eliezer Kaplan, halted funds for the conversion of two vessels, the *Pan*

---

[1]Sachar, p. 290; also Joseph Klarman in Ha'uma (Tel-Aviv), Vol. 57, April/May 1979.

York and the *Pan Crescent* that were being refitted to transport fifteen thousand *ma'apilim* from Romania to Palestine.

The U.S. Government went still further in its cooperation with the British. The American Ambassador to Romania called upon Anna Pauker, the Romanian Minister of Foreign Affairs, and protested against Romania permitting Jews to leave for Palestine. He pointed out to Mrs. Pauker that the U.S. saw this as a hostile act towards the United States, since Britain was its ally, and since this immigration was forbidden under the Mandatory Government's laws. Pauker was at a loss how to react. A long-time Communist, she had disavowed her Jewish ancestry (she was a rabbi's daughter) and was a violent opponent of Hebrew nationalism and Zionism. But she could no better sympathize with the "colonial-imperialist" designs of Great Britain and the United States. The decision was made more difficult for her yet because the key men in the Romanian Communist hierarchy were friendly towards Hebrew aspirations. In the end, the vessels sailed, and Pauker informed the ambassador that the emigration of Jews to Palestine was not an illegal act "since they are returning to their homeland." The matter did not rest there. The British once again used a technique they had exercised during the war years, when they had convinced the U.S. War and State Departments that Jewish emigrants from Nazi lands should not be admitted to Palestine or anywhere else, because so many might be German agents. Now the British disseminated the information that Jewish immigrants from Russia and its allied countries included Communist fifth columnists.

When the two boats from Romania were forced by the British blockade to land on Cyprus, the British actually did find several men who had kept their Communist membership cards. Most people in Iron Curtain countries who hoped for any privileges felt compelled to join the Party. But despite that, there was little chance that these passengers who kept their cards were "agents," for whom such an oversight would have been unlikely.

Nevertheless, *The New York Times* featured a front page story by Herbert L. Matthews, reporting that many of the passengers spoke Russian and were members of the Communist party. Joseph Klarman, a veteran of the Jabotinsky movement who had been deeply involved in the planning for the voyages, also was named in the story as a suspected Communist agent. He filed a libel suit against the *Times* and upon his arrival in New York to pursue the legal action, he was prevailed upon by his employer, J. Landau, the head of the Jewish Telegraphic Agency, to drop the suit, even though he had a good chance of winning it. Landau explained that he had been approached by Rabbi Stephen Wise and told that the case would antagonize the *Times* unnecessarily. The Establishment leaders felt they badly needed the newspaper's support while the debate was going on in the United Nations. Traditionally, the *Times* had taken an anti-Zionist position, but the Establishment was hoping to win its sympathies, or at least its neutrality. Klarman dropped the suit.[1]

Klarman had one more brush with the Establishment regarding the two vessels. Our "old friend" Nahum Goldmann, in a feeble attempt to appease the British, issued a statement to the press that the *ma'apilim* had sailed of their own free choice directly to Cyprus, and that their immediate goal had not been *Aliyah* but merely to leave Romania. Klarman responded with a letter to the Zionist executive: "As an officially authorized and active participant in the *Aliyah* of these fifteen thousand people, I wish to state that Dr. Goldmann's statement is an outright lie . . . an insult to devoted sons and daughters of our people . . . the British are (not) so naive as to believe things that are fictitious . . . I demand that the Executive deny Dr. Goldmann's allegations and ask him to resign from the Executive."

Nothing of the kind happened. The Establishment's simplistic reasoning only helped weaken Zionism's already unpopular stand with the White House and the State Department. The tug of war continued between the "Arabists" in State, the hesitant Secretary Marshall and an increasingly irritated Mr. Truman. With the Cold War emerging as the most important issue confronting the democracies, Truman was becoming fed up with the Arabs, the Jews and the whole question.

The British had made sure that the leaders in Washington were well aware of what was now presented as their common policy— to protect the Western Allies' interests east of the Suez, including Haifa Bay and the oil fields of the Middle East, even if it meant

---

[1] Klarman, Ibid.

abandoning the historic commitment to a Hebrew national home-land. Bevin's moral rationale was the same one Britain had given throughout the war to justify their inaction when faced with the extermination—"the injustice to the Arabs of Palestine." To bol-ster this argument, the British also pointed to Arab military might raising the specter of a Moslem Holy War, which could cause a massacre of the Jewish population and even culminate in an all-out Pan-Arab assault against the British and American inter-ests in the Middle East. The State Department took these apoca-lyptic arguments to heart, and largely threw their weight on the side of the Arabs. Once again, during the coming months, its Near East experts attempted to interest Secretary Marshall in solving the problems by the admission of one hundred thousand immi-grants and then freezing Hebrew national aspirations into a stunted national cultural homeland.

By mid-1947 the Allies' Mediterranean policies were coal-escing. A Truman doctrine for the northeastern Mediterranean was emerging based on a British-American alliance. At the same time Bevin was growing more nervous and uncertain as to a British Palestine policy. The Russians were shrewdly fishing in the troubled waters, catering to both Arab and Jewish interests. President Truman was facing growing unpopularity in the coun-try and both we and a militant Rabbi Silver were not letting up our campaign to force a British departure from Palestine. It all culminated in the U.N.'s General Assembly decision to form UNSCOP. Three months later, the General Assembly received its recommendations.

While in Palestine, several members of UNSCOP, including Ralph Bunche, met with Begin who forcefully presented to them the *Irgun's* rejections of the partition plan, enthusiastically fought for by Weizmann and Goldmann. Begin said: "We cannot give up any part of our country. Instead, the answer is to immediately bring to Palestine all Jews who desire to settle there. This to be carried out by a Provisional Hebrew Government. Once the resettlement is completed, elections could be held to choose a permanent government. Arabs would vote and participate in governing the country." And in New York the HCNL submitted to the U.N. "Ad Hoc" Committee on Palestine a detailed memo-randum with proposals on the creation of "A Hebrew

Republic in Palestine." The HCNL rejected the proposal of partition, asked for immediate free repatriation of all Jews who wish to do so, asked for the ending of the British Mandate and the formation of a Provisional Government.

And in Palestine the *Irgun* and *Lehi* were not giving any respite to the British forces. Following the *Exodus* incident, even the *Haganah* carried out a number of attacks on British radar stations and sank a patrol boat in Haifa Harbor. Once again Ben-Gurion assumed a militant posture and was now calling for British withdrawal from Palestine.

Actually, diplomatically and in public relations the cause and concept of Hebrew independence was doing rather well. In that historic moment, world public opinion and the postwar nations seemed inclined to give Jews what was denied to them for centuries—their country. And uniquely, American and Russian maneuvers coincided although for varying reasons. However, the final battles were still to be fought.

On July 10, 1947, in the midst of mounting political tension and the *Irgun*'s struggle, Begin sent us a scathing letter.[1] He once again rejected Kook and Eri's urgent recommendations that we declare a Provisional Government.

> There will be the need for a government, and there will be the time to form it, and possibly even a constellation of events that will bring about [the unilateral act of] declaring it—if the Agency accepts a modified [Cantonization] plan. Then events will bring together all opposing factions and create the entity that will lead the War for freedom and the integrity of the homeland . . . To rush with such a decisive political step will be to destroy that edifice before it is built.

Once again Begin was putting the emphasis on intensifying the armed struggle while protecting the *Yishuv* from fratricide.

It was at that crucial moment of the rising tide of the resistance that the *Palmach* leadership proposed, and Ben-Gurion approved, a plan to crush us once and for all. Dr. Eldad, a top *Lehi* leader, asserts that a decision was reached to stage a St. Bartholomew style massacre of *Irgun* and *Lehi* men.[2] A list of

---

[1] Direct quotations are from M. Begin's Letters, copies of which are in the writer's possession.
[2] "Ma'aser Rishon"—Hadar Publishing, Tel-Aviv, 1975 (P. 296).

three to four hundred men was prepared for this purpose. Begin and Yalin-Mor were at the head of this list. The plan called for a fast, short invasion of the homes of *Irgun* and *Lehi* men and shooting them on the spot. The plan became known to non-Socialists like Mayor Rokach of Tel-Aviv. Only a last-minute, vehement intervention by Rabbi Silver caused it to be canceled. This horror of a plot was hatched by the same people who, for the past ten years, had preached to us about "thou shalt not kill" and about the "purity of arms."

Begin admitted that he was unable to predict the course the United Nations would pursue (termination of the Mandate or a cantonization plan or the British managing to maintain a modified status quo). The important thing Begin stressed was "I'm not a fatalist. Only one thing will decide the fate of Eretz-Israel—the armed resistance . . . which needs funds and which should have been forthcoming from you during the past year, but have not."

Begin hit hard at our failure to raise substantial funds. He criticized me for not coming through with the $100,000 I had optimistically promised in May, when I watched the growing sympathies for the *Irgun* across the country.

Begin wrote:

> I'm enraged to think that the *Irgun* delegates are not coming across with all possible help . . . which we must have to widen our battle. Do you conceive of the conditions [we face] . . . the boys who come out of the jails are wandering around hungry . . . we lost repeated opportunities to purchase weapons . . . actions were cancelled because of the lack of funds—and only because of that. . . .
>
> These miserable funds mean arms, safe havens for our men, printing of our message. . . .
>
> As to *Aliyah*—$550,000 for two vessels! With such an amount in our hands, we could organize 'a small revolution . . .' If we could have both the vessels and our 100,000 Pounds—well and good. But we received not even a farthing for the battle while [funds are available] for an activity which is mostly demonstrative, [*Aliyah* ending in Cyprus] which has no chance to smash the blockade. It is illogical. I therefore recommend to curtail, although not to cancel, our activities in this direction.
>
> I must conclude with one simple statement—everything, but everything for the front line!

It was a sharp rebuke for our failure to come across with the funds that the growing struggle needed. Personally, I did have doubts about the need for our involvement at that stage of history in *Ha'apalah* work, but was also not sure at what stage the Establishment would once again capitulate, as Ben-Gurion offered in February, *and trade the Agency's Ha'apalah activity against some pitiful British handouts.* The option to end resistance and *Ha'apalah* could not be permitted to rest in the hands of the Jewish Agency. However, meager funds, combined with the steady hammering by Kook and Eri on the need to declare a Provisional Government, plus differences in temperament and style of work in Washington and Paris, caused, in due course, an irreparable schism. It caused an alienation between Begin and key men in the Command and Kook, Eri, 'Irma' Helpren and others. By the end of the year it was at the root of Kook's resignation as chairman of the HCNL and his replacement by Samuel Merlin.

The internal debates, the *Irgun's* unbending opposition to partition and Begin's dire warnings of coming military dangers all took place against the background of fastmoving events in the arena.

Bevin seemed to have erred in almost all his calculations. The Russians were behaving unpredictably. The State Department could not control Truman. The Russians shocked everyone by delivering speeches in the United Nations on "Jewish rights," and on how much the Jews had suffered during World War II. Truman announced America's commitment "to help bring about a redemption of the pledge of the Balfour Declaration and the rescue of at least some of the victims of nazism." Neither the rank and file of the *Haganah* nor the *Yishuv* as a whole, were inclined to "unmask" the resistance. Though the *Haganah* Command made some fleeting attempts to threaten the *Irgun* with a new "season," the *Yishuv* would not join in. The *Irgun* would not be drawn into a fratricidal war, but instead intensified the war on the British. While opposing partition, the *Irgun* declared that if the U.N. would not act promptly to end British interference and sabotage of emerging Hebrew freedom, Hebrew arms would.

Finally, the crowning insult to Bevin came when both Russia and the United States shifted directions, and announced their support for the principle of Hebrew independence.

Though Truman later attributed his decision simply to "independent American policy," it was as if a light had flashed on in his mind, telling him that larger moral issues were at stake.

In 1947, the United States policy reached a crossroads in its Palestine policy. Overruling objections by Secretary Marshall and his colleagues, President Truman instructed the United States delegation in the U.N. to endorse partition. Whatever reasons and explanations were later given for this final decision, we who had labored for the past ten years in the U.S. spreading the message of Hebrew nationhood, felt that it was due less to any personal bias of the President than to the conscience of the American people whom he represented.

VII
From Lake Success to the Hills of Judea

O n November 29, 1947, the United Nations General Assembly
voted thirty-three to thirteen approving the partition of
Palestine into two states, one Arab and one Jewish.

The Arab League reacted immediately. From Aleppo to Aden,
Arab mobs attacked and killed defenseless Jews, burned down
their homes, businesses and synagogues. Within a few days,
attacks also began in Palestine against outlying and isolated
Jewish settlements. Key highways were cut off by armed Arab
bands and tensions rose to fever pitch between the two
communitites.

The State Department quickly recommended a U.S. embargo
on weapons to the Middle East, while the British continued to
supply arms to the Arab League countries. The *Yishuv* had no one
to provide it with weapons. Suddenly, the Jews in Palestine were
as vulnerable as their fellow Jews had been in Europe eight years
earlier. After all the experiences, years under British colonial rule,
and after nearly twenty years of hearing our warnings, the *Yishuv*
not only was psychologically and logistically unprepared for a
war of liberation;[1] the violent opposition of the Pan-Arabists
caught it practically defenseless.

We in the *Irgun* recognized that the moment for which we had
trained and prepared since the early thirties was at hand.

On October 1, 1947, the *Irgun*'s "The Voice of Fighting Zion,"

---

[1]On December 15, 1974, Golda Meir said on the CBS *Face the Nation* program: "Do you
know what our situation was in '48? . . . We were six hundred and fifty thousand, with an
arsenal of fourteen (one four!) hundred guns all over the country in the Kibbutzim and in
the various settlements. . . ."

warned that even if the United Nations granted partition, it would not create an international force to implement it. On the 12th, another broadcast warned that immediately following partition, the British Army would evacuate the areas bordering on the Arab States, leaving the Jews defenseless. At the same time, the sea blockade would continue so the Jews would get no arms or reinforcements.

On November 16, when partition looked imminent, the broadcast was more vehement:

> The public is harboring three illusions fostered by its leaders: One—that the partition . . . will be implemented by peaceful means; two—that if war breaks out in Eretz-Israel, as the result of an attack engineered by British government agents, the United Nations Committee sitting in Jerusalem will soon restore peace; three—that if the United Nations representatives fail in their mission . . . the Security Council will intervene, issue a command, and stop the war! . . . It is essential that the people be called upon to prepare themselves for war and not for repose . . . The creation even of this ghetto inside our Homeland will be carried out amid flames . . . and rivers of blood.

These warnings continued almost daily. On November 30, the day after the partition resolution was passed, our "Voice" said: "The partition of the Homeland is illegal . . . Jerusalem was and will be forever our capital . . . In the war that is surely coming . . . all the Jewish forces will be united."

The leaders of the Jewish Agency continued in their delusion that Britain would abide by the terms laid down by the United Nations, including the opening of a port on February 1 so the *Yishuv* could bring in the supplies needed for its defense. The *Irgun* warned the Agency not to be deluded.

As the Arabs were beginning their attacks, American Jewish leaders appealed to the White House for American military intervention. We in New York felt stunned and humiliated. For how long had we preached and agitated, so that when this moment would come the Hebrew fighters would be ready. Throughout the years, even at the height of the "season," when our men had been kidnapped, tortured and sometimes killed by the *Haganah*, we had restrained ourselves, avoiding a civil war at all costs, because an eventual united nation would need all the men at its disposal for the final battle. With whatever resources we had we had built brick by brick the framework for a Hebrew military which would be ready for exactly this moment in history. Now we had to hear that Jewish leaders had bombarded an irritated Truman with appeals to use American soldiers to save the partition plan!

While Truman shifted his position day to day, depending on developments, the State Department remained Britain's steadfast supporter. The U.S. Consulate General in Jerusalem issued a warning to all American citizens that taking part in the fighting would cause them to lose their United States passports. The State Department also ordered the Treasury to conduct another investigation of Jewish activities to see if funds were being raised in the United States to "smuggle Jewish emigrants unlawfully into Palestine."

The consensus in the British military was that the Jews of Palestine would be no match for Arab military might. As Bevin eloquently put it to Secretary Marshall. "They would get their throats cut." Our longtime friend Frances Gunther visited Palestine with her husband in late 1947. At a dinner party at the High Commissioner's residence, the guests were seated at small tables, one of which the Gunthers shared with General Wavel, another visitor to Palestine. Wavel, unaware of his dinner partners' involvement in the Hebrew struggle, freely discussed the situation in Palestine. "His comments were revealing," Frances Gunther wrote afterwards: "The Jews could not hold out against an attack by the Arab States. It would be only a matter of weeks, after British rule was relinquished, before the British—and American navies—would be called up to evacuate the surviving Jews from Palestine." British officers who employed Jewish civilian help, inquired discreetly whether the latter would be willing to move temporarily to Amman where they would be safe from Arab massacres.

General Sir Gordon Macmillan echoed this sentiment, saying he was convinced that the Arab armies "would have no difficultly in taking over the whole country." Similarly, Field Marshall Montgomery opined that the Jews "had bought it." Both in Whitehall in London and in Government House in Jerusalem, everyone held their breath, expecting a replay of the 1916 massacre of Mussa Dag, in which hundreds of thousands of Armenians had been slaughtered by the Turks.

Britain decided not to rely merely on wishful thinking. To make sure the cataclysm they predicted would actually befall the Jews, they kept weapons coming to Egypt, Iraq and Trans-Jordan justifying their action by the existence of defense treaties, some negotiated even while the debate was still going on in the United Nations. General Taha Hashimi, the Iraqi general in charge of training Arab volunteers in Damascus, later told how Arab leaders had received advance notice of scheduled British evacuations from fortified and strategic posts. When British police abandoned parts of Jerusalem, the Arabs were forewarned. The British sold their properties like the huge Sarafend Camp to the Arabs instead of the Jews. Step by step, the British retreated to their carefully fortified bastions making sure that Jewish forces could not enter strategic areas. The semi-overt *Haganah* was harassed and often disarmed by the British, while British weapons continued to be delivered to Iraq and Trans-Jordan. Choking under the Anglo-American embargo, the *Yishuv* and we in the diaspora were now forced to search for weapons, no matter what laws we had to break. Within one decade there was not going to be a second genocide of the Jews.

Small attempts were made by a few courageous Palestinian Arabs to find ways for peaceful coexistence. The *Lehi* actually had some of its bases in Arab villages. The *Irgun* repeated the assurances that it had made to Palestinian Arabs since its appeal to them in 1944—that it had no enmity towards the peaceful Arab inhabitants, and that they would have full equality in the future Hebrew State. But neither the Arab League nor Bevin would let events take a peaceful course.

The Arab League raised an "Arab Liberation Army" under the field command of Fawzi El Kaukji, the old Arab gang leader from the thirties, who had spent most of the war years in Nazi Germany along with the Jerusalem Mufti. An Iraqi general was appointed commander-in-chief. The League undertook to supply ten thousand rifles and other weapons. Gradually the force grew to over fifteen thousand men, mostly mercenaries from Syria, along with Moslems from Yugoslavia, former SS men, British deserters, anti-Semitic Poles from the Anders Army and Spanish Falangists. The units spread throughout Palestine, establishing positions in Jaffa, Lydda, Ramleh, and taking control of most of the Galilee and the Negev. Haifa and Jerusalem were divided. Through all of this, *Haganah* operations were static, sporadic and mostly defensive. Ben-Gurion later admitted that in November of 1947, the *Haganah* force consisted mostly of three thousand men in the *Palmach* and a back-up of some ninety-five hundred men who had been given two or three hours a week of military field training, and about thirty thousand men and women for defense of settlements and towns. It was in no way ready for field operations or overt action as a regular army.

The *Haganah* historians[1] estimate its weapons on November, 1947 at ten thousand rifles, eight hundred machine guns and thirty-six hundred submachine guns and miscellaneous light mortar and handguns. For a population of six hundred and fifty thousand Jews, at least sixty thousand of whom could easily carry arms in a time of mobilization, this was a long way from adequate. When they should have been preparing militarily, year after year, the Socialist-Cultural Zionist Establishment had instead spent its large resources and brain power pursuing idealistic projects. As late as 1946, Ben-Gurion had reached an agreement with fundraising organizations in the United States: all collected monies would be divided forty percent for settlements and immigration, thirty percent for land acquisitions and thirty percent for the *Haganah*. This thirty pecent figure for the *Haganah*, already dangerously low, was reduced shortly thereafter to ten percent!

The first large orders for rifles were placed in Czechoslovakia in March, 1948. They started arriving in April and May, 1948! This was what the Establishment defined as meeting "all necessary means to the safety of the *Yishuv*," when they denounced and blocked our fundraising activities in the United States.

By early 1948, the British were doing their best to nurture complete anarchy in Palestine. They had let the country's banking, postal and transportation systems collapse, while their policemen and soldiers engaged in unprovoked bombing attacks on Jewish civilians. On Ben Yehuda Street in Jerusalem an explosion killed dozens. Bevin's predictions were coming along nicely. By February, 1948 the very survival of the *Yishuv* was in jeopardy.

Since the early fall of 1947, both the *Irgun* and *Lehi* had

---

[1]Contradicting Golda Meir's statement, above.

concentrated on accumulating weapons. Begin's pressure on us in the U.S. for funds and supply sources intensified; by mid-1947, with a substantial part of our funds, we had purchased our second vessel in the U.S., and began to prepare it to cross the ocean to the Mediterranean. Begin also entrusted us with forming the first *Irgun* cells in the United States for a future source of experienced manpower for Palestine. The Command sent several young men, mostly in their early twenties, to assist me in putting these units together. They all had some combat experience. Across the country we formed cells of four to five persons; each cell worked independently of the others and the members were known only to their immediate supervisors. It was not truly an active military organization, since there was no plan of engaging in military operations in the United States against British or Arab groups. Our chief aim was to prepare a reserve of manpower for the air force and other specialized combat groups in Palestine. We also sought arms and supplies from any and all sources for shipment to Palestine.

These shipments went by regular mail or by ocean freight. We acquired warehouses where the arms were assembled, packed and shipped with great help from Irish and Italian stevedores. We had our share of setbacks; arms caches were discovered and confiscated and some of our young men were arrested. Luckily, Paul O'Dwyer, William O'Dwyer's brother, had extraordinary success in handling the defense of those who were apprehended.

One of our worst failures occurred after we made a down-payment on two Lodestar and four Hudson Class fighter bombers in Canada. We began assembling materials to outfit them, and made preliminary arrangements for their registration under South African ownership. But then a *Haganah* man in New York anonymously phoned the owner, as well as the engineer who was preparing the planes for the trans-Atlantic flight, and advised them that the planes were destined for Palestine and that was the end of the deal. Our advance payment was lost. Furthermore, the Canadian authorities were informed of the incident and from then on more carefully checked all passport applications made by Canadians with flying experience or aircraft-related activities. The denunciation backfired on the *Haganah* since it hurt their activities in Canada more than it hurt ours. To avoid a repetition of this fiasco for all concerned, I asked Eri Jabotinsky to meet with the *Haganah* representatives in New York. They refused to speak with Eri.[1]

By early 1948 we still had a deficit of $150,000 even though more funds came in; funds remitted to Palestine were far short of requirements. Begin did not hesitate to show his disappointment. "Never before did so many fighters expect so much and receive so little." We understood Begin's frustrations, but we felt unjustly reproached—American Jews with means simply had never come through. Our support still came mostly from those whose financial capabilities were limited—the masses, and a small portion of the middle classes.

While the *Irgun*'s battles made its existence and goals widely known across the U.S., they also intensified pressure against us from the Department of Justice, F.B.I., their collaborators within Zionist and non-Zionist groups and from pro-Arab and sometimes anti-Semitic elements in the population. It was as formidable opposition as any group could face and much energy and time was spent by us defending our activities. One incident, somewhat amusing, is still vivid in my memory. We were subjected to censorship by the Pennsylvania Attorney General and the Commissioner of the State Police. They reviewed a film we produced titled "Last Night We Attacked," describing the armed resistance to the British. Quentin Reynolds, a popular foreign correspondent, narrated it. The Pennsylvania authorities licensed the film with two excisions. The narrator could not ask for funds, nor could he refer to "Our Allies in America."

The Palestinian *Haganah* emissaries in the United States, just like their predecessors in the late thirties, exerted all their power to discredit and wreck our fundraising. The Establishment's

---

[1] The New York office of the *Haganah* headed by Teddy Kollek, caused us much trouble. Leonard Slater in *The Pledge*, p. 232, describes one such incident: "Steve Schwartz . . . had heard of a meeting of volunteer pilots . . . recruited by the Irgun . . . [he] led a raiding party . . . on the pretense of reaching some accommodation—they had airplanes, *Irgun* had the crews—they went to the meeting at the Hotel Wellington. The negotiations became recriminations . . . in the excitement, someone stole the Irgun membership list." Presumably the pilots' names and addresses. Our aviation coordinator, in turn, advised me that the man who denounced us in Canada was "Irvin Schwarz." Whether the same person or not, the evil spirit of the 1944 "season" was transplanted, without much soul searching, to New York.

attacks on us in the U.S. and in Europe kept pace with the viciousness of their attacks against the *Irgun* in Palestine: whenever extreme actions were taken against the *Irgun* at home,the campaign simultaneously intensified against us overseas. This new wave of assaults by the *Haganah* led Lankin and Kook to meet with Dr. Sneh, the senior *Haganah* man in Europe. They advised him that unless the *Haganah* cooled its activities against us at home and in the diaspora, we in turn would take selected actions against it, publicizing our reasons. Sneh transmitted this warning to his people in Palestine; a few months later, Kook and Lankin were made to pay dearly for this temerity.

* * *

In January, 1948, Samuel Merlin was appointed Chairman of the HCNL and head of the *Irgun* delegation in the United States. Hillel Kook, who had experienced mounting discord with Begin and within the HCNL, relinquished the chairmanship. The development had been long in coming for many complex reasons, among them an ideological struggle between the command in Palestine, and Kook and Eri Jabotinsky in the diaspora.

It had begun in 1946, over the issue of declaring a provisional Hebrew government. It was to be formed by the joint efforts of the *Irgun* and the HCNL; but disputes developed mostly over timing. Begin demanded careful timing for such a step, and insisted it was the prerogative of "the people on the front line"; Kook and Eri felt Begin was being timid and provincial and asked for creating a government even without Begin's consent. From its side, with the war escalating in Palestine, and the final confrontation coming closer every day, the *Irgun* command asked for more tangible help and less "political gestures." The debate became acrimonious.

At the same time, division grew within the HCNL, at first over what policy to adopt in the event of partition, and later over how to respond to the U.N. resolution before and after its passage. In the meantime Eri was adamant by asking for a full *Irgun* identification with the HCNL's public statements. It was clear that Begin and his colleagues were not inclined to accept it. Eri wrote to

Begin that if the *Irgun* would not extend such backing, then the *Irgun* should organize a "Committee for National Liberation." He said that political facts are being created as important as the Balfour Declaration and that we must be on record with our views on what is being proposed as well as other issues such as elimination of Trans-Jordan from the original mandate. Merlin, on the other hand, seriously doubted that partition would materialize. He argued that the Agency's leadership would collapse under the pressure of events and retreat even from the tokenism of partition. Kook disagreed; Kook went so far as to recommend that once partition was passed, we should accept it as a *fait accompli*, give up our independent activities and merge with the Establishment institutions. By "consolidating with what had been internationally recognized," he felt that we could then press for a revision of the borders. He also believed that by joining the Zionist consensus in accepting the fifty-five hundred mile partitioned State, we could monitor the leadership from within, preventing them from issuing "weekly declarations that they have no claim on Shechem (Nablus) or Jaffa."

I tended to agree with Kook, and so did the majority of the HCNL. But where most of us soon parted ways with him was on the issue of our unconditional commitment to back the *Irgun*'s military struggle with all our resources. Merlin, though, not satisfied with the ambivalent view of Begin and his colleagues towards the HCNL's concepts of political activism, asked us to give top priority, now more than before, to "full harmonization between the fighting resistance and its political representation." I backed Merlin's opposing Kook's concept that the men of the HCNL are "the political leaders of our national revolution [while the *Irgun* leaders are] its technical commanders." I agreed with Merlin's criticism of the elements of bitterness that had crept into the dialogue between Kook, Eri Jabotinsky and the *Irgun* command.

Merlin angrily rejected Kook's suggestion that we join with the Establishment in accepting partition. Merlin almost prophetically retorted: "The Jewish ghetto State government . . . is not going to be composed of people born yesterday . . . Our good old friends in the Jewish Agency are the worst kind of ruthless clique this ugly world ever generated. This will be a government denuded of any power vis-a-vis foreign factors, which will therefore exercise all its evil passions towards an internal minority opposition."

In the following months, just as the *Irgun* had predicted, the battles in Palestine were escalating, and Begin constantly wrote to us demanding funds and supplies. In February of 1948, in a lengthy statement of policy which later proved to be over-optimistic, he wrote us:

> If the effort will be made on your end, we will face up to the decisive battle properly armed . . . The whole country will be liberated . . . Even the *Haganah* will join us to the Jordan . . . Even the asinine partisans now understand that there is no alternative.

The letter went on to say it was vital to tell everyone we could that the U.N. had not provided the international force to carry out its "solutions." The only path to peace was for Hebrew military power to destroy the Arab League's illegal invasion forces, which had rejected international authority in attacking us. Begin recognized that although this was just a legalistic argument, such developments create historic facts. In early March, Begin implored us again: "Two months are left to forge Hebrew diplomacy on the field of battle, at it is not clear whether there will be a '15th of May'[the day the mandatory regime was to end] . . . "We must receive your weekly remittance . . . Funds for us today mean life for those in danger of annihilation . . ."

The letter then dealt with the HCNL's renewed pressure for an immediate declaration of a Provisional Government: "We again dealt seriously with the possibility of forming a political-national entity which would claim the whole country . . . We decided against it. Such a step would precipitate an all-out internal attack on us. You must leave such decisions to us who live with the grim reality of Eretz-Israel."

By April even Ben-Gurion and his *Haganah* Commanders finally awakened to the "grim reality," to the fact that the infant nation was naked and alone in a hostile world. The *Haganah* Chief of Operations, Yigal Yadin, told Ben-Gurion that the *Haganah* could not carry on solely as a defensive militia, but must go over to the offensive. At long last, at essentially the last possible moment, seeing that reliance on "others" was suicidal, the left stripped off its ideological blinders, giving up its fixation with the Socialist "purity of weapons." Now it followed in the footsteps of the Maccabees.

Ben-Gurion began obtaining weapons from any and all sources, mostly from Czechoslovakia. The *Palmach* and other units emerged from their static positions, and went forward to seek freedom with blood and fire.

VIII

A Small Peaceful Village

On Sunday morning, April 11, 1948, I flinched when I read the headlines in New York: "Jews attack village of Deir Yassin. Massacre of civilians reported. *Irgun* and Sternists accused." I read the article fast. The way the *New York Times* described it, Deir Yassin was a "peaceful village" and its "civilian population" had been "massacred by terrorists."

I remembered Deir Yassin well from the late twenties and the last thing I would have called it was a "peaceful village." Way back in 1929, Arab marauders out of the village of Kalandia had attacked Motza, a Jewish settlement since 1894. Bands out of Deir Yassin and Lifta then cut off the Jewish relief force that tried to reach Motza. The Makleff family, one of the oldest, most respected families, was massacred in their home. One of my father's old friends, Broza, lay critically wounded, hovering between life and death for weeks.

In 1936, when I was in charge of an *Irgun* defense position in Givat Shaul, one of the Jewish Jerusalem's outlying suburbs, we continually faced attempted forays into our homes from Deir Yassin. We dug our "illegal" weapons every night and waited, while the Jewish supplementary police repulsed the infiltrators again and again. Months later, we had a defense position in nearby Motza commanded by Hillel Kook, and he often asked my help to transport men to their night duties in Motza. Driving back and forth to Motza from Jerusalem, I spent many hours lying in roadside ditches after ambushes out of Deir Yassin. The "peaceful little village" the *Times* now spoke of, earned itself quite a reputation over the years as a nest for terrorist attacks on the highway and the outlying settlements. Together with Lifta, the Arab village lying to the left of it entering Jerusalem, its "civilian population" tried to choke off traffic to and from Jewish Jerusalem whenever trouble was brewing.

Reading the newspaper I knew something had been "lost in translation." It took me a long stretch of time and many conversations with Mordechai Raanan, *Irgun* Commander in Jerusalem, with Nathan Yalin Mor, the key *Lehi* commander, and with men out of the ranks who had participated in the operation before I was able to put together all the pieces.

It was a far more involved story than the one the *Times* had printed. The first week in April, the Hebrew forces in Jerusalem had learned that Iraqi and Jordanian soldiers, as well as a number of Europeans of various origins, had installed themselves in the surrounding Arab villages. The night of April 2nd, Deir Yassin opened intense fire on the Jewish suburbs of Beit Hakerem and Bait Vegan. The firing lasted all night. For the next several nights running, *Haganah* and *Irgun* troops reconnoitered Deir Yassin; by the seventh of April, the *Irgun* and *Lehi* commanders had decided to attack and occupy the village. This would discourage further night attacks, help secure the highway to Tel-Aviv and consolidate Hebrew control of the western area of Jerusalem.

Because of limited coordination and cooperation between *Irgun-Lehi* and the *Haganah*, the *Haganah* was not asked to join in the operation. When their commander, David Shaltiel, learned about the plans on April 7, he wrote to the *Irgun-Lehi* commanders that he had no objections to the occupaton of the village. However, he warned against destroying it, "since this may lead to the occupation of the ruins by foreign forces." He added that to prevent such foreign occupation, "the *Irgun-Lehi* must stay on and occupy the village."

Some one hundred and twenty men and women were mobilized for the attack, but only one hundred went out to do battle because of a lack of weapons. They had thirty-three rifles, thirty-five *Irgun*-made Sten guns, three Bren guns, pistols, grenades (homemade by the *Lehi*) and only forty rounds of ammunition for the riflemen and one hundred rounds for the Sten guns. The *Irgun* units were led by Ben-Zion Cohen (Ghiora). Yehoshua Goldsmit, fittingly enough a native of Givat Shaul, Deir Yassin's usual target, assisted in the briefing of the combatants. He explained the plan of attack, gave the soldiers the password, then issued his final instructions. No one was to fire unless absolutely necessary; no unarmed people were to be shot at; no property was to be destroyed. The goal was not to kill or pillage, but to occupy the village and secure the highway. All prisoners would be transported towards the Arab lines to the East.

On Friday, the attackers slowly and quietly made their way toward the village in the predawn darkness. By the first light of dawn, somewhat behind schedule, they approached the entrance of the village, preceded by an armored car atop which a loudspeaker began repeating warnings in Arabic to the inhabitants: "The forces of the *Irgun* and *Lehi* are attacking you. Run towards Ein Karem or seek shelter below the village. We come to chase the foreign forces in your villages." The element of surprise had been sacrificed in an attempt to save civilian lives.

Suddenly, the Arab positions opened fire, and the armored car struck an anti-tank ditch and capsized. Hundreds of villagers obeyed instructions and fled for their lives but many stayed behind.

Murderous fire fights ensued. Every house and every stone wall served as a defensive position for the Arabs, while the attackers, exposed, had to charge each individual structure to secure it. The houses were entered by blowing down the doors. If the defenders gave up, they were sent to a stockade behind the fighting lines; if they did not, the house was belabored with hand grenades.

As the attackers gained ground, they found a number of surprises: among the prisoners were a Moslem Colonel from Yugoslavia, a British sergeant, two Iraqi soldiers and other Britons." A store of weapons was discovered: eighteen German rifles, forty pistols and ammunition. More surprises—many of the Arab women who were captured turned out to be men—disguised in peasant women's garb. Eventually thirty such armed "women" were identified.

The battle continued, house after house, courtyard after courtyard, and by 10 A.M. the number of wounded reached forty, though the count was imprecise because the dead lay among the wounded. The stalled armored car was turned into a first aid station, and men were wounded and lost their lives carrying their comrades to the medics. The battle was much fiercer than expected, and it took the attackers time before they could orient themselves. For many it was the first exposure to open battle. Some were veterans of guerrilla warfare, but this was totally different and some were as young as seventeen.

The battle heated up fiercely when the *Irgun* commander was shot by an Arab who emerged from a house carrying a white flag. Angrily the attackers advanced, slowly occupying one house at a time, always warning "Give up! Come out with your hands high!" And usually being answered with heavy fire. After about a dozen houses were dynamited, the inhabitants started coming out more freely. First women, then children, then old men, followed by young men wearing khakis.

By two in the afternoon, most of the houses had been taken, though to the end, the defenders tried different deceptions. Men came out with hands high and then suddenly drew out guns and started firing. These ruses only made things bloodier and more tragic for both sides.

The seizure of the houses continued through Friday, up until the following morning, when at last the house of the village head was taken. It had been fortified and stubbornly defended. The attackers raised the Hebrew flag over the house.

David Shaltiel, the *Haganah* commander, had met with the *Irgun* commander, Mordechai Raanan on Friday afternoon, and they agreed that the village would be taken over by the *Haganah* on Sunday morning. Raanan was anxious to disperse his men back to their bases as soon as it was safe, since the British were quartered in the environs and might take advantage of the concentration of *Irgun-Lehi* forces to settle old accounts. One intelligence report said they might bomb the village from the air. The *Irgun-Lehi* units had suffered excessive casualties, but had no available replacements.

Sunday, the *Lehi* took over the occupation duty. By midnight, the *Haganah* surrounded the village. On Monday morning, a unit of *Gadna*, the paramilitary youth branch of the *Haganah*, marched into the village and faced the bedraggled *Lehi* soldiers.

"We came here," the *Gadna* commander announced "to take in our hands a village that the bandits of the *Irgun-Lehi* desecrated with their barbarous acts . . . to cleanse it from the shame they brought on the Jewish population . . ." The youngsters, fifteen or sixteen years of age were then ordered to train their guns on the *Lehi* men.

Only the intervention of the *Irgun-Lehi* city commanders prevented an ugly, bloody incident. The *Lehi* unit simply marched out, shocked by the betrayals. The Hebrew soldiers had lost five men, and forty-four had been wounded. The Arabs had lost two hundred and twenty people.

By Sunday morning, rumors had already started circulating in town that the "renegades" had committed atrocities in Deir Yassin. A Red Cross representative asked permission to visit the village and the *Lehi* commander unhesitatingly approved his request. The representative roamed through the village unmonitored, accompanied by two Jewish doctors. His final comment was, "As we see, some people were killed by explosives, others by gun shots." He made no mention of atrocities and promised the *Lehi* commander a written confirmation that he had seen nothing untoward. One of the Jewish doctors, Dr. Avigdori, told the *Lehi*: "Come into my office in a day or two and I'll give you a copy of the report on behalf of the three of us." A discussion followed on how to dispose of the dead bodies to avoid an epidemic. The Red Cross man suggested covering the corpses with lye or burning them.

There was no lye. Nothing was done for another day.

The promised document was never produced. When Dr. Avigdori was approached during the following weeks, he finally blurted out: "There is pressure." When asked "from whom?" he answered: "I cannot tell you."

Once the battle for Deir Yassin was over, David Shaltiel launched a wide propaganda attack against the *Irgun-Lehi*. He heralded the offensive with a statement issued on the 12th, which he posted on the walls of Jewish Jerusalem:

> This morning, the men of *Lehi-Irgun* ran away from Deir Yassin and our forces entered the village . . . We were forced to assume this responsibility because the renegades brought about, through their their shameful action, the creation of a new front in western Jerusalem. They chose as their target one of the most peaceful villages . . . during an entire day, they were engaged in the slaughter of women and children simply for murder and pillage . . . When they finished their deeds, they ran away.

These were the words of the same man who, five days earlier, had delivered a written message to the commander of the *Irgun-Lehi* stating: "I have no objection to your carrying out the action on Deir Yassin." The same man who, three days later, when the attack was over, made no complaint about "shameful" acts, but simply agreed that the *Haganah* would take over the occupation and policing of the village. The only condition he had made was that *Irgun-Lehi* should bury the dead. Raanan had refused, stating that his men did not have the means to dispose of the bodies and that they were exhausted and had to be relieved.

One of the worst "horror propaganda" compaigns in history was launched against the "renegades." The Arab and British press jumped at the opportunity and soon far surpassed the smear efforts of the Jewish Establishment. One immediate effect was that all hope was dashed of compromise with those Palestinian Arabs who might have hoped for coexistence with the Hebrew population. For a long while after Deir Yassin, when Arab settlements were attacked, panic broke out and the inhabitants fled generally behind the lines of the Arab Legion. Gradually, their land and deserted homes were taken over by some eight hundred thousand Jews who had also fled their homes in Arab countries where they had resided before Islam conquered the Middle East.[1]

---

[1] On April 9, 1955, a former notable of Deir Yassin, Ahmed Assad, was quoted in the Jordanian paper *El Urdun* as saying: "The Jews did not intend to harm the inhabitants of Deir Yassin. But they had no choice when they met tough resistance and were fired upon from all sides . . . The flight of Arabs from villages and towns was not a result of the massacre of Deir Yassin, but of the exaggerated reports emanating from the Arab leadership."

He should have added "and from the Jewish leadership." Establishment historians perpetuate the tales even today. In his monumental *A History of Israel* (Knopf, Jewish Publication Society, 1976), Howard M. Sachar writes: "The most savage actions of these reprisals took place . . . in Deir Yassin. The Etzel [*Irgun*] and *Lehi* initiated the operation, and the ruthlessness these groups had earlier demonstrated against the British was now applied in even fuller measure against the Arabs. The village was captured, and more than two hundred Arabs, men, women and children, were slain, their bodies afterwards mutilated and thrown into a well . . . the deed was immediately repudiated by the *Haganah* command . . . which arrested the Etzel officers responsible."

Sachar was wrong in almost every detail: The action had never been planned as a "reprisal," but as part of a coordinated military operation, approved by *all* Hebrew Forces, to lift the siege of Jerusalem. Furthermore, no *Irgun* or *Lehi* officers were arrested. Yehoshua Goldsmidt fell a month later in a battle with the Arab Legion. Leah Prisant, the ranking woman officer of the *Lehi* contingent, was killed a few weeks later in an explosion at a *Lehi* arms cache.

Walter Laqueur, makes his comment simply but more sweepingly in his *A History of Israel* (Shocken Books, 1976): "On April 8, most of the inhabitants of the Arab Village

After the Deir Yassin incident, negotiations with the *Haganah* were rougher. Since December, 1947, the *Irgun* had been holding discussions with representatives of the Jewish Agency, working out possible collaboration. The discussions continued despite verbal and physical attacks by the *Haganah* and the Agency on the *Irgun*. There were repeated confrontations and incidents between the *Haganah* and the *Irgun* around the country, including a wave of kidnapping and counter-kidnapping. In early 1948, a *Haganah* unit tossed hand grenades into a crowd in Tel-Aviv which had gathered to hear an *Irgun* fund-raising broadcast in Moghrabi Square.[2]

When *Irgun* officer Yedidiah Segal was kidnapped by the *Haganah*, and then found dead near an Arab village, negotiations temporarily broke down, and just as the *Yishuv* was on the verge of independence, it was once again faced with the specter of a civil war. Yedidiah's mother then told the *Irgun*: "I do not want the shedding of my son's blood to cause a civil war."

On April 15, Begin wrote to us in New York:

> I know that you have made supreme efforts . . . and thanks to you we made progress . . . but there is no limit to our needs, as there is

---

of Deir Yassin . . . two hundred and fifty-four in number, were killed by a combined IZL-Sternist Force." According to Jewish Agency sources, the village numbered three hundred to six hundred people. Arab sources report eight hundred to one thousand. The *Irgun-Lehi* did not kill *most* of the people, and they did not simply walk in and begin slaughtering the way Laqeuer relates.

On April 5, 1968, the Israel Information Services of the Israeli Consulate General in New York issued a "Fact Sheet" on "The Deir Yassin Incident." One "fact" was that the *Haganah* never gave consent for the attack. Another was that the incident was significant, "because it was exceptional . . ."

Collins and LaPierre belabored the subject further in their book *O Jerusalem*, (Simon & Schuster, 1972). They report that the *Irgun-Lehi* practiced "cutting up of little children." When I quoted this to men who had participated in the attack, they said it reminded them of the blood libels of the Middle Ages.

A fascinating element in these "war atrocities" reports by respectable historians and internationally renowned journalists is that they chose to ignore a most startling document published by the Government of Israel's Ministry for Foreign Affairs; Information Division, on March 16, 1969, several years before the above books appeared.

The nine-page document, titled *Deir Yassin*, totally contradicted all previous Establishment statements and gave a version of the events almost identical with the *Irgun* and *Lehi* reports. It concludes: "They [the attackers] had no possibility of knowing beforehand whether any civilians were left in the village, after the evacuation of two hundred before the fighting began. This was no massacre of an unarmed peaceful village population by a military unit as Arab propaganda pretends. The *Irgun* fought and won a battle, there was no aftermath of outrage or brutal excess."

[2]NIV, Vol. VI, p. 124.

no limit to our needs, as there is no limit to the dangers threatening
us . . . it is absolutely excluded for us to form a government at our
own initiative . . . the [Jewish] Agency promises . . . that in one
month—only one month—it will form a government!

. . . once again—if the Agency yields and a government is not
formed—then a government will be formed by us! You in the
diaspora must have confidence in us. For years we walked a
tightrope. We have not fallen. We shall not fall!

Finally, on April 15th, the secret agreement between the
Haganah and the *Irgun* was approved by the Zionist Executive
with thirty-nine voting for and thirty-two (Labor and "new immigrants") voting against. Ben-Gurion steadfastly opposed any
agreement with "the renegades." The agreement was patterned
somewhat on the old United Resistance Movement accord, and
gave the *Haganah* sector commanders overall authority. It
required prior agreement of the *Haganah* for proposed action by
the *Irgun* and accepted the principle of reprisals against British
forces which committed violence against the population. It
included the *Irgun*'s repeated statement that if and when a
government would be established, the *Irgun* would dissolve itself.

One important clause for us in the diaspora was the one that
formally authorized the *Irgun* to continue to raise its funds independently from the Agency and *Haganah*. However, to the end
the *Haganah* men in the diaspora denied the existence of this
clause.

* * *

Although arms and funds were still meager, and though only a
handful of men were on full-time pay with the *Irgun*, the command decided early in April, on its largest single operation—the
capture of Jaffa. The idea was first of all to stop Arab sniping
from the Menshia Quarter which was endangering life in many
parts of Tel-Aviv. Secondly, it was to prevent Egyptian forces
from landing in Jaffa and attempting to reach Jerusalem, splitting
the country and cutting off the Negev. Tel-Aviv was the heart of
the *Yishuv* and Egyptians in Jaffa would pose a grave danger.
Finally, the British still maintained a great number of tanks in
Jaffa, which also represented a great threat to Tel-Aviv. All these

factors taken together made the capture of Jaffa top priority. And it appeared to be within the realm of possibility. Two successful attacks on a British camp in Pardess Hanna on April 4th, and on an ammunition train five days later, had provided the strike force with the minimum arms necessary for the assault.

On April 25th, six hundred *Irgun* men moved out from their staging area, and began a battle that eventually involved some fifteen hundred of their men and women.

The ruined buildings of Jaffa's Menshia Quarter were an excellent defense, fortified and honeycombed with tunnels. British tanks and cannons were positioned behind the Arab lines, while the heaviest weapons the *Irgun* possessed were two two-inch mortars.

It appeared that the British, for their own reasons, were determined to hold on to Jaffa up to the 15th, their projected departure day in May. When the *Irgun* men broke through the Arab lines to the sea and isolated the Menshia Quarter, the British counterattacked. They found more resistance than they anticipated, and flew in reinforcements from Cyprus and Malta. But still they managed to hold the inner city of Jaffa, now mostly deserted, only for a few more days. On May 13th, the city was fully occupied by *Haganah* and *Irgun* units. The *Irgun* had lost forty-two men and four hundred more had been wounded.

The British at last pulled out. No Egyptian landings were made in Jaffa as they were earlier in Gaza and Tel-Aviv was not cut off from the southern part of the country.

By the 11th of May, the leaders of the Agency gathered all their courage and decided to proclaim a Provisional Hebrew Government. In a six to four vote, the "responsible" leaders at long last voted for independence. At 8 o'clock in the morning of May 14th, the British lowered their Union Jack in Jerusalem. By noon, the Declaration of Independence of the State of Israel was broadcast over the radio by Ben-Gurion, the man who only twenty years earlier had taught me that neither a Hebrew majority nor a Hebrew State were our ideal, and that nothing would ever be won by the might of arms.

Begin had promised Ben-Gurion earlier, "if the official leaders set it up (a new government) . . . We shall support it with all our strength."

On Saturday night, May 15th, on the radio station of the *Irgun*, Begin made his announcement to the people of Israel:

> The Hebrew Revolt of these last four years has been blessed with success—first Hebrew revolt since the Hasmonean insurrection that has ended in victory . . .
>
> The State of Israel has arisen . . . the words of your *Irgun* fighters were not vain words: it is Hebrew arms which decide the boundaries of the Hebrew State . . . so it is now, so it will be in the future . . .
>
> You, brother of our fighting family . . . alone and persecuted, rejected, despised . . . tortured . . . cast into prison . . . driven to the gallows, but went forth with a song. You have written a glorious page in history!

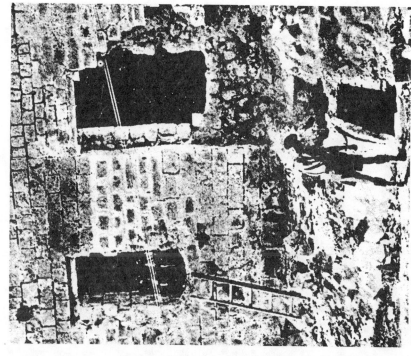

The breaching of the wall (the Acre fortress).

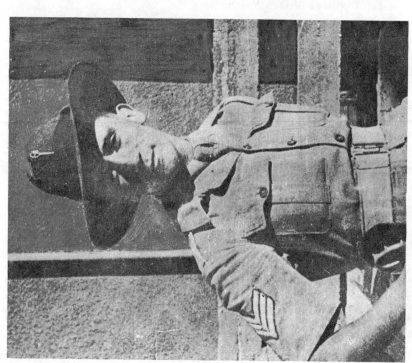

Shimshon (Dov Cohen), commander of the Acre fortress operation.

Deir Yassin's houses. (Courtesy Hadar Publishing, Tel-Aviv)

The "peaceful" village of Deir Yassin.

IX

An LST Named Altalena

My involvement with the *S.S. Altalena* had begun in March, 1947, at the Kingsbridge Veterans Hospital in the Bronx, New York. I was confined to bed with back trouble, while the doctors considered surgery.

On a quiet, snowy afternoon, two visitors arrived, one my old acquaintance Abrasha Stawsky, and the other a man called "Uncle Joe." Though Stawsky had changed his name to Ben Aron Palest (an abbreviation of "Palestine"), he was practically unchanged from when I had first seen him in 1933 in the old courthouse in Jaffa. He was then the main defendant in the Arlosoroff murder trial, the case staged by the Establishment to damage the Jabotinsky movement. Stawsky and the others were ultimately released, but not before the frame-up had gravely injured our credibility, setting back the movement's growth for years.

I did not know Stawsky personally until much later, when our paths crossed in the *Ha'apalah* work. He was a big outgoing man with small squinting eyes, a warm laugh, and a ready wit. At the same time he was a hardheaded business man. He was also fearless when the wellbeing of Jews were in question.

He shook both my hands, grinning from ear to ear. "What a life," he said in his juicy Yiddish, "beautiful nurses, Red Cross girls, shows . . . " We both laughed. Turning to his companion, he said in his heavily accented English: "This is 'Mike' Ben-Ami.[1] He met recently with Begin in Palestine and can tell you about our ideas and Begin's on shipping."

I looked over Abrasha's companion: a man in his fifties, medium height, heavy set, with deeply-lined hard prominent features. Like Abrasha he walked with a waddle, and as the two of them came closer to my bed, they seemed like some sort of vaudeville act.

"Uncle Joe" was introduced to me as a native of Whitechapel, London. He spoke a strange hybrid of Cockney slang with a Yiddish accent, answering Abrasha's questions in English with bits of Yiddish thrown in. Abrasha alternately spoke in Yiddish, Polish and Russian.

Uncle Joe, I was told, was a businessman. He had many interests and even more friends, and was a special admirer of the *Irgun*.

We had a long discussion on the part shipping was to play in our campaign, especially in delivering the survivors in the D.P. camps in Europe. The S.S. *Ben Hecht* affair was not closed yet and I explained to Uncle Joe that the *Ben Hecht* was a legal test case, but that for the future, we were considering vessels that could carry men and weapons to serve the armed struggle. I told Uncle Joe that we were generally leaving it to the *Haganah* to transport unarmed immigrants.

Abrasha cut us short in Yiddish. "What do you have in mind?" I was ready with an answer for him; it had begun forming in my mind during the consultations in Paris and New York in the weeks since I had left Palestine: "Two, fast, thoroughly reconditioned vessels capable of carrying several thousand men each; we will need at least half a million dollars, not including the arms."

Uncle Joe was impassive. "Half a million?" He mused quietly, repeating the figure. Then he looked at me through half-closed eyes: "How can I assure the people who will contribute that kind of money that it will be used only for purchasing vessels—not for political activities or ads and propaganda?"

I personally guaranteed Uncle Joe that any funds designated for *Aliyah* activities would be used for that alone, and that if necessary, Ben Hecht would vouch for their specific use.

---

[1] The nickname the Gunthers gave me years ago and which stayed with me.

We then went into detail about timing and organization. Attempting to convey Begin's urgency during our meeting a month ago, I repeated his comments about how our delegation was "responsible for the fate of our people," and could not afford to let him down. I stressed the importance of speeding up our activities before the ultimate showdown with Britain arrived. We agreed to set up a shipping company as soon as possible. Uncle Joe promised to contact his friends, and to arrange for a number of meetings in New York, Detroit, Chicago and on the West Coast. Hopefully he could help to raise a substantial portion of the monies needed.

Mentioning that most of the funds would be in cash, Uncle Joe explained that even though he was convinced I was an honest man, he would prefer it if his friends knew the monies were remitted directly to Ben Hecht. I did not object, and assured him that Hecht would verify in person that the money had been put to its proper use.

We all shook hands, and after Abrasha said we should share a vodka to celebrate our new partnership, I proposed a Coke out of the vending machine. "We shall name the first vessel after Jabo," said Abrasha.

* * *

Before Uncle Joe came along, the January meetings in Tel-Aviv, Paris and New York had agreed on the purchase of two or more vessels capable of carrying up to forty-five hundred men and a large store of weapons. These were all tentative decisions; we were not sure just how many boats we would purchase, or what proportion of men and weapons would sail on them. The one thing we were sure of was that we wanted to get soldiers and arms to Palestine, and as many of both as possible. Preferably we would seek a large vessel and a smaller, faster one: As a last resort in case of trouble, the large one would take on all the *ma'apilim* and be rammed onto the beach, while the smaller one, with the crews of both vessels, returned to Europe. The bare minimum cost for the two vessels was estimated at over a quarter million dollars, not including the expenses for land transport, assembly camps and food. We already owed $150,000, and worried that we were undertaking too much. Once again I could not help asking myself if this wasn't going to deprive our fighters of resources at the worst possible time? Of course, if we could get weapons to them the undertaking would prove invaluable but where would the funds come from for the arms, once we were done buying the ships?

I called on my old friend Gershon Hakim who had experience in the S.S. *Ben Hecht* operation. We discussed different possibilities for vessels and soon were focusing on surplus U.S. Navy vessels which might be available and in our range. "I'm going up the Hudson to Jamestown, near West Point. There are dozens upon dozens of ex-Navy ships tied up there," said Gershon. "Let's see what's available."

He came back with the news that he had made friends with a Navy petty officer who supervised the maintenance of the moth-balled vessels. Gershon had told him that he was going into business hauling freight across the Caribbean and the man promised to pinpoint a good, solid vessel "to give an ex-GI a break."

The man did indeed give us a break and we ended up making a deposit on an LST (Landing Ship Tanks), a craft used for landing operations in the invasions of Europe and the Pacific Islands. In good condition, LST No. 138, the 1820 deadweight tonner with twin General Motors diesels, seemed to fit the bill. Gershon traveled up the river several times more to look it over and continue negotiations. On one trip he took along Jack Baron, a Palestinian merchant marine officer recently recruited into our ranks.

Finally the decision was reached to conclude the purchase, for $75,000. The Petty Officer promised to throw in free spare parts and tools, and Gershon signed the purchase order on behalf of the newly formed "Three Star Line." An office was opened in mid-Manhattan, and Gershon started recruiting the crew and officers. Stawsky was to supervise the commercial side of the operation.

* * *

In June, when the purchases were under way for the LST and possibly another vessel, we received a long letter from Begin. Begin expressed his initial joy upon learning of our pending purchases, but expressed certain reservations about the plan. The

$550,000 for the overall project, he said, was enough to organize a small revolution by itself. He concluded that if we could have both the money and the vessels, well and good, but that the acquisition of vessels should not go forward at the expense of the armed struggle so we dropped plans for acquiring several vessels.

We wanted to call the LST the *Zeev Jabotinsky*, but the name would have caused us too many difficulties. Someone, possibly Merlin, eventually came up with the name "Altalena," Jabotinsky's pen name as a youth. Hardly anyone in world shipping knew it; it was even doubtful the British would identify it so the name was formally registered.

* * *

By September, after many weeks of work the *Altalena* was almost refitted. Those of us in the middle of the project felt as if we were in a whirlpool. Lankin was complaining to us from Paris about the paucity of funds for the *Irgun* in the diaspora, and Begin was hammering at us about the lack of funds for the homeland. Our people in Washington demanded their periodic allotment, and our weekly, *The Answer*, always seemed to be at the mercy of the printer who had not been paid for weeks.

The battle in Palestine was heightening at a furious pace. After every major crisis in Palestine, we had to counter renewed attacks by the Zionist Establishment and the British, as well as added pressure from the State Department. To keep the armed struggle from being ruined by the slander, we had to keep the public continuously alerted to developments in Palestine. There were still not half a dozen well-to-do Jews in the United States who had made meaningful contributions, though we were gratified by the envelopes bearing single dollar bills which came from New York's east side, south Philadelphia and other "Jewish ghettos" accompanied by notes of encouragement written in Yiddish or broken English. They warmed our hearts and gave us all the moral support we could want. These were the same poor Jews who had been with us since the start.

We tried to keep all negative thoughts out of our heads—the *Altalena* could not be endangered. We had to finish outfitting her and get her out of the country. She had too many potential enemies, and could not stay much longer at her dock at Gravesend in Brooklyn.

* * *

By summer's end, we were making progress recruiting the crew. The emphasis was on security. We placed small ads in the papers under "men wanted," giving a telephone number and a brief mention of the Near East. The initial interviews were conducted by Jack Baron and Joe Kohn, a veteran of the war in the Pacific. Those applicants who made it through the various screenings eventually came to the "Three Star Line" office for final approval by Gershon. I was happy to find among those applicants an old acquaintance from Tel-Aviv. He was a metal worker and an expert boiler maker, Arieh Kolomeitzov. The crew was completed by September. Altogether it numbered twenty-three; later, additional men out of *Irgun* units in Italy would be taken on as sailors.

A captain was chosen, but a few weeks later he had to be let go. Unlike the first captain of the *Ben Hecht*, he was not an alcoholic; he was instead an outright thief. Victor Bennahum, our man in Chicago, sent Monroe Fine to us. He had served in the Navy in the Pacific. Fine, a U.S. citizen, was promptly given preference for the command over Jack Baron, who was still carrying a British Palestine passport. If the British had caught Baron commanding a vessel carrying arms to Palestine, he could have been sent to the gallows. The crew was completed by the end of September.

* * *

In October, 1947, the *Altalena* was ready to sail. We were concerned about reports of visits to the dock by unidentified men, and believed it inadvisable to delay the departure, though there were no clearcut instructions yet from Paris. The diaspora Irgun was not ready with properly trained men. Few weapons had been accumulated in Europe so far, and official obstacles blocked secure legal loading the arms and departure. France and Italy were not showing willingness to cooperate in operations like this; the French had had their fill with the *Exodus* incident. The

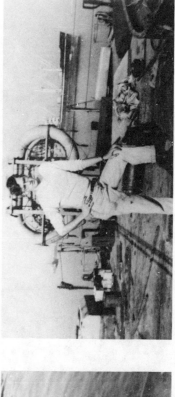

Monroe Fine, Captain of the *Altalena*

Lee C. Archer, member of the crew.

The *Altalena* anchored off Marseilles, April 1948.

Dick Fallon, Irish-American, native New Yorker. Mate. Served in Canadian and U.S. Navy. (Courtesy David Gen).

Loading the *Altalena*. From left: H. Kook, the author, and E. Lankin.

Inspection on the *Altalena*. From left: E. Lankin, Monroe Fine, Joe Kohn, A. Stawsky, and the author.

A training session on the *Altalena*.

dilemma facing us, despite all these drawbacks, was should the *Altalena* sail directly to Europe expecting to load the men and weapons sometime soon? Or should she be kept on this side of the ocean, but outside the U.S.A.?

While we were awaiting developments in Europe, Stawsky suggested we spend several months on local commercial voyages in the western Atlantic to cover expenses, break in the vessel and give the crew time to adjust to their duties. We obtained a temporary certificate of registry from the Panamanian Consul General in Houston, and a Panamanian Master's certificate for Monroe Fine. We covered the insurance and the vessel sailed on its first assignment, carrying a load of potatoes from New Brunswick to Virginia—rather mundane cargo to commemorate Jabotinsky's heritage.

From Virginia the ship proceeded to Florida for lumber. There Gershon went aboard, officially as representative of the owners, unofficially in charge of security and to be in a position to report to New York on any critical developments. Stawsky continued to handle all commercial matters, and flew to visit the ship wherever it put into port. In the meantime, Uncle Joe provided us with donations of canned food, clothing and medicine for the ship's hold, and promised us that his people would make fuel available to us in Europe.

In winter 1947-48, the ship visited Cuba, Italy, France and Casablanca, then returned to the Continent. During the intense internal debates within the HCNL in December, Kook proposed that we put the *Altalena* at the disposal of the Jewish Agency/ *Haganah* to be used to transport six thousand *Olim* and have it anchor at Tel-Aviv on February 1, the day the British were to withdraw from the area. We did not pursue the idea. The British army, incidentally, did not withdraw from neighboring Jaffa till May 14. In February the HCNL transferred control of the *Altalena* to the diaspora *Irgun*. We in New York remained responsible for finances.

In March, 1948, Lankin and the diaspora command began organizing a five thousand man brigade to sail on the *Altalena*. They carried out this phase of the operation overtly, apart from the underground *Irgun*, without concerning themselves about weapons acquisition. A flurry of activity followed: 'Irma' Helpren was put in charge of raising volunteers; a staff of ex-officers was assembled; and weapons negotiations commenced with representatives from Poland. The initial reports sounded encouraging. But as the weeks passed, and the screening of military men went on, it became clear that they would never complete the project in time to keep up with onrushing developments in Palestine.

Begin's appeals for arms and funds assumed a desperate tone, and we considered selling the *Altalena*. Gershon phoned from Genoa and reported an offer of $300,000 for the boat. I asked him to keep the offer open for twenty-four hours. We discussed it in New York and with our people in Paris. The unanimous decision was not to sell, but at the same time, not to divert any more funds intended for Palestine to any new project. From here on, Merlin devoted all his time to the fundraising campaign in the U.S. Stawsky was told to scout up a few more cargoes of bananas to keep the vessel self-supporting.[1]

On March 25, Samuel Ariel submitted a preliminary draft agreement between the French government and the *Irgun*. It looked as if men and arms would be permitted to clear a French port. We agreed that regardless of what the negotiations with the French ultimately produced, *Irgun* men and women would soon assemble near the coast with whatever weapons we could get our hands on. Once we knew exactly when the British blockade was to be lifted, or when we could breach it with reasonable certainty, the *Altalena* would sail.

For all of us in the HCNL, the ALFP, and the diaspora *Irgun*, the *Altalena* became a symbol of respect and love. Bearing our teacher's name, it would carry trained fighting men and an invaluable supply of weapons to our comrades on the battle lines. We told one another that it would sail even if we had to paddle it

---

[1]On February 25, the U.S. Consul General in Marseilles cabled a report on the *Altalena* to State in Washington. He obtained report from the Panamanian consul who routinely visited vessels of Panamian registry. The consul was suspicious of the many U.S. citizens in the crew and suspected a connection with the "Palestine situation." A follow-up dispatch gave an incomplete list of the members of the crew. Then on March 6, the United States Embassy in London reported to State on a visit by a British official (identity deleted) who advised that Peter Bergson's activities in Paris were being monitored by the British. Documents available do not indicate whether the State Department advised the British whatever it knew about the *Altalena*.

across the Mediterranean with wooden oars. However, the fate of the *Altalena* was being decided by others.

* * *

Since December 1946, when Ben-Gurion had assumed the dominant position in the World Zionist Organization and the Jewish Agency, we, especially in the diaspora, perceived his mind was set on several parallel but eventually converging goals: first, to maintain his autocratic control of the Jewish Agency and all other key Jewish institutions; second, to guide the *Yishuv* and the Jewish Agency towards compromise with the British, especially if it would guarantee British physical protection for the *Yishuv*; thirdly consolidate control, eventually eliminating any military or political "dissidence" within and outside the *Yishuv*; fourth, to control and use the newly formed (1948) left wing *Mapam* party as it suited him, exploiting its influence to his best advantage. The ultimate goal was absolute rule over the *Yishuv*, and over whatever national political entity might be forthcoming.

To accomplish this, he had to curb the rising popularity of the *Irgun* in Palestine, and damage the HCNL-ALFP in the United States.

Labor left and right united in its dedication to liquidate the *Irgun*. More indirectly, it also committed itself to neutralizing the centrist and middle class political elements in the *Yishuv*, since, in the face of the rising military threat to the community, they were calling for an accord with the *Irgun*. At the same time, *Mapai* slowly prepared itself for a future showdown on the left with *Mapam* and the *Palmach*. Once the *Irgun* was taken care of with the help of *Mapam*, Ben-Gurion would aim to liquidate the *Palmach* and its semi-independent status. Ben-Gurion stubbornly opposed an agreement with the *Irgun*, saying it would only legalize "divisiveness and rejection of national discipline." He was backed in this by an overwhelming majority of his "moderate" *Mapai* and wholeheartedly by *Mapam*. Representative of this attack was Mordechai Namir of *Mapai* who said he would back the agreement with this group of "gangsters" and "fascists" only if it led "to their disintegration and dissolution." Buoyed by this support, Ben-Gurion went one step further and prior to the U.N.

vote once again sanctioned a small "season," the kidnapping and torture of "dissidents."[1]

Though the Jewish Agency and the *Vaad Leumi* finally voted for an agreement between the armed forces of the *Yishuv,* Ben-Gurion never reconciled himself to it. He urged instead a "civilian militia" to maintain internal law and order. The Zionist-Revisionists who had recently returned to the fold of the World Zionist Organization, were called a "Trojan Horse" of the *Irgun* and not admitted into the newly formed "Security Committee," which oversaw the military effort of the Agency-*Vaad Leumi.*

By spring 1948, the country was in anarchy; the Arabs were staging even more violent attacks on Jews, and the British, though giving signs that they actually might withdraw by the May 15 deadline, still were primed at a moment's notice to reverse field and impose law and order if the United Nations asked. Despite the mounting danger to the *Yishuv,* the negotiations on the agreement between the Establishment and the *Irgun* dragged into their fourth month.

The leader of *Mapam,* Israel Galili, defended Ben-Gurion's opposition to the accord, saying that there was no need for it, since *Mapam* had "information" on the plans and deployment of *Irgun* manpower and thus could "disrupt most of their plans." Since the proposed accord provided Regional *Haganah* Commanders with final say on all military matters, there would have been no need for the "disruption" Galili spoke of. On April 12, when the vote on the agreement took place, *Mapai, Mapam,* and the "New Immigrants" (mostly from Germany) voted against it. Nevertheless, to Ben-Gurion's frustration, the Zionist Executive approved the agreement.

Mapam immediately called for a secret meeting of its political committee on May 3rd, reaffirming its determination to increase its influence over the *Palmach,* and to undermine the new agreement between the *Haganah* and *Irgun.*

When the *Irgun* attacked Jaffa, on April 27, the militant opposition of *Mapam* increased tenfold, and all of labor expressed "frustration and irritation" at the operation. For the first time, hundreds of *Irgun* men had appeared above ground, armed;

---

[1]Niv, Vol. IV, pp. 112-124.

thousands of Tel-Aviv residents, tired of the sniping and the attacks which came from Jaffa, cheered them on. *Mapam* proposed the formation of an armed *Histadrut* militia to put the *Irgun* in its place. Statements from Labor bordered on the hysterical. "The *Irgun*," said Eliezer Prai of *Mapam*, "is not ready yet to do what the Nazis did, but it is capable." Dr. Drabkin said that the *Irgun* was the "avant garde" of "the entire Jewish bourgeoise." Yitshak Lev of *Mapam* agreed, saying that all *Mapam* members in the *Haganah* command were "doing everything in their power to sabotage the agreement." Yitshak Ben-Aharon, another top leader of *Mapam* said: "We have to decide here to shoot or not to shoot—go out to the street and open fire . . ."[1]

As late as May 3, 1948, as the discussions went on, and the nation was on the verge of being destroyed before drawing its first breath, *Mapam* and *Mapai* were bent on wrecking the critical military accord.

The key *Mapam* man in the *Haganah*, Israel Galili, and Levi Eshkol of *Mapai*, the close confidant of Ben-Gurion, were appointed to head all future negotiations with the *Irgun* command. This assured the hardest possible lines since both men were committed to the liquidation of the agreement and the *Irgun*. They would have a lot to do with the final outcome of our *Altalena* operation.

* * *

We received a frustrated letter in New York from Kook, postmarked Paris, April 8, 1948. He reported that despite extensive efforts all over Europe, success in obtaining weapons for the *Altalena* sailing was minimal, though the chances were still there. Stawsky's contacts with professionals were excellent, and Theo Bennahum's business connections also looked extremely hopeful. Kook went on to say that such local opportunities, just like the

---

[1] Such statements by the leaders of *Mapam* were made at a closed meeting, the minutes of which were not made public until years later; the *Mapai* leaders' statements, however, were made during an open meeting of the Zionist Executive, and the minutes were immediately available to the *Irgun* leadership. Within a week, in good faith, the *Irgun* leaders entered into protracted negotiations regarding the *Altalena* with these same *Mapam-Mapai* leaders.

chances for financial support in the States, had improved, though we did not have much yet to show for it. He recommended that Alex Rafaeli leave New York and join him immediately to help the *Irgun* in Europe.

The letter then took on a distressed rueful tone. Kook said that though he felt "deep affection" for Lankin and had "fallen in love" with "Yoel" Amrami, the man in charge of arms purchases, "the results they produce are less than modest . . . their style is amateurish and primitive . . . they waste most of their time in meetings and contacts with people who are valueless . . ."

Kook concluded on a despairing note: "[In view of the deepening crisis] possibly we should consider loading . . . mostly men of military age, and land in Tel-Aviv even before May 15th . . . I doubt whether the local authorities will permit us to load arms on the vessel."

The letter summarized the disappointment we all felt. The final hour was nearing and we still were nowhere near ready. We had come up with neither the weapons and supplies our men in Palestine needed, nor with adequate numbers of trained men to back them in battle. And now Kook was telling us that we might have to sail the *Altalena* to Palestine without a real load of weapons, and with only a fraction of the men we had hoped for! In our admiration and respect for the younger generation's performance in battle, we in the "older" generation had overlooked the fact that they lacked experience, social and political, to deal with officialdom and governmental entities. By April, 1948, our only substantial possibility left on the government level rested with Ariel's efforts to win over the French Foreign Ministry.

We were now to converge towards the front. Alex Rafaeli would leave immediately for Europe, then Merlin would follow, then I would turn over my ALFP functions and my other duties to our friends here and follow, probably first to Italy. Whatever we did, our overriding task was to find arms and get them to Palestine, on the *Altalena* or by any other means of transport.

In the coming weeks Rafaeli would concentrate on his specialty of aircraft acquisition, and I would try to further the progress we had made in recent months with Italian and Irish contacts in the United States. My Italian was rusty, but good enough for negotiations in Naples and the port cities of Sicily. The men with whom we were dealing did not exactly belong to high society but like Uncle Joe they carried weight on the docks of Palermo.

Then on April 30 in Paris, Kook drafted a statement which was approved and signed by Meridor as Deputy Commander of the *Irgun*. The statement was carried by Kook to the U.S. Ambassador in France—Jefferson Caffrey—with the request that it be transmitted to his colleague, the British Ambassador in Paris. If conditions would so require, it would be made public by us on May 10th. It said:

> Spokesmen of the British Government have indicated that they plan to continue the sea and air blockade of the shores of Palestine after May 15, 1948. In this connection the high command of the *Irgun* hereby appeals to free men everywhere to refrain from traveling in ships or aircraft flying the British flag . . . Persons boarding British sea or aircraft will be exposed to deadly peril . . . We feel confident that the peoples and governments of free nations everywhere will fully understand the efforts of the Hebrew Army of Liberation to crush the British Blockade which is a deliberate and diabolical scheme . . . The British Government . . . is encouraging the invasion of Palestine by . . . Syria, Lebanon, Iraq and Egypt [and] the so-called 'Arab Legion' which is a British organized, financed, maintained and officered military formation . . . which has already bombed our sacred and eternal City of Jerusalem.

After recounting British policies during the war and in Palestine "which turned them into Hitler's tacit accomplices," it concluded:

> The Hebrew nation is determined that never again will there be a massacre of Hebrews. If our men, women and children are to die, so will those responsible for their deaths.
> It is . . . the hope of the *Irgun* that the British Government will announce that the air and sea blockade off the shores of Palestine will end on May 15 . . .
> (signed) the High Command of the *Irgun* Zvai Leumi.

Ambassador Caffrey read the statement and then assured Kook that the British Ambassador would be handed it immediately. It was also cabled to Secretary Marshall that same evening.

* * *

Early in May, 1948 as the day approached for the birth of the tiny, truncated Hebrew State, the U.S. State Department enthusiastically encouraged Dr. Nahum Goldmann and Judah Magnes to make one last attempt to induce the Zionist Establishment not to proclaim an independent state in Palestine. Still unable to relinquish the hard line it had followed against Hebrew Statehood for decades, it resorted to scare tactics and pressure to sway the Jews from declaring their independence. Assistant Secretary of State Dean Rusk threatened embargoes and economic cut-offs, intimating that only continuing British tutelage would keep the *Yishuv* from being wiped off the face _. the earth.[1]

Though the *Irgun*, the HCNL and the ALFP were outspoken opponents of the partition scheme, they were even more strongly opposed to a continuing British presence in Palestine. On May 8, Harry Selden and Maurice Rosenblatt of the ALFP Washington office countered the continuous State Department machinations by calling a special conference. The conference was on "United States policy for Palestine and the Middle East." Three senators issued the invitations and then delivered the keynote addresses at the conference. Before the conference met, one of the senators, Wayne Morse, was subjected to the usual pressure from the Zionist Establishment and asked to disavow the conference which he helped sponsor. At the conference he said: "We are only searching after facts . . . We can no longer take a pro-Zionist line on Monday, pro-British on Tuesday, and pro-Arab on Wednesday. We must develop and project an American line."

Senator Dennis Chavez of New Mexico more bluntly repudiated the State Department's policies: "We will fail in our duty if we withhold support from the brave Hebrews who are manning the outposts of American democracy in the Middle East . . . if we continue the immoral and incongruous policy of embargo against those who are victims of aggression . . ."

---

[1]That the U.S. Government encouraged and backed the creation of the Hebrew State and backed its early survival is a long-perpetuated myth. On May 8, Marshall and Undersecretary Lovett warned Sharett that in the case of an Arab invasion, the "Jews must not seek the help of the U.S." Truman recognized Israel once it declared its independence, but immediately imposed an embargo which deprived it of weapons and arms. Later, in the Dulles-Eisenhower years, U.S. policies towards a strong, independent Israel were at best inconsistent and unpredictable. Until the past decade, Israel's military security was based on factors other than U.S. assistance.

Congressman Andrew Sommers offered the most convincing, almost prophetic argument in terms of national security: "Some day, circumstances may arise in which we, the United States, will need a strong and loyal ally in the Middle East. I have no faith in the trustworthiness of any other regime in that region. But I know with absolute certainty that the Hebrew Republic of Palestine will be our friend."

The conference recommended prompt recognition of the Provisional Hebrew Government in Palestine as the lawful authority, "within the boundaries of the original Mandate"; lifting of the arms embargo; and U.S. aid in prompting free immigration. The conference also asked the United States to extend economic aid, and to exercise its influence with other governments to prevent troop movements and other aggressions against the new State.

On the 13th, the ALFP filled Madison Square Garden with twenty thousand people who joined Senator Chavez and Congressmen Sommers and Powell of New York, to demand U.S. recognition of the new State.

* * *

On May 14, 1948 Israel proclaimed its independence. The HCNL's last political act in Washington was to secure the help of Harry I. Schwimmer, an old friend of President Truman, to convince the President not to delay recognition of the new State. At our behest, Schwimmer had already visited the President several times during the past months.[1]

Also on May 15th Hillel Kook, Alexander Rafaeli, Yaakov Meridor, Shmuel Katz and several other leading *Irgun* delegates landed at the small airport on the outskirts of Tel-Aviv, after almost being shot down by the nervous Israelis. Only a few minutes earlier, the Egyptians had completed a bombing run over the city, luckily with very poor results.

On May 16 in New York, the HCNL declared that since part of the national territory had been freed, there was no more need for a liberation movement in exile, and no reason for the liberation

---

[1] Harry Schwimmer visited the President twice prior to May 15. On January 19 and March 25, 1948. On May 8, 1952 Mr. Schwimmer declined making his "contacts with President Truman [which are] privileged," public.

movement in Palestine to remain underground. On May 17 in Tel-Aviv—Kook and Rafaeli held a press conference repeating the statement the HCNL had issued in New York.

Out of the original "six Palestinians," I was the only one left in the United States. I prepared to move to the European headquarters of the *Irgun*; shortly after I would go to Italy and then to Israel. Our mission as *Irgun* emissaries which was conceived and planned back in November, 1938 by Zeev Jabotinsky and David Raziel, was reaching its end, and the *Altalena* named to honor Jabotinsky was meant to be the climax of it.

* * *

In Tel-Aviv on May 16 at 1:00 A.M., *Irgun* headquarters telephoned an invitation to the liaison officer of the Ministry of Defense, to meet with *Irgun* leaders. Eshkol, Galili and David Cohen responded and met with Begin, Landau, Meridor and Katz. The meeting was friendly. The *Irgun* commanders gave the liaison men an update on the *Altalena*, mentioning the shortage of funds needed to complete a number of pending arms purchases. They advised them that in addition to a thousand *Irgun* men, the vessel could carry one to two thousand *Haganah* people and a large load of weapons. In compensation for the use of the vessel, the *Irgun* proposed that it be given funds to acquire additional weapons.[1]

The meeting was being held in accordance with the secret April agreement between the *Irgun* and the *Haganah*. The agreement stated that the *Irgun* could continue its own fundraising and that outside the partition borders, *Irgun* units would continue to operate independently of the *Haganah*. These clauses were subject to further elaboration through continued meetings of the liaison men.

The *Irgun* was ending its independent existence within the borders of the new State; as we had vowed over the years and Begin had said in his broadcast welcoming the declaration of independence the day before: "In that part of the country in

---

[1] The M.O.D. representatives later claimed that the *Irgun* had offered to sell the vessel to them for the proposed amount.

which Hebrew law reigns, there is no need for a Hebrew underground. In the State of Israel we shall be builders and soldiers."

Begin called for the present meeting with the M.O.D. in the spirit of the agreement. As he had said in his public statements, he wanted to keep the Provisional Government fully informed of ongoing *Irgun* activities. At the meeting, there was discussion not only about the *Altalena* but about planes available to the *Irgun* in Canada[1] badly needed by the *Haganah* and also about the shortage of standard caliber ammunition.

The meeting broke up at 3 a.m. Ben -Gurion wrote in his diary their version of the talk (May 16): "Israel and Eshkol were summoned to Begin at 1:00 in the morning. He proposed that they purchase their vessel...with these funds they will purchase arms."

The *Haganah* people in Europe were instructed to investigate proposals for joint use of the *Altalena*. Within a few days, they paid a friendly visit to the *Altalena* in Marseilles. After a thorough inspection of the vessel under Fine's guidance, they remained in contact with Stawsky for several days. Then suddenly contact was cut off. Stawsky and Fine were of the impression that the *Haganah* men were ordered to break off negotiations by their people in Israel. Later the *Haganah* people in Europe claimed that they themselves had decided to keep away from the venture since the *Altalena* was deemed "burnt"—it had lost its cover and was known to the British and probably to the Arabs. This was not the case; as no evidence existed that the vessel was held suspect except by the U.S. About four weeks earlier, the commercial agent of the *Altalena* who knew the vessel was a Panamanian commercial freighter, managed by a Panamanian named "George," approached "George" (our man Hakim) in France and told him about a deal to move six hundred tons of weapons to Syria. Gershon stalled by haggling about the rates, drawing out the negotiations for about ten days. Then, fortunately, the French discovered the cache and confiscated it. In any event, the episode nullified the claim made by the local *Haganah* men that "the *Altalena* was known by the Arabs" in April, 1948. Nevertheless, the M.O.D. in Tel-Aviv and the *Haganah* men in France, after

---

[1]The *Haganah* leaders in Tel-Aviv may or may not have been aware of the *Haganah's* New York men sabotaging our activities with the Canadian owners or other mischief they engaged in, to sabotage our work (Leonard Slater, *The Pledge*, p. 232).

verifying the avilability and suitability of the *Altalena* for the voyage, declined to join in the operation. Later, the M.O.D. explained further "that the *Irgun* was inexperienced in moving boats and arms, especially under the conditions then prevailing. Furthermore, they did not have a coastal settlement which they controlled, nor could they defend the vessel if attacked." The last argument was the only valid one.

When the *Haganah* turned down Begin's invitation to collaborate in the *Altalena* operation, it was agreed that the *Irgun* would act on its own, keeping the M.O.D. informed of developments. Meridor was made head liaison with the newly created Israel Defense Force (the I.D.F.), and the wheels for the integration of the *Irgun* units into the I.D.F. started rolling.

In Paris on the night of May 16, Sam Ariel achieved a breakthrough in his negotiations with Jean Morin, the advisor of Foreign Minister Georges Bidault. The negotiations had lasted months. Back on March 25th, Ariel had submitted a draft agreement proposing collaboration between France and the *Irgun* in training and equipping an infantry division and then transporting it to Palestine by May 15th. In exchange, Ariel, on behalf of the *Irgun*, assured the French Government of the everlasting friendship and loyalty of the Hebrew Republic.

The Foreign Ministry favored the contents of Ariel's memo. Still, France was not about to affix its signature to a formal agreement with an underground resistance organization.

Despite all the good intentions and reassurances, nothing concrete happened for weeks, and the *Altalena* continued to cool its engines in Marseilles. The diaspora *Irgun* kept accumulating modest quantities of arms, some kept back for the *Altalena*. Spurred on by the flurry of events in Israel, Jean Morin advised Ariel that he had broken through the bureaucratic logjam that prevented a positive French decision. He still had in his possession an updated requisition given to him earlier in the month by the *Irgun*, and he assured Ariel that the operation was going through.[1] We had been waiting for a breakthrough like this for many months.

---

[1]Contrary to Ben-Gurion's later statements, our French contacts said in May, 1948 that they had never been approached for arms by representatives of the Israeli Government.

On May 23rd, Bidault advised Ariel that the French Government would give the arms to the *Irgun* as a gift. The arms would be supplied in several shipments. Once the *Altalena* discharged its first load, it would return to France for additional weapons, mostly heavier arms that would probably not be ready for the first, urgent sailing.

The French military began a smooth discreet operation, the details of which were made known to only a few. Short of weapons of their own production, the French assembled mostly weapons of British origin, out of the stores delivered to France during the German occupation. The *Irgun* preferred weapons of British manufacture. The Enfield rifle was the most familiar weapon in the *Irgun* arsenal.

Despite Ariel's glowing mood, doubts still lingered in the Paris headquarters of the HCNL-*Irgun* as to whether the promised weapons would materialize. Too many things could still go wrong.

News from Israel remained nerve-wracking. The belated activism of the *Haganah* which had begun in April, prodded by the *Irgun* offensives in Jerusalem, Jaffa and along the coast, was now counteracted by the invasion of Arab forces. Though the youth of Israel were ready for sacrifice, they lacked weapons, ammunition and training. The casualties were heavier every day.

* * *

On May 27, during my flight to Europe, I read that the Israel Defense Forces (I.D.F.) had been officially established, the name formalized. The *Irgun* then announced within twenty-four hours

---

[1] Recent Zionist-Labor historians, apologists for Ben-Gurion, have said that in giving us these weapons the French were acting as British agents provocateurs. According to labor historian Uri Brenner, "The British-produced weapons were in original packing . . . they were given to the *Irgun* to precipitate a civil war and in the process destroy the new State . . . Georges Bidault and the *Irgun* actually conspired to transport the weapons unbeknown to the Government of Israel."

The amazing thing about these theories is that both the documentary evidence and Ariel, Lankin, Merlin, Kook on the Paris end exist to refute them. Galili, Begin, Meridor and others on the Israeli end are available for testimonies as of this writing. What Labor's historians refuse to admit is that leaders like Bidault and Morin preferred to deal with a movement that had proven its military capability and promised the most effective results. Socialist-Zionism, with its inveterate pacifism, did not fit the bill, any more than it had for the NKVD in Vilna in 1940, or for the Polish Government in 1939.

that its battalions were ready to merge into the national army. Ironically, of the three underground armed forces, only the *Haganah*, the one least committed to a national army, was now historically preserved as an entity, evolving into the *Tzva Hahaganah L'Israel*.

When I reached the HCNL and diaspora *Irgun* headquarters at 18 Avenue de Messine, Kook, Rafaeli and Katz told me that the home forces were choking because they lacked arms and ammunition. We did not know, as Yigael Yadin divulged later, that the field unit of the *Haganah* had only fifteen hundred rifles (and about ten thousand in the Settlements[1]) on November 19, 1947 and no artillery. We did know plenty of other frightening facts: Jerusalem was practically isolated and the old city had been lost. The battle of Latrun had ended catastrophically, and *Irgun* reserves of fifteen thousand or more men could not be mobilized because there were not enough weapons for them. Not only were we losing our last chance to assert sovereignty over the original Mandate area, but because of the historic blindness of the Zionist leadership towards coupling the political with the physical-military the very life of the *Yishuv* was threatened.

* * *

On May 29 in Paris I met with Arieh Ben-Eliezer. We had not seen each other in almost five years. Despite the African detention camps, the Cairo isolation cells, his escape and days as a fugitive, Arieh had hardly changed. Even in critical moments, he could still throw his head back and laugh, or conclude the most somber dialogue by flashing a smile, and saying "Yehie Tov"—"things will turn out all right." He was always this way through all the long years we were friends. His optimism sprang from the conviction that almost everything was achievable through self-sacrifice.

The longer we talked, the more Arieh seemed like his old self. It took almost an hour before I could bring him up-to-date. Finally we reached the part of the conversation that we had been postponing.

Arieh began speaking about the relationship between the

---

[1]He, too, was contradicted by Golda Meir, as above.

HCNL and the *Irgun* and between Begin and Kook. He was disturbed by the conflicts which had led to Merlin taking over the chairmanship of the HCNL and Kook being forced into a "leave of absence" from the *Irgun*. "We should have prevented it. Our forces are so limited already and we're always under attack from the rest of the Zionist world. Did it have to reach the point where Lankin and Kook talk to each other as if they're on opposite sides of the battle?"

I tried my best to give Arieh an objective picture. I was the only one in our original delegation who had bridged the physical gap between the diaspora and Palestine from 1945 to 1948.

I told Arieh that it boiled down to this: Begin, Kook and the rest of the HCNL had all differed about how the war of liberation should develop and be presented to the world. Begin saw the armed resistance in Palestine as the primary front, to be backed with all available means; for him, the HCNL existed specifically to mobilize public, political and physical support for the armed struggle. Hillel and the HCNL, on the other hand, saw the Liberation movement as wider, with military action important, but only part of the political struggle. Some in the HCNL even saw the armed struggle as more symbolic than pragmatic. (As opposed to Begin, who saw *our* efforts as mostly symbolic.) And finally, the greatest conflict between the HCNL and the *Irgun* command had been about the proper timing to declare a Provisional Government, partly in exile and in the underground in Palestine. A year earlier, the HCNL had acceded to Begin's demand that this step be delayed, "since it would only endanger the armed struggle." But even as they gave in, most HCNL members felt we were making a tragic mistake. Now that the State achieved was only a tiny, truncated version of the original Mandate area, they were convinced more than ever that they had been correct.

Arieh listened quietly. Then he said: "I know all that. I have gathered as much from all sides in the past month." Then he took another sip of his drink and said: "But—did it have to get so bitter?"

I told him that there had been a narrowness in perspective on both sides. "Begin had been right that without a relentless physical attack on the British, they would not leave the country; this had been our central credo since the early thirties. Consequently, most of our resources, above all our finances, should have been mobilized to support the front lines."

On the other hand, we in the diaspora felt that all the heroism on the front line could be in vain without our political campaigns in the United States and later in France. Throughout history, many freedom movements had fallen short despite heroic military resistance, precisely because the political battles had not been fought well. Our incessant campaign in the U.S. had given the struggle international and historic dimensions; it was our publicity, we felt, that had allowed the *Irgun* to withstand the British, Zionist Establishment and State Department campaigns against it and against its precepts. Without us the *Irgun* might have been wiped out, and the State of Israel might not have been born.

Still I told Arieh that I had agreed with Begin that avoiding haste was essential; if we had launched the Provisional Government at the wrong time, it would have given Ben-Gurion and other fanatic Socialists a chance to unleash the *Palmach*, or worse, civil war. I told Arieh that I felt Begin had risen to the level of a national leader because of the restraint he had exercised during the dark months of the "season" in 1944-45, as well as in the years thereafter. Thinking of the "season," I began to speak more heatedly; Arieh, listening silently, smiled and patted me on the shoulder: "I agree with most of what you've said. But what could you have done that was not done?" I smiled weakly, and said that if I had known how sour relations with the Command would become, I would have insisted Kook visit Begin in 1947 instead of myself. It would have given them a chance to understand each other.

I added that Eri Jabotinsky and 'Irma' Helpren should also have returned to Palestine and gone underground, joining the High Command, since Begin, Shmuel Katz, Marek Kahn and the others would never have handed over political leadership to the HCNL unless the High Command and the HCNL became practically interchangeable. They were all strong-minded, stubborn men, and only face-to-face dialogues and sharing the dangers in Palestine would have saved the dialogue between them. All along, not securing sufficient funds had been our greatest failure; if Begin had established a rapport with Hillel, Kook's public relations and political proselytizing abilities could have been directed into securing funds and supplies. Instead Kook was granted "a leave of absence" we could not afford during those crucial months and most of our delegation was kept out of the covert activities of the diaspora *Irgun*.

Arieh said: "People underground just can't help but see things differently from those out in the open. If Hillel had been in solitary in Cairo for six months or in the underground in Palestine since 1944, he would have had more respect for tangibles and less for symbols. You don't make gestures when your life hangs in the balance."

Arieh concluded: "What is past is done with. Our work is still not completed. We cannot foresee what will happen in Palestine in the coming weeks." He did not trust the resoluteness of Ben-Gurion and his colleagues. A truce might capitulate Israel into a ghetto entity. Ben-Eliezer added: "The only safe borders are on the Jordan, and Jerusalem cannot be surrendered. There can be no lesser national goals."

* * *

From Paris, I was to leave for Rome to meet a contact man who would be flying there from New York. The two of us would then proceed to Catania for arms discussions. If everything went smoothly, we would receive a substantial supply of weapons immediately. Hopefully I could then proceed straight to Israel with them or ahead of them. Before I left for Italy, Stawsky joked: "You may need a visa." It dawned on me that it might actually be true. I sent my U.S. passport over to the local "Representation des Gouvernement Provisiore de l'Etat d'Israel" and it came back with my new visa. It looked beautiful. The words "Etat d'Israel" were written across it, accompanied by a Star of David. The last time I had seen a Star of David displayed in Europe was on D.P. survivors in southern Germany in April 1945.

I talked once again with Kook, mentioning my pending mission to Italy. I told him that if we shipped the arms directly to Israel, the British might attempt to intercept them.

In his usual self-confident manner, Hillel snapped: "They won't!"

I looked surprised. "How come you're so sure?" I asked.

He half smiled and said: "Because we warned them not to." He proceeded to tell me about the April 30 letter to the British Ambassador in Paris.

I agreed with Kook that such a communication must have left an imprint. By now, the British had learned to take warnings from the *Irgun* seriously. It put my mind more at ease, not only about my prospects in Italy, but also about the *Altalena*.

* * *

On June 2, before leaving Paris for Rome, I visited Sam Ariel at the Hotel Eduard VII. Ariel was in a glowing mood. Jean Morin had invited him for dinner to his home to celebrate the successful culmination of many months of negotiations. Ariel said he had never doubted his efforts would succeed, and when I cautiously inquired why it took so long, he answered: "That's government red tape for you—especially French red tape. After all, it a delicate matter."

"It was a delicate matter," I answered, "three months ago as well. Do you know what having the *Altalena* ready a month or two earlier would have meant for future borders and security?"

Ariel spread his arms as if to say: "I did what I could." I was sure it was the truth.

But if the weapons promised for the *Altalena* reached Israel as late as May 15, the *Irgun* would have pushed forward to achieve safer borders: The Arab Legion, which had crossed the border of Jordan illegally, would have been driven back out of Jerusalem, the Egyptians would have been chased out of the land they had occupied in the south, the invading Iraqi and Syrian forces would have been expelled from the central and northern parts of Palestine. But this had not happened due to circumstances beyond our control, and now we had to make the best of the consequences. The French, our best friends in the world then, nevertheless acted only when their need for a toehold in the Middle East overrode their fear of disturbing the Arabs in their North African colonies—and when they developed enough respect for the *Irgun*.

As I walked back to my hotel I remembered a story Merlin had told me recently about Foreign Minister Bidault. Early in 1946, Merlin had come to Paris to launch the HCNL activities in

France. Armed with introductions from U.S. senators he secured an appointment with Bidault. Merlin was ushered in for a "short interview." He ended up staying two hours. He spoke about the *Irgun*, the HCNL, and the armed struggle. Bidault was well-informed about events in Palestine; the French were still smarting from the way Britain had maneuvered them out of positions of influence in the Near East. The old feud, going back to Napoleon's days and earlier was still very much a part of French geo-political thinking. Recent tensions between DeGaulle and Churchill had not helped.

Bidault revealed a thorough understanding of our struggle for independence. He told Merlin that he supported our movement because it was both historically and morally right; in addition, he said France had an account to settle with Britain, "who had 'screwed' us out of Lebanon and Syria." Bidault finished by saying that Merlin's people were the right people to settle that account.

He then told Merlin about an episode in his life when he was head of the Resistance Council in occupied France. One night in a home in a small provincial town he was settling into bed when suddenly the house was surrounded by Gestapo and S.S. men. Someone had tipped them off about suspicious goings-on. By pure accident there was a Jewish man being sheltered in the same house. As Bidault put it, "the man was a real Jew, with a beard and sidelocks." So, while Bidault hid in a wardrobe, the Jewish refugee was caught. Bidault heard him beg for mercy and he could hear the Gestapo obscenities. "I'll never forget the incident as long as I live. I owe my life to that poor Jew and I want to do something to repay the debt."

On that beautiful May morning in Paris, as I walked down the Rivoli away from Ariel's hotel, I remembered Merlin's story, and found myself wishing that Bidault had acted three months earlier.

* * *

On June 1, in an apartment in Ramat-Gan, a suburb north of Tel-Aviv, Begin, Galili and their aides met to finalize the agreement which would merge the *Irgun* with the Israeli Defense Forces. In accordance with the general mobilization order of the Government, the *Irgun* members would be inducted into the Army and swear allegiance to the State. Special battalions would be established out of the *Irgun* and all weapons would pass into the control of the army; a temporary command composed of *Irgun* officers would function until the induction was completed; separate acquisitions of weapons would cease and all arms sources would be transferred to the army; the *Irgun* would cease to function as an independent military entity within the State of Israel or within areas under its control. This did *not* include Jerusalem, where the *Haganah*, *Irgun*, and *Lehi* would continue to function as independent units.

It was an exciting day for Begin. He signed the agreement with a pen that belonged to Zeev Jabotinsky, and years later wrote: "In exultation and joy I signed the agreement to form a unified Hebrew Army; we had dreamed about this throughout all our years in the underground."

We in the diaspora *Irgun* headquarters were still in the dark about these historic developments. The *Haganah* men in Paris seemed to be acting no differently towards us. Then, three days after the fact, the I.D.F. radio reported that the *Irgun* was now functioning in complete coordination with the army.

* * *

On June 3rd, I spent a day in Rome then took a short journey to Naples. I immediately got in touch with our contacts and found out what I needed to know: Yes, certain facilities were available for moving small vessels out—but it depended on the top men in Sicily. I headed back to Rome that same day to await the arrival of the main contact from New York. Before he came in, I had several phone calls back and forth with Paris. The papers gave a confused picture, mentioning the fighting in one article and hinting at a cease-fire in the next, but no mention was made of what the terms of the cease-fire might be, or how long it might last.

I phoned Ben-Eliezer and Merlin to wish them a good trip to Israel. They were heading there together with "Niko" Germant, another escapee from Eritrea. Germant would then return to Paris with instructions on codes, a port of discharge, and any other last minute arrangements for the *Altalena*. Arieh sounded cheerful on the phone. In code he told me that the men were beginning to arrive, and that "Sam's friends (the French)" were coming through with weapons just as planned. Everything was going well.

* * *

On June 5, the small twin-engined plane chartered by the HCNL landed safely in the tiny airport outside Haifa; on the plane were Merlin, Ben-Eliezer, Germant, the author Arthur Koestler and his wife. Before flying here, they made a short stop in Cyprus, where the British were carefully scrutinizing all transiting planes. Arieh and Germant, the escapees, stayed safely hidden on the plane.

From Haifa, the arrivals rushed to Tel-Aviv. Merlin, Begin and Ben-Eliezer had an emotional reunion—then Begin's first question was "Is the *Altalena* coming and what will she bring?" Ben-Eliezer reported that the French were coming through with weapons, but Begin and his colleagues were still skeptical; they had waited almost a hundred days for news that the *Altalena* was sailing. Week after week, day after day, as the future of the State was being decided on the battlefields, the *Altalena* was still tied to the pier in Marseilles. Countless explanations had been given to Begin about the lack of progress with the purchases, recruitment and training of the men and with the French authorities. So when Ben-Eliezer now told them: "This is it. She is coming," they could not bring themselves to believe it. And Ben-Eliezer did not increase their confidence when he told them we did not know yet exactly what she would carry and wouldn't know until the weapons were actually delivered. He assured them, though, that it looked definite and the weapons would come in any day. Then he concluded: "She is coming with or without the French supplies, so we better start planning for a port of discharge."

Begin explained the June 1st agreement with the *Haganah*-I.D.F.; he wanted to advise the M.O.D. liaison man immediately about this latest news. Ben-Eliezer hesitated. He had gone through years in exile and months in solitary confinement being interrogated by the British—all of this thanks to the Jewish Establishment; he was wary of rushing to them with sensitive information. His clinching argument, though, was that the

French might still delay acting.

After some discussion, Begin at last agreed to await further confirmation of the cargo and the vessel's projected date of arrival before telling the M.O.D. people, who were already fully advised of the vessel's readiness to sail. Once Paris provided the information, the M.O.D. would be told formally.

Marseilles. The first shipments were beginning to arrive at regional French Army warehouses. Ariel phoned Paris from Marseilles advising Lankin that all was progressing well. Paris then cabled a coded message to Tel-Aviv: "Part of the French supplies arrived. Expecting additional by June 7th. Possible departure 7th or 8th."

June 5. Tel Aviv. Germant and Chief of Operations "Giddy" Paglin surveyed the coast from Tel-Aviv to Haifa. A coded map was prepared by zones. Germant would take it back to Paris.

Paris. The diaspora command received conflicting reports from Israel. Some information mentioned that the possibility of a cease-fire seemed stronger. Simultaneously the diaspora command learned of U.S. Intelligence reports which indicated that the Israeli forces were facing defeat. In any case the situation was precarious, and the arms the *Altalena* would carry could definitely tip the scales. With almost a thousand men and women gathered at camps outside Marseilles, and the *Irgun*'s own weapons already on board, the diaspora command decided to chance it and wait a few more days for the French to finish delivering their weapons. A letter was sent to Begin by courier explaining the circumstances, and the reasoning behind the decision to wait. The letter might or might not reach Begin prior to the sailing.

Begin cabled that Germant would be back in Paris on the 9th and he asked to be advised immediately of the vessel's departure.

The press in France and Italy reported that a cease-fire now seemed almost certain for the 11th.

June 8th. Marseilles. There is a heated debate between Lankin and Kook as to who should sail on the *Altalena* to represent the HCNL and the people in the U.S. who had raised the funds making the *Altalena* possible. The compromise—"Mike."

Rome. The phone rang in my room at midnight. "Mike?" The voice was Kook's. "When can you be in Marseilles?" Somewhat surprised, I hesitated. He laughed, "You're going home!"

June 9th. Port du Bouc, 2 A.M. A long column of French Army trucks proceeded silently into the darkened port area. Headlights were dimmed. At the port entrance the convoy stopped. The commanding officer asked for "Monsieur Ariel." Ariel identified himself.

The Captain leading the convoy jumped out, saluted and announced: "This transport is for you. I'm at your disposal. Where should we unload?"

* * *

On June 10th, at noon, I went aboard the *Altalena* for the first time in almost five months. Lankin, Kook, Fine and Stawsky were all aboard.

The cargo was still being loaded. The inexperienced crew members and several dozen *Irgun* men were slowly, unsystematically finishing the task. Fine told me that the day before the French arms arrived, a case of arms belonging to the *Irgun* had broken, or had been broken on purpose, by the North African stevedores. Once the contents became known, the stevedores walked off the pier. To make matters worse, a photographer had been seen filming the French arms as they were being loaded. Now we and the French took stricter security measures. Armed patrol boats circled in the water. Guards were posted around the vessel and on the pier nearby.

I climbed down into the hold. There were several half-tracks, and hundreds upon hundreds of cases of weapons, ammunition and aerial bombs.

After a short conversation with Lankin and Kook, I understood my duties—in case we were boarded peacefully by the United Nations or anyone else, I was to act as spokesman. "On whose behalf?" I asked. "The HCNL!" said Kook. Lankin, not so sure, said, "We will see . . ." I had all the confidence in the world that between Lankin and Fine navigational and military problems would be handled as well as possible. I kept silent, for when my voice might be needed later in the voyage.

We could not complete the loading until sometime tomorrow, so I went back to the Grand Hotel where Abrasha Stawsky was staying in a room next to mine. Abrasha had a free hour and asked me to go shopping with him to buy some toys for his brother's children.

Beset by problems and tensions, with danger all around us, he was remembering that the kids would greet him with "What did you bring us, Uncle Abrasha?"

I joined Ariel, Kook, Claire Vyda, Abrasha and a few others, for a final dinner in Marseilles. We talked about everything except the voyage. Abrasha reminisced about an incident in Marseilles when he was running *ma'apilim* in 1939. He and Elihau Glaser were chartering the *S.S. Parita* and the *S.S. Noemi Julia*, when their owner, Manakulis, insisted that the Rothschilds must guarantee him the safe return of the vessels or their worth in pounds sterling. We laughed, remembering how the N.Z.O. office in London had settled the whole matter by wiring a thousand sterling. The passengers of the *Parita* and *Noemi Julia* made it safely to Palestine and Manakulis lost his two vessels. What a far cry from the friendship the French had extended to us now.

On June 11, just before noon, I went aboard carrying a small handbag I had bought when Abrasha purchased his gifts. At the last minute I had chosen one that could be tied to my back, like the ones French children use for their school books. I had also purchased a small waterproof bag that could protect money and various documents—just in case.

I was assigned a bunk in a small cabin next to the radio room to share with Germant, who had returned from Israel and reached the vessel late the night before. He had brought instructions on the landing spot—the beach off Frishman Street in the heart of Tel-Aviv. When he told me, my heart skipped a beat. Frishman Street was just a few yards away from where Haim Arlosoroff had been assassinated in June, 1933. Abrasha was accused as the assassin.

We had heard now that the U.N. Security Council had passed a resolution calling for a cease-fire, and that Count Folke Bernadotte of Sweden, a high U.N. official, had been appointed mediator: even the British U.N. representative, Sir Alexander Cadogan, had changed his stance and favored the appointment of such a mediator. Whitehall had at last realized that the Jews of Palestine, although bleeding profusely, were going to survive the final bloodletting predicted by Bevin and Generals

Montgomery, MacMillan and Wavell.

None of us, however, gave a serious thought to delaying the departure, cease-fire or not. If there was one, and our sailing caused a confrontation with the United Nations, we could anchor in Haifa or Tel-Aviv and wait out the political negotions.

Paris, June 11. At 10:15 A.M. the *Haganah* representatives cabled to Israel in code: "Yesterday the dissidents loaded their goods on their carrier. Big noise around it. It was all reported in the Communist press . . . the name of the LST, its cargo . . ." And at 12 noon, another open, uncoded cable: "For your information, yesterday the dissidents loaded their cargo on their vessel in Port du Bouc."[1]

A few days earlier, Begin's close advisor, Marek Kahn, had given the Israeli Consul General in Paris a list of the passengers.

"They are going to Israel," the Consul Abraham Goldberg had demanded, "therefore they need an entry permit." With or without permits, the head of the *Haganah*'s intelligence—immigration work, Haim Ben Menachem, had a plan ready for execution to prevent the *Altalena* from sailing. However, the order for him to carry it out was never given.

Port du Bouc. Same day. All throughout Friday afternoon, the loading of clothing, helmets, medical supplies, food and water continued. One thousand folded bunks were loaded at Gershon's insistence, since the voyage could last longer than eight days. Finally, the men came aboard. Eli Tavin directed the embarkation unit by unit, country by country. At the last minute, the Cuban contingent came aboard. They had arrived via New York only two days ago, and almost missed the deadline for medical checkups, security clearance and other formalities. They pleaded and argued with us not to leave without them and finally they were let on, the last group to board.

The French authorities were becoming more and more nervous. They wanted the pilot to take the vessel out before dark. I stood at the railing and watched the final hectic activity preparatory to castoff. Finally, at 8 P.M., as the Sabbath celebration

---

[1]Most direct quotations from Haganah-I.D.F. sources, Labor meetings, Provisional Governments minutes, are based on Shlomo Nakdimon's *Altalena* (Edanim Publishers, Tel-Aviv, 1978).

began in Jewish homes all over Europe, our *Altalena* slowly edged away from the pier.

With only a few friends waving to us, and a few French officials standing motionless on the pier watching our departure, we sailed out over the darkening waters. The thousand men and women and crew crowded the decks singing the *Hatikvah*. A lone pilot's boat trailed us out aways as the lights of Port de Bouc receded in the distance.

That night not many people on board slept. There would be enough time to rest in the days to follow. Lankin, Fine, Stawsky, Germant, Gershon, the radio man, the cooks—all of them were trying to cope with the confusion. Piles of supplies, arms and misplaced personal belongings were scattered everywhere, and no one seemed certain yet about where everyone would sleep. All through the night, the lights burned in the long, vast hold of the LST. The bunks were lined up neatly, and the women were assigned to the cubicles along the vessel's hull. The hospital was organized under the direction of Dr. Lazaroff, and the first aid station was set up immediately.

I had no specific assignment on board and attempted to keep out of the way of the harried command. On the way to my bunk, I paused in the radio room to see if we had established communications with Europe. We had not. Our transmitter near Paris was not functioning. The radio operator attempted to contact Israel and again had no luck. In Marseilles, Bernard Vogel, in charge of spare parts, attempted to purchase replacements for defective tubes for the transmitter. The store owner suspected that he was a Communist assembling an illegal transmitter and the police had been called in. It took some complicated negotiations to get him back to the vessel and the defective tubes were not replaced. He was able to tune into the BBC for the London midnight news, "The ceasefire has gone into effect in Palestine . . . An *Irgun* vessel has sailed from Port du Bouc with arms and hundreds of men."

I went to sleep that night dead tired. I closed my eyes, feeling the thousands of miles separating me from my wife and infant son, privately celebrating my thirty-fifth birthday.

Tel-Aviv, June 12th. The BBC broadcast of the night before was heard in Israel as well and now repeated during the day. Begin was spending the evening, the eve of the festival of Shavuot with his family and friends, among them Ben-Eliezer, Meridor, Paglin and Ziporah Levy. It was their first holiday above ground in years, with no battle sounds in the air. The evening 7 o'clock BBC broadcast repeated: eight hundred men . . . the loading was completed by the Jews after the north African stevedores refused to load . . . Panamanian registry." It sounded much too authentic to be a British ruse. Ben-Eliezer smiled happily, but Begin was concerned. He did not want to be held responsible for breaking the cease-fire, and as soon as he heard the evening broadcast he decided to stop the vessel. Ziporah was immediately sent back to the transmitter and told to broadcast a short message continuously: "Keep away—await instructions." He cabled also to Paris in code: "Wire immediately about the *Altalena*, she cannot return home now. Why did she leave?"

Paris. Katz, now in charge of the Paris headquarters, received Begin's tense cable. After deliberation he proposed to arrange for the vessel to temporarily tie up in a Yugoslav port. Kook, having returned to Paris by car with Mrs. Vyda and Ariel, argued with Katz not to instruct the vessel to go to Yugoslavia. Because it was a Communist-ruled country it would disturb the French. Katz answered that he had his orders. Kook took the next plane to Israel to convince Begin to change his instructions. If worse came to worst, he would settle for having the vessel returned to France.

June 12th. On board, our radio communications were dead. No contact with Paris, no messages from Israel. We knew nothing about all that was going on. Lankin and Fine were concerned about British or even some other nation's torpedoes. Had the London broadcast been aimed at inviting others to attack us? But wasn't this even too much for the British?—first identify us and then blow us up, especially when the *Irgun* had warned them against such agression?

Lankin looked worried, Abrasha smiled a little half-heartedly. With Paris and Tel-Aviv not transmitting, we had no alternative method of communications, nor did we have an alternative landing plan. Unless we established contact and received other instructions before we reached Israeli waters, we would head for Frishman Street.

We were still unaware that the lack of spare parts would affect our radio's operation as seriously as it did. If anyone had second thoughts about our rushed departure, no one seemed inclined to raise them now. In the last few days it was difficult to maintain contact with Israel; the phone and telegraph in Marseilles were practically useless to us. The *Irgun* command's final landings instructions were carried to us by Germant. All that mattered was to move the men and the weapons as quickly as possible, out of Port du Bouc. We were being pressured by the French and by events in Palestine to sail as soon as possible. We read in the French papers that Nathanya had been occupied by the Arabs which meant that the country was cut in half! The consensus at the diaspora headquarters was: get the weapons to Israel immediately.

We did have some misgivings about the safety of the operation tucked away in the corner of the mind. Here we were, almost one thousand people on a potential volcano. I casually inquired how many passengers could swim. Practically none, came the answer. Most of them had never been to sea. Gershon said there were enough life belts for all. I looked for the defensive potential of the vessel in case of attack. The best weapon, I learned, was the captain's ability to take evasive action against torpedoes and air attack.

During the day, mounts for machine guns were welded in place fore and aft. I wondered how many of the men knew how to handle a heavy machine gun. I found out there were only a few. A military police was formed under Joe Kohn, and a "Fifth Platoon" under "Jerry" and "Abe" to spearhead any necessary military action. Most of the men in the platoon were commando and army veterans with considerable combat experience. They were practically the only ones on board who had ever been in regular combat. A few *Irgun* instructors on board had guerrilla experience in Palestine, and a few had served in the British Army.[1]

On Sunday, the second day, some order gradually emerged from the chaos. Duties were assigned, and the *Altalena* started to assume the character of a military transport.

These soldiers of the infant State of Israel may not have been expertly trained in the use of arms, but they had the highest

---

[1] Years later Lankin told me he did think our chances to reach Israel safely were at best fifty-fifty.

morale and commitment. They came from Italy, Austria, Germany, North Africa—the main *Irgun* branches, and most had been recruited and trained in the D.P. camps. They were trained by *Irgun* men from Palestine, and by Jewish Brigade veterans. The Italian contingent appeared to be the most cohesive, the nearest to a regular army unit. Back in Italy, they had covered their own budget with savings, and by selling part of the rations they received in the D.P. camp. They had paid their own transportation to Marseilles.

It was also heartwarming to welcome the North Africans from the Islamic diaspora. The *Irgun* in North Africa operated out of Tunisia, spreading its cells into all other North African countries. These soldiers had also raised their funds and weapons locally. There were also Americans and Cubans aboard and even some British. The diaspora was fully represented. We had people from fifteen countries, a total of eight hundred and twenty men and one hundred and twenty women.

Their movement into France had been organized by Claire Vyda, the head of the Independent Organization of Assistance to War Refugees. It took superhuman efforts, especially after the *Exodus* incident, to overcome the objections of the French Consular and other sundry low echelon bureaucrats. The help and influence of high Paris government officials had been repeatedly required. But almost miraculously, by early June everybody assigned to the *Altalena* was at the assembly points.

The following day, June 13, I raised the point of the men's military experience with Lankin, Joe Kohn and the leaders of the "Fifth Platoon." We decided to use the days before we reached Israel to work on anti-aircraft drills; and to familiarize the men with the lighter machine guns. There was not much more training we could give them in such a limited space, even on the large deck of an LST.

Despite the feverish activity on the *Altalena*, all was really peaceful.

We continued to steam southward, down the west coast of Italy towards Sicily. At Sicily we would turn East toward Eretz-Israel.

And regardless of dangers and uncertainties lurking ahead, there was romance and love aboard. We held a marriage ceremony. Captain Fine, in full white regalia officiated. Zeev and

Monique were married according to civil law ruling the sea. The
ktuva was typed on the vessel typewriter and duly witnessed. The
wedding party went on till myriads of brilliant stars transformed
the sky in a wonderful *Hupa* (wedding canopy). The singing and
dancing lasted late into the night.

New York. Sunday, June 13th. The New York Times carried a
short news item by Reuters, dateline Marseilles. It was tucked
away between a long report on the U.N. sending transport planes
to help the truce supervision mission and a short item from
Tripoli (Libya) about seven Jews who were killed and many
wounded by Arab mobs that attacked the Jewish Quarter.

The Reuters dispatch was headlined:

> 950 SAIL FOR ISRAEL. TWO IMMIGRANT SHIPS SLIP
> FROM LONELY FRENCH HARBORS.
>
> Two Jewish immigrant ships . . . carrying nearly one thousand
> new citizens for Israel . . . [one], the landing craft *Altalena*, left
> Port du Bouc with eight hundred Jewish volunteers and a ship-
> ment of arms.
>
> Almost at the same time the auxiliary schooner *Marie Annic*,
> nationality unknown, with one hundred and fifty men, women and
> children sailed from a lonely breakwater near La Ciotat, twenty-
> five miles west of Marseilles.

Our people in New York read it tensely. They did not understand why the *Haganah* had to send "men, women and children"
to the State of Israel in the dark of the night—unless the *Marie
Annic* too, carried men of military age and arms, both banned
under the June 11 truce.

* * *

June 13, past midnight. I was on deck outside the radio room
where Lankin was again attempting to reach Paris or Israel.
Suddenly a woman's voice signaled the *Altalena*. Lankin recognized it as the voice of Ziporah, his secretary in Paris: "Keep away
. . . Keep away . . . Await instructions." That was all. It left us
stunned. The radio went dead again.

We were at a loss to understand the message. Why couldn't we
land in Tel-Aviv? *Where* was the danger exactly? Lankin radioed
a message to Paris via regular shipping channels. After more
meetings, we chose to sail full speed ahead toward Israel. At this

point, we did not know where else to head but Israel, and our guess was that we would be safe till we approached the shore. We continued making good speed—14 knots per hour. The engines worked perfectly, and we hoped for a renewed radio contact once we neared the coast.

Paris. Dr. Chaim Weizmann read in the papers about "two vessels that left Marseilles with young men and weapons." He sent a scathing cable demanding that Israel adhere strictly to the truce.

Tel Aviv. The Minister of the Interior, Moshe Shapiro, met with Begin. Begin told him that the vessel had sailed without his authorization and that he had sent instructions for the vessel to "stay away."

On board Lankin ordered tightening of food and water rations, though the vessel was carrying enough provisions to last comfortably for two weeks. It did not cause much hardship. The sea was calm, the weather magnificent. The "Fifth Platoon" under Jerry and Abe began an intensive physical fitness regimen. The Captain pursued a zigzag course, changing direction often, but still steadily nearing our destination.

June 14th. An uneventful day and a first chance to estimate what we were carrying. Our gift from the Fench was substantial: five thousand Enfield rifles and four to five million rounds of matching ammunition; six armored half tracks; three hundred Bren guns; one hundred and fifty Spandaus; and several thousand aerial bombs. We also had on board weapons the *Irgun* had bought with its own funds: hundreds of rifles, submachine guns, and bazookas, other anti-tank weapons, a large assortment of smaller guns, ammunition and explosives. And finally we were also carrying fifty cases of arms for the *Lehi* as a courtesy. There was enough all told to arm six battalions.

I walked over to the stern, and staring at the wake, I could not help remembering other voyages through the centuries . . . Yehuda Halevi, eight hundred years ago, had faced terrible storms and countless other hardships sailing to Egypt and then to his beloved Zion. Yehuda Hehassid, 250 years ago, had set forth with his men in sailboats, drifting for months towards Palestine, surviving pirates' raids and innumerable other dangers. And the *Prushim* and *Hasidim* had come in small rickety boats from the Pale. My own grandparents sharing the holds with cattle and rats—all these defenseless, dreaming Jews who had risked their lives and those of their loved ones to return home. The *Altalena*, with its load of soldiers and weapons was the crown of their sacrifices, a symbol that our people would never be defenseless again.

I tore myself out of my reverie. The *Altalena* was still only a tiny speck floating on the sea.

* * *

June 15, Washington, 6 P.M. Secretary Marshall cabled (marked urgent) to Gray, the Consul General in Marseilles, quoting in full the Reuters dispatch in *The New York Times* which named both boats. Then adding "Please telegraph whether these reports are true, and report to Cairo and Jerusalem for information of U.N. mediator."

Cable was repeated to London Paris, and the U.N. Mission in New York. Gray answered:

> Local authorities confirm sailing *Altalena* and *Marie Annic* to Palestine. Authorities state they have no information regarding passengers cargo carried each vessel as dossiers sent Foreign Office Paris last week. Requested [U.S.] Embassy obtain details from Foreign Office and inform all addresses this message. Press reported *Altalena* carried *Hagana* [sic] recruits and arms. Repeated Cairo, Jerusalem.

The State Department, recently so deeply concerned about the safety of the Jews of Palestine, was giving full, wide distribution to the whereabouts of two vessels.

Six hours later Gray followed with a second cable advising that the *Altalena* carried six hundred tons of arms and seven hundred passengers between the ages of eighteen and thirty-five [i.e., of military age banned under the truce] half of which women and children [sic]." Also that a "furious Panamanian Consul" advised *Altalena* carried passengers without proper authorization. Several days later, the Panamanian Consul canceled the *Altalena*'s registration.

Later, the U.S. Ambassador in Jedda (Saudi Arabia) cabled to Washington (copied: Jerusalem, Cairo, Beirut, Baghdad,

Damascus, Haifa) that "Shaikh Yussef Yassin, Deputy Foreign Minister informed me he has heard from Arab League: 'information re *Irgun* ship, given to Bernadotte four days before vessels arrival off Tel-Aviv but he did nothing about it'."

It is unclear as to who leaked State's frantic, widely-distributed cables to the Arab League. The U.S. embassies throughout the Arab countries, someone in the U.N.'s truce commission or did they read the Reuters dispatch?

* * *

June 15. Still no new contact with Paris or Tel-Aviv. We were steaming full speed eastwards. In the dark about the armistice lines, we had no idea if we might stumble into enemy territory. Lankin called in the unit commanders, and plans were evolved in case contact was never established with the shore. The weapons remained in their cases, heavily greased, tightly packed. The piles were covered with canvas, protected from the salty air and sea water. A day before we reached the shore, we would unpack and clean enough weapons to arm the men. The combat-tested Fifth Platoon (also known as the "Anglo-Saxons") and the M.P.'s under Joe Kohn would lead any charge required to secure a beachhead. The training of these units intensified.

Tel-Aviv. Begin received another coded cable from Katz in Paris: "I cabled you yesterday about the *Altalena*. In a day or two, you should be able to contact her. We have no contact with her!"

By now it was clear to the *Irgun* command that the vessel was continuing its course towards Israel. No confirmation had been received from the *Altalena* saying it had gotten the instructions to "stay away." Begin felt that this must be reported to the M.O.D.

June 16. In three days we expected to be off the coast of Palestine. We were south of Greece now, and still had not made radio contact. Nor had we sighted any vessels or aircraft. However, our handful of anti-aircraft units were manned continuously and on full alert.

Tel-Aviv, June 16, 1 a.m. Begin invited Galili, Eshkol and David Cohen to an urgent meeting. It started off on the wrong foot. The *Irgun* guards at the entrance of the Command building refused to let the visitors in. This was quickly cleared up but the visitors were irritated.

Begin, Ben-Eliezer, Meridor, Landau and Paglin represented the Command. They got to the main topic promptly. After an introduction summarizing the history of the *Altalena* from its purchase to its sailing, Begin then posed the critical question: In view of the cease-fire, did the government wish to authorize the vessel to land, or should they send it back to France, or divert it to another port? Begin did not know that the *Haganah* was awaiting its own ship, which was carrying weapons to be discharged at Bat Yam, south of Tel-Aviv, within three days. He also did not know that on the 11th, prior to the departure of the *Altalena*, the European *Haganah* operatives had already cabled all the details they knew about the cargo and passengers the vessel carried, nor about Weizmann's cables about the two vessels, or that the *Haganah* men had a plan all ready to sabotage the *Altalena* prior to its departure.

Begin asked Ben-Eliezer to give the visitors the details on the French arms which should have been delivered to the vessel; he had received this information from Ariel prior to Ben-Eliezer's departure from Paris on June 5th. Ben-Eliezer still had serious reservations about revealing this information to Galili at all. He did not have a rational explanation for his hesitation, but he felt a sense of distrust which he could not shake. He was also disturbed by the discrepancy in attitudes: Begin was friendly, accommodating and polite, while the visitors were arrogant and tense and listened mostly in silence. Merlin, who was present but did not officially participate in the conversation, describes Eshkol's attitude as tough, curt, almost rude. Galili appeared more subtle in his questions and comments. Begin, Landau, and Meridor were grave and friendly. Admitting to hindsight both Ben-Eliezer and Merlin said later that they should have warned Begin and his advisors of an underlying hardened hostility in the attitude of the two top M.O.D. representatives, and that whatever friendly gestures were coming from the *Irgun* were not being reciprocated.

One subject particularly seemed to interest the visitors. They asked more than once about artillery. "No," Arieh answered. "Not on this trip."

Considering the conditions prevailing in the country, Arieh expected a pleased reaction at his report that weapons were coming. But instead Eshkol harshly repeated the warnings of May 15. "You were warned that men and arms should not be combined. The vessel is known all over . . . could she be directed somewhere else?"

The *Irgun* men answered that they had attempted to contact the vessel without success. They read to the visitors the cable exchanges with Paris, and said that it was too late now to stop the vessel. The visitors answered: "We will see . . . we'll try to find a solution." Then Galili asked: "Would you sell us the arms?" Begin, in disbelief, answered: "Sell? We have no financial interest. These arms are holy, they are the Nation's." Galili, amazed, said: "Really, truly?" Galili concluded by saying he would report all of this to the Minister of Defense (Ben-Gurion).

With a smile on his face, Begin said to them as they left: "Well, it was worthwhile bringing you in so late." The visitors didn't reciprocate the smile.

Early in the morning, the I.D.F. made inquiries with the manager of the Tel-Aviv harbor about whether the vessel could discharge quickly and discreetly at the port. He answered yes.

Under June 16, Ben-Gurion noted in his diary the report his men gave him of their meeting with Begin and another with the harbor manager. He listed the full data on the arms and men, then added: "It is not advisable to endanger the port of Tel-Aviv or return the vessel. It should be discharged onto some unknown beach."[1]

By 10 A.M., Galili phoned Begin: "Menahem . . . we agree to the arrival of the vessel." He added: "As quickly as possible."

Begin was elated, and he said as much to Ben-Eliezer. "As long as the government does not see this in a negative light because of the cease-fire, our worries are over." He told Ben-Eliezer that "just the rifles alone" would make all the difference in the world to the army.

Ben-Eliezer's doubts began to subside. It was decided that he would return immediately to Paris to prepare the second voyage with the heavy weaponry.

---

[1]At the State Council, June 23, Ben-Gurion answered a direct question as to when he learned about the arrival of the *Altalena*: "I learned about it on Saturday (the 19th)," meaning *the day of its arrival.*

* * *

June 17. On the *Altalena*, no contact yet. We were still follow-ing a zigzag course at full speed. The sea remained mostly moder-ate and despite some sickness, the daily routine of drills and exercises continued on deck. The vessel's command was tense, but did not let that feeling filter down the ranks.

In just a few days, we would see land. I wondered how far south of Tel-Aviv the cease-fire line was. So far we knew only that it was within artillery distance, and therefore our southern safety zone would be terminated not far below Tel-Aviv. If the Egyptians attacked, it would be out of my hands; my job was limited to deal with the United Nations forces if they accosted us. Whatever happened, the United Nations could not expect us just to wander on the seas. We had not willingly broken the cease-fire—we had sailed before we knew it was in effect. If the United Nations vessels ordered us to put into Haifa, we would probably agree but only for the duration of the cease-fire. When it ended, there would be peace or renewed fighting and we would react accordingly. In any event, our cargo belonged to the State of Israel and could only be held under U.N. control temporarily. Would the U.N. forces insist on boarding us? Before we allowed that we would insist on communications and instructions from Israel. By that time, we certainly would have communications with shore. I could not imagine an armed confrontation with the U.N. Forces; firing on us was probably beyond their authority. There would be a lot of give and take before it came to an armed showdown. If we managed to get to the Tel-Aviv beach unimpeded, the first thing we would have to do is raise the flag of the State of Israel . . . it would have to be discussed more with Lankin and Fine.

Tel-Aviv. Galili was convinced that the *Irgun* was lying about not having contact with us. Unknown to the *Irgun* he ordered a plane to go out at sundown the following day to look for us and pin down our position.

Cohen and Pinchas Vazeh met again with the *Irgun* Command to discuss technical aspects of the unloading. They recommended that the vessel be discharged at Kfar Vitkin, an old, loyal Labor settlement. Begin saw no reason to object. A few days later, Ben-Gurion told the Cabinet: "This is an area we control . . .

therefore, we told them what we did."

Begin asked that I.D.F. men assist in the unloading, and after Galili and Chief of Staff Yadin were consulted, it was agreed upon. Then there was a bone of contention. The *Irgun* suggested that the arms be stored in warehouses with I.D.F. and *Irgun* men guarding them jointly. The representatives of the M.O.D. rejected this. Another meeting was scheduled for the following day.

Washington, D.C. Intense exchanges of memoranda continued between the FBI, the Criminal Division of the Justice Department, State and the Chief of Naval Operations, concerning the *Altalena*. The actual information exchanged has still not been made public.[1]

June 18. We were one day away from Israel. With no new directives from Paris or Israel, the warning "Keep away" seemed more foreboding than ever. Nothing in the BBC news or other news broadcasts indicated unusual developments, but why this continuous silence? On the bridge tension mounted. Would we face an attack from British submarines? Possibly the warning to the British ambassador gave pause to those in the military who may have considered it. The Egyptians? They might attempt an aerial bombing. They could claim we were in the process of breaking the truce. The anti-aircraft units were on full alert. But how good were our gunners? Twenty-two Bren and two Browning machine guns? Not exactly a formidable array of anti-aircraft weapons. One well placed aerial bomb and our precious cargo could blow sky high.

Tel-Aviv. Ziporah had been glued to her transmitter for hours, repeating her coded message without receiving a response from the *Altalena*. Begin was meeting again with Cohen and Vazeh, arranging the details for the discharge procedure. The matter of distribution of the arms came up. Begin proposed that 20% go to the *Irgun* units still functioning in Jerusalem, which was considered "special territory" outside the partition borders. The balance he wanted for the *Irgun* battalions being incorporated into the I.D.F.. Galili agreed to the 20% "for Jerusalem" but rejected the demand that 80% of the weapons go to the *Irgun* Battalion in the I.D.F.. Later he claimed that the first part of the agreement meant

---

[1]FOIA documents, heavily blanked out, in the writer's possession.

weapons for all the different units in Jerusalem. A debate followed; sometimes it became quite heated. Nothing was resolved.

Based on the speed of the *Altalena*, the *Irgun* command estimated that, precluding unforeseen delays, the ship could reach shore by Saturday. Begin sent a written message to Galili advising him of the estimated time of arrival, and again requested help in the discharge.

More phone conversations ensued. Galili kept a rigid stance against allocating arms to the *Irgun* units in the IDF. Begin argued and pleaded, explaining the trying conditions under which the *Irgun* units had operated in the past several months because of the shortage of weapons and ammunition. But Galili insisted on transferring ownership of the weapons to the IDF without any conditions.

The *Irgun* command became embroiled in emotional internal debates. Paglin argued vociferously that "his boys" had to get the weapons. In the end, Begin acceded to him, and repeated his position to Galili. At this point negotiations were deadlocked.

The same day, the process of incorporating the *Irgun* battalions into the I.D.F. was proceeding according to schedule. The battalion's commanders, stationed in Be'er Yakov and Ramlah, informed their brigade commander about the weapons expected from the *Altalena*, urging him to requisition a share of the arms.

June 18. Sabbath eve on board. The observant passengers conducted Sabbath prayer but no Sabbath candles could be lit. Our pulses were quickening now; only one or two more days . . .

Abrasha called me into his cabin and produced a bottle of brandy. "*Shabbat Shalom*!" he said, gulping down a swig. "Well, I should be with my family shortly. I can't wait to see the kids when they spot my presents." And then, almost apologetically for showing a concern for himself: "Do you think the *Mapainiks* (Labor) will give me trouble . . . ?"

June 19, Morning. On deck. The sky and the sea were one connected, changing shade of blue. The day before we had passed south of Crete, and now we were only about two hundred and twenty miles from Israel. Though we tried not to express it, our tension was mounting. We might reach the coast by nightfall.

Lankin, who had made us keep the weapons and ammunition sealed in their crates to facilitate unloading, now met with the unit heads again to consider unpacking part of the arms. We still did not know exactly what points above Haifa or below Tel-Aviv were safe, and the blacked-out towns and villages could easily lead us astray into enemy territory.

I was not thrilled at the prospect of arming the men. Except for the Fifth Platoon and some of the Italian Units, I would not have trusted weapons in the hands of most of the men, especially on a dark night under combat conditions. But I kept my counsel to myself.

Suddenly, we heard our radio signal and the voice of Ziporah. She was coming in loud and clear! As we deciphered the coded messages, our hearts leaped. We were being instructed to proceed to "Kfar Vitkin!" Lankin double- and triple-checked. Yes, Kfar Vitkin! A grin spread across his face. Only a few of us on the *Altalena* appreciated the meaning of this message: we were to land in one of the strongholds of the *Mapai* and the *Haganah*. Even in our *Ha'apalah* days of 1937-40, we had kept away from there, and now, after all the tragedies of the past, our *Altalena* would touch the soil of Israel at a village that would have driven us away like lepers. What better token that we were at last one nation!

"Two Red Lights, vertical. Kfar Vitkin."

The news spread across the vessel. We've made contact with Israel!

A few hours later, more news: At 4 P.M., a plane with a solid star of David, the markings of the Israeli Air Force, was to circle over the *Altalena*. Meridor would be aboard. The plane would drop instructions. The plane never appeared, due to what Ziporah later explained to us were "technical difficulties."

Tel-Aviv. No explanation was given for the "technical difficulties." They could have meant that Galili commenced a retreat from any further good faith negotiations. Was it because he actually believed the *Irgun* was intent on turning against the Government, which would be unthinkable if Begin agreed to bring the vessel to Kfar Vitkin?

Or was Galili motivated by the much more important power struggle in the original *Haganah* hierarchy, between the *Palmach-Mapam* and Ben-Gurion? And was his intent to create a diversion? Except for bits of gossip brought back from Israel, we on the *Altalena* were unaware of this conflict. The *Irgun* command in

Tel-Aviv did not seem much better informed.

The witch's brew was boiling over between the *Palmach* (linked with the *Mapam*) and the Jewish Brigade Veterans and other army veterans—the proteges of Ben-Gurion and *Mapai*. Galili, recently demoted from his position as Chief of Staff, still was acting in the capacity of Deputy Defense Minister to Ben-Gurion, and also promoting the interests of *Mapam*. As such he was thrust into a sensitive position as negotiator between the *Irgun* and Ben-Gurion.

As it turned out, Begin and the rest of the *Irgun* command seemed to be as ignorant of these critical developments as we on the *Altalena* were. They displayed this "innocence" in their dealings with Galili, putting faith in him as the conduit to Ben-Gurion, though they knew he also represented the interests of *Mapam* and the *Palmach*, Ben-Gurion's adversaries. They trusted him to give Ben-Gurion accurate reports on their negotiations with him, though he had various political reasons to do otherwise. There was no excuse for their naivete, for we had known since the "season" in 1944 that the *Palmach*, led by *Mapam* was a prejudiced and embittered enemy. However, Ben-Gurion's hatred toward the "renegades" did not require a special fanning by Galili. It was well-developed for over twenty years.

That afternoon at *Irgun* headquarters, after Ziporah had happily established uninterrupted radio contact with the *Altalena*, Kook and Stawsky exchanged congratulations. Then Kook walked into Begin's room where Begin was on the phone. Meridor and Landau were also present; Meridor gestured to Kook not to interrupt and whispered "Galili." Kook listened. Begin was summarizing his position once again: "20% to the *Irgun* in Jerusalem and 80% to the *Irgun* units in the army." Begin listened with a serious mien and then hung up. Kook exploded. "How can we be so irresponsible? Setting a precedent in our national army that weapons acquired be distributed according to quotas? This is inconceivable! Jerusalem, all right, there is no national authority there. But the army?"

Begin looked around the room. The others expressed ambivalence. A heated conversation ensued. Kook, finally calmed down, urged Begin to amend his message to Galili. At last the group reached a consensus. Begin picked up the phone: "Israel—we have talked things over further . . . we insist on one condition only—20% of the arms should go to the *Irgun* in Jerusalem. The rest goes to the I.D.F. units according to general staff decisions. One more minor condition—when the major allocations of these weapons are made, we would like a representative of the *Irgun* to appear before the units receiving them to inform them where the weapons came from."

Everybody around the room smiled, relieved. To this day, Kook believes Galili never advised Ben-Gurion of this conversation.

* * *

At sundown, we made out the low grayish-blue line of the coast in the distance. For the new *olim* it was a thrilling sight, and great excitement filled the air. To the few of us who were natives and returnees it was a doubly moving experience because for the first time, we were coming home to a free country.

The anti-aircraft crews were at their positions. The unit commanders were busy down in the hold issuing final instructions on baggage and disembarkation procedures. Now that the coast was in sight and a safe disembarkation point chosen, no weapons were to be carried by the men. The Israel Defense Force would provide the proper defensive umbrella.

Our first task was to disembark the men and women. In case of an air or sea attack, the fewer exposed to danger the better; so the units would disembark as quickly as possible, carrying only their personal belongings that could be placed upon the shoulders or carried in one hand.

We were not sure what the disembarkation conditions would be, but Ziporah had mentioned a jetty. Possibly the men would be able to walk off right through the gates on the bow, stepping off the unloading platforms which would be lowered onto the rocks or sand.

Ignoring our security instructions and the possibilities of air attacks or other unknown dangers, the passengers silently swarmed to the railings.

The captain slowed down the engines, since we were planning to stay off shore until dark; the Egyptians, British, or United Nations craft might be cruising near the shore. The anti-aircraft watch continued until the last flicker of light disappeared from the western skies and it finally was pitch black all around us.

By 9 P.M., under complete blackout conditions, we were steaming straight towards the coast. Depth sounding continued until we knew we were very near the shore, yet we still saw no vertical pair of red lights. On the darkened bridge of the *Altalena*, under faint blue lights, I could see Fine poring over his charts. He decided that we should move slowly southward. We traveled for half an hour, then another half hour, holding our breath; we were more nervous about the United Nations patrols based in Haifa than about the Egyptian Navy, since the I.D.F. and its infant Navy was supposed to protect us from any aggressive acts by the enemy. Except for an occasional random light, the shore was nothing but a colossal black mass. We moved silently, almost gliding. Suddenly red lights flickered on and off on the blacked-out coast. We halted. Baron and Germant were lowered into our launch. Shortly, they called back on their walkie-talkie that we were off Tel-Aviv, facing the Reading power station. At least we were not off Gaza, where the Egyptians were in control.

Only a few of us were around the bridge. Most of the crew and passengers were downstairs, tense and silent. The cracking of the walkie-talkies continued and I peered towards Tel-Aviv. I guessed that the beach must be to the right. Suddenly I remembered my first swim with father, then different scenes from my childhood flashed before my eyes. I saw myself in my early years in the *Irgun* training at the mouth of the Yarkon River. And only a few blocks away the cemetery on Trumpeldor Street where my parents' graves were. Flashing on and off in my mind they were like kaleidoscopic pictures.

We turned north. Finally, at 3 A.M., where we had almost given up hope, we spotted the two red lights. Fine rammed the *Altalena* as far onto the sandy shore as it would go, beaching the LST the way it would have been done back in the war.

* * *

Tel-Aviv. That same night the Central Committee of *Mapai* met. Galili called Ben-Gurion and Eshkol away from the meeting and closeted the three of them in a small room. They kept no protocol of the meeting, but later Ben-Gurion said: "On the 19th, I was suddenly advised of the imminent arrival of the *Irgun* vessel." This contradicted his diary entry of the 16th where he had noted: "Galili and Eshkol met yesterday with Begin . . . their vessel will arrive in a day or two . . . carrying five thousand rifles, etc."

Galili later reported that at the meeting with Eshkol and Ben-Gurion, he had advised them that the arrival of the *Altalena* was a conspiracy . . . "the first attempt to establish a separate army in the State . . . They lied to us and did not tell us they were preparing this sort of vessel . . . Suddenly they advised us that the vessel was en route . . . in addition, they refused to turn over the weapons to the army."

Ben-Gurion and his colleagues had actually been officially advised about the vessel's existence back in early May, and *Haganah* intelligence had been reporting on the *Altalena* for months. A year ago in New York, a *Haganah* representative threatened us with having to give up our preparations of the ship or face severe consequences. For the past several weeks we had been reporting to the *Haganah* and then to the government on the status of the vessel, of our readiness to share space, for men and arms. Nothing could have accounted for all their sudden shock and rage, unless they simply never had believed that anything substantial would come of the project. More likely, having failed to interfere with the vessel's sailing from New York, and having failed to sabotage the operation in France because the French would not permit them to, they were desperately determined to turn this venture into a graveyard for a threatening popular political rival.

One possible reason for the furor within Labor was its embarrassment upon learning the volume of the weapons we were bringing in one boat load, without having paid a penny. The *Irgun* was then delivering more weapons than the I.D.F. units possessed even six weeks earlier!

Perhaps this was too obvious a proof that Political Zionism might have been much more foresighted as to historic-military developments of the last decades and would offer better security to the State than the present leadership. A successful landing of the *Altalena* might give a great push to the ambitions of Menahem Begin and his newly announced Herut Party, offering a serious threat to Ben-Gurion's political dominion over the *Yishuv*. Perhaps Ben-Gurion's mind clicked back to the last time the Jabotinsky movement's popularity was gaining fast on Labor; he had stemmed the tide then by crying "political murder!" within twenty-four hours of the death of Haim Arlosoroff. Now their cry was "conspiracy against the State!"[1]

That night Galili advised Begin that since the *Irgun* was still insisting that arms from the *Altalena* be delivered to its battalions in the I.D.F. he and the M.O.D. were discontinuing all collaboration on the discharge of the vessel. Begin shrugged this off, thinking it just another bargaining ploy, and left for Kfar Vitkin. On board, we had no inkling of any of this.

* * *

Sunday, June 20, 4 A.M. Kfar Vitkin. Dawn would break soon. The waves off the jetty near shore were moderate, but still they violently lifted and lowered the few small boats awaiting us. It would take hours to disembark the men, and a lot longer for the cargo. There was no direct foot link from the vessel to the jetty, which was only a makeshift structure suitable for tying up smaller fishing vessels. We were trying to understand how we would accomplish the unloading under such circumstances, when Begin shouted from the shore—"Go back out and come back at night." He was afraid we would be spotted in the daylight, and wanted us to return under cover of darkness. We waved from the open bow gates. Disappointed at both this development and the poor disembarkation setup, but still in high spirits, we pulled the drawbridge up and closed the bow gates. The winches pulled the ship back out toward the anchor dropped farther out. We were afloat again.

We sailed straight out for eight and a half hours to reach safer waters, then made a full 180° turn and headed back east. A calm descended on the vessel. This was the last leg of the voyage, and

---

[1]Ben-Gurion later wrote to the Minister of the Interior, Gruenbaum: "According to information reaching me, the *Irgun* was preparing, with the support of monied individuals in the *Yishuv*, to raise an army of five thousand men. The aims were: 1) the conquest of Jerusalem or another part of the country which would remain in its absolute control and be defended from foreigners and also from Jews; and 2) to prepare the groundwork for taking over the government in the State of Israel by force."

most everyone was resting after the tense night. The anti-aircraft crews on deck were again on full alert. The *Altalena* was quiet except for its steadily-humming engines and the sea looked pure blue. I stretched out on my bunk, attempting to catnap without much success. Instead I relived the past evening's events and one incident struck in my mind. Last night the anti-aircraft commander, a young *Irgun* officer from Palestine, had vehemently protested sailing from Tel-Aviv to Kfar Vitkin; he could not erase from his mind the years of persecution and treachery by Labor. I did not share his feelings, because of my jubilance at being practically home free with our lifesaving cargo. At last we had come back home to our free State. Stawsky came in beaming. Whatever doubts he might have had about the choice of Kfar Vitkin had disappeared. We all had seen the boats of the *Hapoel* (Labor's sports organization), or whatever unit they were, who had come to assist us. "Sure we'll have some problems discharging the heavy crates and the half-tracks," said Stawsky. "But a solution will be found. Elyusha [Lankin] worries too much." At last I drifted into a brief, fitful sleep.

Tel-Aviv. A.M. Unaware that the M.O.D. had surreptitiously sent men by land and by boat to report on developments at Kfar Vitkin, Landau phoned the M.O.D. liaison officer, David Cohen. He advised Cohen that the *Altalena* had reached Kfar Vitkin late last night, before dawn, and had been sent back to sea to prevent its being discovered by the United Nations observers. Cohen answered: "Right decision. Will advise Galili." Landau again asked for help in unloading the half-tracks. Cohen said he would try his best. Before they hung up, Landau again invited representatives of the I.D.F. General Staff to observe the operation. Later Begin phoned Galili, reporting on the past night's events. He informed Galili that the vessel would return at 9 P.M.

Tel-Aviv. P.M. At the regular meeting of the Provisional Government, Ben-Gurion and Sharett decided to advise the ministers, who had been kept in the dark until now, about the developments with the *Altalena*.

Sharett was dramatic: "We are facing the possibility of a breach of cease-fire."[1] Sharett's emphasis on the cease-fire, considering

---

[1] Pinchas Vazeh wrote in his *hamesimah Rechesh*, Maarachot, Tel-Aviv, 1966: "Of course we could not permit ourselves to halt arms shipments to *(continued on the next page)*

Ben-Gurion's earlier instructions to proceed with a speeded-up landing of the *Altalena,* as well as his sanctioning of the breaking of the cease-fire by the IDF's own vessels and planes, was more likely a sham than ignorance. Either Sharett was unaware of the facts or he willingly ignored them, while pointing his finger at the "irresponsible acts" of the "dissidents."

The tension mounted as Sharett described how the *Irgun* occupied an army camp with five hundred men in anticipation of the landing. Sharett said that the vessel was known worldwide, and he read Dr. Weizmann's cable about "the two vessels that sailed from Marseilles with men and weapons." Then he added angrily: "There are not two vessels but we have enough with one.[2] Ben-Gurion joined in: "They carry five thousand rifles, two hundred machine guns, eight hundred men!"

Sharett's anger mounted: "This is anarchy . . . we have invested a lot in this cease-fire . . . The fact is, the *Irgun* continues to exist . . . This constitutes a grave danger."

The ministers were stunned. Neither Sharett nor Ben-Gurion had informed them of the repeated negotiations on the *Altalena* that began in late April.

Ben-Gurion took over the floor from Sharett, waving Galili's written report from that morning: "On June 1, 1948, Begin signed an agreement that the *Irgun* would cease independent arms acquisitions in Israel and overseas . . . A few days later he confirmed that his people abroad were advised accordingly . . . A week later our men advised us that the *Irgun* people in Europe were not in receipt of such instructions and were continuing their activities. When I protested to Begin he apologized, saying that there had been a mix-up in communications, and that it would be corrected.[3]

Israel during the cease-fire . . . when the . . . Arab states were free from U.N. sanctions. We did not sit idly by but increased our armaments" (p. 200).

   "Inco (Marie Annic) and *Altalena*—the first one teaches us how one was to deliver weapons during a cease-fire and blockade; the second, how not to" (p. 201). Obviously, Vazeh did not read *The New York Times* of 6/13/48. Reuter's man in Marseilles was as well informed on the *Haganah's* vessel as he was on the Irgun's."

[2] Obviously, Weizmann was right. Sharett either was ignorant of the facts or was not telling the truth.

[3] In the period from May 29-June 2, when I had been at headquarters in Paris, Lankin made no mention of instructions received from the *Irgun* commanded *(continued on next page)*

Ben-Gurion continued to read Galili's report to the Ministers: "On the 13th Begin suddenly advised me that their vessel was on the high seas . . . (Here it seemed that Galili had confused the date he received the cables from *Haganah* intelligence in Europe with the date of his June 16th meeting with Begin.)

"On Friday, June 18, I received a letter from Begin that the vessel would arrive on Saturday night . . . I answered per [Ben-Gurion's] instructions: a) the arms are to be turned over to the government on the beach. b) We are willing to consider their request that part should be assigned to Jerusalem. [After additional exchanges] Begin advised me that they insisted that though in principle the arms would be at the government's disposal, they would be used to equip the *Irgun* battallions in the Army, and that 20 percent should go to Jerusalem . . .

The situation is sufficiently transparent. They covered up the departure of the vessel. This is why they did not turn over to us their sources of supply . . . They sailed knowing that it would reach shore during the cease-fire . . ."

Then Ben-Gurion concluded: "This . . . is very serious. There cannot be two armies, with Begin doing just as he likes . . . We have to decide if we want to hand over the Government to Begin, or tell him that if he does not stop these actions—we will shoot!"

The weeks of negotiations and agreements were totally ignored in this most crucial report Ben-Gurion presented to the Cabinet.

Not one of the ministers present asked for details on the previous contacts, not one suggested that Begin be invited to appear before the cabinet to give his version of the events. Not one asked if Ben-Gurion had agreed that 20 percent of the weapons would go to the *Irgun* in Jerusalem. No questions were asked at all. Ben-Gurion and Galili, burying their own political hatchets, united to "face the common enemy."

---

to turn over sources of equipment to the *Haganah* in Europe. Even if such instructions had been received, they would not have been instigated before Ben-Eliezer and Merlin reached Israel on June 5th, when the June 1st agreement with the Government for the first time was revealed and explained to them. We had no doubt that within the borders of Israel, the arms we obtained in Europe would be channeled through the Army to our former units. It was our time, labor, and sacrifices and our meager money which made these weapons possible. We never doubted the Army would assist us in transiting weapons to our units in beleaguered Jerusalem, where the *Irgun* continued to exist as a legal, independent entity.

June 20, afternoon. Tel-Aviv, Haifa Road. Begin and Merlin were traveling in Begin's Rover back to Kfar Vitkin. Merlin, in his second week back in Israel, was still acquainting himself with the country. "What is Kfar Vitkin?" he asked.

Merlin, surprised that such a labor stronghold had been designated as the discharge point, mused aloud: "Isn't it dangerous? You know, Menahem, this could be a trap." Begin shrugged off the suggestion impatiently. "Nonsense," he said, and used a derogatory adjective to underline his disdain for the effectiveness of the *Haganah.* Merlin was unhappy that Begin brushed aside his apprehension so easily; but Begin was the legendary commander, whereas Merlin was only a newcomer to Israel. Merlin felt that it was not his place to protest any further. Nevertheless, the uneasiness stayed with him. In the meetings, Galili and Eshkol had behaved like absolute masters of the situation, continuously interjecting epithets like "dissidents" and "renegades," and mixing them with threats like 'We still have accounts to settle with you."[1] Merlin could not forget the call he had gotten a year earlier from the New York *Haganah;* the caller told him that the HCNL-*Irgun* should not become involved in *Ha'apalah* work. "If you don't cease and desist," he told Merlin, "we will see to it that your venture fails." Merlin, in his usual slow, deliberate way, said: "Well, after all, you don't have police or an army to carry out such threats." The man answered: "We will make sure the vessel never reaches Palestine."

Now on the road to Kfar Vitkin, knowing that Ben-Gurion did have an army and police at his disposal, Merlin could not escape his feeling of foreboding. But he was a neophyte in Israeli politics, so he felt behooved to keep silent.

On the beach, small groups of *Irgun* men not yet absorbed into the Army arrived and were assigned duties. Roadblocks were erected to keep away strangers, including United Nations personnel. Several dozen men were assigned to help in the actual discharge. A number of wounded soldiers, now recovering and

---

[1] An abysmal communication gap existed between Begin and Ben-Gurion. In his memoirs of the Jaffa Battle, Begin related that Ben-Gurion came to inspect liberated Jaffa. He reviewed an *Irgun* unit and commented, "I did not know what wonderful youths [the *Irgun*] had." Ben-Gurion actually wrote in his diary: "I reviewed a guard unit of the *Irgun.* They presented arms to me. It may be accidental, but all the unit members had the face of gangsters."

ambulatory, were assigned police duty on the beach. A few trucks were around. There were continuous comings and goings and confusion reigned supreme.

Tel-Aviv. The tense Cabinet meeting continued. Minister Ben-Tov of *Mapam* wanted to know whether warships were available to the Government, and Ben-Gurion answered: "We have vessels that are more or less armed. However, the *Irgun* vessel has superior weapons . . . I know the character of these people . . . I see the danger of the 5,000 rifles, this vessel is better armed than ours . . . Therefore, I'll not expose our ships in a battle with it."

Yadin and Galili were invited to join the nine ministers in session. Sharett inquired whether the Army had the forces to disperse the *Irgun* men. Ben-Gurion answered: "We chose the area because we control it." Then he added enigmatically, "However, I don't know where they will arrive tonight." A strange comment, since he knew the ship was to land at Kfar Vitkin, and since no one had hinted of a change in plans.

Galili settled the "uncertainty": "They will probably land by 9 P.M. at Kfar Vitkin." Galili did not tell the Cabinet that it was Begin who had given this information to Galili himself that morning.

Yadin then said: "We have about six hundred men available." And again Ben-Gurion: "There are 900 men, 5000 rifles and 250 Brens.!"

Yadin indicated that by midnight or early morning he could muster the forces to be in control of the situation.

Ben-Gurion once again: "What they're doing now is child's play in comparison to what they will do tomorrow. Then there will be two States and two armies."

Eight ministers voted to empower Yadin to assemble the necessary armed forces, issue warnings to the *Irgun*, and if unavoidable—use force. Ben-Gurion had put together his case carefully. Nothing would deter him from the course he had embarked upon years ago: liquidation of the opposition he hated and feared most—Jabotinsky's heritage.

* * *

June 20, 8 P.M. It was dark now and we were sailing toward the beach in a straight line. Two red lights shone bright and distinct up ahead. Fine maneuvered the *Altalena* into its final approach, as the disembarkation orders were passed on from person to person. First women would descend, then the men. They would have to be taken off the beach quickly, in case of enemy bombings, or interference by the United Nations. Then the unloading of the arms would commence.

We touched bottom at 9 P.M. about thirty yards away from the beach. The gates opened. I went down to the landing bridge. All we had for the debarking operation were a launch and a few rowboats. I wondered what had happened to the additional boats that had met us the night before.

In a few moments, Begin arrived on the launch. The men and women on board, lined up for debarkation, let out an ear-splitting cheer. The soldiers poured out their affection for their commander, the symbol of the victorious resistance against the occupying power. Tears in their eyes, they touched him, they shook his hand, they called out thank yous, congratulations and endearments.

Begin returned to the beach and the disembarkation began in great confusion, the men pressing forward in a swarm towards the few boats. The organized units seemed to have disintegrated, and I was concerned. The water was at least ten feet deep, there were sizable waves, and the platform was slippery. A similar scene flew through my mind: the collapsing foot bridge on the Neckar Canal in Germany three years earlier, and the soldiers drowning in shallow water.

I stationed myself at the head of the platform, trying to control the surging men. I saw Gershon opposite me to the starboard doing the same. We stood there for almost three hours, permitting only small groups to enter the bobbing boats. Slowly, the few boats carried the men to the beach load after load. It was wonderful to see the men smiling, eager and happy, some clapping each other on the backs, others more somber but all feeling lucky because of the safe arrival to this peaceful, friendly beach. The awaiting buses started up and pulled away as soon as they were loaded.

June 21. Shortly after midnight, all the men were off except the Fifth Platoon which remained to help in the unloading. Some

Irgun men also came in from the shore. The unloading of the cargo began, and that completed my assignment on the *Altalena.* I waved to Gershon and we both left the platform. I walked through the quiet hold, wondering how long it would take to discharge the cargo with so few men and boats, and no heavy cranes to handle the half-tracks. I met with Lankin and Stawsky, and huge grins came onto all our faces. They were heading to the beach to ascertain how the discharge could be speeded up.

I went back to my bunk to pack my small bag, as well as the Russian automatic that Gershon had presented to me as a memento of the voyage. As soon as I had everything together I went ashore.

The first man I stumbled across in the darkness on the beach was Merlin. He looked me over critically, the legs of my trousers rolled up, my hair blowing, the automatic in my belt. "Well," he greeted me, "you look better than at the desk in New York."

I wandered around in the dark watching all the commotion, then settled down to await the dawn when I would find transportation to Nathanya and spend a day or two with my family, catching up on sleep before reporting to *Irgun* headquarters. Perhaps I would then return to France, to pick up the "real stuff," the heavy armaments for the second trip.

I.D.F. Headquarters. Galili and Yadin arrived from the Cabinet meeting. "A strictly personal and secret" order was issued to the commander of the two brigades which include *Irgun* battalions: "Because of the possibility of a rebellion by the [*Irgun*] units, you are to see to it that all preventive measures are undertaken so such a rebellion will not be possible."

Shortly after, Dan Evan, the "Alexandroni Brigade" Commander, instructed his officers: "The purpose of this operation is to force the *Irgun* to turn over to the Army the weapons that arrived on the LST. "From this point on in all communications the *Irgun* was referred to as "the enemy."

Evan soon had a message delivered to Begin giving him ten minutes to surrender the weapons and the men on the beach. As soon as he received it, Begin labeled it "a stupid ultimatum" and sent back a message asking to meet the officer who had signed it. Evan refused. Meridor suggested to Begin: "Let's wait till morning, when we can meet under more pleasant conditions."

Tel Aviv. Two corvettes from the Israeli Navy, the *Wedgwood* and the *Elath*, were ordered to sea to keep watch on the *Altalena* and await further instructions.

By 1 A.M., army units were on the move all around the Kfar Vitkin area. More roadblocks were going up, fortified positions were constructed, guns were dug in.

Sdeh Dov, the small airport outside Tel-Aviv. Boris Senior, a former *Irgun* man and now commander of the airport, was instructed to ready several of his planes for a bombing run of the *Altalena.* Shocked, he stalled and manipulated until he managed to turn the mission into a surveillance flight. He reported sighting the *Altalena* and the corvettes.

On the beach. 3:45 A.M. Fine noticed the two corvettes about a mile and a half away to the west. He radioed the beach, asking who they were. "Don't worry," the answer came. "They are our navy's." The unloading continued. At dawn, Fine identified the white and blue flag flying from the masts of the vessels.

At dawn I came across some old friends from Tel-Aviv. One, Aharon Heichman, an officer from the early days of the *Irgun,* had a cast on his arm. He had been wounded in combat a few days prior to the cease-fire. We were chatting about recent events and mutual friends, when someone came up and said: "Aronchik, there's trouble outside the village. There are army road blocks ... I had difficulty reaching here." Aharon, looking worried, excused himself to go find out what this was all about. I spotted Lankin and asked what was going on, and Lankin said he had already checked with Begin. Begin told him that the government was objecting to the portion of the weapons he had requested for Jerusalem; it would be settled soon, though, he promised, and there was nothing to worry about.

Tel-Aviv. Landau and Amitzur of the *Irgun* command attempted to obtain crane-rafts from the Tel-Aviv harbor to help in the unloading at Kfar Vitkin. The Mayor of Tel-Aviv promised to request these rafts from the director of the port in the morning. If the rafts were available, the *Altalena* might nevertheless have to return to the open sea and return the following night to complete the unloading.

On the roads leading out of Kfar Vitkin, buses were transporting soldiers from the *Altalena* to their camps. This went smoothly without incident, until the last buses encountered army road blocks. Some of the newcomers were puzzled. The last bus had to take a detour through sand dunes.

By early morning, Kfar Vitkin was totally sealed off. The *Altalena* and all the people on the beach were now isolated from the rest of the country.

I was unaware of most of these developments. Daylight came and the slow unloading continued, the few boats shuttling back and forth. The atmosphere began getting a bit tense. I noticed a cluster of men around Begin, Meridor, Paglin and some others I did not know. There were enough men already working on whatever problems we were facing, and I felt it was not my place to get involved in all the discussions.

A few men came looking for me. One, Arieli, I remembered from my young *Betarim* group in the early thirties. He told me he had been in the intelligence section of the *Irgun*, and was now attached to the "Temporary *Irgun* Command" in Tel-Aviv. He was awaiting incorporation into the regular army in a week or two. He settled down on the sand next to me, and when I asked if he knew what was happening, he stopped smiling. "I think it's more serious than the old man sees it. There's going to be trouble, *Tsaroth*." I still did not understand.

He repeated what I knew already—that there was no agreement on the distribution of the arms; he added that the army had given Begin an ultimatum and now had us practically surrounded. Back on Friday, the M.O.D. had withdrawn their promise to help discharge the vessel, and now we were essentially trapped. Begin had sent emissaries to Tel-Aviv to invite press representatives to come witness developments but there was not much we could do.

I was flabbergasted. "How could the situation reach this point?" I asked. "Why were we told 'full speed ahead towards Kfar Vitkin'?"

I went looking for Merlin but I could not find him. Nor could I find Lankin or Stawsky. I was disturbed and disoriented, as if I were entering a strange shadow realm.

A hundred yards away, a tense dialogue was going on between Begin and "Giddy" Paglin, who headed the operation on the beach. Begin asked Paglin why the launch was returning to the vessel with arms, and Paglin said he had ordered it. He intended to bring all the men on the beach back to the vessel. "And then?" asked Begin. Paglin replied: "We can wait out the cease-fire . . . or, land in Gaza or El Arish. We have enough strength to take over an Arab area." Begin emphatically disagreed. "Our problem is with the United Nations. The Army has no bad intentions towards us." Paglin persisted in his line of argument so Begin relieved him of his duties. Meridor took over the command. Paglin said he was leaving the beach.

The sun was high now. I sat at the edge of the water and brooded. All the struggles and privations to get this ship where it was now . . . had we been right in keeping the project alive? I should have supported the suggestion earlier in the year, to sell the vessel and remit the proceeds to Palestine. So much could have been done with those funds.

Paris, June 21. Ben-Eliezer who had returned from Israel on the 19th, wrote a letter to Harry Selden, in New York, lamenting the failures of the past months. He pointed out the amazing feats the *Irgun* had accomplished, using scarcely more than "bare hands." There were "close to five thousand trained men and women" in the ranks, yet only two thousand could be armed, and even then only for "street fighting." In Jerusalem, the *Irgun* faced a continuous confrantation with the *Haganah* who opposed the transfer of arms to *Irgun* units in every way they could, sometimes even with physical force. Nevertheless, Ben-Eliezer said, with almost no weapons, the Jerusalem *Irgun* had accomplished "miracles."

Ben-Eliezer added that the Army itself did not have arms. Ben-Eliezer called this "the greatest scandal" on the part of the leadership, which had failed the nation both in the "practical" and "political" realms. The day after the May 15 British evacuation, Ben-Eliezer wrote, the *Haganah* was still essentially unarmed— "only a few thousand men could be put into action." Ben-Eliezer concluded the letter by saying: "If the *Altalena* had reached the shores of Palestine not later than a month or three weeks ago, the situation in Palestine would be entirely different."

Kfar Vitkin. Off shore, the corvette *Wedgwood* sent a launch to observe the situation on and around the *Altalena*. The launch reported back: "One launch and two rowboats continue slow discharge of the vessel . . . about forty men on the LST . . . about one hundred *Irgun* men on the beach."

There was little drinking water on the beach except for those who shuttled to the *Altalena* to get it. The settlers of Kfar Vitkin were not providing any. Yesterday they had been friendly and hospitable, but it was becoming more and more like the "good old days" of the thirties, and we were being seen again as the "fascist renegades."

The circle around Begin was growing increasingly agitated. Men were constantly coming and going and I tried again to find out what was happening. I came across Kook, who said the situation was very serious. Begin either did not realize or did not want to admit that we had fallen into a trap. Kook told how he had rushed to Palestine to argue against Katz's proposal to divert the vessel to Yugoslavia. Kook had argued to the command for the vessel to return to France, which would have been less likely to upset the French.

Kook sounded bitter to me when he described the negotiations between Begin and the M.O.D. Though the *Altalena* operation had been specifically the HCNL's handiwork, Kook had been excluded from any decision-making role in those discussions, which we realized now were only a sham on the government's part. "We've been had," he said.

I sat hanging my head, with visions of the Arlosoroff trial, of the "season," of the King David incident going through my brain. "It is going to end badly," said Hillel. He told me he was going to leave the beach by simply walking through the army cordon, and suggested I come with him. There was no way I could let myself leave the *Altalena* now, and I declined. I accompanied Kook to the outskirts of the village, where we waved goodbye.

Gershon came by and I told him all I knew. He went to Begin and asked him: "Sir, what are we planning to do?" Begin gave the same answer he had been giving all day: "Don't worry, things will be all right." Gershon said respectfully: "And if no solution is found?" "Then we'll go to Tel-Aviv. We will discharge our cargo there." Gershon was silent a moment and then said: "But Commander—they will shoot at us!" Begin looked at him as if in disbelief and answered: "Jews don't shoot at Jews!"

Gershon went on board and returned with his bag. "What are you doing? You're leaving the *Altalena*?" I asked. Gershon smiled bitterly. "Yes. They are going to kill us." I was shocked, both at his statement and at the sheer fact that he was leaving. He had nursed and watched over the vessel for almost twelve months, and if he could quit like this, we had to be facing frightening probabilities.

I was seriously worried. Could the leaders of the government not have been told clearly that we had rushed here only because we believed the State was in mortal danger? How could such a horrible mix-up have developed in just a few days? Was it a mix-up or really a trap as Arieli had said all along. We had done all the work to gather the weapons, penny by penny, gun by gun—so our units should have first call on them. But now what was our choice? A military confrontation? Whom were we facing? Our own Army! We, a handful of men on the beach, some unarmed and some wounded. We were morally right but in a hopeless military and an unbearable emotional situation with a lot to be lost and very little to be gained.

But how could I presume to argue with Begin, Meridor and the other highly admired commanders who had led us to independence? Besides, in my previous face-to-face meeting, in the correspondence over the past two years, Begin appeared always to be logical, rational. Possibly I didn't understand what was happening.

I went looking for Merlin but could not find him. Hillel had gone. He has lost the ability to communicate with Begin months ago. There was no one else I could talk to. I wished Arieh Ben-Eliezer was here.

A United Nations plane circled overhead. Now we had been pinpointed, so there was no sense going back to sea.

Oved Ben-Ami, the Mayor of Nathanya, arrived with a set of proposals to solve the situation. He left after asking Merlin and Meridor to secure Begin's agreement to the proposals which Meridor did. Begin was still on the vessel. As soon as Ben-Ami left, Meridor seemed more relaxed. Smiling, he said,"Things will work out."

10 A.M. Army Headquarters. Oved Ben-Ami submitted a memorandum to Galili: "Based on my discussions with the concerned in Kfar Vitkin, and with their concurrence, I propose that:

"a) The weapons be transferred to the control of the government.

"b) Thereafter, they should be transferred to stores under joint guardianship.

"c) The demand of the *Irgun* for weapons to be assigned to its battalions in the I.D.F. should be ruled upon in negotiations with the government, with the latter to have the final say.

"The above does not affect points on which you have already reached an accord [the arms for the Jerusalem *Irgun*]."

Ben-Gurion reacted immediately. Irritated that initiatives were originating outside his control, he communicated with Galili at 12:15 P.M.: "I don't know what has happened during the morning. This time there can be no compromising. Either [the *Irgun*] obeys orders—or there is shooting. I'm opposed to any negotiations with them. If we have the forces available, then they're to be used without hesitation immediately."

Tel-Aviv Landau met with Gruenbaum, the Minister of the Interior, giving him a detailed report of all the negotiations on the *Altalena*. Gruenbaum remarked that the report was substantially different from Galili's written report and Sharett's and Ben-Gurion's reports to the Cabinet. Gruenbaum then drafted a letter to Ben-Gurion, in substance repeating Oved Ben-Ami's proposals. However, Greenbaum also proposed that three battalions of former *Irgun* men should be allocated weapons from the *Altalena*. Ben-Gurion gave no response to this message until late that evening, when he said: "First, we have the Cabinet's decision. Second—it's too late."

Kfar Vitkin. 5 P.M. I heard the names of Yadin, Dayan and other high commanders mentioned. It appeared that we were surrounded by the top brass of the I.D.F. We had become the Israeli army's first priority target.

After more consultations on the beach, the atmosphere was grim again. I saw Merlin and Meridor in agitated conversation. Merlin told me he had asked Begin to have the boat sail out of the territorial waters, possibly to seek shelter in Yugoslavia. Begin had rejected his suggestion, instead ordering all the men to line up to hear him give a report on events and announce that the vessel would be moved to Tel-Aviv. The unloading stopped.

8 P.M. The units on the shore formed into an open rectangle; quiet settled on the beach. Begin walked over to the middle of the rectangle and said: "The *Irgun* was again proven right . . ."

This was all I heard. Suddenly, gun fire opened on us from all sides. Machine guns spattered the beach and mortar explosions resounded in the air. Tracer bullets arched overhead. I fell flat on my face. I lay still several moments then slowly raised my head. Men were running towards the perimeter. 'Irma' Helpren, in his white naval uniform with a rifle in his hands, ran by cursing in colorful Russian. 'Aronchik' Heichman, holding both his injured arm and a rifle was running in a different direction. I looked around. Meridor was near the center of the beach shouting orders. I started crawling towards him. I glanced towards the *Altalena*. She was pulling up the landing platform and the gates were closing.

Within a few minutes, we were in a state of uncontrolled siege.

The firing came mostly from inland where the village was, an area shaped like the inside of a horseshoe to the south and east. A semblance of a defense perimeter emerged and the men dug in. With the water to the west, and sand dunes directly behind us, we established a loose defense line.

As the *Altalena* backed out into the sea, I saw the launch move out from the jetty with a number of people on it. The *Altalena* turned slowly southward, as tracer bullets were streaming towards it from the corvettes. The launch came into its shadow and people began climbing up the ladder. Shortly the *Altalena* disappeared from sight, moving south and hugging the shore.

Sporadic shooting continued. There were wounded men lying on the beach near me, some apparently badly hurt. A few medics shouted for assistance and medication, but there was little of either on the beach. Machine gun bursts were coming from everywhere. I was terrified that a mortar shell might hit piles of ammunition crates. Meridor was digging a command post. He had found a flat board and kept pounding with it to tamp down the sand into a defensive parapet. I moved to within ten yards of him, and tried to follow what was happening. Men were running back and forth, barking out reports on the chaotic situation.

I dug my foxhole in the soft, warm sand, and looked for my Russian automatic. It was gone. Then I remembered that I had given it to Ziporah earlier in the morning, thinking I had no use for it. Who was there to shoot at? I had thought.

Sporadic shooting kept erupting, and the calls continued for medics. It was getting dark now.

Young Arieli came looking for me, this time with no trace of a smile on his round, boyish face. He flopped down next to me, keeping his Sten in his lap. Then he brought me-up-to date on events. At the meeting of Begin, Meridor and the others before the shooting, it had been decided to move the *Altalena* to Tel-Aviv, since contact could be established there with various ministers, mayors and the press, and we could break out of the isolation imposed on us in Kfar Vitkin. Whatever plots were brewing in Ben-Gurion's mind could not be carried out in Tel-Aviv, in full view of thousands of people. Tel-Aviv was not a small *Mapai* settlement tucked away in the sand dunes.

"Who is on the boat?" I asked. "Begin, Merlin, Stawsky, Lankin and Ziporah—they all went out on the launch. I hope they made it safely." We fell into silence a few moments, then I asked him quietly if he had read Josephus. "Do you remember." I asked, "the description of the final days in the defense of Jerusalem? After the Romans had captured and burnt most of the city, the Judeans continued to massacre each other in the upper city, and didn't stop until the Romans launched the final assault on the upper city." Arieli looked around at the scene and he understood what I meant. "Doesn't this look like the third destruction of the Temple?" I said.

Arieli did not answer. He sat with his head in his hands. Now it was quiet all around, except for the sounds of moans drifting from the jetty.

* * *

Dawn, June 22. A tenuous, *de facto* cease-fire went into effect; the army at last spoke with Shlomo Ariav and agreed to evacuate the wounded and dead. I walked over to the jetty. Four dead men were laid out, partially covered with blankets. I did not recognize any of them.

Not far away lay the wounded. There again was my old commander and friend, "Aronchik." Blood was oozing out of his cast. "How lucky can anybody be?" he cracked. "I still have one good arm."

By 9 A.M., Shlomo Ariav our medical officer returned from the negotiations on evacuation of the wounded and dead. He

reported to Meridor that the army had mortars and armored cars
with heavy machine guns surrounding us. He whispered to Meridor: "They intend to wipe us out. We must accept a formal
cease-fire." Meridor called for a consultation of the senior officers. We squatted around his position and talked in low voices.
Some suggested we put up a stiff fight, but the majority were for a
cease-fire. As one of them said: "None of us ever intended to fight
against our army or our State. If this is the way they want it—let
them take the arms and choke on them."

Meridor sent Ariav back to accept the army's terms, and command cars were dispatched back to pick up the wounded and
dead. A few hours later, Meridor went to the village and was given
a draft of an "unconditional surrender" document. Meridor con-
tended that neither he nor his men had engaged in any military
action, nor sought armed confrontation—therefore they could
not "surrender." After further arguments, the word "surrender"
was eliminated. As soon as Meridor returned from the village, he
called us together and reported that he had signed the cease-fire
agreement. All arms were to be surrendered to the Army; all men
were to give their names and addresses to the army. Meridor
concluded: "The agreement signed between the *Irgun* and the
army has always been in force; we are part of the army—how
could we fight against ourselves?"

In the center of the village, several tables were put down; there
army officers took down the name of the assembled rag-tag *Irgun*
soldiers, stevedores, clerks and senior commanders.

When my turn came, I silently pulled out my American passport. The bright-eyed, sandy-haired young officer looked at the
picture, not noticing that my birthplace read "Tel-Aviv," and
addressed me in English: "Your address?" "Kate Dan Hotel,
Tel-Aviv," I answered. "Occupation?" "Journalist." I said, the
same answer I had always given the British. I walked away, feeling
like a complete stranger in the new state. At most that young
officer might have been five years old when I had followed David
Raziel climbing the goat path in the Judean desert, where the
seeds of the future army were sown.

I saw Meridor enter a jeep. Two officers were escorting him,
their hand guns drawn. They got in and drove away.

Later in the day, Ben-Gurion distributed the text of the "surrender" document signed by Meridor. In his accompanying letter, Ben-Gurion said that Evan, the Alexandroni Brigade Commander, had informed him that the *Irgun* had opened fire at Kfar Vitkin.

* * *

On the outskirts of Kfar Vitkin I was stopped again. The non-com wanted to know my destination so I said Nathanya, and he instructed me to get into the car on the right. I found myself sitting next to Moshe Hasson, my old comrade from the Jerusalem *Irgun*. Moshe looked at me blankly, without greeting me. The non-com gave the driver a one-word instruction: "Nathanya."

We passed numerous roadblocks and our driver repeated his orders: "Headquarters Nathanya." As we stopped in front of H.Q., the driver said "Please stay till I verify my orders." Suddenly, Moshe, next to me, saw my cousin Yizchak Elroy come out of the building. Yizchak served as a runner for H.Q. Moshe knocked and motioned from the car, unobtrusively pointing towards me. Yizchak sized up the situation quickly. He opened the door of the car and announced loudly: "Come with me." The driver nodded his approval.

Instead of leading me into H.Q., he took me by the arm and walked me half a block down to his father's store. We went in through the front and immediately out the back door, hurried towards his parents' house.

"They're rounding up *Irgun* men all around town," Yizchak said. "I think Moshe is going to be arrested. We better get you out of sight."

We reached the house in a few minutes, and my cousins Shoshana and Shlomo were there to greet me with hugs. "Things are bad in Tel-Aviv," Shlomo said. "We'd better find you a safe place for a few days." He flashed an angry smile. "Just like in the good old days," he said.

We waited until dark, then we walked down the quiet, darkened streets of Nathanya. In one house after another, I could hear Begin's voice on the radio telling the story of the last hours of the *Altalena*.[1]

When the *Altalena* had sailed away from Kfar Vitkin,, the

---

[1] The events that follow were described to me by Lankin, Merlin, Jack Baron and Ziporah Levy-Kessel.

corvettes at first ordered it to proceed to Tel-Aviv. They quickly
countermanded their order and instead ordered the vessel to the
open sea. Lankin and Fine reasoned that out on the open sea they
would be at the corvettes' mercy, so they ignored this second
order. The vessel sailed full speed south, leaving the corvettes
behind. Ben-Gurion noted in his diary that it was a mistake to let
the ship go, and that now the vessel might have "sprung its trap."
She reached Tel-Aviv in the early hours of June 22, approached
the head of Frishman street and promptly impaled herself on the
relics of the *Tiger Hill*, a *ma'apilim* boat beached there eight years
before.

By now, Yadin had mobilized numerous units for the contain-
ment and isolation of the Tel-Aviv beach. Yadin, eventually
assisted by Allon and Rabin, planned a final assault on the
Altalena. Begin and his comrades on board had no idea of any of
this; they were not in contact with Landau at *Irgun* headquarters,
or with anyone else on shore. Actually, as Merlin remembered it,
no one on board had any plan of action.

June 22, A.M. The government was meeting at Ben-Gurion's
headquarters in Ramat Gan. Ben-Gurion, irritable and bad-tem-
pered, was helping to create a tense atmosphere. Almost anything
that anyone proposed, like "smoke bombs" or "boarding the
ship" was quickly rejected. Ben-Gurion seemed fixated on only
one goal: to destroy the vessel.

Tel-Aviv. On shore, the I.D.F. liaison man, David Cohen,
shouted through a loudspeaker that a government representative
was ready to board and arrange the discharge of men and material. The *Altalena* answered that those on board were agreeable, if
members of the *Irgun* command could come aboard first so they
could consult with them. This request was denied.

On board, Begin was asked to put on a hat. "Why?" he asked.
"For your safety," he was told. "So you won't be easily recognized." He waved his hands in disgust, "Nothing will happen!"

Ramat Gan. Ben-Gurion issued the first orders to Yadin to take
the *Altalena* unconditionally, in any way possible. The detailed
order included a timetable, withholding action until 3:30 P.M. At
that time final orders would be issued.

12:15 P.M. Ben-Gurion reported to the special meeting of the
Cabinet: "*Irgun* soldiers have run away from their army units to

join their comrades in unloading the *Altalena* at Kfar Vitkin."
Ben-Gurion then said that as soon as Galili had given the ultimatum to surrender the weapons, the *Irgun* began shooting. Ben-
Gurion then consoled the Cabinet by saying that "the rebellion"
had failed. He ended by announcing that the *Altalena*, was now
commanded by Stawsky, Begin and Meridor (sic).

A lengthy discussion ensued, with Ministers Gruenbaum and
Rabbi Fishman urging negotiations. Said Gruenbaum: "We can
solve the problem in one of two ways: Either we execute Begin,
with or without a trial or we force the *Irgun* to surrender, in a way
that will not create an underground armed resistance [in the
state]. I prefer the latter course."

Sharett then shocked Gruenbaum by denying that there was
ever an explicit agreement on the weapons for Jerusalem. The
percent of the weapons agreed upon for Jerusalem "were never
meant for the *Irgun* units there. The urgent matter is to make [the
Irgun] obey—even [by the use of] arms. Afterwards we can talk."
He added that "Begin, Meridor and Stawsky should be arrested."

Ben-Gurion jumped in wholeheartedly: "Peter Bergson-Kook
is already under arrest as a draft evader. What happened
endangers our war effort . . . this is an attempt to destroy the army
. . . to murder the State."

The uprising now escalated to an attempt to "murder the State"
consisted of some 50 men aboard the *Altalena*, "Fifth Platoon"
men, crew, and a few *Irgun* men who went aboard in Kfar Vitkin.
Small, disorganized groups of men on the Tel-Aviv beach were
wandering around confused and leaderless. There was no central
command of the *Irgun* left anywhere, neither on shore or on the
vessel.

Finally the Cabinet voted six to four not to negotiate with the
Irgun, and seven to two to demand the surrender of the vessel.
Minister Shapiro mused aloud: "We agreed to a 30 day cease-fire
with the Arabs. If this is good for dealing with non-Jews, possible
it is not so bad when dealing with Jews?"

The *Altalena* attempted again to establish contact with the
shore, but had no success. There was a visible build-up of armed
positions on the beach and on roof-tops. Begin and Lankin used
the loudspeakers on the bow to reach the armed men on the shore.
"Don't open fire!" they broadcast. "We brought weapons for

ourselves and for you! We came to fight together. We will not fire! We shall not fight brothers! We brought you arms! Come and take them." There was no reaction from the beach, and uncertain whether or not the appeals were heard, Lankin and Begin decided to send the launch to the beach with a dozen men, weapons, and walkie-talkies and attempt to establish contact with the IDF people. The men would establish a beachhead and try to start a dialogue with the army or the government. The launch made one successful trip to the beach and unloaded its weapons, then returned to the boat for more weapons; now receiving intense fire from all directions. Within minutes, localized battles raged in the streets and along the shore. *Irgun* and *Palmach* men, army units and military police were all trading fire indiscriminately. Machine gun fire began to strafe the *Altalena*. Merlin was sitting on the deck of the vessel next to the radio room, listening to garbled and static-filled communications between the operator and various stations. The confusion among the vessel's command was rampant. All attempts for communications with government representatives or with the *Irgun* Command at the Freund hospital failed. Within minutes bullets hit the radio shack. One hit Merlin's leg and a gaping wound appeared. It was a dum-dum bullet.

The loudspeakers on the *Altalena* went dead. With only sporadic contact with the men on the launch by walkie-talkie, Fine instructed the Fifth Platoon to answer the fire from shore. Begin countermanded the order and immediately stopped the firing.

Casualties on the vessel mounted. Merlin, the first hurt, was bleeding profusely. Then Jerry and Stawsky and others were hurt. A machine gun atop a building on shore was taking a heavy toll of the vessel.

In the streets and along the beach, *Irgun* soldiers wandered without leaders. Men within the army units were also confused, torn between disobeying orders and saving lives, or obeying orders and killing fellow Jews. Another attempt to enlist the air force to bomb the *Altalena* failed. And the army's Kiriati Brigade "was only firing intermittently and half heartedly" at the vessel. *Irgun* men controlled part of Yarkon Street, parallel to the beach.

Now Ben-Gurion gave Yadin the final order: "Undertake all necessary steps to force the vessel to surrender. All forces to be used." Ben-Gurion told Yadin to bring in artillery as well, and named the zero hour: 4 P.M. If the *Irgun* did not surrender the vessel by then, Yadin would be free to unleash an all-out attack. Fine sent Jack Baron into shore with a white flag to arrange for evacuation of the wounded. The *Palmach* headquarters told Baron that they would send help, but even after three hours no boat or doctors were sent to help the wounded.

On the vessel below deck, Merlin was bleeding profusely. He was visited by Begin, who told him that Fine had raised the white flag. Begin was disturbed by this but Merlin told him there was no other way. This only made Begin more distraught. Merlin tried to soothe him, saying there was no sense in becoming charred martyrs. He urged Begin to end the impasse and let them all disembark. Begin did not answer and went back on deck. Moments later, the white flag continued to flutter.

But by now, it was too late. The shooting from shore continued; two small caliber cannons were brought to the beach and the *Altalena* was fixed in their sights. Several men in the artillery's chain of command refused to follow orders, but they were brushed aside, and the new gunners were told: "You are firing on people who rebelled against the State, who want to precipitate a civil war."

The cannons opened fire. Several shells overshot the *Altalena*, and Fine lowered the flag of Israel as another sign of surrender. Still more shells flew towards the vessel. The seventh shell entered the *Altalena* through a ventilator and set afire a pile of clothing. In a few minutes the entire vessel was aflame.

Ben-Gurion's Headquarters. The heads of the major municipalities came to plead with Ben-Gurion to stop the bloodshed. Mayor Rokach of Tel-Aviv said: "They are our children! Yesterday they shed their blood in Jaffa and Jerusalem, and tomorrow they will again, so that we may live."

Ben-Gurion answered: "This is more serious that you imagine. Either there is authority in this country or everyone acts according to his will."

The conversation was at an impasse when a note was passed to Ben-Gurion. He looked up and announced to his visitors: "The shooting has started." He took them out on the terrace, where they saw the smoke rising from the direction of the sea. Mayor

Krinitzi of Ramat Gan, who was with Ben-Gurion on the terrace, said later: "With the arms of the *Altalena* in the hands of those courageous men, the borders of our State would have been different, and Jerusalem, the one behind the walls, would not be in ruins, deserted."

Levi Eshkol reported to the *Mapai* executive: "I felt as if the viper's head had been crushed . . ."

As the *Altalena* blazed and bellowed smoke, the wounded were helped down ropes. Merlin slid down, scorching his hands. Stawsky followed. Both non-swimmers, they were picked up by small boats. Ziporah who could not swim either, put on two "Mae West" life jackets and jumped into the water. The head of the Cuban youngsters, a medical student who had interrupted his studies to volunteer for the defense of his people, and with whom I had established a friendly dialogue on board, was dead. As the vessel was evacuated, Fine ordered that its hold be flooded because the explosives on the ship could destroy a large part of the city. Risking their lives, led by Fine, the crew and officers worked to flood the holds, dousing the fire already burning in the lower hold.

The last of the crew were finally ordered to leave; and even as they were swimming or being rowed to shore, they were shot at continuously. Begin, who had refused to leave the ship until the wounded were evacuated, finally descended. He was picked up by a flat-bottomed boat and rowed to the beach. Lankin, Joe and Fine quickly followed. The *Altalena* was abandoned now, except for two dead Cuban boys, who had fought and argued so hard to be let on board June 11. The flames and explosions now convulsed the vessel.

Nathanya. Exhausted and drained emotionally, I listened to the *Irgun* radio station in a virtual stupor. In a strained, breaking voice, Begin spoke for two hours, venting all the pent-up hurt and outrage that had been accumulating in each of our hearts for so many years.

Begin wept, and thousands wept with him, for all the sacrifices that had come to nothing; for all the fear and frustration we had to live with constantly because of the persecution by our own brothers, for all our heroic children of Israel who had never been thanked or praised, but instead hounded and reviled and

Planes purchased by the *Irgun* (May 1948).

Joe Kohn headed the M.P. unit on the *Altalena*. Fell in the defense of Jerusalem. (Courtesy Ellen Wilf).

The *Altalena* burning on the Tel-Aviv beach, June 22, 1948. (Jabotinsky Inst. Archieves, Tel-Aviv.)

The Author and Major Sam Weiser, with the charred *Altalena* (July 1945).

denounced as criminals; and finally, for the *Altalena*, burning to a cinder in the waters.

All that night, I relived my long sixteen years in the *Irgun*, the long nine years of the Mission to the U.S.A., and the short life of the *Altalena*. I remembered the day Abrasha came to the Veterans Hospital with "Uncle Joe"; the selection and outfitting of LST no. 138, and the slow, painful selection of the crew; the endless struggle to keep her solvent. She was to be our life-saving gift to our people. Denied help by "respectable Jews," we had scraped together pennies from any modest and poor and even outcast Jews to make her fast and solid and dependable. And then the great nation of France had come through.

We had sailed, our hearts pounding with excitement, full of hopes that Jerusalem and the Jordan would soon be ours again, that we would have safe borders and a strong State for generations to come. We sailed bearing our future and our past with us all at once. Abrasha carried toys for his nephew, others carrying faded pictures of their fathers and mothers lost in the *Shoah*. Parents had sent their children to us from Cuba and North Africa, and from what was once the teeming Pale; and we had all sailed together, with one desire—to join our brothers in an hour of mortal danger.

But when we reached our brothers, they destroyed the gifts we brought them and tried to destroy us as well; then slammed the door in our faces as we carried our wounded from hospital to hospital. Abrasha Stawsky was dead, Merlin was badly wounded. And soldiers wearing the emblem of the State, the State we had dedicated our lives to building, were hunting us down in the streets like animals.

In the attacks at Kfar Vitkin and Tel-Aviv, the *Irgun* lost sixteen dead, the I.D.F. three. The I.D.F. and assorted settlements gathered up off the Kfar Vitkin beach eighteen hundred rifles, two million rounds of ammunition; 200 Brens and other weapons; all told, about a quarter of what we had carried.

The *Irgun* was physically and emotionally crushed. Meridor, Lankin, Kook, Amitzur, and Moshe Hasson were incarcerated in the first political jail of the State of Israel. Ben-Gurion had second thoughts about imprisoning Begin, and let him remain free, but Begin's charismatic image as the victorious resistance leader was badly tarnished. The Hebrew Revolution was over.

In the elections to the constituent Assembly in January 1949 in which Begin's *Herut* party expected to get a third of the votes, it received only 11.3 percent. They would remain a small minority opposition for decades. Ben-Gurion's *Mapai* received 34.7 percent of the vote; Galili and Allon's *Mapam* received 14.5. They formed a coalition government which, under Ben-Gurion, ruled Israel for decades. Throughout these years, Galili refused to make public the part he had played in the sinking of the *Altalena*.

In the battles against the invading Arab armies, seventeen of the "rebellious" soldiers from the *Altalena*, including Joe Kohn fell, defending the state.

Post Scriptum
Jerusalem, 1980—Mount Olives

I climbed up to the tombstones of my grandfather Shmuel and his wife Chaya Frieda, where other close relatives are also buried, and where there is also a plaque in memory of my cousin Eliahu who, as a young man in the 1920's, went to sea in the first vessel ever acquired by Palestinian Jews. The vessel disappeared without any trace.

From my family's resting place, I looked out over the sprawling city of peace, Yerushalaim. I saw the Jewish quarter within the Old City, the home of my ancestors for many years, the Temple mount and the Western Wall from which Jews were banned by the Jordanians for two decades. Below, in the Kidron Valley, David danced before the Ark 3,000 years ago. Today, Jerusalem is whole and free again. And my ancestors have come home.

No one has cherished the covenant with Yerushalaim like the ancient—and modern—Hebrews. Assyrians, Babylonians, Persians, Greeks, Romans, Byzantines, Arabs, Crusaders, Mamelukes, Turks—all came and went, but the great-great-grandchildren of Chaya Frieda and Shmuel, of Batya and Zeev Leib again dwell on the land, from the Golan to the Negev, from the coast to the Arava and in Jerusalem.

They arrived here, carrying with them their heritage: From Spain, where Don Isaac Abravanael—an even older ancestor—had pleaded with the arrogant Queen Isabella in 1492 not to expel his people from Spain. They survived the massacres of the 17th century when Bogdan Chmielnitzky swept over the Ukraine and parts of Poland and left hundreds of thousands of Jews dead. From Eastern Europe, they carried with them the heritage of

Habad Hasidism, which taught them how to cope joyfully despite their daily degradation and perils.

My great-grandfather, Schneour Levi, in his Hasidic tradition, said in his last Will and Testament that his advice and guidance to his children had been culled from the books of the holy man, Schneour Zalman, the "Admor" ("master and teacher") of Lyady.

Everything my great-grandfather had passed on to us was rooted in the ethics and common sense of the Habad school of Hasidism, which taught above all a way of life to the common man, and it pointed them towards the physical return to Zion.

It was not exactly the secular Zionism of the latter nineteenth century, but it was the first mass movement in hundreds of years that urged a physical return to the ancestral land. When the sons of both my great-grandparents gathered their families and "ascended" to the sun baked emptiness of Eretz-Israel, they obeyed the teachings of the *Besht,* and they followed in the footsteps of his pupil, Menahem Mendel of Vitebsk, who settled there a hundred years before them. Now it was the proper place for my ancestors to rest even if there had been no peace here for millennia.

* * *

No one people have yearned for peace more than the Jews. For thousands of years it was at the core of their hopes for themselves and mankind. And yet, very few, throughout man's history suffered as much as the Jews. But they failed to learn one cruel truth, that physical strength is a condition for survival and that survival is a prerequisite to a just society. Cultural-Socialist Zionism conceived of an exemplary communal life in Palestine but it did not anticipate the six million dead. The creation of the State came far too late for them; it came almost by accident because of the perseverance of a handful of disciples of Pinsker, Herzl and Jabotinsky.

The short history of modern Israel has not been tranquil, and the new nation will be exposed to grave dangers for years to come. But Israel has relearned some of its age old creeds and understands that, though no nation can live by the sword alone, woe unto it if it does not have one.

Following a short period of embarrassment and guilt in the late 1940's, the non-Jewish world has not become much kinder to the Jews. Having failed to save the Jews of Europe, it now offers advice to Israel on "how to save it from itself." Western political leaders have acquired a concern for "Arab-Palestinian homeless-ness," which is selfishly economic rather than humanitarian. At the same time they ignore that three quarters of the original Palestine Mandate area is now under Palestinian-Arab rule.

The sooner the diaspora Jews and the Hebrew nation recognize these new realities, the stronger they will be.

The Hebrew renaissance offers a painful choice to Jews. They can live in the diaspora, often facing isolation, persecution and ambivalent identities, or they can return to their ancient land and face perils, but with a chance for honorable self-fulfillment and an end to wandering all over the globe. The mere existence of the choice has given back to Jews everywhere the dignity of which their homelessness had stripped them.

* * *

Making my way downhill to the Western Wall, I saw a new mosque. I turned right at the bottom of the hill towards the Old City, past the vividly colored old Byzantine church at Gethse-mane. I walked through the Dung Gate, up past the new excava-tions of David's city to the Wall. Entering under the Wilson Arch to the roofed area in front of the Wall, I headed to a cool corner next to the iron gate. Through the gate I saw the huge Herodian stones stretching north into the darkness.

The different groups of worshippers were forming small, separ-ate minyanim for their own particular evening prayers. In my corner a little old Yemenite was praying devoutly. I spoke to him gently, asking why he had chosen this secluded spot. He answered in his guttural, sing-song Hebrew: "Because it is the nearest to the Holy of Holies of the Temple."

I leaned my head against the cool stones. My little neighbor, son of a tribe exiled from this land 2,500 years ago, spread his arms on the stone wall and closed his eyes in silence. I closed my eyes as well, my hands resting on the stones next to his. The two of us merged into the cold gray stones of our past.

Glossary

AACI. Anglo-American Committee of Inquiry (1946), appointed by Britain and the U.S. to recommend a solution to the strife in Palestine and to the problem of the Jewish Displaced Persons of Europe.

Admor. Acronym for "our master and teacher," referring to a Hasidic rabbi (Heb.).

Ahuzat-Bait. Original name of Tel-Aviv.

Aliyah. Ascent, immigration to Eretz-Israel (Heb.).

Amenu. Our people (Heb.).

Artzenu. Our land (Heb.).

Auto-Emancipation. The title of a book by Dr. Leon Pinsker (1882) calling for the establishment of a Jewish national homeland, where Jews might live like any nation.

Bakshish. Graft (Turkish).

Balfour Declaration. The official statement of the British government issued by Lord Arthur Balfour (November 1917) declaring Britain's "viewing with favor the establishment of a Jewish National Home in Palestine."

Brit Hehayal. A Jewish Veterans Organization founded in Poland (early 1930s) by Zeev Jabotinsky.

Betar. Acronym for Brith-Trumpeldor, the youth organization founded by the Jabotinsky movement (1924).

Bilu. The first Zionist pioneering movement founded in Russia (1882).

Chaverim. Comrades (Heb.).

C.I.D. The Criminal Investigation Department of the Palestine Police.

Da'lal. Town crier (Arabic).

Die Tat. A daily newspaper of the *Irgun* (1938-39) published in Warsaw, Poland (Yiddish).

Diaspora. The area outside Eretz-Israel where Jews live, or those Jews.

El-Al. A student fraternity in the Hebrew University of Jerusalem (1930s).

Fellaheen. Arab peasants (Arabic).

Gadna. Pre-army youth service. Youth units of the *Haganah*, later in the I.D.F.

Glattkopfe. Shaven heads (German); prisoners in German concentration camps whose heads were shaven upon imprisonment.

Ha'apalah. See Ma'apilim.

Habad. A Hasidic movement founded in the late 18th century by Rabbi Schneour Zalman of Lyady (White Russia). Name is an acronym for the Hebrew: wisdom, understanding, knowledge.

Habadnik. A member of the Habad sect.

Hachshara. Training camps in the diaspora, mostly to prepare young people to settle on the land in Palestine.

Haftara. A chapter from the Books of Prophets, read in the synagogue on the Sabbath and holidays.

Haganah. Self-defense militia, created by Zeev Jabotinsky in 1920. Officially the armed instrument of the Jewish population of Palestine, it was controlled throughout its existence (till 1948) by the General Federation of Labor (Histadrut).

Haluka. Charity funds raised in Europe and distributed to indigent Jews in Palestine when it was under Turkish rule.

Halutzim. Pioneers who worked the land, built roads and formed new settlements.

Hamsins. Hot winds blowing from the desert, mostly during the summer months (Arabic).

Hanoar Haoved. A Jewish-Socialist youth labor movement in Palestine.

Hapoel. The sports organization affiliated with the Federation of Labor and often, covertly, with the *Haganah.*

Heshbon Hanefesh. Taking stock, morally.

Hasidism. Populist religious movement founded in Europe in the early eighteenth century.

Hashomer-Hatzair. A Marxist-Zionist movement.

Havlaga. Self-restraint (Heb.) policy of non-retaliation to Arab terror (1936-1939) adopted by the Jewish Agency, Vaad Leumi and the *Haganah.*

HCNL. Hebrew Committee of National Liberation, formed in 1944 by the *Irgun Zvai Leumi* delegation in the U.S.

Herut. *Irgun* underground paper (1942-1948). Later, the political party established in 1948, headed by M. Begin.

Histadrut. The general Federation of Labor, founded in Palestine in 1920, dominiated by socialists of varying Marxist ideologies.

Horah. Folk dance, evolved in the early 1920s, in Palestine.

Hovevei-Zion. Early (pre-Herzl) Zionist movement in Russia, Poland and Palestine.

ICA. Jewish Colonization Association (founded 1891), a philanthropic association assisting economically depressed Jews in Europe or countries to which they emigrated, to acquire productive occupations and agricultural know-how.

I.D.F. Israel Defense Forces, formed upon creation of the State of Israel.

Irgun Zvai Leumi-(Irgun-IZL). The Hebrew underground movement, founded in Palestine in 1931, which fought Arab terrorism and the British occupation. Zeev Jabotinsky acted as Supreme Commander from 1937 to his death in August, 1940.

Jewish Agency. International, non-government body based in Jerusalem, whose aim was to assist the World Zionist organization in matters of economic and social development, originally in Palestine, later in Israel.

"Jewish Establishment." Organizations and moneyed individuals considered to be the spokesmen of the Jewish people.

J.M.O. Jewish Military Organization (Swit-Farband), the non-socialist military resistance organization, in the Warsaw Ghetto (1939-1943).

J.D.C. The Joint Distribution Committee, the American-Jewish relief organization.

Kristallnacht. The Night of Crystals, meaning the night (November 9-10, 1938) when broken glass covered the streets of Jewish neighborhoods in Germany and Austria, after a government-organized pogrom on Jews (German).

Lehi. Lohamei Herut Israel (the Stern Group), the Jewish underground in Palestine which fought the British (1940-1948), organized and led, while he lived, by Abraham Stern.

Ma'apilim. Immigrants who came to Palestine in spite of the British blockade (1937-48) (Heb.).

Malek. King (Arabic).

Mapai. The main labor party of the Jewish community in Palestine; founded in 1930, it dominated the economics and politics of the country between 1933 and 1977.

Mapam. Left-wing labor party, founded in 1948 and aiming at Socialist rule achieved by democratic means.

Ha-Metzuda. The Citadel, the first underground publication of the *Irgun,* published during 1932-1933.

Midrash. Interpretation of the Scriptures.

Mishna. Early oral Jewish laws which form the basis of the Talmud.

Minyan. A quorum of ten adult male Jews, required for congregational prayer.

M.O.D. Ministry of Defense of Israel.

Mufti. Title of religious leader of a Moslem community.

Mukhtar. Village head (Arabic).

Mujiks. Russian peasants.

Olim. Immigrants to Palestine.

Ostjude. Jews from Eastern Europe (German).

Pale. The Pale of Settlement, an area in Russia roughly from the Baltic Sea to the Black Sea where Jews were authorized to legally reside from the late eighteenth century. It was formally abolished when the Czar fell (February 1917) by the provisional Government. At the end of the nineteenth century, about five million Jews lived in the Pale.

Palmach. The striking units of the *Haganah* and dominated by the left wing of Labor.

Plugot Ha'avoda. Two year labor units established by Betar, for national service. Later known as *Plugot Ghius*—national service units.

Piutim. Liturgical poetry (Heb.).

Sabra. Jews born in Palestine/Israel.

Samo-ob-Rona. Self-defense (Russian).

Sanbalats. Traitors (after the name of the satrap of Samaria who opposed Nehemiah's rebuilding of Jerusalem).

"Season." November 1944-October 1945. A campaign organized by the *Haganah-Palmach* to inform on, kidnap and often torture *Irgun* men and women, launched under Ben-Gurion's leadership.

Seifa and Sifra. Book and Sword (Aramaic).

S'gan. Non-commissioned officers in the *Irgun* (Biblical origin).

Shkotzim. Gentile youngsters (Yiddish).

Shochet. Person qualified to perform the slaying of animals according to religious requirements (Heb.).

Shoah. The destruction of European Jews by the Nazis (Heb.).

Talit. Prayer shawl.

Talmud. Ancient Jewish volumes containing the Midrash, the Mishna, and rabbinic commentaries.

Templer. Religious German order founded 1868, which established a number of agricultural settlements in Turkish ruled Palestine.

Tisha B'av. The ninth day of the month of Av, commemorating the destruction of the First and Second Temples.

Tsaroth. Headaches, tribulations (Heb.).

UNSCOP. United Nations Special Committee on Palestine (May 1947). Its purpose was to investigate all questions ... relevant to the "Problems of Palestine," and report to the General Assembly by September 1, 1947, with specific proposals.

U.R.M. The United Resistance Movement, created in November 1945; lasted till August 1946. It coordinated the anti-British military and sabotage actions of the *Haganah, Irgun* and *Lehi.*

Vaad Leumi. National Council representing the Jewish Community of Palestine during the British rule.

W.R.B. War Refugee Board. Created by President Roosevelt's executive order in January 1944 to rescue and assist those who could still be helped in and out of Nazi controlled lands.

Yarmulka. Skullcap worn by observant Jews.

"Yihye beseder." All will be well (Heb.).

Yishuv. The Jewish Community in Palestine prior to the establishment of the State of Israel.

Zagiew. An organization of Jewish provocateurs, recruited by the Gestapo in the Warsaw Ghetto. Liquidated by the Jewish Military Organization.

Chronological Table
From the Land of Canaan to the State of Israel

c. 25th century, B.C.E., Northwest Semites spread through fertile crescent.

c. 18th century: The Patriarchs

c. 1250 Conquest of Canaan under Joshua

c. 1200 Philistines settle in Erez Israel

c. 1125 Deborah

c. 1100 Gideon

c. 1050 Fall of Shiloh, Samuel

c. 1020-1004 Saul

1004-965 David

965-928 Solomon

928-720 Kingdom of Israel

720 Sargon makes Samaria an Assyrian province. Mass deportation of Israelites.

928-586 Kingdom of Judah

586 Destruction of Jerusalem, mass deportation to Babylonia

585? Murder of Gedaliah

538 First return under Sheshbazzar

c. 522 Zerubbabel governor

520-15 Temple rebuilt

458? Second return under Ezra

445 Walls of Jerusalem reconstructed under Nehemiah; Ezra reads the Torah

398? Second return under Ezra

348 Artaxerxes III deports a number of Jews to Hyrcania

332 Alexander the Great conquers Eretz Israel

301 Ptolemy I conquers Eretz Israel

219-17 Antiochus III conquers most of Eretz Israel

217 Ptolemy IV defeats Antiochus III in the battle of Rafah and recovers Eretz Israel

198 Battle of Panias (Banias); Eretz Israel passes to the Seleucids

c. 172 Jerusalem becomes a *polis* (Antiochia)

168 Antiochus IV storms Jerusalem; gentiles settled on the Acra

167 Antiochus IV outlaws the practice of Judaism; profanation of the Temple; the rebellion of the Hasmoneans begins

166-60 Judah Maccabee, leader of the rebellion, victorious over several Syrian armies

164 Judah Maccabee captures Jerusalem and rededicates the Temple

161 Judah Maccabee defeats Nicanor and reconquers Jerusalem; treaty between Judah and Rome

160 Judah Maccabee falls in battle against Bacchides; Jonathan assumes the leadership; Guerrilla warfare

152 Jonathan high priest

142 Simeon assumes leadership; Demetrius II recognizes the independence of Judea; renewal of treaty with Rome

141 Simeon captures the Acra

140 Great Assembly in Jerusalem confirms Simeon as ethnarch, high priest, and commander in chief

134 Simeon assassinated

134 Treaty with Rome renewed

134-32 War with Antiochus VII; Jerusalem besieged; treaty between John Hyrcanus and Antiochus VII

107 John Hyrcanus' sons capture Samaria

67-63 Civil war between Hyrcanus II and Aristobulus

63 Pompey decides in favor of Hyrcanus II. Temple Mount besieged and captured by Pompey

63-40 Hyrcanus II ethnarch and high priest. Judea loses its independence

48 Caesar confirms Jewish privileges

40 Parthian invasion

37 Jerusalem captured by Herod

19 Temple rebuilt

4 B.C.E.-6 C.E. Archelaus ethnarch

4 B.C.E.-34 C.E. Herod Philip

4 B.C.E.-39 C.E. Herod Antipas

531

Beginning of 1st cent. d. of Hillel
6 C.E.-41 Judea, Samaria, and Idumea
   formed into a Roman Province
   (Judaea) under a *praefectus*
26-36 Pontius Pilate *praefectus*
30 Jesus crucified; d. of Shammai
37-41 Crisis caused by Caligula's insistence
   on being worshiped as deity
41-44 Agrippa I
66 Beginning of revolt against Rome
67 Vespasian conquers Galilee; the Zealots
   take over in Jerusalem
c. 70 Destruction of Qumran community
70 Siege of Jerusalem; destruction of the
   Temple
70 Sanhedrin established at Jabneh by
   Johanan b. Zakkai
73 Fall of Masada
132-35 Bar Kokhba war
135 Fall of Betar; Aelia Capitolina established; Akiva executed
c. 125-38 Persecutions of Hadrian
c. 140 Sanhedrin at Usha
c. 170 Sanhedrin at Bet She'arim
c. 200 Sanhedrin at Sepphoris
c. 210 Redaction of the Mishnah
c. 220 d. of Judah ha-Nasi
c. 235 Sanhedrin at Tiberias
351 Jews and Samaritans revolt against
   Gallus; destruction of Bet Sh'earim
363 Julian the Apostate allows Jews to
   start rebuilding the Temple
c. 365 d. of Hillel II
c. 385 d. of Gamaliel V
c. 390 Jerusalem Talmud completed
425 Patriarchate abolished
614-617 Jewish rule established in Jerusalem under the Persians
632 Heraclius decrees forced baptism
638 Jerusalem conquered by the Arabs
762-67 Anan b. David lays the foundation
   of Karaism
921-22 Dispute between Erez Israel and
   Babylonia over the calendar
1099 Jerusalem captured by crusaders
1187 Jerusalem captured by Saladin
1210-11 Settlement of 300 French and
   English rabbis
1244 Jerusalem captured by the Khwarizms
1516 Erez Israel conquered by the Turks
c. 1561 Joseph Nasi leases Tiberias from
   the sultan
1564 Joseph Caro's Shulhan Arukh
   published
1569-72 Isaac Luria in Safed
1700 Judah Hasid and his group arrive in
   Jerusalem

1777 Menahem Mendel of Vitebsk and his
   group of Hasidim settle in Galilee
1799 Napoleon's campaign
1808-10 Disciples of Elijah Gaon settle in
   Erez Israel
1831 Erez Israel taken by Muhammad Ali
1839 Citizenship to Turkish Jews
1840 Damascus blood libel; restoration of
   Turkish rule in Erez Israel
1852 Confirmation of "Status Quo" in
   Holy Places
1870 Mikveh Israel founded
1878 Petah Tikvah founded; d. of Judah
   Alkalai
1881 Ben-Yehuda arrives in Erez Israel
1882 Beginning of First Aliyah (Bilu);
   Rishon le-Zion founded
1883 Beginning of Baron Edmond de
   Rothschild's help to Jewish settlements
1884 Gederah founded
1890-91 Large number of immigrants from
   Russia
1890 Rehovot and Haderah founded
1904 Beginning of Second Aliyah
   Vaad ha-Lashon organized; Habimah
   Theater founded
1906 Hebrew high school established in
   Jaffa; Bezalel founded
1909 Deganyah founded; Ha-Shomer
   organized; Tel Aviv founded
1916-18 Three Jewish Battalions formed
   by British
1917 The British capture Jerusalem
1918 Zionist Commission appointed
1919-23 Third Aliyah
1920 British Mandate over Palestine; Tel
   Hai falls; Arabs riot in Jerusalem
1920-25 Sir Herbert Samuel High
   Commissioner
1920 *Haganah* founded by Jabotinsky
1921 Arabs riot in Jaffa
1922 Churchill White Paper eliminates
   Trans-Jordan from area pledged as
   Jewish National home
1923 Mandate confirmed by League of
   Nations
1924 Technion opened in Haifa
1924-32 Fourth Aliyah
1925 Hebrew University in Jerusalem
   opened
1929 Arabs riot in Jerusalem; Massacres in
   Hebron and Safed
1931 MacDonald's letter; split in the
   Haganah; Irgun Zeva'i Le'ummi

founded

1933-39 Fifth Aliyah; immigration from Germany

1933 Chaim Arlosoroff murdered

1936 Palestine Symphony Orchestra established; Arabs riot; Arab strike

1937 Peel Commission proposes partition of Palestine

1937 Split in *Irgun*. *Irgun-Betar* launch "illegal immigration"

1938 Wingate organizes special Jewish units to fight Arab terrorism

1939 MacDonald White Paper

1940 d. of Zeev Jabotinsky (Aug. 4); Lohamei Herut Israel (*Lehi*) founded

1944 *Irgun* declares revolt against British occupation

1944 *Irgun* and *Lehi* strike at the British; Jewish Brigade organized (fights in Italy); Hebrew Committee of National Liberation formed in Washington D.C.

1945 Bevin's declaration on Palestine; "Illegal" immigration intensified; Struggle against the British intensified; Cooperation between *Haganah, Irgun* and *Lehi* (URM)

1946 Anglo-American Committee publishes its conclusions; *Irgun* blows up the King David Hotel; the British deport "illegal" immigrants to Cyprus

1947 U.N. General Assembly decides on partition of Palestine; Beginning of Arab attacks

1948 January—The "Arab Liberation Army" invades Palestine, attacks Jewish settlements. Jordanian and Iraqi units cross into Palestine

1948 May 14—Proclamation of the State of Israel. Five Arab states invade Israel, cross international borders of Palestine. President Truman recognizes the State of Israel but includes it in the Middle East arms embargo.

1948 June 22—Ben-Gurion orders the destruction of the *Irgun*'s L.S.T. *Altalena*

1948 December 13—Trans-Jordan annexes Judea and Samaria, including the walled city of Jerusalem, in violation of the U.N. resolution on partitioning Palestine and internationalizing Jerusalem. (Jordan formalized its act on Apr. 24, 1950)

1949 First Knesset opens; Chaim Weizmann first president of Israel; Ben-Gurion prime minister; cease-fire agreements with Egypt, Lebanon, Transjordan, Syria; Israel member of UN; 240,000 immigrants

1950 Western Powers guarantee existng borders (1949 cease-fire line) in the Middle East, Law of Return, mass immigration

Appendix A
The Eastern Mediterranean
As Administered by Turkey at the Turn of the Century

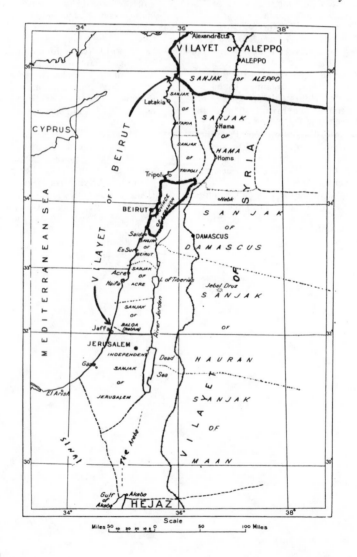

At the turn of the nineteenth century, the area the British would later define as Palestine was desolate and sparsely populated. Visitors to the country described their impressions thus: "a hopeless, dreary, heart-broken land . . . inhabited only by birds of prey and skulking foxes"—Mark Twain. "Bare as a desert . . ."—Churton. "Here is one of the most remarkable and best situated countries in the world, without a population, without resources, without commerce"—A.G.H. Hollingsworth. "Ruined towns in every direction . . . There was not a tree in sight as far as the eye could see . . ."—J.S. Buckingham.

The eighteenth century had seen Bedouin tribes from Hedjaz (the Bani Zidani and Bani Sacher) move to the northwest and spread west of the Jordan to the Galilee. The Bani Harawa from Egypt, Egyptian mercenaries and slaves from North Africa (Moghrabis, who preferred emigration to French rule), added to the polyglot character of the region.

By 1840, the population of Palestine was estimated at 150-200,000. Forty to sixty percent spoke Arabic, twenty to thirty percent Turkish or Circasian, the balance being Jewish, Druse, and of other backgrounds. During this time, immigration of tribes from as far away as Mesopotamia, and others of Turkoman origin, added to the diversity. Thousands of Moslems from the Caucasus and Crimea sought refuge from Czarist rule by fleeing to Palestine as well.

By mid-century, Jews were settling in the cities, and the tribesmen on the land. Lack of unity or common background among the population made it hard to govern and often led to anarchy in the countryside. In the 1830's, the Egyptian ruler Muhamad Ali was forced to import Egyptian tribesmen to settle the southern part of the country to quell uprisings and halt banditry.

The Jews were the first to show a political interest in the region. Other groups with their own political motivations such as the British-Protestant, French-Catholic, and Russian-Orthodox began at about this time to stake their claims as well. Palestinian-Pan Arab sentiments began to surface only much later, in 1919. They drew strength from Moslem notables (effendis) who rose to prominence when municipal councils were formed in 1857, and from the minority Christian-Arabs whose economic and social positions were being threatened by Jewish immigration.

Appendix B
The McMahon Letter

This letter was sent by Sir Henry McMahon, the British High Commissioner for Egypt, to the Sherif Hussein[1] in reply to his request for a clearer definition of the terms under which he was willing to start a rebellion against the Ottoman Empire:

"October 24th, 1915

"The districts of Mersina and Alexandretta and portions lying to the west of the districts of Damascus, Hama, Homs, and Aleppo, cannot be said to be purely Arab, and should be excluded from the proposed limits and boundaries. With the above modifications and without prejudice to our existing treaties with Arab chiefs, we accept those limits and boundaries, and in regard to those portions of the territories in which Great Britain is free to act without detriment to the interest of her ally France, I am empowered in the name of the Government of Great Britain to give the following assurance and make the following reply to your letter:

"'Subject to the above modifications, Great Britain is prepared to recognise and support the independence of the Arabs within the territories included in the limits and boundaries proposed by the Sherif of Mecca.'

"Henry McMahon."

---

[1] King of Hedjaz, head of the Hashemite dynasty.

Appendix C

Agreement Between Emir Feisal and Dr. Weizmann

(January 3, 1919)

His Royal Highness the Emir Feisal, representing and acting on behalf of the Arab Kingdom of Hedjaz, and Dr. Chaim Weizmann, representing and acting on behalf of the Zionist Organisation, mindful of the racial kinship and ancient bonds existing between the Arabs and the Jewish people, and realising that the surest means of working out the consummation of their national aspirations through the closest possible collaboration in the development of the Arab State and Palestine, and being desirous further of confirming the good understanding which exists between them, have agreed upon the following Articles:

Article I

The Arab State and Palestine in all their relations and undertakings shall be controlled by the most cordial goodwill and understanding, and to this end Arab and Jewish duly accredited agents shall be established and maintained in the respective territories.

Article II

Immediately following the completion of the deliberations of the Peace Conference, the definite boundaries between the Arab State and Palestine shall be determined by a Commission to be agreed upon by the parties hereto.

Article III

In the establishment of the Constitution and Administration of Palestine all such measures shall be adopted as will afford the fullest guarantees for carrying into effect the British Government's Declaration of the 2nd of November, 1917.

Article IV

All necessary measures shall be taken to encourage and stimulate immigration of Jews into Palestine on a large scale, and as quickly as possible to settle Jewish immigrants upon the land through closer settlement and intensive cultivation of the soil. In taking such measures the Arab peasant and tenant farmers shall be protected in their rights, and shall be assisted in forwarding their economic development.

Article V

No regulation nor law shall be made prohibiting or interfering in any way with the free exercise of religion; and further the free exercise and enjoyment of religious profession and worship without discrimination or preference shall forever be allowed. No religious test shall ever be required for the exercise of civil or political rights.

Article VI

The Mohammedan Holy Places shall be under Mohammedan control.

Article VII

The Zionist Organisation proposes to send to Palestine a Commission of experts to make a survey of the economic possibilities of the country, and to report upon the best means for its development. The Zionist Organisation will place the aforementioned Commission at the disposal of the Arab State for the purpose of a survey of the economic possibilities of the Arab State and to report upon the best means for its development. The Zionist Organisation will use its best efforts to assist the Arab State in providing the means for developing the natural resources and economic possibilities thereof.

Article VIII

The parties hereto agree to act in complete accord and harmony on all matters embraced herein before the Peace Congress.

Article IX

Any matters of dispute which may arise between the contracting parties shall be referred to the British Government for arbitration.

Given under our hand at London, England, the third day of January, one thousand nine hundred and nineteen.

Chaim Weizmann.
Feisal ibn-Hussein.

Reservation by the Emir Feisal

If the Arabs are established as I have asked in my manifesto of January 4th addressed to the British Secretary of State for Foreign Affairs, I will carry out what is written in this agreement. If changes are made, I cannot be answerable for failing to carry out this agreement.

Feisal ibn-Hussein.

Appendix D
Feisal-Frankfurter Correspondence
Delegation Hedjazienne, *Paris, March 3, 1919.*

Dear Mr. Frankfurter: I want to take this opportunity of my first contact with American Zionists to tell you what I have often been able to say to Dr. Weizmann in Arabia and Europe.

We feel that the Arabs and Jews are cousins in race, having suffered similar oppressions at the hands of powers stronger than themselves, and by a happy coincidence have been able to take the first step towards the attainment of their natural ideals together.

We Arabs, especially the educated among us, look with the deepest sympathy on the Zionist movement. Our deputation here in Paris is fully acquainted with the proposals submitted yesterday by the Zionist Organization to the Peace Conference, and we regard them as moderate and proper. We will do our best, in so far as we are concerned to help them through: we will wish the Jews a most hearty welcome home.

With the chiefs of your movement, especially with Dr. Weizmann, we have had and continue to have the closest relations. He has been a great helper of our cause, and I hope the Arabs may soon be in a position to make the Jews some return for their kindness. We are working together for a reformed and revived Near East, and our two movements complete one another. The Jewish movement is national and not imperialist, and there is room in Syria for us both. Indeed I think that neither can be a real success without the other.

People less informed and less responsible than our leaders and yours, ignoring the need for cooperation of the Arabs and Zionists have been trying to exploit the local difficulties that must necessarily arise in Palestine in the early stages of our movements. Some of them have, I am afraid, misrepresented your aims to the Arab peasantry, and our aims to the Jewish peasantry, with the result that interested parties have been able to make capital out of what they call our differences.

I wish to give you my firm conviction that these differences are not on questions of principle, but on matters of detail such as must inevitably occur in every contact of neigbouring peoples, and as are easily adjusted by mutual good will. Indeed nearly all of them will disappear with fuller knowledge.

I look forward, and my people with me look forward, to a future in which we will help you and you will help us, so that the countries in which we are mutually interested may once again take their places in the community of civilised peoples of the world.

Believe me,

Yours sincerely,

(Sgd.) Feisal.

5th March, 1919.

Royal Highness:

Allow me, on behalf of the Zionist Organisation, to acknowledge your recent letter with deep appreciation.

Those of us who come from the United States have already been gratified by the friendly relations and the active cooperation maintained between you and the Zionist leaders, particularly Dr. Weizmann. We knew it could not be otherwise; we knew that the aspirations of the Arab and the Jewish peoples were parallel, that each aspired to reestablish its nationality in its own homeland, each making its own distinctive contribution to civilisation, each seeking its own peaceful mode of life.

The Zionist leaders and the Jewish people for whom they speak have watched with satisfaction the spiritual vigour of the Arab movement. Themselves seeking justice, they are anxious that the just national aims of the Arab people be confirmed and safeguarded by the peace Conference.

We knew from your acts and your past utterances that the Zionist movement—in other words the national aims of the Jewish people—had your support and the support of the Arab people for whom you speak. These aims are now before the Peace Conference as definite proposals by the Zionist Organisation. We are happy indeed that you consider these proposals "moderate and proper," and that we have in you a staunch supporter for their realisation. For both the Arab and the Jewish peoples there are difficulties ahead—difficulties that challenge the united statesmanship of Arab and Jewish leaders. For it is no easy task to rebuild two great civilisations that have been suffering oppression and misrule for centuries. We each have our difficulties we shall work out as friends, friends who are animated by similar purposes, seeking a free and full development for the two neighbouring peoples. The Arabs and Jews are neighbours in territory; we cannot but live side by side as friends.

Very respectfully,

(Sgd.) *Felix Frankfurter.*

His Royal Highness Prince Feisal.

Appendix E
The Shrinking Jewish National Home

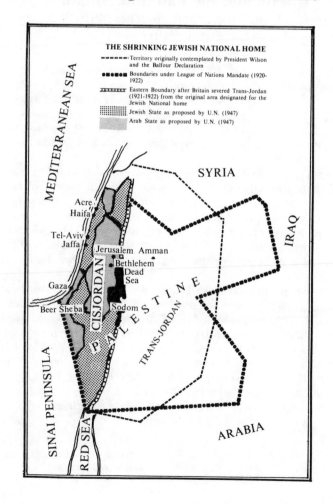

THE SHRINKING JEWISH NATIONAL HOME

- - - - - Territory originally contemplated by President Wilson and the Balfour Declaration
●■●■●■ Boundaries under League of Nations Mandate (1920-1922)
⊥⊥⊥⊥⊥⊥ Eastern Boundary after Britain severed Trans-Jordan (1921-1922) from the original area designated for the Jewish National home
Jewish State as proposed by U.N. (1947)
Arab State as proposed by U.N. (1947)

Appendix F

Britain and the Palestine Mandate
Excerpts from Articles and Speeches of the 1930's by
Lt. Col. Henry J. Patterson, D.S.O.[1]

On May 17, 1939, The British Government issued a White Paper
nullifying, in effect, the Balfour Declaration of November, 1917, which
pledged the establishment of a Jewish National Home in Palestine. It
involves a betrayal hatched by a blind junta of bureaucrats in the
Colonial Office in London, nourished by anti-Jewish prejudices, and
carried into effect by the most inept government Britain has had since
1776.

I am speaking from intimate knowledge going back to 1918 when I say
that the policy of sabotaging the Jewish National Home, of rousing
Arab terror, of flaunting an Arab nationalist cause in Palestine, was
deliberate on the part of certain key British officials misusing their
position to deceive their own government and people. The chief responsibility for the Palestine betrayal lies squarely on the shoulders of British
officials, who in betraying the Jews have also betrayed the British
people.

The Jewish aid to the British Empire was indeed responsible for the
charter of Jewish nationhood in their ancient homeland which was
embodied in the famous Balfour Declaration issued in 1917. At that time
we were in dire peril on all fronts. Lord Balfour, Lloyd George and
others, with a blare of trumpets, blazoned forth to the people of Israel
the world over the promise of the restoration of a Jewish state in
Palestine. The Jews responded nobly to the dazzling bait. A Jewish
Legion was soon fighting in Palestine under Allenby. Jewish soldiers
died in Palestine in the firm belief that they gave their lives so that Israel
might live once again in the land of its forefathers.

---

[1]Commander of the Zion Mule Corps in the Gallipoli campaign (1916) and of the 38th
Royal Fusiliers Battalion (first of three Jewish Battalions) which participated in the
liberation of Palestine from Ottoman rule (1918).

Again and again I witnessed these gallant men of Zion going to their death, singing joyously. They said they were glad to die for England because she had promised to help them rebuild their old homeland. These Jewish soldiers lie side by side with their British comrades in the great military cemeteries throughout Palestine, but no Arab will be found there. For no Palestinian Arab lifted a finger during the war to drive out the Turkish oppressors.

During the war, when Jewish soldiers gave their lives to liberate Palestine, the Arabs of Palestine fought and spied for our enemies and their taskmasters, for the Turks. They murdered and looted in our back areas where they could do so with safety to themselves. The fellaheen (peasants) of the Holy Land did not know of such a thing as Arab nationalism, and when Colonel Lawrence, aided by millions in gold, induced the Arabs of the Hedjaz to revolt against the Turks by holding out hopes for future Arab independence, the Arabs of Palestine remained quite indifferent to this temptation. It meant nothing to them.

Similarly, the Arab leaders in the surrounding territories accepted as a matter of course that Palestine should become the National Home of the Jews. Faced with the hope of independence over a huge expanse of territory, over 1,150,000 square miles, with a population of 10 to 14 million people (or, if Egypt be included in the calculation, a territory of 1,500,000 square miles and a population of 24 to 28 million people), the fate of Palestine did not at all bother them. They never considered it an Arab country properly speaking. This attitude was made more natural by the traditional contempt with which the desert Arab looked upon the fellaheen of Palestine, whom he did not consider as of the same racial stock.

More than once I had the pleasure of meeting the late King Feisal, the great spokesman for the Arabs in the Western world, and the son of King Hussein of the Hedjaz. I conferred with him in Damascus, in London, and in his own palace at Baghdad. He was a noble soul, kind, patient, just. We spoke of Palestine, and he expressed his pleasure that the Jewish people were returning to it and prospering in their own homeland. Never did King Feisal drop a hint to me that the Jews were poaching on Arab rights in any way in Palestine.

The First Anti-Semite

I saw the beginning of this policy of knifing the Jewish National Home while I was commanding the Jewish Legion in Palestine during and after the World War. Shortly after the Armistice, while stationed in Palestine, I read in the Egyptian papers a report that General Bols would be appointed governor of Palestine. I had known General Bols, who was the chief of staff to Field Marshal Allenby, for two years. I had found him to be the most rabid anti-Semite I had ever met. He had used his position on every occasion to prejudice the interest of the Jewish battalions in Allenby's army and to attempt to set the Commander-in-Chief's mind against the Zionists as much as possible. I regarded his projected appointment as first governor of the Jewish National Home, pending the settlement of the question of the country's administration at the Peace Conference, as nothing short of a catastrophe. I therefore took the first train for Cairo, where Dr. Weizmann, the Zionist leader, was then staying. I called upon him and asked him if there was any truth in the report of the proposed appointment of Bols. Weizmann confirmed it, upon which I observed:

"If Bols is appointed Governor of Palestine, he will get every anti-Semite in the Colonial service that he can lay his hands on from as far as the Sudan and India, and will fill the administration with them. If you give him this much of a start, you will never see your National Home."

Dr. Weizmann, with a smile of superior knowledge, replied:

"I fear you exaggerate, Colonel, I found General Bols a most charming gentleman. I have just had a two hours' conversation with him."

General Bols got the appointment. He proceeded to fill the administration of the executors of the trust of a Jewish Palestine with anti-Semites, many of whom remained in their positions for years, and permeated the Palestinian Government with a spirit of antagonism to the Zionists, a spirit which soon infected certain Arab politicians. . . .

Terror and Its Reward

The reign of terror which broke out anew in 1936 was the inevitable fruit of fifteen years (since 1921) of encouraging rebellion and assassination. During the period of murder and outrage that ensued, the Mufti of Jerusalem was allowed to go through the country urging his fanatical followers to organize and defy the government of which he was a paid servant. Lawlessness reached such a pitch that many decent Arabs asked, "When will the government act?" The law-abiding Arabs suffered severely alongside the Jews. Arab peasants were robbed, Arab shopkeepers were terrorized and responsible Arab leaders were murdered by the paid assassins of the Mufti.

The Jews could, of course, have protected themelves if they had been allowed to do so. British officials would not allow this. And the Arabs knew it. The restraint shown by the Jews under the greatest possible provocation has been hailed as a splendid tribute to their steadiness and discipline; but it also acted as an incentive to the Arab terrorists who, according to War Office figures, never numbered more than 1,500 at the height of the depredations.

The course of official sabotage in Palestine is well marked by the periodic outbreaks of terror, and their political consequences.

The first Arab riots occurred in 1920. Following the outburst, the Jewish battalions were demobilized, and henceforth the Zionist settlers in their Homeland had to rely on Englishmen and Arabs for the protection of their threatened life and property.

The next outbreak occurred in 1921. The result of this tragic episode was the cutting off of Transjordan from Palestine and the subjection of Jewish immigration to permanent restrictions despite the explicit undertaking to facilitate Jewish immigration into Palestine under the terms of the Balfour Declaration.

After the bloody massacres of 1929, a White Book was published by the British Government inaugurating restrictions on land settlement by Jews in the whole of Palestine. And this was put into effect despite the declaration by the Mandates Commission of the League of Nations that the responsibility for the riots lay with the British officials.

After the riots of 1933, the restrictions for the acquisition of land by Jews were further tightened.

The 1939 White Paper

Since the reign of terror which commenced in 1936, immigration has been curtailed to a minimum, in spite of maximum needs for a Jewish place of refuge. And now, under the British White Paper of May, 1939, it is proposed to turn over the whole of Palestine to the Arabs, to nullify the Balfour Declaration, to turn its provisions and promises upside down, and to restrict even the civil rights of the Jewish population which will have to remain a minority forever. The Jews are consoled, however, by the promise of a British "guarantee" of their status.

The progressive subversion of the Jewish National Home denoted by the various riots was no freak of fate or history. It was the result of a deeply laid plan. In every outbreak of terrorism, high officials of the British Administration were implicated.

It should be stressed that on the whole British governments have tried to live up to the Balfour Declaration, but were adversely influenced by the permanent officials of the Colonial Office. Our Cabinets did not initiate anti-Zionist policies; they were pressed by the career men of the civil service to adopt these policies. Somehow, up to the latest White Paper, the various Cabinets managed to save at least something from the attacks of the Colonial officials bent on destroying the whole of the Jewish effort. Generally, therefore, the Cabinets have appeared as fighting a rear-guard action for the Jewish Homeland, slowly and reluctantly giving way to the insistence of the Colonial Office.

Of all post-war Colonial Secretaries, only two—Lord Passfield and Mr. Cunliffe-Lister—were indifferent to Zionism. All others—Mr. Churchill, the Duke of Devonshire, Mr. Amery, Mr. Thomas, Mr. Ormsby-Gore, and Mr. Malcolm MacDonald,—entered upon their functions with a definite friendliness toward the great task which they faced in Palestine. And yet every single one of them, once in office, found himself obliged to yield to some extent to the insistence of the permanent officials, and to introduce some additional obstacles in the path of the Jews.

Lord Samuel

With the exception of the recently appointed High Commissioner, Sir Harold MacMichael, I knew all of the chief guardians of the British trust in Palestine. It must be said in all fairness that, just as Dr. Weizmann shared responsibility for the appointment of the anti-Semitic General Bols as governor of Palestine, a tremendous share of responsibility for all that has happened since lies with the first High Commissioner, Sir Herbert Samuel, himself a Jew. His main preoccupation seemed to be to prove to his non-Jewish friends that he was entirely free from any prejudice in favor of his own race. An outstanding British official in Palestine came and told him frankly that he was entirely out of sympathy with the Balfour Declaration, and offered his resignation.

"Never you mind," said the Jewish High Commissioner, admiring his own impartiality, "just carry on."

The official carried on, and became the main inspirer of militant anti-Jewishness in Palestine.

I vividly recall the impression made upon me by Sir Herbert Samuel in Jerusalem when I discussed with him the great promise of the Jewish National Home. To him, the Zionist effort was not practical politics as he saw it. I went away feeling that I had spoken to a man blind in one eye. The eye which was open looked upon the Prime Ministership of Great Britain. The blind eye was turned upon Palestine.

Perhaps the feeblest High Commissioner Palestine ever had was General Wauchope, a cultured and kindly man. He ruled over Palestine from 1931 to 1938. He had been full of good intentions when he assumed hs post. Once, while in Palestine, I asked Sir Arthur why the National Home was not making better progress. He reluctantly admitted in reply:

"I came to Palestine full of hope and enthusiasm for the Jewish National Home, but was told to go slow."

Had the British Administration displayed the least bit of goodwill towards the effort which it had undertaken to "facilitate" and to "encourage," the Jewish State would now be a reality. In peaceful understanding with neighboring Arab States, to the great economic advantage of the Arabs of Palestine, that country would have already served as an element of stability in the East, and as a reservoir for those countless Jewish refugees whose plight now complicates and aggravates the international situation. As it is, the world remains saddled with the tragic problem of the wandering Jew, and the record of Britain in Palestine is blackened by one of the most cynical pages in the world's history.

To a certain extent, the Jews are themselves to blame for this situation. Ever since the appointment of General Bols, the ineptness of Zionist leadership has been manifest. In those days, the Government in London was still wholeheartedly committed to the principles of the Balfour Declaration. It would have been a simple matter for the Zionist

organization to have prevented the appointment of an anti-Jewish official to the chief office in Palestine. Yet the Zionist organization, headed
by Dr. Chaim Weizmann, a British subject—a condition which is in
itself a grave error,—was already obsessed by the idea that the more
"moderate" they were in their relations with the British authorities, the
more the British would respect their aims. The truth, of course, was that
the less the Zionist pressed, the more the anti-Zionist functionaries of
the Colonial Office were encouraged to subvert the Balfour Declaration.

The greatest political minds among the Jews of that period pointed
out the triple need of the time: Max Nordau, in Paris, emphasized the
need to transfer bodily 500,000 to 1,000,000 Jews within a brief period in
order to constitute without delay the Jewish majority and the Jewish
State. (The feasibility of such a transfer was proved some years later
when almost 1,500,000 Greeks were moved from Asia Minor to Greece
under the supervision of the League of Nations in a little over one year.)
Louis D. Brandeis, in Washington, urged the need of attracting to
Palestine a stream of private investments and private initiative, to insure
the speedy development of the country and the rapid absorption of large
masses of immigrants.

Weizmann and the other Zionist leaders did none of these things: they
decided on a small "selected" immigration, rather than on a rapid
mass-immigration; they refused to import into Palestine "the evils of
capitalism" and restricted their settlement to the little that could be
achieved on the basis of charitable contributions; they dismissed "militarism" as unworthy of Jewish ethics and went on to build a Jewish State
under the protection of Arab policemen and English soldiers. And
getting wind of the Colonial Office's dislike of the prospect of a Jewish
majority in Palestine, some of these leaders obligingly modified their
very aims and declared that what the Jews required was not a place to go
to, but merely a "spiritual center."

The Colonial Office Cabal

Palestine should never have been put under the jurisdiction of the
Colonial Office. The mouthpiece of this group is the well-known London publication, "Great Britain and the East." In and around these
Colonial Office circles, has been fathered that twenty-year-old sabotage
of the National Home which has dogged the steps of all Jewish endeavor
in Palestine.

Perhaps Sir Ronald Storrs should be included in this group. During
the first pogrom in 1920, while he was Governor of Jerusalem, he
ordered all the gates of the old City to be closed for three days, well
knowing that inside fanatical mobs were murdering and raping a helpless and unarmed Jewish community. No assistance, neither military nor
police, was allowed to enter the City to quell the murderers' outburst. Sir
Ronald was undoubtedly the most astute and polished Civil Servant we

have had in Palestine, and for many years, despite his 1920 record, he contrived to beguile the majority of the Jewish leaders.

Two members of this group showed their hand too clearly: General Bols, Governor of Palestine during the pogrom of 1920, and Mr. Harry Luke, acting High Commissioner at the time of the pogrom of 1929. Public opinion, aroused by their flagrant dereliction of duty in connection with these pogroms, compelled the Colonial Office to dismiss them. What followed, however, was a most unusual procedure with respect to officials found to be grossly inefficient: both were promoted. General Bols received a governorship in the West Indies, Mr. Luke—a knighthood and the Lieutenant-Governorship of Malta. Here we have obvious proof of the fact that both gentlemen were merely carrying out Colonial Office policy. . . .

Although the Mandate for Palestine enjoins the Government to "encourage . . . close settlement by Jews on the land including state lands and waste lands, not required by public purposes," what do the facts show? They show that out of the land fund in the hands of the government, 72 per cent have passed into Arabic possession, while only 5.3 per cent were leased or concessioned to Jews. Altogether the Jews of Palestine, *forming 30 per cent of the population, own but 5 per cent of the land.*

Pan-Arabism

The so-called pan-Arab movement is a huge bubble. The economic prerequisites, the cultural conditions for Arab solidarity simply do not exist except in the minds of a handful of irresponsible agitators and another handful of corrupt Arab politicians.

Are Jews Determined?

When I am asked whether the Jews will ever establish a homeland for the millions of their persecuted brethren, I can only reply that with each passing year the difficulties mount. Measures which would have been adequate a few years ago to carry out that aim would not be adequate today. More and more determination will be needed on the part of the Jews if, despite the time lost, they still want to create a country of their own. Do they possess this determination? I wonder. Generations of life in the ghetto and in fear of oppression have endowed Jews with many talents, spiritual, intellectual and commercial. It seems to me that they have deadened their political talents. Will they master the art of acquiring a country, an art which requires some finesse, but mostly will power, courage and perseverance?

Appendix G

Samples of Advertisements
Placed Across the U.S.A.—1942/1948

The first ad we published: N.Y. Times (1/5/42)

JEWS FIGHT FOR THE RIGHT TO FIGHT

"The vast majority of the members of the human race are on our side. Many of them are fighting with us, all of them are praying for us." —Franklin Delano Roosevelt.

The Jews of Palestine and the stateless Jews of the world do not only want to pray—THEY WANT TO FIGHT!!!!

"ANY NATION, ANY MAN WHO FIGHTS AGAINST NAZIDOM WILL HAVE OUR AID." —*Winston Churchill.*

200,000 JEWS OFFER THEIR SERVICES.

What are the Jews doing in this war?

In England, the United States and in Russia this question has an easy answer:

They are fighting.

But there are thousands upon thousands of Jews who are not fighting.

135,000 Fearless Palestinian Jews registered as volunteers for war service as soon as the war broke out. They want to defend their homeland and their very lives from attack by aggressors.

They are still waiting to be called to the colors.

Then there are the stateless Jews, the disinherited Jews, the ones driven from their homes by the great and evil violence of the Axis Powers.

They are scattered in every part of the world, young and courageous, who have only one dream—to fight under a flag that will carry them against the armies of Hitler.

They were the first victims of Hitler's hatred and aggression. Their relatives, their people are the most persecuted, the most starved, the most tortured under Hitler's yoke; they paid and are paying an actual human suffering infinitely more than any other people on earth.

They are eager to fight back and to avenge.

There is still another category of Jews—from countries not yet involved in the war—from South America and the Middle East. They feel that they, too, should have a part in the world struggle to defeat the enemies of civilization.

All of them are convinced that the Jewish people's place in on all the fronts where the democracies are fighting for those very foundations of society whose Magna Charta is the Bible.

They all want to unite in their own Freedom Army and to fight under their own Liberty Flag, under the supreme Allied Command.

There is nothing unprecedented in this demand: Jewish Legions fought in the last World War and participated in conquering Palestine.

To urge the materialization of this demand a Committee For a Jewish Army was organized and inaugurated on December 4, 1941, in Washington, D. C., a committee composed of men from all walks of American life who passionately believe in the victory of democracy and through that victory, in a better world for all, regardless of race or creed.

This Committee believes that with America's entrance into the war against the Axis, the question of a Jewish Army, based on Palestine, has become a direct and vital concern to the United States, since this army, 200,000 strong,

Will consolidate the Allied positions around the Suez Canal;

Will release a considerable part of the Anzac forces from the Middle East for combat in the Pacific, and thus

Will strengthen the defenses of this hemisphere.

In these historic days when the greatest leaders and animators of world democracy, President Roosevelt

Prime Minister Churchill, are deliberating the vital problems of world strategy, this Committee wants to express its conviction that the organization of a Jewish Army will be of great strategic importance to the strength of the United Nations and an additional proof that this titanic struggle will be decided not solely by brute force, but by principles of justice and honor.

Churchill gave expression to this conviction in these immortal words:

"Without honor we could neither hope nor deserve to win this hard war."

Therefore, this committee feels that humanity, Christianity, the very ideals for which we are fighting this war, are embodied in the demand for a Jewish Army.

It is the conviction of this Committee that the Jewish flag must fly in this ultimate clash, that will probably be fought out in the Middle East, over the evangelic hills of Galilee.

This Committee demands the right for the Jews to go and fight for freedom under the walls of Jerusalem.

This Committee demands that the Jews be not slaughtered in Palestine as helpless children, but that they will be trained and will be given arms in their hands—arms, airplanes, tanks and guns

This Committee demands that the Jewish People be heard, that the Jewish People takes its place in the ranks of free peoples of the earth.

This Committee demands that the Jews the world over should be given a chance to express and to demonstrate that solidarity with the great American nation which became the standard bearer of the fight for freedom and justice everywhere and for everyone. This chance should be given to them by enabling them to form an army of Palestinian and stateless Jews, who will fight side by side with the American people and her allied nations

Many American strategists and many of America's most far-seeing statesmen are already convinced of the rightness of this plan and have endorsed it. Secretary of War Stimson has wired to the inaugural session of this Committee the following encouraging and inspiring words:

"Free men everywhere are arming for the defense of democracy. I send my best wishes for the success of your movement."

A powerful and courageous army ready to give its life for the ideals that mark the Allied cause lies waiting to be born.

The Committee asks that men and women of all creeds come to its aid by a determined effort in the creation of this first great modern Jewish Army.

With your help and cooperation the Jewish Army will be victorious. It will be victorious not only in the interest of the Jewish people but also in the interest of world democracy. Because ours is a struggle for right and justice—and right and justice are indivisible—they should be for all and everywhere.

COMMITTEE FOR A JEWISH ARMY

NATIONAL HEADQUARTERS

285 Madison Avenue   New York, N. Y.

LEx. 2-7646

Washington Office: Willard Hotel

REGIONAL OFFICES:

Philadelphia, 716 Walnut St.
Chicago,   139 No. Clark St.

HELP MAKE THE JEWISH ARMY A REALITY NOW!

THE AIM:

To bring about, by legal means and in accordance with the laws and foreign policy of the United States, the formation of a Jewish Army, based on Palestine, to fight for the survival of the Jewish people and the preservation of democracy. This army, composed primarily of Palestinian Jews and refugees as well as of volunteers from free countries, will fight on all required battlefields side by side with the United States, Great Britain, and the other Allied nations.

I wish to help the Committee in its work for the formation of the Jewish Army. My contribution is enclosed.

Name _____

Address _____

City _____ State _____

Make Checks Payable To:
Committee for a Jewish Army

549

THE NEW YORK TIMES, TUESDAY, FEBRUARY 16, 1943.   L+   11

ADVERTISEMENT   ADVERTISEMENT   ADVERTISEMENT

FOR SALE to Humanity
70,000 Jews

Guaranteed Human Beings at $50 a Piece

Roumania is tired of killing Jews. It has killed one hundred thousand of them in two years. Roumania will now give Jews away practically for nothing.

SEVENTY THOUSAND JEWS ARE WAITING DEATH IN ROUMANIAN CONCENTRATION CAMPS:

Roumania Will Give These 70,000 Jews to the Four Freedoms for 20,000 Lei ($50) a Piece. This Sum Covers All Transportation expenses.

COMMITTEE FOR A JEWISH ARMY
OF STATELESS AND PALESTINIAN JEWS

To The FOUR FREEDOMS
Care United Nations' Leaders.

February 16, 1943

My Dear Noble State of Mind:

I know you are very busy, too busy perhaps to read the story on the left hand side of this page.

For that reason I am writing an ad. Ads are easier and quicker to read than stories.

Your admirer,

Ben Hecht

RUMANIA WILLING TO TRANSFER 70,000 JEWS TO PALESTINE

Loss of Faith in Germany's Victory Seen in Rumanian Proposal

[small column of text]

ROUMANIA OFFERS TO DELIVER THESE 70,000 ALIVE TO PALESTINE

Attention Four Freedoms !!!

NO SPIES WERE FOUND AMONG THE 300,000 JEWS WHO CAME TO PALESTINE SINCE HITLER ASSUMED POWER IN GERMANY
THERE WILL BE NO SPIES SMUGGLED IN AMONG THESE JEWS.
(IF THERE ARE YOU CAN SHOOT THEM)

Attention Humanity !!!

PALESTINE'S ARABS WILL NOT BE ANNOYED BY THE ARRIVAL OF 70,000 JEWS THE ONLY ARABS WHO WILL BE ANNOYED ARE THE ARAB LEADERS WHO ARE IN BERLIN AND THEIR SPIES IN PALESTINE.

Attention America !!!

THE GREAT ROUMANIAN BARGAIN IS FOR THIS MONTH ONLY!
IT IS AN UNPRECEDENTED OFFER!
SEVENTY THOUSAND SOULS AT $50 A PIECE!
The Doors of Roumania Are Open! Act Now!

The four million Jews of Nazi-held Europe can be saved from the fate of their two million brothers already exterminated.

The Germans have dared to undertake this process of annihilation because they knew that the Jews are defenseless and forgotten.

The great, humanitarian people of the United States and Great Britain must be made aware of the facts.

To that end the Committee for a Jewish Army of Stateless and Palestinian Jews has launched an intensive campaign to arouse the conscience of humanity and to demand that something be done NOW, WHILE THERE IS STILL TIME, to save the remaining Jews of Europe.

The principal demand of the Committee is that the United Nations immediately appoint an inter-governmental committee to formulate ways and means of stopping this wholesale slaughter of human beings.

You are part of the collective conscience of America: this conscience has never been found wanting. Join in this fight! You can help spread this message to your friends. You can write to your Congressmen. You can make contributions for the further distribution of messages like these to all the people of the United States. In this way, you, with the force of your indignation, of your wrath, and of your action, you can help save European Jewry!

Committee for a Jewish Army

of Stateless and Palestinian Jews

National Headquarters • New York, 535 Fifth Ave. • Murray Hill 2-7237

I want to support your campaign to save European Jews by action—not pity, and to help publicize your messages through the press, the radio and public meetings throughout the country. I am glad to enclose my check in the amount of

$ ....

Name ....

Address ....

PLEASE MAKE YOUR CHECK PAYABLE TO THE COMMITTEE FOR A JEWISH ARMY OF STATELESS AND PALESTINIAN JEWS, 535 FIFTH AVE., N. Y. C.

NEW YORK JOURNAL-AMERICAN • • *America's Greatest Evening Newspaper* • • MONDAY, MARCH 15, 1943

Advertisement   Advertisement   Advertisement

Mr. HULL–Mr. EDEN–ALLIES FOR HUMANITY, CAN YOU NOT HEAR THE MESSAGE OF YOUR PEOPLES?

Action–Not Pity, Can Save Millions Now!

THE VOICE OF AMERICA

". . . We shall no longer witness with pity, alone, and with passive sympathy, the calculated extermination of the ancient Jewish people by the barbarous Nazis . . ."

(From the preamble of the Proclamation on the moral Rights of the Stateless and Palestinian Jews)

[list of names]

MADISON SQUARE GARDEN, MARCH 9, 1943

The Jews in Europe are not just other victims in the array of peoples that fell prey to Hitler's aggression. The Jews have been singled out, not to be conquered, but to be exterminated. To them Hitler has promised—and is bringing—Death.

For too long have we stood silent before the awesome spectacle of an entire people being put to death.

At last we have broken our silence. We have come awake. We have become gradually aware that with our passive attitude and our silence we, too, have had a share in the responsibility for the massacres in Europe. Our frightened whispers have grown and our repeated appeals to the conscience of the world aroused multiplied echoes throughout the length and breadth of the freedom-loving world.

The whispers have grown into a great shout. Tremendous mass manifestations have taken place in New York, throughout the United States and in Great Britain. This process of awakening conscience was climaxed last Tuesday by the Memorial, "We Will Never Die," where under our auspices, two overflow audiences of more than 50,000 persons gathered to cry out their indignation as well as their call for immediate and stern action.

The people of the free world have become aware that mere statements of sympathy and pity on the part of the governments of the United Nations are to the criminal German mind a "carte blanche" to go on with the slaughter. And the people have spoken!

What can be done? What do the people demand that their governments do?

First of all they must impress the Germans that the governments of the United Nations have decided to change their present policy of passive sympathy and pity to one of stern and immediate action, that a way will be found to stop the murdering hands of the Nazi assassins.

The inauguration of such a new policy would logically result in the immediate appointment of an intergovernmental commission of military experts for the task of finding ways and means to stop the wholesale slaughter of the Jews in Europe.

This new policy would naturally result in the immediate utilization of existing possibilities to transfer Jews from Hitler-dominated countries to Palestine or any temporary refuge as well as the initiation of further possibilities along these lines.

And above all, such a new policy on the part of the United Nations would logically result in enabling those Palestinian and stateless Jews who have managed to escape the European Hell to fight back, in their own Army—200,000 strong—under the flag of David.

Suicide squads of the Jewish Army would engage in desperate commando raids deep into the heart of Germany. Jewish pilots would bomb German cities in reprisal.

A Jewish Army would participate in the imminent invasion of the European continent, and thus will help to win the war.

These, in essence, are the demands of the manifold manifestations of public opinion throughout the free world.

Mr. Hull—Mr. Eden—allies for humanity, can you not hear the message of your people?

It is in our hands, *not in Hitler's*, to save the remaining four million Jewish survivors of the greatest massacre the world has ever seen.

There is no time left for long conferences—lest we would confer on the disposal of four million additional corpses.

It is in our hands to save those whom Hitler has not yet destroyed. Do it now. Do it now before the "Four Freedoms" become a hated rattle in the throats of the last remnants of a dying people.

Mr. EDEN!

We appeal to you and to your Government.

There are practical possibilities to rescue tens of thousands of human beings from Roumania, Bulgaria, Hungary and other countries.

It is up to you whether they will be rescued or handed over to death.

The remnants of appeasement must not stem the way to save human lives now.

Open the gates of Palestine to the persecuted and tortured Jews of Europe, or grant them temporary refuge wherever possible.

Act now, before death slams the door on all humanity.

NO AMERICAN CITIZENS are wanted as soldiers in the Jewish Army. 300,000 Americans of Jewish ancestry are fighting in the Armed forces of the United States, where millions of men of all creeds have joined the struggle.

THE VOICE OF ENGLAND

[list of names]

WHO is America? WHAT is the U. S. A.? The answer is — YOU. That's the credo of Democracy. That's the genius of America. It's Your Voice that calls the Main Event. Call it. Shout it Out Loud. Demand Action against the German Massacre of the Jews.

You are part of the collective conscience of America; this conscience has never been found wanting. Join in this fight! You can help spread this message to your friends. You can write to your Congressmen. You can make contributions for the further distribution of messages like these to all the people of the United States. In this way, you, with the force of your indignation, of your wrath, and of your action, can help save European Jewry!

COMMITTEE FOR A JEWISH ARMY
OF STATELESS AND PALESTINIAN JEWS
535 FIFTH AVENUE, NEW YORK, N. Y.
MUrray Hill 2-7237
National Chairman, HON. EDWIN C. JOHNSON, U. S. Senator, Colorado

I want to support your campaign "save European Jewry by action—not pity." To help publicize your messages through the press, the radio and public meetings throughout the country, I am glad to enclose my check in the amount of

$ . . . .

Name . . . .

Address . . . .

PLEASE MAKE YOUR CHECK PAYABLE TO THE COMMITTEE FOR A JEWISH ARMY OF STATELESS AND PALESTINIAN JEWS, 535 FIFTH AVE., N. Y. C.

THE WASHINGTON POST   TUESDAY, APRIL 20, 1943   X••••

TO THE GENTLEMEN AT BERMUDA ★ . . .

"On the field of battle soldiers die . . .

on the field of massacre <u>civilization</u> dies!"

That's why the massacre of European Jews must be stopped NOW

THE VOICE OF AMERICA

". . . We shall no longer witness with pity alone, and with passive sympathy, the calculated extermination of the ancient Jewish people by the barbarous Nazis . . ."

(From the preamble of the Proclamation on the moral rights of the Stateless and Palestinian Jews)

Major Gen. Charles J. Bolte
Rear Admiral Charles A. Bolte
Rear Admiral Richard S. Byrd
Maj. Gen. Pat Casey
Major Gen. William Crozier
Major Gen. Robert F. Davis
Rear Admiral Keith Denbie
Rear Admiral George W. Denny
Major Gen. Charles E. Farnsworth
Brig. Gen. Robert E. Fox
Brig. Gen. Ira A. Haynes
Admiral A. J. Hepburn
Major Gen. Ben B. Hickman
Major Gen. C. R. Kilbourne
Rear Admiral E. J. Marquart
Rear Admiral W. F. Santelmann
Gen. Edward M. Lewis
Major Gen. Marshall Magruder
Maj. Gen. Edw. M. McCandlie, Jr.
Brig. Gen. George W. McIver
Major Gen. Monroe C. Kerth
Admiral H. E. Maine
Brig. Gen. J. Ross Piper
Brig. Gen. John F. Preston
Maj. Gen. Charles M. Reynolds
Lt. General H. S. Harmon
Rear Admiral Horace Borris Farwell
Rear John H. Rumbold (Ret.)
Gen. Morris Reitman (R.J.)
Lt. General A. W. Reynolds
Gen. Frank P. Ross, Pres.
Rear Admiral Harris Borris Farwell
Brig. Gen. J. Spaulding (R.J.)
Gen. James J. Evans (Ret.)
Rear Admiral Harold (Mil.)
Gen. William G. Colbern (Ret.)
Brig. Gen. Calvin (No.)
Gen. Lestie Johnson (Col.)
Lt. Gen. William W. Brown (R.J.)
Gen. William Garner (R. Det.)
Rear Amiral W. Maxwell (Mass.)
Col. George H. Morrison (Tenn.)
Lt. General Sherwin (Tenn.)
Gen. George H. McAllister (West.)
Rear Admiral C. Taft (Ohio)
Gen. Albert S. Thomas (Cape)
Gen. Charles W. Tobin (R. A.)
Rear Admiral H. Chandler (R. A.)
Gen. James A. Wagner (N. Y.)
Rear Admiral J. D. Wright (R. A.)
Gen. Robert F. Wagner (N. Y.)
Col. Joseph C. Green (Col.)
Rear Admiral S. Wilson (Texas)
Gen. Alexander Milo (Fla.)
Rev. Charles D. Brooks
Dr. H. A. Atkinson, Chm.
Dr. J. Alexander de Chin
Past Mayor of New York
Fiorello H. La Guardia
Hon. William R. Castle, Former Amb.
Frank R. Kent
Gov. Herbert H. Lehman (N. Y.)
Hon. Kent S. Thomas
Hon. Elmer Thomas, Senator of Okla.
Hon. Guy M. Gillette, Senator of Iowa
Hon. Robert F. Wagner, Senator N. Y.
Hon. James M. Mead, Senator N. Y.
Hon. Edward R. Burke
Hon. Warren R. Austin, Senator Vt.
Hon. Tom Connally, Senator Texas
Hon. Carl Hayden, Senator Arizona
Hon. Dennis Chavez, Senator New Mex.
Hon. Burton K. Wheeler
Hon. Pat McCarran, Senator Nevada
Hon. Harry S. Truman, Senator Mo.
Col. Frank Knox, Secretary of Navy
Henry L. Stimson, Secy. of War
Cordell Hull, Secretary of State
Frances Perkins, Secy. of Labor
Henry A. Wallace, Vice-President
Jesse Jones, Secy. of Commerce
Harold L. Ickes, Secy. of Interior
Claude R. Wickard, Secy. of Agric.

THE VOICE OF ENGLAND

"The Jews only symbolize what Hitler would do to the British if he gets the chance. If the refugees were British, American or Russian, the United Nations would be up and doing some thing despite all difficulties." —
Manchester Guardian, Feb. 9, 1943.

Lord Wedgwood
Lord Horder
Sir Norman Birkett
Dr. Cosmo Gordon Lang, Archbp. of the Church of England
Eleanor Rathbone, M.P.
Alfred Edwards, M.P.
Mr. Boothby, Commander R.N.
Ivor Thomas, M.P.
Sir Patrick Hannon, M.P.
Capt. Victor Cazalet, M.P.
J. M. McGovern, M.P.
Rt. Hon. T. S. Green, Chm. of TUC
Hon. Winston Churchill, Prime Minister
Herbert Morrison
Anthony Eden, Foreign Secy.
Clement Attlee
William Temple, Archbishop of York
Viscount Samuel
Rt. Hon. Arthur Greenwood, M.P.
Reinhold Niebuhr
Walter Nash
The National Committee for Rescue from Nazi Terror, representing all Trades Unions and Churches

LAST week, in Constitution Hall, a Mass Memorial for the two million murdered Jewish children, women an dmen of Europe was attended by Diplomatic Envoys of forty nations, by members of the United States Supreme Court, by members of the Cabinet, by hundreds of Senators and Representatives, and many hundreds of other leading government officials.

The memorial service, "We Will Never Die," written by Ben Hecht and organized by this Committee, recorded before the eyes of our government not only the ruthlessness of the German's slaughter of an innocent People, but also Democracy's guilt —the guilt of indifference.

At the close of the service, Official Washington listened to these words spoken by two of America's greatest actors, Paul Muni and Edward G. Robinson:

"Was it the Germans alone?" . . .

"Other people have been villainously slain by the Germans in the effort to reform them, subjugate them, silence them or frighten them. The Germans have no such program for the Jews. They desire neither their reform, nor subjugation. They desire only their extermination. Death to all Jews is their cry!

"Who thus condemned the Jews? Who thus robbed an honorable people not only of life but of their fair name? Was it the Germans alone? It was the Germans who spoke and killed. But there are other ways of passing sentence than by speech and deed. There is the way of silence. As much by the silence of the world as by the howl of the German posse has the Jew been condemned.

"We are more than a nation at war, more than an arsenal, more than a battle line. Above and beyond the valor of our working and fighting millions, America is a dream of justice, a light held aloft to the sacred ways of humanity. We have brave soldiers who are fighting to victory. But the massacre of the unarmed civilians is beyond the reach of their guns. The dream and the Mediterranean are their battle front and they are honorably engaged in it. The massacre of Europe is our battle front —and we are not honorably engaged on it."

"We Do Not Use Our Weapons" . . .

"In the historic halls of this city many great deeds and dreams have been forged. We ask that the silence of these halls be broken again. We ask for a second front against the crime of Europe's murder, a front of soldiers, tanks and planes. But a second front of the human spirit against massacre.

"Our valiant soldiers are using to the last ounce of their power the weapons given them. But we who hold the weapons of morality —the cry of wrath and outrage, the words of righteousness which more than armor have made the shape of the world —we do not use our weapons. We betray our victories for not winning them in the name of the decencies for which they are fought. The dead and dying who litter the steps of civilization had only one cry —Remember us. Speak for us, they said, before you become too guilty in your silence even to mourn us. Speak for us and give not only the Jews, but give mankind back its fair name."

★ ★ ★

On the completion of the service, Edwin C. Johnson, United States Senator from Colorado, and National Chairman of the the Committee for a Jewish Army of Stateless and Palestinian Jews, addressed the audience. This, in part, is what he said:

"They CAN Be Saved!" . . .

"We must save the five million remaining Jews who stand out first on the murder docket of the Nazi book-keepers! They can be saved. It is a hard task, but not harder —indeed it is a great deal easier —than many another task humanity has faced and conquered.

"The problem itself is basically simple. Mass Jewish men, women and children can be saved merely by opening the doors of their hell-trap. The satellite nations of Hitler are willing and ready to release these people now, if only someone will accept them."

"It Is Sinful to Keep the Gates Closed" . . .

"And so long as the United Nations are not offering more practical and more immediate places of refuge, it is sinful to keep the gates of Palestine closed to them. There is little point in debating changes in our immigration laws. There is no time to arrange with reluctant, far-off countries to take in these desperately heart people, when Palestine, but a stone's throw from the slaughter pens of Central Europe, is pleading for the privilege of accepting them.

"Then, too, there are other Jews —stateless and domiciled but who have made their escape from Europe —who ask only the right to fight Hitler as Free Jews side by side with other Free Nationals. They ask the right to die as soldiers —not as victims."

"Until they be given the right to die usefully and bravely, as Jews on the field of battle, the world will continue to look upon them as victims to be pitied, not a people to be honored."

"The Dual Tragedies . . ."

"The dual tragedies —the Jews of Europe victims of brutality and the Jews of Palestine victims of politics —demand an immediate and adequate humanitarian answer. These dual tragedies have brought a new and natural grouping of a down-trodden people into a new national entity.

"This natural grouping —yea, this new nation must be deemed by us a fellow nation of the family of nations, entitled to all rights and dignity accorded other peoples. We must recognize it as a fellow-belligerent in our common war for survival.

"We have no more to say to the good hearts and great minds who have honored us with their presence here tonight. We leave the matter in their hands. May Almighty God guide us in righteous action!"

★ GENTLEMEN AT BERMUDA:

You, who meet today as delegates from Great Britain and the United States, to discuss the "refugee" problem of Europe — remember this:

The hope of salvation for millions of European Jews, now being tortured and agonized, is in your hands.

The fair name of democracy and the sincerity of the Four Freedoms, hang upon your deliberations and derision.

Remember this as you sit in Bermuda.

Every day, every hour, in which you deliberate dooms living children, women and men to helpless death in Europe. ACTION is called for. ACTION—not pity. ACTION—not "exploratory" words. As you will talk, people will die because you have not yet come to ACTION.

The action can be . . . must be . . . simple and swift. It is encompassed in the following program, which asks only the will to save the European Jews, to be successful.

THE PROGRAM OF <u>ACTION</u> (. . . not pity!)

There can be no real ACTION until a practical MACHINERY FOR ACTION is set up by the United Nations. Thus the first concrete step to be taken is . . . :

The immediate creation of a United Nations Agency, of military and diplomatic experts, with full authority to determine and effectuate a realistic and stern policy of action, to save the remaining millions of Jewish people who are marked for cold-blooded slaughter by Hitler.

There are two broad areas in which this Agency can immediately begin to operate:

1. Immediate utilization of all *existing* possibilities of transfer of Jews from German-dominated countries to Palestine or to any temporary refuge; and the initiation of all further possibilities in this program.

2. The immediate creation of a Jewish Army of Stateless and Palestinian Jews, including "Suicide" Commando Squads which will raid deep into Germany, and Air Squadrons for retaliatory bombing.

THE COMMITTEE FOR A JEWISH ARMY OF STATELESS AND PALESTINIAN JEWS

NATIONAL OFFICES:

2317 15th St., N.W., Washington, D. C.
535 Fifth Ave., New York City

National Chairman
EDWIN C. JOHNSON
United States Senator, Colorado

National Director
PETER H. BERGSON

I want to support your campaign "To rescue European Jewry by action—not pity." help publicize your message through the press the radio and public meetings throughout the country. I am glad to enclose my check in the amount of

$ ....

Name ....

Address ....

PLEASE MAKE YOUR CHECK PAYABLE TO THE COMMITTEE FOR A JEWISH ARMY OF STATELESS AND PALESTINIAN JEWS, 2317 15TH ST. N.W. WASHINGTON, D.C.

Reprinted from The New York Times, May 4, 1943

To 5,000,000 Jews in the Nazi Death-Trap Bermuda Was a "Cruel Mockery"

When Will The United Nations Establish An Agency To Deal With The Problem of Hitler's Extermination of a Whole People?

THE VOICE OF AMERICA

"... We shall no longer witness with pity alone, and with passive sympathy, the calculated extermination of the ancient Jewish people by the barbarous Nazis ..."

(From the preamble of the Proclamation on the moral rights of the Stateless and Palestinian Jews.)

SOMEHOW, through invisible, underground channels, one ray of shining hope might have penetrated the ghettos of Europe. A rumor might have spread and grown into a whisper among the agonized Jews of Hitler's hell. A whisper telling of deliverance from torture, death, starvation and agony in slaughter-houses. This ray of hope and this whisper were expressed in one word: Bermuda!

The rumor told of representatives of the United States and Great Britain, the leading champions of the United Nations, the protagonists of the Four Freedoms, assembling to save the hunted and tortured Jews in Europe. On the deliberations of this small convention on an Island in the Atlantic were focused all the hopes of the doomed Jews of Europe; those, too, of the free well-meaning people the world over. Men and women of good will everywhere at last believed that the United Nations had decide d to do something about the unprecedented disaster of a people put to death.

Wretched, doomed victims of Hitler's tyranny! Poor men and women of good faith the world over! You have cherished an illusion. Your hopes have been in vain. Bermuda was not the dawn of a new era, of an era of humanity and compassion, and of translating pity into deed. Bermuda was a mockery, and a cruel jest.

THIS is not our definition. It is the definition of the London Sunday "Observer"—one of the most influential and important newspapers in Great Britain.

Not only were ways and means to save the remaining four million Jews in Europe not devised, but their problem was not even touched upon, put on the agenda, or discussed. More than that—the name "Jews" was banished from the vocabulary of this convention, as PM's foreign editor, Alexander Uhl, reports: "It was regarded as almost improper to mention even the word Jew."

But not only the attention of the victims of Nazi atrocities and of their friends the world over was concentrated on the meeting at Bermuda. Hitler, too, was concerned with the United Nations' reply to his challenge to the extermination of the Jewish population in Europe. Alas! To him Bermuda was again convincing proof that the United Nations were neither ready nor willing to answer his threat with action. They were continuing to give him "carte blanche" in his extermination process, exactly as in the pre-war days they permitted him to deal with Jews in Germany, with Austria and Czechoslovakia, thus paving the way for aggression, invasion, and war.

Can it be possible that the United Nations do not understand that should Hitler succeed in exterminating the Jews as a people, they by their silence will pave the way to the extermination of the Czechoslovak, Polish, Greek or even the French peoples?

Now we are witnessing a variety of attempts to justify the Bermuda failure, to wrap it in secret formulae, such as "no dealing with Hitler," or "not to interfere with the prosecution of the war," or "not to undertake anything which should prolong the war," etc. All this is just throwing sand into the eyes of public opinion. All this has nothing to do with the real facts and the harrowing truth.

The facts, plain and simple, are the following:

(a) This is a specific problem of Jewish disaster. Hitler did not (as yet) decree the extermination of all the peoples of Europe, he decreed the extermination of the Jewish people in Europe and this process of extermination is unabated and steady. Two million or more have been put to death already!

(b) Five million Jews in Europe still live. The governments of Roumania, Hungary and Bulgaria, all satellites of Germany, are willing to release their Jews any time the United Nations are willing to take part in the deliverance. By doing so, they hope to find grace and pardon in the eyes of the United Nations whom they consider as the inevitable victors in this world struggle.

(c) The United Nations have taken no advantage of these offers. They have prevented them for one reason: the British government has prevented them, fearing that public opinion will demand that these refugees be admitted into Palestine—a practical place of solution only a few days away from the Axis countries by short water route, train or even bus, where the new Hebrew Nation awaits them with open arms.

The Jewish Problem Is Not a Refugee Problem

With the Bermuda Conference a thing of the past, not having even discussed the problem of the extermination of the Jewish people in Europe, now, more than ever, it is clear that we are dealing not only with a *refugee problem*, but with the *Jewish problem* of Europe. These two problems should not be confused. They are entirely distinct. Democracy cannot connive with the slaughter of millions of innocent civilian people—the Jews in Europe. There are ways and means to stop Hitler's wholesale murder and to evacuate those who can be evacuated. But no one has been assigned to deal with this tremendous problem. What is necessary is that the machinery for action be created. The United Nations, which have uttered so many words of pity must now *do* something if these words of pity are to be more than empty lies. They must create a United Nations Agency composed of military and diplomatic experts, which should have full authority to define and effectuate a realistic and stern policy of action, to save the remaining millions of Jewish people. This Agency or Commission will deal, not with refugees outside Hitler's reach, but with the Jewish people under his yoke today.

A Program of Action (. . . Not Pity!)

There are two broad areas in which this Agency can begin to operate without delay or procrastination.

1. Immediate utilization of all existing possibilities of transfer of Jews from Hitler-dominated countries to Palestine or to any temporary refuge and the initiation of all further possibilities in this program.

2. The immediate creation of a Jewish army of stateless and Palestinian Jews, including "suicide" Commando squads and Air Squadrons for retaliatory bombing, which will raid deep into Germany, thus participating as an entity in the war and bringing their message of hope to Hitler's victims.

Join the Crusade for Decency

The crime of Europe calls for the mobilization of every shred of righteousness and spiritual power left in the world. On the field of battle soldiers die, On the field of massacre civilization dies. The thunder of civilization against the swastikist antics of the German government is the only chance of stopping the German crime against life. Such a thunder unleashed by our own representatives and by all the nations that serve the cause of God would strike terror into the souls of the German people.

Therefore we dedicate ourselves to this fight and we call upon every American to join hands with us in this crusade for humanity and decency.

Every citizen is part of the collective conscience of America; this conscience has never been found wanting. Demand action from your government against the German massacre of the Jews.

THE VOICE OF ENGLAND

"The Jews only symbolize what Hitler might do to the British if he gets the chance. If the refugees are British, American or Russian, the United Nations would be up and doing something despite all difficulties."—*Manchester Guardian, Feb. 9, 1943.*

Lord Horsley
Lord Winster
[... list of names ...]

COMMITTEE FOR A JEWISH ARMY OF STATELESS AND PALESTINIAN JEWS

NATIONAL CHAIRMAN:
Hon. EDWIN C. JOHNSON, United States Senator, Colorado

NATIONAL HEADQUARTERS

535 FIFTH AVENUE, NEW YORK, N. Y.   MUrray Hill 2-7237
2317 FIFTEENTH STREET, N. W., WASHINGTON, D. C.   ADams 0640

REGIONAL OFFICES

Pennsylvania Division
16 Walnut St., Philadelphia, Pa.

New England Division   *South Western Division*
393 Washington St., Boston, Mass.   1300 Congress St., Houston, Tex.

Mid Western Division   *Pacific Coast Division*
139 No. Clark St., Chicago, Ill.   616 W. 8th St., Los Angeles, Calif.

I want to help your campaign "Save European Jews by action—not pity." You have my support in carrying out right through the press, the radio, and in public meetings throughout the country, as well as in your endeavors in Washington and London capitals of the United Nations.

Name _____

Address _____

PLEASE MAKE YOUR CHECK PAYABLE TO THIS COMMITTEE FOR A JEWISH ARMY OF STATELESS AND PALESTINIAN JEWS, 535 FIFTH AVE., N. Y.

Appendix H

Resolutions of the
Emergency Conference to Save the Jewish People
(New York City, July 20-26, 1943)

Senator Edwin C. Johnson of Colorado, the Chairman of the Committee for a Jewish Army, issued the call for An Emergency Conference To Save The Jews of Europe.

The following served as honorary chairmen of the conference:

Dean Alfange	Sen. Edwin C. Johnson (Colo.)
Louis Bromfield	Philip Murray
Van Wyck Brooks	Harrison E. Spangler
Waldo Frank	Rex Stout
Sen. Guy M. Gillette (Ia.)	Sen. Elbert D. Thomas (Utah)
William Green	Bishop Henry St. George Tucker
Arthur Garfield Hays	Hendrick Willem Van Loon
William Randolph Hearst	William Allen White
Herbert Hoover	Samuel Zemurram
Secretary Harold L. Ickes	

PREAMBLE

In this global war in which we are engaged and which will decide the fate of humanity for generations, human tragedies have occurred on an unprecedented scale. But the plight of the Jewish people in Europe stands out unique. Non-Jews in Axis-dominated countries undergo unbelievable sufferings, enslavement, semi-starvation and death. But Jews alone have been singled out for mass destruction as a people.

Their complete extermination is the professed policy of Germany. Moreover, the escaped patriots of occupied countries have been enabled, by the formation of auxiliary fores of the United Nations, to partake in the battle against Hitler's armies on other fronts. This opportunity for resistance preserves the moral dignity of peoples. But the Jews alone have been deprived of this opportunity.

Here is a challenge to the moral sense of mankind which cannot be shirked save by gross violation of the dictates of justice and charity toward our fellow-man. Moreover, the very dignity of mankind is at stake. Action cannot be postponed till after the war. In the case of the Jews rehabilitation after the war will come too late. There may be only corpses to rehabilitate.

Today, the question that confronts humanity is whether the rulers of Germany, who have already exterminated two million Jews, noncombatants all, shall be allowed to destroy the remaining four million Jews

554

in Europe.

To prevent this mass slaughter is not only consistent with our professed war aims. It is an inescapable obligation of the United Nations, a test case of the integrity of their purpose.

Principles Evolved As Guide to Action

There are many precedents for such action of rescue in the midst of the war. A number of political refugees have been admitted on a temporary basis to America and other countries. The population of Greece was saved from starvation under arrangements made with the Axis countries.

Conscious of the possibility which a civilized humanity would bear were it passively to watch the continued slaughter of the Jews of Europe, the Emergency Conference is compelled to state that none of the steps undertaken by the United Nations, none of the agencies created by them to date, has served to save the doomed Jews of Europe to any appreciable extent.

The Conference has, therefore, probed into ways and means of saving these human beings from impending doom. It has sought for methods of achieving this end, which would be at once feasible and effective, and which would not conflict with the prosecution of the war.

As a result of its deliberations, the Emergency Conference has arrived at these three basic conclusions:

1. That saving the Jewish people of Europe constitutes a specific problem which should be dealt with as such, and not as part of the general refugee problem.

2. That most of the four million surviving Jews in Europe can be saved from annihilation prior to the cessation of hostilities without detriment to the successful prosecution of the war.

3. That a specific governmental agency should be created for that purpose.

American Government Asked to Take Lead

The following are the specific recommendations of the Conference:

I.—Governmental Agency

The Government of the United States is urged to create an official agency specifically charged with the task of saving the Jewish people of Europe.

The other United Nations should be invited to participate in this agency, with a view to its ultimate conversion into a United Nations agency: but, because of the urgency of the problem, action should not be postponed pending the adherence of other nations.

II.—Treatment of Jews in Axis Countries

1. The satellite Governments of the Axis should be urged through the intermediary of the International Red Cross of the neutral countries, or of the Vatican, to guarantee treatment of Jews in accordance with the minimum standards guaranteed to other inhabitants. These minimum standards should particularly include freedom from execution without just cause or on a discriminatory basis, freedom from forcible deportation, equal food rations and equal access to medical and health resources. The carrying out of this undertaking should be supervised by the International Red Cross or by neutral Governments mutually agreed upon.

There are good grounds for the belief that the satellite Governments of Germany, convinced as they are of the inevitable defeat of the Axis, will agree to this request.

2. If necessary, importation of limited quantities of food and medical supplies should be permitted into Axis-held territory with a view to providing the Jews the same amount of nourishment as is received by non-Jews. These supplies should be distributed under the supervision of the International Red Cross or of neutral Governments, following as far as possible the precedent established in feeding the people of Greece.

III.—Emigration of Jews From Axis-Held Territory.

All Axis countries should be urged through the intermediary of the International Red Cross of neutral Governments or of the Vatican to permit Jews to leave the territory controlled by the Axis.

IV.—Refuge In Non-Belligerent Territory

1. The non-belligerent countries in Europe—Sweden, Ireland, Portugal, Spain, Switzerland and Turkey—should be urged to grant temporary asylum to all Jews escaping Axis-controlled territory. The Governments of the United Nations should undertake to assist in feeding and clothing these refugees, and should further undertake to make arrangements for their evacuation from the non-belligerent countries of refuge during hostilities, and within a reasonable period after the cessation of hostilities.

2. The Goverments of the United Nations are urged to operate their foreign exchange controls so as to make possible financial assistance to Jewish refugees in non-belligerent territory.

V.—Refuge In Territory Controlled By United Nations

1. Every Government and authority associated with the United Nations should be urged to grant temporary asylum in territories under

its control to all Jews who may escape or have escaped Axis-contrlled territories, and whom it may be impracticable to maintain in non-belligerent territory; it being understood that such admission shall not constitute a claim to permanent residence after the end of hostilities.

2. Special attention should be paid to the practicability of the admission of Jewish refugees to Palestine. Indeed, Palestine is close to Axis-controlled territory, it can be reached without diverting shipping space; its Jewish community has repeatedly expressed readiness to welcome an unlimited number of Jewish refugees; and the country has already proven its capacity to absorb Jewish refugees in large numbers.

The opening of Palestine to Jewish refugees from Axis-held territories is particularly important since the continued prohibition of their entry into Palestine, internationally designated as the Jewish National Home, serves as precedent for other United Nations and neutral countries in similarly barring their entry.

3. All non-belligerent countries should be requested to grant transit facilities to all Jewish refugees from Axis-controlled territory who might be en route to any territory controlled by the United Nations, whether as refugees, as immigrants, or as repatriates.

VI.—Transportation

The following facilities, available at present without interference with the war effort of the United Nations, should be made use of in transporting Jewish refugees from Axis controlled territory to their places of refuge:

1. Road and rail communications operating between Axis held territory and Turkey and between Turkey and territory controlled by the United Nations.

2. Road and rail communications operating between Spain, Switzerland, Sweden and Axis-controlled territory.

NOTE: Experts associated with the relief and transportation panel of the Emergency Conference estimate that available neutral shipping alone can transport 50,000 persons per month from European countries. The number of people which can be transported by rail and road exceeds this figure many times.

3. Neutral shipping at present lying idle in United States ports.

4. Idle tonnage of neutral registry in other ports.

VII.—Military and Punitive Measures

1. In line with the announced policy of the United Nations that all atrocities and crimes against humanity committed by the Axis Powers be met with just reprisals immediately, and with punishment of the guilty after the war, it should be specifically declared that such reprisals and punishment will also be inflicted for any atrocities and crimes com-

mitted by Axis countries against the Jews.

2. This policy should be officially brought in the notice of the Axis Government and —through the use of the radio, leaflets, and other appropriate means—to the knowledge of their populations.

3. More particularly, all Axis Governments and authorities should be informed that they will be held strictly accountable for the death through murder, torture, deportation, starvation or denial of medical help of all Jews in territories under their control.

4. The same policy of just reprisals, already applied by the United Nations, should be immediately extended to any authenticated case of anti-Jewish atrocities.

5. Special use should be made in such reprisals, and in the most dangerous military operations against the Axis in general, of available Jewish man-power not yet included in the armed forces of the United Nations.

Attention is called in this connection in the fact that there is already in existence a Jewish Palestinian military force consisting of approximately 23,000 persons.

It is also estimated that there are available perhaps 100,000 stateless Jews outside of the United States who have not been used for military service, many of whom have had previous military training.

It is, therefore, recommended that full military use of this source of man-power be made, preferably in Jewish military units.

NOTE: The experts associated with the Military Affairs Panel of the Emergency Conference go on record unanimously to the effect that the recommendations made herein to rescue the Jews of Europe will not cause any adverse military repercussions or in any way impede the war effort of the United Nations. In fact, they will greatly help the war effort.

VIII.—Public Opinion.

In addition to the above measures urged upon the Governments of the United Nations, it is essential that public opinion in America be fully and frankly informed of the facts of the situation:

The extent and horror of the special tragedy endured by the Jewish people of Europe, and them alone, in being marked by the Nazis for mass slaughter.

The desperate urgency of their need for help;

The common responsibility of the peoples of the United Nations to end this blood-bath; and

The many avenues of rescue actually available which could be put to immediate use by the Governments of the United Nations.

IX.—Organization.

The Emergency Conference resolves to transform itself into an Emergency Committee to Save the Jewish People of Europe, to further the policies herein recommended and to continue in function until the emergency is over.

More particularly, the Committee shall submit the above recommendations to the President and other public officials of the United States, shall seek to secure the co-operation of the Congress of the United States, and shall call for the continued support of the American people.

* * *

Ex-President Herbert C. Hoover, at the closing session, addressed the entire nation over the Columbia radio network:

"This Conference which is endeavoring to find unity of views and constructive solution to the suffering and persecution of the Jews in Europe. There is no language which will either portray their agonies or describe their oppressors. But I propose to discuss it tonight, not in emotional terms, but in practical ones. To find relief for them is one of the great human problems of today. It requires *temporary measures* and *long view measures*. There should be more systematic temporary measures. There are groups of Jews who have escaped into neutral countries of Europe. They and any other refugees from the persecution of Fascism should be assured of support by the United Nations. This should go further. Definite *refugee stations* should be arranged in these *neutral countries* for those who may escape. But these measures should be accompanied by arrangements to *steadily transfer them from these refugee stations in neutral countries to other quarters.*

"There is another direction of temporary aid to these distressed people. For two years I have urged the systematic *food relief* of the starving women, children and unemployed men in the occupied countries. That would have included several million Jews. Relief was refused on the ground that such action would aid the Germans. We proposed conditions that would have prevented that. Relief, however, was finally permitted to one of these countries, that is, Greece, under the exact conditions which we stipulated. Does not this experience warrant its extension to other countries?" . . .

The First Lady, Eleanor Roosevelt, sent the following message:

"No one in this country will withhold any help that can be extended and I send every good wish to your Committee which is trying to save the Jewish people of Europe. It is hard to say what can be done at the present time but if you are able to formulate a program of action, I am sure that the people of this country, who have been shocked and horrified by the attitude of the Axis Powers toward the Jewish people, will be more than glad to do all that they can to alleviate the sufferings of these people in Europe and to help them reestablish themselves in other parts of the world if it is possible to evacuate them."

Henry Morgenthau, Jr., Secretary of the Treasury, wrote:

"It is my earnest hope," he wrote, "that out of your Emergency Conference will come a specific plan to relieve the critical situation which exists among the Jewish people who are facing complete extinction in Hitler's Europe. Certainly every effort must be made to stop the slaughter which can be expected as the final gasping gesture of the dying Nazi regime. As we all know, if anything is to be done, it must be done quickly, for the corrupt leaders of Fascism must recognize fully that the day of final reckoning is not far off."

Wendell L. Willkie regretted that he would not be in New York during the Conference but sent the following:

"The increasing military advances of the United Nations armies, the repeated bombing attacks upon Axis strongholds—the turning of the tide—doubtless will provoke Hitler to unloose a fresh outburst of savage destruction upon the helpless Jewish people of Europe and once again make them feel the full force of his blind hate. The time has come when the fate of millions of our fellow human beings must be determined. Hitler's ruthlessness has placed the challenge squarely before each person alive today. No one can remain aloof from the solemn obligations of living in a critical period of history. No one is exempt from individual responsibility. Each person has learned the answer to the age-old question: 'Am I my brother's keeper?'

"Truly the last hope of the enslaved Jews of Europe rests with the people of the United Nations. It is they who must put an end to the mass slaughter and provide a means for evacuating the remaining Jews to places where decency and hope still exist. The creation of a United Nations Agency, the aim of your Emergency Conference, is one with which I am in complete agreement. Surely everyone will respond vigorously to the call for the creation of such an agency."

President Roosevelt, in a telegram dated July 15th, stated:

"I am glad to transmit a message from the Honorable Cordell Hull, Secretary of State, which has my full concurrence. You are aware of the interest of this Government in the terrible conditions of the European Jews and of our repeated endeavors to save those who could be saved. These endeavors will not cease until Nazi power is forever crushed."

The message Cordell Hull sent, read:

". . . I take particular note that the object of the Conference is to seek methods by which the Jewish people of Europe may be saved from the massacre to which they are being subjected.

"The rescue of the Jewish people of Europe, and of other peoples likewise marked for slaughter by Nazi savagery, is under constant examination by the State Department, and any suggestion calculated to that end will be gladly considered. An intergovernmental agency has been created designed to deal with these problems. You will readily realize that *no measure is practicable unless it is consistent with the destruction of Nazi tyranny*;[1] and that the final defeat of Hitler and the

---

[1]Emphasis added.

rooting out of the Nazi system is the *only* complete answer. This Government, in cooperation with the British Government, has agreed upon *those measures* which have been found to be practicable under war conditions and steps are now being taken to put them into effect."

Dr. Max Lerner, chairman of the Resolutions Committee, after reading them in open session, stated in the name of the Conference:

"We welcome the messages to the Conference by President Roosevelt and Secretary of State Hull. Both are motivated by the noblest concern for human suffering and the dignity of man, in this war for survival. Both are generous and sympathetic. . . . At the same time, we wish to state our earnest conviction that the Inter-Governmental Agency, as well as the other steps taken to date, have been *catastrophically* inadequate to cope with the magnitude of the problem, and that no appreciable saving of lives has resulted from them. The problem of the European Jews is centrally the problem of those Jews *still remaining in Axis-held territory* and especially and uniquely marked for destruction as a people by Nazi Germany. Only a *governmental agency* specifically charged with the task of saving the Jewish people of Europe and given sufficient authority to act, an successfully accomplish the task.

"We of the Conference do not believe that our work has been completed. It has just begun. The Conference has, therefore, decided to become the Emergency Committee to Save the Jewish People of Europe. We shall continue our efforts within the framework of a victory with unconditional surrender, until the job is done."

* * *

Some members of the panels:

International Relations

Dr. B. Akzin
Rep. Emanuel Celler
Charles Davila
  Former Ambassador to Romania
Julio A. Del Vayo
  Former Min. of Foreign Affairs, Spain
Rep. Samuel Dickstein
Dr. Emil Lengyel
Dr. Max Lerner
Dean George W. Matheson

Edgar Ansel Mowrer
Dr. C. Pergler
  Dean, National Univ. Law School
Count Carlo Sforza
  Leader of Free Italian
  Anti-Fascist Movement
Rep. Andrew L. Somers
Johann Smertenko
  Free World
Paul Weill
  France Forever

Relief and Transportation

Laird Archer
  Foreign Dir., Near Eastern Foundation
Silas B. Axtell
  Maritime Attorney
Edward Corsi
  Chairman, State Industrial Board (N.Y.)
Mrs. Marion A. Dougherty
  Chairman, Fighting French Relief
Perrin Galpin
  Food for Small Democracies
Dr. Conrad Hoffman
  U.S. Exec., War Prisoner's Aid
Major W. W. Hoffman
  Chairman, Belgium Relief

Hon. Herbert Hoover
Mrs. Sturgis Jenkins
  Maple Leaf Fund
Dr. Kenneth Miller
  United Czechoslovak Relief
Thomas J. Watson
  President, Unalted Yugoslav Relief
Gabriel A. Wechsler
Dr. Maurice William
Mrs. Zosja Wojciechowski
  Relief Dept., Polish Embassy
Samuel Zemurray
  President, United Fruit Company

Military Affairs

Sir Norman Angell
Thomas H. Johnson
  N.E.A., Military Correspondent
Dr. Emil Lengyel
Fletcher Pratt
  Radio Commentator

Major Paul C. Raborg
  I.N.S., Military Correspondent
Admiral Yates Stirling, Jr.
  U.N. Navy (Retired)

Public Opinion

M. Berchin
Mrs. John Gunther
G. W. Johnstone
  Blue Network
Dorothy Kenyon
Lawrence Lipton
Elsa Maxwell
Tristram Walker Metcalfe
  President, Long Island University
Abe Miller
  Secretary-Treasurer, A.C.W. of A.
Herbert S. Moore
  Trans-Radio Press
Dorothy Parker

Curt Riess
John Selby
A.P.
Lisa Sergio
K. Shridharani
Lyman Beecher Stowe
Arthur Szyk
Sigrid Undset
Walter White
  Exec. Secy., Natl. Assoc. for the Advancement of Colored People
Max Zaritsky
  President, United Hatters Union

Religion and Churches

Archbishop Athenagoras
  Greek Orthodox Church
Rabbi Philip David Bookstaber
  Former National Chaplain,
  Jewish War Veterans
Rabbi Aaron Decter
  Philadelphia

Rev. Charles A. McAlpine
Rabbi Harold Mashioff
Michael Potter
Rt. Rev. Henry St. George Tucker
  Presiding Bishop, Episcopal Church
Bishop Herbert Welch

Appendix I

The Proclamation
(with a free translation)
Issued by the Irgun then headed by Menachem Begin,
in June 1944, to the Arab Population of the Land
called Palestine.

רה כך

الى جيراننا العرب !

لذ ان الشعب العبري ...
ان الحركة العسكرية الوطنية العبرية ... في وفلسطين ... من جنوب
ا... بالسلام الحديث عازب المكومة المالئة المكومة التي ...
هائمة على ساد الشعب العبري العظيم الخالد.
ان شعب العرب حرب الوطن ... الآن في ... امره ولكنا ...
وتعلم من حين ال ال اخر روما روما.

يا ايها الجيران العرب ! ... غلف العرب ... شعب ... ايا لانا لا
... ايضا ان ... من زلزال كبيرين ... لا ان اي هذه البلاد
لاعلان لو طردتم من اراضيكم ومن هذه البلاد بما سكنوت.
ان فلسطين موطن بكم ايضا بل ولاولادكم وحدكم وللاجين من اخوانا
اليهود الطرودين في الجم الاراضي ولا يجدون المياة الا في هذه البلاد.

اعطوا ايها الجيران ! ... المكومة العبرية فيه تمكن الماوة
... المدنية وتكون ... سلمى ... النابة ... جول ... العكومية ال...
وتكون الاماكن المقدسة ... تحت ... المكومة العبرية
جامع اكتناب العلم والثقافة ولا يكون اي في بلاد الكتاب النفس ولا...
الاخرى ال معكم وسترم ايره علاج كل درجة انابية وتعلم زراعتكم
وستعكم وسيود ... جا من خيام ... وستكون لنا وانا ال ...
...

يا ايها الجيران العرب ! ان المكومة المالئة لن ترض بكل هذا وانا
زد التمرين ... زد المكومة جعل ... ينا وضعينا ... ان تكون هي
هي سلط ... وتملكن ... في البيء ... وهي ... ونيد اخوتنا
اليهود. في هذات العلا والورود.

انا ان نسمع ولا نقت النظرة لابال المكومة وقد ... المكومة باماننا ... هذ
... وام انة العربية واحطنا عطة ... المركزية بالرغم من كونها بالعرب بن عطة البرلس
وام عنك لاجل رام ال ... وقد ... مرين في ... وما ايضا ل ... نشكل
وقد عينا على مدينة القدس ولى حبا وام ... زرع ... ضد السكان العرب ايضا.
لهذ طريقنا الان ول السعيل ال شا ان.

... فاعتبروا ايها العرب من الاسئة ال المهربين لا تضلوا ...
اليهود ولا تهبوا اموالهم لانكم اذا رفتم ... على اليهود نحطم
قطع عنه اليد وسطة سلاحنا ونظن انكم تحتتم جهة جهة ال اسلامكم
ما هي قوة الشباب العبري الخالد.

... اعلم ال ما غنا لكم سيبرود السلام والسكون بن الحسين ال الاب
...سنى ... هذه البلاد المنسة ... ما انقرها وتعمل في جمع غزورها ومن
زراعتنا وصناعتا وتقدم ح ... جيع الامر وكما ... سهيدة ال هذه البلاد
نمره لهذا المرء وللاخوة.

يا ايها العرب انا لنه اليكم يد السلام والاخوة الواهبة!

الحركة العسكرية الوطنية العبرية

562

This war that we are waging is not aimed against you. We do not consider you enemies—we want to see you as good neighbors. We do not come to annihilate you or to drive you off this land, the land that you are now living on. In Eretz Israel there is enough room for you also and also also for your children and grandchildren and also for the millions of Jews who have no other raison-d'etre.

The Hebrew government will give you full, equal rights. Hebrew and Arabic will be the two recognized languages. There will be no discrimination between Jew and Arab in government positions or communal employment. The Holy places of the Arabs will be under their jurisdiction.

The Hebrew government will make it possible for you to gain education and there will not be any discrimination in the land of the Bible. There will not be any exclusion in your villages and cities. Wages for employees will reach the scale of European counterparts. There will be a great development in your agricultural undertakings. You will build houses where now you have tents. The electric development will reach into every one of your settlements. The Hebrew government will be a partnership house to all of us and peace will reign and a good neighborly relationship which can include the neighboring Arab countries.

It depends upon you and your consideration. If you agree and you will not listen to the agitators, peace and tranquility will result between our two nations forever. Together we will build this Holy Land; together we will reap its treasures and fruits; together we will develop agricultural and industrial aims. We will meet with all the freedom-loving countries of the world in order to live with justice and freedom for a prosperous and honorable life.

Our Arab neighbors!—we stretch out our hand to you in peace and brotherly love—Do not discard it!!

Appendix J
Letter of
Senator Guy M. Gillette, President of the ALFP,
appealing to Dr. Chaim Weizmann to form a Provisional
Government of the Hebrew Republic of Palestine.

December 10, 1946

Dr. Chaim Weizmann,
President of the World Zionist Organization,
Care of The World Zionist Congress,
Basle, Switzerland

Dear Dr. Weizmann:

Permit me on this fiftieth anniversary of Zionism to extend to you and to the World Zionist Congress the greetings of the American League for a Free Palestine and to express the appreciation of the civilized world for the achievements of your organization. At the same time may I venture to suggest that the moment has arrived to bring to a conclusion the present phase of Zionism as embodied in the World Zionist Organization and take the next and inevitable step in the fight for Israel's freedom.

It is in no sense an adverse reflection upon the leadership of the Zionist movement during all these years but on the contrary it is a tribute thereto that Zionism has reached the point where it should enlarge the scope of its activities.

It was indeed a master stroke to conceive of a World Zionist Congress whose primary purpose it should be to awaken the conscience of the nations to the plight of Jews everywhere. The noble purposes of Zionism have, without question, quickened the sensitiveness of the modern world to the tragic history of the Jewish people. So successfully has this been brought about that concrete political action is now indicated. Accordingly, with the greatest respect, I offer the following suggestions:

(1) That the Twenty-second World Zionist Congress proclaim that the aim of Zionism has been attained and that the existence of the Hebrew Republic of Palestine is now a fact and that accordingly a new

governmental structure should replace that of the present World Zionist Organization, the Jewish Agency for Palestine, and the World Jewish Congress.

(2) That those members of the Zionist Congress who are eligible to serve in a provisional government of the Hebrew Republic of Palestine immediately dedicate themselves to the formation of such a government. That government could assume all the functions of government as practiced during the war by the various exile regimes; but its provisional nature must be emphasized since its function will end with the early establishment of a duly elected constitutional government which would grant the fullest equality of right to all its citizens irrespective of creed or national derivation.

The Jewish Agency for Palestine would, of course, hand over to the Provisional Government all its prerogatives and assets, as would the Hebrew Committee of National Liberation, and the Zionist movement, reorganized on a non-sectarian basis, would pledge and give maximum assistance to the Provisional Government. The present Zionist Congress could thus announce the fulfillment of its mission, that it would be the last of its kind since further such congresses would not only be futile but would perpetuate the abnormal ghetto existence of the Jews which Zionism sought to eliminate.

Of course, leaders of the Zionist movement such as yourself, Dr. Silver, and others who are British or American citizens would not necessarily be excluded from personal participation in the government if they are called upon and willing to serve. They would, however, necessarily have to terminate their allegiance to their respective countries and identify themselves with the Hebrew nation.

That the members of the Congress, as men of good will, pledge themselves to the support of those valiant patriots who are now fighting so heroically to drive the aggressor from their country.

As you know, the tentative proposal to effect a provisional government now being drafted by the Hebrew Committee of National Liberation meets with the complete approval of the American League for a Free Palestine, of which I have the honor to be President.

There are, as you will recognize, historic precedents for the above Plan originally suggested by the Palestine Resistance. You will immediately recall the Brooklyn-born De Valera who expatriated himself to join in the fight for Irish freedom. We here have in mind the Americans of Czech ancestry who gave up their citizenship to participate in the provisional government of Czechoslovakia when formed in Pittsburgh. Of course we all recall a period in the history of my country when large numbers of patriots were impelled to renounce their former political allegiance in their devotion to the ideal of liberty.

Surely the Hebrew people in their desperate struggle have every right to look to you and your colleagues for that moral and spiritual assistance which is so necessary in a battle against an unscrupulous adversary with vastly superior material strength. I, on my part, am doing everything possible to mobilize my countrymen, Jews and non-Jews alike, to that end. I am confident that nothing could so reinforce the determination of the Hebrew people at this time as a solid front in the great democracies of the world in their behalf.

I should be most grateful if you would have these proposals presented before the Congress regardless of your personal reaction to them. I pray that the Almighty may give the delegates the wisdom and the courage necessary to undertake this drastic action. There comes a time when it is no longer virtuous to exercise limitless patience. Indeed it is immoral when it is exercised at the expense of so much suffering by others.

We of the American League for a Free Palestine pledge our total strength and complete support to the Provisional Government of the Hebrew Republic of Palestine once established and should be most happy to join hands with a reorganized non-sectarian Zionist Organization in an all-out effort to end the world's ignoble tragedy of its sins against the glorious ancient Hebrew people.

With every good wish, I am,

Faithfully yours,

Guy M. Gillette
President

Appendix K

"Liberal" America Welcome to Menahem Begin

(The N.Y. Times, November 29, 1948, Letters to the Editor)

The text of the open letter, sent on the eve of a dinner (11/29/48) at the Hotel Waldorf-Astoria in New York:

We have seen your name listed on the reception committee for Mr. Menachem Begin, leader of the Irgun Zvai Leumi. We assume that you are interested, as we are, in the advancement of peace, the strengthening of the United Nations, and American support of humanistic, as opposed to totalitarian elements everywhere.

Therefore, we wonder whether you are fully informed on the career of the man and the organization to which you have lent the backing of your name.

It is one thing to support Jewish immigration and settlement in Palestine. It is one thing to support a humanitarian movement to aid refugees. It is quite another thing to support a terroristic band, whose acts have horrified supporters of Zionism and have been repudiated by the authorities of Israel.

Do you know that Mr. Begin's terrorists were responsible for the bombing of the King David Hotel? Do you know that they kidnapped and garrotted two British sergeants and booby-trapped their bodies?

Do you know that Irgun forces, in an act of calculated terrorism, massacred 250 inhabitants, women and children included, of the village of Deir Yassin? Do you know that as a result of this and similar horrors there are now almost half a million refugees from the fighting in Palestine, scores of whom die daily from exposure and hunger?

Do you know that Mr. Begin and his followers assert their intention of flouting the United Nations by conquering not only all of Palestine but Trans-Jordan and other Arab territories as well?

Do you know that this program runs counter to United States

policy, and to the positions taken by the Republican and Democratic party conventions?

Finally, do you know that the Irgun, here masquerading under the front of "democracy," is in fact a totalitarian-minded group, as reactionary as the fanatical Moslem Brotherhood? And that it uses the funds it gets from gullible Americans to buy arms from Soviet Russia?

You owe it to yourself and to your fellow-citizens to investigate the true record of Mr. Begin and his Irgun—and, having investigated, to withdraw your support as publicly as it was pledged.

We trust that you will favor this communication with a reply.

(Signed)—The Rev. Dr. Henry Sloane Coffin of Lakeville, Conn., former president of Union Theological Seminary and former moderator of the Presbyterian Church in the United States, Father John La Farge of New York, well known Catholic editor, and Rabbi Morris Lazaron of Baltimore, member of the Central Conference of American Rabbis and a director of the American Association for the United Nations.

Appendix L

The Jewish "Establishment" Followed Suit

(The N.Y. Times, December 4, 1948, Letters to the Editor)

New Palestine Party

*Visit of Menahem Begin and Aims of
Political Movement Discussed*

To the Editor of The New York Times:

Among the most disturbing political phenomena of our time is the emergence in the newly created state of Israel of the "Freedom Party" (Tenuat Haherut), a political party closely akin in its organization, methods, political philosophy and social appeal to the Nazi and Fascist parties. It was formed out of the membership and following of the former Irgun Zvai Leumi, a terrorist, right-wing, chauvinist organization in Palestine.

The current visit of Menachem Begin, leader of this party, to the United States is obviously calculated to give the impression of American support for his party in the coming Israeli elections, and to cement political ties with conservative Zionist elements in the United States. Several Americans of national repute have lent their names to welcome his visit. It is inconceivable that those who oppose fascism throughout the world, if correctly informed as to Mr. Begin's political record and perspectives, could add their names and support to the movement he represents.

Before irreparable damage is done by way of financial contributions, public manifestations in Begin's behalf, and the creation in Palestine of the impression that a large segment of America supports *Fascist elements in Israel*, the American public must be informed as to the record and objectives of Mr. Begin and his movement.

The public avowals of Begin's party are no guide whatever to its actual character. Today they speak of freedom, democracy and anti-imperialism, whereas until recently *they openly preached the doctrine of the Fascist state*. It is in its actions that the terrorist party betrays its real character; from its past actions we judge what it may be expected to do in the future.

Attack on Arab Village

A shocking example was their behavior in the Arab village of Deir Yassin. This village, *off the main roads* and surrounded by Jewish lands, *had taken no part in the war*, and had even fought off Arab bands who wanted to use the village as their base. On April 9 (The New York Times), *terrorist bands attacked this peaceful village*, which was not a military objective in the fighting, killed most of its inhabitants—240 men, women and children—and *kept a few of them alive to parade as captives* through the streets of Jerusalem. Most of the Jewish community was horrified at the deed, and the Jewish Agency sent a telegram of apology to King Abdullah of Trans-Jordan.

But the terrorists, far from being ashamed of their act, *were proud of this massacre, publicized it, widely, and invited all the foreign correspondents present in the country to view the heaped corpses and the general havoc at Deir Yassin.*

The Deir Yassin incident exemplifies the character and actions of the Freedom Party.

Within the Jewish community they have preached an admixture of ultra-nationalism, religious mysticism, and racial superiority. Like other Fascist parties they have been used to break strikes, and have themselves pressed for the destruction of free trade unions. In their stead they have proposed corporate unions on the Italian Fascist model.

During the last years of sporadic anti-British violence, the IZL and Stern groups *inaugurated a reign of terror in the Palestine Jewish community*. Teachers were beaten up for speaking against them, adults were shot for not letting their children join them. By gangster methods, beatings, window-smashing, and wide-spread robberies, the terrorists intimidated the population and exacted a heavy tribute.

The people of the Freedom Party have had *no part in the constructive achievements in Palestine*. They have reclaimed no land, built no settlements, and only detracted from the Jewish defense activity. *Their much-publicized immigration endeavors were minute, and devoted mainly to bringing in Fascist compatriots.*

Discrepancies Seen

The discrepancies between the bold claims now being made by Begin and his party, and their record of past performance in Palestine bear the imprint of no ordinary political party. This is the unmistakable stamp of a Fascist party for whom terrorism (against Jews, Arabs, and British alike), and misrepresentation are means, and a "Leader State" is the goal.

In the light of the foregoing considerations, it is imperative that the truth about Mr. Begin and his movement be made known in this country. It is all the more tragic that the top leadership of American Zionism has refused to campaign against Begin's efforts, or even to expose to its own constituents the dangers to Israel from support to Begin.

The undersigned therefore take this means of publicly presenting a few salient facts concerning Begin and his party; and of urging all concerned not to support this latest manifestation of fascism.

Isidore Abramowitz, Hannah Arendt, Abraham Brick, Rabbi Jessurun Cardozo, Albert Einstein, Herman Eisen, M.D., Hayim Fineman, M. Gallen, M.D., H. H. Harris, Zelig S. Harris, Sidney Hook, Fred Kabush, Bruria Kaufman, Irma L. Lindheim, Nachman Majsel, Seymour Melman, Myer D. Mendelson, M.D., Harry M. Orlinsky, Samuel Pitlick, Fritz Rohrlich, Louis P. Rocker, Ruth Sager, Itzhak Sankowsky, I. J. Schoenberg, Samuel Shuman, M. Unger, Irma Wolpe, Stepan Wolfe.

New York, Dec. 2, 1948.

---

[1]Note: Emphasis added throughout—Ed.

Appendix M
American League Supporting Irgun
Dissolved Here
(From the N.Y. World Telegram, 11/30/48)

Announcement of dissolution of the American League for a Free Palestine was made today.

Mr. Begin, who plans to oppose Premier David Ben-Gurion in the forthcoming Israeli elections, was greeted by former Rep. William S. Bennet, past vice president of the Sons of the American Revolution; Paul O'Dwyer, brother of the Mayor; Arthur Szyk, the cartoonist, and Frank Kingdon, the columnist.

Announcement of the end of the American league, which has been bitterly opposed by leading Zionist groups and condemned by the British government, came last night.

Ben Hecht, co-chairman, told 1200 guests at a dinner in the Waldorf-Astoria Hotel, at which Mr. Begin was guest of honor, that the league's job was done, adding its story "ends at least as nicely as a Jewish story can end.

"Against the calumny of its own people," Mr. Hecht said, *"against the pitiless skulduggeries of British propaganda and against the thousand-to-one power of the British army, Irgun fought for the right of Jews to strike back at their destroyers and oppressors."*

Appendix N

Report to the Secretary of the Treasury on the Acquiescence of this Government in the Murder of the Jews.[1,2]

January 13, 1944

One of the greatest crimes in history, the slaughter of the Jewish people in Europe, is continuing unabated.

This Government has for a long time maintained that its policy is to work out programs to save those Jews of Europe who could be saved.

I am convinced on the basis of the information which is available to me that certain officials in our State Department, which is charged with carrying out this policy, have been guilty not only of gross procrastination and wilful failure to act, but even of wilful attempts to prevent action from being taken to rescue Jews from Hitler.

I fully recognize the graveness of this statement and I make it only after having most carefully weighed the shocking facts which have come to my attention during the last several months.

Unless remedial steps of a drastic nature are taken, and taken immediately, I am certain that no effective action will be taken by this Government to prevent the complete extermination of the Jews in German controlled Europe, and that this Government will have to share for all time responsibility for this extermination.

---

[1] Excerpted from a report to Treasury Secretary Henry Morgenthau, Jr., prepared by Josiah DuBois Jr., in collaboration with the Treasury's General Counsel Randolph Paul and Foreign Funds Division Chief John Pehle. Secretary Morgenthau presented his own version of a memorandum, culled mostly from the DuBois document, to F.D.R. on January 16, 1944. Five days later, and only a few days before the Senate was to vote on the U.S. Senate Resolution 203 (Gillette-Rogers), F.D.R. created, by executive order, the War Refugee Board. Josiah DuBois stated later that he advised the Secretary that if the report is not presented to F.D.R. and acted upon, he will resign and make it public.
[2] Emphasis added throughout.

The traic history of this Government's handling of this matter reveals that certain State Department officials are guilty of the following:

(1) They have not only failed to use the *Governmental machinery* at their disposal to rescue Jews from Hitler, but thave even gone so far as to use this Governmental machinery to prevent the resue of these Jews.

(2) They have not only failed to cooperate with *private organizations* in the efforts of these organizations to work out individual programs of their own, but have taken steps designed to prevent these programs from being put into effect.

(3) They not only have failed to facilitate the obtaining of information concerning Hitler's plans to exterminate the Jews of Europe but in their official capacity have gone so far as to surreptitiously attempt to stop the obtaining of information concerning the murder of the Jewish population·of Europe.

(4) They have tried to cover up their guilt by:

(a) concealment and misrepresentation;

(b) the giving of false and misleading explanations for their failures to act and their attempts to prevent action;

(c) the issuance of false and misleading statements concerning the "action" which they have taken to date.

Although only part of the facts relating to the activities of the State Department in this field are available to us, sufficient facts have come to my attention from various sources during the last *several months* to fully support the conclusions at which I have arrived.

(1) *State Department officials have not only failed to use the Governmental machinery at their disposal to rescue the Jews from Hitler, but have even gone so far as to use this Government machinery to prevent the rescue of these Jews.*

The public record, let alone the facts which have not as yet been made public, reveals the gross *procrastination and wilful failure to act* of these officials actively representing this Government in this field.

(a) A long time has passed since it became clear that Hitler was determined to carry out a poliy of exterminating the Jews in Europe.

(b) Over a year has elapsed since this Government and other members of the United Nations publicly acknowledged and dennounced this policy of extermination; and since the President got assurances that the United States would make every effort together with the United Nations to save those who could be saved.

(c) Despite the fact that time is most precious in this matter, State Department officials have been kicking the matter around for over a year without producing results; giving all sorts of excuses for delays upon delays; advancing no specific proposals designed to rescue Jews, at the same time proposing that the whole refugee problem be "explored" by this Government and Intergovernmental Committees. While the State Department has been thus "*exploring*" the whole refugee problem, without distinguishing between those who are in imminent danger of death and those who are not, hundreds of thousands of Jews *have been allowed* to perish.

As early as August 1942 a message from the Secretary of the World Jewish Congress in Switzerland (Riegner), transmitted through the British Foreign Office, reported that Hitler had under consideration a plan to exterminate all Jews in German controlled Europe. By November 1942 sufficient evidence had been received, including substantial documentary evidence transmitted through our Legation in Switzerland, to confirm that Hitler had actually adopted and was carrying out his plan to exterminate the Jews. Sumner Welles accordingly authorized the Jewish organizations to make the facts public.

Thereupon, the Jewish organizations took the necessary stand to bring the shocking facts to the attention of the public thrugh mass meetings, etc., and to elicit public support for governmental action. On December 17, 1942, a joint statement of the United States and the European members of the United Nations was issued calling attention to and denouncing the fact that Hitler was carrying into effect his oft-repeated intention to exterminate the Jewish people in Europe.

Since the time when this Government knew that the Jews were being murdered, our State Department had failed to take any positive steps reasonably calculated to save any of these people. Although State has used the devices of setting up inter-governmental organizations to survey the whole refugee problem, and calling conferences such as the Bermuda Conference to explore the whole refugee problem, making it appear that *positive action* could be *expected*, in fact *nothing* has been accomplished.

Before the outcome of the Bermuda Conference, which was held in April 1943, was made public, *Senator Langer* prophetically stated in an address in the Senate on October 6, 1943:

"As yet we have had no report from the Bermuda Refugee Conference. With the best good will in the world and with all latitude that could and should be accorded to diplomatic negotiations in time of war, I may be permitted to voice the bitter suspicion that the absence of a report indicates only one thing—the lack of action.

"Probably in all 5703 years, Jews have hardly had a time as tragic and hopeless as the one which they are undergoing now. One of the most tragic factors about the situation is that while singled out for suffering and martyrdom by their enemies, they seem to have been forgotten by the nations which claim to fight for the cause of humanity. We should remember the Jewish slaughterhouse of Europe and ask what is being done—and I emphasize the word 'done'—to get some of these suffering human beings out fo the slaughter while yet alive.

". . . Perhaps it would be necessary to introduce a formal resolution or to ask the Secretary of State to report to an appropriate congressional committee on the steps being taken in this connection. Normally it would have been the job of the Government to show itself alert to this tragedy; but when a government neglects a duty it is the job of the legislature in a democracy to remind it of that duty. . . . It is not important who voices a call for action, and it is not important what procedure is being used in order to get action. It is important that action be undertaken."

Similar fears were voiced by *Representatives Celler, Dickstein, and Klein. Senator Wagner* and *Representative Sadowski* also issued calls for *action.*

The widespread fears concerning the failure of the Bermuda Conference were fully confirmed when Breckinridge Long finally revealed some of the things that had happened at that Conference in his statement before the Committee on Foreign Affiairs of the House on November 26, 1943.

After Long's "disclosure" *Representative Celler* stated in the House on December 20, 1943:

"He discloses some of the things that happened at the so-called Bermuda Conference. He thought he was telling us something heretofore unknown and secret. What happened at the Bermuda Conference could not be kept executive. All the recommendations and findings of the Bermuda Conference were made known to the Intergovernmental Committee on Refugees in existence since the Evian Conference on Refugees in 1938 and which has been functioning all this time in London. How much has that committee accomplished in the years of its being. It will be remembered that the Intergovernmental Committee functions through an executive committee composed of six countries, the United States, the United Kingdom, the Netherlands, France, Brazil, and Argentina. True, no report of the Bermuda Conference was made public. But a strangely ironical fact will be noted in the presence of Argentina on this most trusted of committees, Argentina that provoked the official reprimand of President Roosevelt by its banning of the Jewish Press, and within whose borders Nazi propagandists and falangists now enjoy a Roman holiday. I contend that by the very nature of its composition the Intergovernmental Committee on Refugees cannot function successfully as the instrumentality to rescue the Jewish people of Europe. The benefits to be derived from the Bermuda Conference like those of the previous Evian Conference can fit into a tiny capsule."

One of the best summaries of the whole situation is contained in one sentence of a report submitted on *December 20, 1943*, by the Committee on Foreign Relations of the Senate, recommending the passage of a Resolution (S.R. 203) favoring the appointment of a commission to formulate plans to save the Jews of Europe from extinction by Nazi Germany. The Committee stated:

"We have talked; we have sympathized; we have expressed our horror; the time to act is long past due."

The Senate Resolution had been introduced by Senator Guy M. Gillette in behalf of himself and eleven colleagues, Senators Taft,

Thomas, Radcliffe, Murray, Johnson, Guffey, Ferguson, Clark, Van Nuys, Downey and Ellender.

The House Resolutions (H.R.'s 350 and 352), identical with the Senate Resolution, were introduced by Representatives Baldwin and Rogers.

The most glaring example of the use of the machinery of this Government to *actually prevent the rescue of Jews* is the administrative restrictions which have been placed upon the granting of visas to the United States. In the note which the State Department sent to the British on February 25, 1943, it was stated:

"Since the entry of the United States into the war there have been no new restrictions placed by the Government of the United States upon the number of aliens of any nationality permitted to proceed to this country under existing laws, *except for the more intensive examination of aliens required for security reasons.*"

The exception "for security reasons" mentioned in this note is the joker. Under the pretext of security reasons so many difficulties have been placed in the way of refugees obtaining visas that it is no wonder that the admission of refugees to this country does not come anywhere near the quota, despite Long's statement designed to create the impression to the contrary. The following *administrative* restrictions which have been applied to the issuance of visas since the beginning of the war are typical.

(a) Many applications for visas have been denied on the grounds that the applicants have close relatives in Axis controlled Europe. The theory of this is that the enemy would be able to put pressure on the applicant as a result of the fact that the enemy has the power of life or death over his immediate family.

(b) Another restriction greatly increases the red tape and delay involved in getting the visa and requires among other things two affidavits of support and sponsorship to be furnished with each application for a visa. To each affidavit of suport and sponsorship there must be attached two letters of reference from two reputable American citizens.

If anyone were to attempt to work out a set of restrictions specifically designed to prevent Jewish refugees from entering this country it is difficult to conceive of how more effective restrictions could have been imposed than have already been imposed on grounds of "security".

It is obvious of course that these restrictions are not essential for security reasons. Thus refugees upon arriving in this country could be placed in internment camps similar to those used for the Japanese on the West Coast and released only after a satisfactory investigation. Furthermore, *even if we took these refugees and treated them as prisoners of war, it would be better than letting them die.*

Representative Dickstein stated in the House on December 15:

"If we consider the fact that the average admission would then be at the rate of less than 88,000 per year, it is clear that the organs of our

Government have not done their duty. The existing quotas call for the admission of more than 150,000 every year, so that if the quotas themselves had been filled there would have been a total of one-half million and not 560,000 during the period mentioned.

"But that is not the whole story. There was no effort of any kind made to save from death many of the refugees who could have been saved during the time that transportation lines were available and there was no obstacle to their admission to the United States. But the obstructive policy of our organs of Government, particularly the State Department, which saw fit to hedge itself about with rules and regulations, instead of lifting rules and regulations, brought about a condition so that not even the existing immigration quotas are filled."

Representative Celler stated in the House on June 30:

"Mr. Speaker, nations have declared war on Germany, and their high-ranking officials have issued pious protestations against the Nazi massacre of Jewish victims, but not one of those countries thus far has said they would be willing to accept these refugees either permanently or as visitors, or any of the minority peoples trying to escape the Hitler prison and slaughterhouse.

"Goebbels says: 'The United Nations won't take any Jews. We don't want them. Let's kill them.' And so he and Hitler are making Europe Judenrein.

"Without any change in our immigration statutes we could receive a reasonable number of those who are fortunate enough to escape the Nazi hellhole, receive them as visitors, the immigration quotas notwithstanding. They could be placed in camps or cantonments and held there in such havens until after the war. Private charitable agencies would be willing to pay the entire cost thereof. They would be no expense to the Government whatsoever. These agencies would even pay for transporation by ships to and from this country.

"We house and maintain Nazi prisoners, many of them undoubtedly responsible for Nazi atrocities. We should do no less for the victims of the rage of the Huns."

Again on December 28, he stated:

"According to Earl G. Harrison, Commissioner of Immigration and Naturalization Service, not since 1862 have there been fewer aliens entering the country.

(2) *State Department officials have not only failed to cooperate with private organizations in the efforts of those organizations to work out individual programs of their own, but have taken steps designed to prevent these programs from being put into effect.*

The best evidence in support of this charge are the facts relating to the proposal of the World Jewish Congress to evacuate thousands of Jews from Rumania and France. The highlights relating to the efforts of State Department officials to prevent this proposal from being put into effect are the following:

(a) *On March 13, 1943*, a cable was received from the World Jewish Congress representative in London stating that information reaching London indicated the possibility of rescuing Jews provided funds were put at the disposal of the World Jewish Congress representation in Switzerland.

(b) *On April 10, 1943*, Sumner Welles cabled our Legation in Bern and requested them to get in touch with the World Jewish Congress representative in Switzerland, whom Welles had been informed was in possession of important information regarding the situation of the Jews.

(c) *On April 20, 1943*, a cable was received from Bern relating to the proposed financial arrangements in connection with the evacuation of the Jews from Rumania and France.

(d) *On May 25, 1943*, State Department cabled for a clarification of these proposed financial arrangements. This matter was not called to the attention of the Treasury Department at this time.

(e) This whole question of financing the evacuation of the Jews from Rumania and France was first called to the attention of the Treasury Department *on June 25, 1943.*

(f) A conference was held with the State Department relating to this matter *on July 15, 1943.*

(g) *One day after this conference, on July 16, 1943, the Treasury Department advised the State Department that it was prepared to issue a license in this matter.*

During this five months period between the time that the Treasury stated that it was prepared to issue a license and the time when the license was actually issued delays and objections of all sorts were forthcoming from officials in the State Department, our Lagation in Bern, and finally the British. The real significance of these delays and objections was brought home to the State Department in letters which you sent to Secretary Hull on November 23, 1943, and December 17, 1943, which completely devastated the "excuses" which State Department officials had been advancing. On December 18 you made an appointment to discuss the matter with Secretary Hull on December 20. And then an amazing but understandable thing happened. On December 18, the day on which you requested an appointment with Secretary Hull, the State Department sent a telegram to the British Foreign Office expressing astonishment with the British point of view and stating that the Department was unable to agree with that point of view (in simple terms, the British point of view referred to by the State Department is that they are apparently prepared to *accept the possible—even probable—death of thousands of Jews in enemy territory because of "the difficulties of disposing of any considerable number of Jews should they be rescued").* On the same day, the State Department issued a license notwithstanding the fact that the objections of our Legation in Bern were still outstanding and that British disapproval had already been expressed. State Department officials were in such a hurry to issue this license that they not only did not ask the Treasury to draft the license (which would have been the normal procedure) but they drafted the license themselves and issued it without even consulting the Treasury as to its terms. Informal discussions with certain State Department officials have confirmed what is obvious from the above mentioned facts.

Breckinridge Long knew that his position was so indefensible that he was unwilling to even try to defend it at your pending conference with Secretary Hull on December 20. Accordingly, he took such action as he felt was necessary to "cover up" his previous position in this matter.

(3) *State Department officials not only have failed to facilitate the obtaining of information concerning Hitler's plans to exterminate the Jews of Europe but in their official capacity have gone so far as to surreptitiously attempt to stop the obtaining of information concerning the murder of the Jewish population in Europe.*

The evidence supporting this conclusion is so shocking and so tragic that it is difficult to believe.

The facts are as follows:

(a) *Sumner Welles as Acting Secretary of State requests confirmation of Hitler's plan to exterminate the Jews.* Having already received various reports on the plight of the Jews, on *October 5, 1942,* Sumner Welles as Acting Secretary of State sent a cable (2314) for the personal attention of Minister Harrison in Bern stating that leaders of the Jewish Congress had received reports from their representatives in Geneva and London to the effect that many thousands of Jews in Eastern Europe were being slaughtered pursuant to a policy embarked upon by the German Government for the complete extermination of the Jews in Europe.

(b) *State Department received confirmation and shocking evidence that the extermination was being rapidly and effectively carried out.* Pursuant to Welles' cable of October 5 Minister Harrison forwarded documents from Riegner confirming the fact of extermination of the Jews (in November 1942), and in a cable of January 2 1943 (482) relayed a message from Riegner and Lichtheim which Harrison stated was for the information of the Under Secretary of State (and was to be transmitted to Rabbi Stephen Wise if the Under Secretary should so determine). *This message described a horrible situation concerning the plight of Jews in Europe.* It reported mass executions of Jews in Poland; according to one source *6,000 Jews were being killed daily;* the Jews were required before execution to strip themselves of all their clothing which was then sent to Germany; the remaining Jews in Poland were confined in Ghettos, etc.; in Germany deportations were continuing; many Jews were in hiding and there had been many cases of suicide; Jews were being deprived of rationed foodstuffs; no Jews would be left in Prague or Berlin by the end of March, etc.; and in Rumania 130,000 Jews were deported to Transnistria; about 60,000 had already died and the remaining 70,000 were starving; living conditions were indescribable; Jews were deprived of all their money, foodstuffs and possessions; they were housed in deserted cellars, and occasionally twenty to thirty people slept on the floor of one unheated room; disease was prevalent, particularly fever; urgent assistance was needed.

(c) *Sumner Welles furnishes this information to the Jewis organizations.* Sumner Welles furnished the documents received in November to the Jewish organizations in the United States and authorized them to make the facts public. On *February 9, 1943* Welles forwarded the horrible message contained in cable 482 of January 21 to Rabbi Stephen Wise. In his letter of February 9 Welles stated that he was pleased to be of assistance in this matter.

Immediately upon receipt of this message, the Jewish organizations arranged for a public mass meeting in Madison Square Garden in a further effort to obtain effective action.

(d) *Certain State Department officials surreptitiously attempt to stop this Government from obtaining further information from the very source from which the above evidence was received.* On February 10, the day after Welles forwarded the message contained in cable 482 of January 21 to Rabbi Wise, and in direct response to this cable, a most highly significant cable was dispatched. This cable, 354 of February 10, read as follows:

"Your 482, January 21

"In the future we would suggest that you do not accept reports submitted to you to be transmitted to private persons in the United States unless such action is advisable because of extraordinary circumstances. Such private messages circumvent neutral countries' censorship and it is felt that by sending them we risk the possibility that steps would necessarily be taken by the neutral countries to curtail or forbid our means of communication for confidential official matter.

Hull (SW)"

Although this cable on its face is mot innocent and innocuous, when read together with the previous cables I am forced to conclude it is nothing less than an attempted suppression of information requested by this Goverment concerning the murder of Jews by Hitler.

Although this cable was signed for Hull by "SW" (Sumner Welles) *it is significant that there is not a word in the cable that would even suggest to the person signing it that it was designed to countermand the Department's specific requests for information of Hitler's plans to exterminate the Jews.* The cable appeared to be a normal routine message which a busy official would sign without question.

I have been informed that the initialled file copy of the cable bears the initials of *Atherton* and *Dunn* as well as of *Durbrow* and *Hickerson*.

(e) Therefore Sumner Welles again requested our Legation on April 10, 1943 (cable 877) for information, apparently not realizing that in cable 354 (to which he did not refer) Harrison had been instructed to cease forwarding reports of this character. Harrison replied on April 20 (cable 2460) and indicated that he was in a most confused state of mind as a result of the conflicting instructions he had received. Among other things he stated: "May I suggest that messages of this character should not (repeat not) be subjected to the restriction imposed by your 354, February 10, and that I be permitted to transmit messages from R more particularly in view of the helpful information which they may frequently contain?"

The fact that cable 354 is not the innocent and routine cable that it appears to be on its face is further highlighted by the efforts of the State Department officials to prevent this Department from obtaining the cable and learning its true significance.

The facts relating to this attempted concealment are as follows:

(i) Several men in our Department had requested State Department officials for a copy of the cable of February 10 (354). We had been advised that it was a Department communication; a strictly political communication, which had nothing to do with economic matters; that it had only had a very limited distribution within the Department, the only ones having anything to do with it being the European Division, the Political Advisor and Sumner Welles; and that a *copy could not be furnished to the Treasury.*

(ii) At the conference in Secretary Hull's office on December 20 in the presence of Breckinridge Long you asked Secretary Hull for a copy of cable 354, which you were told would be furnished to you.

(iii) By note to you of December 20, Breckinridge Long enclosed a paraphrase of cable 354. This paraphrase of able 354 specifically *omitted any reference to cable 482 of January 21*—thus destroying the only tangible clue to the true meaning of the message.

(iv) You would never have learned the true meaning of cable 354 had it not been for the fact that one of the men in my office whom I had asked to obtain all the facts on this matter for me had previously called one of the men in another Division of the State Department and requested permission to see the cable. In view of the Treasury interest in this matter this State Department representative obtained cable 354 and the cable of January 21 to which it referred and showed these cables to my men.

(4) *The State Department officials have tried to cover up their guilt by:*

(a) *concealment and misrepresentatiion.*

In addition to concealing the true facts from and misrepresenting these facts to the public, State Department officials have even attempted concealment and misrepresentation within the Government. The most striking example of this is the above mentioned action taken by State Department officials to prevent this Department from obtaining a copy of cable 354 of February 10 (which stopped the obtaining of information concerning the murder of Jews); and the fact that after you had requested a copy of this cable, State Department officials forwarded the cable to us with its most significant part omitted, thus destroying the whole meaning of the cable.

(b) *the giving of false and misleading explanations for their failure to act and their attempts to prevent action.*

The outstanding explanation of a false and misleading nature which the State Department officials have given for their failure to work out programs to rescue Jews, and their attempts to prevent action, are the following:

(i) The nice sounding but vicious theory that the *whole* refugee problem must be explored and consideration given to working out programs for the relief of *all* refugees—thus failing to distinguish between *those refugees whose lives are in imminent danger* and those whose lives are not in imminent danger.

(ii) The argument that various proposals cannot be acted upon promptly by this Government but must be submitted to the Executive Committee of the Intergovernmental Committee on Refugees. This Committee has taken no effective action to actually evacuate refugees from enemy territory and it is at least open to doubt whether it has the necessary authority to deal with the matter.

(iii) The argument that the extreme restrictions which the State Department has placed on the granting of visas to refugees is necessary for "security reasons". The falsity of this argument has already been dealt with in this memorandum.

The false and misleading explanations, which the State Department officials gave for delaying for over six months the program of the World Jewish Congress for the evacuation of thousands of Jews from Rumania and France, are dealt with in your letter to Secretary Hull of December 17, 1943.

A striking example is the argument of the State Department officials that the proposed financial arrangements might benefit the enemy. . . .

In this particular case, the State Department officials attempted to argue that the relief plan might benefit the enemy by facilitating the acquisition of funds by the enemy. In addition to the fact that this contention had no merit whatsoever by virtue of the conditions under which the local funds were to be acquired, it is significant that this consideration had not been regarded as controlling in the past by the State Department officials, even where no such conditions had been imposed. Thus, in cases involving the purchase, by branches of United States concerns in Switzerland, of substantial amounts of material in enemy territory, State Department officials have argued that in view of generous credit supplied by the Swiss to the Germans "transactions of this type cannot be regarded as actually increasing the enemy's purchasing power in Switzerland which is already believed to be at a maximum". It is only when these State Department officials really desire to prevent a transaction that they advance economic warfare considerations as a bar.

(c) *the issuance of false and misleading statements concerning the* "action" which they have taken to date.

It is necessary to go beyond Long's testimony to find many examples of misstatements. His general pious remarkes concerning what this Government has done for the Jews of Europe; his statement concerning the powers and functions of the Intergovernmental Committee on Refugees; his reference to the "screening process" set up to insure wartime security, etc., have already been publicly criticized as misrepresentations.

A statement which is typical of the way Long twists facts is his remark concerning the plan of a Jewish agency to send money to Switzerland to be used through the International Red Cross to buy food to take care of Jews in parts of Czechoslovakia and Poland. Long indicates that the Jewish agency requested that the money be sent through the instrumentality of the Intergovernmental Committee. I am informed that the Jewish agency wished to send the money immediately to the International Red Cross and it was Long who took the position that the matter would have to go through the Intergovernmental Committee, thereby delaying the matter indefinitely. Long speaks of an application having been filed with the Treasury to send some of this money and that the State Department was supporting this application to the Treasury. The facts are that no application has ever been filed with the Treasury and the State Department has at no time indicated to the Treasury that it would support any such application.

The most patent instance of a false and misleading statement is that part of Breckinridge Long's testimony before the Committee on Foreign Affairs of the House (November 26, 1943) relating to the admittance of refugees into this country. Thus, he stated:

". . . We have taken into this country since the beginning of the Hitler regime and the persecution of the Jews, until today, approximately 580,000 refugees. The whole thing has been under the quota, during the period of 10 years—all under the quota—except the generous gesture we made with visitors' and transit visas during an awful period."

Congressman Emanuel Celler in commenting upon Long's statement in the House on December 20, 1943, stated:

". . . In the first place these 580,000 refugees were in the main ordinary quota immigrants coming in from all countries. The majority were *not* Jews. His statement drips with sympathy for the persecuted Jews, but the tears he sheds are crocodile. I would like to ask him how many Jews were admitted during the last 3 years in comparison with the number seeking entrance to preserve life and dignity. . . . One gets the impression from Long's statement that the United States has gone out of its way to help refugees fleeing death at the hands of the Nazis. I deny this. To the contrary, the State Department has turned its back on the time-honored principle of granting havens to refugees. . . . Long says that the door to the oppressed is open but that it 'has been carefully screened.' What he should have said is 'barlocked and bolted.' By the act of 1924, we are permitted to admit approximately 150,000 immigrants each year.

During the last fiscal year only 23,725 came as immigrants. Of these *only 4,705 were Jews* fleeing Nazi persecution. . . .

"If men of the temperament and philosophy of Long continue in control of immigration administration, we may as well take down that plaque from the Statute of Liberty and black out the 'lamp beside the golden door.'"

(signed) R. R. P.

Selected Bibliography

Abel, Ernest L.: *The Roots of Anti-Semitism*. Farleigh Dickinson University Press, New Jersey, 1975.

Ahimeir, Abba: *Selected Writings*. 4 vols. Ahimeir Publishing Committee, Tel-Aviv, 1974 (Heb.).

Amitzur, Ilan: *America, Britain and Palestine*. Yad Izhak Ben-Zvi Publications, Jerusalem, 1979 (Heb.).

Antonius, George: *The Arab Awakening: The Story of the Arab National Movement*. G. P. Putnam's Sons, New York, 1946.

Arendt, Hannah: *Eichmann in Jerusalem*. Penguin Books, New York, 1977.

Bein, Alex: *Theodor Herzl*. Jewish Publication Society, Philadelphia, 1951.

Begin, Menachem: *The Revolt*. Story of the Irgun. Henry Schumann, New York, 1951.

Beit-Zvi, S. B.: *Post-Ugandian Zionism in the Crucible of the Holocaust*. Bronfman Publishers, Tel-Aviv, 1977 (Heb.).

Ben Elissar, Eliahu: *Diplomacy of the Third Reich and the Jews, 1933-1939*. Edanim Publishers, Jerusalem, 1978 (Heb.).

Ben-Gurion, David: *We and Our Neighbors*. Davar Press, Tel-Aviv, 1931.

———, *Memoirs*. The World Publishing Co., New York, 1970.

Ben-Zvi, Izhak: *Eretz-Israel Under Ottoman Rule*. Bialik Institute, Jerusalem, 1962 (Heb.).

Blum, John Morton: *The Morgenthau Diaries, Years of War (1941-1945)*, Houghton Mifflin Co., Boston, 1967.

Briscoe, Robert: *For the Life of Me*. Little Brown and Co., Boston, 1958.

Canaan, Haviv: *Gallows in Nathania*. (The Hanging of the Two British Sergeants.) Hadar, Tel-Aviv, 1976 (Heb.).

Cohen, Geula: *Woman of Violence*. Memoirs of a Young Terrorist, 1943-1948. Rupert Hart-Davis, London, 1966.

Crum, Bartley C.: *Behind the Silken Curtain: A Personal Account of Anglo-American Diplomacy in Palestine and the Middle East.* Simon & Schuster, New York, 1947.

DeHaas, Jacob: *History of Palestine.* MacMillan, New York, 1934.

Documents on German Foreign Policy 1918-1945. Series D vol. VI. The Last Months of Peace, March-August 1939. London, Her Majesty's Stationery Office, 1956.

Documents on the Holocaust. (Selected Sources on the Destruction of the Jews of Germany and Austria, Poland and the Soviet Union.) Yad Vashem, Jerusalem, 1978. (Documents translated into Hebrew.)

Druks, Herbert: *The Failure to Rescue.* Robert Speller & Sons Publishers, Inc., New York, 1977.

———, *The United States and Israel, 1945-1973.* Robert Speller & Sons Publishers, Inc., New York, 1979.

Dubois, Josiah E. Jr.: *The Devil's Chemists.* Beacon Press, Boston, 1952.

Eldad, Israel: *Maaser Rishon.* Hadar Publishing Corp., Tel-Aviv, 1975 (Heb.).

Feingold, Henry L.: *The Politics of Resue.* Rutgers University Press, New Brunswick, New Jersey, 1970.

Friedman, Saul S.: *No Haven for the Oppressed.* Wayne State University Press, Detroit, 1972.

Gilbert, Martin: *Auschwitz and Allies.* Holt, Rinehart & Winston, New York, 1981.

———, *Exile and Return: The Struggle for a Jewish Homeland.* London, 1978.

Gilead, Haim: *Under the Shadow of the Gallows.* Hadar Publishing Corp., Tel-Aviv, 1978 (Heb.).

Gitlin, Jan: *The Conquest of Acre Fortress.* Hadar Publishing Corp., Tel-Aviv, 1974.

Gurion, Itzhak: *Triumph on the Gallows.* Brit Trumpeldor of America, 1950.

Haber, Eitan: *Menahem Begin, the Legend and the Man.* Delacorte Press, New York, 1978.

Hanna, Paul A: *British Policy in Palestine. American Council on Public Affairs*, Washington, 1942.

Hecht, Ben: *Child of the Century.* The New American Library (Simon & Schuster). New York, 1954.

———*Perfidy.* Julian Messner, Inc., New York, 1961.

Herzl, Theodor: *The Jewish State.* Herzl Press, New York, 1970.

Hess, Moses: *Rome and Jerusalem.* Bloch Publishing Co., New York, 1945.

Hilberg, Raul: *The Destruction of European Jews.* Quadrangle Books, Inc., Harper & Row, New York, 1961.

Hirschler, Gertrude and Eckman, Lester S. *Menahem Begin.* Shengold

Publishers, Inc., 1979.

Jabotinsky, Eri: *My Father, Zeev Jabotinsky.* Steimatzky's Agency, Ltd., Tel-Aviv, 1980 (Heb.).

Jabotinsky, Zeev (Vladimir): *The Collected Writings.* 13 vols. Eri Jabotinsky Publisher, Tel-Aviv, 1958 (Heb.).

————, *Prelude to Delilah.* Jabotinsky Foundation, New York, 1945.

————, *The War and the Jew.* Dial Press, New York, 1942.

Katz, Doris: *The lady was a Terrorist.* Shiloni Publishers, New York, 1953.

Katz, Samuel: *Days of Fire.* W. H. Allen, London, 1968.

Kelly, J. B.: *Arabia, the Gulf and the West.* Basic Books, Inc., New York, 1980.

Knee, Stuart E., *The Concept of Zionist Dissent in the American Mind, 1917-1941.* Robert Speller & Sons Publishers, New York, 1979.

Koestler, Arthur: *Promise and Fulfilment: Palestine 1917-1949.* MacMillan, London and New York, 1949.

————, *Thieves in the Night: Chronicle of an Experiment.* MacMillan, London and New York, 1946.

Lankin, Eliahu: The *Story of Altalena.* Hadar Publishing Corp., Tel-Aviv, 1967 (Heb.).

Lazar, Haim (Litai): *Af Al Pi.* Jabotinsky Institue, Tel-Aviv, 1957 (Heb.).

Levine, Nora: *The Holocaust.* Thomas Y. Crowell Co., New York, 1968.

Manuel, Frank E.: *The Realities of the American-Palestine Relations.* Public Affairs Press, Washington, D. C., 1949.

Mark, Ber: *Uprising in the Warsaw Ghetto.* Schocken Books, New York, 1975.

Meridor, Yaakov: *Long is the Road to Freedom.* Achiasf, Jerusalem, 1950 (Heb.).

Mery, Jacques: *Laissez Passer Mon Peuple* (The Story of the S.S. Ben Hecht). Editiones de Seuil, Paris. 1974.

Morse, Arthur D.: *While 6,000,000 Million Died.* Ace Publishing Corp., New York, 1968.

Mosse, George L. *Toward the Final Solution.* Howard Fertig, New York, 1978.

Nakdimon, Shlomo: *Altalena.* Edanim Publishing, Jerusalem, 1978 (Heb.).

Nordau, Max: *Collections of Addresses to Zionists and Congresses.* Scopus Publishers, Inc., New York, 1941.

Niv, David: *The Irgun Zvai Leumi,* 6 vols. Hadar Publishing Corp., Tel-Aviv. 1980 (Heb.).

Ringelblum, Emmanuel: *Notes from the Warsaw Ghetto.* Schocken Books, New York, 1974.

Sachar, Howard M.: *History of Israel.* Alfred A. Knopf, New York, 1976.

Samuel, Horace B.: *Unholy Memories of the Holy Land.* L. and V. Woolf, London, 1930.

———, *Revolt by Leave.* New Zionist Press, London, 1936.

Schechtman, Joseph B.: Jordan, *A State that Never Was.* Cultural Publishing Corp., Inc. New York, 1968.

Schechtman, Joseph B.: *The Jabotinsky Story.* 2 vols., Thomas Yoseloff, New York, 1956.

Sereni, Enzon and Ashery, R. H.: *Jews and Arabs in Palestine:* Hechalutz Press, New York, 1956.

Shapiro, David: *The Role of the Emergency Committee for Zionist Affairs as the Political Arm of American Zionism 1934-1944.* Ph.D., at Hebrew University, Jerusalem (1979) (Heb.).

Shavit, Yaakov: *Open Season.* The Confrontation Between the "Organized Yishuv" and the Underground Organization (I.Z.L. and Lehi) 1937-1947. Tel-Aviv, Hadar Publishing Corp., 1976 (Heb.).

———, *Revisionism in Zionism (1925-1936).* Yariv, Inc., Tel-Aviv, 1978 (Heb.).

Shay, Abraham: *The Milk Cans Roared.* (The Bombing of British Headquarters at King David Hotel). Hadar Publishing Corp., Tel-Aviv, 1977 (Heb.).

Shmulevitz, M.: *Beyamim Adumim.* Tel-Aviv, 1949 (Heb.).

Sykes, Christopher: *Cross Roads to Israel.* Collins, London, 1965, World Publishing, Cleveland 1965.

Tavin, Eli: *The Second Front (Irgun Tzvai Leumi in Europe, 1946-1948).* Ron Publihsers, Tel-Aviv, 1973 (Heb.).

Van Paassen, Pierre: *Forgotten Ally.* Dial Press, New York, 1943.

Wasserstein, Bernard: *Britain and the Jews of Europe, 1939-1945.* Oxford University Press, New York, 1979.

Wdowinski, David: *And We Are Not Saved.* Philosophical Library, New York, 1963.

Wedgwood, Josiah: *The Seventh Dominion.* Labour Publishing Co., London, 1928.

Weinshall, Yaakov: *The Blood That is in the Basin.* (The Life Story of Abraham Stern). Hamatmid, Tel-Aviv, 1956 (Heb.).

Weismandel, Rabbi Michael Dov: *Min Hametzar.* Published Anonymously (Heb.).

Weizmann, Chaim: *Trial and Error.* Hamish Hamilton, London, 1949; Harper & Row, New York, 1949.

Wyman, David S.: *Paper Walls: America and the Refugee Crisis, 1938-1941.* Unviersity of Massachusetts Press, Amherst, Mass. 1968.

Yalin-Mor, Nathan: *The Fighters for the Freedom of Israel.* Shikmonah, Inc., Jerusalem, 1975 (Heb.).

Zaar, Isaac: *Rescue and Liberation.* Bloch Publishing Co., New York, 1954.

Ziff, William: *The Rape of Palestine.* Longmans, Green & Co., New York, 1938.

PUBLICATIONS, ARTICLES, MONOGRAPHS, RESEARCH PAPERS

American Zionist Emergency Council (1943-1948), Minutes of meetings, Zionist Archives and Library, New York.

Amrami, Yaakov: *Practical Bibliography*. (Nili; Brit Habiryonim; IZL: LEHI). Hadar Publishing, Tel-Aviv, 1975 (Heb.).

The Answer, 1943-1948. Complete set of issues at Yale University, Sterling Memorial Library, Manuscripts and Archives, Palestine Statehood Committee Papers. Also at: Institute of Mediterranean Affairs, New York, New York.

Ben-Eliezer, Arieh: *Incomplete Ms. of autobiographical memoirs.* Jabotinsky Institute, Tel-Aviv, (108 pp.).

Berman, Aaron: *Abba Hillel Silver: Zionism and the Rescue of European Jews.* Masters Essay, Columbia University, 1976.

————, *The Hebrew Committee of National Liberation and the Rescue of The European Jews.* Division III. Hampshire College, Massachusetts. April, 1975.

Beit-Zvi, S. B.: *Sensitive Matters.* A critic of a Yad-Vashem Symposium on the destruction of Hungarian Jewry. Sha'arim, Tel-Aviv, 3/27/81 (Heb.).

Documents on the Holocaust. Edited by Arad, Gutman and Margaliot. Yad Vashem, Jerusalem, 1978.

Feinstein, Marcia: *The Irgun Campaign in the United States for a Jewish Army.* Submitted for graduate degree, City University of New York, 1973.

Gelber, Yoav: *The Zionist Diplomacy and the Fate of the Jews of Europe 1939-1942.* In Yad Vashem Studies vol. 13, Jerusalem, 1979.

Gottlieb, Michael: *American Zionist Emergency Council and the Emergency Committee to Save the Jewish People of Europe.* Research Paper, Yale, 1975.

Greenberg, Hayim: *Bankrupt.* Originally in *Yiddishr Kemfer*, February 1943 (Yiddish). Reprint *Midstream*, March 1964.

Grobman, Alex: *What Did They Know? The American Jewish Press and the Holocaust* American Jewish History, vol. LXVIII, no. 3; March 1979.

Hecht, Reuben: Interview on Rescue Work in Switzerland (1944-45). *Herut* (Daily) Tel-Aviv, September 6, 1955 (Heb.).

Jabotinsky, Zeev: *Evidence Submitted to the Palestine Royal Commission.* New Zionist Press, 1937.

Katz, Yaakov: *The Holocaust: Was it Predictable?* Tefuzot Hagolah; vol. XVII, no. 75-76 (Heb.).

Klarman, Joseph: "The Truth on the mass Ha'apalah from Romania: The Two Pans." Hauma, #57, May 1979 (Heb.).

Laqueur, Walter: *Hitler's Holocaust: Who Knew What, When and How?* Encounter, July 1980.

Matzozky, Eliyho: The *Response of American Jewry and its Represen-tative Organizations (November 1942 and April 1943) to Mass Killing of Jews in Europe.* Masters project, Bernard Revel Graduate School, Yeshiva University, 1979.

———— , An Episode: *Roosevelt and the Mass Killing.* Midstream, August/September 1980.

Matz, Eliyho: Poltical Action vs. Personal Relationship, Midstream, April 1981.

Metzuda and Herut (Published in the underground): Complete facsim-ile set. Hadar Publishing, Tel-Aviv, 1978 (Heb.).

Michman, Dan: Zeev Jabotinsky—"Evacuation and Foreseeing the Extermination." Kivunim, no. 7, May 1980. Public Information Section, W.Z.O. (Heb.).

Morgenstern, Arieh: The United Rescue Committee (Va'ad Ha'hat-zalah) and its Activities. Yalkut Moreshet, vol. XIII. June 1971. Israel (Heb.).

Morgenthau, Henry Jr.: *The Morgenthau Diaries* (The Refugee Run-around). Colliers, November 1, 1947.

Nedava, Joseph, (Ed.): *Compilation of Articles on Zeev Jabotinsky, The Man and His Teachings.* Publishing Section of the Ministry of Defense, Jerusalem, 1980 (Heb.).

———— , *Who created the State.* Haumah, no. 58, Sept. 1979, Tel-Aviv (Heb.).

———— , *Predicting History and the Oncoming Extermination* (Heb.).

Netanyahu, Ben-Zion: *In the Twilight* (A critique of the HCNL's Hebrew and Jew distinction. Bitzaron, New York, Vol. X, No. VIII, June 1944 (Heb.).

Peck, Sara E.: *The Campaign for an American Response to the Nazi Holocaust* (1943-1945). Journal of Contemporary History (London and Beverly Hills); vol. 15, 1980.

Pinsky, David E.: *Cooperation Among American Jewish Organizations in Their Efforts to Rescue European Jewry During the Holocaust.* (1939-1945). Ph.D. New York University, 1980.

Sampolinsky, Meir: *The Anglo-Jewish Leadership, the British Government and the Holocaust.* Ph.D. Bar Ilan University, Ramat Gan, 1977 (Heb.).

Seligman, Max: *On the Arlossorof-Stawsky Trial.* Tel-Aviv, Ma'ariv, 1/25/81 (Heb. Daily).

Slutzki, Yehuda: *Publication of Stenographic Report. Berl Katznel son on Meeting with Jabotinsky.* September 1939.

Trepman, Paul: *The Holocaust.* A Critique of Lucy Dawidowicz' *The War Against The Jews. Midstream,* June/July 1977 (letters to editor).

The Truth About the Warsaw Ghetto Uprising. By the World Leader-ship of Betar, Tel-Aviv, 1946 (Heb.).

Vago, Bela and Mosse, George L. (Eds.): *Jews and Non-Jews in Eastern Europe, 1918-1943.* John Wiley & Sons, New York, 1974.

Wasserstein, Bernard: *The Myth of "Jewish Silence". Midstream, New York, August/September 1980. For rebuttal, see letters to editor, Midstream, March 1981.*

Yalin-Mor, Nathan: *A Zionist Underground Under Soviet Auspices.*
  • Included in *Bleter Fun Yiddish Lite* (Yiddish and Hebrew.) Menorah, Tel-Aviv, 1974.

Yehoshua, A. B. *Between Right and Right.* Doubleday, New York, 1981.

NOTE: Pertinent documents are also available at:
  Morgenthau Diaries, F.D.R. Library, Hyde Park, New York (mostly declassified).

  U.S. Justice Department, F.B.I. and State Department (mostly declassified). Obtainable at the respective Departments under the Freedom of Information Act. (Pertinent documents are available at Institute of Mediterranean Affairs, New York, New York.)

  Harry S Truman Library, Independence, Missouri (64050).

  British Government documents on file at the Jabotinsky Institute, Tel-Aviv, and the Institute for Mediterranean Affairs, New York, New York. Originals at the Public Record Office, London.

Index

(Excluding Family)